PHL

5406000128271

KT-550-750

Craft, Industry and Everyday Life: Wood and Woodworking in Anglo-Scandinavian and Medieval York

By Carole A. Morris

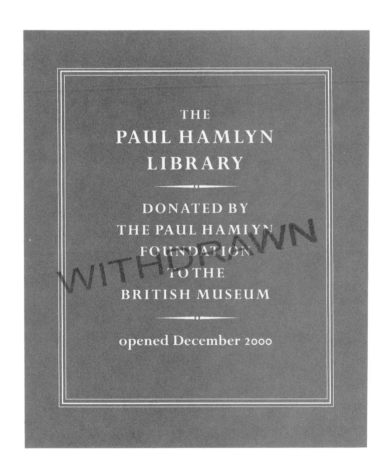

THE
PAUL HAMLYN
LIBRARY

DONATED BY
THE PAUL HAMLYN
FOUNDATION
TO THE
BRITISH MUSEUM

opened December 2000

WITHDRAWN

Published for the York Archaeological Trust by the
Council for British Archaeology

2000

This book is dedicated to my father, Ernest Chapman,
who was always interested in the project
but who died in 1990 before it was completed

THE
BRITISH
MUSEUM
THE PAUL HAMLYN LIBRARY

WITHDRAWN

942.843 MOR

Contents

List of Figures

List of Tables

Volume 17 Fascicule 13

Craft, Industry and Everyday Life: Wood and Woodworking in Anglo-Scandinavian and Medieval York

By Carole A. Morris

With contributions by J.A. Spriggs, D.M. Goodburn and P. Walton Rogers

Key words: Anglo-Scandinavian, boxes, bowls, buckets, casks, coopering, cups, face-turning, lathe, lathe-turning, medieval, spindle-turning, stave-built, timber, tools, tubs, vessels, wood, wooden artefacts, woodland management, woodworking, York

Introduction

The material discussed in this fascicule, together with copies of all appropriate records, will be deposited at The Yorkshire Museum, York, under the Museum and YAT accession codes 1976–81.7 (16–22 Coppergate), 1982.22 (Coppergate watching brief), 1987.21 (22 Piccadilly), 1973–79.13.X (Bedern south-west), 1978–80.14.II/IV (Bedern north-east), 1973–6.13.I/II (Bedern Foundry), 1974–5.13.III/IV (Bedern south-west, long trench).

Archaeological Introductions to the Sites

Excavation at 16–22 Coppergate

By R.A. Hall

The site and the recovery of evidence

The site of 16–22 Coppergate lies on the spur of land between the Rivers Ouse and Foss. It is bounded to the west by Coppergate, a street leading towards the only bridge across the Ouse in the medieval period, and to the east by the banks of the Foss (Fig.962, **1**).

The excavation took the form of a continuous archaeological campaign of five years and four months during 1976–81. Resources were provided principally by the Ancient Monuments Inspectorate of the Department of the Environment (now English Heritage), the Manpower Services Commission, the British Academy and a host of private individuals and corporations.

The data recovered have been attributed to six broad periods; the evidence presented here relates to the Roman and post-Roman centuries, and in particular the 9th–14th/15th centuries. During this time the site was sub-divided into four tenement plots which, in general, were more densely occupied as time passed.

The characteristics of the demolition site that was handed over for investigation, notably the varying extent of modern intrusions, coupled with the logistics of excavation and the continual financial uncertainties, dictated the strategy and tactics employed throughout the excavation process. Anglo-Scandinavian deposits were revealed below modern cellars within a few days of excavation commenc-

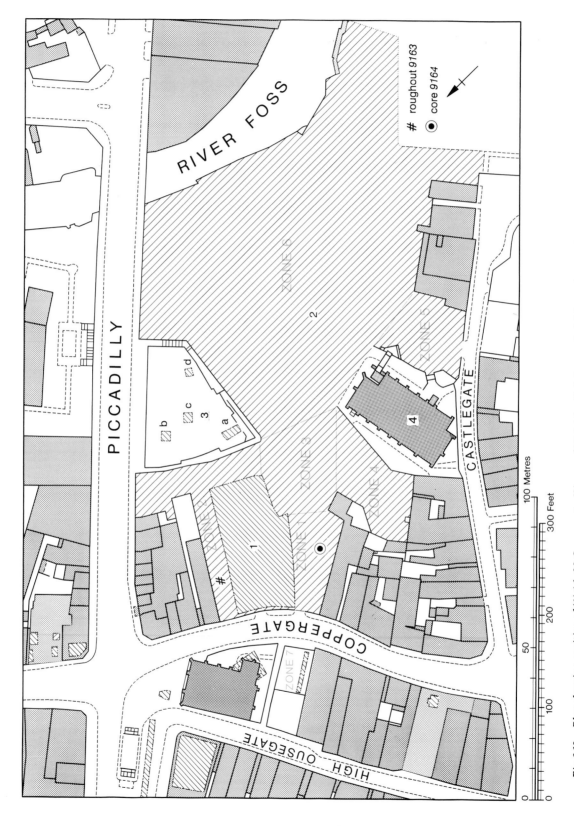

Fig.962 *Plan showing position of (1) 16–22 Coppergate; (2) area of Watching Brief, zones 1–7 (shown in green) and findspots of 9163–4; (3) 22 Piccadilly, a–d correspond to Trenches 1–4; and (4) St Mary, Castlegate. (Based on the 1982 Ordnance Survey 1:1250 National Grid Plans. Reproduced from Ordnance Survey mapping on behalf of The Controller of Her Majesty's Stationery Office, © Crown copyright. MC 012225.) Scale 1:1250*

ing, yet elsewhere on the site late medieval deposits were still being investigated two years later.

During the redevelopment of 1981–3 a continuous watching brief over an extended area, running down to the present edge of the River Foss (Fig.962, **2**), was maintained under the direction of N.F. Pearson. The results of this exercise are incorporated into the summary given below (pp.2083–4).

Mid 10th century to late medieval deposits were investigated over the entire excavated area, which comprised c.1000m². Owing to a shortage of funding, the earliest levels, dating from the Roman period to the early/mid 10th century (i.e. up to and including what is described below as Period 4A), were not examined right across the c.1000m² open in the subsequent levels. Instead, a strip measuring approximately 20 × 7·5m across the Coppergate street frontage and a contiguous strip up to 12m wide and 37m long, running down the southern half of the site towards the River Foss, were excavated to natural soils (Fig.963, p.2078).

Layers attributable to Periods 1 and 3 were recorded throughout these strips. A well-defined Period 2 horizon existed only in the street frontage strip; elsewhere, because of stratigraphic interruptions and an overall thinning of these earlier layers as they ran eastwards from the street frontage, Period 2 contexts could not be isolated with certainty. Therefore, although some deposition of soil must have taken place throughout Period 2, remains of this period are shown as of limited extent. Similarly, the Period 4A horizon, while extending right across the frontage, could not be traced convincingly down the southern strip beyond a point where diagnostic features petered out. It is thus conceivable that a small amount of soil build-up which took place during Period 4A on that part of the southern strip to the east of the limit of identifiable 4A features has been subsumed into Period 4B, which was investigated over the entire excavated area.

For reasons outlined below (p.2081), the deposits designated as Period 5A were limited in extent to the front part of the site. Deposits of Period 5B were traced across the entire area excavated. Deposits of Period 5Cf and 5Cr were limited front- and rearmost portions of the excavation respectively, and no contemporary levels could be stratigraphically iso-

lated in the central part of the excavation. Layers of Period 6, a designation that encompasses all deposits of the Anglo-Norman to post-medieval/early modern eras, covered the entire excavated area except where removed by more recent disturbances (Fig.964, pp.2080–1). As noted above, structures which could be attributed to Period 6 were not in evidence at the modern street frontage, but structures were found across the rest of the excavated area. Survival of these remains was affected in places by modern (19th and 20th century) disturbance, particularly that related to occupancy of part of the site by Cravens, the Victorian and later sweet factory.

These variations in the size of area excavated must be borne in mind in any chronological/quantitative analysis of the artefactual evidence.

Site history and a summary (Figs.963–4)

The earliest occupation on the site, designated Period 1 (Table 191), was in the Roman era. At that time the legionary fortress lay 160m to the north-west; the immediate vicinity was certainly occupied by temples, and it probably also contained a variety of commercial establishments. Evidence for Roman buildings constructed of both timber and stone was recovered, but the functions of these structures could not be deduced. The site also contained a small late Roman cemetery. The admixtures of silt, clay and loam which characterised soil conditions associated with Period 1 did not permit the survival of any organic-based artefacts except the very fragmentary remains of some wooden coffins and items made of osseous material.

There seems no reason to suppose that Romano-British activity continued here beyond the conventional date of c. AD 400 or shortly after, and from then until the mid 9th century the site seems to have been unoccupied (Period 2). This period was marked stratigraphically by the accumulation of up to 1m of grey silty clay loam soils; there was no evidence for structures, domestic or otherwise. All of the pottery in these layers was Roman with the exception of a small quantity of Anglo-Scandinavian sherds which are believed to be intrusive; the contexts from which they were recovered were adjacent either to upstanding baulks incorporating later material, or to later, down-cutting features which may have been the source of obviously later sherds. Although, once

Table 191   Summary of archaeological development at 16–22 Coppergate

Period	Date	Characteristics
1	late 1st–late 4th century or later	Roman timber and stone buildings; late Roman cemetery. Limited survival of organic materials
2	5th–mid 9th century	Apparent desertion. Homogeneous loamy deposits which did not preserve organic materials
3	mid 9th–late 9th/early 10th century	Rubbish disposal, suggesting occupation close by. Post/stake and wattle alignments, possibly boundaries. Organic materials preserved only in pit cuts
4A	late 9th/early 10th century–c.930/5	Realignment of boundaries, suggesting that Coppergate was laid out by this period. Possible buildings at Coppergate frontage. Organic materials preserved mainly in pit cuts
4B	c.930/5–c.975	Four tenements distinguishable, with post and wattle buildings at Coppergate frontage. Evidence for iron-working and other trades on a commercial scale. Organic-rich deposits nearer to Coppergate; organic content thinning to zero towards River Foss
5A	c.975	Near Coppergate frontage only. Layers between structures of Periods 4B and 5B; probably mixture of occupation deposits, dump deposits and soil from 5B semi-basements
5B	c.975–early/mid 11th century	Perpetuation of boundaries. Introduction of sunken-featured structures in double row at street frontage. Organic-rich deposits as in Period 4B
5Cf	mid–later 11th century	Organic-rich deposits at street frontage, associated with buildings which survive only in Tenement D
5Cr	mid–later 11th century	Post-built structure closest to River Foss sealed by earliest in a succession of dump deposits. Little organic material surviving
6	later 11th–16th century	No remains surviving at street frontage, but area to rear increasingly built up above later dump deposits. New methods of building and rubbish disposal, leading to reduction in organic content of deposits

again, soil conditions would not have preserved organic-based artefacts other than those made of osseous material, the dearth of other, more durable, artefactual evidence for contemporary activity indicated that this absence reflects accurately the site's apparent desertion at this time. A later 8th century helmet, found only 9m beyond the perimeter of the excavation during construction work in 1982, lay within a wood-lined shaft. This was, perhaps, a mid–late Anglian well, and may possibly relate to a contemporary settlement nucleus, either on the ridge now represented by Nessgate/Castlegate or around what may be an early ecclesiastical foundation at St Mary, Castlegate (Fig.962, **4**). The final backfilling of the shaft is dated to the Anglo-Scandinavian period on the basis of a characteristic suite of accompanying palaeobiological remains (pp.870–81, *AY* 17/8); a wooden churn dasher found with it is discussed on p.2277.

Above the clean grey loams which mark the four and a half centuries interpreted as Anglian desertion of the site, a band of dirtier grey silty clay loams was recognised, and into these was cut a series of features. One of the earliest of these features was a sequence of hearth/oven/kiln bases represented by a horizontal setting of re-used Roman tiles, perhaps used in glassworking. An archaeomagnetic determination of 860 ± 20 was obtained from these features. This is the single most precise indication of the date when renewed use of the site (Period 3) began, although it allows no more than the approximation of mid–late 9th century. It is not possible to determine whether a date of c.840, c.860 or c.880 is more likely, and therefore impossible to relate the inception of the period with conviction to either a definitely pre-Viking (i.e. pre-866) or post-Viking date. It does seem, however, that the assemblage of Anglian pottery from the site (just under 200 sherds) is best seen as in a direct typological and thus chronological succession with that from the Anglian occupation site at 46–54 Fishergate (AY 7/1; AY 16/6, 650–1) where occupation is thought to have ceased in the mid 9th century.

Apart from one porcupine sceat of c.720–40, found in an 11th century layer at the river end of the site, all nine of the other identifiable Anglian coins from the site are of 9th century date (four of Eanred c.810–41; five of Æthelred II 841–4, 844–8: AY 18/1, 51–3). All were found in contexts stratigraphically later than that with the archaeomagnetic determination of 860 ± 20. Such coins were certainly available for hoarding in the reign of Osberht, the last pre-Viking king of Northumbria, and they occur in coin hoards found in York which may be interpreted as a response to the Viking attack of 866. Such coins might even have continued in use in York until Viking kings began minting coins c.895.

The writer interprets this evidence as indicating that activity and settlement in this area, on anything but an occasional and sporadic basis, recommenced in the middle of the 9th century. There is no stratigraphic or artefactual evidence, for example, no stratified 8th century sceattas like those from 46–54 Fishergate (AY 7/1, 17) to indicate that there was protracted Anglian activity before that time.

Other features in this period included several pits containing domestic debris, and some pits also contained human skeletal remains. The latest features of this period were a series of post-holes, some apparently forming alignments at an angle to the later tenement lines, and an accompanying cobble spread at the south-west of the area. It is conceivable that these features represent the remains of a building, although this is not certain. This entire horizon, Period 3, is tentatively dated c. AD 850–900 on the basis of a combination of archaeomagnetic and numismatic evidence; in later periods, dendrochronological data provide a greater level of chronological precision.

Sealing the post-holes, cobble spread and other features of Period 3 were deposits into which wattle alignments were inserted. These anticipated the alignment of the subsequent tenements and structures, but do not themselves form obviously coherent structures. The alignments and both their underlying and associated layers and features are assigned to Period 4A and dated c. AD 900–930/5. Characteristic of the layers of this period were dark grey silty clay loams, very similar to those of Period 3, but differentiated by the inclusion of patches of grey clay, brown ash, scatters of charcoal and occasional very small fragments and slivers of wood. These conditions, like those of Period 3, were not particularly conducive to the survival of organic artefacts.

The next phase on the site, Period 4B, is marked by the division of the area into four tenements, designated A–D (Fig.963), and if the street Coppergate was not in being before it must have been laid out at this time. The tenements were defined by wattle fences, whose lines fluctuated only very slightly over the succeeding millennium; towards the River Foss end of the site, however, there was no trace of any continuation of the fences discovered nearer to Coppergate. Whether this should be attributed to the nature of the soil conditions in this area, or whether tenement divisions never extended this far, is not clear. Each tenement contained buildings of post and wattle construction, positioned with their gable-ends facing the street. All had been truncated towards their front by the subsequent widening of Coppergate; the greatest surviving length was 6·8m and they averaged 4·4m in width. The buildings on Tenements A and B had been substantially disturbed by the digging of semi-basements for the Period 5B buildings, but those on Tenements C and D were very largely intact. The buildings had to be repaired or replaced frequently, for they were vulnerable to fire as well as to natural decay, but successive refurbishments varied little in their dimensions and position. Hearths were found on the long axes of the buildings in Tenements B, C and D; any trace in A was destroyed by later intrusion, and even in B only vestiges remained. In C and D the hearths measured up to 2·4 × 1·3m and consisted of a clay base, sometimes resting on a stone slab underpinning, and surrounded by a revetment of horizontal timbers, limestone rubble or re-used Roman tiles. Discolouration of the clay base by burning was quite restricted, and the large size of

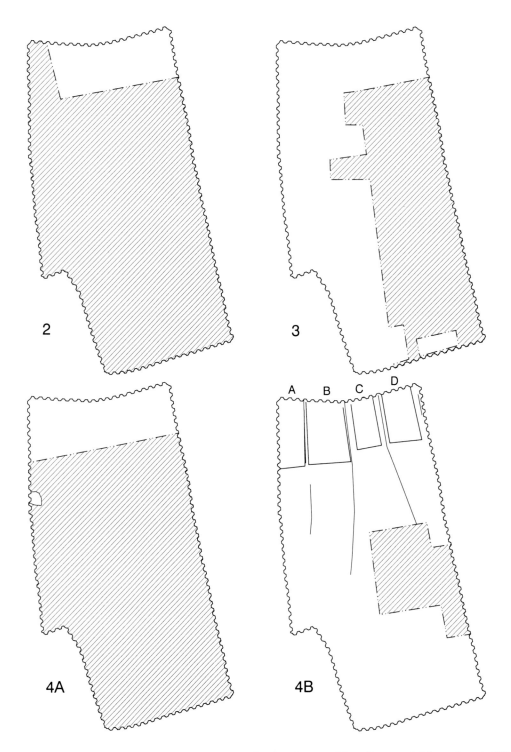

Fig.963 *(above and facing) Plans of the site at 16–22 Coppergate showing the area of deposits excavated for each period (Periods 2–5). The variation is due either to restricted excavation or to the limited occurrence or survival of the relevant deposits. Scale 1:500*

the hearth appears to reflect a desire for a margin of safety for embers rather than the size of the fire itself.

Only one rank of buildings stood in each tenement and their lengthy backyards were not built up but used for rubbish disposal and other ancillary functions. Although sometimes difficult to differentiate, a sequence of superimposed layers built up within each building. Their accompanying artefacts allow the activities within each tenement to be followed with varying degrees of assurance. Metal-

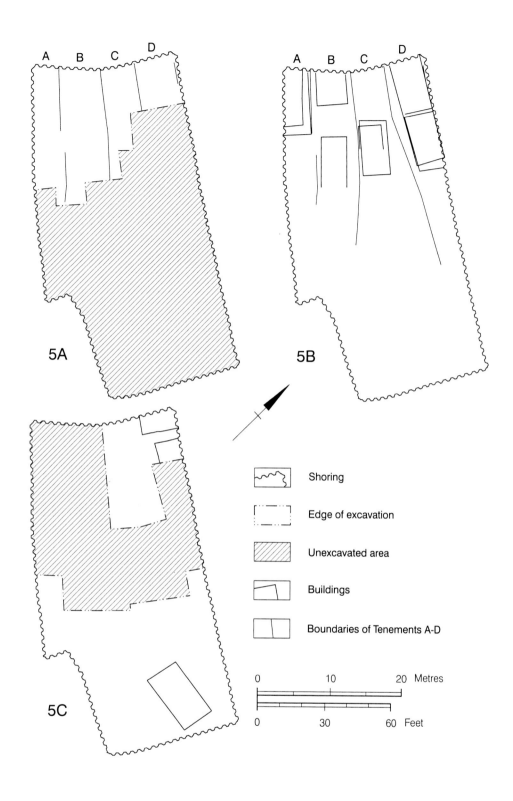

5A

5B

5C

	Shoring
	Edge of excavation
	Unexcavated area
	Buildings
	Boundaries of Tenements A-D

0   10   20   Metres

0   30   60   Feet

working seems to have been the predominant activity, with the manufacture of items in iron, copper alloy, lead alloy, silver and gold. A notable feature was the quantity of crucibles recovered with their important corroborative evidence for the range and variety of metalworking techniques (*AY* 17/6; *AY* 17/7). Occupation was evidently intensive, generating organic-rich occupation deposits which accumulated

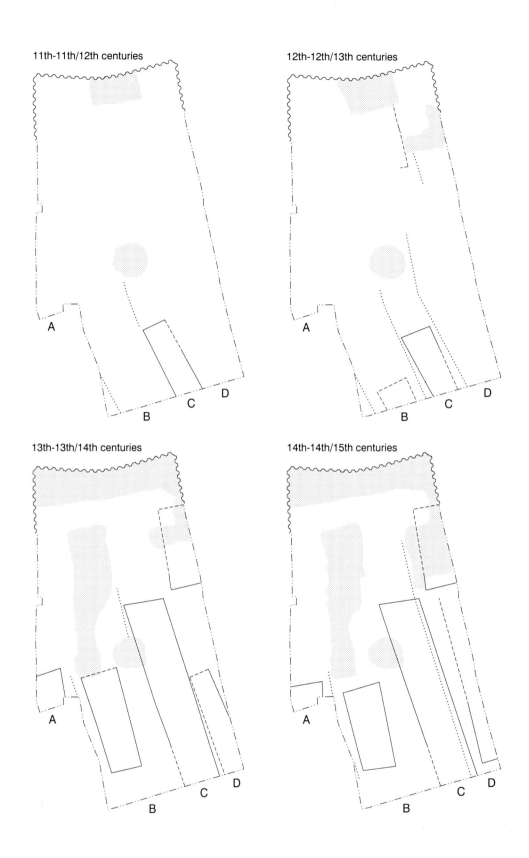

Fig.964 *(above and facing) Plans of the site at 16–22 Coppergate showing the area of deposits excavated for Period 6. Scale 1:500. The insertion of perimeter shoring after the removal of most Period 6 deposits slightly lessened the excavated area*

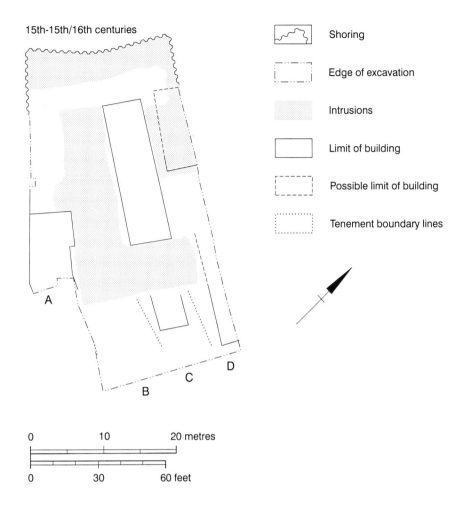

15th-15th/16th centuries

Shoring

Edge of excavation

Intrusions

Limit of building

Possible limit of building

Tenement boundary lines

0   10   20 metres

0   30   60 feet

rapidly, in particular in and around the buildings, and which accounted for a continual rise in ground level. Deposits which were rich in organic remains extended to approximately half-way down the excavated area in the direction of the River Foss. From this point their organic component lessened until, in the south-easternmost quarter of the excavation furthest from the Coppergate street frontage, organic materials other than bone and antler did not survive except in the fills of pits and other cuts.

In the later 10th century the remains of the latest phase of post and wattle structures at the street frontage were covered to a depth of up to 1m. This horizon, which was not traced in the yard areas behind the buildings, is interpreted partly as occupation deposits, partly the upcast from digging out the sunken structures of Period 5B, and partly as a deliberate dump of make-up or levelling material. Some of it thus accumulated very quickly, probably within a period of weeks or months, and contained a mixture of material of c.975 and before.

The dating of Period 5A is assisted by the dendrochronological analysis of timbers from the immediately succeeding plank-built semi-basement structures of Period 5B. These were erected at the Coppergate end of each tenement, sometimes in two closely spaced ranks; as in Period 4B, organic-rich deposits were concentrated in the vicinity of these buildings, and the organic content of the deposits decreased riverwards. As in the buildings of Period 4B, successive layers and lenses of silty loam usually characterised the superimposed internal deposits. Manufacturing continued at this period, although new trades were practised. It is argued in this report (pp.2203–4) that the structure on Tenement C in Period 5B served as a lathe-turner's workshop.

On Tenement D sufficient overlying stratification remained undisturbed to show that the latest of the Period 5B sunken buildings was eventually replaced by structures built at ground level. The chronology of these subsequent buildings is imprecise: they can be assigned only approximately to the mid 11th century. They and their associated stratification are designated as belonging to Period 5Cf. A series of approximately contemporary mid 11th century levels was also identified at the rear of the site, associated with and sealing a post-built structure, the latest timber of which has been dated through dendrochronology to 1013–58 (AY 8/4 in prep.). These levels, which did not preserve their organic component, are designated Period 5Cr. They were themselves covered by a series of dumps of very dark grey silty clay loam interleaved with evidence for sporadic activity, and dated to the Norman period.

Within the Anglo-Scandinavian stratification there is clear evidence from coins and pottery for the displacement of objects from the context where they were originally deposited and their redeposition in later, often appreciably later, layers. The principal mechanism of this movement was the cutting of pits, wells and the like, and, more particularly, the digging out of the sunken element in the Period 5B buildings, which penetrated earlier levels and redistributed the soil removed from them. In the case of the precisely dated coins it can be seen that, in the Anglo-Scandinavian levels, coins sometimes occur in contexts dated 75–100 years later than their striking (AY 18/1, 24), although their wear patterns do not suggest circulation for this length of time and there is no evidence that they were hoarded. Less precisely, but none the less clearly, study of the pottery from Anglo-Scandinavian levels has shown, for example, that sherds both of Roman wares and also of handmade middle Saxon type which are unlikely to have been produced after c. AD 850–900 are found residually throughout the era, another testimony to the redistribution of earlier material (AY 16/5, fig.144).

Period 6 incorporates all later activity on the site, most of it datable to c.1100–1500. At the Coppergate street frontage, no buildings survived later than those attributed to Period 5Cf. The earliest surviving building of Period 6 was a late 11th/12th century post and wattle structure incorporating a hearth at the rear of Tenement C (Fig.964, p.2080). It adjoined the only length of contemporaneous property boundary which could be identified. Other, probably structural, features attributed to this time include a hearth and a group of large posts at the excavated rear limit of Tenement A.

In the 12th–12th/13th century (Fig.964) the building at the rear of Tenement C was replaced with a series of superimposed post and wattle structures incorporating hearths/ovens. This complex, which stood within well-defined fenced property boundaries that could be traced towards the middle of the site, is tentatively interpreted as a bakery or malting house. The end of a post and wattle structure on the adjacent Tenement B was also recorded, as was a further set of possibly structural features, including hearths, at the rear limit of Tenement A. A very fragmentary possible structure, represented by a post alignment, was noted towards the front end of Tenement C.

The tenement plots were occupied more extensively in the 13th–13th/14th centuries, although the only evidence for buildings on Tenement A was, once more, from its rear, where a series of post-holes and sill walls defined a structure (Fig.964). Towards the rear of Tenement B a building was erected which had its principal uprights supported by padstones; alongside it a cobbled surface providing an access way replaced and extended over the fence line that had earlier separated Tenement B from Tenement C. A relatively long building, constructed on pile-cluster foundations, now stood on Tenement C; it is unclear whether it extended to the riverside limit of excavation, or whether a separate structure occupied that part of the tenement plot. Meanwhile, at the riverward end of Tenement D, there is some evidence for a structure represented most tangibly by a line of posts to the north-east of a series of deposits which have the characteristics of internal floors. It is the combination of these two sets of features which define the structure shown on Fig.964. Towards the Coppergate end of the plot a stone-built structure with substantial horizontal timber foundations underpinning the rear wall may also have been erected within this period.

A very similar layout of buildings was maintained into the 14th–14th/15th centuries, although most individual structures were rebuilt during this time (Fig.964). A new building represented by post-holes now occupied the rear of Tenement A, and the Tenement B padstone building was also rebuilt. The long building on Tenement C continued in use initially but was then demolished; an alley surface was laid down between it and the building on Tenement D. Later, a ditch, redefining the Tenement C–D property boundary, was cut within the limits of the earlier long Tenement C building. Evidence for a contemporary building over the rear of Tenement D was now unequivocal, with the construction of a rubble sill wall. The stone cellared building nearer the frontage may have remained in use.

The latest coherent archaeological evidence is dated to the 15th–15th/16th century. A much more substantial, stone-built, structure was now erected in the centre/rear of Tenement A; its full extent is not known. More recent disturbance has removed contemporary stratification from most of Tenement B, and there was no trace of any building within the undisturbed portion at the riverward end of this property. A new, relatively long building represented by rubble sill walls was built at the centre/front of Tenement C, and there were also robbed out traces of another, smaller structure nearer to the river, with a ditch defining the property boundary to one side and a wall to the other. The earlier Tenement D buildings continued in use at this time.

A series of dendrochronological and archaeomagnetic determinations provide a fairly precise chronology for a majority of the buildings; ceramic and numismatic data support and extend this information.

Although the number and size of these buildings varied throughout the late medieval and early post-medieval centuries, their intermittent presence sealed the deposits below and temporarily protected them from damage caused by intrusive pits. Furthermore, the introduction both of levelling deposits before the erection of some of the buildings, and of dump deposits which indicate the disposal of a quantity of rubbish in a single event, served to raise the ground level and offer some protective cloak or masking against erosion and disturbance. Conversely, changes in building techniques and materials, notably the increasing use of stone and then brick wall footings, and tiled roofs, contributed to a gradual diminution in the amount of organic debris being generated and deposited on the site during the late medieval period. From the 13th–13th/14th centuries onwards,

access alleyways rather than fence lines sometimes marked the boundaries of tenement plots. Concomitantly, these stone surfaces also sealed underlying deposits, temporarily protecting them from intrusion and degradation. None the less, the digging of wells, cess-pits and other features throughout the medieval and post-medieval centuries did bring some earlier material to the surface.

The structures and strata recorded in the Coppergate excavations will be published in *AY* 6, 7, 8 and 10. Biological evidence from the Anglo-Scandinavian deposits has been published in *AY* 14/7 and the Anglo-Scandinavian animal bones have been published in *AY* 15/3; biological evidence from medieval deposits will be published in *AY* 14 and the medieval animal bones have been published in *AY* 15/5. The Anglo-Scandinavian pottery has been published in *AY* 16/5 and the medieval pottery will appear in a subsequent fascicule in *AY* 16. A series of artefact reports is being published in *AY* 17. The post-Roman coins and numismatica are included in *AY* 18/1. Roman coins will appear in *AY* 18/2. Once all the Anglo-Scandinavian structures, artefacts and environmental data have been studied and published, a synthesis of the entire assemblage will be produced.

The Watching Brief

By N.F. Pearson

The Coppergate watching brief embraced the whole of the 2·02ha area of the Coppergate Shopping Centre redevelopment from the Castlegate frontage in the west to Piccadilly at the east. Observations were also made in the areas of 16–22 Coppergate not explored during the main excavation campaign, that is, strips to the west, east and south of the open area (Fig.962, 2, p.2074). A watch was also kept at 14 Coppergate, where the rear of the property was redeveloped in 1984 only after the construction of the rest of the shopping centre had been completed. Recording also took place to the rear of the former Market Tavern, 24 Coppergate, where a medieval building on the Coppergate street frontage was refurbished as part of the development.

Observation and recording was carried out in often adverse conditions during ground preparation and building works undertaken by Wimpey Construction plc. The ground preparation works were undertaken largely by machine, under archaeological supervision. Where significant archaeological deposits were disturbed, work was suspended to allow recording, or, where appropriate, small-scale excavation. To facilitate recording, the redevelopment area was split into discrete zones (Fig.962).

The main archaeological discoveries for the watching brief can be summarised as follows.

The principal Roman features encountered included the fragmentary remains of a largely robbed-out stone building recorded between the Coppergate excavation and 14 Coppergate (Zone 1). This has tentatively been interpreted as a warehouse, on the basis of its proximity to the River Foss. In the helmet pit area (Zone 3), four pits were excavated in addition to a linear feature. In the Fossbank area (Zone 6), a red gritstone wall was observed briefly during machine clearance. It was well constructed with individual blocks measuring 0·8 × 0·6 × 0·4m. No other associated material was seen and although it was clearly structural in nature its north-east/south-west alignment precludes it from being interpreted as a river wall.

The only feature from the site which may be attributable to the Anglian period is the pit containing the Coppergate helmet and churn dash *4421* (see p.2277).

From the Anglo-Scandinavian period, the west wall of Structure 5/1 (Period 5B), which had already been excavated during the main excavation, was uncovered in the area between the Coppergate excavation and 14 Coppergate (Zone 1). Associated tenement boundaries and pits were also recorded. Between the Coppergate excavation and the Market Tavern public house (Zone 2), further well-preserved timber buildings and associated features, attributed to Periods 4B and 5B, were recorded.

The recorded medieval Period 6 features included structural remains, fence lines, the outer defences of York castle, and parts of the cemetery of All Saints, Pavement. There was also evidence for riverside reclamation, including some boat timbers re-used as a revetment of the bank of the King's Pool (see report on pp.2379–82). From the post-medieval and early modern periods the most significant discoveries were part of the cemetery of St Mary, Castlegate (Fig.962,

4, p.2074), traces of the canalisation of the River Foss, and part of the footings for the Victorian prison in the Castle Yard.

Excavation at 22 Piccadilly

By R. Finlayson

When the site of the ABC Cinema at 22 Piccadilly was to be developed an excavation was carried out in 1987 to examine, in four trenches, some of the material which would be destroyed by the new development (Fig.962, **3**, p.2074). The excavation lay to the south-east of the tenements excavated on Coppergate, in an area between them and the River Foss. From these limited areas of excavation some interpretation of the changes in topography and depositional regimes relating to the River Foss could be made. Trench 4 was within the course of the River Foss prior to its canalisation in or after 1793. A steeply sloping bank of natural sandy clay in Trench 3 is likely to have been a part of the river bank. Trenches 1 and 2 were located to the west of this bank and demonstrated intensive occupation of the area from the 1st century to the 16th century; later deposits had been truncated by the foundation of the ABC Cinema (Table 192). Many of the deposits were dumps and build-up material containing domestic and industrial waste which provided important information about craft activities, the utilisation of resources, diet and living conditions.

Roman activity comprised what was probably a drainage ditch, aligned at right angles to the modern day River Foss. The cut silted up and filled with a variety of material c.280 (*AY* 16/8).

During the 9th–12th centuries there were a series of attempts to make the area close to the Foss usable. Periods when the area was in use and timber features were built were interspersed with periods when activity declined. Flood deposition, the decay of vegetation and the dumping of domestic and industrial waste material all resulted in an accumulation of deposits. Particular evidence was found of the glass industry, small pelt preparation, horn and antler working, and butchery on a commercial as well as a domestic scale.

The first timber feature in Trench 1 was a fence parallel to the present course of the River Foss. This

Table 192 Summary of archaeological development at 22 Piccadilly

Period	Date	Description
Natural		Sandy clay
1	Roman	Riverine deposition, drainage ditch at right angles to the Foss, silting of ditch and dumping
2	9th century	Small pit and fill, riverine deposition, fence parallel to the Foss, dump and build-up material, two fence lines at right angles to each other, peaty and silty clay build-up and dump
3	10th century	Riverine deposition, silty clay, organic build-up and dump, timber revetment of river bank, silty clay, organic build-up and dump
4.1	975–early/mid 11th century	U-shaped timber revetment and wattle fence on river bank, silty clay and organic build-up and dump, fence
4.2	later 11th century	Renewal of intersecting fences, organic build-up and dumped large sawn timbers, timber revetment of river bank, silty clay build-up and dump
4.3	mid–late 12th century	Riverine deposition, compact peat build-up, small pit cuts, river bank timber revetment, silty clay build-up and dump, clay levelling on river bank
5.1	13th century	Pit cut with organic fill, drainage channel, soak-away?, peaty build-up, levelling
5.2	early–mid 14th century	Clay and peaty build-up and dump, rubbish pits
6	15th–early 16th century	Drainage? cut, organic build-up and dump, pit cut, barrel-lined well
7	15th century–modern	Levelling, concrete

fence was no longer in use when a dump and build-up of organic material (1058) covered the whole area. Environmental evidence suggests the area was wet grassland, and associated pottery is consonant with a 9th century date. A further series of fences (1040 and 1059) were constructed with two elements aligned parallel to the River Foss, and an alignment intersecting them at right angles. Pottery in associated dump and build-up deposits also dates from the first half of the 9th century.

In Trench 3 there were indications of an attempt at revetment to try to prevent soils slumping towards the sloping bank in the second half of the 10th century. A second phase of constructional activity in Trench 3 is represented by wattle which broadly followed the con-tour of the land, forming an open U shape. A similar U-shaped construction was found on the south-west bank of the River Ouse at North Street (YAT 1993.1), and also dated to the 11th century.

In Trench 2 timber fences and revetments indicate that some land management and manipulation of the course of the River Foss is likely to have taken place during the late 10th–early 11th century. There was evidence for the natural accumulation of material, for a deliberate raising of the ground surface, for fences and for possible revetments, but there was evidently continued periodic waterlogging of the area. Dumped material included concentrations of smashed crucibles with glass making waste, a number of glass beads and antler waste.

A broadly similar series of activities and structures was continued into the later 11th century. Glass beads, numerous worked goat horncores, antler waste, two bone skates, an increased amount of crucible waste, and a dump of large sawn timbers were recovered from this material and reflect the continuation and range of craft activity. A series of revetment timbers found closer to the river in Trench 3, and a fence line in Trench 1, both dated to the same period.

In the 12th century the area continued to be used for the disposal of rubbish and debris although glass industry waste ceases to appear. However, the soil now included a higher proportion of inorganic material, including demolition debris, although peaty deposits also continued to accumulate.

The area continued to be used for the disposal of domestic and industrial waste throughout the medieval period, with some evidence for drainage in the form of cuts and a large soakaway. The latest significant feature found on the site was a cask-lined well dating to the 15th or 16th century (see *9190–2, pp.2238–9*). Later deposits had been truncated by the foundations of the ABC Cinema.

Excavations at the Bedern

By R.A. Hall

The Bedern, an area of notorious slums in the 19th century, lies c.105m south-east of York Minster. The name survived into the 1970s as that of a minor street, formerly a cul-de-sac, approached through a medieval gatehouse fronting on to Goodramgate, and giving access to the obvious remains of Bedern Chapel and the considerably less obvious traces of a medieval stone and timber hall. These three structures were the only survivals from the College of the Vicars Choral of York Minster. The college was established in 1252. The office of Vicar Choral derived from the obligation upon absentee canons to appoint personal deputies to take their place in the choir of York Minster. Throughout the 14th century the college housed 36 vicars but it began to decline from the end of the 15th century. In 1574 the vicars ceased to dine in common, although the college was not formally dissolved until 1936.

An important documentary archive provides evidence for diverse aspects of the college, both as an institution and as a group of men (with, after the Reformation, wives and families) living a communal life (Harrison 1952; Tringham 1993). However, much remained undocumented about the college's topographical and structural development, and about the daily lives of the vicars. In 1968 Lord Esher, in his study, recommended that the existing light industrial usage of the area be replaced by housing. York City Council subsequently purchased land in the Bedern and promulgated redevelopment of the vicinity. It was this which prompted the initiation by York Archaeological Trust of a campaign of excavations which eventually lasted from 1973 to 1980.

The total depth of stratification hereabouts, and the nature of Roman–early Norman occupation and activity, was tested in excavations of a long trench (see below), and beneath some modern cellars (*AY 3/3; AY 14/5*). The upper levels of the long trench contained a sequence of deposits and structures which can often be firmly linked either with those in the area to the north-east occupied by the Vicars Choral or those to the south-west in the area occupied by a foundry. Clay-loam layers dating to the 11th and 12th centuries were seen, however, only in the long trench. Here too was evidence for the robbing of the Roman fortress wall in the 12th century, and for a series of pits, clay floors and other features indicating 12th century occupation (Period 1A).

The largest portion of available resources and effort was devoted to the precinct of the College of the Vicars Choral, as defined on the 1852 Ordnance Survey map of York. In total, an area of 2,500m² was investigated, representing about 30% of the estimated college precinct at its maximum extent. Various parts of the site were designated different area codes (Fig.965). These are used in the catalogue and may be summarised as follows:

Bedern long trench (1973–5.13.III/IV; SE 60545207)
Bedern Foundry (1973–6.13.I/II; SE 60515208)
Bedern Trench V (cellar) (1976.13.V; SE 60545212)
Bedern Trench I (cellar) (1976.14.I; SE 60575216)
Bedern south-west (1976–9.13.X; SE 60535209)
Bedern north-east (1978–9.14.II; SE 60535213)
Bedern north-east (1979–80.14.IV; SE 60555212)
Bedern Hall (1980.13.XV; SE 60525211).

Modern deposits were usually machined off; excavation by hand then continued to a fairly uniform

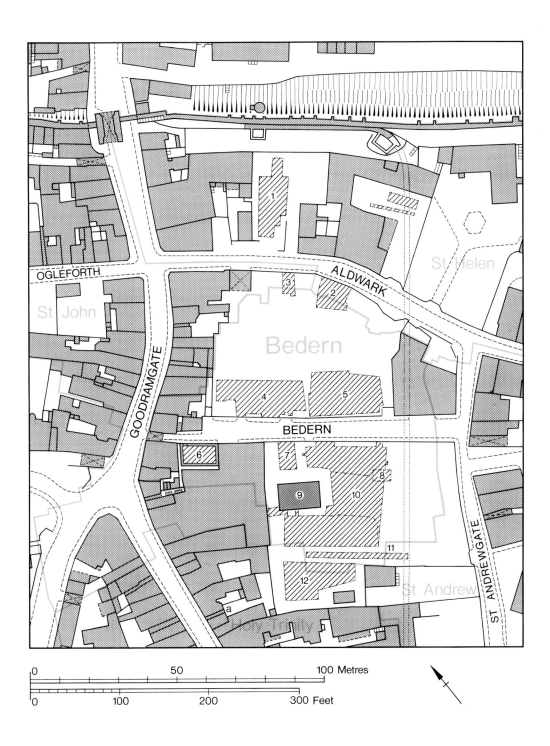

Fig.965 *Plan showing the location of excavations, and building recording, in the Bedern area. The outline of the parish boundaries (in green) defining the precinct of the College of the Vicars Choral is based on the 1852 Ordnance Survey map. (1) 1–5 Aldwark, 1976–7.15; (2) 2 Aldwark, 1978–80.14.III; (3) Cellar, 1976.14.I; (4) Bedern north-east, 1978–9.14.II; (5) Bedern north-east, 1979–80.14.IV; (6) Bedern Chapel, 1980.20.I/II/III; (7) Cellar, 1976.13.V; (8) Cellar, 1976.13.VI; (9) Bedern Hall, 1980.13.XV; (10) Bedern south-west, 1976–9.13.X; (11) Bedern long trench, 1973–5.13.III/IV; (12) Bedern Foundry, 1973–6.13.I/II. (Based upon the 1982 Ordnance Survey 1:1250 National Grid Plans. Reproduced from Ordnance Survey mapping on behalf of Her Majesty's Stationery Office, © Crown copyright. MC 012225.) Scale 1:1250*

Table 193 Summary of phasing at sites within the College of the Vicars Choral at Bedern (including Bedern long trench, Bedern south-west, Bedern north-east)

Note: Periods 6–8 have been sub-divided into phases as follows: Period 6, Phases 1–3; Period 7, Phases 1–4; Period 8, Phases 1–3

Period	Date
Period 0	Roman
Period 1A	11th–12th century (applies only to the long trench)
Period 1	early–mid 13th century
Period 2	mid–late 13th century
Period 3	mid–late 13th century
Period 4	late 13th century
Period 5	early 14th century
Period 6	mid–late 14th century
Period 7	late 14th–early 15th century
Period 8	mid 15th–early 17th century
Period 9	mid 17th century onwards

depth of 1·5m below the modern ground surface. This self-imposed limit was designed to allow the recording of all deposits which would be destroyed by the redevelopment campaign. Fortuitously, this depth of strata encompassed all archaeological remains from the 13th century onwards and thus included the entire span of the archaeological record for the College of the Vicars Choral. Virtually all material was recovered by hand, the excavation pre-dating the introduction of routine riddling/sieving on York sites.

During the first half of the 13th century it appears that the Bedern was subject to light agricultural usage, with a series of drainage gullies and ditches representing property boundaries running back from Goodramgate, and some slight garden structures (Period 1). In the mid 13th century this land was acquired by the college, which erected its first buildings on either side of an open courtyard, running back from Goodramgate, which was to become the Bedern Close. On the north-east side of the close (Areas II and IV; Fig.965, **4**, **5**) a large building — the great hall — was constructed; on the south-west side a stone building and a smaller timber-framed struc-

ture were built (Period 2). As the college expanded the vicars required more accommodation. A second hall was constructed along the south-west side of the close, although this appears to have been short-lived, and a smaller structure was built behind it (Period 3). By the late 13th century (Period 4) there were further buildings at the south-west end of the Bedern. In the early 14th century the chapel was constructed and there were major changes to the buildings on the south-west side of the close (Period 5). In the second half of the 14th century the college reached the peak of its prosperity; the great hall was rebuilt, apparently to provide separate residences; new individual residences were also built on the south-west side of the close (Period 6). There was major building activity throughout the precinct from the late 14th to the early 15th century (Period 7), creating a second courtyard to the south-west, and coinciding with attempts to revive the corporate life of the college. The great hall was now rebuilt in stone, and a new stone-built communal hall was constructed southwest of the close, with adjacent service accommodation, kitchen block, archive room and college gardens. The chapel was enlarged and a number of new houses were built. A bridge may also have been built across Goodramgate at this time. A stone wall now marked the limit of the precinct to the south-east, whilst the south-western development of the college was constrained by the continued presence of a medieval foundry. From the mid 15th to the early 17th century (Period 8) there was less new building work although the existing structures continued to be modified as the vicars increasingly lived elsewhere and sub-let their houses to lay tenants. During the post-medieval period the Bedern became a notorious slum (Period 9).

Analysis of the record of complex floor deposits has shown that there was considerable reworking of many contexts, and much disturbance of earlier layers by subsequent activities. None the less, the development of the buildings — their sub-divisions, rebuildings and renovations — can be clearly traced. Furthermore, they can normally be dated to within 50 years, and sometimes can be equated with building campaigns precisely dated on the basis of documentary evidence. Medieval buildings survived, albeit in increasingly remodelled forms, until the early 17th century. By the mid 17th century, however, many of the medieval buildings had been demolished and replaced.

Some buildings within the college precinct, such as the chapel, continued in collegiate use into the post-medieval period. As the number of vicars in the college shrank, and as the remaining vicars increasingly lived outside the precinct, more buildings in the Bedern were put to secular uses. This post-medieval/early modern stratification was often recorded to different standards from those employed when dealing with the medieval strata, depending upon the nature, integrity and perceived value of the deposits.

Bedern Foundry

An area of medieval and post-medieval industrial activity adjacent to the college precinct was also examined in detail (SE 60515208; *AY* 10/3; Fig.965, **12**), concentrating on a former narrow lane running off Goodramgate. From the mid–late 13th century to the late 15th–early 16th century the site was occupied by a complex of workshops, which were frequently repaired, remodelled or rebuilt. Many of them were associated with walls, pits and hearths. This occupation and activity was separately phased, and was designated Periods 1–5. From Period 2, late 13th–early 14th century onwards, deposits of clay mould fragments and other casting debris were sometimes found. These indicate that founding was carried out, and that the foundry's main products were cauldrons and other domestic vessels. Structures with substantial stone sill walls were erected c.1300 and remained in use throughout the 14th century (Period 3); c.1400 all the buildings in the foundry complex were rebuilt and the alleyway was both extended and linked, via a 90° continuation, to the property of the adjacent College of the Vicars Choral (Period 4). In the later 15th–early 16th century (Period 5) there was another phase of building development; the earlier ground plan was, however, retained. During Period 6 (mid 16th–mid 17th century) metalworking furnaces and hearths were replaced by a series of ovens, and the deposition of foundry waste ceased. Some parts of the complex apparently became derelict, but the remainder functioned as a bakery, a usage attested in the name Baker's Lane. From the mid 17th to the 20th century (Period 7) light industrial usage dominated the area.

Table 194 Summary of phasing at Bedern Foundry

Period	Date range
Period 0	Late 12th–early 13th century
Period 1	Mid–late 13th century
Period 2	Late 13th–early 14th century
Period 3	14th century
Phase 1	Early 14th century
Phase 2	Early–mid 14th century
Phases 3–5	Mid–late 14th century
Phase 6	Late 14th century
Period 4	15th century
Phases 1–2	Early 15th century
Phases 3–4	Early–mid 15th century
Phases 5–9	Mid–late 15th century
Period 5	Late 15th–early 16th century
Phase 1	Late 15th century
Phases 2–4	Late 15th–early 16th century
Period 6	Mid 16th–mid 17th century
Period 7	Mid 17th–20th century

Bedern Foundry has been published in *AY* 10/3. Roman occupation in the Bedern area has been discussed in *AY* 3/3. The coins have been published in *AY* 18/1; the pottery will be published in *AY* 16. The considerable number of re-used architectural fragments from the excavations have been published in *AY* 10/4 and the structural report for the site will be published in *AY* 10/5 forthcoming. Historical research on the tenemental history of the Bedern area will be published in *AY* 20.

Introduction to the Wooden Material

This work is the definitive study of over 1,500 wooden objects, and woodworking tools of both wood and iron, recovered from 16–22 Coppergate and the subsequent watching brief at the Coppergate development site, from 22 Piccadilly and from the Foundry and College of the Vicars Choral sites at Bedern. An iron socketed tool found in 1906 on a site at the corner of Coppergate and Castlegate has also been included (9183) since it was identified by the author as a lathe-turner's hook-ended tool, and is not only an extremely rare find but also valuable evidence for the study of woodworking in Coppergate. This report deals mainly with small portable domestic and utilitarian artefacts and the waste products of their manufacture. The artefacts are either those produced by woodworking craftsmen who specialised in object production and sale, or those which were home-made for domestic use. It does not include larger structural timbers from buildings or other large-scale wooden features, which will be published in *AY* 8/4 and *AY* 10/6, but these should be considered alongside the material published here to obtain a more complete view of the woodworking craftsmen of Anglo-Scandinavian and medieval York, their materials and level of technology. Some accessories of buildings such as panels, door fastening mechanisms, shingles and window openings are included here because they have been found singly on the York sites, unassociated with a particular building or structure.

The wooden finds range in date from Anglo-Scandinavian (c.850–1066) to later medieval (15th–16th century), together with a handful of post-medieval objects. Although wooden objects have been found in small quantities at other sites in York (see Benson 1906; Richardson 1959; Waterman 1959; Wenham 1972; *AY* 17/3; *AY* 17/4), those found at 16–22 Coppergate form an unprecedented collection, not only from York but from any site at any period in Britain. In the British Isles, contemporary wooden finds in the same quantity and of similar quality have only been found in Dublin, another thriving Viking Age city, but only a very small number of these have ever been published (e.g. Lang 1988). The author has examined many of the Dublin wooden artefacts and has discussed some of them elsewhere (Morris 1984), but in this fascicule, wherever possible, they are compared and contrasted with those from Anglo-Scandinavian York. Similar comparisons have been made with wooden artefacts from other major British sites where smaller amounts of waterlogged wood have been preserved, such as London, Winchester, Perth, Beverley, Hull, King's Lynn, Gloucester and Exeter, and Lissue, Lagore, Ballinderry and Cork in Ireland (Fig.966). The author's unpublished Ph.D. thesis (ibid.) contains an exhaustive corpus of wooden material excavated from British archaeological sites before 1984 dating from AD 400–1500 and much of that material has been used in this report.

Fig.966 (facing) *Map of Britain and Ireland showing the main sites referred to in the text*

1. The Biggings, Papa Stour, Shetland
2. Birsay, Orkney
3. Perth
4. Carlisle
5. Durham
6. York
7. Beverley
8. Hull
9. Meols
10. Norton Priory, Runcorn
11. Nantwich
12. Tong
13. Shackerley Mound
14. Weoley Castle
15. Leicester
16. King's Lynn
17. North Elmham
18. Norwich
19. Thetford
20. Sutton Hoo
21. Ipswich
22. Waltham Abbey
23. London
24. Oxford
25. Shakenoak
26. Gloucester
27. Winchester
28. Pevensey
29. Portchester Castle
30. Southampton
31. Exeter
32. Lissue
33. Lagore
34. Dublin
35. Ballinderry
36. Cork

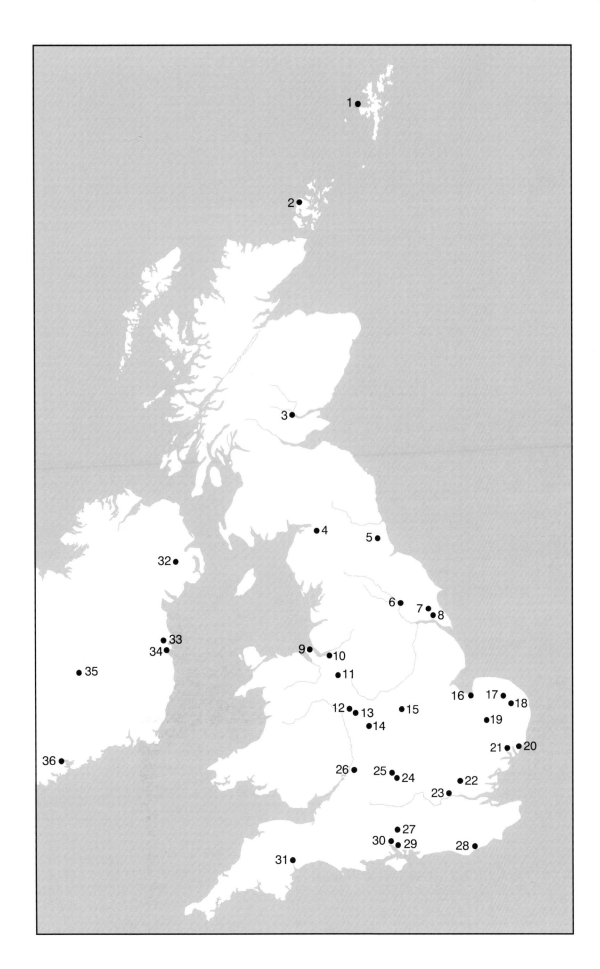

Fig.967   Complete bucket 8742 inside cask 8766 during excavation at 16–22 Coppergate. Scale unit 10cm

Similar comparisons and syntheses have been made by studying the York wooden artefacts in relation to those excavated from the major trading centres of north-west Europe where wood has survived in any quantity, most of which would have had trading contacts with York at this time. Viking period and medieval sites such as Hedeby and Lübeck in Germany; Trondheim, Oslo and Bergen in Norway; Lund and Birka in Sweden; and Novgorod in Russia have produced many artefacts which have been included here (Fig.968). Although most of the research for this report was completed by the author in 1993, she has examined much wooden material excavated since this time and, where relevant, has included some of it in the discussion of the York material.

In York, wooden objects represent a broad spectrum of life and occupations, showing that there were few domestic, craft, leisure, personal or constructional activities which did not involve the use of small woodwork in some way. The wooden objects and woodworking tools found on the six sites are used to illustrate wood technology, and the management of wood as an essential and versatile raw material used by different woodworking crafts from the 9th century onwards in York.

16–22 Coppergate has produced many types of wooden workshop waste from the lathe-turning craft which made bowls and cups for domestic use. Nearly half of the wooden finds from the site were waste

Conservation of the Wooden Artefacts

By James A. Spriggs

Introduction

The sites considered in this work have in common the presence of deeply stratified highly organic waterlogged anoxic deposits which produced, in all, over 1,500 recorded wooden artefacts. These finds varied greatly in their method of production, original purpose, size, wood species and condition prior to deposition. Extended periods of burial left the material in a soft and much weakened state, typified by reduced cellulose content and elevated water content. This is mainly caused by the aqueous hydrolysis of the more soluble components of the wood cell structure, often exacerbated by fungal and bacterial action early in the post-deposition period (Blanchette and Hoffmann 1993, 111). Many of the indigenous wood species such as alder, willow, hazel, field maple and ash are represented in the collection, most of which degrade in a similar way and to a similar extent to each other; all were recovered heavily degraded, water-swollen and in a fragile state. Only those objects made from yew (*Taxus* spp.), oak (*Quercus* spp.) and box (*Buxus* spp.) can be singled out as being considerably better preserved. Despite the extent of degradation in many of the objects, surface details such as tool marks, decoration, graffiti, and signs of use and wear, were all preserved to a remarkable degree.

On-site retrieval

The extreme fragility of much of this material, and the damage caused by drying during and immediately after excavation, required a series of protocols to be established and followed by the excavation team, finds staff and others who would be handling the wood (Clarke 1976). Conservation staff were continually called out to assist with the lifting and 'First Aid' treatment of wooden finds, and establishing storage systems for the many objects, while they were still wet (Spriggs 1980).

Amongst the more complex artefact types encountered were the medieval barrel-lined wells which, being large composite objects, required special excavation, recording and lifting procedures. Three of these structures were found on the sites in question (*8763, 8765* and *8767* from 16–22 Coppergate; *9190–2* from 22 Piccadilly; *9214–16* from Bedern Foundry) and all were lifted for recording and eventual conservation. In each case, the barrels were emptied of their fills, and the staves dismantled from the inside; they were labelled sequentially on the inside surface of the upper ends as they were removed so that their correct order and orientation could be maintained. The withy hoops remained behind, embedded in the surrounding matrix; being extremely soft and fragile they could only be extracted in fragments after having been recorded and labelled in situ.

An attempt was made to retrieve a set of 38 hoops together as a single unit. These belonged to barrel *8766* which was emptied of its fill, and the 20 staves labelled and removed from the inside in the normal way. The intention was to conserve the split hazel hoops intact, prior to rebuilding the barrel with the staves, conserved separately, from the inside. Once the staves had been removed from the interior in the normal manner, the inside space was insulated and packed out with liquid expanding polyurethane foam (Jones 1980). The outside of the barrel with the split hazel bindings was excavated bit by bit, and the exposed bindings were bound with gauze bandage to secure them to the foam core. The intention was to lift the bindings in sections by slicing through the foam core horizontally where there were convenient spaces between the bindings. The operation had to be abandoned, however, when heavy rain flooded the site, and the buoyancy of the foam core caused major disruption to the fragile bindings.

Temporary storage

Pending conservation, wooden objects were stored wet, wrapped in a double layer of plastic with surplus water and kept in plastic boxes in a cool, dark store. Larger items were immersed in polythene-lined tanks, built for the purpose (Spriggs 1980, 21). Since much of the waterlogged material had to be stored for several years prior to conservation, the use of biocides was routine, orthophenyl phenol ('Topane') and a dichlorophen ('Panacide') being the two in most regular use. Staff were aware of the potential hazards of these materials, and wore protective clothing, especially gloves, to handle both the chemicals and the objects.

Attention was paid to the need to use the most weatherproof, non-fading and water-resistant labelling which would survive in these wet conditions over extended periods, tests being carried out, for example, on the best types of marker pens (Jones, Jones and Spriggs 1980).

Conservation

Although the study of the Coppergate collections for publication was clearly a long way in the future, there were pressing reasons for conserving at least a selection of the more spectacular finds soon after excavation. The high public profile of the excavations required material to be on hand for media occasions, temporary exhibitions and, ultimately, for the Jorvik Viking Centre and Yorkshire Museum displays. There was also the fear that material might suffer if kept wet in store for too long. Conservation therefore commenced soon after the start of the excavations, albeit in a somewhat ad hoc manner.

Constraints of space and conservation facilities at the first laboratory of the York Archaeological Trust (YAT) in St Mary's Gatehouse made this work difficult. Adequate facilities were only available with the move to new laboratory premises in Galmanhoe Lane in 1981, by which time much of the waterlogged material from Coppergate had already been in temporary storage for several years. These laboratory premises were fitted out and equipped specifically to deal with the product of the Coppergate and contemporary excavations, one building being dedicated to the conservation of wood and other waterlogged materials (Spriggs 1982) (Fig.969).

By the mid 1970s, conservation staff at YAT had experience of stabilising small wooden items, as well as other waterlogged material such as leather, using techniques currently in vogue. The principal aims were to remove the water from the degraded wood structure whilst maintaining dimensional stability and, above all, surface detail. The consolidation of the fragile wood structure was also considered an important feature of any treatment, to ensure that the object was robust enough to be stored and handled safely. The appearance of the wood was another

major consideration, as it was assumed that much of this material would be required for display as well as for study. The removal of ingrained silt and occasionally concretions necessitated the use of acids and chelating agents which also had the effect of lightening the colour of the wood. The final concern was to ensure that the collection would remain stable, and not suffer damage from fluctuating environmental conditions in essentially uncontrolled stores. The three main techniques used, discussed below, seemed to fulfil these criteria.

Stabilisation techniques

Impregnation with hot polyethylene glycol polymer (p.e.g.), adapted as necessary from the traditional form of application (Organ 1959), was the technique most commonly used in the United Kingdom prior to the mid 1970s. At YAT, the process was first applied in a laboratory drying oven, the maximum length of wood treated in this way being limited to c.0·5m. After the move to the Galmanhoe Lane premises, some of the larger artefacts, particularly the oak elements of the larger stave-built vessels, were tank treated in hot p.e.g., along with the structural timbers from Coppergate (Spriggs 1982) (Fig.969).

A second treatment extensively used at the YAT laboratories was the 'acetone/rosin' method. In its classic form (McKerrel et al. 1972) it was only suitable for small items up to 200mm in length owing to safety and other practical considerations. Special equipment was designed and commissioned by YAT conservators to overcome some of the hazards associated with the technique.

By 1978, batches of wooden objects were being sent to Bradford University to be freeze-dried (Ambrose 1971). Two years later, YAT had its own freeze-drying unit, with a 0·75m long chamber which further extended the size and volume of material that could be treated (Fig.970).

Each of the three stabilisation processes had its own particular advantages and limitations, but the decision as to which should be used on any occasion was determined by the requirements of the individual object.

The hot p.e.g. technique was applied almost exclusively to objects made of oak and the results were satisfactory, with only one or two exceptions. The technique appeared to have a successful stabilising effect on the wood, once all the water had been replaced with the polymer. The dark colour imparted by the waxy p.e.g. polymer was not considered seriously to detract from the appearance of the wood surface as waterlogged oak is normally already black in colour. The type of objects most commonly made from oak, such as stave-built vessel fragments, seldom bore much surface detail that might suffer from the wiping away of excess polymer from the surface. Requiring little equipment and being relatively safe and simple to apply, the technique lent itself to the treatment of slightly larger objects than would otherwise be possible, spades and staves for example. The hot p.e.g. technique proved particularly suitable in

Fig.969   *Plan of the wet wood laboratory, fitted out in 1981 to provide necessary access, space and facilities for the conservation of waterlogged organic archaeological materials. The laboratory was equipped with lifting and handling facilities for the larger items; storage for materials, equipment and artefacts awaiting treatment; good plumbing and drainage for washing and sieving; and ample electrical installations for the heated p.e.g. tanks and other equipment. An analytical laboratory was provided for detailed recording, the microscopic examination of samples, and to house the freeze-dryer. Lagged and heated tanks of two sizes were constructed for the treatment of wood with p.e.g.*

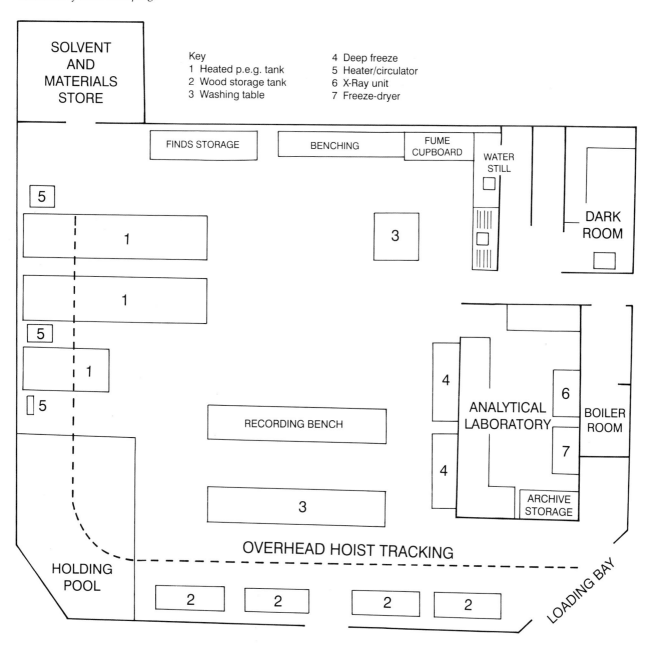

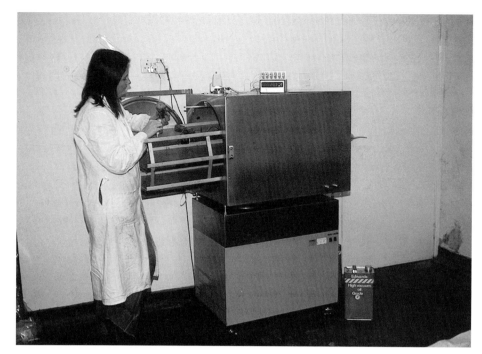

Fig.970 The Heto CD12 freeze-dryer in use for the sublimation of water from small wooden artefacts. The chamber is shown with the sliding rack unit extended for trays of finds to be loaded. The base unit contains the vacuum pump and a water vapour condenser with a working capacity of 6 litres of ice. A multi-channel electronic thermometer (visible on top of the chamber) is used to monitor the progress of freeze-drying via needle probes inserted into sample objects.

the case of a box lid of woven willow rods (*8931*) that was lifted intact from site (Fig.971), but was badly distorted due to uneven compaction in the surrounding burial matrix. After treatment it was possible to resoften the wax in the basketry by warming and to flatten the lid gradually through the application of even pressure from above. Once the facilities became available, most of the smaller oak artefacts were treated by freeze-drying (see below).

The acetone/rosin treatment was in regular use throughout the period that these wood collections were being conserved. Despite the high cost of the colophony rosin and solvent, and the hazards associated with handling and heating the rosin/solvent mix, the results of the treatment were considered highly satisfactory. Until the advent of freeze-drying, it was used as the alternative to the hot p.e.g. process. It lent itself particularly to the treatment of the many fragile objects, such as bowl fragments, combs, barrel hoops and bentwood objects such as the decorated box (*8935*) recovered during these excavations. Colophony rosin provides considerable consolidation to a fragile wood structure and renders the objects hard but somewhat brittle. Being pale in colour, the rosin imparts a light slightly glossy appearance to a degraded wood surface which is visually pleasing, the lightness in colour

of the wood often assisted by the bleaching effect of the acid pre-treatment. The consolidatory effect of the rosin on the broken edges of fragmentary objects such as the many cups and bowls in the collection assisted greatly with their reconstruction.

The process also lent itself to the stabilisation of composite objects which could not be dismantled. The discovery of a complete iron-bound bucket (*8742*; Figs.1066–7, p.2225) precipitated the need to design a special gas-tight stainless steel container in which to apply the acetone/rosin treatment to such a large object. The equipment was subsequently adapted to take a number of smaller items by providing tiered stainless steel shelving that could be inserted into the container. The bucket stave with hoops and dome-topped iron studs (*3033*) and the iron knives with wooden handles (e.g. *2812, 2898, 2938*) were successfully treated this way, the solvent-based treatment system and non-hygroscopic rosin being sympathetic with the needs of the iron components.

Despite the advantages of the acetone/rosin treatment, it has seldom been used in the YAT laboratories since 1988 on safety grounds. There is, additionally, some question as to the long-term stability of the treatment (Esteban et al. 1998).

Fig.971 Box lid 8931 *in situ before being lifted intact. Scale unit 1cm*

In 1979 a freeze-drying unit was acquired (Fig.970). Freeze-drying is the final part of a multi-stage treatment which offers considerable flexibility to suit a broad range of object types and conditions. Apart from the initial capital expense of the equipment, a treatment regime based on freeze-drying is low-cost in terms of materials and ancillary equipment and, above all, is low-risk as no solvents are used. As the quantity of p.e.g. polymer required to stabilise the wood can be relatively small, the result of the treatment is sometimes very different from that produced by the previous two treatments described. The wood tends to be light in weight, normally light in colour (unless it is oak), and the surface can look rather porous and dry. Despite the advantages of fine preservation of form, detail and colour, freeze-dried wood can often be extremely fragile. Post freeze-drying, surface consolidation with a high molecular weight p.e.g. polymer was often necessary to provide a little extra strength and to enhance the surface appearance for display purposes. Ultimately, over two-thirds of the wooden artefacts from the sites under consideration in this report were stabilised by freeze-drying, particularly good results being obtained with the 301 examples of centre waste from turning cups and bowls, and individual items such as the boxwood syrinx (*9038*), the inlaid oak saddle bow (*9020*), and the large poplar trough (*8915*).

Prior to 1989 many wooden objects had been treated by acetone/rosin, but after that date the majority were freeze-dried. Only composite objects of wood and iron continued to be treated by the acetone/rosin method. This was because the p.e.g. polymer involved in freeze-drying is not compatible with moisture-sensitive archaeological ironwork. Freeze-dried wood of non-oak species tends to be physically fragile and requires careful handling and a high standard of packaging, but the p.e.g. polymer it contains makes it environmentally stable in the conditions normally prescribed for an archaeological store (Anon. 1984).

Reconstruction

In many instances, wooden objects recovered in fragments required adhering so that the original shape of the object could be reconstructed. This was particularly so in the case of the many turned wooden vessels which, being thin-walled, were prone to crushing once buried. It was found that the all-purpose cellulose nitrate adhesive 'HMG' was perfectly adequate, and many early reconstructions using this adhesive have withstood the test of time. Some objects to be joined required extra support. Wooden dowelling was used to bridge the two halves of the wooden forked tool (*8970*) and a filled epoxy resin 'Plamur C' (Spriggs 1991) was used to fix the join. This same adhesive was used to fix the various fragments of the sluice (*9061*), which was also reinforced with brass dowelling and gapfilled with 'Bondafiller SL' (Spriggs 1981), a microsphere-filled polyester paste (Fig.972). Other fillers, such as 'AJK dough' (Plenderleith and Werner 1971, 341), were used to make up missing areas and fill cracks as the nature and condition of the individual object dictated.

Special mounts and storage boxes were provided for the support and protection of many of the more fragile items, such as the decorated composite box-lids *6964* and *8930*. The mounts for these two items were fabricated from perspex, designed to allow the objects to be displayed.

Packaging

The post-conservation packaging and storage of artefacts from these excavations varied over the years, as budgets and attitudes dictated. Much of the early packaging was both inadequate and badly maintained, so in 1995 a major repackaging pro-

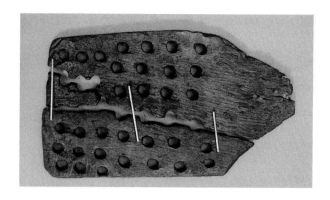

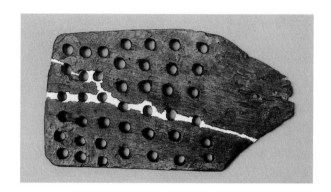

Fig.972 *Sluice* 9061 *before and after gapfilling. Actual length 480mm*

gramme became necessary to bring the whole wood artefact collection, and its supporting records, up to the same standard. Remedial conservation was carried out on the few items that had suffered damage in the intervening years, and every object was provided with the necessary level of support, padding and protection, labelling and documentation. This major collection of ancient wood artefacts is now in an optimum state for long-term storage for future generations to research and admire.

Acknowledgements

Credit is due to Conservation staff, students and volunteers who, over the years, assisted with the immense task of conserving these collections. Particular thanks are due to Julie Jones for her considerable contribution to the work, and to Dr Allan Hall for undertaking the many wood species identifications.

Craft and Industry

Woodland Exploitation, Woodworking Tools and Techniques

Wood was an essential and versatile raw material for Anglo-Scandinavian and medieval York. The study and interpretation of over 1,500 wooden objects found during excavations at 16–22 Coppergate, the Coppergate watching brief, 22 Piccadilly and the Foundry and Vicars Choral College sites at Bedern are vital to our understanding of the technology and resources used from the 9th century onwards in York to convert and shape timber from living trees to finished artefacts. Woodworking was arguably the most important Anglo-Scandinavian and medieval craft in York, including many individual specialist trades, and was responsible for the vast majority of structures, vehicles and portable domestic objects. This fascicule is concerned with the latter.

Wooden artefact production can be seen as a two-stage process involving woodland management to provide correct sizes and species of raw material, and then conversion from tree to object using various types of woodworking tools and techniques.

Woodland management

Craftsmen had strong preferences for particular sizes, species and forms of wood/timber. There was conscious selection, and each craft exploited the properties of different types to enable its finished products to satisfy the demands placed upon them. Woodworking crafts, therefore, are inevitably linked at any period with the history of woodland exploitation and management. It is important to view woodland as an owned and managed resource.

Wood and timber

To craftsmen, wood and timber are different types of material and the distinction is practical since each is the product of different exploitation methods. Timber can be used for large beams and planks for structural work and is usually obtained by felling individual trees; wood is smaller in size at less than 600mm in girth or about 280mm diameter (Rackham 1976, 23), provides roundwood, boards, poles, rods, blocks and billets for small artefact crafts, and is normally produced by coppicing and pollarding. Crafts-

men making small artefacts need constant supplies of material and this allows wood to be replenished without woodland or forest being destroyed.

The various methods of producing different types of underwood and timber are described elsewhere (Rackham 1976, 20–2; 1980, 3–5). Woodland management would have varied from owner to owner and through time, but trees to supply the right size of material could have been produced in various ways. Small timber or standard trees were allowed to grow individually in plantations or among underwood coppice. Coppice trees were sometimes allowed to stand for several rotations before being felled to provide larger material (Rackham 1980, 3). Documents rarely give information about the sizes of trees used (ibid., 145) and it is the wooden artefacts themselves which show that craftsmen were not only selecting particular species, but also sizes and forms of wood.

Size and age of roundwood are important for the study of exploitation and some of the artefacts themselves give clues as to the size of roundwood used to make them. To give some examples, 90% of the lathe-turned vessels found at Coppergate were made from roundwood measuring 260mm in diameter or less (Rackham's 'underwood'), but vessels such as *8583* had required alder up to 360mm in diameter. Alder roundwood less than 160mm diameter was used to make bracket *9052*; poplar roundwood over 400mm in diameter was used to make trough *8915*; boxwood roundwood at least 170mm in diameter had been used to make syrinx *9038*, and over 120mm in diameter to make bowl *8578*. The age at which wood was cut down was related to the size needed, and medieval coppice cycles varied enormously (Rackham 1980, 139–40, figs.10.2 and 10.3). Size of roundwood relative to age can also be influenced by the speed of growth. Many of the oak, ash and maple objects found at Coppergate have measurable ring growth which can give a rough guide as to whether the tree was relatively fast- or slow-grown. For example, ash tool handle *8989* has less than two rings per 10mm, oak cant stave *8770* and ash hoop *8852* had only two rings per 10mm, oak box base *8934*, ash frame/rack *9057* and maple turned lid *8638* had three rings per

10mm, oak churn dash *8919* had between four and five rings per 10mm, oak stool seat *8947* had five rings per 10mm and oak wedge *8175* had eight rings per 10mm. These were made from young fast-grown trees. In contrast, oak offcut *8667* had 20 rings per 10mm, oak lid *8867* had 25 rings per 10mm and perforated oak block *9131* had 43 rings per 10mm. These were made from trees which had grown slowly. Ash bowl *8606* was made from roundwood 180mm diameter, probably 100 years old. Eighty growth rings over 60mm show that the tree enjoyed relatively fast growth to begin with (10 rings over 20mm), then it slowed down considerably over its later years (70 rings over 40mm).

Selection of species

Certain use-groups of species can be derived from the artefacts showing the distinct preferences of craftsmen making different items, for example alder, ash and field maple for turning wooden vessels. Species selection is described in the relevant artefact sections below.

Forms of wood/timber

Three forms of wood were selected to make artefacts: naturally occurring forms, roundwood and splitwood. Naturally occurring forms such as branch junctions were often selected for their curvature and strength. Oak bracket *9049*, maple bracket *9047* and possible rake handle *8694* were made from such pieces. Roundwood trunks and branches were sometimes used without splitting. Large cylindrical vessel *8923* and bucket *8924* were hollowed from a single large roundwood length of poplar 590mm diameter and a length of alder, willow or hazel 304mm diameter respectively; unfinished pin *8952* was made from a small yew branch; flax pounders *6642* and *6643* were carved from lengths of willow and alder roundwood respectively; mattock head *8974* was made from a length of ash roundwood squared off along two edges; gaming pieces *9033* and *9037*, and spindle-turned objects such as bowling ball *9041*, vessel roughouts *8196–8*, and unfinished and finished cups *8200–2* and *8613–37* were made from various sizes and species of roundwood. Roundwood rods were used to make ladder rungs *8983* and heddle rod *6655*, and smaller coppiced roundwood rods were used for basketry items such as *8909–13*.

Most wooden objects, however, were made of splitwood which had been radially or tangentially converted. Face-turned vessels such as *8534–5, 8537– 60, 8563, 8566–9, 8571–7, 8579–610* and *8612*, rake head *8977*, ladder uprights *8980–1* and troughs *8915– 17* were made from split half-sections. Small cleft, wedge-shaped sections and billets were used for items such as spoons *8895–9* and *9174*, spatulae *8902– 5*, mattock and rake heads *8972–3, 8975–6* and *8978– 9*, and pegs *9067–9* and *9072*. Scutching knife *6644*, pot-lids *8878–89*, basket bases *8907–8* and *8914*, garderobe seats *8949–50* and *9176*, combs *8961–2*, all the staves from stave-built vessels, and shovels and spades *8964–9* are examples of objects made from narrower boards, while very thin split laths were used for lath-walled boxes *8935–6* and split sections of rods were used for stave-built vessel hoops *8850– 65*.

Conversion

Conversion is one of the most important features to identify on any artefact; it involves woodworking tools and techniques which varied through time and were linked to the technological development of the society which made the artefact.

Primary and secondary conversion

Fig.973 shows examples of cross-section drawings of different types of primary and secondary conversion from tree trunk to shapes of wood used for various artefacts. This could have been done by radial splitting (Fig.973a), or tangentially by splitting or sawing (Fig.973b). The terminology described here has been used throughout this fascicule and in the catalogue, and alternative descriptive terms are given in brackets to allow the Coppergate pieces to be compared with those in other publications using slightly different terms.

In the primary conversion by radial splitting, roundwood or whole stem can be made into half-section (halved), quarter-section (quartered), or radially split section (radially faced). In the secondary conversion, roundwood can be squared (boxed heart), and sections made into squared halves (boxed halves), squared quarters (boxed quarters) or squared sections, or they can be irregularly shaped depending on the intended outline of the artefact.

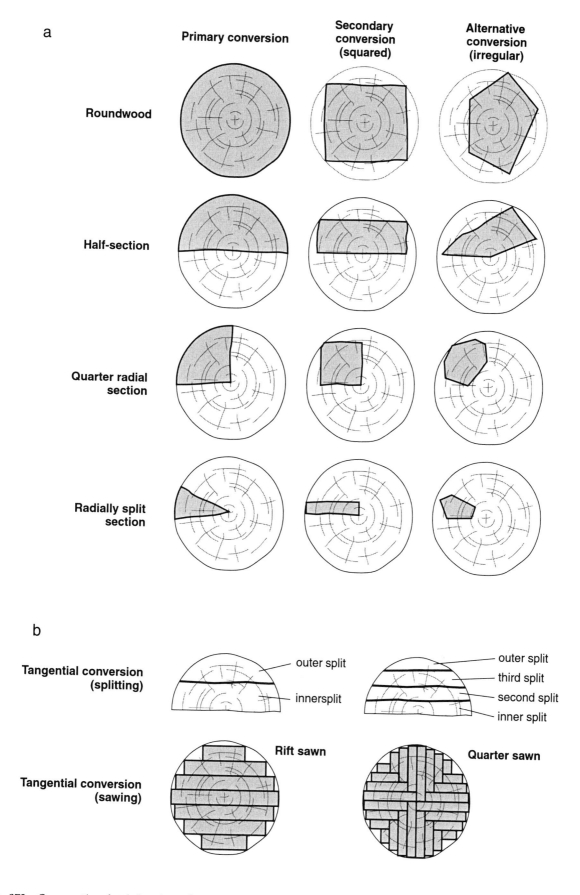

Fig.973 *Cross-section sketch drawings of primary and secondary conversion of wood: (a) radial; (b) tangential*

Tangential conversion by splitting usually involves splitting the roundwood first in half, then each half into two sections, then each section into two again, and so on, across the grain. Tangential conversion by sawing is usually in parallel sections across the roundwood (rift sawing) or by quarter sawing.

Most conversion of wood for artefacts was done by radial splitting, but some objects from Coppergate were made from tangentially converted pieces, showing that this technique was practised in York from the very earliest Anglo-Scandinavian settlement on the site (Period 3) right through to Period 6, using various species of wood. The objects include items of oak (garderobe lid *8951*, wedge *8175*, sluice *9061*, shovel *8968*, stool seat *8948*, block *9143* and base *8790*), hazel (roperunner *9024*), ash (object *9142*, lathwalled box *8936*, spatula *8905*), willow (strips *9141*), pine (stave *8730*, base *8771*), alder (bread peel *8922*), boxwood (comb *8961*), birch (bracket *9046*), Pomoideae (block *8646*) and yew (staves *8727*, *8732*, *8735* and disc *9140*).

Tools

Each stage of conversion can involve a different set of woodworking techniques and hence a variety of tools, some of which have been found on the Coppergate sites. Most are metal tools, but some (e.g. *8173–88*) are themselves made of wood. The Anglo-Scandinavian iron tools have been discussed in relation to metalworking in *AY* 17/6 (pp.527–37). All the Anglo-Scandinavian and medieval woodworking tools found are discussed below in relation to the various conversion techniques in which they were used.

The quality of the bladed tools available to Anglo-Scandinavian and medieval woodworkers in York must have been determined by contemporary levels of ironworking, but the actual tools found cannot be taken to represent the whole range used, as some of them would have been specialised and probably costly to make, and consequently rare. The evidence for the use of certain types of tools which have not been found on the site can be seen in tool marks on some of the wooden artefacts. Wooden wedge *8185* has the characteristic chatter marks made by a drawknife (see Fig.976, p.2107), weaving comb *9179* has the marks of a saw with set teeth, and pine panel

9062 has a tripartite outline made by a moulding iron (see Fig.1174, p.2373). Hammers, possibly claw hammers, would also have been required for driving iron nails into wooden objects such as box lid *8930*, stave *3033* and bucket *8742*.

Woodworking tools are usually of two types: all-purpose tools in a general woodworking kit, and very individual tools made for and used by perhaps only a single craft such as *9183* for lathe-turning (Fig.1014, p.2163) or *2259* for coopering (Fig.982, p.2114). All-purpose tools such as the axe, chisel, mallet, auger, and perhaps the adze and the billhook, were used in many different ways by the layman and the specialist. Also, since the constant sharpness of the cutting edge is the most important feature of a woodworking tool, a whetstone (or other sharpening implement) was the woodworker's most vital accessory. Whetstones of all kinds have been found on the Coppergate sites (*AY* 17/14), and although individual finds cannot be ascribed definitely to a woodworking use, they must be considered in terms of this craft as well as for their petrology, shape and usefulness for sharpening domestic knives.

Felling and splitting

Axes and wedges for felling, hewing and splitting would have been used by all woodworking craftsmen to prepare suitable pieces of wood for use in both building trades and the crafts which made small domestic objects. Although there is some evidence for the use of hand saws on some of the York pieces (e.g. weaving comb *9179*, lid *8930*, syrinx *9038*, combs *8961–2* and frame/rack *9057*), there is little convincing evidence among surviving tools and documentary references that trees were regularly sawn down or wood sawn into planks and boards until the later medieval period in Britain.

Axes (Figs.974a and 975)

The axe has always been the woodworker's basic tool, and a master craftsman could fell a tree, split sections of roundwood, roughly shape pieces of timber and smooth planks by using only an axe. Felling and shaping were usually done with different types of axe.

2253 is probably a general-purpose woodworking axe and *2255* is part of the blade edge of a felling

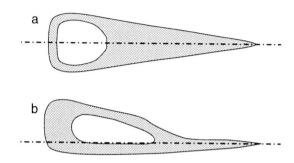

Fig.974 *Longitudinal cross-sections of axes for (a) felling, (b) shaping*

axe. Both are Anglo-Scandinavian in date. The most important features of a felling and hewing axe is its weight and a double-bevelled cutting edge. Felling axes also normally have a fairly straight blade which is symmetrical and thick in cross-section (Fig.974a); profile shape is less important. Darrah considers that such an axe weighing 2kg would be a light axe (1982, 220), most useful for felling and for cutting joints. Although both are incomplete, 2253 and 2255 would fall within this category. Axes with a narrow, thick blade like 2255 have been found at two other sites in York — in the Coppergate 'A' deposit excavated by Benson and probably dating to the 10th century (Benson 1906, 73, pl.III), and in an 11th century context at Baile Hill (Addyman and Priestley 1977, 139, fig.10, 5). Two other similar axes found in Ipswich,

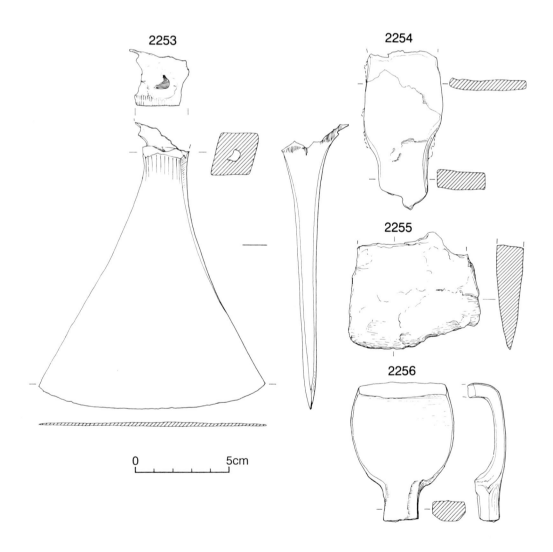

Fig.975 *Iron axes from 16–22 Coppergate: 2253 and 2255 were probably used for felling, 2254 and 2256 for shaping. Scale 1:2*

2105

Suffolk, are probably 9th–11th century in date (unpublished, Ipswich Museum R1938.80). Other thick-bladed, double-bevelled felling axes of a similar date, with blades symmetrical about the longitudinal plane, have been found at Exeter, Devon (Goodall 1984b, fig.189, 1), in the Hurbuck hoard, Co. Durham (Wilson 1976, fig.6.1a), in the Nazeing hoard, Essex (Morris 1983b, fig.1b), at North Elmham, Norfolk (Goodall 1980, fig.266, 49), Thetford, Norfolk (Goodall 1984a, fig.117, 12), and Underhoull, Shetland (Small 1964–6, fig.11).

If present, another noticeable feature of this sort of axe would be the length of its handle. A felling axe needs a long handle to facilitate the swing, absorb the impact shock and provide a distance between the worker and tree. The axe illustrated by Darrah (1982, fig.12.7) has a handle 0·9m long. By comparison, the complete oak handle of the 11th–early 12th century T-shaped axe from Milk Street, London (Pritchard 1991, fig.3.14), is only 420mm long. This is definitely a shaping axe not a felling tool, and shows that the length of the handle, if it survives, can be an indicator of the major use of an axe rather than just a study of the general morphology of the head.

Wedges (Fig.976)

Wood, especially unseasoned oak, from which many objects were made, can be split easily along the principal planes of weakness which follow the medullary rays, that is, radial splitting (Edlin 1949, pls.91–2; Darrah 1982, 220), or by splitting tangentially across the grain. Splits are normally started by driving seasoned oak wedges into the side of the trunk near one end, and continued by driving wedges in further along (ibid., 221). In radial splitting, half-sections are then split into quarter-sections, quarters into eighths and so on, using wedges (see Fig.973a). In tangential conversion, half-sections can be split into an outer and inner split, then each of these is split again (see Fig.973b). Thick-bladed axes with sturdy butts could also have been used as wedges for splitting, and some axes are found with their butts heavily burred or crushed by hammering. Neither 2253 nor 2255 has a surviving butt end which could have indicated if they had been used for splitting. However, some of the thirteen wooden wedges (8173–85) and four iron wedges (2257 and 8170–2) found at 16–22 Coppergate could have been used for splitting wood.

All thirteen wooden wedges are identifiable as oak, the species usually selected for wood-splitting wedges because of its durability and strength, and all of them are Anglo-Scandinavian in date. 8173–4, 8178–9 and 8183–5 were themselves made from radially split oak sections (cf. Darrah 1982, figs.12.1–2); 8175 is unusual since it is made from a tangentially split piece. 8183 and 8185 have rounded tips, whereas 8178–9 and 8184 have facet cuts from one side to the tip as seen in profile. 8174 and 8185 have compression damage (ibid., fig.12.4). All the iron wedges 2257 and 8170–2 have burred heads damaged by hammering. Only 2257 is Anglo-Scandinavian; the other three iron wedges date from Period 6.

Wooden and iron wedges to compare with those from Coppergate have been found at various sites. Wooden wedges were found at 6–8 Pavement, York (Fig.77, 484–6, AY 17/3), in mid 6th–mid 9th century layers at Ballinderry Crannog 2, Co. Westmeath (Hencken 1942, 60, fig.26, W9), at the bottom of a 9th century well at North Elmham (Wade-Martins 1980, fig.108, 19–20), in a late 11th century deposit at New Fresh Wharf in London (Pritchard and Morris 1991, fig.3.130, 384) and at Århus in Denmark (Andersen et al. 1971, 155, EVQ). Iron examples include a 6th century wedge from grave 233 at Sarre in Kent (Wilson 1968, fig.2f), three 10th–11th century ones from Christchurch Place in Dublin, Ireland (Morris 1984a, W104), an early–mid 9th century iron wedge from St Aldates, Oxford (Goodall 1977, 142), two possibly Anglo-Saxon wedges from Stanton Chair in Suffolk (Morris 1984a, fig.163, W108), a small iron wedge dated to c.1090–3 from Winchester Cathedral Green, Hampshire (Goodall 1990, fig.60, 405), and another from grave 968 at Birka in Sweden (Arbman 1940a, Taf.185, 14).

The size of the wedge may have been determined by the species and size of timber to be split. Small wedges such as 2257, 8171 and 8173–4 could have been used to split small boards or staves, the larger ones such as 8175, 8179, 8183 and 8185 to split small tree trunks into sections. Some small wedges were used to split the top of a tool handle and secure the tool head, and others were used to widen the ends of trenails and pegs (e.g. 8944, 9067 and 9069). Wooden wedges are very efficient and, since iron wedges were probably more expensive to produce, they may have been considered unnecessary by Anglo-Scandinavian woodworkers for most splitting tasks. All of the iron

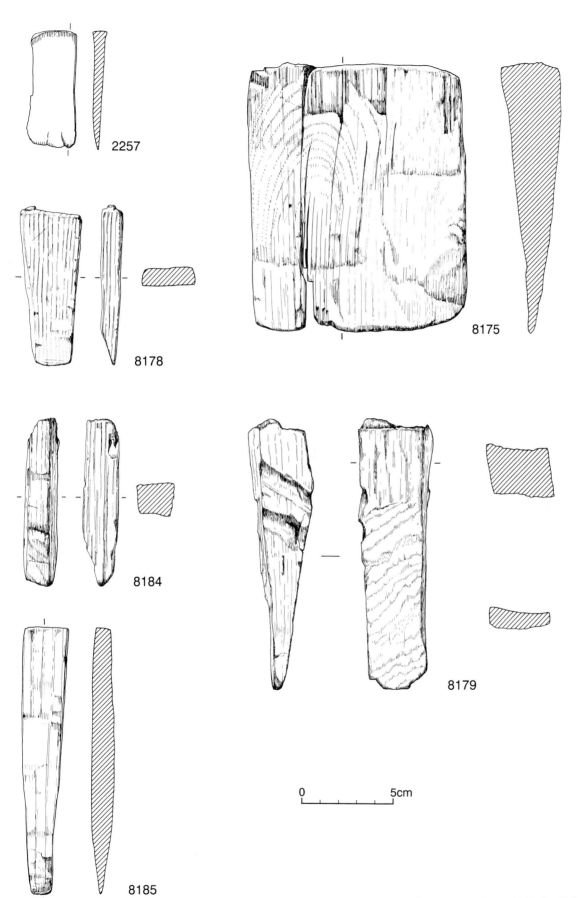

Fig.976 *Iron wedge 2257 and wooden wedges 8175, 8178–9, 8184–5, all from 16–22 Coppergate. Scale 1:2*

2257

8175

8178

8184

8179

8185

0   5cm

wedges are also small. None of the iron wedges from Coppergate measures over 100mm in length, and the comparative tools listed above are only 37–95mm long.

Shaping

Most wooden artefacts made from felled and split timber have been further shaped with other wood-working tools to create the finished product.

Axes (Figs.974b and 975)

Simple squaring up, smoothing and shaping of roundwood and split sections was done with shaping axes. As with felling axes, the most important feature of these tools is not necessarily morphology, although a distinct series of T-shaped axes dating from the 8th century onwards in England were intended mainly for shaping. The salient features of any shaping axe are a thin blade (which is often wide and exaggerated, especially in medieval and later examples), and a blade edge which is sharpened or bevelled on one side only.

2254 and *2256* are probably broken neck and socket fragments of originally T-shaped Anglo-Scandinavian shaping axes. Another broken T-shaped axe was found in Parliament Street, York (Waterman 1959, fig.5, 7). The T-shaped axes have at least as much cutting edge as later medieval wide shaping axes (e.g. Ward Perkins 1940, fig.13, 1–3 and 5, fig.14, 1–2) but are lighter and more economical of metal. They are ideally suited to shaving the faces of planks, beams and boards because the long cutting edge allows a large broad shaving to be removed and so minimises the raggedness left on either side of the cut, and requires fewer cuts to complete the shaping.

There are eleven dated T-shaped axes to compare with *2254* and *2256*. Most are broken, and the complete or reconstructed examples vary in size from blade lengths of 138mm to 357mm, but all originally had narrow necks and long T-shaped blades. They include a 7th–8th century axe from Île Agois, Jersey (Morris 1984a, W14), an 8th–9th century axe from St Neots, Cambridgeshire (Lethbridge and Tebbutt 1933, fig.3,1), an 8th century axe from Six Dials, Southampton, Hampshire (Morris 1984a, fig.155, W13), a 9th century axe from the Crayke hoard, N. Yorkshire (Sheppard 1939, 279–80), a late Saxon axe

from Hauxton, Cambridgeshire (Hughes 1888–91, pl.vi), three late 9th–early 10th century axes of different sizes from the Hurbuck hoard (Wilson 1960, fig.11), an 11th–early 12th century axe from Milk Street, London, with its original oak handle (Pritchard 1991, fig.3.14), and two 11th–12th century axes from Winchester (Cunliffe 1964, fig.54, 4; Goodall 1990, fig.58, *391*). Twenty-two other undated examples have been found at various sites in England, most in London (Morris 1984a, figs.156–7, W23i–xxii).

2256 has a very narrow neck, a feature also seen on the T-shaped axes from Hurbuck and Winchester, and on examples from Banham in Norfolk, Cliveden in Buckinghamshire and Geddington in Northamptonshire (Morris 1984a, fig.156, W23i and fig.157, W23iv–v). The different forms and sizes of T-shaped axes may be related to the shaping required. Earlier forms have more crescentic blades, later types have exaggerated, perpendicular T-shapes (ibid., 199–200, fig.9.2b). One unfortunate feature of all T-shaped axes, however, is the tendency for the arms to break off. The breaks on *2254*, *2256* and the Parliament Street axe could have been caused by their misuse for chopping or felling, by pulling them awkwardly out of cuts or splits, or by metal fatigue.

Shaping can be carried out using axes with double-bevelled edges, but the cuts then start at a steep angle (Darrah 1982, figs.12, 19–20) making them more ragged and giving a dimpled surface. Side axes or broad axes (those with a single-bevelled edge) cut at a shallow angle. The surface produced is smoother and the cuts less ragged because there is a flat face edge next to the wood. An 11th century axe from the Nazeing hoard with a flaring asymmetrical blade (Morris 1983b, fig.1, c) and a 7th century axe found in 1938 in mound 3 at Sutton Hoo (Bruce-Mitford and Ashbee 1975, fig.66) are definitely side axes with single-bevelled cutting edges. The broken 11th–12th century T-shaped axe from Milk Street, London, whose surviving wooden handle curves markedly to the right (when looking down on the butt) to keep the woodworker's right hand clear of the wood which he was shaving on his left, is also a side axe, as is a late 4th–early 5th century bearded axe from Hardown Hill in Dorset (Evison 1968, fig.2b). Although it was found with spears, this is a woodworking axe whose butt is burred over with hammering, and whose head is asymmetrical in cross-section, with the main socket set to one side of the blade. The blade edge was probably sharpened on one side only. 2256 also displays this asymmetry in cross-section (Fig.974b).

Slice (Fig.977)

2258 is a slice or heavy-duty paring chisel with a circular, flanged socket for a long wooden handle and a small, flaring symmetrical blade sharpened only on the upper (socket) side. The blade now curves downwards slightly in cross-section. It dates from the earliest phase of Anglo-Scandinavian occupation on the Coppergate site (Period 3).

This type of tool is often omitted from discussions of woodworking tools, and archaeological examples are often interpreted as spuds, hoes, celts or even side-hafted axes/adzes. Although some artefacts of this kind could be agricultural tools, seven tools found in England and Denmark (including 2258) were probably for woodworking. The others are three 6th century tools from Anglo-Saxon graves at Bifrons in Kent (Baldwin Brown 1915, pl.xxix), Sarre (Brent 1868, pl.xi) and Soham in Cambridgeshire (Leth-

bridge 1933, fig.3,1), a 13th century tool from Assize Court South in Winchester with fragments of the original wooden handle (Goodall 1990, fig.59, 394), an undated tool from Thames Street, London (Manning and Saunders 1972, fig.5, 18), and a Viking/early medieval tool from Århus (Andersen et al. 1971, 252, EAA).

The main feature of a slice (which would not be as important for an agricultural tool) is a single-bevelled cutting edge which is clearly present on 2258 and the tools from Winchester and Århus. The Bifrons, Sarre, Soham and London tools do not have well-preserved blade edges, but deserve to be considered here as slices because of their similarity to the other three. The slice was often used in boat building (McGrail 1977, 62–4), but would also have been used as a paring chisel for smoothing and shaping surfaces by cutting along the grain. It was pushed along the grain of the piece being worked, rather than being hit with a mallet. The downward-curving blade of 2258 suggests it could have been used for smoothing curved surfaces, whereas the parallel-sided blade of the Århus tool made it ideal for paring grooves.

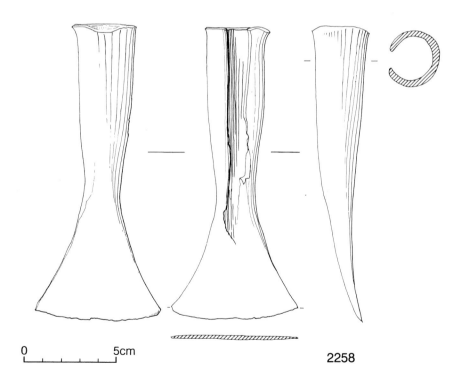

0 _____ 5cm

2258

Fig.977 Iron slice 2258 from 16–22 Coppergate. Scale 1:2

Paring chisel and hand gouges (Fig.978)

Woodworking chisels are nearly always tanged or socketed for a wooden handle. Different types of chisels would have been required to cope with many shaping operations in small artefact crafts, from cutting and smoothing surfaces to hollowing out notches, holes, mortices and joints; they would have been used for functional and decorative carving and also for lathe-turning. Toolmarks from chiselling can be seen on many of the wooden finds from Coppergate, for example, shovel blade *8968*, stave-built vessel hoop *8864*, lid *8866*, and tub staves *8751–2* with D-shaped handle holes.

2143 is an 11th century paring chisel with a thin, flaring triangular blade and a narrow tang which is now bent to one side but would originally have been straight. Paring chisels like this were designed to be pushed along the wood grain by hand to provide a smooth surface finish. There are no later medieval parallels for this tool, but several similar tools with tangs and rounded or triangular blades have been found on 5th to 7th century Anglo-Saxon sites in England. These are a 6th century chisel from grave 83 at Little Wilbraham, Cambridgeshire (Neville 1852, pl.39, 28), four chisels from the 5th–7th century settlement at West Stow, Suffolk (West 1985, fig.241, 21 and 23), and one from the 6th century settlement at Sutton Courtenay, Oxfordshire (Leeds 1923, fig.1,

D). It is possible that *2143* is also earlier in date and was residual in a Period 5Cr context.

2269 and *2270* are Anglo-Scandinavian hand gouges designed to do similar tasks to firmer and carving chisels. *2270* could have been hit with a wooden mallet and used to cut along or across the grain. Both have tangs for wooden handles, but *2269* has its tang bent perpendicular to the gouge blade, then bent back to lie in the same plane but offset by 20mm, a feature which may have helped to keep the woodworker's hand at a distance from the object he was working on. This tool would have worked more efficiently if pressure had been applied by hand rather than by using a mallet. Hand gouges with curved blade edges were ideal for cutting grooves or channels in wooden objects such as the pine panel *9063*, hollowing out awkward shapes and for carving or hollowing joints. Other woodworking gouges with curved blade edges are a 6th century gouge from grave 86 at Finglesham in Kent (Swanton 1973, 173), a possibly 9th century socketed gouge from the Crayke hoard (Sheppard 1939, 280), a 7th–11th century socketed gouge from Lagore Crannog, Co. Meath (Hencken 1950, fig.42, 171), an 11th century socketed gouge with the remains of its wooden handle from Fishamble Street, Dublin (Morris 1984a, fig.160, W64), and an unsocketed gouge with a solid burred head and U-shaped gouge blade from the 11th century Nazeing hoard (Morris 1983b, fig.3e).

Mallet (Fig.979)

8186 is a cylindrical Anglo-Scandinavian willow mallet head with a hazel handle. Its circular ends are worn, compressed and burred from use. Two wooden mallets were found in the Coppergate 'A' deposit, possibly dated to the 10th century (Benson 1906, 73), and a fourth mallet from York, found in Clifford Street and now in the Yorkshire Museum, has a round face at one end and a chisel-like tail at the other. Mallets from other sites include a 10th–11th century one from Ballinderry Crannog 1 (Hencken 1936, fig.35, E), a 6th–9th century example from Ballinderry Crannog 2 (Hencken 1942, fig.27), four Viking period (probably 11th century) mallets from three sites in Dublin (Morris 1984a, fig.165, W139i–iv), two 7th–11th century mallets from Lagore Crannog (Hencken 1950, fig.83, W3), and a late 11th–early 12th century maple mallet head from Milk Street, London (Pritchard and Morris 1991, fig.3.127, 373).

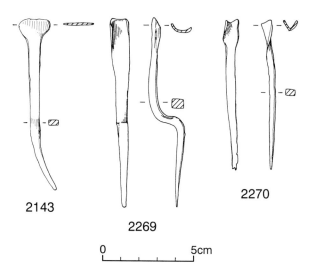

2143

2269

2270

0   5cm

Fig.978 Iron paring chisel 2143 and iron hand gouges 2269–70, all from 16–22 Coppergate. Scale 1:2

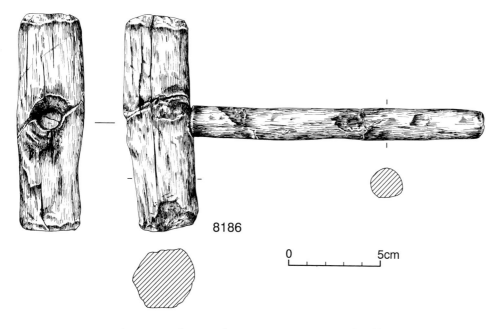

Fig.979 *Anglo-Scandinavian mallet 8186 from 16–22 Coppergate, with willow head and hazel handle. Scale 1:2*

Wooden mallets were indispensable tools for both general-purpose woodworking and specialised crafts. They were used in most circumstances where a wooden object needed to be struck repeatedly and where a metal hammer would damage the wood, for example, posts being driven into the ground, wedges into a split, pegs into holes, tenons into mortice holes and especially the wooden handles of firmer, mortice and carving chisels. A lathe-turner who assembled the wooden components of his lathe in woodland (see p.2117) would have used a wooden mallet.

Boring holes

There is archaeological and pictorial evidence that several types of boring tools were used by Anglo-Saxon, Anglo-Scandinavian and medieval woodworkers for making holes in timber and artefacts. Technologically, these are of two types — the bow-drill and the auger — although the actual iron boring bits used to cut the holes would have been very similar in both types.

Bow-drills (Fig.980)

The bow-drill has an iron bit fixed into a stock, and the whole assembly can be rotated by a taut string in a frame (the bow). It has been said that the only representations of Roman boring tools are bow-drills

(Goodman 1964, 161), and that after the Roman era the bow-drill was little used by woodworkers who preferred the more powerful breast augers and brace (ibid., 162).

It is difficult to be certain whether any of the fifteen iron spoon and twist bits found at Coppergate (*1843, 8189–93, 2260–8*) were for use with bow-drills. There are none, for instance, with a square middle section for a grooved wooden stock to take the bow-string like that on a 12th–13th century bit from Novgorod (ibid., fig.162). *8187*, however, could be part of an Anglo-Scandinavian alder stock for a very small drill bit. It has a circular head with a deep groove cut around it for the bow-string. A shaft of circular cross-section below the head is broken, however, and has no trace of a metal bit or tang hole.

8188 is a small medieval yew bow made from a rod of rectangular cross-section which tapers slightly towards each end and has rounded triangular terminals with notches cut below them as shoulders to hold the bow-string, which has not survived. It could have been used with a drill bit or to operate a small bow-powered lathe, a device for which there is evidence at Coppergate in the Anglo-Scandinavian period (see pp.2142–5). Four other possible bows for bow-drills include two objects from a 9th century pit at Portchester Castle, Hampshire (Cunliffe 1976, fig.143,

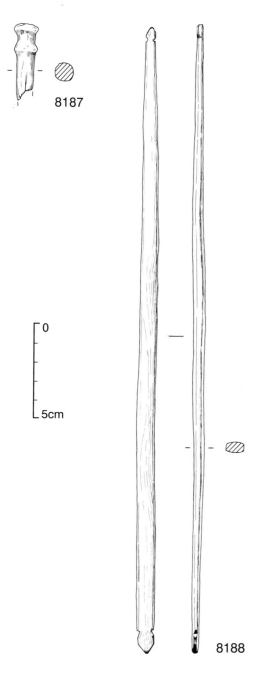

Fig.980 *Bow-drill parts 8187–8 from 16–22 Coppergate. Scale 1:2*

high speed. These would have influenced the wood-worker in any choice of bow-drill over auger. Very small bits for making holes such as those around basket base *8906* (which were only 5mm diameter) and on delicate objects such as the syrinx *9038* could be controlled better with a bow-drill than an auger. Large holes such as those on stool seat *8948* (36mm diameter) and one stave of cask *8765* (27mm and 57mm diameter), however, would have required large bits which were far too heavy to have been manipulated by a bow. Bow-drills may also have been used on other materials such as bone, antler, jet and amber.

Augers

Augers had iron spoon or twist bits with oval or lozenge-shaped tangs to fit into one of three types of wooden handle. The first type was a transverse handle such as that found with a 13th century bit from Mileham, Norfolk (Wilson 1968, 147). An 11th century T-shaped wooden handle found at Christchurch Place, Dublin, is possibly an unused handle of this type (Morris 1984a, fig.165, W144), and a 13th century auger from Ragnildsholmen, Sweden (Goodman 1964, fig.165), illustrates the general type. The second was a brace handle such as a fine holly example from Queen Street, Exeter, dated to c.1300 (Allan and Morris 1984, fig.175, 31), which employed the principle of a crank. The third was a breast-stock as illustrated in the Bayeux Tapestry (Wilson 1985, pl.36). This illustration, a breast auger in the collections of the Nordiska Museet (Arwidsson and Berg 1983, fig.4) and a 19th century breast-stock illustrated by Goodman (1964, fig.176) show how simple iron bits such as those found at Coppergate could have been mounted in elaborate wooden stocks to create a powerful drilling tool where the power used for turning the bit is separated from the direct pressure on the tool (ibid., 172). Iron collars found with the spoon bits from the Mästermyr, Sweden, tool chest dated to c.1000 suggest they were used with a breast-stock (Arwidsson and Berg 1983, 34).

A boring tool's efficiency in cutting a clean, true hole of the required size is most important to the craftsman. Bits were presumably made, therefore, to the craftsman's exact specification. The set of five spoon bits from the Mästermyr tool chest reflects this precision. The diameters of their cutting ends vary by increments of only a few millimetres at a time and measure 12, 17, 20, 29 and 32mm.

90–1), which were found in the same context as three lathe-turned waste cores and a hook-ended lathe-turning tool, a 13th century bow from Århus (Andersen et al. 1971, 260, BLG) and a small bow from Custom House, London (Morris 1984a, fig.164, W129).

The important features of a bow-drill are its reciprocating motion, low torque (turning force) and

Spoon bits (Fig.981)

Thirteen spoon bits ranging in date from Period 4A to Period 6 have been found at 16–22 Coppergate. The form of such tools changed very little between the 5th and the 19th century, suggesting a high degree of conservatism in an efficient and powerful hand tool. They have curved or straight sides, a rounded point and are spoon-shaped in cross-section. The sides and end are sharpened, and they cut when rotated, but do not usually leave a large central core of shavings as do the parallel-sided straight shell bits which are later medieval in date. The rounded ends of spoon bits leave characteristically round-bottomed holes in artefacts not completely perforated such as lathe-turned cores with mandrel hole cup centre marks (e.g. *8451, 8456, 8458–9* in Figs.1008–9, pp.2151–2).

Makers of small wooden artefacts would have required various sizes of spoon bit. The lathe-turner, for example, would require the cup centre holes in his roughout bowls to correspond to his mandrels; the basketmaker using a solid wooden basket base would need holes the same size as his upright rods. Spoon bits would have been used to cut holes in the wooden separate-bladed shovels, rake heads, mattock and mallet heads, pot-lids, cask, tub and bucket staves, churn dashers, heddle cradle, stool seats, rope-woods, musical instruments, roof shingles, spouts, spindle whorls, and saddle bow found at the various York sites. Mortises were begun with spoon bits and finished with chisels, adzes and/or twybils; large holes were created in garderobe seats by first making a ring of holes with a spoon bit, then chiselling out the central waste disc (see *8684* and *8689*, Fig.1064, p.2222).

The surviving Anglo-Scandinavian spoon bits would have cut a range of hole sizes from 9mm (*2268*) to 35mm (*2263*) diameter. These are comparable to the measurements of 32 spoon bits ranging from the 5th to 11th century in date (Morris 1984a, 209, figs. 163–4), which were 140–451mm long and would have cut holes 8–30mm in diameter. The two medieval spoon bits from Coppergate which can be measured cut holes 8mm (*8190*) and 12mm (*8189*) in diameter. The wooden objects themselves have holes ranging from 5 to 57mm diameter and some, such as stake *9157* (Fig.1186, p.2390) and lathe-turned cores with mandrel-hole centre attachments (e.g. Figs.1004–9,

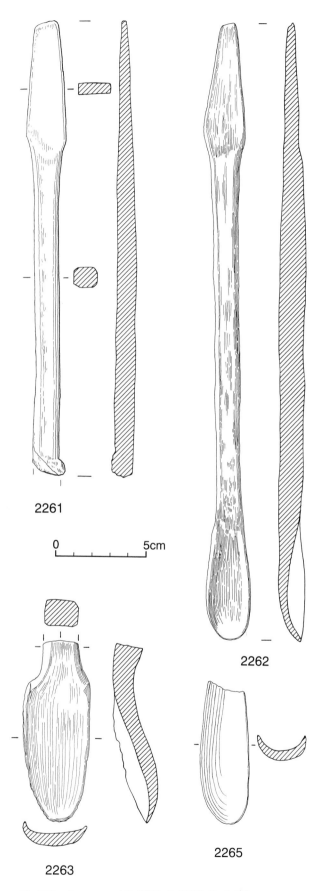

2261

0   5cm

2262

2263

2265

Fig.981   Iron spoon bits 2261–3, 2265. Scale 1:2

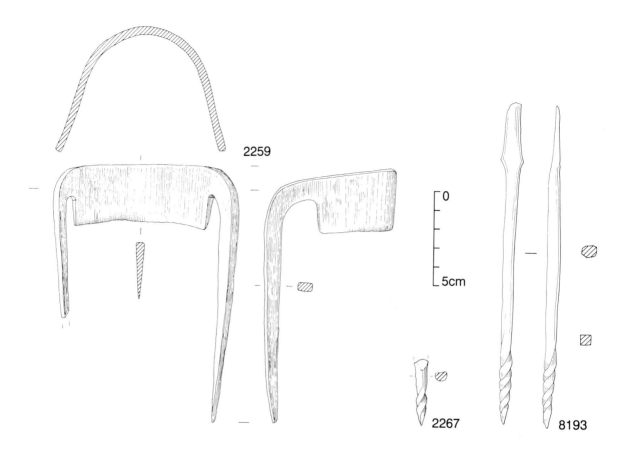

2259

2267

8193

Fig.982 *Fragment of an iron gimlet 2267, complete iron gimlet 8193 and round shave 2259, all from 16–22 Coppergate. Scale 1:2*

pp.2147–52), have round-bottomed holes made by spoon bits.

Gimlets/twist bits (Fig.982)

Tools like the Anglo-Scandinavian fragment *2267* and complete medieval tool *8193* are rare. They are not true twist bits which remove shavings from the cutting point, but gimlets for making starting cuts for spoon bits to enlarge into holes. A 6th–8th century iron fragment found with Anglo-Saxon deposits in a Romano-British ditch at Shakenoak Farm in Oxfordshire could be a similar gimlet or a reject from making one (Brodribb and Hands 1972, fig.42, 194), and other Viking Age examples have been found (Rygh 1885, 417; Petersen 1951, fig.124). An example of a 15th/16th century twist bit/gimlet set in a transverse horn handle was found at The Biggings, Papa Stour (Morris 1999, 190, fig.114, 1617), and indicates the probable type of handle originally used with *2267* and *8193*.

Specialised tools

Specialised tools useful only for certain techniques would have been made or commissioned by individual woodworking craftsmen.

Round shave (Fig.982)

2259 is a tool designed to smooth and shave along the grain of curved objects such as the jointed edges of staves on the inside of a circular stave-built vessel. Round shaves are still a vital part of a cooper's toolkit (Kilby 1971, pl.47c), and it is likely that *2259* was used by an Anglo-Scandinavian cooper in York. The idea that this type of tool was used for hollowing out the interior of solid wooden vessels (e.g. Roesdahl et al. 1981, 123; Arwidsson and Berg 1983, fig.5, b) is misleading in the context of tools found in Britain, as there is no archaeological evidence for Anglo-Saxon, Anglo-Scandinavian or medieval circular bowls being hollowed with a shave. On the contrary, almost every circular wooden bowl of this period was lathe-turned. In addition, the angle at which the tangs of *2259* are set, parallel to the cutting edge, would make it difficult to use along the grain for hollowing a bowl, and almost impossible across the grain.

In England two other round shaves have been found in a sunken-featured building in the Anglo-Saxon settlement at Mucking (Morris 1993b, 70, fig.153.2) and in a 10th–11th century context at Saddler Street, Durham (Carver 1979, fig.13). Round shaves were also found in the Mästermyr tool chest (Arwidsson and Berg 1983, pl.27, 54) and at Framstad in Norway (Petersen 1951, fig.114).

Lathe-turners' tools

8237 is an ash support for a lathe-turner's tool-rest; *9183* is a lathe-turner's hook-ended iron. Both are discussed in the section on lathe-turning at Coppergate (Figs.987 and 1014, pp.2120 and 2163).

The Craft of Lathe-turning, Lathe-turned Vessels and Manufacturing Waste

Any Anglo-Scandinavian or medieval household, whatever its place in the social order, would have had a large range of wooden vessels and utensils for storing, preparing, presenting and consuming food and drink, and for many other domestic purposes. Carved open-topped vessels such as handled bowls and dishes have been found at various Scandinavian sites (e.g. Hedeby, Schleswig-Holstein, in Schietzel 1970, Abb.5), and a carved vessel (*8918*) is discussed on pp.2275–6, but such carved vessels are very rarely found on Anglo-Scandinavian and medieval English sites where nearly all circular open-topped wooden vessels (bowls, dishes, cups etc.) were lathe-turned and would have been obtained from a specialist woodworking craftsman. The larger vessels were normally used as dairy and kitchen wares, whilst the smaller ones were used extensively as tablewares.

The archaeological evidence from York for lathe-turning is excellent in its quantity and variety, and survives in the form of manufacturing debris (roughout blocks *8194–9, 9163*, unfinished vessels *8200–3* and waste products *8204–36, 8238–533, 9164, 9184–5*), tools (a cutting tool *9183* and part of a lathe *8237*), and finished vessels *8534–642, 9165–8, 9202–6, 9226–31*, complete, broken, repaired and re-used.

Detailed research and quantitative analysis of the finds, carried out in conjunction with experimental work since 1978 on a reconstructed lathe, have enabled the author to reconstruct in detail some of the manufacturing techniques used by the lathe-turners in 9th to 11th century York, as well as many different types and sizes of vessels they made, the species of wood they selected to make them and the tools they used.

Turning on a pole-lathe is a skill acquired gradually by experience, and a craft which had to be taught and learned if a living was to be based on it. The lathe-turner's tools and raw materials could not have been acquired easily on an ad hoc basis. All the vessels found in York, therefore, would have been manufactured by skilled craftsmen and not home-made. They would have been bought from craftsmen or traders by those who needed them.

Techniques of manufacture, experimental work and reconstruction

The pole-lathe

The pole-lathe used in Anglo-Scandinavian and medieval York had a reciprocating rather than a continuous rotary motion. At present, there is no archaeological or documentary evidence that any rotary type of lathe was used for wood-turning in medieval Britain.

Evidence for the use of pole-lathes at this period comes from the turned vessels themselves and from manuscript illustrations. The pole-lathe's reciprocating motion leaves characteristic discontinuous, spiralling tool grooves on the wooden vessels and waste products. These can be seen on any vessel turned on a modern version of a pole-lathe and were present on all the Anglo-Scandinavian and medieval pieces from the York sites considered in this report. The author has examined most of the lathe-turned vessels excavated from British sites dating before 1500, and all have the same distinctive tool marks consistent with manufacture on a pole-lathe.

The earliest examples of lathe-turned wooden vessels in Britain come from Late Iron Age sites such as Glastonbury Lake Village, Somerset (e.g. Bulleid and Gray 1911, fig.67). Roman lathe-turned wooden vessels are rare as most Roman bowls and cups were made from pottery, but finds from British sites show that some wooden vessels were made. Three spindle-turned birch or Pomoideae cups and a very rough face-turned, flat, oak platter, for example, were found in a well at a Roman villa at Dalton Parlours in West Yorkshire (Morris 1990a, fig.137, 58–61). Lathe-turning waste products were found in Roman Castleford (Morris 1998, fig.153, 11–13) and spindle-turned lids were found in the Blackfriars boat, London (Marsden 1966, fig.19). In Anglo-Saxon, Anglo-Scandinavian and medieval Britain, however, lathe-turning was undoubtedly the most important craft in the production of domestic tablewares, a claim well supported not only by archaeological evidence from York and many other sites but also by documentary references.

Fig.983 Drawing of painted glass window in Chartres Cathedral showing a wood-turning lathe (from Gille 1956, fig.585)

little alteration through long periods of time' (Wheeler 1927, 23).

The following description (and Figs.985–6) outlines the terminology used throughout this section and forms the basis for the reconstructed pole-lathe used by the author and discussed below. It is a composite device constructed from parts which can be fixed together and taken apart again. In Anglo-Scandinavian York this would have been an important property in a device which may often have had to be transported to different sources of raw material in woodland and set up in situ there. At other times turners may have used more solid, permanent lathes in their workshops in Coppergate. The component pieces could all have been made of wood except for the metal centre points. The horizontal bed could have been either a single block of wood with four solid legs, or two horizontal beams fixed to two or four solid uprights. The former would have had a slot cut vertically through it, the latter a slot between the two beams. Either arrangement would take two

There are three important illustrations of European wood-turning lathes dating before 1500. These are a painted miniature dated c.1250 in Volume II of the Bible Moralisée in the Bibliotheque Nationale, Paris (front cover illustration) (MS Lat 11560, fo.84), a 13th century painted glass window in Chartres Cathedral (Fig.983) (Gille 1956, fig.585) and a page from the Mendel Bruderbuch in the Stadtbibliothek, Nürnberg, dated to c.1425 (Fig.984) (Treue et al. 1965, pl.33; MS Mendel I Amb. 317, fo.18v). The Paris and Nürnberg manuscripts undoubtedly show pole-lathes. The Chartres window depicts a lathe, but the details are indistinct. There is no clear pole, but it might be seen end on since there is a loop at the end of the thong leading up from the work, above the turner's head.

Turners continued to use pole-lathes down to the 20th century. George William Lailey turned wooden bowls using a pole-lathe on Bucklebury Common in Berkshire until 1956 (Myres and Dixon 1988; Geraint Jenkins 1978, pls.52–5), and in 1949 men were still turning chair legs in the Chiltern beechwoods using pole-lathes (Edlin 1949, 33–4). This continuous use of a device over at least two millennia in Britain 'illustrates the conservatism of the civilian craftsman, who evolves an adequate tool and retains it with

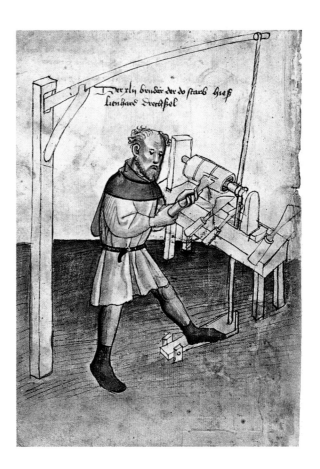

Fig.984 Lathe-turner in the Mendel Bruderbuch, c.1425

2117

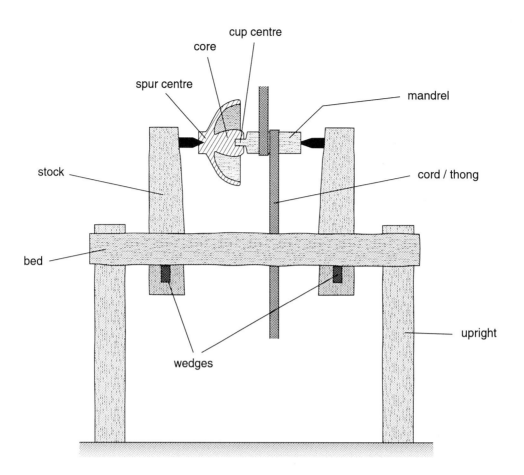

Fig.985 *Side view of a pole-lathe*

stocks or solid uprights which could be fixed in the bed by wedges. At least one of the stocks must have been adjustable to vary the space between them according to the size of the piece being turned. This is usually referred to as the tail-stock, the other being the head-stock. The mandrel is a cylindrical rod which acts as a drive shaft in face-turning (see below). The diameter of the particular mandrel used would vary, depending on the size of the bowl being turned. This variation in a turner's set of mandrels can be seen in those used by Joseph Hughes of Armagh (MacManus 1983, pl.6). The author uses mandrels of 50–60mm diameter to turn vessels up to 250mm diameter. The mandrel's diameter will determine the minimum top diameter of the upstanding core left in a face-turned vessel when the inside turning is complete. Pole-lathes probably varied in detail from turner to turner and through the centuries. The reconstruction here does not attempt to show an actual Anglo-Scandinavian lathe, but is as simple as a pole-lathe can be to represent the least complex device which could have existed.

Any pole-lathe has four essential attributes. Firstly, two metal centre points which are fixed into the stocks and point towards each other along a horizontal axis, to serve as pivots on which the material being turned can be rotated. In the case of spindle-turning, a single piece is worked between the points. In face-turning, a separate mandrel is fixed rigidly, either to the base of a vessel (the spur centre), or to the open end (the cup centre). This entire assembly then rotates on the metal points. The second essential attribute is a means of rotating the work on the metal points. A rope or thong is fixed above the lathe to the end of a pole. This can either be a sapling in situ or, more often, a cut pole fixed at the other end and supported by a fulcrum (for example, as shown on the lathe in the 15th century Mendel Bruderbuch; Fig.984). The thong is looped around the single piece of wood or mandrel and passes through the bed to a treadle or stirrup below. The arrangement of the thong around the mandrel is such that when the treadle is depressed with the foot, the edge of the worked material nearest the turner moves down-

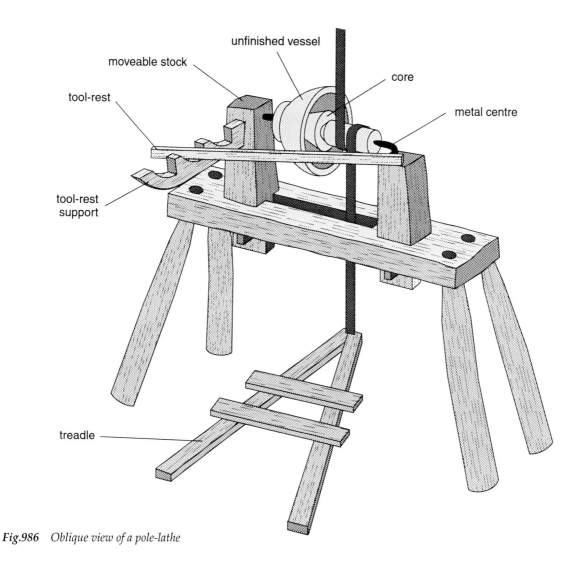

unfinished vessel

moveable stock

tool-rest

core

metal centre

tool-rest
support

treadle

Fig.986 *Oblique view of a pole-lathe*

wards (the cutting stroke). This bends the pole which keeps the thong taut. When the treadle is allowed to rise, pulled up by the pole, the worked material is rotated in the opposite direction (the return stroke). The overall action of the material on the lathe is therefore reciprocating. Thirdly, the lathe must be rigid, whether it is set up temporarily in woodland or as a permanent fixture in a workshop. Finally, it is essential that the lathe possesses a rest on which to support the cutting tool. During the cutting stroke, the downward force on the working end of the turner's gouge or chisel as it removes wood is very great, and the tool could not be held firmly in the turner's hands alone. A tool-rest is necessary to act as a fulcrum for the tool, and needs to be as close to the work as possible. On the return stroke, the cutting tool is withdrawn slightly from the work.

The lathe in Fig.986 has a tool-rest support with three V-shaped notches cut into the upper long edge. It represents the ash object *8237* found in levels dating to Period 5B at 16–22 Coppergate (Fig.987). This object was almost certainly a turner's tool-rest support, and the bar which formed the actual tool-rest could have been moved towards or away from the work and fitted into one of the notches according to the size of the work. One end of the support had straight shoulders cut perpendicular to the grain, and a rod of circular cross-section to fit into a hole in one of the stocks. An old Welsh pole-lathe described by Peate (1935, 12–13) had a tool-rest support with many notches similar to *8237*. The Welsh National Folk Museum at St Fagan's, Cardiff, still possesses two such supports, but instead of rods they have holes through their ends to secure them to the lathe. They

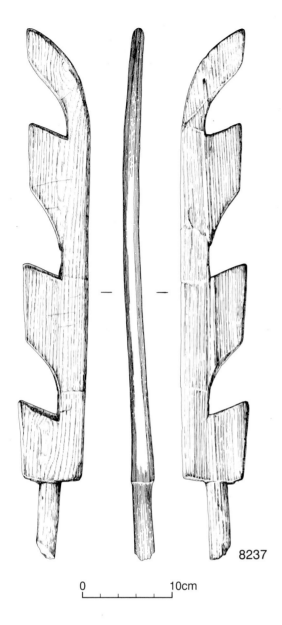

Fig.987   Tool-rest support 8237 from 16–22 Coppergate.
Scale 1:4

0 [_____] 10cm

Scandinavian in date, contemporary with the intense lathe-turning activity in Coppergate discussed below, but *9052* is medieval and probably post-dates most of the lathe-turning on the site. Unlike *8237*, these objects could also have functioned as door latch brackets (see pp.2361–5).

Experimental work

Before anyone can hope to appreciate fully the sophistication of a society and its material culture, he must be able to understand the craft skills and processes used to manufacture its artefacts, and the patterns of exploitation and preparation of the raw materials. A study of the finished artefacts alone or a mere appraisal of the form and dimensions of the workshop waste cannot provide this understanding. The author therefore reconstructed a pole-lathe, learnt the rudimentary turning skills needed to work it competently, and then manufactured bowls from raw material to finished product in order to answer the many questions arising from the archaeological evidence from the York sites.

In 1978, when the experimental work began, Gwyndaff Breeze at the Welsh National Folk Museum was using a pole-lathe to manufacture bowls and offered much valuable advice. In the absence of any archaeological evidence other than *8237* for the form of pole-lathe which the Anglo-Scandinavian turners would have used in York, the form of the reconstructed pole-lathe was based on the lathes in the Paris and Nürnberg manuscripts and the Chartres Cathedral window (see p.2117), and surviving folk examples, although some of the latter are constructed in ways which would have been beyond Anglo-Scandinavian and medieval technology, including the use of massive metal bolts. These lathes include the Borrisokane, Co. Tipperary, lathe in the National Museum of Ireland (Ó Ríordáin 1940), Joseph Hughes's lathe in the Ulster Folk and Transport Museum (MacManus 1983, pl.5), the Lailey lathe in the Museum of English Rural Life at the University of Reading (Geraint Jenkins 1978, figs.52–3; Myres and Dixon 1988, pl.XIXb), the Wellington, Shropshire, lathe (Edlin 1949, pl.21), and the lathe used by Breeze at the Welsh National Folk Museum (Fig.989; Geraint Jenkins 1978, fig.50).

Initially, the experimental lathe was built to be transportable, and hence was not as heavy and solid

are also much longer than the York piece and need to be supported at the other end, whereas *8237* would have needed no support. The author reconstructed a tool-rest support identical to *8237* in size and species and it has functioned well on her pole-lathe (Fig.988) since 1978, showing no sign of wear or strain, and needing no support other than a hole in the headstock. *8237* is the only unequivocal part of an actual lathe dated before 1500 known to have survived in Britain, although six other simple wooden brackets (*9046–50, 9052*) could have functioned as supports for a one-position tool-rest. *9046–50* are Anglo-

Fig.988 *(above) The author at work on her pole-lathe*

Fig.989 *(right) Gwyndaff Breeze using his pole-lathe at St Fagan's*

as some of the folk lathes listed above which would have been permanent fixtures in workshops. It was constructed with two constraints in mind: the materials available to the Anglo-Scandinavian craftsman and the levels of technology and competence presumed to be within the scope of Anglo-Scandinavian society — no massive iron screw bolts. Solid, heavy, permanent lathes would have been required to turn heavy roughouts for bowls of large diameters. The majority of both Anglo-Scandinavian and medieval wooden bowls measured less than 260mm in diameter (see Fig.1030, p.2179) and could have been made on lighter, transportable pole-lathes.

The large body of waste material from the manufacturing processes of lathe-turning found at 16–22 Coppergate, on the Coppergate watching brief site and at 22 Piccadilly (8194–236, 8238–533, 9163–4, 9184–5) formed the basis for the author's experimental work which was carried out at the same time as the study of all the excavated material. The techniques used by Anglo-Scandinavian turners to produce wooden bowls and cups from tree to finished product are detailed here using combined evidence from the artefacts themselves and the experimental work. The terminology used in the text when referring to the waste products of lathe-turning is outlined here. A core is a roughly cone-shaped object which was left when the wood was cut from the inside of a vessel; base waste is a disc-like object which was removed from the external base of a face-turned vessel; end and middle waste are cylindrical pieces which were left at the ends of a spindle-turned object or at the base of a spindle-turned vessel.

Face-turning and spindle-turning

There are two basic ways in which the wood grain can be aligned during turning: perpendicular to the axis of rotation, that is face-turned, a method used for manufacturing small to very large bowls (8534–612, 9165–8, 9202–6, 9226–31); and parallel to the axis of rotation, that is spindle-turned, a method for producing much smaller turnery such as cups (8613–37), lids (8638–42), solid knife and tool handles (8986, 8996–7, 8999, 9001), spindles (6649), bobbins and whorls (6650–1), small cylindrical boxes (8940), gaming pieces, musical instruments and bowling balls (9036, 9040–1), and furniture components. These two alternative methods of face- and spindle-turning require wood in different forms for their roughouts. Face-turning usually needs split half-sections of

roundwood, whilst spindle-turning requires lengths of roundwood poles or split billets roughly shaped to cylinders. In both cases the diameter of the roundwood must be at least as great as the intended diameter of the vessel to be turned.

Face-turning: raw material to roughout
(Fig.990a–e)

Fig.990 shows the likely stages of preparation from tree to roughout for a face-turned vessel. These are simplified and by no means represent all the variations which occur archaeologically. For example, different types of centre attachment were used and the mandrel could have been attached to either the cup centre or spur centre of the roughout. These are discussed below.

The selected roundwood trunk would have been cut into sections according to the intended diameter of the bowl. For example, if the bowl diameter was to be 250mm, then the turner would require roundwood of slightly more than 250mm diameter (Fig.990b). In general, the section would then have been split in two through the heart and most of the actual centre heart cut away to reduce the chance of cracking in the eventual bowl rim (Fig.990c and d). Some lengths were split into unequal 'halves'. For example, 8386 is a face-turned waste core from a bowl which was turned from a block greater than a half-section which contained the heart of the tree, whereas bowls 8537 and 8552 were definitely made from blocks split or cut down to form less than half-sections of the tree. The block would probably then have been shaped with an axe to the rough form of the vessel (Fig.990e). 8195 from Period 5B is an alder offcut from preparing a roughout for face-turning (Fig.991). It is a fragment from the side of a length of half-section timber which still has bark adhering to the outside and has plainly visible axe marks. A roughout ash block with similar faceting was excavated from a late 14th century cistern at Whaddon in Buckinghamshire (Stamper 1979, fig.11, 17). This had been made from a split half-section, but the bowl shape had not yet been formed. In a letter written in 1936, Frank and Joseph Hughes of Armagh described how they shaped their roughouts for the pole-lathe with a hatchet, taking one and a half to two hours on each one (MacManus 1983, 44). Earlier in the letter it is implied that the roughouts they were taking so long to shape were 18–24 inches (c.450–600mm) in diameter. The time taken to shape one of these roughouts

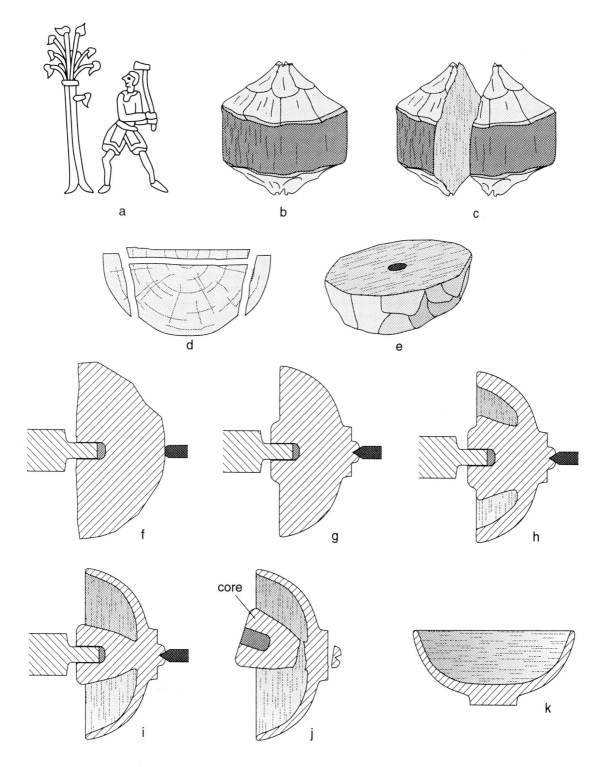

Fig.990 *Stages of preparation of a face-turned bowl from tree to finished product*

must have been much greater than for most of the face-turned vessels made in Anglo-Scandinavian York, 90% of which measured under 250mm in diameter (see Fig.1001, p.2144). This must also have been the case with most vessels made throughout Anglo-Saxon and medieval Britain, where 80% measured 90–260mm (see Fig.1030, p.2179) and very large bowls were exceptional. An accurately cut roughout would have made the actual turning much easier and quicker.

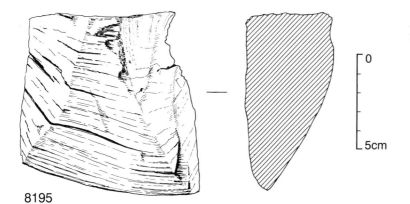

Fig.991 Alder offcut waste 8195 from preparing a roughout for face-turning. Scale 1:2

0

5cm

8195

Complete roughouts for face-turning have not been found at York. This is very significant since, if all the processes in the manufacture of a bowl from raw material to finished product were being carried out on the Coppergate and 22 Piccadilly sites, one would have expected at least one or two roughouts at various stages of manufacture, along with lengths of roundwood or split sections, to have survived in the same ideal conditions that preserved 301 waste cores. The lack of roughouts may show either that there was very little wastage due to roughouts being rejected before the turning stage, or perhaps that the roughouts were converted several stages along the bowl-making process before being brought into the urban workshops at Coppergate. This would imply that roughout manufacture and possibly preliminary turning on a portable lathe was carried out away from the site (such as in the woodland where the raw material was obtained), and the semi-finished vessels were then brought into the workshops in York to be finished and sold. The majority of face-turned waste products found on the Coppergate site would support this theory since, apart from the alder offcut *8195*, all the cores and base waste and the unfinished face-turned vessel *8203* are discards at the stage after a vessel is finished and are therefore waste products of the later stages of bowl manufacture, possibly from semi-finished vessels. Two-stage turning is also suggested by certain centre mark patterns on cores (pp.2131–2).

In order to test the practicality of the technique, the author partially turned some green alder roughouts of approximately 200–250mm in diameter using a mandrel hole centre attachment. The external walls, rim and base were completely finished, and the internal cutting was started, leaving a hollow of several millimetres and an incipient core. She then left the mandrel/bowl assemblies for a week to dry in the air. After this time, as the wood had begun to dry out, two basal cracks had opened up in the end grain of one bowl, neither reaching the rim. After a few weeks, the cracks had almost closed up again. The complete assemblies were remounted on the lathe after six months, and the bowls completed, needing very little reshaping to make them circular again, since the solid roughout had not seasoned to a very marked oval shape as a completed unseasoned bowl might have done.

The most important fact to emerge from this experiment was that when roughouts were prepared from green wood in the woodland they could have been partially turned, then kept in moist conditions and not allowed to dry out until the vessels had been completed to prevent cracking. Although there is no direct evidence for this in York, roughouts have been found in wet contexts on several other sites showing that turners made conscious attempts to keep their roughouts from drying out. Some of these waterlogged contexts were not actually in settlements, but on the edge of them, where there were naturally wet conditions. An unturned alder roughout with a partially hollowed interior was found in a waterlogged pit on the edge of a fen next to the 4th–early 5th century settlement at Wijster in the Netherlands (Van Es 1967, 133, pl.15, 2), four partially hollowed maple roughouts from the 3rd century terp settlement at Paddepoel, Netherlands, were found in the immediate vicinity of the settlement (Van Es 1968, 240–2, figs.21–4), and two alder roughouts were found in an area north of the 'river' next to the 9th–10th century crannog at Lagore (Hencken 1950, 156–8, fig.77A). Many undated unturned roughouts have also been found in Irish bogs, suggesting that Irish lathe-turners practised a technique of making roughouts and then keeping them artificially wet before mounting them on the lathe (Morris 1984a, L79–L86). These include one of alder from Derreen, Co. Clare, two from Derryaroge, Co. Longford, two of hazel from Doonmaynor, Co. Mayo, six of ash from Inchin Lough, Co. Kerry, ten from Muckanagh, Co. Mayo, and eleven from Roebuck, Co. Cavan, all found sunk into peat bogs at depths of 0·9–3·0m. If the turners in York prepared their roughouts in the nearby woodland, they would either have had to keep the roughouts or partially turned bowls wet before or after bringing them into the city workshops, or there must have been almost no time lapse at all between the cutting of timber, preparing of roughouts and the actual turning of the bowls. If they prepared the roughouts in the woodland, no rejects would ever have reached the workshops in Coppergate and this would explain the lack of face-turning roughouts on the site.

There are several sources of evidence which suggest that medieval bowl-turners (including those in York) used green, unseasoned timber for their bowls, unlike some of the recent pole-lathe bowl-turners who used large roughouts of air-dried timber. Many turned wooden bowls found in excavations are not perfectly circular, but oval, with their longer axis along the grain. When bowls are turned green, they always become slightly oval as they dry out and their rim edge also has a tendency to curve slightly in profile. Two wooden bowls with curved rim profiles are shown on a table at a feast in Venice in a manuscript dated to c.1300 (Bodleian Library MS Douce 178, fo.225v). The illustrator appears to have drawn (perhaps exaggeratedly) exactly what he saw, since this curved profile can occur in any size of circular wooden bowl when it is turned green and then allowed to season.

Also, several medieval documents show that turners in Wales and Yorkshire made some of their bowls in woodland where they presumably set up pole-lathes, cut green timber and worked it unseasoned (see p.2193). The timescale suggested by all the manuscript references is a short period of working, not involving cutting down trees to season the logs, or air drying the roughouts for long periods of time. This is different from the seasoning programmes carried out by more recent pole-lathe turners such as Lailey, who is said to have seasoned wood for up to five years (Sparkes 1977, 18). The much larger, more valuable bowls which needed a solid lathe and more time and effort to turn them are more likely to have been made from seasoned wood.

Roughouts with flat or slightly hollowed centres have been found on other sites, including two 9th–10th century alder ones from Lagore Crannog and a 12th century one from Lübeck in Germany (Neugebauer 1953–5, Taf.XXVII, 9). Some of the roughouts found on continental rural sites dating from the 2nd to the 5th century had been taken a stage further than these. The four maple roughouts from 3rd century Paddepoel, the 4th–early 5th century alder roughout from Wijster and three 2nd–3rd century examples from Feddersen Wierde in Germany (Haarnagel 1979, Taf.42, 1, 2 and 5) had part of their bowl centres cut away with a chisel or hand adze, leaving rough upstanding cores in the middle. Those from Feddersen Wierde also had roughly shaped bases. The eleven roughouts found at Roebuck (Lucas 1953–4, fig.2) had also been partially hollowed by hand. It is interesting that wood had been cut out in this way, since the author's experimental work has shown that when the vessel is less than 250mm diameter it is much quicker, in general, to remove wood by turning than to hollow by hand. A possible explanation is that with the reciprocating motion of a pole-lathe, the angular momentum of the roughout must be overcome every time the direction of motion is reversed at the end of each stroke. For small bowls (c.150mm diameter) this is not a great problem, but since the moment of inertia is proportional to the fifth power of the radius of the bowl (assuming constant proportions), it increases very rapidly. For example, a roughout of c.250mm diameter has approximately thirteen times the angular momentum of one of the same proportions measuring 150mm diameter if rotating at the same rate. The problem of angular momentum can be alleviated if as much wood as possible can be removed from a large roughout before turning, which could explain why the roughouts discussed above had been partially hollowed by hand. Two of the Feddersen Wierde roughouts were 336 and 367mm in diameter, and at least one of the finished bowls found on the same site was 414mm diameter (Haarnagel 1979, Taf.42). Any of these roughouts could represent the variety of forms manufactured by the Anglo-Scandinavian turners in York, but which have not survived.

Roughouts could have been prepared with the base of the vessel towards the outside (sapwood) or inside (heartwood) of the tree. Although no complete roughouts for face-turned bowls have been found at York, surviving face-turned cores, unfinished and finished bowls from York and other sites show that the former technique was the one most commonly used. This represents a practical, economic choice on the part of the Anglo-Scandinavian turners. Experimental turning has shown that fresh, green wood turns much more easily than well-seasoned wood, but if a bowl is turned green, the stresses produced in the drying out process (which cause radial shakes or cracks from the outside in roundwood) sometimes cause the rim to crack at the weakest points where the grain runs directly through it (in the end grain). This occurs more often when the base is at the heartwood. If a bowl is turned green and the base is at the sapwood, the same stresses build up in drying out, but the rim is less likely to crack. Also, very fine hairline cracks have a tendency to close up again if the roughout has been prepared in this direction. The crucial factor in avoiding cracking in bowls during or after manufacture must have been the Viking craftsman's intimate knowledge of the qualities of the individual piece of timber he chose each time. He would always have tried to select roundwood which was less likely to develop shakes along the radial lines of weakness. He would also have considered some of the natural growth features in the roundwood, such as large knots or spiralling grain which were undesirable. Only one unfinished face-turned bowl (8203) was found on the entire Coppergate site (see Fig.996, p.2135). It is dated to Period 5B and was found in a floor level of Structure 5/6 on Tenement C. The fact that the bowl was never finished strongly suggests that the building was used as a turner's workshop. The turning of this particular alder bowl had been completed, including the removal of the mandrel and core, but the rough area left on the internal base where the core had been broken out and the small knob on the external base, with a metal point centre mark from the spur centre on the lathe, had not been removed. The bowl had been rejected because it had developed an unrepairable split in the rim and the bowl wall had distorted out of shape. The lack of excavated wasters and rejects from the Coppergate site emphasises the high level of woodland skill and knowledge possessed by the Anglo-Scandinavian turners.

Whatever their form, a mandrel would then have been attached to the centre or base of the prepared roughout (Fig.990f). There is very little evidence to suggest how the turners centred the mandrel in the roughout. Most would probably have been centred by eye and the roughout then turned down to its initial circular outline. On a very large vessel, however, it would have been more critical to get the centring correct to save a lot of time and effort in the initial turning. 8371 (Fig.1007, p.2150) is a fragment of a core 111mm in diameter which dates to Period 3 and must have come from a very large alder bowl. The circular hole for the mandrel was augered in the centre of a cross made by two intersecting grooves cut into the top of the roughout, presumably to act as a centring device. Four similar nicks on core 8459 could have been for centring (Fig.1009, p.2152), and 8425 (Fig.1008, p.2151) is a smaller alder core whose metal plate centre was fixed in relation to an incised cross which survives on the top of the core, perhaps yet another centring device.

Centre marks: face-turning and spindle-turning (Fig.992)

Marks in base waste, end waste and cores (8204–35, 8238–530, 9164, 9184–5) indicate the types of centre attachments used at the end of the mandrels and as pivot points for face-turning and spindle-turning on the lathes in 9th–11th century York. Only three types seem to have been used: mandrel hole, multiple metal plate and single metal point centres. Cores from other British sites show that at least six types of centre attachments were in use, some with restricted distributions, and these and the corresponding marks made in the cores are illustrated schematically in Fig.992. Mandrel hole, metal plates, bar and plate, metal pins and multiple metal points (Fig.992a–e) were all used in face-turning when the mandrel had to be firmly fixed to either spur or cup centre, whereas a single metal point (Fig.992f) is a pivot point mark and occurs on all spindle-turned waste products and occasionally on face-turned base waste. The very small square, lozenge-shaped, triangular and rectangular marks are related to spindle-turning using a bow-powered lathe (Fig.992g–i). Tables 198–9, 201 and 203 (pp.2155–7) show the number of examples

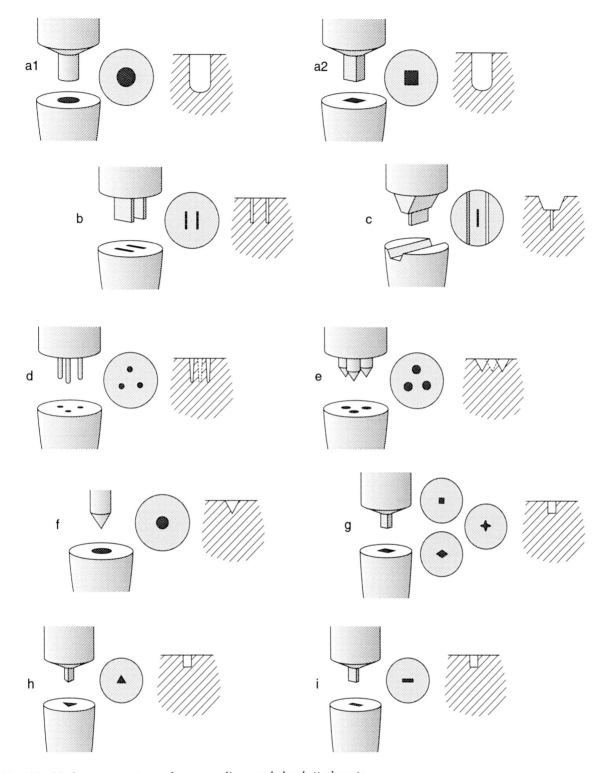

Fig.992   Marks on core centres and corresponding mandrel end attachments

of each type of centre attachment mark found on the cores from 16–22 Coppergate in relation to turning technique, core shape, species and period respectively.

In face-turning, the mandrel hole type of mark is produced where the end of a wooden mandrel is formed into a cylindrical shape to fit into a circular augered hole in the roughout bowl centre or base

(Fig.992 a1). Sixty-one cores from 16–22 Coppergate and one from 22 Piccadilly had mandrel hole cup centres, including *8371* from Period 3, which, along with other turning waste found in Period 3 contexts and discussed below, suggests that vessel-turning was being carried out on or near to the 16–22 Coppergate site as early as the second half of the 9th century. Table 203 (p.2157) shows that this type of centre attachment was used continuously throughout the life of the site from Period 3 onwards, with large concentrations of cores in Periods 4B and 5B.

Some cores have mandrel holes with rounded bottoms showing the profile of the spoon bits used to drill the holes, for example, *8461* which has a well-rounded bottom to a hole 52mm deep. Sometimes the tenon on the end of the mandrel and the hole in the vessel centre were other than circular (Fig.992 a2), for example, *8289* from Coppergate which dates to Period 5B, an early 7th century core from the monastic settlement on the Isle of Iona (Barber 1981, fig.33, 444 1) and a late 9th century core from a well pit at Portchester Castle (Cunliffe 1976, pl.XXa; Morris 1984a, fig.129, L95i) had squared mandrel hole centres, whilst a late 12th century core from Perth in Scotland had a D-shaped mandrel hole (ibid., fig.132, L111iii). At first sight, this type may not seem to be efficient, especially in its ability to remain firmly fixed in the cup centre. It is not a method which continued to be used on pole-lathes by English and Welsh bowl-turners in recent years. However, the author's experimental work has shown it to be an excellent method when turning green or slightly seasoned timber. Indeed, the mandrel's tenon can become so firmly embedded in the core of a green bowl that it is difficult to remove after the bowl is finished and the core/mandrel assembly removed from the bowl. This difficulty is illustrated by a 10th century alder core from Brook Street, Winchester (Keene 1990, fig.377, *4454*), which had a fragment of a circular cross-sectioned hazel rod embedded in the mandrel hole centre when it was found. This could be part of the original mandrel which broke off when the turner was removing it from the core.

If the mandrel became so embedded in the core that it simply could not be pulled or twisted out, it would have to be knocked out by striking the side of the mandrel with a wooden mallet. A fragment of the side of the core would tend to shear off or the core would be broken in two, leaving two character-istic fragments but releasing the end of the mandrel. In experimenting with embedded mandrels, the author was able to remove them in this way, producing two pieces of core. Sometimes the largest piece retained all the foot and most of the walls with a complete hole profile, whereas the smaller fragment was usually a piece of core wall with part of the hole profile above the rounded bottom. *8346*, an alder core from Period 5B, is a large piece with a scar where a smaller fragment, which does not survive, sheared off. A core found at Odell in Bedfordshire in a well dated by dendrochronology and radiocarbon to c.580 (Morris 1982, fig.14.4, A4) and an early 7th century core from Iona (Barber 1981, fig.33, 444 1) are very similar. They show that this must have been a common technique. Many cores with mandrel hole centres are found in fragments or halves suggesting that they had to be forcibly removed from the mandrel, for example, *8273, 8374, 8391, 8414, 8456, 8461* (Figs.1007–9, pp.2150–2). Another core, *8443*, survives in two conjoining fragments split across the central hole. Other fragmentary cores with mandrel hole centre marks include examples from Portchester Castle (Cunliffe 1976, pl.XXa), Milk Street, London (Morris 1984a, fig.129, L96), and Whitefriars, Norwich (Morris 1982, fig.14.4, A5).

The Odell core shows that the mandrel hole type of centre attachment was used as early as the 6th century in Anglo-Saxon England, and a core from King's Lynn, Norfolk, is evidence for its continued use in Britain at least as late as the 14th century (Clarke and Carter 1977, fig.171, 15). Other cores with this type of centre attachment have been found at Granville Street, Southampton, where a truncated conical core with a large circular mandrel hole had been re-used in an 8th century stave-built cask (Holdsworth 1976, fig.20), at a 9th century Irish rath at Lissue, Co. Antrim (Morris 1984a, L94vii), in late Anglo-Saxon levels at Milk Street in London (ibid., fig.129, L96) and Whitefriars, Norwich (Morris 1982, fig.14.4, A5; Ayers and Murphy 1983, fig.20.3), in Viking Age levels at Hedeby (Schietzel 1970, Abb.3, 2, 3 and 5) and Christchurch Place, Dublin (Morris 1984a, L99viii), and in 12th century Lübeck (Neugebauer 1953–5, Taf.XXVIa).

Of the 62 York cores with mandrel hole centre marks, 46 were alder, twelve field maple and one birch, showing that the Anglo-Scandinavian turners preferred alder for face-turning vessels using this method with maple a second choice (Table 201, p.2156).

The commonest type of centre attachment used for face-turning in Anglo-Scandinavian York was the multiple metal plate (Fig.992b). One hundred and twenty cores with two parallel slits in their centre have been recovered from 16–22 Coppergate, dating from Period 4B onwards, and one from 22 Piccadilly, dating to early–mid 11th century. Table 203 shows that this type of centre mark was used for face-turning vessels throughout the life of the Coppergate site with a concentration in Period 5B. It seems to have been used contemporaneously with the mandrel hole centre, but the evidence from the cores suggests that the metal plate centre was more popular by Period 5B. Table 201 shows that there seems to have been no preference for one of these two centre marks over the other when using a different species of wood. The cores with metal plate centre marks reflect the same pattern of species selection as those with mandrel hole centre marks since 106 of the 120 cores were alder, eleven were field maple and one yew, reinforc-

ing the suggestion that the Anglo-Scandinavian turners in York preferred alder for face-turning vessels, with maple as second choice.

Although the Coppergate excavations did not recover any actual mandrels, examples of this type must have had two sharpened metal plates fixed into their ends which were driven into the roughout cup or spur centre, producing a pair of parallel slits in the centre of the core or base waste (Fig.992b). The scattergram in Fig.993 illustrates the wide range of slit lengths and separations on the York cores and base waste, and suggests that many different mandrels with this type of centre attachment had been used whilst this area of Coppergate was a centre of lathe-turning activity. Almost all the slits on cores and waste were parallel to the grain of the wood showing the turner's conscious decision to follow the grain. Core *8276* and base waste *8208*, however, have slits set at an angle to the grain.

A 14th century core from Shackerley Mound in Shropshire had an offset pair of metal plate slits (Mor-

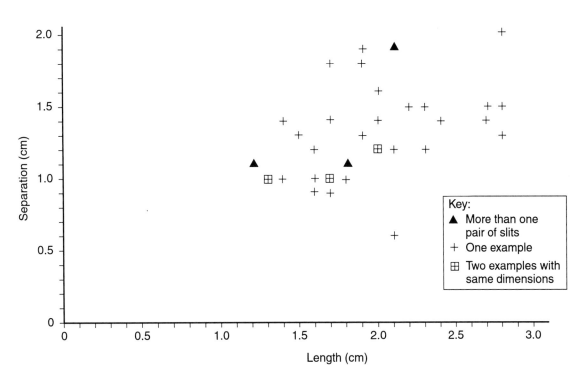

Fig.993   Scattergram of slit lengths and separations of multiple plate centre attachments

ris 1987, fig.10, 6), the mandrels used on the pole-lathe at St Fagan's have three metal plates, and Joseph Hughes of Armagh used mandrels with four metal plates instead of two (MacManus 1983, pl.6). Pieces of base waste from excavations in Novgorod, Russia, have various patterns of slits representing four or more metal plates, sometimes arranged in a square (Kolchin 1989, pl.123, 1–3). All the examples show how different turners used variations in the numbers and positions of plates, but all were equally effective.

The bar and plate type (Fig.992c) has so far only been found on 24 cores from the 7th century monastic site on Iona (Barber 1981, figs.31–3). No cores with a centre mark of this type have been found in York. The Iona cores had remains of chiselled slots presumably to receive a bar at the end of the mandrel into which was fitted a single metal plate. This, like the multiple plate variety, would have been driven into the chiselled slot in the roughout cup centre. Only one core from York (8309; Fig.1005, p.2148) had chiselling marks in the top where some hollowing had been done before seating the cup centre attachment. This, however, was a two-plate centre similar to all the others used in York.

The limited distribution of the bar and plate type suggests a local tradition which was not sufficiently useful to spread widely elsewhere. The single plate by itself may not have transferred torque from the mandrel, and the mandrel end had to be cut to a rectangular/pyramidal bar to engage in the chiselled slot. Six contemporary cores found on Iona had mandrel hole or metal point centre marks (Barber 1981, fig.33, 447/78, 119, 129, 444/1, 6 and 260/12) showing that other types of centre attachments or pivot points were also being used there in the early 7th century.

The multiple metal pin (Fig.992d) and multiple metal point (Fig.992e) types are very rare and only occur on single 13th century cores from Nantwich, Cheshire, and Perth (Morris 1984a, fig.132, L110ii and L111ii).

Judging from the lack of face-turned waste cores with a single metal point centre mark, either at Coppergate or on any other British site, and the very small number of pieces of face-turned base waste with a mark from a firmly fixed mandrel (8208–13,

8216–17), the majority of Anglo-Scandinavian turners seem to have preferred to arrange their work with the mandrel fixed firmly in the cup centre.

Single holes from single metal point type centres (Fig.992f) are found on spindle-turned waste products such as cores (e.g. 8238–44, 8249–52, 8258–9, 8480–94) and end waste (8219–27, 8232–3) where the roughout itself was rotated on two pointed metal centres. The excavations at 16–22 Coppergate produced 98 cores with marks of this type, dating from Period 4A onwards and continuing throughout the life of the site. Cores with this type of centre mark have been found on many other sites, including an unstratified alder core from Parliament Street, York, and a core dated to c.1300 found at Blake Street, York (Morris 1984a, fig.132, L103 and L114), four 7th century alder cores from Iona (Barber 1981, fig.33, 447/78, 119, 129 and 260/12), 7th century cores from Lagore Crannog (e.g. Hencken 1950, fig.84, W169), two 9th century cores from Portchester Castle (Cunliffe 1976, pl.XXa; Morris 1984a, fig.129, L95i–ii), thirteen Viking Age cores from High Street, Christchurch Place and Fishamble Street, Dublin (ibid., fig.129, L98–L100), 13th century cores from Cork, Ireland (Hurley 1982, fig.16.3, 7 and 8), Crown Car Park, Nantwich (Morris 1984a, fig.132, L110i), and Cuckoo Lane, Southampton (Platt and Coleman-Smith 1975, fig.229, 1645–6), and a 15th century core from Whitecross Street, London (Morris 1984a, fig.132, L108). All of these cores and those from Coppergate came from vessels which had been spindle-turned.

No surviving face-turned cores have metal point centre marks (Table 198, p.2155), although metal plate centre marks on some pieces of base waste (e.g. 8208–13) and the finished bowl 8608 show that some of these cores must have been produced. Only on rare occasions is this type of mark found on other face-turned items such as base waste (8214–15) or an unfinished bowl (8203), suggesting that on most vessels the turner left little or no base waste by turning down the sustaining knob of wood with the metal pivot point centre to unrecognisable fragments. The knob surviving on the unfinished bowl 8203 gives an impression of how small this base waste may have been.

Four spindle-turned cores (8322, 8333, 8460, 8505) and one piece of face-turned base waste (8214) dating from Periods 4B, 5A and 5B (Figs.995 and 1009) have metal point centre marks in the centre of small circular depressions. These depressions measure 9–14mm across in the spindle-turned cores and 20mm in the face-turned base waste. They must have been made by the end of the metal bar from which the metal centre point projected. This would have helped to prevent the metal centre point digging its way deeper into the bowl centre or base.

Most metal point centre marks are circular and reflect the conical form of the metal point which acted as a pivot point on the lathe. Nine spindle-turned cores and one piece of end waste, however, are unusual in having metal point centre marks which are not circular (Fig.992g–i). Seven have squared, star-shaped or lozenge-shaped cross-sections (*8221, 8259, 8359, 8366, 8482, 8502, 8514*), *8350* has a very irregular cross-section, while *8331* and *8363* have triangular and rectangular cross-sections respectively. *8502* is also unusual in that it had a larger V-sectioned hole which had been plugged with a piece of wood before the small lozenge-shaped mark was made into the plug (Fig.1009). Technologically, these marks are difficult to explain, since they cannot have been made by centres on which the roughout pivoted; they suggest that some form of mandrel was attached in the centre of the end grain of the roughout, a method which is usually unnecessary in spindle-turning where the entire roughout pivots on two metal point centres. These ten pieces date from Periods 4B, 5A and 5B, showing that whatever turning technique was involved in producing them, it was not simply an experimental technique used at one period and then discontinued. The type of turning which probably produced them is discussed on pp.2142–3.

V-sectioned holes from single metal point centres vary greatly in width and depth, showing that a variety of metal centres were used, perhaps on different sized lathes. The hole on core *8318* is 20mm, those on cores *8322* and *8361* are 12mm deep, whilst those on cores *8322* and *8369* are very wide. Some holes, on the other hand, are small and neat with hardly any depth at all, e.g. *8315, 8321, 8360, 8480–1, 8492*, three of these cores being recovered from the same context. The hole in core *8339* was worn to one side, perhaps because the roughout had been loose between the two centres and there had been lateral movement on one of the metal points. There is hardly a trace of a hole on core *8332*. One of the possible reasons for these differences is the length of time that any particular roughout was on the lathe: a large

roughout for making more than one vessel would have more time to wear a wider deeper hole than a very small roughout for one vessel.

Using evidence from all 106 cores with metal point centre marks, a different picture of species selection emerges (Table 201). When spindle-turning their vessels, the turners appear to have preferred field maple, with alder and birch as second and third choices, but with at least six other species being used as well in small quantities.

Six cores have no visible evidence to indicate which type of centre attachment was used (*8281, 8355, 8372, 8430, 8495, 8526*). Very small slits or holes in wood may be obscured or may close up when an object is buried in the ground; for example, core *8365* had a metal plate centre mark of two slits but they are now so fine as to be almost indistinguishable. There are several other reasons which may explain the lack of evidence on cores. *8355* is a small curved conical object which may not actually be a core (Fig.1007, p.2150). It is very small and regular with a smooth circular top with no trace of a centre mark. Also, its clear end grain with medullary rays, large spring vessels and close but distinct annual rings make it very definitely identifiable as oak, a species not suitable for turning on a pole-lathe and hardly ever used by turners throughout history for either spindle- or face-turning. There are no other oak cores or vessels from the Coppergate site or other sites in York. *8355* is more likely to have been a bung or stopper, although it is possible it was a spindle-turned core whose metal point centre mark has been obscured or cut off. A fragment of a spindle-turned oak cup was found at 6–8 Pavement (Fig.75, *466*, *AY* 17/3). The other five cores with no centre marks are either fragmentary or broken at the top, with the part of the core which normally displays the centre mark missing. The shape of *8495*, and the fact that it is spindle-turned, suggest that it had a metal point centre mark. The other four are face-turned, and could have had either mandrel hole or metal plate centre marks.

Most centre marks are still approximately central in the top of the core, even allowing for shrinkage and distortion in the ground. At least seven cores, however, have centre marks which are very obviously off-centre: *8253, 8273, 8387* and *8457* (mandrel hole centre marks); *8280, 8304* and *8338* (metal plate centre marks). One possible explanation is that roughouts were partially turned green (perhaps the outside and the beginning of the inside of a vessel), then a period of time elapsed during which a certain amount of drying out occurred with accompanying shrinkage from the circular outline. When they were remounted on a lathe, without repositioning the mandrel, they would have to be turned down to circular again, and this may sometimes have resulted in the mandrel centre being offset from its original position. The author has produced cores with offset centre holes in this way, suggesting that two-stage turning of a vessel was at least possible. The offset mandrel hole centre in core *8253* is now positioned near the edge of the core (Fig.1004, p.2147). The vessel from which this core came was turned from burrwood, which has no real grain direction, so the shrinkage may have been quite substantial.

Other centre marks which may reinforce the idea of two-stage turning occur on at least ten cores with metal plate centres. *8313, 8344, 8395, 8426, 8431–2* and *8464* have two sets of parallel slits where the mandrel has been removed and repositioned. *8290, 8436* and *8468* each have three sets of parallel slits where the mandrel has been removed and repositioned twice.

Face-turning: roughout to finished product (Fig.990f–k)

The roughouts of most of the face-turned vessels made on the Coppergate site were fixed to the lathe with the end of the mandrel as the solidly fixed cup centre, and a metal pivot point at the spur centre (Fig.990f, p.2123). Once this had been done, the roughout had to go through various stages of manufacture to turn it into a finished bowl (Fig.990g–k). Most of the face-turned waste found in Anglo-Scandinavian York was produced at one of these stages; at any stage, mistakes or accidents could have caused a piece to be discarded.

The author's pole-lathe (see Fig.988, p.2121) has a moveable tail-stock higher than the solidly fixed head-stock. The metal pivot centre in the head-stock is L-shaped and protrudes from the top of the stock, with the pivot point aligned along the lathe axis. The metal centre in the tail-stock is fixed exactly opposite the latter, into the side of the tail-stock. After mounting the roughout and mandrel assembly in several positions, the author found it easier initially to mount the roughout with the mandrel rotating on the tail-stock centre, and the base of the roughout on

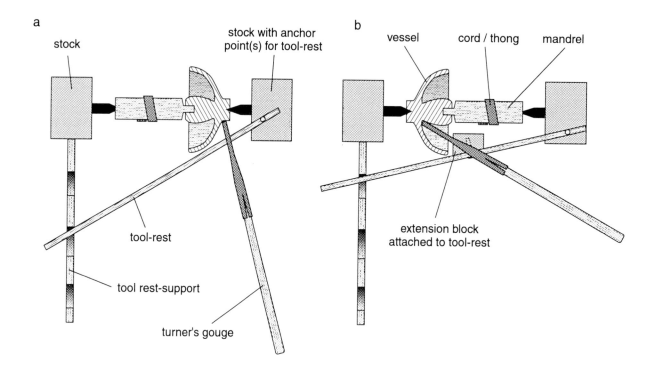

Fig.994   Overhead view of tool-rest: (a) for turning base; (b) for turning interior

the head-stock centre. The replica of the tool-rest support 8237 is mounted in the tail-stock, perpendicular to the main axis of the lathe. A bar which serves as a tool-rest is then fastened at one end by a nail or peg driven through it and into the top of the head-stock, whilst the other end rests in one of the notches in the tool-rest support. This positioning can be seen in overhead view in Fig.994a. Most of the external shaping of the vessel can be carried out without moving the tool-rest, and one turner can stand to the right of the tool-rest support, operating the treadle and cutting the bowl at the same time. Although we can never be certain how the Anglo-Scandinavian turners mounted their rough-outs, there are limits as to how 8237 can be fixed and used successfully on a lathe, and the method suggested here is a tried and tested one.

First, the turner shaped the outside of the vessel completely, and prepared the rim as much as possible from the external side (Fig.990g). The rim was the most vulnerable part of the vessel throughout its manufacture and fragments spalling off the rim meant that the vessel would either have to be re-shaped or discarded. This was less likely to happen if the rim was partially shaped while the centre of the roughout was still solid. Some of the rim shapes discussed below with the vessels themselves (see Fig.1017, p.2166) show how and when the turner created their shape. The base of the bowl, including any edge shapes or footrings, was also turned at this stage, as was any turned decoration in the form of encircling grooves, singly or in sets, or ridges separated by grooves.

9165 from the Coppergate watching brief site is a large medieval alder bowl 298mm in diameter, which has a wide unturned facet on its external wall where a shaping cut on the roughout has not been turned down. Similar random external facets can be found on other medieval bowls from Bedern (9226), Lurk Lane, Beverley, E. Yorkshire (Foreman and Hall 1991, 175, fig.121, 948), Greyfriars monastery, Bristol, Avon (Morris 1984a, fig.134, L129vii), King William Street, London (ibid., fig.143, L175), and Stamford, Lincolnshire (ibid., fig.146, L199iii, iv and vii). They are the remnants of the cuts used to shape the roughout which have not been completely removed. They are evidence that turners were making roughouts with a high degree of accuracy, leaving little to be removed to make the vessel circular.

When the outside of the bowl was completely finished, the wood would have to be cut from the inside of the bowl (Fig.990h–k). If the turner had positioned the tool-rest support as suggested, he would have found it very difficult to turn the inside of the bowl if the mandrel and bowl assembly were left in the same position. Not only would he have to stand to the left of the tool-rest support and lean over it in a very uncomfortable position, but he would probably not be able to reach the treadle easily, and the distance between the tool-rest bar and the centre of the bowl would be too great for him to control the cutting tool. It is very important when turning on the pole-lathe to position the tool-rest and support the cutting tool as close to the working surface as possible. In her experimental work, the author overcame all these problems by turning the mandrel and bowl assembly through 180 degrees so that the internal bowl centre now faced the fixed head-stock. The tool-rest support was left in the same position, but since the distance between the tool-rest bar and the working surface was now too great, a separate block of wood was added to the front of the bar to provide a better tool-rest near the bowl centre. This arrangement can be seen in overhead view in Fig.994b. If they used tool-rest supports like 8237, the Anglo-Scandinavian turners in York would perhaps have had different sizes of blocks, according to the size of the bowl being turned. It is also possible, of course, that for turning the inside of the bowl they used a completely different tool-rest system for which no evidence has survived.

When turning the inside of the vessel, an upstanding core of wood was left to sustain the assembly until all the necessary shaping had been done. Many cores were excavated from the Coppergate sites and are discussed in a separate section below. When the inside was complete, the mandrel/bowl assembly would be taken off the lathe and the core removed from the vessel. With face-turned bowls, the author found that the most efficient method of removing a core was to place the bowl between the knees (in a kneeling position), being careful to cushion the rim of the bowl nearest the ground, and detach the core with a single blow from a wide-bladed chisel. This method leaves a single flat scar at the bottom of the core which can be seen on most of the York face-turned cores, especially the truncated varieties. If the core came out whole, the mandrel could then be removed from it and re-used. Only one face-turned core from York, 8316 (Fig.1006, p.2149), has multiple fac-

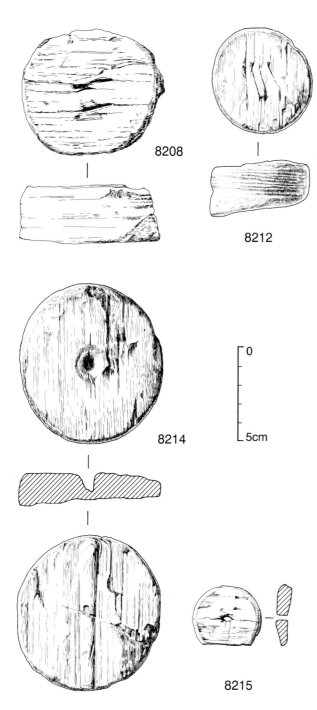

core, and the base would be smoothed off by either chiselling or axeing away any small knobs or cutting off any larger discs of base waste. *8204–18* (Fig.995) are fifteen examples of face-turned base waste cut from vessels at this stage of manufacture, including twelve alder, one field maple and one willow. Several very small shavings (*8204*) were all found in the same Period 4B context. These represent the very fragmentary pieces of waste which must have been cut from the base of most vessels. A similar thin willow shaving fragment (*8206*) is possibly the same kind of waste. Some bowls have rough, shallow discs on their external base where a small disc of base waste has been cut off, but the bowl base has not been smoothed down (*8541, 8571–2, 8595, 9203, 9205, 9229–30*). *8595* is a very roughly turned vessel and may even have been a reject. The shallow discs on these eight bowls measure 15–50mm in diameter. The other thirteen more substantial examples of base waste, dating from Periods 4B to 6, show that the bowls they were cut from had bases 38–92mm in diameter. These dimensions are reflected in the base measurements of complete vessels found on the site. Base waste *8208–13* and *8216–17* show that mandrels with two metal plate attachments had been fixed at the base of these vessels, whereas *8214–15* have V-sectioned holes produced when using the metal pivot points described above. The other three pieces of base waste (*8205, 8207, 8218*) have no visible centre attachment marks, probably because they are so fragmentary.

On rare occasions a bowl retains the rough disc of wood on the internal base where the core came out, e.g. *8580*, a face-turned alder bowl which had clearly had a disc of base waste removed and had been used over a long enough period of time to have become worn underneath, but had never had the internal disc cleaned off. *8571*, a maple bowl 216mm in diameter, has internal gouge marks running perpendicular to the grain showing where a waste disc 35mm in diameter, left after the removal of a core, had been properly removed.

8203 is the only unfinished face-turned bowl found at 16–22 Coppergate, dating from an intensive period of lathe-turning activity in Period 5B (Fig.996). It is a rare survival and not only provides valuable information about Anglo-Scandinavian face-turning techniques, but could also indicate the presence of a turner's workshop on tenement C in Period 5B, since it was found embedded in a floor

Fig.995 Base waste from 16–22 Coppergate in the form of discs cut from the bottom of face-turned bowls after turning: 8208, 8212, 8214–15. Scale 1:2

eted cuts from a chisel or gouge at its base, suggesting that it was either chiselled out of the bowl, or cut in this way after removal from the bowl.

After the core had been removed, the inside of the vessel would be cleaned and shaped by chiselling out any remaining roughness at the base of the

level. Its internal bottom has a circular rough area 38mm across (measured along the grain) indicating the diameter of the bottom of the core which was broken out. This is useful in providing a relationship between the diameter of the bowl (110mm) and the diameter of the bottom of the core which the turner left before removing the core. The turner would aim to leave as wide a core base as was technically possible without endangering the integrity of the vessel when he removed the core. In face-turning, due to the nature and direction of the grain which runs across the core, it is possible to leave wider core bottoms than in spindle-turning, where the grain runs down the core. Table 195 (p.2153) shows that 83% of the face-turned cores (153 out of 184) were truncated shapes with wide bottoms, whereas only three out of 112 spindle-turned cores were truncated (*8301, 8396, 8463*) and none of these had bottom measurements over 20mm.

8203 also retains a small knob of base waste which was never removed. This knob is only 25mm in diameter in the centre of a bowl base which is 56mm across. It is perforated by a metal point centre mark 10mm deep and 6mm wide where it enters the knob. The hole is slightly deeper than the height of the knob and a small indentation would have been left in the centre of the bowl's base if the knob had been cut off. Such marks can be seen on finished bowls *8572, 8592, 9167, 9227–9* where the holes in their bases are too small to have been complete metal point centre marks. Unfinished bowl *8203* was presumably discarded before it was finished because it split and distorted beyond repair.

Unfinished lathe-turned bowls are rare finds. The only other unfinished face-turned bowl to have been excavated on an English site came from a late 14th century cistern deposit at Whaddon (Stamper 1979, fig.11, 3). This was larger than the York bowl, measuring 205mm in diameter, and made of ash. It also had a small external base knob which had not been cleaned off, and it had been discarded along with a block of ash which had not yet been formed into a bowl roughout, and fragments of one willow and six ash bowls (ibid., 66, fig.11). Another unfinished bowl

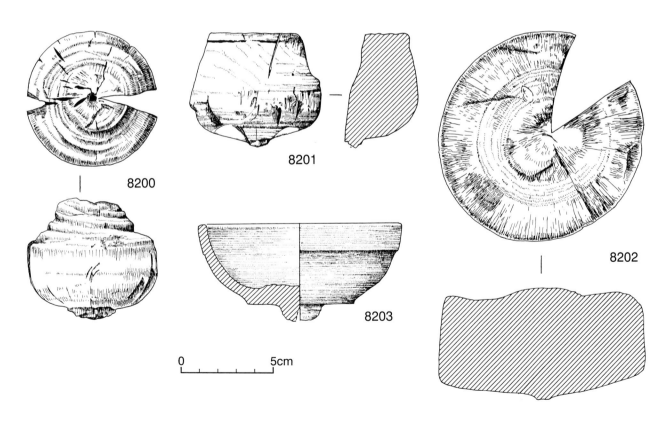

8200

8201

8203

8202

0   5cm

Fig.996   *Unfinished spindle-turned cups 8200–1; unfinished spindle-turned bowl 8202; unfinished face-turned bowl 8203, all from 16–22 Coppergate. Scale 1:2*

was found in Lübeck (Neugebauer 1953–5, Taf. XXVIIb), in a context dated to c.1100 which produced other lathe-turning waste in the form of cores, end waste and a roughout (ibid., Taf.XXVIa–c and XXVIIa). The Lübeck unfinished bowl had an extremely shallow profile with straight sides, and short cylindrical 'cores' in the inside and on the base. It is possible that it was a roughout which was never turned on the lathe.

An alternative technique for face-turning vessels which produces a different type of base waste to that already discussed is demonstrated by pieces of 13th to 15th century base waste found at Novgorod (Kolchin 1989, pl.123, 1–3). A mandrel with a metal plate centre attachment had been fixed to the base of the roughout, the exterior of the vessel was turned, leaving a long cylindrical piece of base waste as wide as the eventual vessel base, the inside of the bowl was then completely turned, and finally the turner cut into the base cylinder from the side, creating the vessel's base at the same time as parting the base waste from the vessel (ibid., pl.123, 12).

Spindle-turning: raw material to roughout

Preparing roughouts for spindle-turning bowls or cups would have been very different to preparation for face-turning, and the size and diameter of raw material chosen would have depended on factors such as the number of vessels a turner intended to manufacture from one roughout. The standard raw material was a length of unconverted roundwood, slightly larger than the intended vessels, which would have its bark removed and be shaped to a rough cylinder. 8194 is a length of debarked birch roundwood 150mm diameter, with its ends sawn across. It may have been an offcut from a longer piece, or it may have been intended as a roughout for a single vessel c.150mm diameter, which was never completed. 9163, found on the Coppergate watching brief site, is a very small Anglo-Scandinavian field maple roughout cylinder, only 60mm in diameter, whose sides and ends had been shaped with an axe. It may have been 'centred' on a lathe since there are small V-sectioned centre holes in each end, but there are no toolmarks to show that it had ever been turned on a lathe. This roughout may have been too small to spindle-turn a vessel, but could have been used for spindle-turning a small solid object. This may also

be true of the medieval ash roughout 8199 which is a narrow cylinder 30mm in diameter with two deep V-sectioned holes in its ends (Fig.997).

Sometimes the heartwood was used as the centre of the cylindrical roughout, where it would be mounted between two metal pivot point centres on the lathe. This centring can be seen in many items found at 16–22 Coppergate, including cores (e.g. 8244, 8314, 8317, 8506, 8512), cups 8615 and 8631 (Figs.1031–2, pp.2180–1), box 8940 (Fig.1124, p.2297), roughout 8198 (Fig.997) and end waste 8224–5 (Fig.1000, p.2141). Using a slightly different method, turners prepared their roughouts with the centre of the tree offset from the centre of the bowl, and the holes for the two metal pivot point centres on the lathe would be positioned up to 10–15mm away from the centre of the tree. Evidence for this off-centring comes from many of the spindle-turned cores (e.g. 8238, 8240–1, 8250, 8323–4, 8330, 8342, 8484, 8518), roughout 8197 (Fig.997), end waste 8226 and 8229 (Fig.1000), and a yew cup 8633 (Figs.1032, 1038). The dating of the objects suggests that both methods were used from the earliest years of Anglo-Scandinavian turning on the 16–22 Coppergate site (e.g. birch cup 8615 from Period 3 has its centre close to the heart of the tree, whereas ash core 8238 from Period 4A has its centre at least 10mm away from the centre), and that both methods continued in use throughout the 10th and 11th centuries (Periods 4B to 5B).

In both methods the complete piece of roundwood would have been used to make one or more vessels with a similar diameter to the original tree. Some cores and vessels, however, suggest that roughouts for spindle-turning were sometimes made from sections of larger roundwood which may have been converted by splitting through the centre into two halves or splitting tangentially into two unequal parts, e.g. cores 8513–14, cups 8625, 8628 and 8630, end waste 8224 and lid 8642. The split section would then have been shaped into a rough cylinder as before. This method appears to have been used contemporaneously with the other two, at least from Period 4B onwards. The pieces of roundwood chosen for splitting down to make all three cups, the lid and the roughout which produced the end waste 8224 would originally have been 200mm or greater in diameter and thus suitable for face-turning, so the turners must have made a conscious selection of these particular pieces for spindle-turning into small items rather than larger

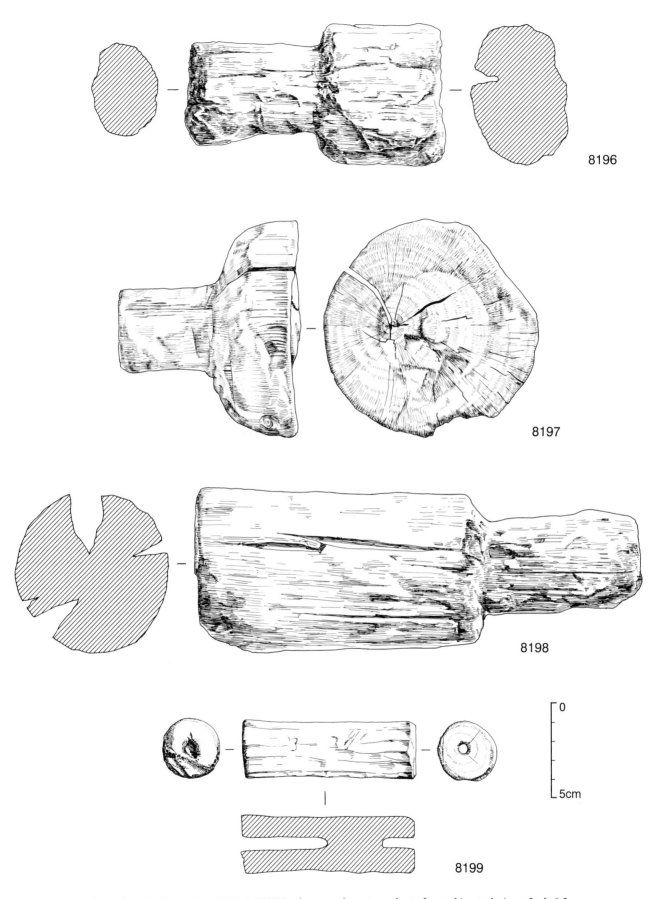

Fig.997 *Roughouts for spindle-turning 8196–9. 8197 is also an end waste product of a stacking technique. Scale 1:2*

8196

8197

8198

8199

0

5cm

bowls. Roundwood of the same species of field maple, alder and small quantities of others such as birch, yew, ash and pomoideae were selected for all three methods. In spindle-turning, the quality rather than the species of the timber must have played the dominant part in its selection, where features such as large knots, incipient radial splits and spiralling grain may have caused only a part or a section of a piece of roundwood to be rejected and the rest used.

When face-turning vessels, the mandrel (which acts as a drive shaft around which the rope or thong is passed) and roughout are separate items which are fixed together and mounted on the lathe as an assembly. The whole assembly then rotates on two metal pivot point centres. When spindle-turning vessels, however, a separate mandrel is not necessary. The complete roughout rotates on the centres and part of the roughout itself can accommodate the rope or thong. Rejects and spindle-turned waste products recovered from 16–22 Coppergate show that Anglo-Scandinavian turners in York had at least two methods of preparing and working roughouts to accommodate the rope.

In the first method (Fig.999a), a narrow projecting cylinder was shaped at one end of the length of roundwood roughout, whose diameter was smaller

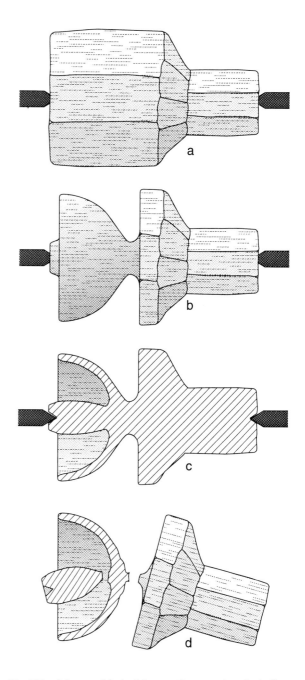

Fig.999 (above and facing) Stages of preparation of spindle-turned bowl from roughout to finished product: (a)–(d) single vessel; (e)–(h) stacking technique leaving basic end waste; (j)–(m) stacking technique leaving collared end waste

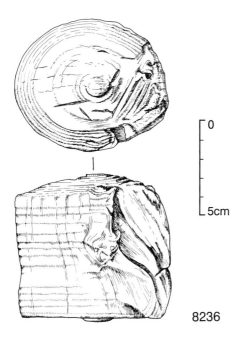

8236

Fig.998 Alder middle waste 8236 from 16–22 Coppergate. Scale 1:2

than the roughout itself. This narrow cylinder acted as a mandrel. Two unturned roughouts with these 'mandrels', 8196 and 8198, have been excavated from the 16–22 Coppergate site (Fig.997). Both are field maple dating from Period 5B; 8196 has a shallow dimple in the centre of the larger end where perhaps it was centred on a lathe. The narrow cylinders are

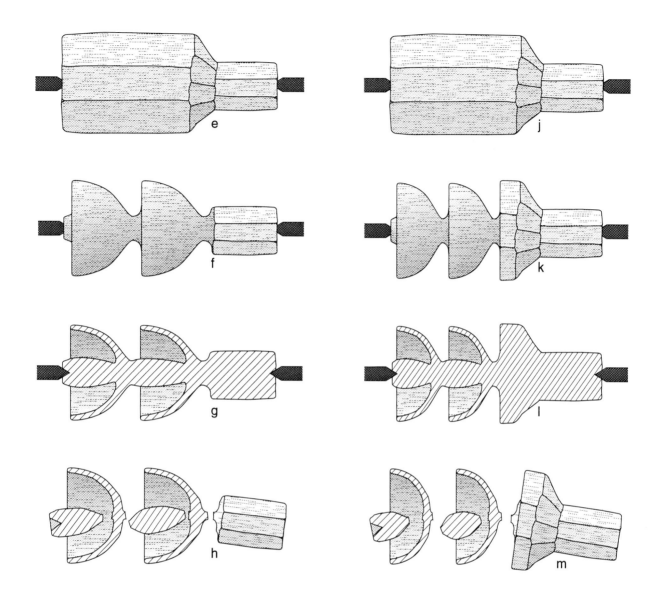

both 53–4mm in diameter. Sixteen pieces of spindle-turned end waste in the form of cylinders, with or without larger 'collars', are also evidence of this method (*8219–28, 8230–5*; Fig.1000). They are field maple, alder and birch, and date from Periods 3 to 5B. All the narrow cylindrical parts measure between 38 and 65mm in diameter, and accord well not only with those on roughouts *8196* and *8198*, but also co-incidentally with the diameter of the mandrels the author uses in face-turning today for vessels up to 250mm in diameter. Fig.999e and j shows how a longer roughout could have been used to produce more than one vessel, a stacking technique which will be described below.

The second method of accommodating the rope is demonstrated by *8236* which is a piece of middle

waste from the spindle-turning of at least two objects (not necessarily vessels) and was originally part of a faceted alder cylindrical roughout 82mm in diameter, dating from Period 4B (Fig.998). Each end has turning lines and a central knob where finished objects have been detached, whilst the sides have wide smooth grooves round the circumference to accommodate the cord attached to the pole and treadle. These grooves would have been artificially created by the turner to anchor the cord, rather than being produced by the cord as wear marks in the wood. The grooves must have anchored the cord sufficiently so that it did not keep slipping over the edge towards the base of the object being turned. Another possibility is that the cuts which detached the finished objects were only made at the final stage, thus limiting the chances of the cord fouling up.

Spindle-turning: roughout to finished product (Fig.999)

Small holes were made in the ends of a roughout which would then have been mounted between two centres on the lathe so that it could pivot freely on the two metal points. *8223* is a piece of end waste from spindle-turning which still retains fragments of an iron metal point in situ (Fig.1000). It is possible that this is part of a metal point from the lathe which became embedded in the end of the roughout and was discarded along with the waste. The two methods used by Anglo-Scandinavian turners to accommodate the rope around a roughout, and described above, are shown in Fig.999a, e and j. The diagrams here reconstruct the probable techniques used to turn the roughouts into finished vessel(s).

First, the turner shaped the outside of the vessel(s) completely, in some instances leaving a collar which would prevent the rope fouling up with the cutting tool as the external base was shaped (Fig.999b). Three pieces of end waste (*8220*, *8224* and *8234*), produced after the finished vessel(s) had been separated from the rest of the roughout, have such collars which give them a mushroom-shaped appearance (Fig.1000). They date from Periods 3, 4B and 5B, showing that this technique was a successful one used continuously from the mid–late 9th or early 10th century, the earliest phase of Anglo-Scandinavian turning on the site, right through to perhaps the mid 11th century. A similar piece of end waste with a small collar was found on a Viking Age site at Christchurch Place in Dublin (Morris 1984a, fig.133, E122:15443) showing that turners there were not only spindle-turning vessels but also using similar techniques to their fellow craftsmen in York. Other pieces of end waste (*8219*, *8221–3*, *8225–9*, *8231*, *8233*) do not have collars, and although they could have been waste products of either spindle-turning bowls or other products such as handles, they all fall within the same range of diameters as the collared ones. *8229*, a very flat cylinder 103mm in diameter, is an unusual example (Fig.1000).

As with face-turning, the turner would then have prepared the rim as much as possible from the external side as it was the most vulnerable part of the vessel, and also completed the base shaping and any turned decoration in the form of grooves or ridges. *8200–1* are two unfinished spindle-turned cups which were discarded before internal shaping began because they had become useless in the turning proc-

ess (Fig.996). *8200*, dating from Period 3, and therefore part of the earliest evidence for turning on the site, would have been a small cup with a globular profile, typical of the small Anglo-Scandinavian drinking vessels produced on the site for 200 years (see pp.2179–82). It has a single metal point centre mark in the middle of an incipient core, and must therefore have been turned either from a roughout intended for a single vessel or at the very end of a longer roughout intended for several vessels. The vessel walls are smoothly turned and a small squared base had been formed, but the sides of the core had been only roughly turned and a rim had not been shaped. This, along with two splits and a fragment broken from the external surface, suggests that the turner decided not to proceed any further with this vessel, and parted it from the roughout or end waste, leaving a knob at the spur centre. *8201* is a fragment from a similar unfinished cup dating from Period 4B. Its external surface had been completed even to the point of pigment being applied into a single decorative groove. The rim had been formed and a flat surface turned at the cup centre. Since only a fragment remains, there is no surviving evidence for a cup centre attachment, but a basal knob indicates it had been turned down this far. It is possible that the fragment sheared off the half-finished vessel and spoiled it.

When the outside of the vessel was finished, the wood was turned from the inside, leaving an upstanding core to sustain the centre until all the necessary shaping had been done (Fig.999c). Sometimes, even at this stage, the vessels were vulnerable. *8202*, also dating from Period 4B, is an unfinished larger bowl with almost vertical sides and convex bottom (Fig.996). Small knobs at both spur and cup centre indicate that this vessel was probably one of several made from a large roughout. The outside shaping had been completed, and internal shaping had been started, leaving an incipient core, but two fragments split from the sides had caused the spoiled vessel to be parted off and discarded.

The collared and straight pieces of end waste *8219–35*, the middle waste *8236*, and the unfinished vessels *8200–3* have knobs which show that they have been parted off on the lathe itself rather than the whole piece being taken off the lathe from between the two centres and then both core and end waste removed. The bottom of the vessel would then have to be cleaned up and the core removed as in face-turning. Maple

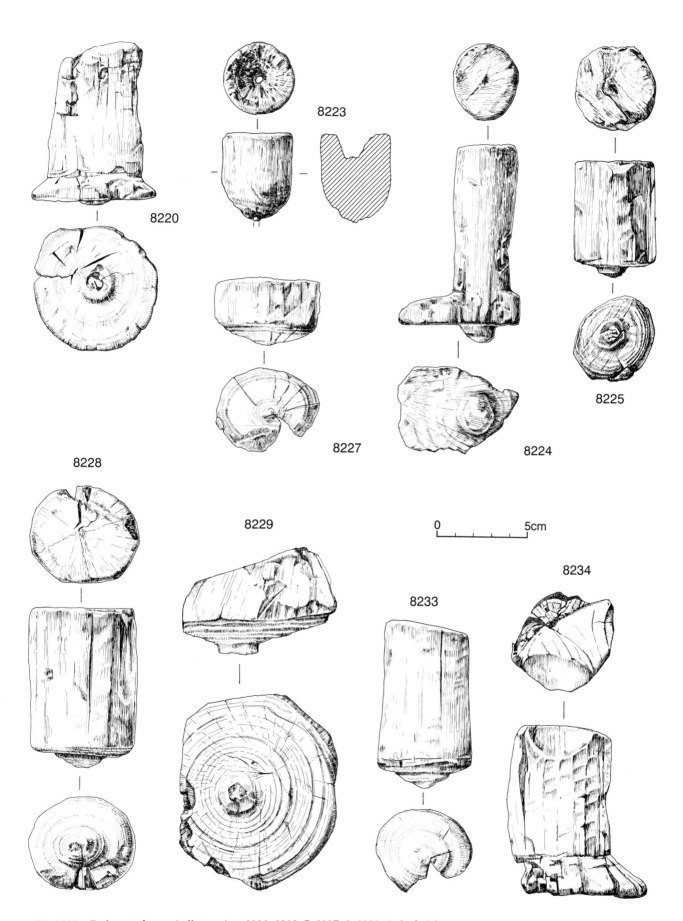

8223

8220

8227

8224

8225

8228

8229

8233

8234

0   5cm

Fig.1000 *End waste from spindle-turning: 8220, 8223–5, 8227–9, 8233–4. Scale 1:2*

cup *8624* still has rough central knobs on the external and internal base where the core and end waste were removed but not cleaned off (Fig.1031). Spindle-turned cores *8334* (Fig.1006) and *8512* have very clear faceted chisel marks where they have been cut from the vessel after removal from the lathe.

Certain pieces of waste suggest that Anglo-Scandinavian turners in York used a stacking method of spindle-turning several vessels from one long roughout (Fig.999e–m). A roughout with a narrow projecting cylinder to act as a mandrel, but whose main section was substantially longer than a roughout for a single vessel, would have been mounted on the lathe between two centres (Fig.999e and j). The external profiles of two or more vessels would then have been shaped, leaving a gap between the base of one and the cup centre of the next (Fig.999f and k), and either a basic or collared end waste. Each section would have been separated by a narrow neck which would form the base knobs when parted off. The interior of each vessel would then have been turned, leaving upstanding cores inside each one to sustain the work (Fig.999g and l). When all the vessels were finished and separated, there would be at least three types of waste: an ordinary core from the first bowl with a metal point centre; one or more middle cores with no centre mark, but perhaps a roughly turned top and bottom; and a piece of basic or collared end waste (Fig.999h and m).

Middle cores such as *8531–3* are best explained as waste products from spindle-turning using a stacking method (Fig.1010, p.2153). These were from birch and maple vessels dating from Period 4B and a birch vessel from Period 6. Other wasters which can only have come from the stacking technique are unfinished maple bowl *8202* which has knobs at both spur and cup centre (Fig.996), and maple roughout/ waster *8197* dating from Period 5B which has a projecting cylinder and a roughout bowl shape which has a knob at the cup centre where the next bowl in the stack has been removed (Fig.997). This bowl was never turned, perhaps because of a deep facet cut into its side making it too small. If the core from Period 6 is not residual, these pieces show that stacking techniques were used in Coppergate from at least c.930 into the medieval period.

The York pieces are the earliest evidence for this technique. As yet, the only other evidence for turn-

ers stacking vessels in this way are two later medieval middle cores from the late 14th century moat at Shackerley Mound (Morris 1987, fig.10, 5) and the 15th–16th century moat fill at the Hall Garth site, Beverley (Morris 1984a, fig.132, L115ii), but future finds may indicate it was a fairly common turning method much earlier.

Spindle-turning using a bow-powered lathe

Nine spindle-turned cores (*8259, 8331, 8350, 8259, 8363, 8366, 8482, 8502, 8514*) and a piece of end waste (*8221*) have metal point centre marks which are neither circular in plan nor V-shaped in cross-section. Instead, they have very small lozenge-shaped, triangular, rectangular or irregular holes in their end grain.

These ten pieces are different from all the other spindle-turned waste products. Eight of the cores are very small, measuring only 25–31mm in height, from level with the rim of the vessel to the internal base, and they must have come from the turning of small, shallow cups or very small bowls. Two of the holes can be measured: *8366* with a lozenge-shaped hole 9mm deep (Fig.1007, p.2150), and *8363* with a rectangular slot only 7mm deep. If these tiny holes are the marks made by centre attachments in separate mandrels, they are far too small to have been able to transfer torque on the same scale and in the same way as the larger firmly fixed centre attachments in face-turning on the pole-lathe already described. These ten pieces of waste may, however, be rare and valuable evidence for wood-turning in Anglo-Scandinavian York using very small-scale apparatus compared to the larger pole-lathe. This may have taken the form of a strap-powered or bow-powered lathe or even a very small pole-lathe.

The earliest representation of any lathe is a strap-powered device illustrated in an Egyptian tomb dated to c.300 BC (Lefebvre 1923, pl.x). The work is a long probably spindle-turned piece (not a vessel) positioned between two centres, and is being reciprocated by an assistant who sits on the opposite side of the lathe-bed to the turner, holding the two ends of a strap which is wrapped around the work. If he pulled the ends of the strap alternately, the work would revolve towards and then away from the turner as in a pole-lathe. The turner would then cut on the equivalent of the pole-lathe's down stroke.

This technique was still being used for bowl-turning in Ethiopia at least up until the 1960s (Boothby and Boothby 1980, 12–13). A bow-powered lathe works similarly in that the two ends of the strap are wrapped around the work, then fastened to the ends of a curved length of wood to form a bow. Moving the bow back and forth reciprocates the work. It is possible that either of these reciprocating methods could have been used in Anglo-Scandinavian York, a period when there is certainly evidence for small-scale turning in other materials including amber (*AY* 17/14), antler (Fig.940, *7733*, *AY* 17/12), bone (Waterman 1959, fig.19, 16; Fig.940, *7900*, *AY* 17/12), ivory (*7889*, ibid.) and limestone (Fig.102, *690*, *AY* 17/4) to make rods, gaming pieces and spindle whorls. Other small lathe-turned tools of bone, for example, styli or parchment prickers and thread-reels, have been found in medieval York (Figs.925, 930–1, *AY* 17/12), suggesting that small-scale turning of this type continued in use.

Although it dates from Period 6, *8188* (see Fig.980, p.2112) could be a small yew bow for either a bow-powered lathe or a bow-drill, and is further evidence that bow-powered woodworking tools, including lathes, could have been used at Coppergate for turning small objects in wood and other materials. Similar small wooden bows have been found on other sites. These include two late 9th century examples from Portchester Castle (Cunliffe 1976, 224, fig.143, 90–1). One is a complete wooden rod with an expanded perforated head at one end with a peg in a circular hole, while the other end has an all-in-one-piece branch carved into a peg-like projection and both 'pegs' are perforated by small holes for a cord which would have stretched between them parallel to the rod. The other Portchester bow is a fragment of an expanded terminal similar to the first. Both these tools were found in the same pit as four lathe-turned bowl/cup cores and a hook-ended tool suggesting that they may all have come from a turner's workshop. Another 13th–14th century bow was found in Århus (Andersen et al. 1971, 260, BLG). It was a wooden rod 283mm long with a square cross-section in the middle and rectangular cross-sections at both ends which were perforated by small holes for the cord. Future finds may help to shed more light on the tools and techniques involved in the use of bows for turning.

Using evidence from the cores (and some vessels), it is possible to suggest how and why small vessels were made on a bow-powered lathe. A bow-lathe has many advantages over a large pole-lathe. If there was a demand for very small turned cups and bowls, it would have been economical and practical to have used small pieces of timber with as little waste as possible. Bow-lathes would have used small rough-outs, provided a very rapid spin with the work moving through many revolutions forward before the back stroke, and a high degree of control and precision. They would have been ideal for the scale of work involved in producing small vessels and also very tiny solid objects.

Could the centre marks in the nine Coppergate cores and end waste *8221* have been made by centre attachments that were intended to remain firmly fixed in the roughout and provide enough torque to rotate it? Let us consider a small vessel or roughout with a diameter of 100mm. The moment of inertia (MOI) of a vessel/roughout with a diameter of 150mm is over seven times that of the one measuring 100mm diameter. The difference becomes even greater in a vessel/roughout measuring 200mm diameter whose MOI is 32 times that of the 100mm one (assuming the vessels/roughouts are the same shape). Starting with an even smaller vessel or roughout of only 70mm diameter, the MOI of a vessel/roughout with a diameter of 150mm is 45 times that of the one measuring 70mm, one of 200mm has an MOI of 190 times and one of 250mm has an MOI of 581 times that of the one measuring 70mm. This makes it very possible that on a small lathe, very small spikes with lozenge-, square-, triangular- or rectangular-shaped cross-sections could be have been used on the ends of small mandrels to act as fixed centres and provide enough torque to turn a roughout without the centre moving or becoming loose, provided the diameter of the work was quite small.

A small 8th century rectangular object with truncated corners found on the market place site at Ribe in Denmark, where a variety of crafts were carried out, has been interpreted as a 'carrier' for a lathe, or a fixed centre point to be attached to the cup centre of roughouts (Jensen 1991, 27). It originally had three iron spikes placed centrally in a row, but only the middle one survives. The object may have been mounted in the end of a wooden mandrel for a bow-powered lathe.

The frequency diagram in Fig.1001 shows the measurable diameters of all the lathe-turned vessels

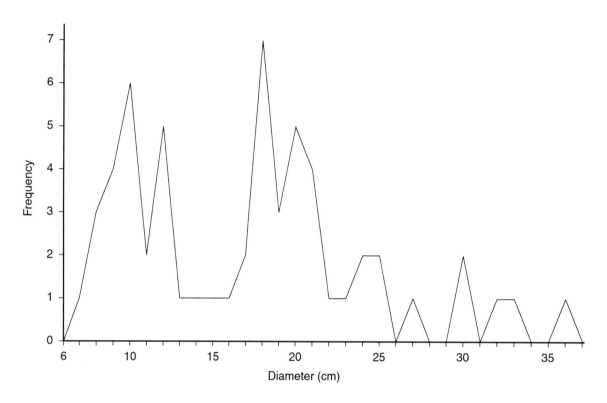

Fig.1001 *Frequency diagram of measurable diameters of all lathe-turned vessels from Coppergate*

found on the Coppergate sites. All of the larger vessels would have been turned on the pole-lathe. Seventeen spindle-turned cups have diameters of 76–126mm, and two unfinished spindle-turned cups (*8200–1*) have diameters of only 72 and 76mm (Fig.996). Some of these vessels with very low MOIs could certainly have been turned on a small bow-powered lathe with fixed mandrels. Unfortunately, neither of the unfinished cups has evidence of fixed centres: *8200* has a 12mm deep V-sectioned cup centre and no spur centre mark, although there is a well-formed base 26mm diameter which could have been cut across, and *8201* is only a fragment with no surviving cup centre and a knob at the spur centre.

Why would the Anglo-Scandinavian turners choose to use fixed centres in spindle-turning when it is possible to revolve the entire roughout between two circular metal point centres? One possible reason is that a bow-powered lathe cannot cope with large heavy roughouts, and in order to cut down the weight, some roughouts were prepared from lengths of roundwood without leaving a projecting cylinder for the bow to wrap around as the cord in a pole-lathe. Secondly, if a bow was moved horizontally without restraint, its end may have had considerable

lateral freedom of movement making it difficult to control the cord on the mandrel. A special mandrel (perhaps with restraining ridges between which the bow-string moved and with a much smaller diameter than the usual roughout cylinder in spindle-turning) would have solved both problems, but would require a fixed centre in spindle-turning.

The third reason is illustrated by Fig.1002a–b which shows overhead views of how a roughout may have been mounted on a bow-lathe between two centres with the bow cord wrapped around a separate mandrel. A fact that becomes immediately apparent is that the turner cannot cut on the same side of the assembly as the mandrel since the bow needs clearance on both sides of the lathe and would prevent the cutting tool from reaching the work. It would have been essential for the turner to have cut on the opposite side to the mandrel for each stage of the turning, that is the outside and the inside of the bowl, even if an assistant used the bow while the turner worked on the vessel. This is made possible by having a separate mandrel. In Fig.1002a, the turner uses the stock as a tool-rest and cuts the inside of the bowl. In this position, the mandrel with its spike is fixed to the spur centre of the vessel and leaves a correspond-

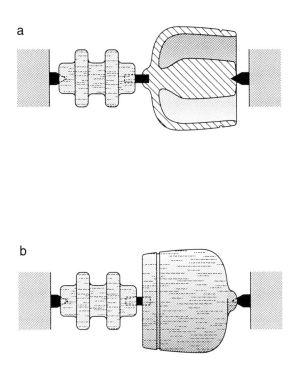

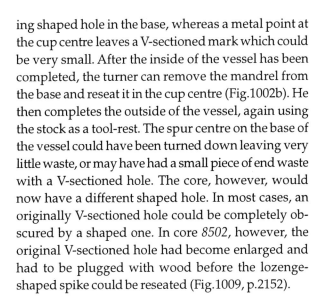

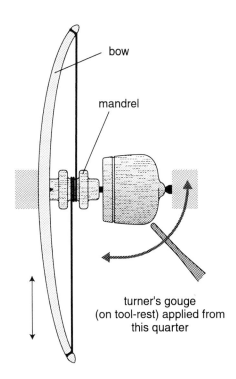

bow

mandrel

turner's gouge
(on tool-rest) applied from
this quarter

Fig.1002 Overhead views of mounting a bow-lathe: (a) to complete the inside of the vessel; (b) to complete the outside of the vessel

ing shaped hole in the base, whereas a metal point at the cup centre leaves a V-sectioned mark which could be very small. After the inside of the vessel has been completed, the turner can remove the mandrel from the base and reseat it in the cup centre (Fig.1002b). He then completes the outside of the vessel, again using the stock as a tool-rest. The spur centre on the base of the vessel could have been turned down leaving very little waste, or may have had a small piece of end waste with a V-sectioned hole. The core, however, would now have a different shaped hole. In most cases, an originally V-sectioned hole could be completely obscured by a shaped one. In core *8502*, however, the original V-sectioned hole had become enlarged and had to be plugged with wood before the lozenge-shaped spike could be reseated (Fig.1009, p.2152).

In Fig.1002, the inside of the bowl was turned first. If the processes had been reversed, with the outside turned before the inside, the resulting core would have had a V-sectioned hole which obscured the original shaped one. Cores with V-sectioned holes may result from spindle-turning on either a bow-powered lathe or a pole-lathe. Cores with fixed mandrel marks, however, are almost certainly evidence for the former. Small cores with very small V-sectioned holes, e.g. one maple and two birch cores

(*8321, 8480–1*) all found in the same context, are examples of the type of waste which could have come from a bow-powered lathe (Fig.1009).

Cores and other waste (Tables 195–208)

The function of cores from inside face-turned or spindle-turned vessels has already been described (pp.2122, 2133, Figs.990, 999). The 301 cores found at 16–22 Coppergate, the Coppergate watching brief site and 22 Piccadilly display a variety of shapes and sizes, at least twelve different wood species, and many different features which can give information about some of the tools and processes used in York to manufacture turned wooden vessels. This is the largest quantity of lathe-turned waste cores found on any site in Britain at any period, and they are sufficiently well preserved to allow quantitative analyses, the results of which are presented in Tables 195–208, pp.2153–8.

Tables 195–204 are related matrices using five important variables: shape, method of fixing centre attachments, species, period and whether face-turned or spindle-turned.

The range of shapes displayed by cores from Coppergate and other sites is illustrated in Fig.1003

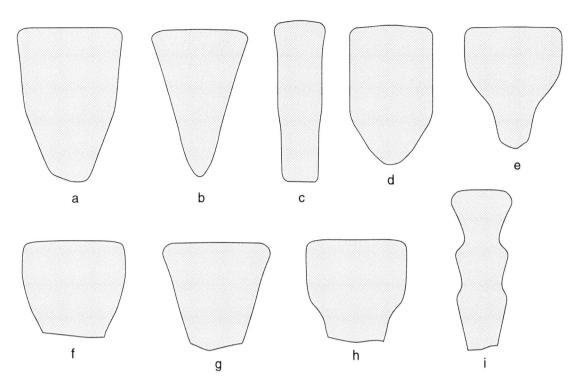

Fig.1003 *The nine basic core outline shapes: (a) curved conical; (b) conical; (c) cylindrical; (d) cylindrical and conical; (e) S-shaped; (f) truncated curved conical; (g) truncated conical; (h) truncated S-shaped; (i) irregular*

and all nine basic outlines are found in Anglo-Scandinavian York, although it is accepted that the difference between some of them is very arbitrary. Different shapes could have been the result of making different sizes of vessel, of face-turning or spindle-turning, of a repeated process, of using the same tool etc. Important facts emerge from some of the matrices which may help to explain this variation in shape.

Table 195 (p.2153) gives the incidence of different shapes produced by face-turning or spindle-turning. Many of the face-turned cores have truncated shapes with wide rather than pointed bases, and were produced when the turner reduced the risk that the core would break before his work was finished by leaving a wide base. He needed to remove less wood than for a bowl with a conical or curved conical core and the method was therefore economical of time. However, whereas in general the latter cores could either be parted off the lathe or snapped off easily at their points, the truncated cores needed extra effort and skill to remove them cleanly after the assembly had been removed from the lathe. Some truncated cores have 'feet' where they were not removed with an absolutely straight cut and brought some of the underlying wood with them, leaving a deeper scar in the internal base of the vessel, e.g. *8246, 8277, 8306*

and *8309* (Fig.1005). The foot is particularly marked in *8306* and *8309*. Most of the cores with feet came from Period 5B or 5C. There are 184 face-turned cores from Coppergate, only 31 of which have narrowed or pointed bases, showing that the Anglo-Scandinavian turners preferred to leave wide core bases when face-turning. The same table shows that of 112 spindle-turned cores, only three are truncated, turners preferring to create either narrowed or pointed cores when spindle-turning. This choice is also connected to the nature of the wood and its grain direction, since it is much more difficult to remove a core with a wide base if cutting across the grain, which would be the case if the vessel were spindle-turned. In addition, many spindle-turned vessels had very narrow or even globular profiles, which would also have hindered the removal of a core with a wide base, as described above. Thus, most truncated cores were face-turned and most narrow and pointed cores were spindle-turned.

There seem to have been two basic groups of spindle-turned core shapes. One was the conical and curved conical group (62 cores), which varied in size from tiny cores such as *8353* which is only 35mm in diameter and 26mm long (Fig.1007), to long cores such as *8334* which is 89mm long and 47mm in di-

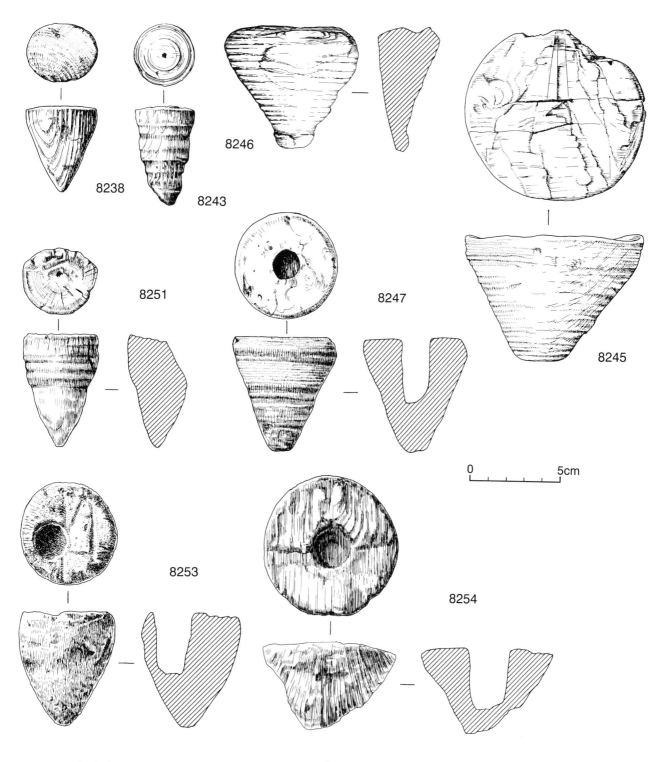

8238

8243

8246

8245

8251

8247

8253

8254

0   5cm

Fig.1004 *Conical cores 8238, 8243, 8245–7, 8251, 8253–4, all from 16–22 Coppergate. Scale 1:2*

ameter. The cores in this group most probably came from vessels with rounded profiles, but varying in size. The second group is of narrow cylindrical, cylindrical and conical, and irregular cores, some of

them over 75mm long, which were almost exclusively spindle-turned, and probably came from narrow and sometimes deep, straight-sided or globular vessels.

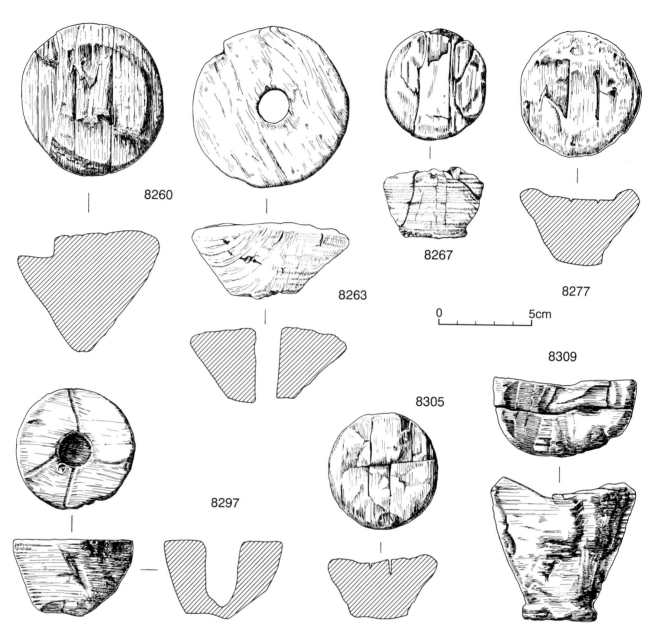

Fig.1005 *Conical core 8260; truncated conical cores 8263, 8267, 8277, 8297, 8305, 8309, all from 16–22 Coppergate. Scale 1:2*

Table 196 (p.2154) gives the incidence of different shapes produced in various species and clearly shows that alder and field maple, the two main species selected by Anglo-Scandinavian turners in York, were used to turn many types of vessels, producing all the nine shapes of cores. Birch is the only other species to display a significant range in core shapes, with four different types. Although curved conical cores were mainly produced by turning in alder and field maple, this shape was produced by turning in at least nine different species, including one which is oak. The seven species other than alder and field maple

were all spindle-turned, a feature which is explained below in relation to Table 200 (p.2156).

Table 197 (p.2154) shows which shapes were produced at different periods. All but 37 of the 301 cores found on the Coppergate and 22 Piccadilly sites were firmly dated to between c.930 and the mid 11th century, and these 264 cores include all nine shapes. Five of the other 37 were undated and five more were Anglo-Scandinavian but not attributable to any particular period. The overwhelming conclusion is that although there was lathe-turning from the earliest

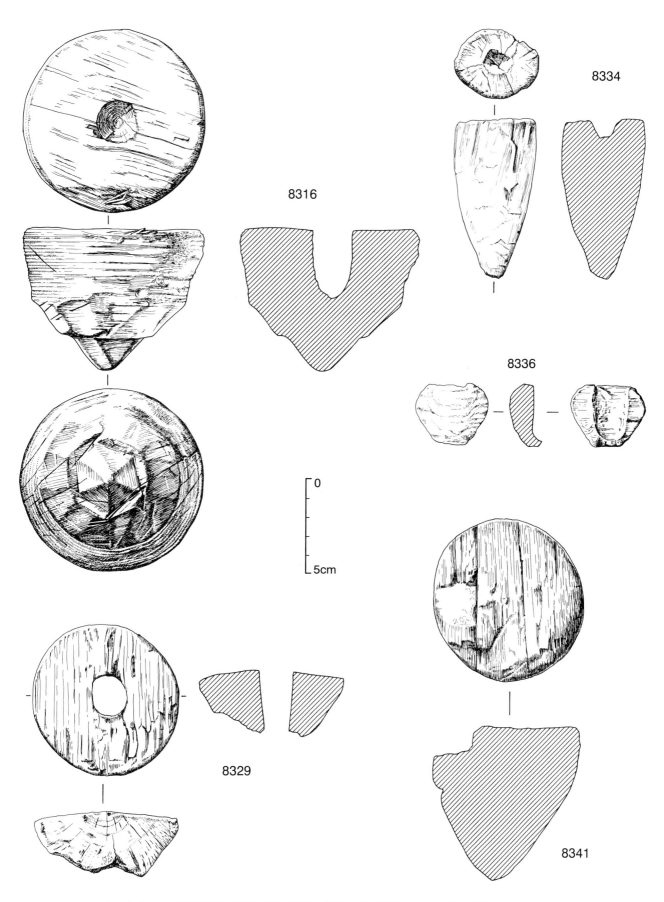

Fig.1006 *Curved conical cores 8316, 8329, 8334, 8336, 8341, all from 16–22 Coppergate. Scale 1:2*

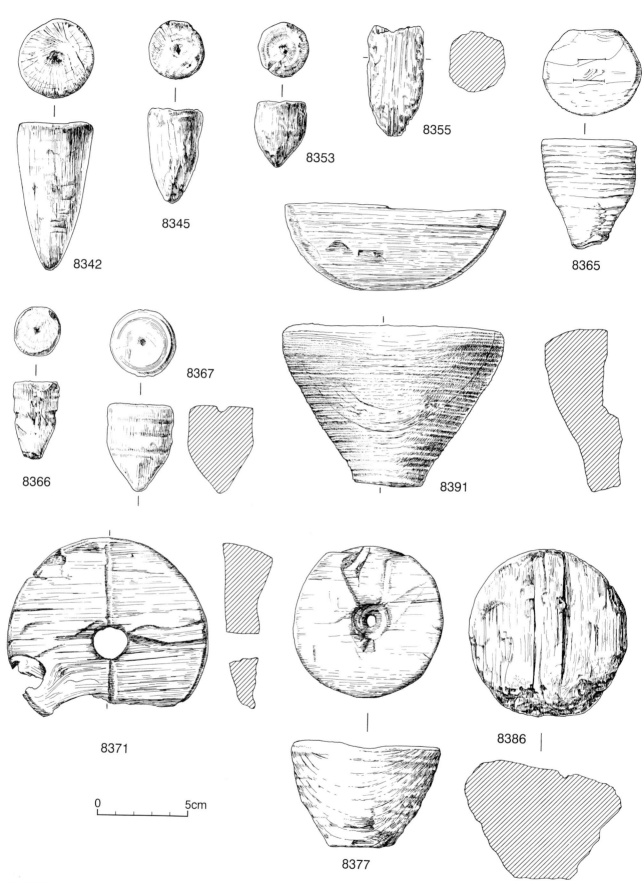

8355

8353

8345

8342

8365

8367

8366

8391

8371

8386

8377

0   5cm

Fig.1007 *Curved conical cores 8342, 8345, 8353, 8355, 8365–7; truncated curved conical cores 8371, 8377, 8386, 8391, all from 16–22 Coppergate. Scale 1:2*

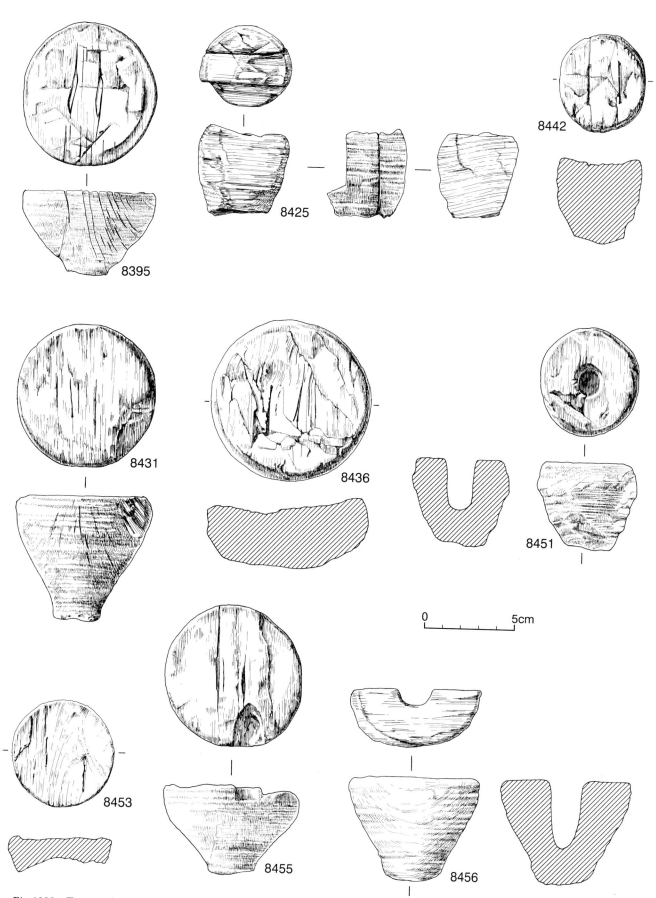

Fig.1008 *Truncated curved conical cores 8395, 8425, 8436, 8442, 8451, 8453; S-shaped cores 8431, 8455–6, all from 16–22 Coppergate. Scale 1:2*

8442

8425

8395

8431

8436

8451

8453

8455

8456

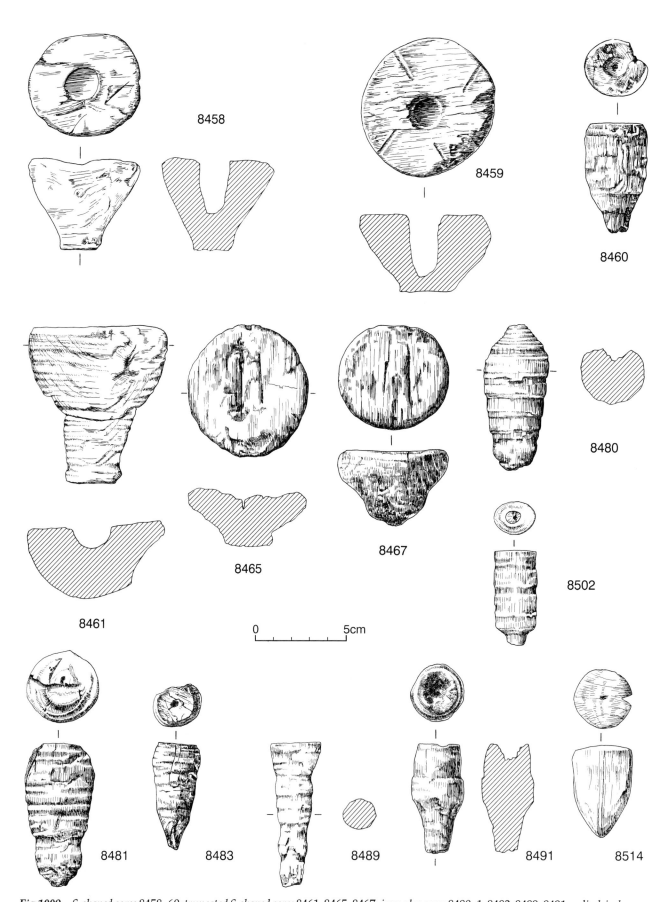

Fig.1009   *S-shaped cores 8458–60; truncated S-shaped cores 8461, 8465, 8467; irregular cores 8480–1, 8483, 8489, 8491; cylindrical core 8502; cylindrical and conical core 8514, all from 16–22 Coppergate. Scale 1:2*

Anglo-Scandinavian occupation of the area in the mid–late 9th century, lathe-turning on a commercial scale was carried out on or near Coppergate mainly from c.930 to the early–mid 11th century; since all nine core shapes are represented, a wide range of vessels must have been produced. The deposits dated to Period 5C are limited in extent (see Fig.963, p.2079), so the fourteen cores from these deposits suggest that lathe-turning may have continued in the mid–late 11th century. In addition, there are no late 11th–16th century deposits surviving in the street frontage areas where the majority of cores were found, so the nine cores dated to Period 6 may also represent a continuation of lathe-turning in the area.

Table 197 also shows that 222 out of the 301 cores were of only four types — conical, curved conical and their truncated versions. These four shapes, however, have been found in layers dating to Periods 3–6, and must have been produced from the earliest Anglo-Scandinavian settlement in the area right through to the medieval period. When turning between two centres on a pole-lathe, it is very important to be able to create the desired vessel profile and also to be able to avoid the tool shaft rubbing against the vessel rim or the core, a problem not encountered on modern lathes where the face-plate method can be used. These four core shapes are those usually produced when turning wide-mouthed bowls and cups with rounded profiles where there is little or no restriction at the mouth for inserting tools to undercut the core or thin down the walls; they must therefore represent the majority of vessels which were being turned in Coppergate, both face-turned and spindle-turned (pp.2165–86).

The S-shaped and truncated S-shaped cores are probably variations of the curved conical types, with

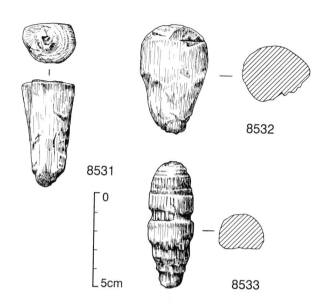

Fig.1010 *Middle cores 8531–3 from a spindle-turned stacking process, all from 16–22 Coppergate. Scale 1:2*

greater emphasis on the undercutting of the core when nearly all of the internal shaping was completed creating an incurving narrower core base. This must be linked to the turner's need to be both economical with time and be able to remove the core easily as already discussed. There are 27 of these cores (including one from 22 Piccadilly), only two of which were spindle-turned, and all but one (undated) are dated between Periods 4B and 5B.

Table 198 gives the incidence of the various types of centre attachments used in face- and spindle-turning. Apart from four cores on which there is either no surviving traces (and three on which there is no available evidence at all, either face-turned or spindle-turned), all the face-turned cores were firmly fixed to the mandrel by attachments in the

Table 195   The incidence of different core shapes at 16–22 Coppergate produced by face-turning or spindle-turning: C conical; TC truncated conical; CC curved conical; TCC truncated curved conical; SS S-shaped; TSS truncated S-shaped; I irregular; CYL cylindrical; C/C cylindrical and conical; ? shape unknown

	C	TC	CC	TCC	SS	TSS	I	CYL	C/C	?	Total
Face-turned	9	53	13	82	6	18		1		2	184
Spindle-turned	15	1	47	1	1	1	14	16	16		112
?										3	3
Total	**24**	**54**	**60**	**83**	**7**	**19**	**14**	**17**	**16**	**5**	**299**

Table 196 The incidence of different core shapes at 16–22 Coppergate produced in various species of wood

	Alder	Maple	Hazel	Holly/Lime	Yew	Birch	Poplar	Willow	Elder	Ash	Pomoideae	Not Identifiable	Oak	Total
C	10	12								1		1		24
TC	43	9										2		54
CC	20	29	1	1		4	1		1	1		1	1	60
TCC	73	7			1	1						1		83
SS	5	2												7
TSS	16	2										1		19
I	4	7				3								14
CYL	5	10						1			1			17
C/C	5	6				4					1			16
?	3					1						1		5
Total	**184**	**84**	**1**	**1**	**1**	**13**	**1**	**1**	**1**	**2**	**2**	**7**	**1**	**299**

form of multiple metal plates or a carved cylinder on the end of the mandrel, leaving a pair (or pairs) of slits or a circular augered hole respectively. The multiple metal plate type was the one most commonly used. Apart from three cores on which there are no surviving traces, 98 of the spindle-turned cores have V-sectioned holes made by single metal point centres, eight have lozenge-, triangular- or rectangular-shaped holes made by fixed metal point centres and three were middle cores from the stacking technique and were therefore never fastened to a centre.

The frequency of centre attachment types occurring with various core shapes is shown in Table 199. Multiple metal plate and mandrel hole centre marks survive on 182 face-turned cores, the majority of which were truncated conical, truncated curved conical and truncated S-shaped in outline. V-sectioned single metal point marks survive on 98 spindle-turned cores, the majority of which fall into the two groups already discussed — conical/curved conical, and cylindrical/cylindrical and conical/irregular, as do the fixed single metal point centres with various shapes.

Table 197 The incidence of each core shape produced at different periods at 16–22 Coppergate

	3	A/S	4A	4B	5A	5B	5Cf	5Cr	6	?	Total
C			1	11	2	8		1		1	24
TC		1		2	1	40	4	3	2	1	54
CC		1	1	13	6	33		2	3	1	60
TCC	1	1		20	3	50		4	2	2	83
SS				2	1	4					7
TSS				2	1	15				1	19
I				8		5			1		14
CYL				10		7					17
C/C				4	1	10				1	16
?				1		4					5
Total	**1**	**3**	**2**	**73**	**15**	**176**	**4**	**10**	**8**	**7**	**299**

2154

Table 198 The number of examples of each type of centre attachment mark found on the cores from 16–22 Coppergate in relation to turning technique

	=	O/□	●	◆/▲/▬	Middle	NO	?	Total
Face-turned	119	61				4		184
Spindle-turned			97	9	3	3		112
?							3	3
Total	119	61	97	9	3	7	3	299

Key to Tables 198–9, 201, 203

=	multiple metal plate
O/□	mandrel hole
●	rotational single metal point
◆/▲/▬	fixed-shape metal point
Middle	middle core
NO	no evidence
?	unknown

The information provided by Table 200 is extremely important in showing patterns of deliberate selection and exploitation of particular species for different vessels and methods of turning. On the evidence of the cores, the most commonly chosen species for turned vessels was alder (*Alnus glutinosa*), with field maple (*Acer campestre*) second. Both were used for face-turning and spindle-turning, but whereas alder was used to turn most face-turned vessels, field maple was preferred for spindle-turned vessels. Based on core evidence, face-turned vessels were almost exclusively turned from alder and field maple in Coppergate, with only two other species identified as single examples of yew and birch cores. On the other hand, spindle-turned vessels were mainly made of field maple, alder and birch with small numbers of other species such as hazel, holly or lime, poplar, willow, elder, ash, Pomoideae (e.g. apple, pear, rowan, hawthorn) and oak represented as well. The statement made by MacGregor about cores from Coppergate, that 'Eight cores were found . . . all of them ash' (1978, 51), has been proved to be incorrect in the light of more recent species identification of the York cores by Allan Hall. MacGregor referred to three illustrations of Coppergate cores (ibid., fig.33, 7–9), *8251, 8334* and *8464*, two of which are field maple, the other hazel. Only two out of 299

Table 199 The number of examples of each type of centre attachment mark found on the cores from 16–22 Coppergate in relation to core shape

	=	O/□	●	◆/▲/▬	Middle	NO	?	Total
C	3	6	13	1	1			24
TC	40	12	1			1		54
CC	6	7	39	5	1	2		60
TCC	53	27	1			2		83
SS	1	5	1					7
TSS	15	3	1					19
I			12	1	1			14
CYL		1	14	1		1		17
C/C			15	1				16
?		1				1	3	5
Total	119	61	97	9	3	7	3	299

Table 200 The incidence of face-turned and spindle-turned cores at 16–22 Coppergate produced in various species of wood

	Alder	Maple	Hazel	Holly/Lime	Yew	Birch	Poplar	Willow	Elder	Ash	Pomoideae	Not Identifiable	Oak	Total
FT	156	23			1	1						3		184
ST	27	61	1	1		11	1	1	1	2	2	3	1	112
?	1					1						1		3
Total	**184**	**84**	**1**	**1**	**1**	**13**	**1**	**1**	**1**	**2**	**2**	**7**	**1**	**299**

Table 201 The number of examples of each type of centre attachment mark found on the cores from 16–22 Coppergate in relation to species of wood

	Alder	Maple	Hazel	Holly/Lime	Yew	Birch	Poplar	Willow	Elder	Ash	Pomoideae	Not Identifiable	Oak	Total
=	106	11			1							1		119
O/□	46	12				1						2		61
●	25	53	1	1		9	1		1	2	1	3		97
◆/▲/━	2	6									1			9
Middle		1				2								3
NO	4	1						1					1	7
?	1					1						1		3
Total	**184**	**84**	**1**	**1**	**1**	**13**	**1**	**1**	**1**	**2**	**2**	**7**	**1**	**299**

Table 202 The incidence of cores of various species at different periods at 16–22 Coppergate

	Alder	Maple	Hazel	Holly/Lime	Yew	Birch	Poplar	Willow	Elder	Ash	Pomoideae	Not Identifiable	Oak	Total
3	1													1
3/4/5	2	1												3
4A										2				2
4B	39	26				5		1			2			73
5A	6	7							1			1		15
5B	116	46	1			7						5	1	176
5Cf	4													4
5Cr	9											1		10
6	2	3		1		1	1							8
?		5	1		1									7
Total	**184**	**84**	**1**	**1**	**1**	**13**	**1**	**1**	**1**	**2**	**2**	**7**	**1**	**299**

Table 203 The nun.ber of examples of each type of centre attachment mark found on the cores from 16–22 Coppergate in relation to period

	3	3/4/5	4A	4B	5A	5B	5Cf	5Cr	6	?	Total
=		2		8	2	89	4	7	2	5	119
O/□	1			21	4	30		2	2	1	61
●		1	2	36	7	46		1	3	1	97
◆/▲/▬				2	2	5					9
Middle				2					1		3
NO				4		3					7
?						3					3
Total	**1**	**3**	**2**	**73**	**15**	**176**	**4**	**10**	**8**	**7**	**299**

cores from Coppergate were in fact made of ash. The information about species gleaned from these core analyses and surviving vessels (Tables 211–12, pp.2194–5) must also correct another previously published and misleading statement, that in the later Viking Age 'many types of wood were used to make these bowls and cups, with ash, yew and maple probably the most common' (Hall 1984, 78). They should be replaced by alder, field maple and birch in that order.

Table 201 supports the data already given in Table 200 where the face-turned cores with solidly fixed cup centres are mainly alder and field maple, and the spindle-turned cores with either V-sectioned or lozenge-shaped centre holes are mainly alder, field maple and birch with small numbers of other species. In the face-turned group, there seems to have been no particular advantage to using either alder or field maple with either the multiple metal plate or mandrel hole type centre attachments.

Tables 202–4 chart the species of wood, the methods of fixing the centre attachments and face-turning or spindle-turning technique in various periods to ascertain whether there were any trends in exploitation of raw material or turning techniques over time. In Table 202, alder and field maple appear to have been the most popular species throughout the entire life of the site, emphasising their suitability for turning and for the purposes for which the vessels were made (see pp.2155, 2194–6). Although it occurs in much smaller quantities, birch also seems to have been popular throughout the Anglo-Scandinavian period and into the medieval. Other species are present in very small numbers at all periods and do not represent any particular pattern of planned exploitation. Tables 203–4 show that both face-turning and spindle-turning and all the types of fixing centre attachments found on the York cores appear to be used over the entire life of the site, with obvious concentrations in Periods 4B and 5B when the largest amount of evidence survives. This must indicate the conservatism of the craftsmen in their use of well-developed tools and techniques.

Tables 205–8 take the analyses a stage further and combine cores with other waste products so that the

Table 204 The incidence of face-turned and spindle-turned cores at 16–22 Coppergate in relation to period

	3	3/4/5	4A	4B	5A	5B	5Cf	5Cr	6	?	Total
FT	1	2	1	30	6	121	4	9	4	6	184
ST		1	1	43	9	52		1	4	1	112
?						3					3
Total	**1**	**3**	**2**	**73**	**15**	**176**	**4**	**10**	**8**	**7**	**299**

Table 205 The incidence of face-turned waste products at 16–22 Coppergate in relation to period

	3	A/S	4A	4B	5A	5B	5Cf	5Cr	6	?	Total
Cores	1	2	1	30	6	121	4	9	4	6	184
Base Waste				2	2	10			1		15
Roughout/Offcut						1					1
Unfinished Vessel						1					1
Total	**1**	**2**	**1**	**32**	**8**	**133**	**4**	**9**	**5**	**6**	**201**

Table 206 The incidence of spindle-turned waste products at 16-22 Coppergate in relation to period

	3	A/S	4A	4B	5A	5B	5Cf	5Cr	6	?	Total
Cores		1	1	43	9	52		1	4	1	112
End Waste	2			7	1	7					17
Middle Waste				1							1
Roughouts						3			1		4
Unfinished	1			2							3
Blank?				1							1
Total	**3**	**1**	**1**	**54**	**10**	**62**		**1**	**5**	**1**	**138**

Table 207 The incidence of face-turned waste products at 16–22 Coppergate in relation to species of wood

	Alder	Maple	Hazel	Holly/Lime	Yew	Birch	Poplar	Willow	Elder	Ash	Pomoideae	Not Identifiable	Oak	Total
Cores	156	23			1	1						3		184
Base Waste	12	1						1				1		15
Roughout/Offcut	1													1
Unfinished Vessel	1													1
Total	**170**	**24**			**1**	**1**		**1**				**4**		**201**

Table 208 The incidence of spindle-turned waste products at 16–22 Coppergate in relation to species of wood

	Alder	Maple	Hazel	Holly/Lime	Yew	Birch	Poplar	Willow	Elder	Ash	Pomoideae	Not Identifiable	Oak	Total
Cores	27	61	1	1		11	1	1	1	2	2	3	1	112
End Waste	4	11				2								17
Middle Waste	1													1
Roughouts		3								1				4
Unfinished		3												3
Blank?						1								1
Total	**32**	**78**	**1**	**1**		**14**	**1**	**1**	**1**	**3**	**2**	**3**	**1**	**138**

entire residues of face-turning and spindle-turning techniques (a total of 339 individual items) can be looked at over time and in relation to species selection.

Tables 205–6, which show the incidence of various waste products at different periods, reinforce the situation suggested by Table 204. Adding other types of waste to the cores shows emphatically that face-turning and spindle-turning were used concurrently over the entire life of the site, with concentrations in Periods 4B and 5B. In addition, the two pieces of end waste 8219–20 and the unfinished cup 8200 are firmly dated to Period 3 and extend the definite use of spindle-turning for vessels back to the earliest Anglo-Scandinavian period on the site.

Tables 207–8, which show the different species of various types of waste products, reinforce the situation suggested by Table 200. Adding other types of waste to the cores shows without doubt that alder was the most commonly chosen species (202 of 339 items), with field maple second (102 of 339 items), and 35 other pieces made from ten other species. Apart from the medieval ash roughout 8199 (which was certainly not a vessel roughout), all the non-core spindle-turned waste products are of the three main spindle-turned species suggested by Table 200: field maple, alder and birch. Also, the non-core face-turned waste reinforces the idea that face-turned vessels were almost exclusively turned in alder.

Tools

The turner's most important tool was the lathe itself, and both pole-lathes and bow-powered lathes are discussed above (pp.2116–20 and 2142–5). The only surviving part of a lathe is 8237, the ash tool-rest support from Period 5B, although 9045–50 and 9052 are also possible tool-rest supports or brackets. The only metal parts of the lathe would have been the pointed centres on the lathe and the metal centre attachments on mandrels. If these were found in isolation, they might not be identified as lathe parts because they would simply resemble headless nails or flat rectangular blade fragments.

The Anglo-Scandinavian turner, like other woodworking specialists, needed to convert wood as a raw material from the growing tree to the finished article in various stages. Each stage involved a different set of woodworking techniques and hence a variety of tools. He had to turn trees into roughouts before he could begin his specialised work on the lathe. His toolkit, like that of his more recent counterpart, must have contained many ordinary woodworking tools such as axes, augers, chisels, mallets, knives, drawknives, hones and perhaps even saws in some instances. In addition, turners using lathes with two centres, such as pole-lathes and bow-powered lathes, have always had some distinctive tools designed for specific purposes. As well as cutting tools such as strong, open-ended gouges and chisels, they had hook-ended irons for cutting back the interior walls of a vessel and undercutting the core. Smaller or larger hooks were necessary for different tasks.

The quality of the tools available to the Anglo-Scandinavian and medieval turners in York would have been determined by contemporary levels of metalworking technology and the manufacturing skills of the blacksmiths who would have made their metal tools. The quality of blade steel available for woodworking tools in Anglo-Scandinavian York was very high (cf. analyses of axe 2255 and spoon bit 2265, Tables 85 and 87, AY 17/6). The number of specialised tools surviving, however, is always likely to be very low because they were valuable items unique to one craft, were resharpened constantly and used to exhaustion. The surviving collection of tools is in no way representative of the actual range used.

Felling, hewing and splitting axes and wedges would have been used by turners to prepare suitable lengths of wood for roughouts. Although four axes (2253–6), thirteen wooden wedges (8173–85) and four iron wedges (2257, 8170–2) have been found on the Coppergate site, dating from Periods 3 to 6, none can be directly attributed to wood-turners. Tools such as these would have been part of the turner's general kit. 2255–6 are probably felling axes. The small birch blank 8194, which is 255mm in diameter, almost certainly had its ends sawn across and shows that turners were using saws to make straight cuts across small tree trunks as early as the middle of the 10th century (Period 4B).

Simple shaping of roughouts would also have been done with shaping axes, knives, mallets and chisels. Offcut 8195, roughouts 8196–9, unfinished cup 8200 and most of the cylindrical pieces of spindle-turned end waste have axe cuts on some of their external surfaces, and end waste 8232 has possible knife cuts from shaping. Axe 2253 could have been used for shaping although its blade edge is sharpened on both sides. *8186* is a small woodworking mallet found in a pit dated to Period 4B (see Fig.979, p.2111). Its ends are well worn and compressed with use, and it could have been used with a chisel for tasks such as shaping roughouts, and cleaning internal and external bases after core removal. Mallets would also have been necessary for assembling the various wooden parts of portable lathes and especially for the constant securing, positioning and repositioning of wooden wedges holding the moveable stocks of the lathes. Only three small paring chisels/gouges have been found on the Coppergate site (*2143, 2269–70*), two Anglo-Scandinavian and one medieval in date. *2143* and *2269* could have been used with a chisel for light shaping work, including tasks such as cleaning after removing a core from a vessel.

Augers would have been essential tools, especially for making circular holes in the centre of roughouts needed in face-turning when the mandrels had shaped cylindrical ends corresponding to the size of the holes drilled. Sixty-one face-turned cores from Coppergate and one from 22 Piccadilly have circular mandrel hole centre marks, 59 of which can be measured and show that the York turners used augers which could cut holes of 14–24mm diameter. These are shown in the frequency graph in Fig.1011. The majority of cores with this type of centre attachment

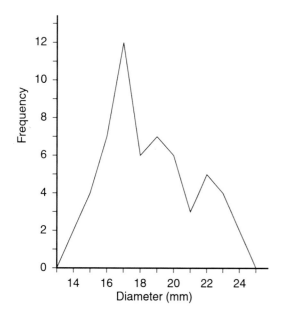

Fig.1011 *Frequency diagram of auger hole diameters in cores*

were found in layers dating to Periods 4B and 5B, but it was used from the earliest period of Anglo-Scandinavian turning in Period 3, right through to the medieval period, with a full range of auger diameters represented at most periods. The seriograph in Fig.1012 shows, however, that there was a greater tendency in Period 4B to use larger augers which made holes over 20mm diameter (and therefore correspondingly large mandrel ends would have been used) than in Period 5B, when the majority of cores have holes under 20mm diameter.

Some of the holes in cores can give more information about the types of augers used and the ways in which they were used. At least sixteen cores have holes with straight sides and clearly rounded bottoms indicating that the bits used in the augers had rounded ends (*8253, 8336, 8370, 8374, 8376, 8388–9, 8391, 8394, 8400, 8414, 8420, 8443, 8457–8, 8461*). Six bits found on the Coppergate site have rounded ends — *2262–5* from Period 4B, and *8189–90* from Period 6, which would have cut holes 24, 35, 12, 27, 12 and 8mm in diameter respectively. According to the diameters of the holes in cores, only *2262* could possibly have been used by a turner to cut similar holes since the others are either too large or too small (see Fig.1012). Coincidentally, both cores with holes 24mm diameter (*8261* and *8384*) came from contexts dating to Period 4B. Only core *8263* has a hole with tapered sides showing that a tapered auger bit had been used to drill it (Fig.1005, p.2148). A tapered spoon bit with a pointed end, *2266*, was found on the Coppergate site. It would have cut a hole only 13mm diameter, whereas the core hole was 17mm in diameter. Both were found in contexts dating to Period 5A, however, showing that these tools were being used in Coppergate by that time.

Three cores, *8316, 8389* and *8462*, have nicks in the sides of the holes which indicate that the auger was turned in a clockwise direction.

Once a roughout had been mounted on the lathe, the shaping would probably have been done using solid open-ended bowl gouges with U-shaped cross-sections, sharpened on the end with a single bevel under the cutting edge. These may have been similar to those used in bowl-turning in recent years on a pole-lathe, treadle lathe or electric-driven lathe (Fig.1013). Unfortunately, no undisputable turner's gouges have been found at the 16–22 Coppergate or

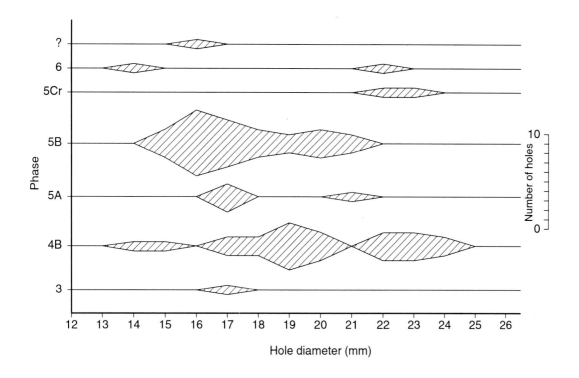

Fig.1012   Seriograph of auger hole diameters in cores

Piccadilly sites, despite the fact that the whole area must have been used for the turning craft for over 200 years. Although some of the thirteen spoon bits found on the site have been sharpened at the ends as well as down their sides (e.g. *2264* and *2266*), they are not the sort of tool which could have been used for bowl-turning where a wide, straight or curved cutting edge needs to be constantly sharpened and cut back, gradually reducing the blade length over time. Also, a bowl-turning gouge is not sharpened along its side as are spoon bits such as *2262–3* and *2265*. Certain tools have been identified as fragments of spoon bits even though they have little or no spoon end surviving, e.g. *2260–1* and *2265*, and it is possible that these may have been more like open-ended gouges when complete.

If tools had survived with their wooden handles intact, they would have been much more informative. Turners' gouges are characterised by very long, thick, solid wooden handles into which the tang of the tool is set longitudinally. These long handles were necessary to hold the tool steady and overcome the kick back caused by the reciprocating rotation. Rotary lathes do not always require such handles, and this difference can be seen in more recent pole-lathe

tools and rotary-lathe tools (Edlin 1949, pls.21 and 60). The bowl-turner in an illustration in the Bible Moralisée de Saint Louis (Paris Bibl. Nat. MS 11560, fo.84; front cover) is using such a gouge on the outside of a bowl, although the angle at which he is holding the tool is probably contrived for the manuscript illustrator's sake, as is the lack of a tool-rest. This illustration dates to c.1250. The tangs of augers, including spoon bits, are usually set perpendicularly to a transverse wooden handle.

A type of turner's chisel not found in the Coppergate excavations but which was used in other parts of late Anglo-Saxon England is represented by an 8th–9th century tool found in Bevois Street, Southampton (Addyman and Hill 1969, fig.24, 12; Morris 1982, fig.14.5C, 1). It has a fine, narrow, parallel-sided blade with a rectangular cross-section and a circular guard between blade and tang which would have butted against the wooden handle. It is sharpened on only one side of the cutting edge which is 6mm wide. The blade is worn down on one corner, and this asymmetrical pattern of wear can also be seen on a similar undated chisel from Northampton (ibid., fig.14.5C, 2). These chisels would probably have been used for spindle-turning handles such as *8995* or *8999*

2161

Fig.1013 *Lathe-turning tools for the St Fagan's pole-lathe*

(Fig.1142) or for cutting grooves on bowls and chair rails such as those from Winchester (Biddle 1990, fig.131, *3486*) and Eastgate, Beverley (Morris and Evans 1992, fig.95, 648), not for shaping the external and internal walls of vessels. A related tool is an undated open-ended gouge from Colchester, Essex (Morris 1982, fig.14.5, 3), which also has a circular guard, and may represent the kind of tool used in bowl-turning.

Most bowls and pieces of turning waste have traces of the non-decorative turning lines produced by the gouges. Even after a vessel has been used over a long period of time, these grooves can still be prominent, suggesting that the vessel surfaces were not artificially smoothed down with abrasives after turning. Some cores, such as *8367* (Fig.1007), have very fine turning lines, hinting at the fineness and sharpness of the gouge's cutting edge.

Hook-ended cutting irons were specialised tools useful for specific tasks in turning a vessel, and would only have been made by special commission for lathe-turners. One such tool (*9183*) was found in the Coppergate 'A' deposit in excavations at the corner of Coppergate and Castlegate in 1906, and was published in a photograph in the excavation report (Benson 1906, 73, pl.II). It was not then recognised as a lathe-turning tool, and nothing found in excavations up to this date had revealed that the Coppergate area was one connected with the turning of wooden vessels. The tool is now in the Yorkshire Museum Collections (YORYM: 551.48) and is published here for the first time as a lathe-turning tool (Fig.1014). It is in extremely good condition, considering that it has not undergone a modern programme of conservation, and the cutting edge is preserved. It is a one-piece tool with a flanged circular socket for a wooden handle which does not survive. The shank is a bar of iron/steel with a circu-

hooked end similar to the Coppergate tool but the hook is set at the end of a straight shaft. Examples are illustrated by Charles Holtzapffel (1846, 514, figs.368–71) and John Jacob Holtzapffel, who calls them straight-stemmed hook tools (1881, 24, fig.27). Various kinds of straight-stemmed hook tools were also used in Germany where different sized tools were called *Ausdrehhaken* or *Krummeissel* (Spannagel 1940, Abb.112–114, 116), and similar *crochets de tourneur* were used in the Forests of the Auvergne in France from at least the 17th century (Desvallées 1976, pls.1 and 2). All of the straight-stemmed hooked tools seem to have been used for hollowing out the inside of bowls whether on a lathe between two centres or on a more modern lathe with a face-plate. Those illustrated by Charles Holtzapffel were sharpened from the point around the hook, sometimes on the upper and lower edges. Similar double-edged turning hooks used in Sweden are described by Rudstrom as low-speed tools which were gouges with their cutting edge oriented at 90 degrees to the length of the tool (Rudstrom 1983, 93–4, fig.5). He also adds that a bent or an angled handle facilitates holding the tool at an efficient safe edge angle.

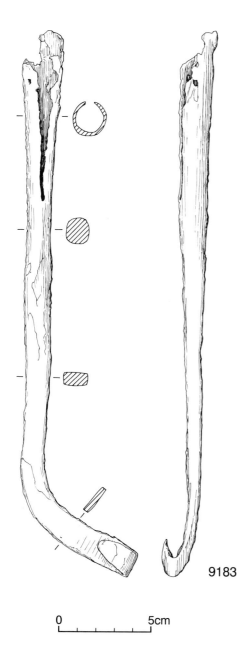

0   5cm

9183

Fig.1014 Hook-ended cutting iron 9183 found during excavations at the corner of Coppergate and Castlegate in 1906. Scale 1:2

lar cross-section which is flattened towards the cutting edge into a rectangular cross-sectioned bar. The last 90mm of the shank is bent at approximately 70 degrees from the rest, and the extreme 25–30mm of the tip is thinned into a blade edge and curves back on itself to form a hook. The sharpened cutting edge is positioned along the top of the hook.

Various types of hook-ended tool can be used for different tasks in lathe-turning. One type has a

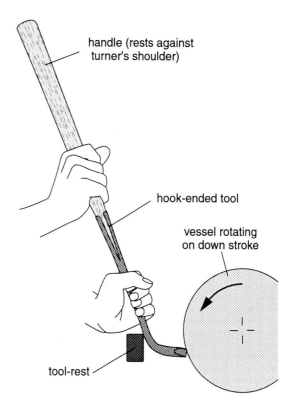

handle (rests against turner's shoulder)

hook-ended tool

vessel rotating on down stroke

tool-rest

Fig.1015 Diagram showing how hook-ended tool 9183 could have been used in lathe-turning

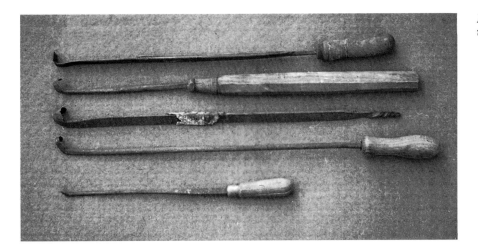

Fig.1016 *Old Welsh turning tools with hooks similar to 9183*

Although *9183* has a similar hooked end to all these tools, it is difficult to compare it with them because of the unusual angle at which the hooked cutting edge is set relative to the main handle. The bend or angle suggested by Rudstrom would leave the tool handle in the same plane as the hook so that the tool could be held and supported on a tool-rest horizontally. *9183* has its handle set in a different plane with an angle of 110 degrees between the bar with the hook and the handle (Fig.1015). This would mean that the small bar with the hook would have to be supported horizontally on a tool-rest whilst the handle was held almost vertically. This seems an awkward position for the turner to adopt, but may have been used for internal shaping on specific vessels. The only tools the author has found which are directly comparable with *9183* are four hooked irons lent to her by a dealer in old tools who said they were old Welsh turning tools (Fig.1016). These also had handles set at an angle to the cutting edge which would have required them to be held vertically.

Only one other hook-ended lathe-turning tool has been found in excavations in Britain. This is a 9th century iron socketed tool with a circular flanged socket and a rectangular cross-sectioned shaft whose end curves round to form a hook. It was found at Portchester Castle in the same pit as four lathe-turned cores and two bow-drills (Cunliffe 1976, 200, fig.135, 41 and pl.XXa). Its end is very corroded and it is impossible to identify a cutting edge. Unlike *9183*, it would have had a straight handle like the old English, German, French and Swedish tools described above.

A second type of hooked tool which has not been found at any period archaeologically and which is not related to the function of *9183* was used to make nested bowls from the same large roughout, smaller bowls being turned one from within the other to save both material and time. These tools, by extension from John Jacob Holtzapffel's description of the straight-stemmed type, should be called curved-stemmed hook tools. He described a method of nesting bowls where straight-stemmed hooks were held horizontally and used to make a series of grooves one or two inches deep across the face of a large roughout whose external profile had already been finished (Holtzapffel 1881, 24, figs.25–6). These grooves were sufficiently distant from each other to leave the edges of the bowls the appropriate thickness. Curved-stemmed hooked tools (ibid., fig.27) would then be used to carry the grooves further and deeper, at curves corresponding to the curvatures of the different bowls. The turner would have needed to use a series of curved-stemmed hooked tools with shafts still more curved until the grooves were cut to the required depths and shapes. It is uncertain when turners began using this method, but there is no evidence from tools, waste products or vessels to suggest that it was used by Anglo-Scandinavian or medieval turners in Britain who seem to have face-turned one vessel from one roughout. The stacking method used by Anglo-Scandinavian turners in York when spindle-turning some vessels (p.2142 and

Fig.999) is another method which would have helped to save time.

Turners in Britain and Germany in more recent times have used curved-stemmed hooked tools to make nested bowls, giving us models of what these tools would look like if found archaeologically. Their form reinforces the idea that *9183* was not used for nesting bowls. The Lailey family's hooked tools, last used by George William Lailey (1869–1958) to turn nested bowls at Bucklebury, are now housed at the Museum of English Rural Life at the University of Reading. Some of these were George's own tools, but others had been inherited from his grandfather, William (1782–1871) (P. Dixon, pers. comm.), putting the method of nesting back to the early 19th century if not earlier. The Museum of English Rural Life has photographs of Lailey and some of his nested bowls and curved-stemmed hooked tools (Fitzrandolph and Hay 1926, 54; Sparkes 1977, 17–19), and a photograph of Robert Jordan of Wellington with his pole-lathe, tools and a set of nested bowls was published in the *Wellington Journal* and *Shrewsbury News* in May 1937 (Edlin 1949, pl.21). David Fankhauser, a bowl-turner in Zillertal, Germany, also used curved-stemmed hooked tools to make nested bowls (Spannagel 1940, Abb.347–51).

The most important property of a lathe-turning tool is its razor-sharpness, especially when used with a pole-lathe without constant rotary motion. A hone or some form of grindstone to keep the cutting tools sharp would have been in constant use. Many hones were found on the Coppergate sites (*AY* 17/14) but none could definitely be identified as lathe-turners' hones as opposed to purely domestic ones. In addition, there are 29 circular grindstones, each with a central hole for an axle, which may have been used to sharpen woodworking tools. A similar 11th century object was found in Viking Age Dublin (O'Brien 1978, 41).

The products of the lathe-turners

In archaeological reports, circular open-topped lathe-turned wooden vessels have been variously called bowls, basins, dishes, plates, platters, trenchers and cups, with no consistency as to shape, size or use. The shapes and sizes of archaeological examples are extremely varied, and it is likely that the names given to them by those who made and used them depended on their shape, size, function and perhaps the materials they were made from. Except in a very general sense, we should not attempt to assign specific names to excavated examples. In an 11th century Anglo-Saxon manuscript commonly referred to as the 'Gerefa', which is an adjunct to the 'Rectitudines Singularum Personarum' (Cambridge Corpus Christi College MS CCCLXXXIII, fo.102), there are at least six Old English words which may refer to this type of vessel — *dixas, beodas, bleda* and *melas* which are probably different sorts of bowls, *stelmelas* which are probably bowls with handles, and *cuppan* or cups (Cunningham 1910, 572–3). All these are among the utensils the 'wise reeve' ought to provide for the Anglo-Saxon manor. In medieval England, makers and users of turned wooden vessels also made distinctions between types, since many different terms are used in manuscripts to describe them, for example, in Latin in 12th–13th century manuscripts — *discis* (dishes), *platellis* (platters), *salseriis* (saucers), *scutellis* (bowls) and *ciphis* (cups) (Morris 1984a, MS238–9). Although there are no documents which refer to Viking Age wooden vessels in Britain, the variety of archaeological material suggests that different shapes and sizes would also have had their own names as they were some of the commonest items in Anglo-Saxon, Anglo-Scandinavian and medieval households, used for many different purposes, some now lost to us.

Bowls and cups

Lathe-turned vessels excavated from Coppergate and Bedern include 94 bowls (*3534–612, 9165–8, 9202–6, 9226–31*), 25 cups (*8613–37*) and five lids (*8638–42*). For future research and in order to make the comparative study of these and all other wooden lathe-turned vessels easier, a consistent terminology should be used to describe their appearance and therefore the techniques used to make them. Fig.1017 illustrates the eight profiles, twelve rim forms and five base outlines found on most turned vessels. Most can be seen on the Coppergate vessels and involved differing levels of skill or different techniques to produce them. The vessels in the catalogue have been described using this terminology.

The majority of turned vessels which would normally be referred to as bowls have rounded profiles (Fig.1017, 2) and rounded rims, represented by at least 65 profiles and 51 rim examples from Coppergate and Bedern. Some have shallow rounded shapes, e.g. *8572, 8579* and *9231*, and can be almost

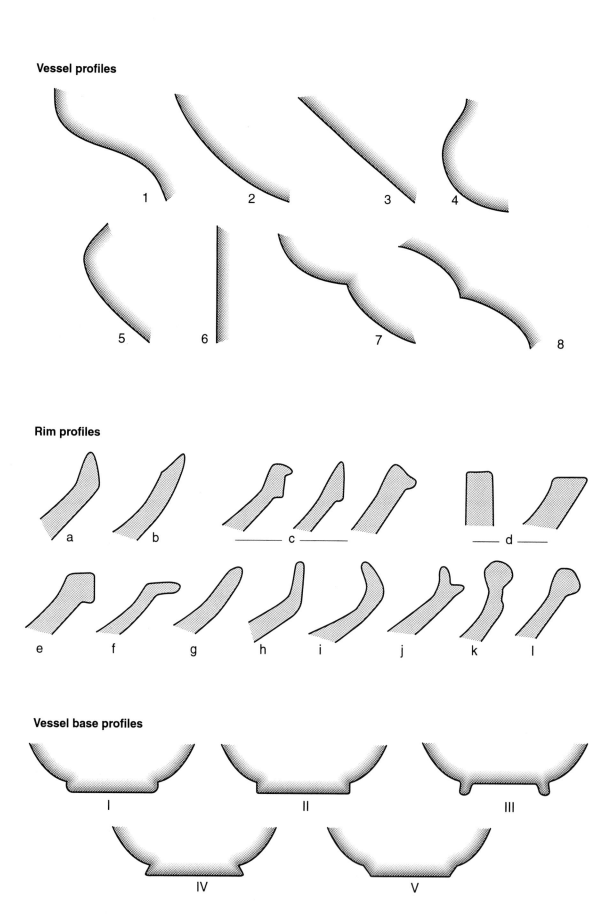

Fig.1017 *Turned vessel shapes: vessel profiles, rim profiles and base profiles*

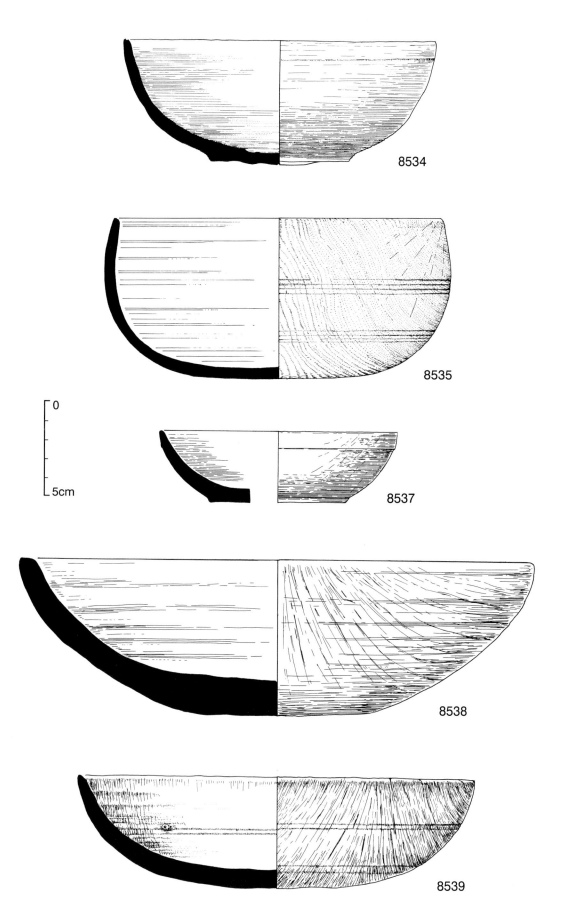

Fig.1018 *Lathe-turned bowls from 16–22 Coppergate 8534–5, 8537–9. Scale 1:2*

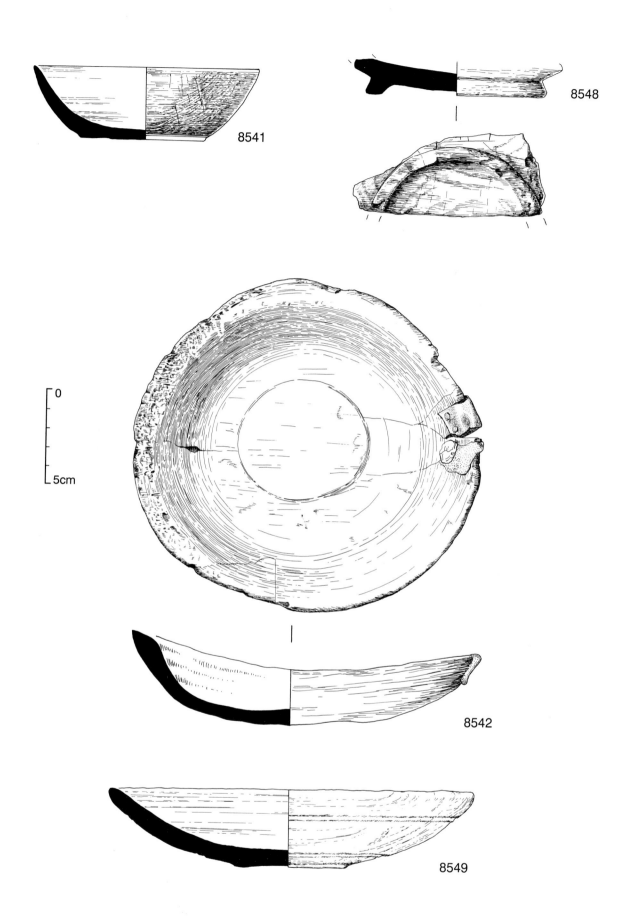

8548

8541

0

5cm

8542

8549

Fig.1019 *Lathe-turned bowls from 16–22 Coppergate 8541–2, 8548–9. Scale 1:2*

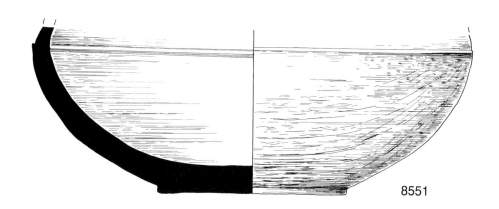

8551

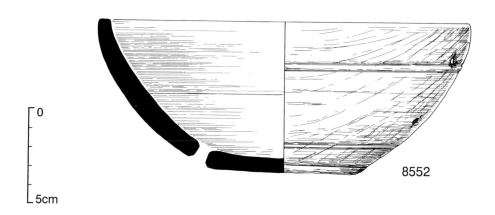

0

5cm

8552

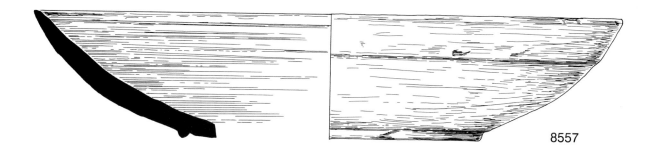

8557

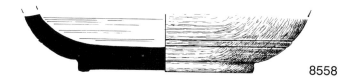

8558

Fig.1020 *Lathe-turned bowls from 16–22 Coppergate 8551–2, 8557–8. Scale 1:2*

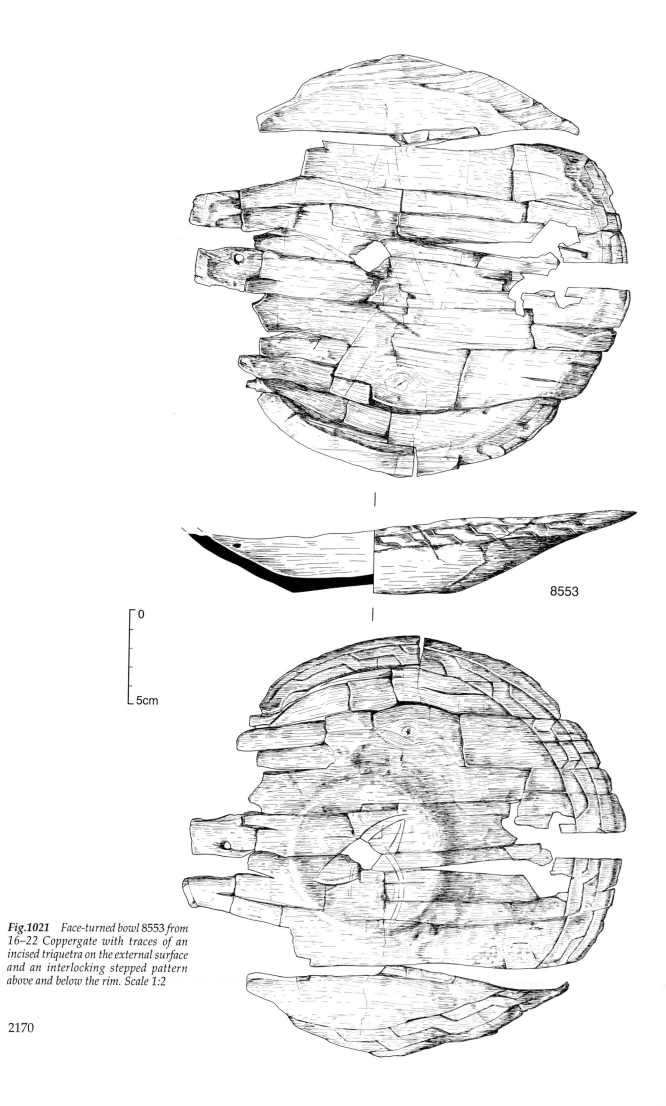

8553

Fig.1021 *Face-turned bowl 8553 from 16–22 Coppergate with traces of an incised triquetra on the external surface and an interlocking stepped pattern above and below the rim. Scale 1:2*

0

5cm

2170

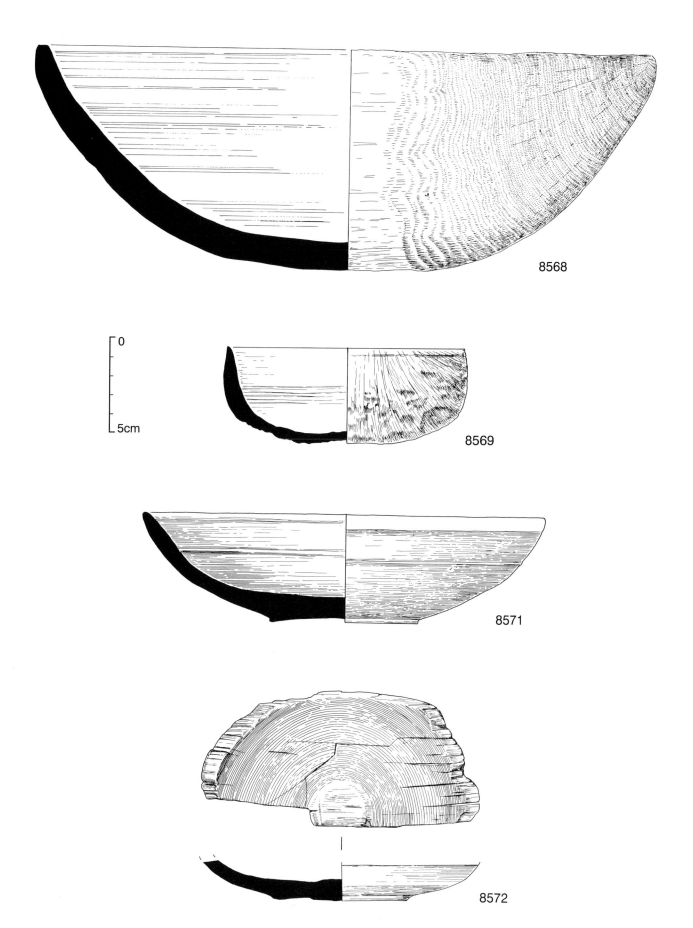

Fig.1022   *Lathe-turned bowls from 16–22 Coppergate 8568–9, 8571–2. Scale 1:2*

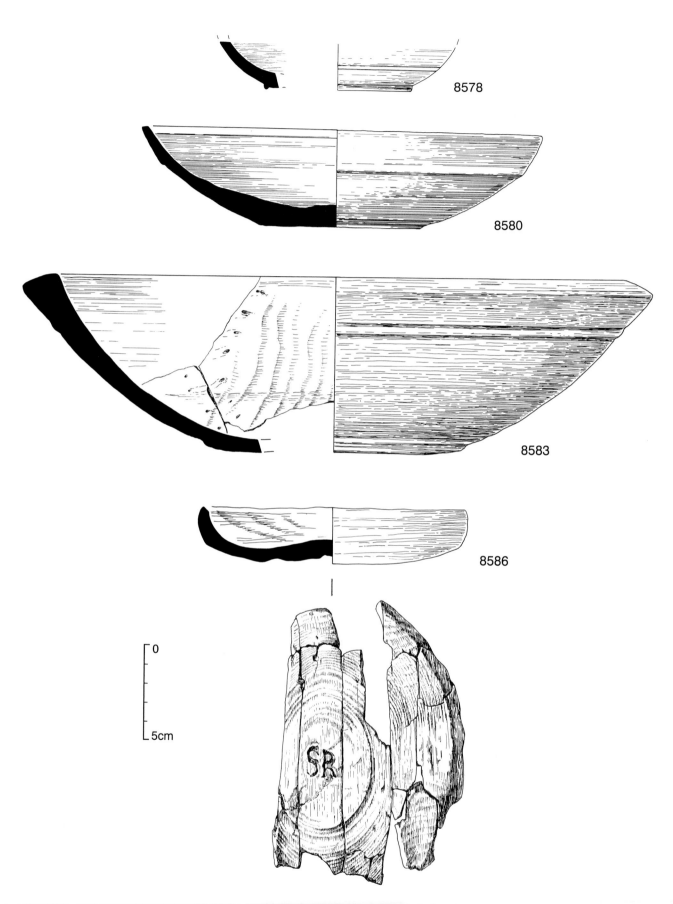

8578

8580

8583

8586

0
5cm

Fig.1023 *Lathe-turned bowls from 16–22 Coppergate 8578, 8580, 8583 and 8586. Scale 1:2*

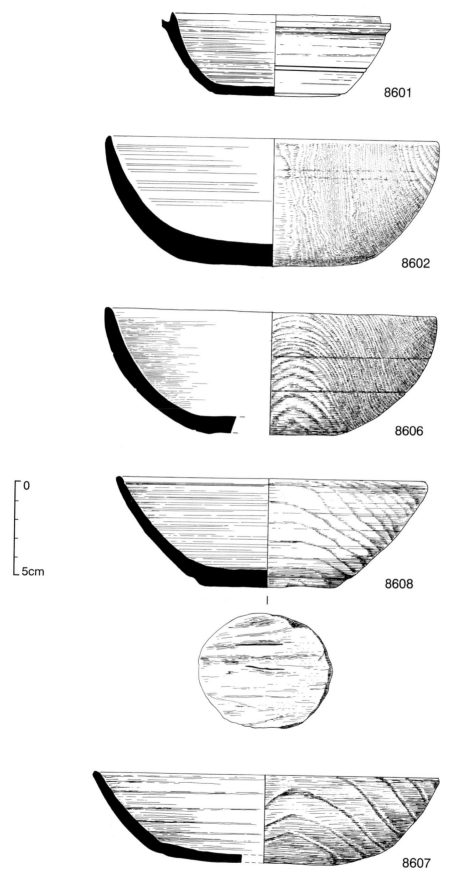

8601

8602

8606

0

5cm

8608

8607

Fig.1024 *Lathe-turned bowls from 16–22 Coppergate 8601–2, 8606–8. Scale 1:2*

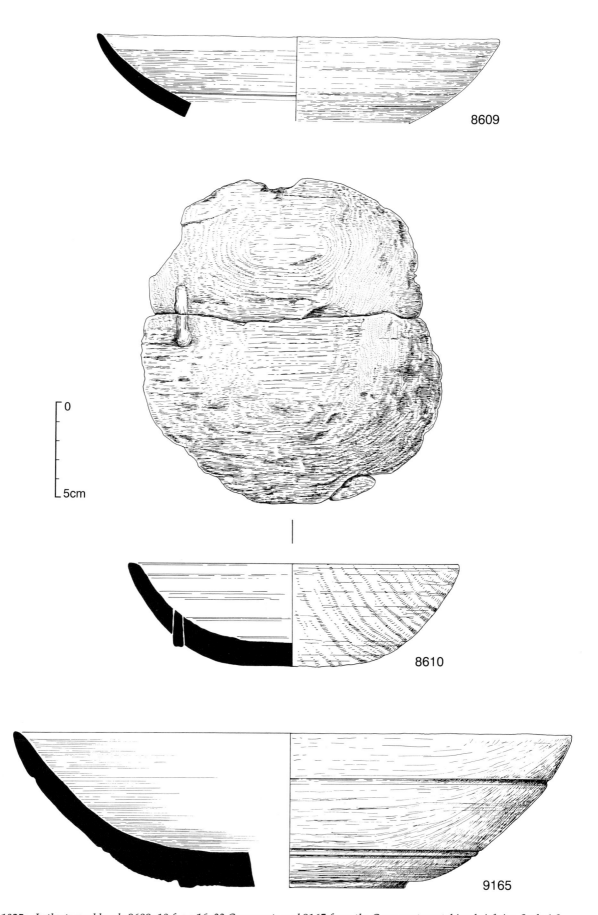

0

5cm

8609

8610

9165

Fig.1025 *Lathe-turned bowls 8609–10 from 16–22 Coppergate and 9165 from the Coppergate watching brief site. Scale 1:2*

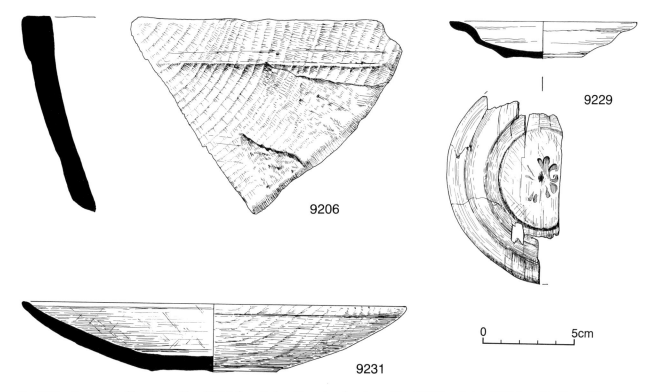

Fig.1026 *Fragment of face-turned bowl 9206 from Bedern Foundry; face-turned bowl 9229 and plate 9231 from the Vicars Choral site at Bedern. Scale 1:2*

plate-like, whereas others such as *8534–5* are deeper. Some have more unusual profiles that are S-shaped (Fig.1017, 1; *8569* and *9229*), straight-sided (Fig.1017, 3; *8553, 8591* and *9227*) or stepped (Fig.1017, 7 and 8; *8593* and *9203*). The smaller, more compact vessels which would usually be referred to as cups have more distinct profiles that are vertical (Fig.1017, 6; *8613, 8621* and *8636*), inturned (Fig.1017, 5; *8586*) or globular (Fig.1017, 4; *8614–20, 8622–6, 8628–35, 8637*).

Most of the wide rounded shapes were made using face-turning techniques, whilst most of the vessels with vertical and globular shapes were made by spindle-turning.

Thinned, pointed and elaborately moulded rims are difficult to produce without the turners' gouges snagging and spoiling the rim, especially when cutting the inside. In general, the thinner the rim, the finer the vessel would appear, hence certain turners used a chamfering technique (Fig.1017a–b) to create the appearance of a thin rim without the need for reducing the thickness of the main bowl walls. Six vessels from Coppergate have thinned rims: *8599–600* and *8606* were thinned on the outside, while *8555,*

8622 and *8628* were thinned on the inside. Three vessels, *8569, 8591* and *8633*, have rounded rims which are almost pointed (Fig.1017g), and another three, *8537, 8557* and *8580*, have moulded rims, grooves and ridges having been used to create a 'lip' effect (Fig.1017c). There are also squared rims on vessels *8577, 8583, 8596* and *9230* (Fig.1017d), everted rims on *8553, 8592, 8618, 8620, 8628, 8635, 9227* and *9229* (Fig.1017e–f), inturned rims on *8586* and *8626* (Fig. 1017h–i), a beaded rim on *8614* (Fig.1017k–l) and flanged rims on *8551* and *8601* (Fig.1017j). The flanged rims are functional, providing seatings for matching turned lids such as *8638–9* or *8641*. Lids matching *8551* and *8601*, however, have not been found at Coppergate.

Some vessels have no distinct shaped external base for the bowl to sit on when placed on a flat surface. Twenty-two of the Coppergate and Bedern vessels have flat bottoms (e.g. *8538, 8597* and *8637*), sixteen have rounded bottoms (e.g. *8535, 8547* and *8628*), and *8569* has a concave bottom. Others, however, have a turned base which is often only a few millimetres deep, but projects below the bottom of the bowl. The commonest base is flat with rounded

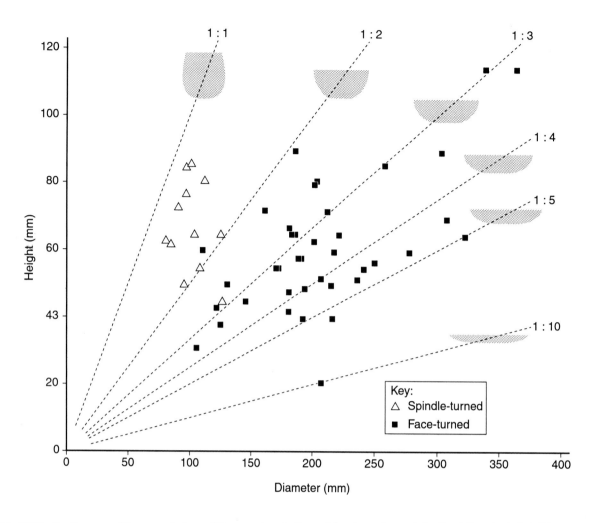

Fig.1027 *Scattergram of the general shape of Coppergate spindle- and face-turned vessels (ratio of diameter to height)*

edges (Fig.1017 I) and is found on 27 of the Coppergate and Bedern vessels, e.g. *8537, 8583* and *9167.* Seven vessels (e.g. *8598, 8617, 8619*) have flat bases with squared edges (Fig.1017 II), nine vessels (e.g. *8540, 8557–8, 9165*) have hollowed footring bases with squared or chamfered edges (Fig.1017 III), seven vessels (e.g. *8534, 8622, 9229*) have flat bases with angled edges (Fig.1017 IV), and *8584* has a flat base with a chamfered edge (Fig.1017 V). Sometimes the turner emphasised the junction of the vessel walls and base with a deeply cut groove, as on *8543* and *8591* from 16–22 Coppergate, *9168* from the Coppergate watching brief site and *9231* from Bedern.

The scattergram in Fig.1027 shows the ratio of diameter to height (that is, general shape irrespective of profile) of the 59 Coppergate vessels which can be measured, regardless of date. All but two of the face-turned vessels fall between the ratio lines of 1:2 and

1:6, irrespective of size, an area on the graph representing vessels which were between twice and six times as wide as their height. These are vessels which would usually be referred to as bowl-shaped. The exceptions are *8616* which falls between the 1:1 and 1:2 lines and in shape belongs with the spindle-turned vessels described below, and *8591* which falls on the 1:10 line and would usually be referred to as a platter or plate because it is so flat and shallow. All but one of the spindle-turned vessels (*8626*) fall between the ratio lines of 1:1 and 1:2, an area on the graph representing vessels which were less than twice as wide as their height. These are vessels which would usually be referred to as cups. In shape, *8626* belongs with the face-turned vessels already described.

The diameters of the spindle-turned vessels fall between only c.75 and 130mm, whereas the diameters of the face-turned vessels vary from c.105 to

360mm. This suggests that the vessels made by the two distinct turning techniques were deliberately intended to be different, not only in shape but in size.

In terms of shape, size and method of manufacture, Fig.1027 shows two distinct groups of vessels. This also indicates production of vessels for at least two different functions although within each group vessels presumably had a variety of related uses. Taking all the variables into consideration, we can refer to the mainly face-turned group as bowls and the mainly spindle-turned group as cups.

Evidence to support the idea of two distinct groups comes from the cores. The scattergram in Fig.1028 shows the ratio of diameter to height of 296 of the Coppergate cores, irrespective of date, although at Coppergate only nine cores were found in medieval (Period 6) levels. There are two distinct groups of cores. One group of long, narrow cores

measuring 20–40mm wide and 40–90mm long, fall mainly between the 3:1 and 1:1 lines. The other group, which have a wide variation in size, fall mainly between the 1:1 and 1:3 lines. Although there can be no fixed correlation between the shape of a core and the final vessel shape, it is still possible to suggest that many of the first group of cores were probably produced while manufacturing narrow, deep, vertical-sided or globular vessels (cups), and many of the second group were probably produced while making wider, more rounded vessels in a range of sizes (bowls). Moreover, the scattergram shows that the first group are mainly spindle-turned, the latter mainly face-turned, which correlates well with the groupings in the vessel scattergram (Fig.1027).

Among the cores, there is less correlation between diameter to height ratio and face-turning or spindle-turning technique. The diameter of the core is more relevant, since the spindle-turned cores from Copper-

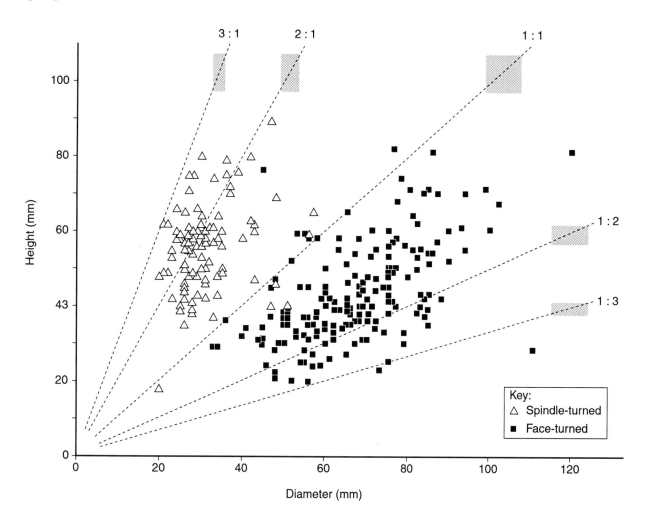

Fig.1028 *Scattergram of the general shape of Coppergate spindle- and face-turned cores (ratio of diameter to height)*

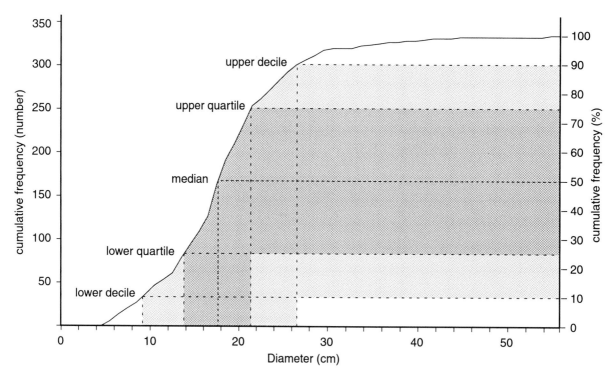

Fig.1029 *Cumulative frequency diagram of diameters of all measurable vessels from Coppergate*

gate measure between 20 and 51mm, whereas the face-turned cores measure between 40 and 120mm; if pot-lid *8881* (a piece of lathe-turning waste or a reject roughout) was originally a core, it would push the maximum diameter of the cores up to 140mm. Thirty-four face-turned cores measure over 80mm in diameter, and were probably produced in the manufacture of relatively large bowls (*8371* and *8391* measure 111mm and 120mm in diameter respectively; Fig.1007, p.2150). *8881* may have come from the production of a wide, very shallow vessel.

The frequency diagram in Fig.1001 (p.2144) shows the distribution of the diameters of measurable vessels from Coppergate. It has two distinct peaks showing that there were two common sizes of lathe-turned vessels made and used in York, the first measuring between 70 and 130mm diameter, but most commonly around 100 or 120mm, the second measuring between 160 and 220mm diameter, but most commonly around 180 or 200mm. The first group are the cups and the second group are the more common sizes of bowls.

The cumulative frequency diagram in Fig.1029 shows that approximately 90% of the bowls found at

Coppergate have diameters of less than 250mm. Some of the remaining 10% are very large, for example *8557* (320mm), *8568* (335mm) and *8583* (360mm), but these are exceptional, and only six vessels catalogued here measure 300mm or more, one of these being from the Bedern site. The Coppergate examples date from the entire period of lathe-turning on the site from Periods 3 to 6 and must represent a size of bowl which, although rare, had a certain function in the household.

The Coppergate figures compare well to those produced for a sample of 338 vessels dating from 400–1500 from sites all over Britain (Fig.1030, which is reproduced from Morris 1984a, figs.8.11a–b). 90% of these bowls measured less than 260mm in diameter, indicating the size of roundwood most often used for turning bowls, and the commonest size of cups and bowls in everyday use throughout Anglo-Saxon and medieval Britain. These were the essential tablewares for drinking and eating. Only 5% of the bowls which survive from this 1100-year period were greater than 300mm in diameter, most of them medieval in date (ibid.). An early example, excavated from the 1st–3rd century settlement at Feddersen Wierde, measured 414mm in diameter (Haarnagel

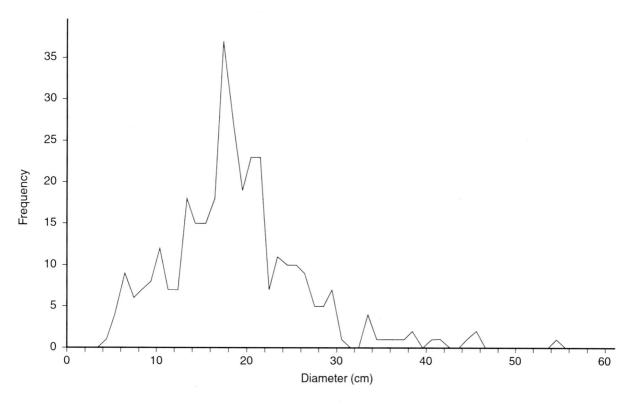

Fig.1030 *Frequency diagram of measurable diameters of all lathe-turned vessels from sites in Great Britain dating from AD 400 to 1500*

1979, Taf.42, 10). A 14th century alder bowl excavated from the moat at Shackerley Mound measured 370mm in diameter (Morris 1987, 26, fig.10, 7), two bowls excavated from the High Street site in Perth measure 442mm and 457mm in diameter (Morris 1984a, fig.141, L191i and iii), whilst 15th century bowls from Scale Lane, Hull, E. Yorkshire, and Greyfriars, Bristol, measure 407mm and 452mm respectively (Armstrong 1980, fig.28, 48; Morris 1984a, fig.140, L129xii). An early 14th century bowl purporting to measure 550mm diameter was excavated from the fill of a well on the site of the Bank of England in London (Dunning 1937, 416–18, fig.2), but does not survive. All these bowls are large, heavy, thick-walled vessels, usually with squared rims, and similar examples were still being made on a pole-lathe in the 20th century (Sparkes 1977, 19). Such vessels were used as dairy bowls, butter bowls and cream bowls. An illustration in the late 14th century Italian 'Tacuinum Sanitatis' (Osterreichische Nat. Bib. Vienna MS s.n. 2644, fo.61v) shows a woman selling butter from a very large wooden bowl. Pinto considered such large bowls as the universal type which had for centuries been used in the kitchen for mix-

ing, in the dairy for milk and at table for serving stews (Pinto 1949, 29). The six large bowls from Coppergate and Bedern and the medieval bowls from other sites almost certainly had similar uses.

The first of the two common sizes of turned vessel shown on the frequency diagram in Fig.1001 (p.2144) could be described as 'cups' because of their size and shape. Table 210 (p.2187) shows that all cups date from Periods 3–5B and are therefore Anglo-Scandinavian. No medieval spindle-turned vessels have been found at Coppergate, although four of the nine cores from Period 6 are spindle-turned (*8368–9, 8492, 8532*). It is possible that these small globular and vertical-sided wooden cups were a peculiarly Anglo-Scandinavian style of drinking vessel, or one inherited from the local Anglian population, whose popularity did not continue very long in medieval York. Lathe-turned wooden cups of this shape are very rare in Britain on any site, all the surviving examples dating from the 12th century or earlier (Morris 1984a, L17–35 and L219–22; Spearman 1995, figs.55–6). They were made as early as the Roman period in Britain; two typical fruitwood examples

2179

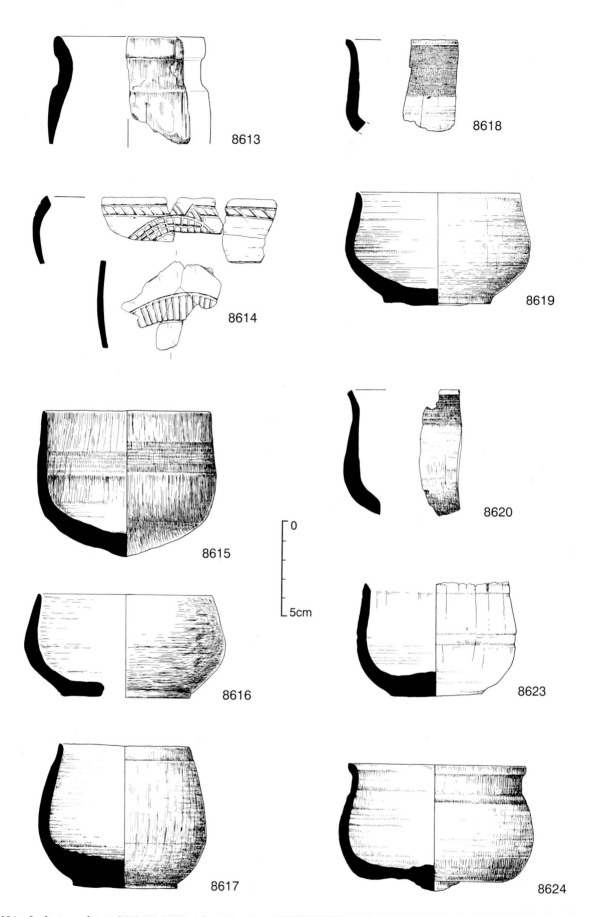

8613

8618

8614

8619

8615

8620

8616

8623

8617

8624

0

5cm

Fig.1031 *Lathe-turned cups 8613–20, 8623–4 from 16–22 Coppergate. Scale 1:2*

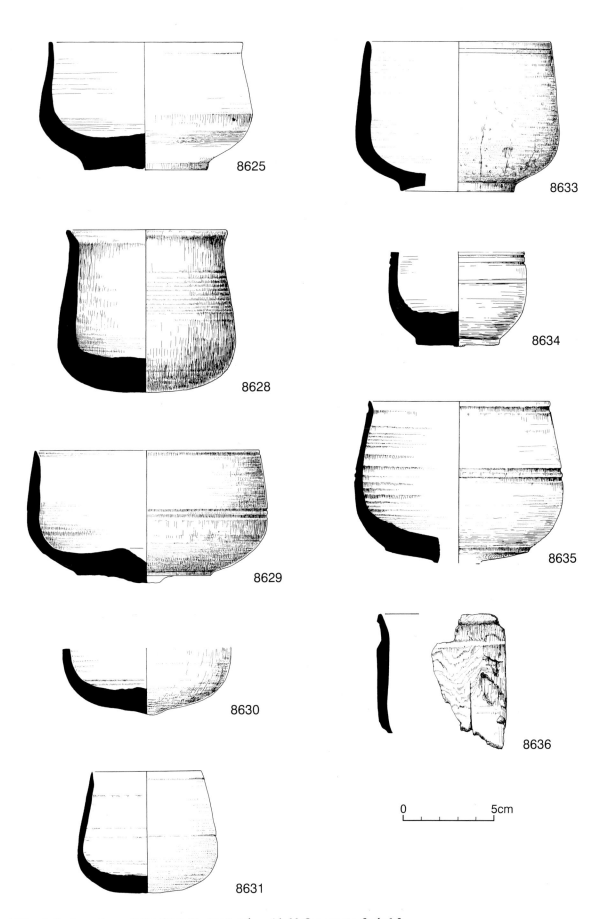

8625

8633

8628

8634

8629

8635

8630

8636

8631

0   5cm

Fig.1032   *Lathe-turned cups 8625, 8628–31, 8633–6 from 16–22 Coppergate. Scale 1:2*

were found in a 3rd–4th century well at Dalton Parlours (Morris 1990a, 224, fig.137, 58 and 60). There
was a definite Anglo-Saxon tradition for making and
using small lathe-turned wooden cups. Globular or
vertical-sided wooden cups, often with combinations
of decorative metal rim mounts, rim bands, rim clips
and triangular vandykes have been found in late 6th–
8th century Anglo-Saxon graves (Morris 1984a, 173–
4). The rims of these vessels have diameters of
45–105mm. The high degree of skill required for their
manufacture, and the precious metals often used for
rim mounts, suggests that this type of vessel was
probably a prestige item. A reference in the 10th century Will of Wynflaed to a gold-adorned wooden cup
(OE *goldfagen treowena(n) cuppan*) and two wooden
cups ornamented with dots (OE *twa treowanan ges-
plottode cuppan*) (Whitelock 1930, 13 and 15) shows
that the Anglo-Saxon tradition of making turned
wooden cups continued in England into the Viking
Age and they were probably still being made by
Anglo-Saxon turners in York when the Danish settlers arrived in the 9th century. Two pieces of spindle-
turned end waste (*8219–20*) and an unfinished
spindle-turned cup (*8200*) date from Period 3 at
Coppergate, the earliest period of Anglo-
Scandinavian occupation on the site. Fragments of
spindle-turned cups have also been found in Anglo-
Scandinavian levels at 6–8 Pavement (Fig.75, *463–6*,
AY 17/3).

Such small globular cups (in wood or another
medium) may already have been fashionable with
the Danish settlers, as shown by a globular silver
parcel-gilt cup found in 1850 in a hoard at Lejre in
Denmark (Graham-Campbell 1980, 19, fig.63). This
cup was only 59mm in diameter, smaller than the
smallest wooden cup from Coppergate, but may have
been used for consuming a very strong drink made
of fermented fruit juices (Fell 1975). Many small silver cups from Danish sites, such as Lejre, Ribe and
Fejø, vary in size (Roesdahl 1982, pl.24). They may
have been used to drink *bjórr*, a sweet, strong, rare
drink which was probably a strongly fermented cider (ibid., 120). The small capacity of some of the
wooden cups from Coppergate suggests they may
have been used for the same purpose. Small spindle-
turned wooden cups were also found in Viking
graves at Birka, for example, in grave 523 which also
contained two wooden bowls decorated with metal
rim clips (Arbman 1940a, 157–60, Taf.214–16). Small
globular and straight-sided glass cups, also found in

Viking graves at Birka, are the same vessels in a different medium (ibid., Taf.189 and 193–4).

Parallels for the spindle-turned cups from York,
although rare, have been found in Orkney and on other
late Saxon or Saxo-Norman sites in England, showing
that they were still traditional among British turners
until the 12th century. For example, a spindle-turned
alder cup with an everted rim, thinned on the inside,
and a hollow footring base was found at Burray in
Orkney in the 19th century, containing part of the Viking Age Burray silver hoard (Spearman 1995). It was
deposited c.997–1010 and, although an accurate reconstruction is not possible, it was probably c.85–90mm
high and 100–110mm diameter and therefore very
similar in dimensions, shape and date to cups such as
8633 (Period 5B; Figs.1032 and 1038, p.2186). A 12th
century maple cup from Saddler Street, Durham
(Carver 1979, fig.15), and an 11th–12th century yew
cup from Brook Street, Winchester (Biddle 1990,
fig.126, *3390*), are also very similar to the yew cup *8633*
from Coppergate. An 11th–12th century alder cup from
Westgate Street, Gloucester (Morris 1979, 200, fig.17,
18), has an S-shaped, globular profile with three external decorative turned grooves, both features which
can be seen on wooden cups used at the table in an
11th century illustration in Aelfric's Paraphrase of the
Pentateuch and Joshua (British Library MS Cotton
Claud. IV, fo.35v) (Fig.1033) and in a 13th century
French illustration (Bodleian Library MS Bodley 207b,
fo.5201–2, 2). It is very similar to cups *8620* and *8628*
from Coppergate.

The excavated vessels show that the form we rec-
ognise as a cup was still being made in the 12th century, but there are no surviving examples dated to
later centuries, despite many references to wooden
cups in later documents. For example, in the early
13th century John de Garlande records 'cups are
made of maple, plane, box, aspen' (Hume 1863, 309);
at Methley, W. Yorkshire, in the Waterton household
in 1417–18, eight dozen wooden cups were purchased
for the specific use of stews/baths (Le Patourel 1976,
170); and in 1522, at the election feast of the Drapers'
Company, green pots of ale and wine with ashen cups
were set before the guests at every mess, but they
had gilt cups for red wine and ipocras (Chauffers
1850, 30).

It is possible that in later medieval England, vessels referred to as wooden cups were no longer al-

Fig.1033   Wooden cups in an 11th century manuscript illustration (British Library MS Cotton Claudius IV fo.35v)

Fig.1034 (left) Drinking bowl from a 13th century Flemish manuscript (Bodleian Add. MS A46 fo.1)

Fig.1035   (above) Drinking bowl and lidded vessel from a 14th century Flemish manuscript (Bodleian MS Douce 6 fo.62)

Fig.1036 *Wooden vessels being used for the preparation and serving of food, from the 14th century Luttrell Psalter (British Library Add. MS 42130 fo.207v)*

ways made in the familiar cup shapes of the Anglo-Saxon and Anglo-Scandinavian periods. Several manuscript illustrations suggest that people also drank from wooden vessels which looked more like small bowls, but which the users may still have referred to as cups. For example, on the 11th century Bayeux Tapestry, at a feast at Harold's manor at Bosham in W. Sussex, a man drinks from a wooden bowl which has a decorative groove and possibly a metal rim mount (Stenton 1957, fig.4; Wilson 1985, pl.3); at a feast in the 14th century Luttrell Psalter, people drink from bowls (British Library Add. MS 42130, fo.208); in a 13th century Flemish manuscript a man sits in front of a fire and drinks from a bowl (Bodleian Library Add. MS A.46, fo.1); and in a 14th

century Flemish manuscript a man holds a lidded vessel in one hand whilst drinking from a bowl in the other (Bodleian Library MS Douce 6, fo.62) (Figs.1034–5).

Apart from the Anglo-Scandinavian cups and the shallow medieval platters *8591* and *9231*, all the other turned vessels from Coppergate and Bedern have a remarkably consistent 'bowl' shape, regardless of size. Table 209 shows that wooden bowls such as these date from all the periods of Anglo-Scandinavian and medieval occupation on the sites. They would mainly have been tablewares for eating and drinking or kitchen and dairy wares for preparation, serving and displaying of food, as shown in the Luttrell

Table 209   The incidence of face-turned and spindle-turned bowls at 16–22 Coppergate in relation to period

	3	4A	4B	5A	5B	A/S	6	?	Total
Bowls									
FT	4		14	3	23	2	29	2	77
ST									0
Burrwood					2				2
Not analysed	1				2		1		4
Total	5		14	3	27	2	30	2	83

Psalter (British Library Add. MS 42130, fo.207v; Fig.1036). Illustrations in medieval manuscripts suggest they could have had many other uses, however, including catching blood, feeding livestock and begging (Luttrell Psalter c.1340, British Library Add. MS 42130, fos.61, 166v and 186v), as lids for other vessels (Egerton Genesis c.1310–20, British Library Egerton MS 1894, fo.4v), and even for bathing children (French late 13th century, Bodleian Library MS Douce 118, fo.135) (Fig.1037).

Other indications as to use come from the bowls themselves. Many bowls from Coppergate have internal surfaces stained with a dark, shiny patina which comes from an accumulation of grease and scorching from heated contents (e.g. *8542*, see Fig. 1041, p.2190). The shallow platter *8591* contains a dark organic residue with vegetable matter and hair, including human hair. Five vessels have very prominent knife cuts either on external (*8597*) or internal (*8538, 8577, 9167, 9231*) surfaces where they have been used as chopping bowls/boards. Many fragments are scuffed, cut, gouged, worn and abraded showing that the bowls have been very well used in domestic contexts and are not simply rejects from turners' workshops in Coppergate (e.g. *8559, 8567, 8569*). *8552* has a small hole 8mm square in the wall which has been deliberately chiselled from both sides, and *8559* has a roughly cut hole through its wall at the junction with the base; perhaps these allowed the bowls to be used as strainers. Bowls may also have been used in industrial or medicinal contexts as shown by a 15th century ash bowl from Greyfriars monastery in Bristol whose wooden walls retained globules of mercury, a metal which might have been used for gold refining (Hodges 1964, 93), gilding or as an emetic (Morris 1984a, fig.134, L129iii).

Lathe-turned bowls and cups from Coppergate and Bedern were decorated in various ways, the most common being lathe-turned grooves, either external or internal, singly or in groups, for example on cups *8629, 8633–5* and bowls *8547, 8574* and *8583*. Raised ridges, either singly, between grooves or in groups were also used to decorate vessels and can be seen on bowls *8584, 8587* and *9205*. One of the rarest form of decoration to survive is applied pigmentation, but three of four surviving 'painted' vessels from England have been found at Coppergate, all dating from Period 4B. The unfinished spindle-turned cup *8201* has an external groove into which pigment has been

Fig.1037   Large bowl used for bathing a child, from a late 13th century French manuscript (Bodleian MS Douce 118 fo.135)

added (Fig.996), and cups *8618* and *8620* have possible areas of dark staining or pigment in bands below their external rim edges (Fig.1031). The fourth vessel, dated by radiocarbon to approximately the same period (AD 972 ± 170), was found in a field drainage ditch at Stafford (Robinson 1973). It is a small beechwood bowl only 87mm in diameter with three external grooves, two filled with deep red/purple pigment. The spinning top *9042*, also dating from Period 4B, had red pigment, possibly haematite, applied to its external surface.

Certain species of wood may have been chosen as decorative in themselves because of their very distinctive grain patterns or colours. This is almost certainly the case with the finely turned yew cup *8633* whose shiny red colour and whorled grain pattern would have given it a splendid appearance (Fig. 1038). The alder bowl *8564*, a 10th–11th century bowl from Southgate Street, Gloucester (Morris 1984a, L151), a 9th–10th century cup/bowl from Eastgate Street, Gloucester (Morris 1983a, fig.118, 3), an 11th century maple cup/bowl from Winchester (Keene 1990, fig.296, *3414*) and a Saxo-Norman bowl from Hemington, Leicestershire (Morris forthcoming b), were all made from burrwood with a very speckled and whorled grain pattern. Such a pattern (as opposed to deliberate additional decoration) could ex-

Fig.1038　*Yew spindle-turned cup 8633. Actual height 81mm*

plain the 'cups decorated with dots' in the 10th century Will of Wynflaed (see p.2182).

None of the vessels from Coppergate have any surviving decorative metal fittings, although cup *8613* (Fig.1031) has a deep external groove 15mm wide which may originally have been a seating for a metal band.

Two forms of decorative carving, incised lines and relief carving, have been found on wooden vessels from York. Incised lines forming patterns were used to decorate *8553* (Fig.1021), a face-turned alder bowl 240mm in diameter, and *8614*, a spindle-turned ash cup whose dimensions cannot be reconstructed (Fig.1031). *8553* had an unusual flat everted rim, 18mm wide, above and below which had been carved an interlocking step pattern. It also had what may have been a triquetra motif carved in double outline on its external base, a pattern also found on saddle bow *9020* and a bowl from Christchurch Place, Dublin (Morris 1984a, L146iv). Fragments of two lathe-turned bowls of a similar size, with the same unusual flat everted rim decorated with incised geometric patterns, were found at the Viking site of Hedeby (Jankuhn 1943, Abb.85–6). *8614* had almost vertical walls with a slightly incurving rim. Three rim fragments have incised decoration in the form of two parallel lines with diagonal hachures between them, below which are two curved lines with the space

between them divided into squares. Seven wall fragments have further incised lines. A fragment of a spindle-turned cup found at 6–8 Pavement (*466*) was decorated with relief carving in imitation of basket-work (Fig.75, *AY* 17/3). This vessel was made of oak, a species which is unusual in the context of turned vessels, but which is excellent for relief carving. In contrast to the wealth of wooden objects found in Viking Age Dublin which are decorated with incised or relief carving (Lang 1988), very few of the wooden objects found in either Anglo-Scandinavian or medieval York are decorated, making these two vessels quite special. *8553* may even have been repaired to prolong its life. Other carved decorated wooden pieces from York include a lath-walled box *8935*, a possible box handle *8932*, three pins *8952* and *8958–9*, three gaming pieces *9033*, *9035* and *9037*, a saddle bow *9020*, an oak panel *9064*, a knife handle *9195*, two spoons (Waterman 1959, 85, fig.15, 1–2) and a disc *9147*.

Many examples of turned wooden vessels to compare with the Coppergate finds have been excavated from British and Irish sites dating from the 5th to the 15th centuries. According to research up to 1984, over 170 early Anglo-Saxon wooden vessels were represented by wood fragments, metal rim mounts and metal repairs (Morris 1984a, L1–70, fig.8.17), and over 420 vessels dating from the 8th to the 15th centuries survived as wooden fragments, some virtually complete and including 30 vessels from Coppergate (ibid., L123–218, fig.8.18, where details of all these vessels may be found). Further excavations and research since the 1984 survey have greatly increased the total number, perhaps to approximately 600 vessels, with new discoveries from sites such as Lurk Lane (Foreman and Hall 1991, 175) and Eastgate in Beverley (Morris and Evans 1992, fig.92), Shrewsbury in Shropshire, Windsor in Berkshire (Morris 1993c, fig.28, 17 and 18) and Barnard Castle in Co. Durham, as well as further finds from sites in York, Winchester, London and Perth. The species and diameters of these finds reinforce the situation presented in Figs.1001 and 1030 (pp.2144 and 2179).

Lids (Fig.1039)

The five turned wooden lids found at 16–22 Coppergate, *8638–42*, are all Anglo-Scandinavian, dating from Periods 3 to 5B. They are similar to the cups in that they are all spindle-turned and none have been found in medieval contexts in York (Table 210).

Table 210   The incidence of face-turned and spindle-turned cups and lids at 16–22 Coppergate in relation to period

	3	4A	4B	5A	5B	5Cf	5Cr	6	?	Total
Cups										
FT		1								1
ST	3	1	13	2	5					24
Total	3	2	13	2	5					25
Lids										
FT										0
ST	1	1	2		1					5
Total	1	1	2		1					5

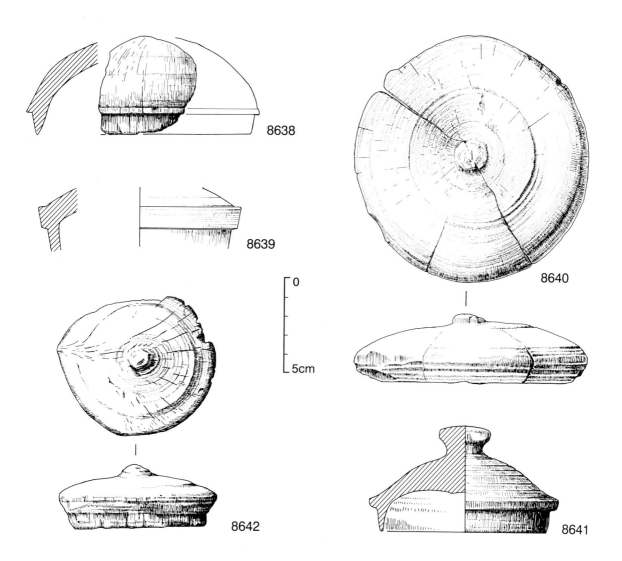

Fig.1039   *Spindle-turned lids 8638–42 from 16–22 Coppergate. Scale 1:2*

There are two distinct types of turned wooden lids, a dichotomy which may have a functional explanation. The first type, represented by *8638–9* and *8641* from 16–22 Coppergate and *467* from 6–8 Pavement (Fig.75, *AY 17/3*), are finely turned lids with hollow interiors and flanged rims which were made to fit onto wooden bowls, jars or boxes of various sizes with correspondingly shaped rims to interlock with the flanges on the lids. *8641* is the most complete and has a disc-like handle grip. Bowls *8551* and *8601* have flanged rims to act as lid seatings. These are both face-turned vessels and *8601* is medieval in date, showing that the fashion for wooden bowls with fitted lids continued in York past the Anglo-Scandinavian period (Figs.1020 and 1024, pp.2169 and 2173). A complete 14th century lid and bowl set found in Hanover, Germany, suggests how the York lids may have been used (Dunning 1937, fig.3, 3 and 4). Similar hollowed lids have been found in Viking Age levels at Hedeby (Schietzel 1970, Abb.2, 1–3), in Dublin (Morris 1984a, fig.150, L225i–ii), in the Irish crannogs at Lagore (Hencken 1950, fig.78, W72) and Lissue (Morris 1984a, fig.150, L227), and in London (Dunning 1937, fig.2, 8). Lidded bowls of a similar shape to surviving wooden examples sometimes appear in medieval illustrations, for example in the 14th century Luttrell Psalter (British Library Add. MS 42130, fo.90v).

The second type, represented by *8640* and *8642* from Coppergate, are solid with flat bottoms and sloping upper surfaces, and their sides angled inward towards the bottom. These lids are cruder and more roughly made than the hollowed type and could have been used either on wooden bowls or jars or on other vessels such as pottery jars where the angled sides would allow the lids to act like corks. Both have traces of a knob on their upper surface, more likely to have been where the end waste was removed in the turning process than remains of broken handles. A complete 13th century lid and bowl set with a handled lid of this type was found at High Street, Perth (Morris 1984a, fig.151, L238). The bowl was globular with an inturned rim which allowed the lid to sit like a cork. Similar 14th century lids have been found at Tong Castle (Wharton 1978, figs.8, 7 and 11, 3) and Shackerley Mound (Morris 1987, fig.10, 8–9) in Shropshire, but *8640* and *8642* are the earliest turned solid lids of this kind to be found in Britain. They may have been used in a similar way to the carved wooden pot-lids *8878–89* (pp.2262–5).

Both types of wooden lid differ markedly from pottery lids used on jars with lid seatings. These were rare and used mainly on early Saxon cremation urns and later medieval jars (Jope 1949). Chipped stone discs may also have been used to cover small wooden or pottery vessels (e.g. *9736, 9738, 9742, AY 17/14*).

Other turned items

At least twelve other wooden objects found at Coppergate were the products of lathe-turners. All were produced using spindle-turning techniques on lathes which could cope with small, lightweight objects.

8940 is a fragment of a medieval cylindrical box which would originally have had a matching lid. There are four turned medieval tool handles: *8999* is a poplar or aspen handle for a socketed tool, *8997* and *9001* are turned yew handles for tools and *8996* is an ash handle. Ten wooden knife handles were found at the York sites under consideration here, but all of them except the medieval *9219* from Bedern Foundry were carved, not lathe-turned. A medieval Rosaceae spindle (*6649*), a medieval poplar or alder whorl for a spindle wheel (*6650*) and an Anglo-Scandinavian yew bobbin (*6651*) are fine, smooth, lathe-turned items for textile production. Turners also produced small items for games and pastimes, such as the ash bowling ball *9041*, yew gaming piece *9036* and alder musical instrument fragment *9040*, all from medieval contexts. *9147*, from an Anglo-Scandinavian context, is a decorated disc which could have been sawn from a turned cylinder.

Repair of turned vessels

Wear, abrasion and thick layers of dark staining on vessel surfaces suggest that they often had long and useful lives. This is a feature common to bowls from many sites other than York, for example, the 9th century bowl discarded in a mill pool at Tamworth in Staffordshire was very worn and abraded before it was thrown away (Morris 1992, 104–7). Some were also repaired to close splits or cracks and thus prolong their lives. Wooden lathe-turned vessels can develop splits for various reasons: if they are turned green they sometimes develop a rim split as they season, and if dropped on a hard surface they crack along the grain, and can sometimes even split in half. Even when it is split, a bowl or cup can be repaired and continue to be used; archaeological and docu-

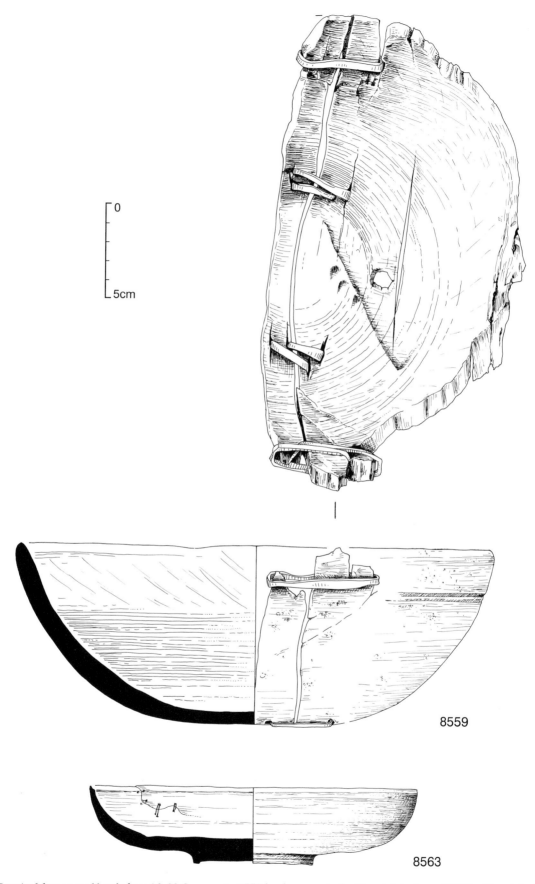

0

5cm

8559

8563

Fig.1040   *Repaired face-turned bowls from 16–22 Coppergate: 8559 has been repaired with metal staples and 8563 with metal wire stitching. Scale 1:2*

Fig.1041   *Bowl 8542 from 16–22 Coppergate, repaired with a metal rim clip riveted in place; internal grease and residue is also clearly visible*

mentary evidence shows that this was a widespread practice in Anglo-Saxon, Anglo-Scandinavian and medieval England (Morris 1984a, 176–8 and 185–6). John de Garlande, an early 13th century writer, records that 'menders of cups say they can repair with brazen or silver thread' (Hume 1863, 309).

Three common repair techniques are found on bowl and cup fragments from Coppergate — metal staples (*8539, 8542, 8553, 8559, 8610* and *8636* dating from Periods 4B–6; Figs.1019, 1025 and 1040), metal rim clips (*8542* from Period 4B; Fig.1041) and metal wire stitching (*8563* and *8583* from Periods 5B and 6; Figs.1023 and 1040). Staples and stitching were used to bind together a linear crack, rim clips were used to cover and close small splits in the rim. A fourth method, using very fine organic stitching made from strands of an undeterminable plant species, was used to repair a crack in an ash bowl found in a pit dated to Period 3 (*8535*). This is an extremely rare repair technique not found on any other vessel from Britain, and here used on a vessel dating to the earliest period of Anglo-Scandinavian occupation in Coppergate. Organic stitching as a manufacturing technique can be found on lath-walled boxes such as *8935* (see Fig.1122, p.2294), also dating to Period 3, and an almost identical box found in Hedeby (see Fig.1121,

p.2293). The stitching on bowl *8535*, however, is much finer than that used on either box.

Repairing with metal staples was an effective method which had been used on wooden bowls at least since the early Anglo-Saxon period in England. Repair staples are often found in Anglo-Saxon graves, a striking example being a set of nine copper alloy staples in grave 37 at Lyminge, Kent, in a line stretching away from the head (Warhurst 1955, 25–6, fig.11, 3). They were all clenched and had almost certainly repaired a long linear crack in a large bowl.

Bowls with metal staples were pierced by small holes straddling the crack before the staple was put in, drawn tight and clenched to close the crack. These staples were used to repair ash, alder, maple and birch bowls from Coppergate. *8539* has a small hole containing metal salts but no surviving staple, *8542* has the corroded remains of an iron staple probably used to repair a crack before a later rim clip was added, and *8553* has a hole but no surviving staple. *8559* is a large birch bowl, 256mm in diameter, which has a dark stained interior and very well worn and gouged internal and external surfaces. In antiquity it split in half and was repaired by four iron staples, three clenched on the inside, then split again before being discarded. *8610* is a similar worn and abraded ash bowl which split in half and was repaired by an iron staple clenched on the inside (Fig.1025). Other bowls found in York have been repaired using the same method. A 10th–11th century maple bowl measuring 230mm in diameter and repaired with three iron staples clenched on the inside was found in a brushwood raft on the riverside embankment at Hungate (Richardson 1959, 86, fig.20) and two large bowls reconstructed to c.300–350mm in diameter, both repaired with iron staples, were found at 11–13 Parliament Street (Figs.104–5, *969–70, AY* 17/4). A large medieval ash bowl 330mm in diameter, found at Aldwark (Morris 1984a, pls.VI–VII, L213ix), had been repaired using two techniques — three iron staples, two clenched on the inside and one on the outside, along a crack across the bottom, and three lengths of copper alloy wire stitching to sew a crescent-shaped crack in the bowl wall (Fig.1042). Bowls repaired with similar staples have been found in Viking Age Dublin at Christchurch Place (ibid., L146ii, iv and v), late Anglo-Saxon London (ibid., fig.142, L172xxv) and 10th century Winchester (Keene 1990, fig.296, *3411*).

Bowls with wire stitching were also pierced by very small holes straddling a crack before the stitching was put in, drawn tight, then finished off to close the crack. A crescent-shaped split in *8563* had been closed with copper alloy stitches in individual loops, whereas a split in bowl *8583* was originally repaired by continuous stitches of iron wire. Only a fragment of this flattened wire with an oval cross-section now survives near the bowl rim. Small fragments of a bowl found in Viking Age Dublin at Christchurch Place had also been repaired with copper alloy wire (Morris 1984a, L146vi).

8542 is repaired with a rectangular rim clip made of tin (with small amounts of lead and zinc) bent over a crack in the rim and held on by a rivet either side of the crack (see Fig.1041). Such clips were made to fit the bowl rim shape before they were fixed and would never be hammered into shape on the bowl. Rim clips found in early Anglo-Saxon graves often retain only a fragment of the wooden bowl but the outline and rim shape of the bowl are preserved in the cross-section of the clips. It is even possible that if a vessel split in seasoning, the turner might have repaired the crack with a metal rim clip and still traded it as a 'second'. Rim repair clips occur on wooden cups and bowls in early Anglo-Saxon graves (e.g. Morris 1984a, 177–8, L36–70) and many of these have been discussed elsewhere (Morris 1994, 31–2).

Why were vessels repaired? Wooden bowls seem to have been cheap to produce in rural areas where raw material was plentiful and available to turners. For example, at Crondall Manor in Hampshire in 1248, platters were bought at different times during the year at either sixteen for 1d or eight for 1d, presumably two different types or sizes (Baigent 1891). In towns they were possibly more expensive since a turner would have to travel to woodland or import raw material to make his bowls. Vessels may therefore have been repaired to defray expense. For some settlements, the wares of itinerant turners may have been available only at periodic markets (cf. Geraint Jenkins 1978, pl.49 for a 20th century example), and this could have been a crucial factor, requiring that bowls be repaired until new ones could be purchased. It is also possible that even in towns such as Anglo-Scandinavian and medieval York which presumably had some resident turners, the manufacture of bowls was a seasonal occupation, and that wood was only cut at certain times of year. This would also help to explain why evidence for other crafts has been found in and around structures which were almost certainly used at some time as lathe-turners' workshops (cf. *AY* 17/6 for ironworking, *AY* 17/7 for non-ferrous metalworking, *AY* 17/12 for bone and antler-working, and *AY* 17/14 for jewellery making using amber and

Fig.1042   *Detail of repaired medieval ash bowl from Aldwark*

jet). Vessels may have been repaired because of their sentimental value or because they were attractive or intrinsically valuable. The large bowls measuring over 250mm have already been shown to account for only 10% of the Coppergate vessels, and also 10% of all the wooden turned vessels surviving from Britain between 400 and 1500 (see Fig.1030, p.2179). They are also the most difficult and time-consuming vessels to make (e.g. pp.2122 and 2125), and would certainly have been expensive and valued. It is not surprising, therefore, that many of the repaired bowls such as *8559* and those from Aldwark and Parliament Street are large ones. Wooden bowls such as that from Aldwark and *8542* must have been perceived as valuable since they were repaired at least twice.

Woodland exploitation by the lathe-turning craft

Lathe-turners, just like other woodworking craftsmen, had strong preferences for particular species and forms of raw material. There was conscious selection, and lathe-turners in York exploited the properties of certain species to ensure that their products satisfied the demands placed upon them. Studying the artefacts produced by one of its crafts helps to reconstruct a part of Anglo-Scandinavian and medieval society in York and it is important to look at the exploitation patterns and sources of raw material as well as analysing the techniques, tools and finished products.

Lathe-turners in Anglo-Scandinavian York seem to have made a conscious choice to make cups by spindle-turning using lengths of *roundwood* without splitting, and a variety of sizes of bowls by face-turning using *splitwood*, in this instance roundwood converted into half-sections by splitting longitudinally along the grain. Rackham makes a distinction between 'timber' and 'wood', traditionally different types of raw material for craftsmen, and produced in different ways (see p.2101). He defines 'wood' as roundwood less than c.600mm in girth or c.280mm in diameter. Since the largest face-turned bowl found at Coppergate measures 360mm in diameter (*8583*), and the two commonest sizes of vessel are much smaller than this (see Fig.1001, p.2144), the York turners were certainly using much raw material well within Rackham's definition of wood, and which could have been obtained from coppiced woodland, a method of exploitation which has been fully described elsewhere (Rackham 1976, 20–2; 1980, 3–5), or from standard trees within coppiced woodland or hedgerows.

Crafts such as lathe-turning, which require constant supplies of material, need wood to be replenished without woodland being destroyed, and they tend to cull roundwood of small diameters. The age of the wood cut for turning in York was related to the size needed. Coppice cycles in medieval English woodland varied enormously (Rackham 1980, 139–40). Some were strictly regulated, with wood cut in regular cycles of several years, for example, a five-year cycle in the 1356 survey of Hardwick Wood in Cambridgeshire, whereas others were cut very irregularly (ibid., fig.10.2). In eastern England, coppice cycles from the 13th to 20th centuries varied from four to 25 years (ibid., fig.10.3), and the latter could, if necessary, have provided wood large enough to turn wooden bowls. Some of the material used to turn the larger bowls found at Coppergate may have been cut from small timber or standard trees allowed to grow individually in plantations or woodland amongst underwood coppice. Many of the smaller vessels could have been made from coppice trees allowed to stand for several rotations and then felled to provide larger material (a method described in Rackham 1980, 3). *8578* is a very exceptional face-turned vessel made from boxwood (*Buxus sempervirens*), measuring over 120mm in diameter, an unusually large size of roundwood for this particular species, probably taken from a very mature tree.

Documents rarely give information about the sizes of trees used (ibid., 145), and it is the products themselves which show that craftsmen were not only selecting particular species, but also regular crops of uniform sizes of wood. This pattern of exploitation by turners is not confined to Anglo-Scandinavian and medieval York. An analysis of the diameters of a sample of 338 lathe-turned wooden vessels dating between 400 and 1500 found on sites all over the British Isles (Fig.1030, p.2179) shows a similar distribution to the analysis of the York vessels (Fig.1001, p.2144), with a peak at c.180mm and 80% of the vessels measuring 90–260mm in diameter.

It is very important to consider how and where craftsmen in York obtained wood for making artefacts. From at least the Anglo-Saxon period in England, wood was a valuable resource which was owned, sold and bought. Woodland management and the use and sale of wood (and timber) probably varied from place to place and through time, but Rackham (1980, 137) has shown that trade and transport of wood was essential in Anglo-Saxon and medieval England since many areas had no woodland and others had more than they could use.

There are no Anglo-Saxon or Anglo-Scandinavian documents which can give us information about the rights of woodworking craftsmen to cut wood, but later documents are more informative and show that in medieval England and Wales craftsmen and individuals acquired wood for making artefacts in various ways. Most woodland was privately owned but products of management were sold, such as the underwood from 11 acres of the 80-acre Hayley Wood near Ely in Cambridgeshire which was worth 5s an acre in 1356 (Rackham 1975, 26). Craftsmen or individuals could rent or own land which included woodland, and the wood which the land produced was used for small artefacts. For example, in the second quarter of the 14th century, Jordan le Tournour shared the rent of a virgate of land in Yateley from the manor of Crondall, and we can presume the land provided at least some of his raw material (Baigent 1891).

Royal or manorial courts issued licences to craftsmen who paid a fee to work in the woodland or forests which the courts administered. In the early 13th century, turners paid 1s 8d to make dishes and woodwork in the forest between Taff and Cynon, and other workers paid 1s to make dishes in the forest (PRO Minute Accounts 1202/8 Glamorgan and Senghenith). In 1331, fees were paid to the Wakefield Manor Court, W. Yorkshire, for individuals to cut wood (Court Rolls, Manor of Wakefield 5 Edw III). In the royal forests, foresters-in-fee paid the king a rent and bought the rights to the 'cheminage' or freedom to cut wood along the forest roads. They could also charge others who wanted to cut wood in the forest, but usually only those who had licences to buy wood to sell elsewhere (Stenton 1952, 116). Medieval turners in York could have obtained wood in some or all of these ways.

It would have been expensive in terms of cost, time and effort for turners to transport underwood over long distances to work into finished products elsewhere. Unlike constructional and rare timber which was widely transported, underwood was less valuable in relation to its weight and was seldom fetched long distances (Rackham 1982, 213–14). It was almost certainly more economical for turners to do most of their work in the woodland and forest, taking the necessary tools and devices with them, and then to transport the finished or semi-finished products away to finish and sell. Manuscripts definitely refer to turners working *in* the woodland. For example, in the early 13th century turners worked in the forests between Taff and Cynon (above), in 1329 William and Rose le Tournour were attached at Wakefield Manor Court for making dishes in the lord's woodland without warrant (Court Rolls, Manor of Wakefield 3 Edw III), and 23 separate cases of illegal use of wood in Sowerby Wood were recorded consecutively in the Wakefield Court Rolls in 1337. Laws governing woodland were strict and affected individuals and craftsmen alike. Wood must often have been difficult to obtain legally since offences of the vert, or illegal use of timber and underwood in medieval forests and woodland, are common in court documents.

Although pollen analyses of urban archaeological deposits have been deemed 'unprofitable' (Godwin and Bachem 1959), investigations in the rural hinterland of Anglo-Scandinavian York have provided important environmental information for the woodworking crafts carried out in the city. Pollen analyses at Askham Bog, two miles outside modern York, show that there was a mosaic of arable and pasture land with areas of woodland, coppice and heath near the city (Kenward et al. 1978, 58 and fig.37). Alder and hazel are prominent species in the pollen diagrams. Coppiced alder was also used in large quantities for wattle stakes in the Anglo-Scandinavian town, suggesting a readily available source of the species (ibid., 60). Alder carr could be found along the River Ouse at York until recent times (Radley and Simms 1971) and some probably existed on land bordering the Rivers Foss and Ouse in the Viking Age. Lathe-turners from Anglo-Scandinavian and medieval Coppergate could have obtained supplies of suitable raw material close to the urban centre.

Pollen analyses have been carried out near two other pre-Conquest sites where lathe-turned waste and/or vessels have been found. Fragments of two lathe-turned hazel bowls were found on the 6th–8th century site of Dinas Emrys in Gwynedd (Savory

1960, 69). A pollen diagram of deposits in a silted-up pool on the site shows that the settlement had been surrounded by a dense hazel thicket (ibid., fig.10, 75–6). The vessels were probably made from hazel cut near the settlement and worked nearby. Wood was preserved in waterlogged ditches on a late 6th–early 7th century monastic settlement on the island of Iona, including fragments of three lathe-turned bowls and 31 cores (Barber 1981, figs.29–33). This workshop waste showed that turners had worked on or near the settlement. The bowls and 29 of the cores were alder, but the pollen diagram of deposits in the ditch where they were found shows oak and ash as the dominant species in the area, with birch, willow and hazel secondary (ibid., fig.41). Alder is present, but only in small quantities (ibid., 346–7). The pollen in the ditch may only reflect the immediate local environment, and the alder used for turning may have been brought from elsewhere on the island; if so, this shows that there was deliberate selection of alder over species plentifully available very close to the settlement which were also used for turning at this period.

The native woodlands of Anglo-Saxon and medieval Britain would have had a rich variety of species managed within them. Rackham suggests that in eastern England alone any one of at least fourteen native trees can predominate locally (1976, 32). Since woodworking crafts such as lathe-turning selected certain species for their products, it is possible that some sections of woodland in which these species predominated would be the sources of raw material for specific crafts. Place name evidence suggests this was possible, for example, the element 'holt' in place names seems to be a special term relating to the growing of a predominant species (Gelling 1984, 196–7). Some English place names with this element have species or products within them such as Alderholt, Aisholt (ash), Bircholt, Buckholt (beech), Wiggenholt (wych elm), Knockholt (oak), Sparsholt (spears) and Throckenholt (trestles).

The species of the lathe-turner's waste products and vessels can be used to reconstruct patterns of exploitation, especially changes or conservatism over long periods of time. The use-group of species for lathe-turned vessels in Anglo-Scandinavian and medieval York has already been analysed in connection with the cores (Tables 196 and 200–2), relating the species to core shape, face-turning or spindle-turning, method of fixing the centre attachment and period respectively. Information has also been gleaned from combining the cores and other waste products (Tables 207–8), relating face-turned and spindle-turned cores to species in turn. Both these analyses related species to manufacturing techniques. The use-group of species is also analysed for the vessels (Tables 211–14), relating separately the species used for cups, bowls and lids to face-turning or spindle-turning, and period. The important conclusions to be drawn from these tables are that alder, field maple, ash and birch were the four main species in the York use-group, with small amounts of

Table 211 The incidence of face-turned and spindle-turned cups and lids at 16–22 Coppergate in relation to species of wood

	Alder	Ash	Birch	Maple	Pomoideae	Willow	Box	Yew	Not Identifiable	Total
Cups										
FT	1									1
ST	8	1	1	12				1	1	24
Total	9	1	1	12				1	1	25
Lids										
FT										0
ST	1			3					1	5
Total	1			3					1	5

Table 212 The incidence of face-turned and spindle-turned bowls at 16–22 Coppergate in relation to species of wood

	Alder	Ash	Birch	Maple	Pomoideae	Willow	Box	Not Identifiable	Total
Bowls									
FT	35	23	3	10	1		1	4	77
ST									0
Burrwood	1			1					2
Not analysed						1		3	4
Total	**36**	**23**	**3**	**11**	**1**	**1**	**1**	**7**	**83**

other species. All four were used for bowls and cups, and were both spindle-turned and face-turned. On the evidence of cores alone, alder was preferred for face-turning and field maple for spindle-turning vessels. Several documents which refer to the species of turned vessels complement the archaeological evidence. In a 13th century copy of a possible 6th century manuscript of the Gorchan of Tudfwlch, a separate lay associated with the Gododdin of Aneirin, there is a reference to 'the bitter alder-wood cup' (Jackson 1969, 153); there is an early 13th century reference to cups of maple, plane, box and aspen (see p.2182); in 1337 William Tournour cut alder for making dishes in Sowerby Wood (Yorks. Archaeol. Soc. MS 759/1340, 82–3); and in 1522 ashen cups were used to drink ale and wine at the Feast of the Drapers' Company (Chauffers 1850, 30).

The use-group of species used for turning in the British Isles over the thousand year period between the 6th and 15th centuries is compared to that for York in Tables 215–16 using vessels and cores respectively. Some of the evidence is limited in date range; for example, only 27 of the 412 cores are medieval, but cores and vessels together (a total sample of 831 items) give a coherent picture of preferences for cer-

Table 213 The number of bowls found at 16–22 Coppergate in relation to species of wood and period

	Alder	Ash	Birch	Maple	Pomoideae	Willow	Box	Not Identifiable	Total
Bowls									
3	2	1		1				1	5
4A									0
4B	9			2				3	14
5A	2	1							3
5B	12	3	1	6	1	1	1	2	27
A/S	1	1							2
6	9	16	2	2				1	30
?	1	1							2
Total	**36**	**23**	**3**	**11**	**1**	**1**	**1**	**7**	**83**

Table 214   The number of cups and lids found at 16–22 Coppergate
in relation to species of wood and period

	Alder	Ash	Birch	Maple	Yew	Not Identifiable	Total
Cups							
3	1	1	1				3
4A	1			1			2
4B	6			6		1	13
5A	1			1			2
5B				4	1		5
6							0
Total	**9**	**1**	**1**	**12**	**1**	**1**	**25**
Lids							
3				1			1
4A						1	1
4B	1			1			2
5A							0
5B				1			1
6							0
Total	**1**	**0**	**0**	**3**	**0**	**1**	**5**

tain species and changes in this selection through time. Overall, the main species are alder, field maple, ash, birch, beech and hazel, although many others were used in small quantities. From the 6th to early 11th centuries, the most favoured species was alder, with maple second in importance, then hazel, birch and ash. Small quantities of at least eleven other species were also used. Alder is resistant to splitting once it is shaped and seasoned, and it is durable in wet conditions, ideal for vessels which would hold liquids, both food and drink, dairy products etc. The vessels dated to the 11th to 15th centuries, however, indicate a major change. The range of species remained similar, but ash became the most commonly chosen, with alder second in importance, then birch and beech, with smaller amounts of poplar and elm. Seven of the eleven medieval vessels from Bedern were ash, two maple, one alder and one birch.

This change in the selection of species must reflect a change in exploitation patterns of wood used for turning in pre- and post-Conquest Britain. It is possible that turners obtained more of their raw material from more mature standard ash trees: *8606* is a medieval bowl measuring only 180mm in diameter but was manufactured from a tree whose growth rings show it to be over 100 years old. Ash has a much coarser texture than either alder or field maple, but when it is turned with the heartwood at the cup centre a very attractive striped grain pattern can be achieved. Although ash is a harder species to turn than alder or maple, the Anglo-Scandinavian turner was perfectly capable of cutting fine bowls from ash, elm and even oak. No turners' gouges have been excavated from 16–22 Coppergate and it has not been possible to gain a metallographic analysis of the hook-ended tool *9183* from Benson's excavation in 1906, but metallographic analyses of other Anglo-Scandinavian woodworking tools from Coppergate such as the axe *2255* and spoon bit *2265* (p.536, Fig.209, *AY* 17/6), plus many other blades (pp.591–9, Fig.246, *AY* 17/6), show that quality blade steel made by skilled blacksmiths was available in this period for making extremely sharp and efficient turn-

Table 215   The use-group of species used for turning in the British Isles between the 6th and 15th centuries compared to that for York: vessels

| | 6th century–Viking Age | | 11th–15th century | |
	York	Other Sites	York	Other Sites
Vessels				
Alder	36	14	9	24
Maple	28	25	2	6
Ash	7	6	16	139
Birch	2	2	2	15
Yew	1	1		1
Pomoideae	1	5		2
Willow?	1	5		2
Box	1	1		
Oak		2		6
Elm		1		6
Beech		2		13
Elder				1
Hazel		17		5
Sweet Chestnut		1		
Poplar		3		8
Total	**77**	**85**	**29**	**228**

Table 216   The use-group of species used for turning in the British Isles between the 6th and 15th centuries compared to that for York: cores

| | 6th century–Viking Age | | 11th–15th century | |
	York	Other Sites	York	Other Sites
Cores				
Alder	182	45	2	1
Maple	81	1	3	
Ash	2	1		
Birch	12	1	1	
Yew	1			
Pomoideae	2			
Willow	1	2		
Oak	1	1		
Elder	1			
Hazel	1	3		3
Sycamore				1
Poplar			1	2
Holly/Lime			1	
Not Identifiable	7	40		12
Total	**291**	**94**	**8**	**19**

ing tools. The analyses in Tables 215–16 were based on cores from 26 sites and vessels from 87 sites all over the British Isles, so the medieval figures were not biased in the favour of geographical areas where ash may predominate as a species.

Turners all over Britain (including York) shifted towards ash as first choice for wooden tableware from the mid 11th century onwards but many bowls were still made of alder, including some of the larger ones such as a 14th century bowl measuring 370mm in diameter found at Shackerley Mound (Morris 1987, fig.10, 7). Ash was not a new choice of species, however, and had been used to make both spindle-turned cups and face-turned bowls in York since Period 3. An article suggesting that, nationally, alder was the commonest material used for medieval bowl manufacture is misleading, and was based on a sample of only 45 vessels (Barber 1984, 125).

Turners' workshops in Coppergate

Wood-turners were vital members of any community, supplying essential tablewares, and other wares for the kitchen and dairy. Like most craftsmen working in urban centres in late Anglo-Saxon, Anglo-Scandinavian and medieval Britain, they probably had their own or shared workshops with working and living accommodation. The excavation at 16–22 Coppergate produced many types of workshop waste, showing that this area was a thriving manufacturing quarter of York from at least the later 9th century onwards, with many crafts other than woodworking carried out in the vicinity (textiles, *AY* 17/5; ironworking, *AY* 17/6; non-ferrous metalworking, *AY* 17/7; bone and antler working, *AY* 17/12; amber and jet, *AY* 17/14). Moreover, much of this craft waste was found in and around a series of wattle structures in Period 4B and a different series of plank-built semi-basement structures in Period 5B. Even allowing for the fact that small wooden objects are very mobile and may have been displaced from the contexts where they were originally deposited, it should be possible to look at the distributions of lathe-turners' waste products, unfinished vessels and the lathe component *8237* in relation to these structures and other features at various periods, and try to establish whether any of the structures could have been lathe-turners' workshops.

The period plans of the site at 16–22 Coppergate in Figs.1044–56 show the distribution of cores, end waste, middle waste, base waste, roughouts and unfinished vessels (both spindle-turned and face-turned), and the distribution of cups and bowls, in Periods 3–6. The composite period plans in Fig.1057–63 show the distribution of spindle-turned and face-turned evidence, highlighting that both techniques were used by turners working on or near the site, and throughout all periods.

In Period 3, there is definite evidence in the form of one large face-turned core, two pieces of end waste and an unfinished spindle-turned cup to suggest that a good range of lathe-turning processes were being carried out in the area of 16–22 Coppergate from the mid–late 9th to early 10th century (Fig.1043). Also, the distinctive small, spindle-turned cups already described (pp.2179–82) were definitely being made in Coppergate from the earliest period of Anglo-Scandinavian settlement on the site (Fig.1050). The waste products are widely distributed over the southern end of the site where organic remains were preserved in Period 3 layers, and a similar scatter of bowls and cups, some repaired and stained, also suggests domestic occupation close by in Period 3.

Although soil conditions in Period 4A were not particularly conducive to the survival of organic artefacts, two spindle-turned ash cores (Fig.1044) and two spindle-turned cups found at the western end of the site near the street frontage (Fig.1051) suggest that lathe-turners were still working in the area c.900–935, and still producing the small cups made in Period 3.

In Period 4B, when the area was divided into four tenements (designated A–D) defined by wattle fences, there is evidence for a great deal of lathe-turning activity. A total of 73 cores (43 spindle-turned), four pieces of base waste, seven pieces of end waste, one piece of middle waste, one blank for spindle-turning, and two unfinished spindle-turned cups were dated to Period 4B, giving an almost comprehensive range of waste products from many lathe-turning processes (Fig.1045). The cores were widely distributed, mainly over tenements B–D, both inside and outside the wattle structures at the front of each tenement. A small number of cores were also found on tenement A, two coming from the boundary line between the structures on tenements A and B. A large number of contemporary cores were found in pits 22557 and 25379, inside the structure on tenement C. A large number of pits were cut in and around the

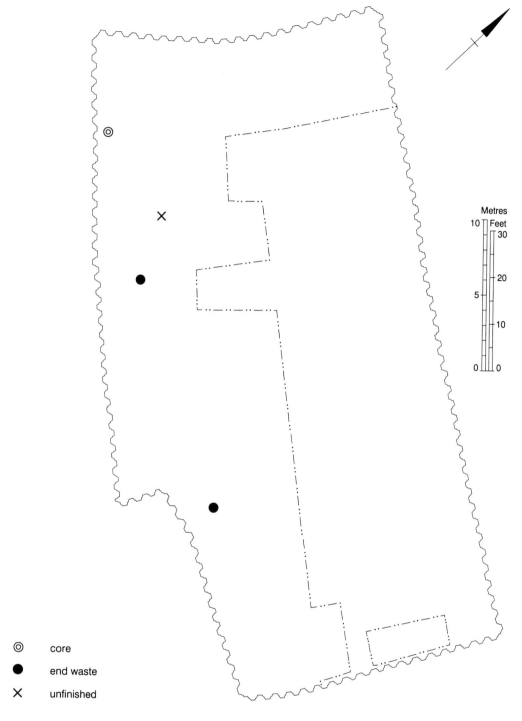

◎   core

●   end waste

✕   unfinished

Fig.1043   *Distribution plot of cores and other waste types in Period 3*

structures at this time; many cores were found behind the structures but not in pits. A small group of cores found at the north-eastern corner of the site at the far end of tenement D show that waste products from this craft were deposited well beyond the street frontage. Only cores were found inside the structures. The birch blank *8194*, and two unfinished cups *8201–2* were found behind the structure on tenement B, while the end, middle and base waste was found mainly behind the structures on tenements B and D.

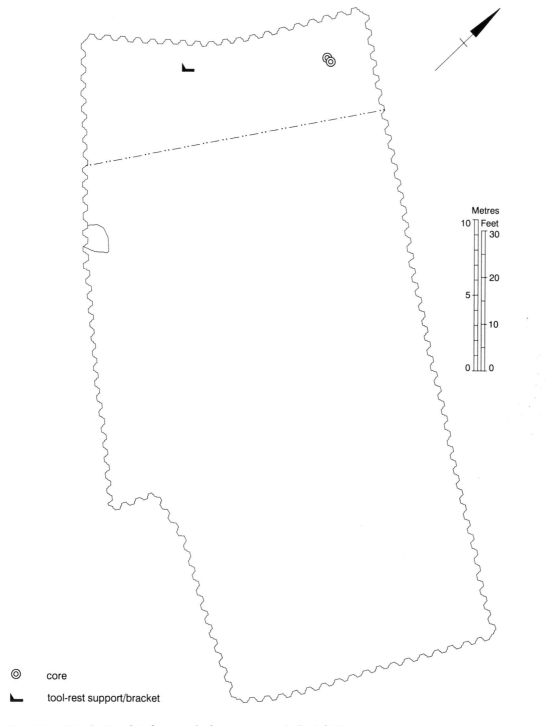

◎   core

∟   tool-rest support/bracket

Fig.1044 *Distribution plot of cores and other waste types in Period 4A*

It is almost certain that at some time over the 40-year period between 930/5 and 975, lathe-turners worked in and behind the structures on each of the four tenements, but mainly on tenements B–D, with a marked concentration of different types of waste on tenement B. It is not possible to be certain whether this was on a permanent or seasonal basis, but the evidence presented elsewhere (p.2191) suggests that seasonality may have played a major role in the lathe-turning craft.

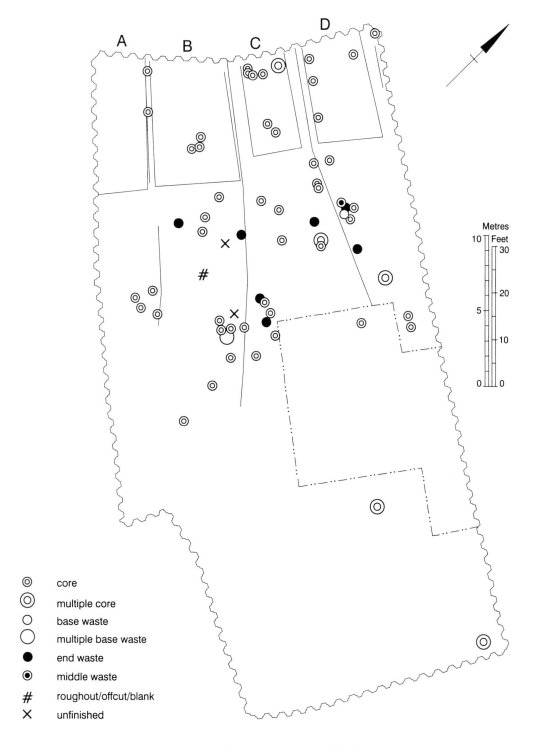

Key (legend):

◎ core
◉ multiple core
○ base waste
◯ multiple base waste
● end waste
◉ middle waste
roughout/offcut/blank
✕ unfinished

Fig.1045 *Distribution plot of cores and other waste types in Period 4B*

Fifteen cores, both spindle-turned and face-turned, one piece of end waste and two pieces of base waste were found in Period 5A layers dated to c.975, between the structures of Periods 4B and 5B. The cores were widely distributed over tenements A–D,

but the end and base waste was found on tenements B and D (Fig.1046).

In Period 5B, when the wattle structures of Period 4B were rebuilt in a completely new style of

2201

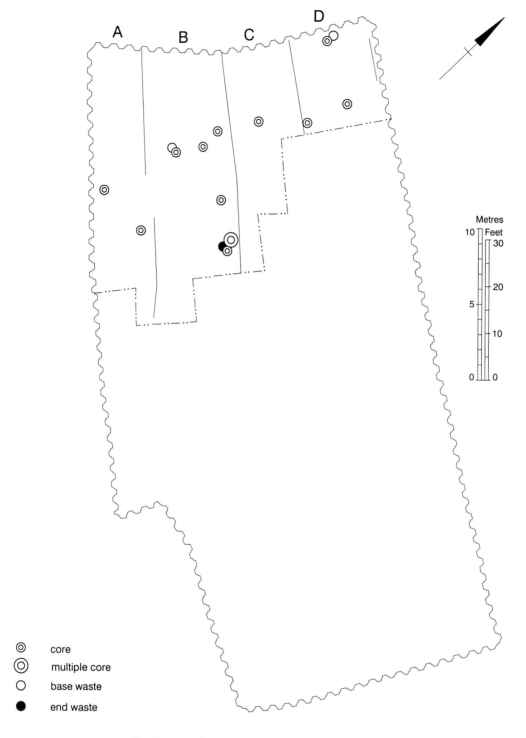

◎ core
◉ multiple core
○ base waste
● end waste

Fig.1046 *Distribution plot of cores and other waste types in Period 5A*

plank-built semi-basement structures, sometimes in a double row, near the street frontage, there is again evidence for a great deal of lathe-turning activity lasting from c.975 until the early–mid 11th century. A total of 173 cores (52 spindle-turned), ten pieces of base waste, seven pieces of end waste, three rough-outs, an offcut from making a roughout, and one un-finished face-turned bowl were dated to Period 5B, giving a comprehensive range of waste products from lathe-turning processes, as in Period 4B. The cores were again widely distributed over all four tene-ments, both inside and outside the structures (Fig.

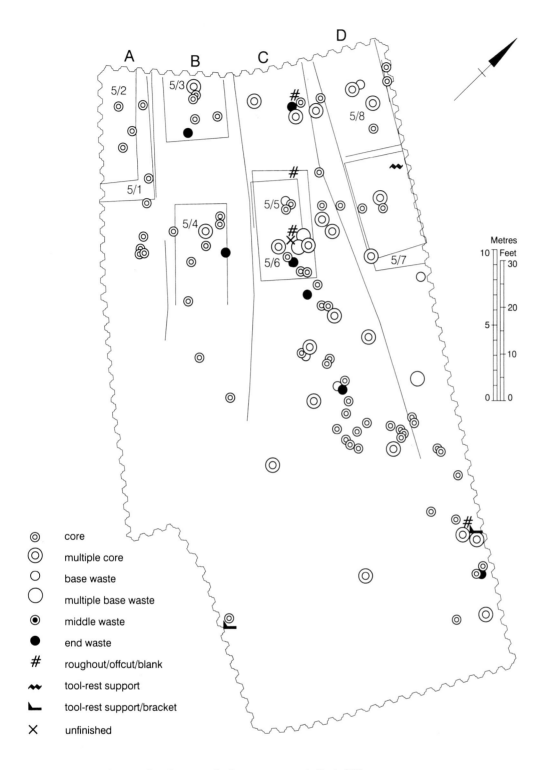

A   B   C   D

5/2
5/3
5/8
5/1
5/5
5/4
5/6
5/7

Metres
10 ⌐⌐ Feet
         ⌐ 30

         ⌐ 20
5 ⌐
         ⌐ 10

0 ⌐⌐ 0

◎   core
◎   multiple core
○   base waste
◯   multiple base waste
◉   middle waste
●   end waste
roughout/offcut/blank
⌁   tool-rest support
⌐   tool-rest support/bracket
✕   unfinished

Fig.1047   Distribution plot of cores and other waste types in Period 5B

1047). Single pieces of end waste were found inside the front and back structures on tenement B, but the majority of cores and other waste products were concentrated on tenements C and D.

On tenement C there was a large concentration of cores behind the single structure, along with two pieces of base waste and two pieces of end waste. Unfinished bowl *8203* was found inside the struc-

2203

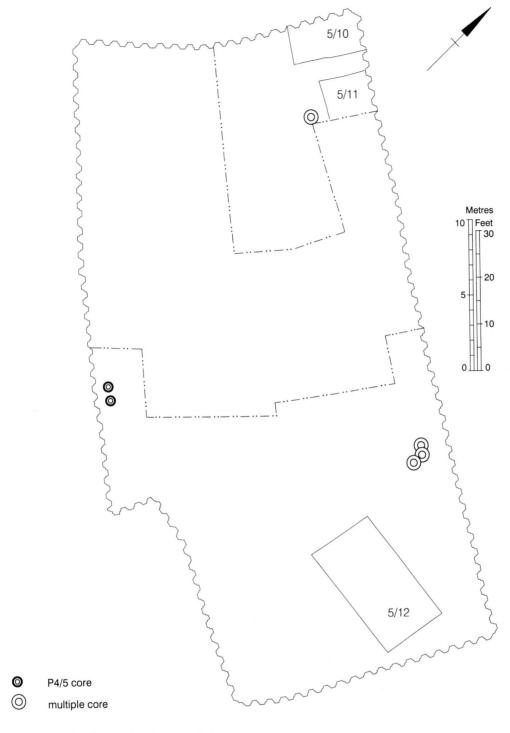

Fig.1048 *Distribution plot of cores and other waste types in Period 5C and Period 4/5*

ture, along with roughout *8198*, several pieces of base waste and one of end waste. Further finds in front of the same structure included roughout *8196* and a further piece of end waste, making this structure a very firm candidate for being a lathe-turner's work-shop at some time in Period 5B. There is also a heavy concentration of finished bowls and cups in and around this structure in Period 5B (Fig.1054).

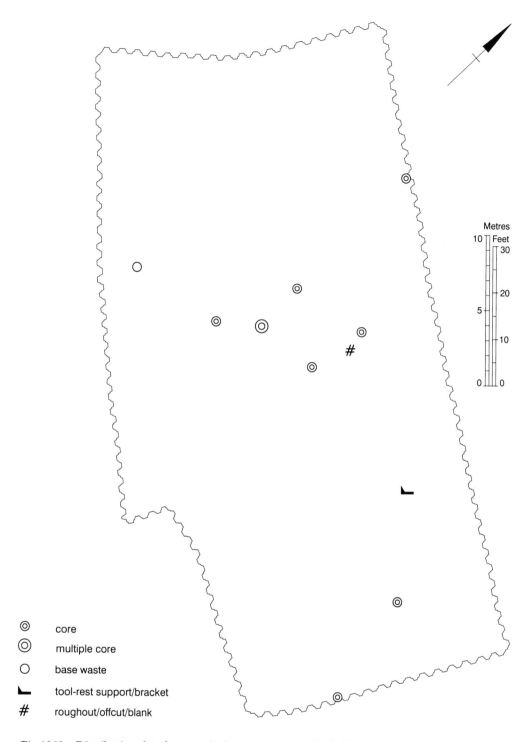

◎   core

◉   multiple core

○   base waste

└   tool-rest support/bracket

roughout/offcut/blank

Fig.1049   *Distribution plot of cores and other waste types in Period 6*

On tenement D there was a noticeable gap in the core distribution, with none at all being found over a stretch of at least 10m of ground immmediately behind the long partitioned timber structure at the front of the tenement. Beyond this, however, there was a large concentration of cores towards the extreme north-eastern corner of the site, just as there had been in Period 4B, showing that on tenement D some waste products from turning were deposited towards the end of the tenement, well behind the street frontage. Per-

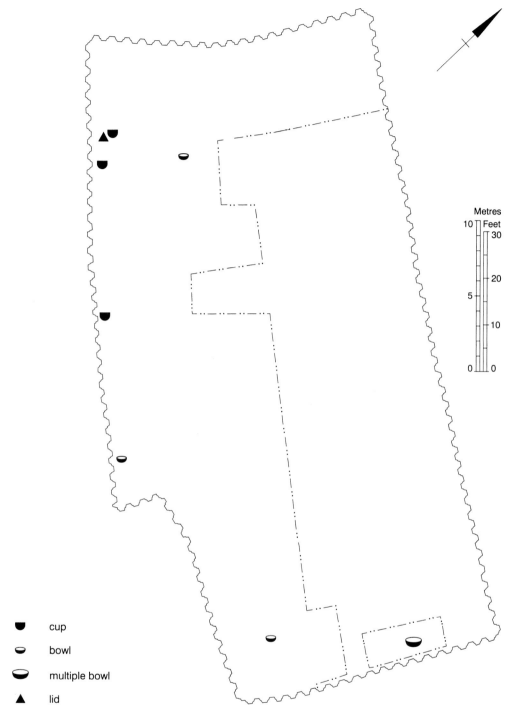

Fig.1050 *Distribution plot of cups, bowls and lids in Period 3*

haps at some time in both periods turners may have worked outside the structures, at the far end of their tenements, or perhaps they simply used the end of their yards as a dumping ground. Further evidence for the concentration of lathe-turning activities on tenement D comes from *8237*, the only certain piece of a lathe found on the whole site, which was discovered inside the rear half of the partitioned structure, and a piece of base waste found inside the front half of the structure. More base waste was found further down the tenement, along with *8195*, an offcut from preparing a roughout for face-turning, *8197*, a roughout or

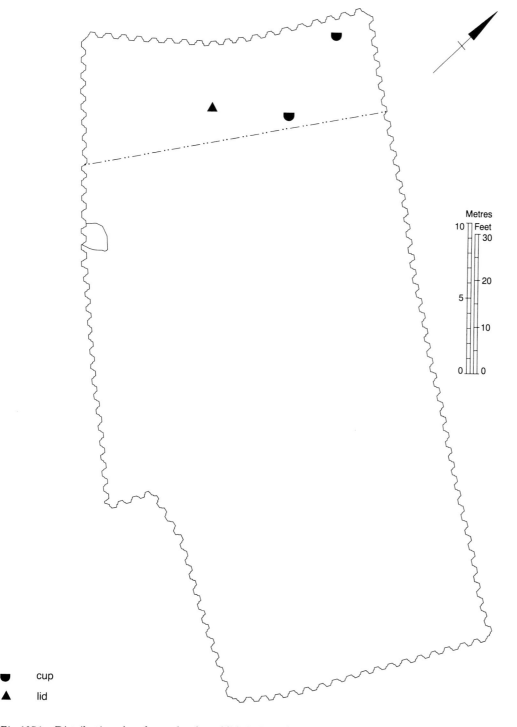

cup

▲ lid

Fig.1051   *Distribution plot of cups, bowls and lids in Period 4A*

reject from the spindle-turned stacking technique, and a piece of end waste. The structure on tenement D would have almost certainly been used as a turner's workshop at some time in Period 5B.

In Period 5C, around the mid–later 11th century, there is still evidence that lathe-turners were working on the site. A group of four cores were all found in pit fill 14069 towards the street frontage, just out-

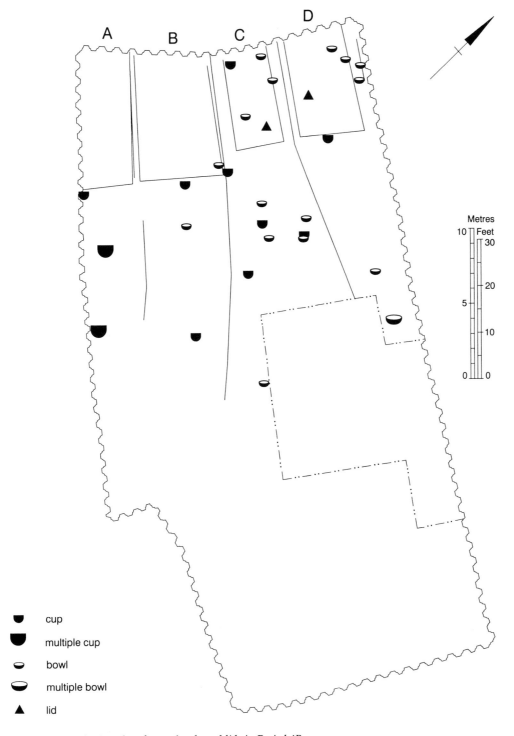

Fig.1052 *Distribution plot of cups, bowls and lids in Period 4B*

side the rear of two stuctures built at ground level on what had been tenement D in Period 5B (Fig.1048). The appearance, size and species of these cores is almost identical, suggesting that they were discarded from bowls made by the same turner at the same time, a craftsman possibly working in one of the structures

found. Seven more cores were found towards the rear of the site, on what had been tenement D, to the west of another post-built structure.

There are nine cores (one a middle core from the spindle-turned stacking technique), a piece of base

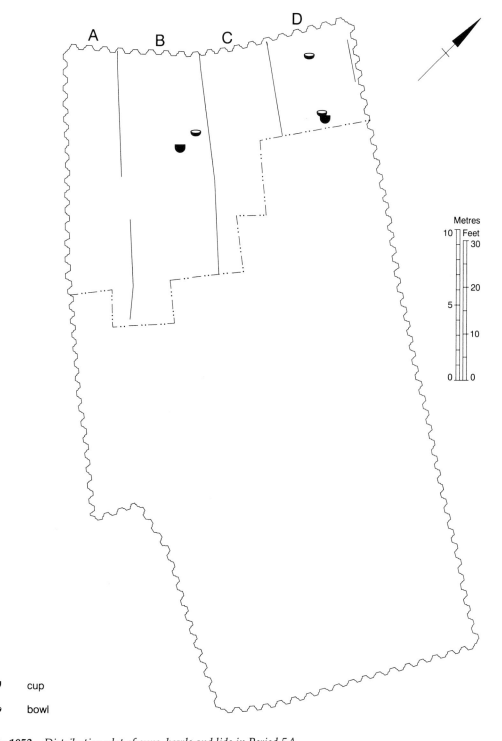

Fig.1053 *Distribution plot of cups, bowls and lids in Period 5A*

waste, a roughout (*8199*) and a possible tool-rest support (*9052*) dated to Period 6 (Fig.1049), a pitifully small amount of waste for the whole medieval period of later 11th to 16th centuries, which is represented by good amounts of lathe-turned bowls and

other wooden items across the parts of the site where medieval occupation had survived (Fig.1056). Apart from two cores found at the extreme eastern end of the site, the rest of the pieces were found in a band across the middle of the site behind the street front-

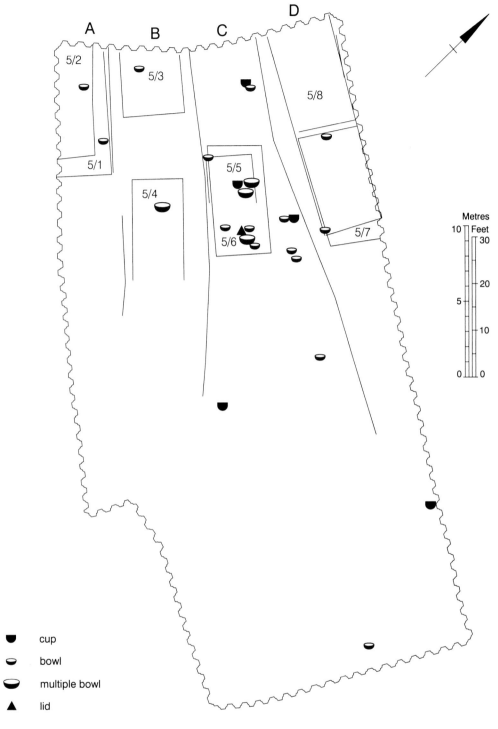

Fig.1054 *Distribution plot of cups, bowls and lids in Period 5B*

age structures of the previous periods. The low number of medieval lathe-turning waste products from the site may be due to the fact that modern intrusions have destroyed virtually all the deposits later than the 11th century right across the street frontage (see Fig.964, pp.2080–1), which may have contained more appreciable amounts of lathe-turners' waste products if these craftsmen had been working on the site. There seems to be clear evidence from pottery and coins, however, that many objects were displaced

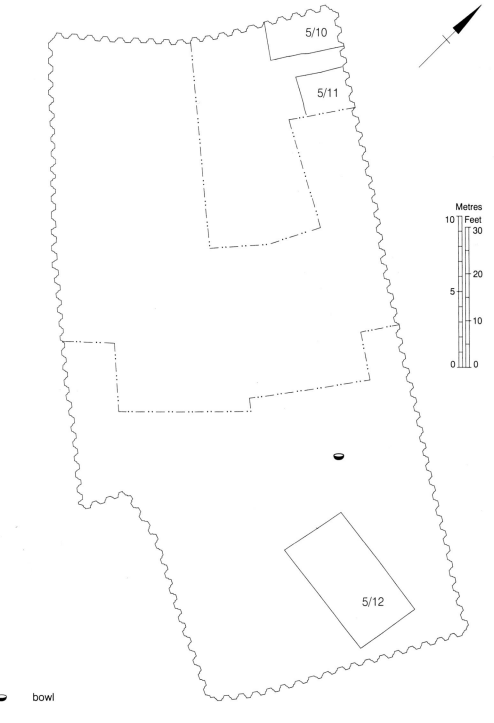

5/10

5/11

5/12

Metres
Feet
10
30

20

5

10

0   0

bowl

Fig.1055 *Distribution plot of cups, bowls and lids in Period 5C*

from their original contexts and redeposited in later layers by the cutting of features. If lathe-turning had ceased to be a common activity in the Coppergate area, the twelve items from Period 6 layers could have been redeposited from earlier layers. The survival of

two cores (*8369* and *8532*) at the extreme south-eastern end of the site, however, where there is intense medieval activity in an area which had previously been open land, suggests that there may have been medieval turning, albeit on a much smaller scale than in

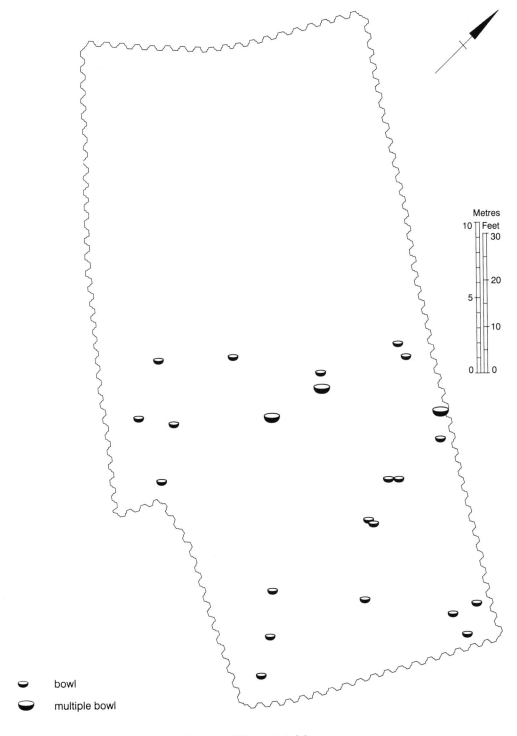

bowl

multiple bowl

Fig.1056 *Distribution plot of cups, bowls and lids in Period 6*

the Anglo-Scandinavian period. Also, *8369* is the only poplar core found on the entire site, a species which was not used for any of the Anglo-Scandinavian or medieval vessels from the site, but which was used for medieval vessels on other sites (Table 215, p.2197).

Fellows-Jensen (1979, 7) has suggested that the name Coppergate comes from two Old Scandinavian elements, *koppari* a rare word whose original meaning must have been 'maker of wooden vessels', from *koppr*, a cup or vessel for holding liquid, and *gata*

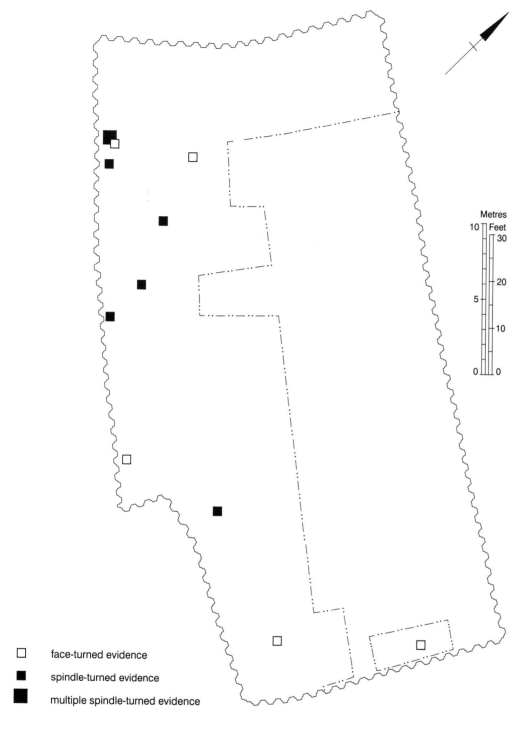

☐　face-turned evidence

■　spindle-turned evidence

■　multiple spindle-turned evidence

Fig.1057　Distribution plot of face-turned and spindle-turned evidence (both waste and vessels) in Period 3

meaning 'street'. Although it is first recorded as a street name in York in the 12th century (ibid.), the overwhelming evidence presented here shows that there had been lathe-turners' workshops on the site of 16–22 Coppergate since at least Period 3 and that there was a logical reason for the street name to have had its origins much earlier than the 12th century. The archaeological evidence for 'cup-turners' as op-

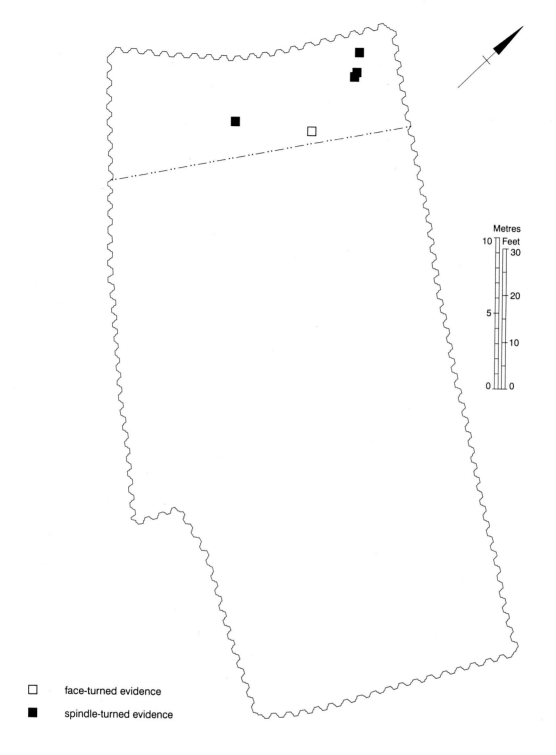

□ face-turned evidence

■ spindle-turned evidence

Fig.1058 Distribution plot of face-turned and spindle-turned evidence (both waste and vessels) in Period 4A

posed to merely 'vessel-turners' is very conclusive, since excavations have uncovered quantities of small globular drinking cups, vessels which may have been a speciality of the street and were made from the mid–late 9th–early 10th century onwards (Figs.1031–2, 1050–4).

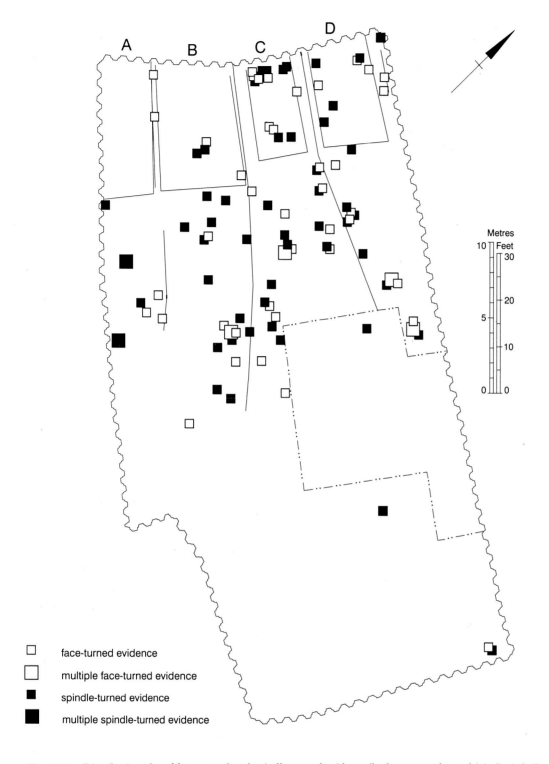

□ face-turned evidence

□ multiple face-turned evidence

■ spindle-turned evidence

■ multiple spindle-turned evidence

Fig.1059   *Distribution plot of face-turned and spindle-turned evidence (both waste and vessels) in Period 4B*

Archaeological evidence for further turners' work-shops has been found at two other sites in the Coppergate area. The hook-ended iron *9183* was found in an excavation at the corner of Castlegate and Coppergate (Benson 1906, 73, pl.II), while core *9164* and roughout *9163* were found on the Copper-gate watching brief site (see Fig.962, p.2074, for findspots). It is interesting that a woodworking tool

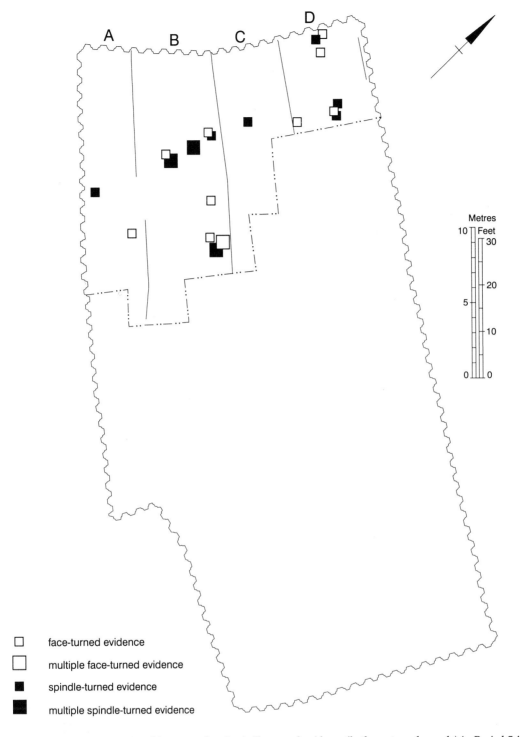

Metres

Feet

10

30

20

5

10

0

0

☐ face-turned evidence

☐ multiple face-turned evidence

■ spindle-turned evidence

■ multiple spindle-turned evidence

Fig.1060   Distribution plot of face-turned and spindle-turned evidence (both waste and vessels) in Period 5A

called *kopparajarn* is mentioned in the Icelandic 'Saga of St Olaf' (Fellows-Jensen 1979, 7). This would logically be a 'cup-turner's iron', perhaps like *9183*, and certainly the type of tool the turners in Coppergate would have used.

Turned wooden vessels were probably produced in large numbers by the Coppergate workshops (either in the woodland, in the town, or a combination of both). If one workshop produced 1,000 vessels in a year (a very conservative estimate), in the 200 years

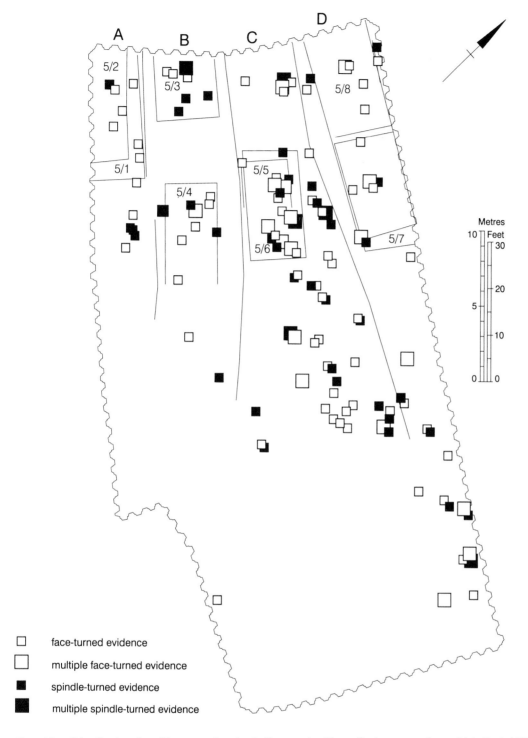

Fig.1061 *Distribution plot of face-turned and spindle-turned evidence (both waste and vessels) in Period 5B*

of Anglo-Scandinavian occupation on the 16–22 Coppergate site the total output of four workshops would have approached one million vessels. The actual numbers could have been very much greater. Since objects such as cores would be very useful as fuel and, like most discarded wooden objects, probably ended their lives as firewood, the 301 surviving cores from Coppergate and 22 Piccadilly could represent at least these one million vessels, a survival rate of only one in approximately every 3,500 made.

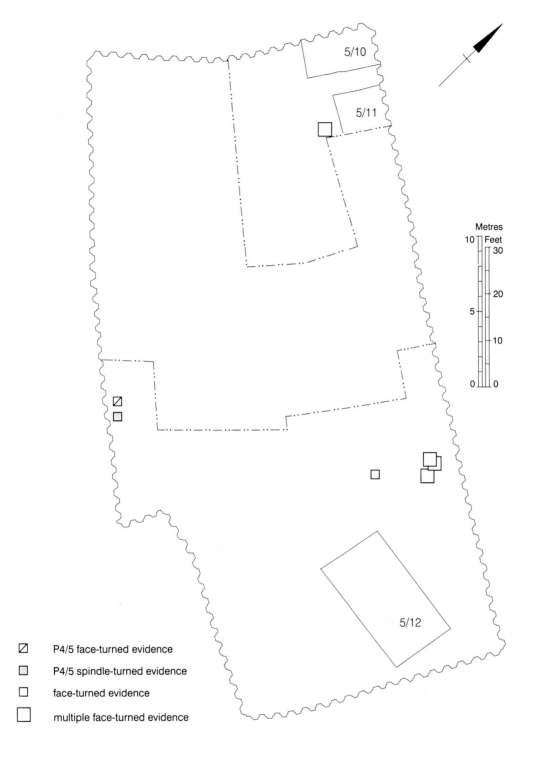

5/10

5/11

Metres
10 Feet
30
20
5
10
0   0

☑   P4/5 face-turned evidence

☐   P4/5 spindle-turned evidence

☐   face-turned evidence

☐   multiple face-turned evidence

5/12

Fig.1062   *Distribution plot of face-turned and spindle-turned evidence (both waste and vessels) in Period 5C and Period 4/5*

In 1066 there were approximately 1,875 *mansios* (tenements with dwellings) in York, implying that the total population was a minimum of c.10,000 (Darby and Maxwell 1962, 154) and probably much greater.

If each household had a wide variety of domestic wooden vessels, and we make the conservative assumption that each inhabitant would have used up one vessel a year on average, the total number of

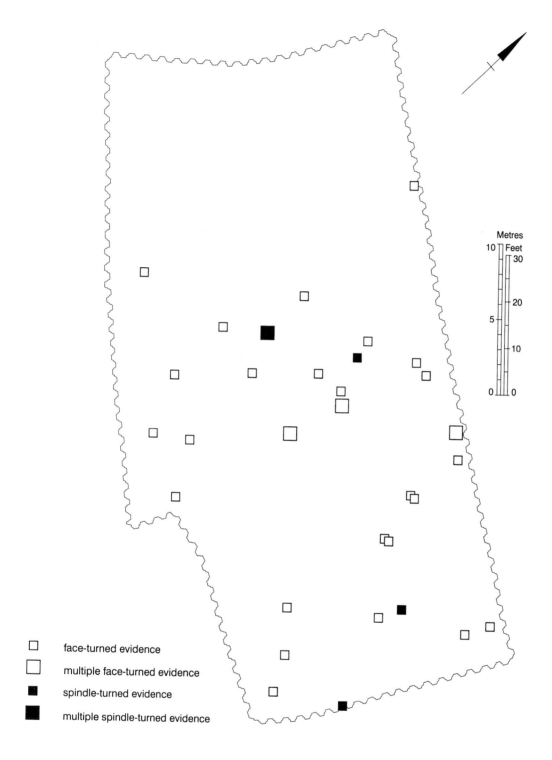

Fig.1063 *Distribution plot of face-turned and spindle-turned evidence (both waste and vessels) in Period 6*

bowls produced by workshops in over 200 years in 9th–11th century York would have been nearer two million. Since vessels could be produced in large quantities by small numbers of craftsmen, most, if not all, of the turners who made vessels in Anglo-Scandinavian York could have lived and worked in the Coppergate area.

Turners'/owners' marks on lathe-turned vessels

Deliberate symbols or marks found on turned vessels are usually incised, stamped or branded. Four bowls found on the Coppergate or Bedern sites have such marks on their external bases. The earliest is *8553*, dating to Period 4B, which has traces of what may be an incised triquetra in double outline (Fig.1021, p.2170). A late 13th–early 14th century bowl from the Bedern Foundry, *9203*, has a simple incised cross, *9229* from a mid 15th–early 17th century layer at the College of the Vicars Choral site at Bedern has a stamped or branded four-armed florid cross (Fig.1026, p.2175), and *8586* from the 16th–19th century stone-lined well at Coppergate was branded with the initials 'SR' (Fig.1023, p.2172). Marks found on lathe-turned bowls dating from the 11th to 15th centuries have been illustrated elsewhere (Morris 1984, fig.8.21).

Marks such as these are probably of two kinds — turners' marks or owners' marks, usually placed on the bottom of bowls, sometimes on the side. It is not always possible to determine which type of mark has been used unless there are two different types on one bowl, as on a bowl from Monkgate, Hull (ibid., fig.138, L158xx), or when the mark occurs on various different wooden items in one context, as on several bowls with the heart symbol of the Douglas family found at Threave Castle, Dumfries and Galloway (Good and Tabraham 1981, fig.14).

In 1346–7 London turners were summoned before the Mayor and Aldermen and given injunctions to have personal marks placed on the bottom of every measure (Letter Book F, City of London, fo.134), al-though these were probably official measuring containers and not domestic bowls. Girling noted that merchants' marks were used in England as early as the late 13th century (Girling 1964, 9). The archaeological evidence from turned vessels, however, suggests that turners could have been using personal marks as early as the 11th century. These include an incised pentacle on an 11th–12th century bowl from Gloucester (Morris 1979, fig.17.17), an incised inverted 2 on a bowl from Milk Street, London (Morris 1984a, fig.142, L172xxviii), two incised triquetras on a bowl from Christchurch Place, Dublin (ibid., L146iv), and two incised S-shapes on a 12th–13th century bowl from Reading (ibid., fig.144, L193ii). If the triquetra mark on *8553* dated to the 10th century is a turner's mark, it could be the earliest example yet found in Britain. The majority of marks, however, date from the 13th to 15th centuries, the period when craftsmen's guilds were developing fast and becoming more important.

In a household which had many wooden vessels, personal or household marks were probably used. The 'SR' mark branded into *8586* was also found on rake *8977* and a fragment *8694* recovered from the same well. The florid cross mark on *9229* and the simple cross on *9203* could be either turners' or owners' marks. Two sets of three bowls found in different pits on Southampton sites each have their own incised mark. One has 'A' symbols, the other conjoined triangles. Each pit also contained other bowls with different symbols. The bowls are in closed groups and the marks are either turners' marks, several bowls being a single turner's work, or owners' marks, each symbol the mark of a person or household (Platt and Coleman-Smith 1975, figs.227–8).

Fragments and Offcuts

Ninety-five wooden small finds from 16–22 Coppergate, the Coppergate watching brief site, Bedern and 22 Piccadilly are either small chips, offcuts and waste pieces from woodworking, unidentifiable fragments, or naturally occurring pieces of wood which may or may not have been worked. Some have tool marks which are usually facet cuts made by shaping with an axe. The species of wood of these fragments are mainly those one would expect from studying the finished products found on the site, for example, oak, alder, ash and maple. All the pieces are grouped here according to the primary conversion of the wood, further subdivided by period.

Thirty-five items were made from radially split sections of wood. Many of the pieces are offcuts of oak which result from the secondary conversion of a radially split oak section into a finished product such as a plank or board, and have faceted surfaces and edges, and traces of axe-cut tool marks. These include *8651* and *8653* (Period 4B), *8663*, *8665*, *8668*, *8675–6* and *8678* (Period 5B), *9188* from the early–mid 11th century at Piccadilly, *8697*, *8699*, *8718* and *8721* (Period 6), and *9208*, *9210–11* from medieval levels at the Bedern Foundry site. Similar oak offcuts from woodworking, but with augered or chiselled holes (hole dimensions given in brackets), include *8648* from Period 4B, *8658* from Period 5A (23mm), *8669* from Period 5B (over 65mm; Fig.1064), *8685* (32mm) and *8687* (23mm; Fig.1064) from Period 5C, and *8690* (14 × 12mm), *8700* (23mm) and *8704* (14mm with trenail 35mm long; Fig.1065) from Period 6. Radially split offcuts of other species include *8650*, a willow piece from Period 4B, *8657*, a maple block with an augered hole 30mm diameter from Period 5A, and four pieces from Period 6, *8703*, an alder half-section with a 'groove' 10mm wide, *8713*, an alder fragment with 30–40 copper alloy rivets embedded in it (Fig.1065), *8716*, an ash fragment with an iron nail, and *8720*, a birch offcut with three faceted sides and the fourth cut straight across. *9209*, from the Bedern Foundry site, is an ash offcut of radially split section from a prepared length of wood. Some of the fragments may have been offcuts from the working of re-used pieces of wood, hence the holes, nails, rivets and pegs.

8694 (Fig.1065), from Period 6, was an alder or hazel branch split into quarter section, with a fragment of side branch, the main stem branded with the letters 'SR'. It may have been part of the handle of toothed rake *8977*. *8698*, also from Period 6, comprised eighteen offcut rods made from radially split timber which is smooth-grained and hard. All have faceted sides and one end which is sawn straight across; the other ends are either broken or faceted.

8684 and *8689* are two unusual items from the working of radially split oak planks which were found in different Period 5C contexts (Fig.1064). They were the waste products of the technique of making large circular holes in boards such as garderobe seats *8949–50* and *9176* (see pp.2304–8). No Anglo-Scandinavian seats of this kind have yet been found, and *8684* and *8689* could have come from the production of another type of object. An offcut similar to the York pieces, however, dated to the 9th–11th centuries, was found in the settlement at Hedeby and is now on display at the Wikinger Museum there.

9186 is a small 10th–11th century oak offcut from a tangentially converted block, found on the 22 Piccadilly site.

Thirteen objects were made from roundwood. *8644* may have been part of an alder hurdle from Period 3. *8654* is a willow offcut from Period 4B in the form of a faceted cylinder with shoulders sloping steeply to a narrower faceted knob fragment (Fig.1064). Although it has a similar profile to a piece of lathe-turning end waste, it is not from lathe-turning. There are six fragments from Period 5B, three of which may have been produced by the debarking of roundwood or the whittling of roundwood during secondary conversion. *8664* is an oak offcut with one surface rough with traces of bark, the other smooth; *8681* includes fragments and slivers which appear to be waste from the whittling of ash roundwood, and *8673* is a bark fragment cut straight across at one end. *8670* is a naturally occurring L-shaped piece with a curved grain, *8679* is an oak or sweet chestnut piece of roundwood with whittled sides and *8680* is a charred roundwood ash fragment. *8688*, from Period 5C, is a faceted roundwood cone-shaped maple offcut with a roughly pointed broken end and a faceted knob at the wider end, but it is not a lathe-turned core or piece of end waste (Fig.1064). There are four roundwood offcuts of different spe-

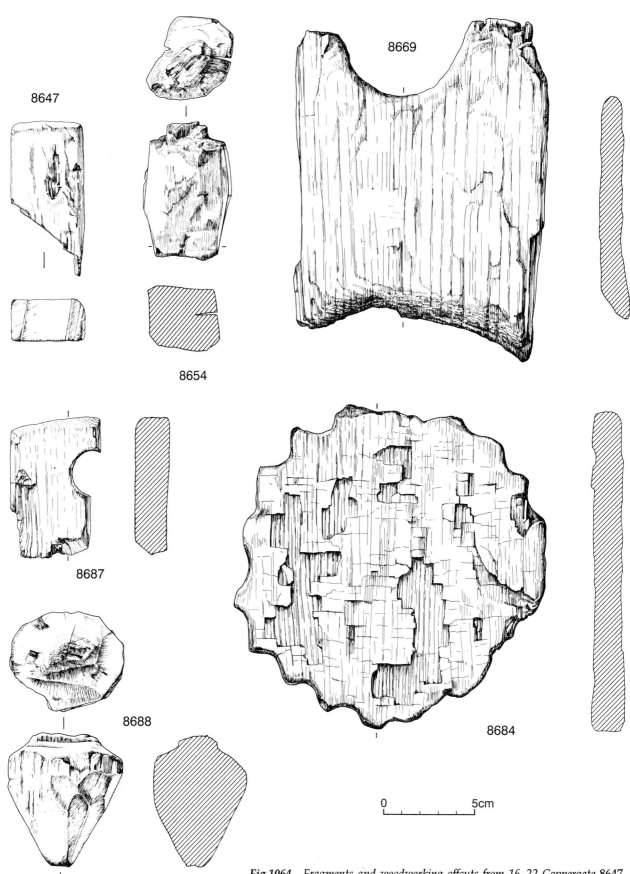

Fig.1064 *Fragments and woodworking offcuts from 16–22 Coppergate 8647, 8654, 8669, 8684, 8687–8. Scale 1:2. 8684 may represent the waste product of the technique of making large circular holes in boards for garderobe seats*

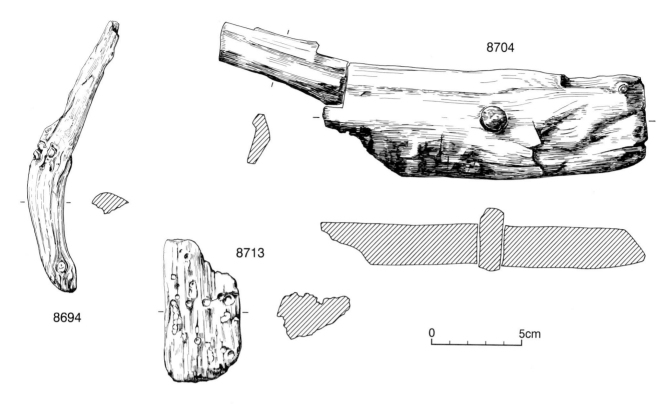

Fig.1065 *Fragments and woodworking offcuts from 16–22 Coppergate 8694, 8704, 8713. Scale 1:2*

cies from Period 6: *8692* is an oak fragment with a facet at one end; *8693* comprises three lengths of alder or birch roundwood with the bark in situ, one piece of which has a faceted cut; *8696* is a length of elder roundwood with a naturally hollowed centre (no pith remains) and an oblique facet cut at one end; and *8708* includes two ash offcuts, one cut down from roundwood or a half-section, the other roughly square in cross-section with truncated corners.

Naturally occurring pieces which may have been discarded in the working of wood on the Coppergate site included a thorn of blackthorn or hawthorn from Period 3 (*8645*), an ash burr from Period 5A (*8656*) and a possible burr fragment from Period 6 (*8722*), a poplar knot from Period 5B (*8672*), and pieces of bark from Periods 5B (*8677*), 5C (*8686*) and 6 (*8706*).

It was not possible to be certain of the primary conversion of the majority of fragments. *8643* and *8646* are two Pomoideae offcuts from Period 3. *8647* is an alder offcut with an axe cut from Period 4A (Fig.1064). Three pieces from Period 4B are *8649* with associated iron fragments, *8652* and *8655*. Twelve fragments were found in Period 5B or equivalent con-

texts: *8659, 8666–7* and *8671* are oak offcuts and chips (*8671* included a fragment of a lathe-turned bowl of unidentified species); *8660, 8662, 8674* and *8682* are alder offcuts and fragments; *8683* is an ash fragment; and *8661* and *9169* are unidentifiable species, the latter associated with a fragment of iron. *9187* is an oak offcut fragment with blue vivianite residue found in a 10th–11th century layer at 22 Piccadilly. Seventeen fragments were found in Period 6 contexts: *8691, 8695, 8701, 8705, 8707, 8709–11* and *8719* are oak offcuts; *8723* is a wood fragment associated with leather; *8702* is a wood fragment with iron; and *8712, 8714–15, 8717* and *8724–5* are fragments of unidentifiable species. *8726* (with an iron nail 60mm long) was recovered from an unstratified context. *9207, 9212* and *9232* from Bedern are a yew offcut, a carbonised fragment and a small unidentified shaving respectively.

It is important to record and/or publish information about fragments and offcuts; as research into wooden artefacts and woodworking tools and techniques progresses, what is one researcher's 'fragment' may one day turn out to contain another researcher's vital information. This has been proved in the case of *8684*.

Coopered Vessels

Many different kinds of stave-built (or coopered) vessels would have been found among the large range of wooden containers and utensils the Anglo-Scandinavian and medieval household used for domestic chores and the storage, preparation and consumption of food. These were made of narrow staves of wood bound together in a circular form by either wooden or metal bands. Stave-built vessels complemented lathe-turned wooden bowls and cups, pottery jars, jugs and cooking pots, and metal cooking vessels in the household. Stave-built containers were also used for commercial purposes, especially the transportation of goods.

At the sites under consideration the archaeological evidence for Anglo-Scandinavian and medieval coopering is as excellent in its quantity and variety as that for lathe-turning. Apart from one unfinished bucket stave 8745, however, it survives only in the form of the coopers' finished products rather than a combination of manufacturing debris and products. These products are mainly different sizes of buckets (3033, 8727–45, 9189, 9233), tubs (8746–63) and casks (8764–8, 9190–2, 9214–16), and individual caskheads or vessel bases (8769–827, 9170–1, 9213), incomplete staves (8828–49, 9172–3), hoops (8850–65), lids (8866–70), battens (8871–2, 9217), spouts (8873–5) and spigots (8876–7) from various vessels.

There would have been no amateur coopers (Kilby 1971, 15). Coopering, like lathe-turning, is a skill acquired gradually by experience, and a craft which had to be taught and learned if a living was to be based on it. The coopers' specialised tools and raw materials could not have been acquired and used on an ad hoc basis to make do-it-yourself stave-built vessels; all pieces of stave-built vessels found in York, therefore, were made by skilled coopers and bought from craftsmen or traders by those who needed them. Apart from the medieval unfinished stave 8745, there is no evidence that coopers were making stave-built vessels in workshops in the Coppergate area, and all the coopered objects found were probably made elsewhere. They are either discarded pieces of vessels or complete vessels in situ where they were used. At least some of the staves found on the site may have been made in woodland areas. Documentary references show that by the 14th century coopers were

manufacturing buckets in woodland areas, presumably cutting the staves in situ rather than bringing raw materials back to a workshop. In 1337 Roger and William Couper and their two serving men illegally manufactured large wooden buckets called collokes in Sowerby Wood on the Manor of Wakefield (Yorks. Arch. Soc. MS 759/1340, 82–3, Court Rolls, Manor of Wakefield), whereas in 1338 a cooper called Jevan Saer paid 1s 1½d for a licence to make 'boketts' for nine weeks in Welsh forests (Court Rolls Portfolio 192/4 Llanover 12 Edw III).

Coopering has an advantage over carving or lathe-turning in that the diameter of any vessel is not limited by the gross dimensions of the timber available. Fairly narrow staves can be made either from riven or tangentially converted planks of small trees, then built up into larger vessels. In the case of stave-built casks, the qualities of strength, watertightness and ease of movement by rolling, for instance, can be added to size.

Coopers have traditionally made three categories of stave-built vessels. Wet coopered casks were watertight for fermented liquids. By the 11th century, at least, these were bellied, that is, much wider at the girth than the ends, and considerable skill was involved in their manufacture. Dry coopered casks were made to hold dry goods or non-fermented liquids. These could be less watertight, more straight-sided than 'wet' casks, and less skill was involved in their manufacture. The vessels made by white coopering were usually straight-sided, open-topped vessels such as buckets and tubs.

Each of these three branches of the craft was not necessarily the work of a different craftsman. A wet cooper might make all three types of vessel, but a white cooper could have plied his trade without the knowledge of how to construct a wet cask. This is important when considering the Anglo-Scandinavian and medieval vessels, the craftsmen who made them and the skills required. The species of wood used and the ways they were converted into staves are also important since different branches of coopering sometimes required different species and forms of timber.

Buckets

8727–45 are either complete buckets, single staves or groups of staves from the same vessel. Most of them are from vessels described here as buckets which are generally open-topped, straight-sided containers with handles joined to two opposed staves. They were products of white coopering, were made in a large range of sizes and were probably the most widely used domestic stave-built vessel in Anglo-Saxon, Anglo-Scandinavian and medieval Britain, a recent study showing a wide distribution over most of the country (Morris 1984a, fig.7.10). Bucket stave fragments *9233* were found in pit 25 on the site of the College of the Vicars Choral at Bedern. This pit contained 10th century pottery. The three Anglo-Scandinavian yew vessels from Coppergate *8727*, *8732* and *8735*, and willow vessel *3033* with its elaborate tinned iron nails and Y-shaped iron strips, may have been mainly decorative and prestigious items, but most of the oak buckets were ordinary domestic containers. Yew stave *8727* has a dark reddish-brown stained internal surface, probably from its original contents; since it is only 159mm high, it could even have been a drinking vessel. It is fortunate for our understanding of the construction techniques used to make them that many of the larger buckets, like

Fig.1066   Complete bucket 8742. Actual height 424mm

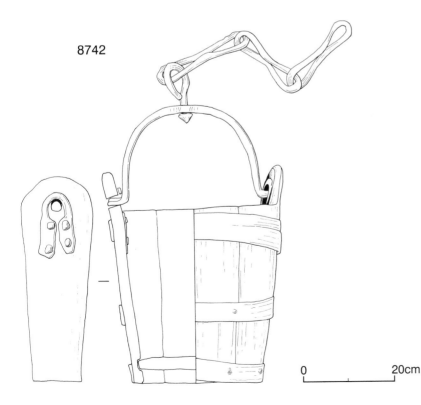

8742

0   20cm

Fig.1067   Complete bucket 8742 from 16–22 Coppergate. Scale 1:8

2225

8742, have been found in wells. The waterlogged layers in wells provide favourable conditions for preserving wood, and buckets such as 8742 which have been lost or abandoned in their well (in this case the cask 8766) tend to be found more or less complete, a condition which is rare among stave-built finds from other contexts. Both cask and bucket are dated to the early 15th century (see Fig.967, p.2092).

8742 is probably the most perfectly preserved complete medieval bucket found on any site in Britain (Figs.1066–7). It is wider at the top, and has nine radially split oak staves and a single-piece circular base with rounded edges in situ in an angular U-shaped basal groove. Two staves have raised rounded upper ends perforated by augered holes, each reinforced on the inside by an iron escutcheon fixed by four iron nails. A curved iron handle with straight, horizontal ends is fixed through the holes, and the centre of the handle has a hole through which is fitted an iron swivel device with a closed loop. Three figure-of-eight links of iron chain are attached to the swivel. Three iron hoops 40mm wide encircle the bucket, the middle one with an iron nail below it. Buckets to compare with 8742 have been found in medieval wells at Almondbury Castle in W. Yorkshire (Morris 1984a, fig.100, C142), Weoley Castle in the West Midlands (ibid., C161), Bramford in Suffolk and Brightlingsea in Essex (Erith 1972, fig.6, 1 and 3), Castell-y-Bere in Gwent (Butler and Dunning 1974, fig.10), Taunton in Somerset (ibid., fig.12), Duffield in Derbyshire (ibid., fig.13), Billingsgate Buildings in London (Rhodes 1980, fig.84), Seaford in Sussex (Freke 1978, fig.13) and Tong in Shropshire (Wharton 1978, fig.13).

Complete staves which have a groove at the lower end and a shaped rim at the upper end were parts of various types of open-topped vessels, not casks. Some of them (e.g. 8730 and 8734) have holes in raised lugs above the rim edge where handles were attached and are definitely parts of vessels which are referred to here as buckets. If a stave has no such distinguishing features, it is not always possible to be certain that it came from a bucket with a handle joined to two opposed staves. Some may have belonged to stave-built bucket-like containers which had only one handle grip (e.g. the two vessels shown on the floor in the late medieval illustration in Fig.1087), some of the larger ones could have belonged to tubs (see below),

and some of the smaller ones could have been parts of stave-built jugs or drinking vessels.

Nearly all of the bucket staves found at Coppergate are oak, 8727, 8732 and 8735 are yew, 8730 is pine and 3033 is willow, all species which could have been obtained and worked locally. 8740 and 9172, which comprises four staves with broken ends which could be parts of a bucket or cask, however, are made of *Abies alba* or silver fir, a species which is not native to Britain and which was only introduced in the post-medieval period (Edlin 1949, 129). 8740 was recovered from a late 12th–13th century context. Two 13th century buckets with silver fir staves were also found in Lund in Sweden (Mårtensson and Wahlöö 1970, fig.73), and, since this species has also not been native to maritime north-west Europe since the last Ice Age (Casparie and Swarts 1980, 270, fig.186), all the finds of silver fir at Coppergate and Lund must either have been imported from areas where silver fir is a native species, or were made in these towns from wood cut down and re-used from larger imported artefacts. The latter is more likely since it is known that casks of silver fir were manufactured in the Upper Rhine and Alpine regions by the Romans, some being exported up the Rhine as far as Britain. Examples of Roman silver fir casks, which probably originally brought imported wine, have been found used as well linings at Silchester, Hampshire (Hope and Fox 1899, pl.VIII), and Roman buckets of silver fir found in a well at Skeldergate in York (pp.47–50, Fig.26, AY 17/2), at *Vindolanda*, Northumberland (Birley 1977, 24), and at Silchester (Boon 1974, 86) show that Roman casks of silver fir could provide good raw material for making vessels such as buckets. Several casks of silver fir were also used as well linings on the late 7th–9th century site of Dorestad in the Netherlands and the 9th–11th century site at Hedeby, which must have been imported to these sites, presumably from the Upper Rhine Alpine region. They show that the construction of silver fir casks and an export trade in wine via the Rhineland continued after the Roman period. The import of wine in such casks may have continued into the medieval period in York and Lund, providing raw material to make buckets.

Staves were manufactured from either thin radially split or tangentially converted boards, their edges cut and shaped with a broad shaping axe. Most of the Anglo-Scandinavian and medieval bucket staves from

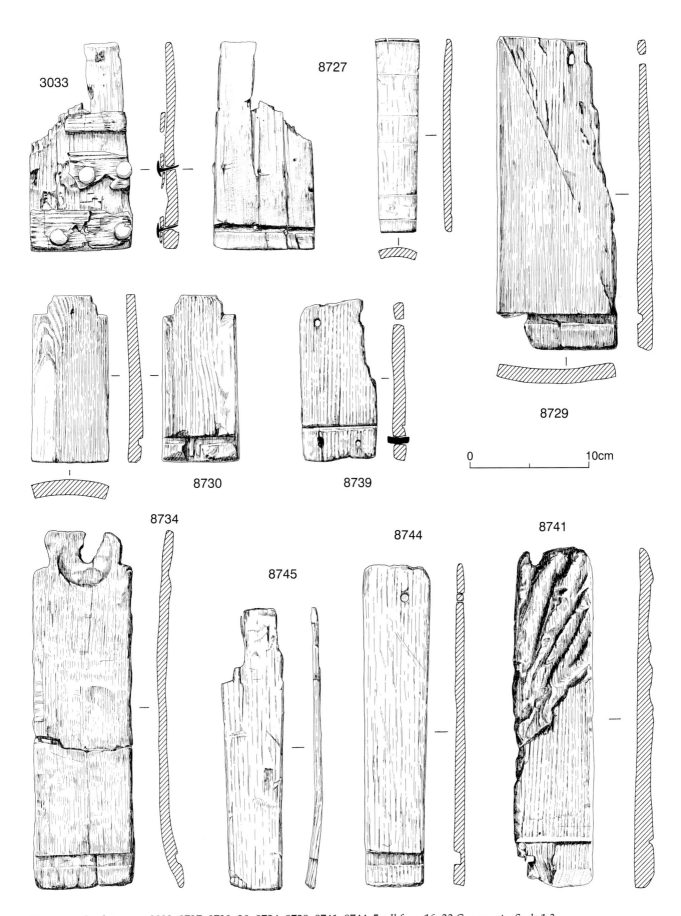

3033

8727

8729

8730

8739

8734

8745

8744

8741

0   10cm

Fig.1068   *Bucket staves 3033, 8727, 8729–30, 8734, 8739, 8741, 8744–5, all from 16–22 Coppergate. Scale 1:3*

Coppergate were made from radially split oak boards, but *3033* is a radially split willow stave. Bucket staves from other late Anglo-Saxon and medieval British sites were all made from radially split boards, mainly oak (Morris 1984a, fig.10.5). Four Anglo-Scandinavian staves from Coppergate, however, were unusual in that they were made from tangentially converted boards — *8727* (Period 3), *8732* (Period 4B) and *8735* (Period 5B) are yew and *8730* (Period 4B) is pine. The only other tangential bucket staves from a British site were oak, alder and ash staves from various buckets found in a Roman well at Dalton Parlours (Morris 1990a, 206–21, figs.124ff). This type of stave which was tangentially sawn or split (as opposed to being cleft radially along the principal planes of weakness which follow the medullary rays in roundwood) may have been common in Roman Britain because Roman woodworkers were well acquainted with large two-man pit saws which were ideal for tangentially sawing large planks and staves, but which may not have been commonly used again in post-Roman Britain until the 15th century. The four Anglo-Scandinavian tangential staves may have been tangentially split rather than sawn. Other tangentially converted small objects of this period found in York have been discussed on p.2104, and tangential conversion was used on the planks of the sunken buildings at Coppergate in Period 5B (*AY* 8/4 in prep.).

Staves usually have chamfered long edges to make an accurate, probably watertight, join. The chamfers could have been made with an axe, drawknives, planes or even a cooper's jointer (Kilby 1971, pl.4). There are very marked chamfered edges on Anglo-Scandinavian staves *8729–30* and medieval staves *8741* and *8743*.

In any vessel, the component staves usually vary little in thickness, but can vary considerably in width. Narrow staves would be inserted with the wider ones to make the perfect circular form of the desired diameter. Bucket *8733* has fragments of five staves which vary in width from 69–118mm (Fig.1069). Complete buckets of this period have between six and nineteen staves, as shown by buckets from Lund (Mårtensson and Wahlöö 1970, fig.73) and Ballinderry Crannog 1 (Hencken 1936, fig.13) respectively, but average ten to fourteen staves. The complete medieval buckets from Coppergate have nine (*8742*) and thirteen staves (*8744*).

Most buckets were either parallel-sided as *3033*, *8728–31*, *8734* and *8737–41*, or wider at the top as *8727*, *8742*, *8744–5*. Much rarer are staves which indicate that a vessel was wider at the bottom such as *8733*, *8735*, three staves of a 13th century vessel found in Cork (Hurley 1982, fig.16.4, 2), and a 7th–10th century vessel found in a souterrain at Larne, Co. Antrim (Waterman 1971, fig.7, 5 and 9).

The basal grooves of the staves found at Coppergate were squared or V-shaped in cross-section. *8745* is an unfinished bucket stave and no groove had been cut in it. Staves *3033*, *8729–31*, *8733*, *8736–7*, *8740* and *8743–4* have neat squared grooves, staves *8727–8*, *8732*, *8735*, *8739* and *8741* have neat V-sectioned grooves, but the groove on *8728* is roughly chiselled. Where complete, buckets like *8742* and *8744* have a neat continuous groove with little deviation from stave to stave; this indicates the use of a tool similar to a modern cooper's croze (Kilby 1971, fig.12), which cuts a continuous groove equidistant from the ends of the staves. No such tool survives from Anglo-Saxon or Anglo-Scandinavian England, but a possible medieval croze found at Meols in Merseyside (Morris 1984a, fig.166, W150) indicates the form of such tools. It is a three-piece iron tool 131mm long and 73mm wide. A socketed iron frame with a rectangular cross-sectioned handle or tang has sides which are bent over to form the flanged socket. A cutting blade with seven teeth is moveable inside the frame and an iron wedge can fix the blade in position. A Viking period stave from Dublin had two basal grooves, either because the basal groove had to be re-cut, or more likely because it was re-used with a refitted base. This feature is also found on a broken stave from Exeter which may be a cask or open-topped vessel stave (Allan and Morris 1984, fig.177, 69) and on Roman bucket staves from Dalton Parlours (Morris 1990a, fig.130, 10). Casks often had their heads refitted after being refilled.

Some staves such as *8740* taper markedly in profile towards a very thin rim edge. Staves found at Coppergate have rounded (e.g. *8727*, *8729–30*) or pointed (*8732* and *8737*) rim edges. Medieval stave *8738* has a possible foot below the bottom edge. The foot has a flat bottom edge and sloping sides. Other buckets, such as those found in a 12th century well at Taunton Castle (Butler and Dunning 1974, fig.12), in a bog at Ty'r Dewin in Gwynedd (Evans 1905, figs.2–4) and in a medieval well at Conway Castle in

Gwynedd (Butler and Evans 1979, 93), also have shaped extensions on certain staves which extend below the bottom edge and would have acted as feet.

Buckets 8733 (possibly two vessels) and 8742 have single-piece circular bases associated with staves, each with squared edges to fit into squared basal grooves (Fig.1069). Medieval stave 8738 has a narrow linear basal groove which retains a fragment of oak base and fibrous caulking material. Most bucket bases which survive in association with their staves are circular and made from a single flat board, such as those found with two buckets from a 13th century well at Almondbury Castle, and a late 12th century

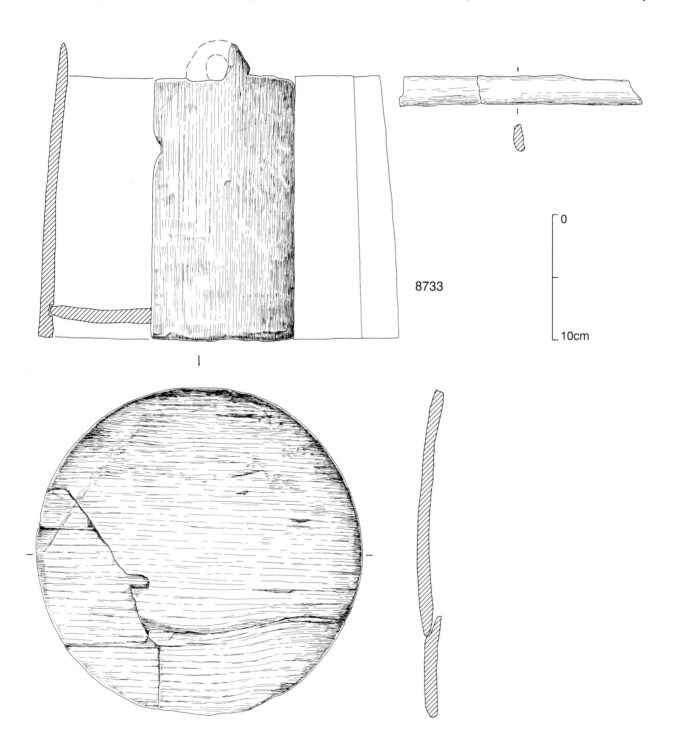

8733

0

10cm

Fig.1069 Bucket 8733 from 16–22 Coppergate. Scale 1:3

bucket at Duffield Castle. Most have squared or rounded edges. The base of a 13th century bucket from the well at Castell-y-Bere was plano-convex in cross-section. Some bases are of two-piece construction such as those found with a Saxo-Norman bucket at Billingsgate Buildings in London and a 13th–14th century bucket from a well at Seaford. Any of the single- or multiple-piece Anglo-Scandinavian and medieval stave-built ends found at Coppergate which did not have vent holes to identify them firmly as caskheads could have been bucket bases (e.g. *8769*, *8771* and *8806*). *9189*, from 22 Piccadilly, is probably too thick to have been a caskhead and is more likely to have come from a 15th century bucket like *8742*. *8790* has three or four peg holes cut into the squared base edge, suggesting it may have been a bucket base, or a base for a lath-walled vessel.

Buckets were bound with either wooden or metal hoops and these two binding materials were in use contemporaneously in medieval Britain (Morris 1984a, 140). Whatever they are made of, the hoops used to bind bucket staves together are structural parts of the vessel.

All the Anglo-Scandinavian bucket finds from York for which there is any evidence of the material used for binding, were bound with wooden hoops, and there are no fragments of iron from Anglo-Scandinavian levels at Coppergate which can be interpreted as bucket hoops. Anglo-Scandinavian yew staves *8727* and *8732* have bands of discolouration or pressure marks in the positions where hoops were originally fixed (Fig.1068). The bands on *8727* were 28, 22 and 20mm wide, and on *8732* they were at the top and bottom the stave. Bucket *8733* had tangentially split wooden hoops 23mm wide and 9mm thick (Fig.1069). Oak bucket stave *8739* has two holes 5mm diameter, one 78mm above the basal groove, one below the groove, and a third rectangular hole with an iron nail below the groove, all presumably for pegs or nails to fasten the hoops to the bucket (Fig.1068). Two staves of medieval bucket *8744* have circular holes 7mm diameter just below the rim edge, one with a peg made from a split billet of wood (Fig.1068). Willow stave *3033* would originally have been part of an elaborately decorated Anglo-Scandinavian vessel 168mm high (Fig.1068). It has fragments of three ash lath hoops 32mm wide in situ, two still attached to the external surface by four tinned iron nails. The lower hoop had its ends overlapped and nailed. A

further two nails associated with the stave held Y-shaped iron strips in place, probably near the rim of the vessel, although they are now unattached. Many medieval buckets from other sites also have wooden hoops including those from Castell-y-Bere, Seaford, Billingsgate Buildings in London, and Lund. The hoops are usually fastened together and fixed to buckets by wooden pegs. Holes for wooden pegs are visible on the staves of the buckets from Almondbury, London and Castell-y-Bere.

8742 and the buckets from Duffield, Bramford, Brightlingsea, Taunton, Tong and Weoley Castle were bound with iron hoops. Apart from iron-bound buckets and tubs found in 6th and 7th century Anglo-Saxon graves, however, there is little archaeological evidence to suggest that stave-built vessels, and buckets in particular, were commonly bound with iron hoops before the mid 12th century (Morris 1984a, 139). Iron hoops were either forged into a circle as the three on *8742*, or nailed as on the 14th century bucket from Tong Castle. It is possible that iron hoops were used mainly on medieval well buckets for greater strength and durability. They were certainly more expensive than wooden-bound buckets; in the 14th century iron-bound well buckets cost an average of 4½d, with one costing 8d in 1373 (Rogers 1866, 552), whereas wooden-bound dairy buckets cost only 2¾d (an average based on 31 documentary references before 1350), with two costing 3¼d after 1350 (ibid., 526). The iron-bound buckets from Coppergate, Bramford, Brightlingsea, Tong Castle and Weoley Castle were all found in wells.

Most buckets have two opposing staves which rise above the rim edge and are perforated by circular, D-shaped or square handle holes. Anglo-Scandinavian staves which have raised lugs above the rim edge are *8730* which has a stepped outline (Fig.1068), a stave from bucket *8733* which has the remains of a rounded lug with sloping sides (Fig. 1069), and *8734* which has a rectangular lug with sides sloping inward slightly, perforated by a hole 13mm diameter (Fig.1068). A stave with a similar raised lug and a fragment of wooden handle were found in the Gokstad ship in Norway, buried c.900–5 (Nicolaysen 1882, pl.8, 2).

The metal escutcheons found on *8742* and the bucket from Tong Castle assume the role of hole reinforcements to prevent premature enlarging and splitting of the hole, since the ends of an iron handle would wear through the wood quite quickly. An arc-shaped depression on raised stave *8734* below the perforation was probably worn into the wood by the movement of the end of the bucket handle (Fig.1068). Less common handle features on medieval buckets are metal escutcheons attached to two opposing staves, such as those found on the buckets from Duffield and Brightlingsea whose metal loops protrude above the rim edge and provide attachments for the ends of the handle. Single escutcheons of this type have also been found in a 9th century level in a well pit at Portchester Castle (Cunliffe 1976, fig.131, 15) and in a late 13th–early 14th century layer between two cask-lined wells at Waltham Abbey, Essex (Huggins and Huggins 1973, fig.12, 46). This type of escutcheon was commonly used on Roman buckets such as examples from Dalton Parlours (Morris 1990a, 218 and 221). Roman coopers did not favour the method of using two perforated raised opposed staves for the bucket handle and it seems that this method was much more popular in Anglo-Saxon, Anglo-Scandinavian and medieval Britain. Where a more or less complete bucket is found, such as those from Billingsgate Buildings and Larne, a handle stave is often missing, indicating that these staves were possibly prone to being pulled out.

Bucket handles were either iron or organic. The former are solid curved handles with hooked or straight ends as found on *8742* and the buckets from Brightlingsea, Castell-y-Bere, Duffield, Weoley Castle and Tong Castle. Organic handles were sometimes wooden such as a curved yew handle from Ballinderry Crannog 1 (Hencken 1936, fig.36F) and one from a bucket in the Gokstad ship burial which was attached to the perforated lug on the bucket stave by a separate horizontal wooden peg which slotted through holes in the lug and the end of the wooden handle (Nicolaysen 1882, pl.8, 2). There were also rope handles, as found on a late 12th century bucket from Lübeck (Fehring 1980, Abb.8 and 16), and straight wooden rods as illustrated in the late 14th century Wenceslas Bible (National Library Vienna Cod.2759, fo.30). Wooden rods may have been removable handles which could have been slipped through the perforations on opposed raised staves on vessels to lift them and then be taken out. Rope does not

Fig.1070 Well bucket with chain from a 15th century manuscript (Corpus Christi Oxford MS 161 fo.11)

Fig.1071 Well bucket with chain from a 15th century manuscript (Corpus Christi Oxford MS 161 fo.28)

Table 217 The volume, weight and type of binding of *8742* from Coppergate and eight other medieval buckets

	Volume in litres (gallons)	Weight in kg (lb)	Bands
Ty'r Dewin	3.0 (0.7)	3.0 (6.6)	Copper Alloy
Almondbury I	13.0 (2.9)	13.0 (28.6)	Wood
Duffield	14.0 (3.1)	14.0 (30.8)	Iron
Almondbury II	15.0 (3.3)	15.0 (33.0)	Wood
York (*8742*)	16.0 (3.5)	16.0 (35.2)	Iron
Taunton	19.5 (4.3)	19.5 (42.9)	Iron
London	22.0 (4.8)	22.0 (48.4)	Wood
Castell-y-Bere	23.0 (5.1)	23.0 (50.6)	Wood
Tong Castle	26.0 (5.7)	26.0 (57.2)	Iron

survive as well as wood, even on waterlogged sites, and many of the otherwise complete buckets such as *8733*, *8744* and the examples from Almondbury, Lund, Seaford, Taunton, three fragmentary buckets from Castell-y-Bere (Butler and Dunning 1974, 100–1) and Billingsgate Buildings in London may have lost rope handles which could originally have been held in place with knots outside the handle holes. No handles other than the iron one on *8742* have survived in York.

The iron handle on *8742* (Figs.1066–7) has a central hole through which is fixed an iron swivel with a closed loop and three figure-of-eight links of iron chain. Similar swivelling devices are found on buckets from Brightlingsea, Weoley Castle and Tong Castle; the Weoley bucket also has three links of chain. The devices allow the lifting chain or rope to swivel freely if necessary to prevent it becoming twisted, but the weight of a full bucket pulling down against the head of the device would tend to keep it still as it was being raised. An early 15th century English illustration of an iron-bound bucket with a chain like that on *8742* and the Weoley bucket shows an iron handle with a U-shaped kink where the end of the chain would have slotted and held the bucket in a fixed position (Figs.1070–1). Although no lifting gear or structures were found associated with the well in which *8742* was found, these late 15th century illustrations show a simple levered lifting pole from which a bucket is suspended on three links of chain (Fig.1070), and a pulley suspended from a horizon-

tal pole over which is a longer chain with more links (Fig.1071).

The iron handle, swivel, chain links, hoops and escutcheons on *8742* are forged objects, the products of a sophisticated ironworking tradition. *8742* and the bucket from Tong Castle give some information as to the order of assembly of such buckets. Their rigid iron handles with straight or hooked ends could not have been fitted into already complete buckets. They must, therefore, have been fitted into the perforated staves before these were clamped together by the iron bands. The iron parts of a medieval well bucket such as *8742* must have been fitted onto the staves during the construction process by a cooper. The cooper may have acquired the iron components from a blacksmith and completed the vessels himself, or he may have been a craftsman with knowledge of both skills.

The volume of *8742* and eight other more or less complete medieval buckets are shown in Table 217. The capacities range from 3–26 litres (0·7–5·7 imperial gallons); when full, the contents would have weighed up to 27·3kg (60lb). Since most are constructed of oak which itself is a heavy wood, the largest bucket from Tong would have weighed about 31·8kg (70lb) when full. The potentially heaviest buckets were not all bound with iron. Two of the largest from Castell-y-Bere and London were bound with wooden hoops, suggesting that this method is as efficient as the use of metal hoops for making stave-built buckets.

Tubs

A tub refers here to a type of open-topped stave-built vessel which did not usually have a separate carrying handle attached to two opposed staves like the buckets described above and, in general, is characterised by its large height and/or diameter.

8746–63 are eighteen finds (some consisting of more than one stave) from Coppergate, most of which measure over 350mm in height and belonged to substantial vessels. Four Anglo-Scandinavian staves from different contexts were made to be lifted by gripping two raised staves in both hands. *8751–2* (Period 4B) and *8760* (Period 5B) have shaped lugs above their rim edges perforated by large D-shaped handholds measuring 65 × 65mm, 71 × 59mm and 70 × 58mm respectively (Fig.1074). Each measures over 500mm in height. *8755* is a fragment of a similar stave (Period 5B) with a D-shaped handhold. These staves are unique among wooden finds anywhere in Britain and would have belonged to very large tubs. An early 15th century illustration of a man and woman filling such a tub with liquid from another vessel

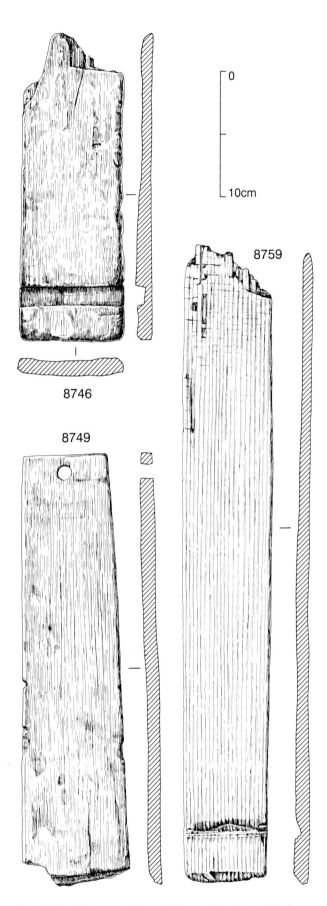

Fig.1073 *Tub staves 8746, 8749 and 8759 from 16–22 Coppergate. Scale 1:3*

Fig.1072 *Large wooden tub with handle holes, from an early 15th century English manuscript (Corpus Christi Oxford MS 161, fo.136)*

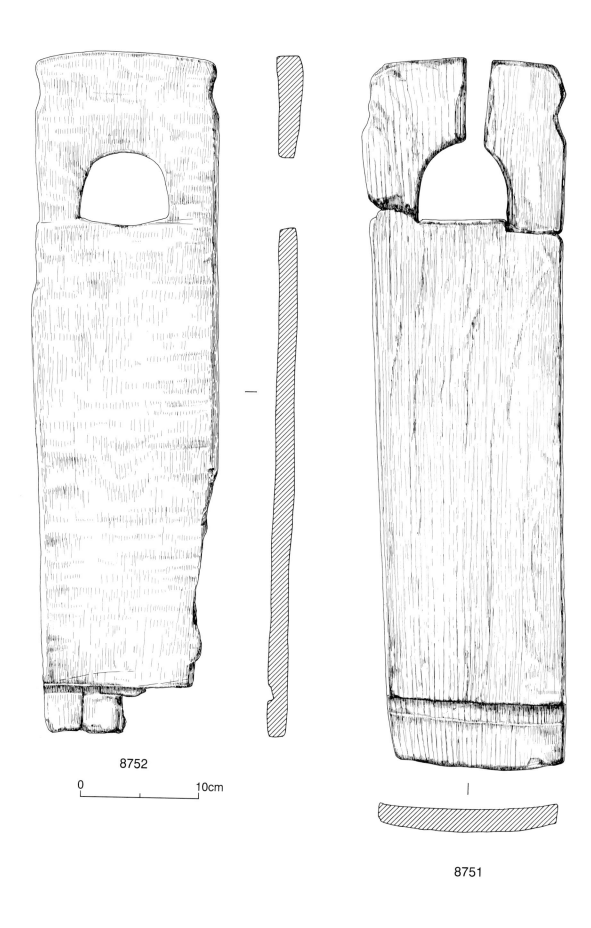

8752

0   10cm

8751

Fig.1074   *Tub staves from 16–22 Coppergate with large handholds 8751–2. Scale 1:3*

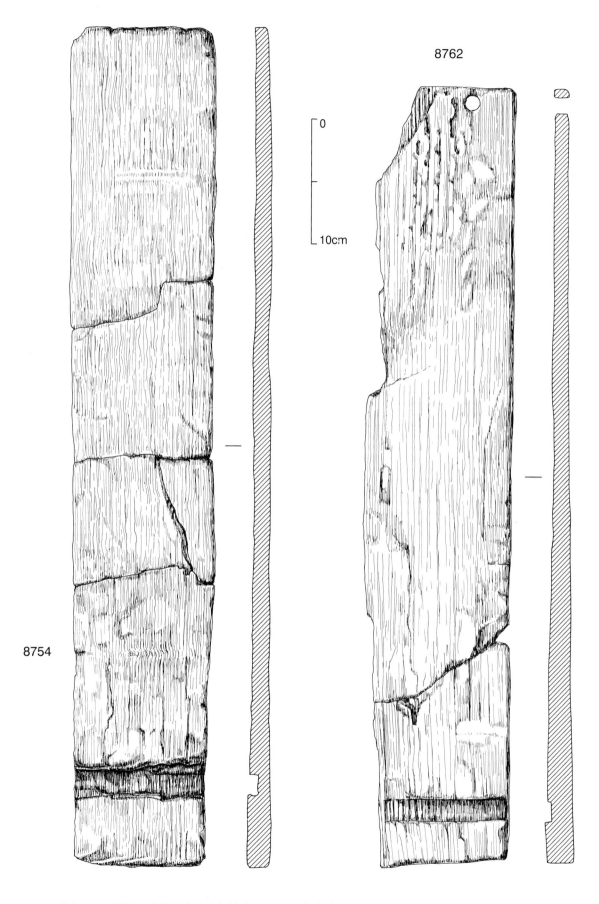

8762

8754

0

10cm

Fig.1075 *Tub staves 8754 and 8762 from 16–22 Coppergate. Scale 1:3*

shows what they would have looked like (Fig.1072). Medieval illustrations show that some tubs were made without any provision for handles or lifting (e.g. Black 1992, pl.34; British Library MS Harley 2838, fo.37). Other tubs, although very large in diameter, were quite shallow (e.g. Black 1992, fig.47; British Library Add. MS 24098, fo.27v).

Most of the other fourteen finds may have belonged to similar vessels, but they are described in the catalogue as tub/bucket staves because they have no definitive features such as the handholds.

One of the largest tubs, 8763, was found in the three-tier medieval cask-lined well 11534 from Coppergate, and may have been a cask cut down to make a tub before it was used in the well, or may have been a large tub re-used in the well. It has eighteen staves with squared rim edges, is 600mm high and was approximately 500–600mm in diameter (distortion in the ground prevented the diameter being assessed accurately). Small circular holes in some of the staves below the groove could have been for attaching an organic hoop or a batten. Similar tub staves were re-used to line a 15th century well at Covehithe in Suffolk (Durbridge 1977–8). The other Coppergate staves range between 247 and 680mm in height, and two have features which indicate how they would have been lifted. 8762, the second largest tub stave found in York, measuring 620mm in height, has an 11mm diameter circular hole near the rim edge. Anglo-Scandinavian stave 8749 is also perforated below the rim by a handle hole 11mm diameter (Fig.1073) and two similar incomplete oak staves with handle holes were found at 9 Blake Street in York (YAT 1975.6, sf681 and sf692). Just as for some buckets (see p.2231), a wooden rod may have been used as a removable handle in these holes.

Some features of tub staves are similar to those on bucket staves and imply the same techniques of manufacture. All the staves 8746–63 were made from radially split planks of oak except 8759, an Anglo-Scandinavian silver fir stave, which may have come from the same source as the silver fir bucket staves described above, and 8761 which was tangentially split oak. The tubs had various profiles; some were parallel-sided (8747, 8750, 8756–7 and 8759–60), some wider at the top (8751–2, 8754 and 8761–3) and some wider at the bottom (8746, 8748–9 and 8758). 8746, 8750–2, 8754, 8756 and 8761–2 have neat, squared

basal grooves, whereas 8747 and 8757–9 have asymmetrical V-sectioned grooves and 8763 has symmetrical V-sectioned grooves, all probably cut with a croze. The squared grooves of staves 8750–1, 8754, 8756 and 8761–2 are very wide and crisply cut, measuring 12–20mm wide. The rim edges of 8747–8 were pointed in cross-section, while those on 8750, 8754, 8756–7 and 8762–3 were squared or roughly rounded. Staves such as 8751, 8756 and 8759 had carefully chamfered long edges.

Some of the large cants and middle staves which have no features to identify them definitely as caskheads may have been part of tub bases. These include 8780, 8788 (Period 4B), 8803, 8808, 8811–12 (Period 5B) and 8822 and 8826 (Period 6) which would have come from bases measuring between 400 and 600mm in diameter.

Other tubs to compare with those from York include a 9th–10th century stave and two wooden hoops from a rath at Seacash in Co. Antrim (Lynn 1978, fig.10, 1–3), a large 9th century tub with 20 staves, four loop handles at the cardinal points held on by rim clips and hoops of openwork carved whalebone found in the Oseberg ship burial in Norway (Brøgger and Shetelig 1928, pl.12), and a late 13th century stave from High Street, Perth (Morris 1984a, C298). Large iron-bound stave-built tubs with iron loop handles were placed in wealthy 6th–7th century Anglo-Saxon graves such as those at Morningthorpe, Norfolk (ibid., fig.99, C136), Sutton Hoo, Suffolk (Bruce-Mitford and Ashbee 1975, figs.88–9), Taplow, Buckinghamshire (Stevens 1884, 64), and Sleaford, Lincolnshire (Thomas 1887, pl.25, 1), but these were rare items, probably with great value in terms of prestige, and possibly used for mixing wine or strong liquors (Morris 1984a, 137). The tubs to which staves 8746–63 belonged were more likely to have been domestic containers with a wide variety of uses.

Manuscripts show that various types and sizes of tubs and vats were used for such tasks as treading grapes, bathing, dying cloth, washing clothes, holding mortar for building work, for milking cows, holding wine or ale, and soaking fish (e.g. Morris 1984a, MS185–94). A late 13th century tub found at Rumney in Glamorgan had the remains of barley within it and was possibly used for animal fodder (ibid., C299), whilst a 14th century tub found deliberately set up in a river channel at St Aldates, Oxford, could have been used for storing live fish (Morris 1984b, 74–6, microfiche E04). Apart from *8763*, found in the cask-lined well, none of the York tub staves were found in contexts which indicated their use.

Casks

Casks were double-ended enclosed 'packing cases' with staves bound together in most instances by wooden bands, and sealed by caskheads set in grooves at each end. Casks were most widely used commercially, but many would also have had domestic uses. They were strong, hardwearing, variable in size, could be watertight if necessary and were easily moveable by rolling. Archaeological evidence from York and other British sites survives either in the form of single staves or parts of caskheads, or as more or less complete vessels without their caskheads used as well or latrine linings. Without the latter type of find, there would be significant voids on the distribution map and gaps in our knowledge of medieval cask making. Study of cask finds from Britain up to 1984 recorded 44 more or less complete examples from well linings, including *8766* from Coppergate; these, along with single staves and caskheads, have a wide distribution over England and Scotland with

Fig.1076 *9216, lower cask of a three-tier cask well from Bedern Foundry. Scale unit 10cm*

Fig.1077 *9215, the hoops of the middle cask of a three-tier cask well from Bedern Foundry, seen from inside. Actual height 1·34m*

Casks *8765*, *8767* and tub *8763* were found together on the Coppergate site in a three-tier cask-lined well dated to the early 15th century. The larger cask *8767* was placed on a frame of two rectangular oak timbers 1·06m long, set at right angles with their centres overlapping in a halved lap joint. The staves of *8763*, which ended its life cut down as a tub with squared rim edges but which may originally have been a cask, were found above *8767*. Above the staves of *8763* were other baulks of wood supporting the smaller cask *8765* whose capacity was much less than that of *8767* (see Table 218, p.2241).

Another three-tier cask-lined well dated to the 14th century was found at the Bedern Foundry site in York (*9214–16*; Figs.1076–7). Two more or less complete casks and the fragments of a third were positioned one above the other as a continuous well lining. The capacities of the two nearly complete surviving casks from the Bedern site well can be estimated (see Table 218), the middle one of the three being somewhat smaller than the lower cask. A third three-tier cask-lined well dated to the 15th–early 16th century was found at 22 Piccadilly (*9190–2*; Figs. 1078–9). As at Bedern, two more or less complete casks and the fragments of a third were positioned one above the other as a continuous well lining. Also as at Coppergate and Bedern, the lower cask of the

fewer finds from Welsh sites (Morris 1984a, 142–9 and fig.7.12).

8766 was a single cask used to line a well dated to the 15th century. Well bucket *8742* was found abandoned inside this cask (see Fig.967, p.2092). *8768* was probably another single cask used to line a well dated to the mid 14th century, but the five staves of *8764* were found in a fill of the stone-lined well 4976 and could either have been discarded in the well or been part of the well furniture. Cut-down casks were sometimes used as well buckets; for example, a cask fitted with an iron handle for use as a well bucket was found at Weoley Castle (now in the City of Birmingham Museum), and the well at Carisbrooke Castle on the Isle of Wight still has a cask as a well bucket.

Fig.1078 *9190, upper cask of a three-tier cask well from 22 Piccadilly. Scale unit 10cm*

Fig.1079   Detail of staves from 9192, lower cask of a three-tier cask well from 22 Piccadilly. Scale unit 10cm

three, *9192*, was larger than those above it. *9191–2* were unusual in that the majority of the staves were tangentially converted rather than the more normal radially split staves. The presence of knots in the staves may suggest a more inferior timber had been used than was normal in cask construction, but these casks were not primarily intended for use in the well since they have bungs and bung holes and holes near the ends of some staves to fasten battens (cf. Fig.1079, top right).

A very useful written account of the cost of the materials and labour for constructing a cask-lined well similar to the three mentioned above, but actually in the vicinity of the Bedern site, appears in the Vicars Choral Chamberlains' Roll for 1401 (UN20

P.SM; Spriggs 1977, 13–14). Materials bought include four *tonnes* (a type of cask) for 8s, *garthes* (wooden hoops) for 2s 6d, 500 *dublespykyng* (nails) for 2s 1d, boards, ropes, boring tools and many more items. It was obviously a major undertaking for which the total cost of materials was 37s 5d, and the total cost of the labour was 45s 11d, including labourers, a carpenter, a tiler, a paver and four others, taking six weeks to complete. The type of cask mentioned in the written account is a *tonne* (tun), which we know in 1707 contained 252 customary gallons (Table 219, p.2242). Casks found in York which approximate to this capacity are *9216*, the lowest of the three Bedern casks; *8767*, the lowest of the three Coppergate casks; and *9192*, the lowest of the Piccadilly casks (Table 218). The *garthes* referred to in the document could have been extra hoops for reinforcing the inside of the casks in the ground. Such internal hoops were found in *9191–2*; moreover, extra reinforcement also seems to have been provided by nails, hammered from the inside, helping to fasten either the internal or external hoops (e.g. on *9190–2, 9215–16*).

Casks used to line wells have been found at other sites in York including two at Union Terrace, positioned one above the other (YAT 1972.18, sf1006, AY 11/1, 17, pls.Va–b; Webster and Cherry 1973, 173), one at Aldwark (YAT 1976.15, sf1871; *AY* 10/2, 74–5, pl.XXIV) which was used as a well shaft lining below a timber-framed well, and one at Feasegate, where a cask bound with wooden hoops was used to line a 12th–13th century well (Dyer and Wenham 1958, pl.3c).

Most Anglo-Saxon, Anglo-Scandinavian and medieval casks were circular in cross-section, although evidence survives to show that some were oval, such as *8783* (Period 4B), an 11th–12th century cask found in a pit at Pevensey Castle, E. Sussex (Dunning 1958, fig.4), and an early 13th century cask with at least thirteen staves and an oval caskhead from Norton Priory in Runcorn, Cheshire (Morris 1984a, pl.III, C268).

A cask's shape, and the skill needed to manufacture it, depended on the intended contents. Most dry-coopered casks need not have been watertight and could therefore have less bulge. Certain dry goods such as fish, however, could require watertight casks, but not necessarily as strong as those used to contain fermenting liquids such as wine and ale. The latter were wet casks which often had distinguishing features such as vent holes in heads or staves. The complicated process of manufacturing watertight, bellied casks is described in detail by Kilby (1971, 20–41). Archaeological evidence suggests that bellied casks with a bulge where the sides were bowed in profile, such as *8765–8, 9190–2* and *9214–16*, were common in medieval Britain, and illustrations of two different sizes of bellied cask in the Bayeux Tapestry (Wilson 1985, pl.38) show that they were also used in the Norman world at least by the second half of the 11th century. However, there is little surviving evidence as yet to suggest that bellied casks were commonly made and used in Anglo-Saxon or Anglo-Scandinavian Britain.

No complete casks were found in Anglo-Scandinavian levels at 16–22 Coppergate, although *8777, 8785, 8787, 8792* (Period 4B), *8793, 8795, 8797, 8799* (Period 5A) and *8802, 8804–5* and *8810* (Period 5B) are parts of Anglo-Scandinavian caskheads from vessels whose profile cannot be reconstructed. Fragments of a 10th–11th century caskhead with a vent hole found at Hungate, York (Richardson 1959, 86), and four Viking period caskheads from Christchurch Place in Dublin, two with battens, similarly shed no light on the shape of their casks. Fragments of other Anglo-Saxon casks such as a 10th–11th century caskhead from Saddler Street, Durham (Carver 1979, fig.15, 148), and a large battened 10th century caskhead 420mm diameter from Brook Street, Winchester (Keene 1990, fig.298, *3427*), give no clues as to the profile of the casks they were used with. A complete cask stave from the Irish crannog at Lagore was listed or tapered towards each end, suggesting it came from a bellied cask, but it was found unstratified. Complete casks used as well linings in the 9th–11th century settlement at Hedeby (e.g. Elsner 1990, 32, Abb.4) were tapered slightly towards the ends.

There seems to be positive evidence that casks with straighter sides were made in Anglo-Saxon England. An 8th century oak cask with hazel or willow bands, found as a well lining at Chapel Road, Southampton, had seventeen staves which appeared to belong to a straight-sided vessel. The staves were dated by dendrochronology and were made from timber felled after 704, probably in England (Morris 1984a, 144 and C257). A late 9th century oak straight-sided cask with an ash hoop was found as a lower lining in the shaft of well 280 at Lower Brook Street, Ipswich. Dendrochronological analysis shows that fourteen of its seventeen staves match timbers from the Graveney boat, Kent, and suggest that it was made in England, although the other three staves match well with timbers of German origin (Keith Wade, pers. comm.). Another possible straight-sided cask was found as part of a late 8th–early 9th century well lining at North Elmham (Wade-Martins 1980, pls.33–5). Twenty 'staves' survived only as organic stains but were outlined by black vertical lines. Some medieval casks such as *8764* were also more or less straight-sided.

Staves of wet-coopered casks have to impart no unwanted flavour to the contents and must be hardwearing, capable of bending without cracking when 'fired' (a heating process used in manufacture), impervious to liquid, yet ring-porous to allow liquors to breathe and mature (Kilby 1971, 70). Oak has all these qualities, and it is not surprising that all surviving Anglo-Scandinavian and medieval cask staves from York and other sites are made of oak. The staves of casks *8765–8, 9214–16* and most of the caskheads/bases *8769–827, 9170–1* and *9213* were made from radially split planks since the medullary rays in oak run radially and provide a layer impervious to liquid contents. *9191–2* had many tangentially converted staves.

Several features on staves allow reconstruction of manufacturing techniques used by coopers. Staves on medieval casks *8765–8, 9190–2* and *9214–16* are listed or tapered towards each end to allow a wider girth and narrower ends on the cask. Most have been shaved along their long edges. The chamfer on the edge of 20th century cask staves is made with a jointer, an upturned plane down which the staves are pushed, and such a tool could well have been used to list medieval and earlier staves.

Some York staves, for example on *8764–5, 8767* and *9215–16*, have been hollowed on the internal surface at each end. This feature can also be seen on staves of medieval casks from Covehithe (Morris 1984a, fig.108, C238), Exeter (Allan and Morris 1984, fig.178, 71), Threave (Good and Tabraham 1981, fig.16, 165–6) and Waltham Abbey (Huggins and Huggins 1973, fig.16). It allows the caskheads to be snapped into position more easily from above the groove, but is not a technique used by 20th century coopers who have a heading vice which screws into the head and enables it to be pulled up into the groove from below (Kilby 1971, pl.19). Hollowing was probably an equivalent medieval technique, perhaps in the absence of such a tool.

Staves such as *8765–6, 9190–2* and *9214–16* have markedly chamfered chimes where the very ends of the staves have been cut obliquely. This feature is also noticeable on staves of the medieval casks from Covehithe, Exeter, Threave and Waltham Abbey already mentioned, and also on a cask from Norwich (Morris 1993a, 95). This chamfering is created by to-

Table 218 The number of staves, dimensions and capacities of tubs and casks from York and elsewhere in Britain (r, R and H refer to the measurements used in the two formulae for calculating cask capacities shown in Fig.1080; cust = customary; imp = imperial)

	No. Staves	dimensions						in^3		cust		gallons imp		wine	
		mm			inch										
		r	R	H	r	R	H	(a)	(b)	(a)	(b)	(a)	(b)	(a)	(b)
York (*8768*)	14	265	299	740	10.4	11.8	29.1	11295	11747	49	51	41	42	52	54
Carlisle	18	290	364	632	11.4	14.3	24.9	13011	13982	56	61	47	50	60	65
York (*8765*)	20	245	320	1110	9.65	12.6	43.7	17083	18575	74	80	62	67	79	86
Waltham Abbey I	25	292	337	1150	11.5	13.3	45.3	21844	22879	95	99	79	83	101	106
Perth	18	385	435	1050	15.2	17.1	41.3	33880	35250	147	153	122	127	157	163
Exeter III		353	458	1260	13.9	18.0	49.6	39941	43345	173	188	144	156	185	201
Exeter IV		394	458	1260	15.5	18.0	49.6	43919	46105	190	200	159	166	203	213
York (*9215*)	22	380	440	1340	15.0	17.3	52.8	43261	45358	187	196	156	164	200	210
Hull III		353	420	1580	13.9	16.5	62.2	45362	47963	196	208	164	173	210	222
York (*8766*)	20	360	477	1400	14.2	18.8	55.1	47314	51662	205	224	171	187	219	239
Waltham Abbey II	21	384	454	1450	15.1	17.9	57.1	48916	51621	212	223	177	186	226	239
Exeter I	24	436	481	1233	17.2	18.9	48.5	49732	51353	215	222	180	185	230	238
York (*9191*)	22	375	475	1450	14.8	18.7	57.1	50442	54355	218	235	182	196	234	252
York (*8767*)	22	375	525	1400	14.8	20.7	55.1	54854	60841	237	263	198	220	254	282
Norwich	20	455	495	1350	17.9	19.5	53.1	58429	60064	253	260	211	217	271	278
York (*9216*)	26	425	494	1470	16.7	19.4	57.9	59615	62580	258	271	215	226	276	290
York (*9192*)	21	425	502	1480	16.7	19.8	58.3	61095	64454	264	279	221	233	283	298

Table 219 The names given to casks of various capacities according to date of manufacture

	1413	1420	1440	1488	1707	Modern
Tun					252	
Butt (Pipe)					126	108
Puncheon						72
Hogshead						54
Barrel	30	30 (36)	30 (18.5)	36	63	36
Kilderkin (Half Barrel)		15 (18)	15	18		18
Firkin	7.5			9		9
Pin						4.5

day's coopers with a chiming adze (Kilby 1971, 28–9), and it is possible that a similar tool was used on the medieval casks. The continuous croze groove cut in each end of the staves of *8765–7, 9190–2* and *9214–16* was V-shaped in cross-section, whereas the grooves on *8764* were narrow and squared. The former is more commonly found, and the edges of most caskheads are chamfered to fit easily into such a groove after the cask was assembled. These continuous croze grooves were cut with a cooper's croze similar to the one found at Meols and described above (p.2228).

The number of staves used to manufacture large casks varied. *8768* had fourteen, *8765* and *8766* had twenty, *9192* had 21, *8767, 9191* and *9215* had 22, *9190* had 25 and *9216* had 26 staves. Most medieval casks had between 18 and 26 staves (Table 218). Every cooper presumably knew the number of staves, lengths, widths and thicknesses needed to manufacture specific sizes of cask (Kilby 1971, 20–1) and by varying the head and girth diameters and the height accordingly could vary the capacity. Varying the dimensions even by a small amount, especially on very large vessels, can change the capacity by tens of gallons (ibid., 61–4). For archaeologically excavated casks, this fact means that it is essential to have very accurate internal dimensions in order to estimate capacities, and, even when this is possible, to use these figures very tentatively, since waterlogging and compression or distortion in the ground may have altered a cask's shape and size.

A cask's capacity could potentially indicate the commodities it might have held since strict rules were laid down by the medieval Coopers' Guild as to the capacities of casks, especially of ale and beer barrels (a barrel being a specific size of cask). For example, in 1413 the Court of Aldermen in the City of London tried the case of a fishmonger, Richard Bartlott, who had secretly constructed in his own house as many as 260 vessels, barrels and firkins of wood not pure, sawn from the middle and of untrue measure. Barrels should have held 30 gallons, but these held 28; firkins held 6·5 instead of 7·5 gallons (Letter Book I, City of London). Different sized casks had different names, some of which have continued in use until the present day. Table 219 shows how their capacities could vary according to when they were manufactured and what they contained.

A complicating factor is the lack of a standardised gallon from the medieval period until the present day. There have been four gallons with different capacities — the wine gallon of 216 cubic inches (used at least in 1297), the Winchester gallon of 268 cubic inches (used at least in 1497), the customary gallon of 231 cubic inches (legalised in 1707 but probably used long before this time) and the modern imperial gallon of 277 cubic inches (Huggins and Huggins 1973, 182). It would be misleading to use imperial gallons for capacities of medieval casks such as *8765–8, 9190–2* and *9214–16*. The wine gallon might be a more useful measure for some of the medieval casks in Table 218 which may originally have been made to contain wine.

Two methods have been used for calculating the volumes of excavated casks from York and other sites and are shown in Fig.1080. One treats the cask as two truncated cones base to base; the other assumes the convex wall of the cask is a trigonometric curve roa

$$\text{Volume} = \frac{\pi H}{3}(R^2 + Rr + r^2)$$

b

$$\text{Volume} = 2R^2\pi\left(\frac{H}{4} + \frac{\sin BH}{4B}\right)$$

$$\text{where} \quad B = \frac{2}{H}\,\text{acos}\left(\frac{r}{R}\right)$$

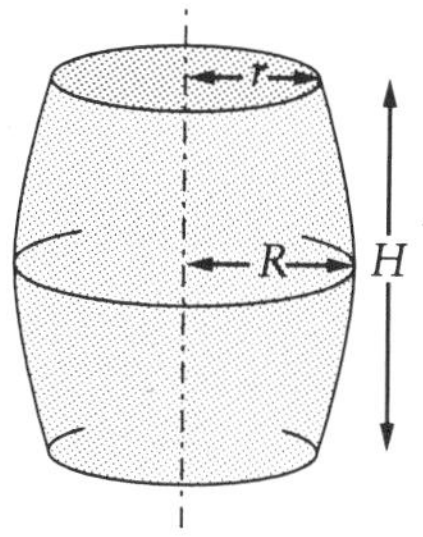

Fig.1080   Two formulae used for calculating cask capacities

tated about a central axis. The former probably underestimates the capacity, while the latter is probably more accurate, but since all the caveats about the shape and size of excavated casks must apply, both calculations should be viewed only as estimates to be used comparatively rather than as individually accurate measures. Six medieval casks have capacities which seem to fall within 20–30 customary or wine gallons of each other, and were probably originally casks holding similar amounts. They are *8766* from Coppergate, *9191* from 22 Piccadilly, *9215* from Bedern, and others from Scale Lane, Hull (Armstrong 1980, fig.8), Waltham Abbey (Huggins and Huggins 1973, fig.16, F146) and Goldsmith Street, Exeter (Allan and Morris 1984, fig.178, 71). Four other casks dating from the later medieval period are larger than these six, but themselves have capacities which also seem to fall within 20–25 customary or wine gallons of each other, and were also probably originally casks holding similar amounts. These are *8767* from Coppergate, *9192* from 22 Piccadilly, *9216* from Bedern, and one from Westwick Street, Norwich (Morris 1993a, 95). All these ten casks, but the latter four in particular, approximate to the size of cask which in 1707 held 252 customary gallons and was referred to as a tun. Although tuns (or tonnes) are referred to in various medieval documents, their capacity is unknown (Morris 1984a, 149). In 1363, for example, Edward III granted the Vintners' Company the exclusive privilege of trading in the wines of Gascony. The Gascons themselves were forbidden to sell wine except in tuns or pipes (Letter Book G, City of London). Other types or sizes of cask referred to in medieval documents include kympes, dolea, barrels, firkins, kilderkins and cades (Morris 1984a, 149). Many of the smaller caskheads such as *8775*, *8805* and *8809* would have belonged to the smaller range of cask sizes.

Stave-built casks must have been the almost universal packing cases for larger quantities of a wide range of commodities. Excavated casks probably used for fermented liquors are evident from their bung holes and vent holes (as described below). Liquors contained in medieval casks included wine, beer, ale, cider and perry, whereas dry casks were used to contain items such as fish, broken food/alms, salt, quarrels, wheat, oil and soap, and for cleaning armour (Morris 1984a, 149).

Larger stave-built casks of various sizes were relatively very expensive wooden craft-made items compared to turned or smaller stave-built vessels. Although in 1370 the bailiff of Wye purchased tuns and pipes at about 9d each (Rogers 1866, 619), and an aletonne and a barrel in the bankrupt stock of Robert and Alice le Cuver in 1310 were valued at 8d each (Letter Book D, City of London), on average in the early 14th century casks cost 1s 7d each, one costing as much as 2s 10d (Rogers 1866, 548). Using these prices as a rough guideline as to the cost of new stave-built casks, it is almost certain that the four tonnes bought in 1401 at 2s each to make a cask-lined well at the College of the Vicars Choral, Bedern, were new vessels and not old, re-used ones which had outlived their usefulness as containers (see p.2239).

Caskheads, vessel bases and battens

8769–827, 9170–1 and *9213* are parts of the heads, ends or bases of stave-built vessels, ranging in diameter from only 120mm (*8805*; Fig.1981), to over 727mm (*8776*; Fig.1082). Depending on the size of a cask, bucket or tub, heads and bases were of single- or multiple-piece construction. Single discs like the base in bucket *8742*, two-piece heads like *8792* and three-piece heads are most usual, but larger heads had as many as four to six component staves, for example, caskheads from Queen Street, Exeter (Allan and Morris 1984, fig.179, 78), and Queen Street and High Street, Hull (Morris 1984a, fig.111, C275–6). The arc staves are cants, the others are middles (Kilby 1971, 38). The multiple-piece heads and bases were often dowelled together with wooden cylindrical dowel pegs set into holes augered into the straight edges of the cants and middles. Dowel holes for wooden pegs can be seen on the Anglo-Scandinavian pieces *8782*, *8788*, *8797*, *8799* and *8811–12*, those on *8812* being 48mm long and 10mm in diameter, while iron pins were used in the edge of the medieval stave *8824*.

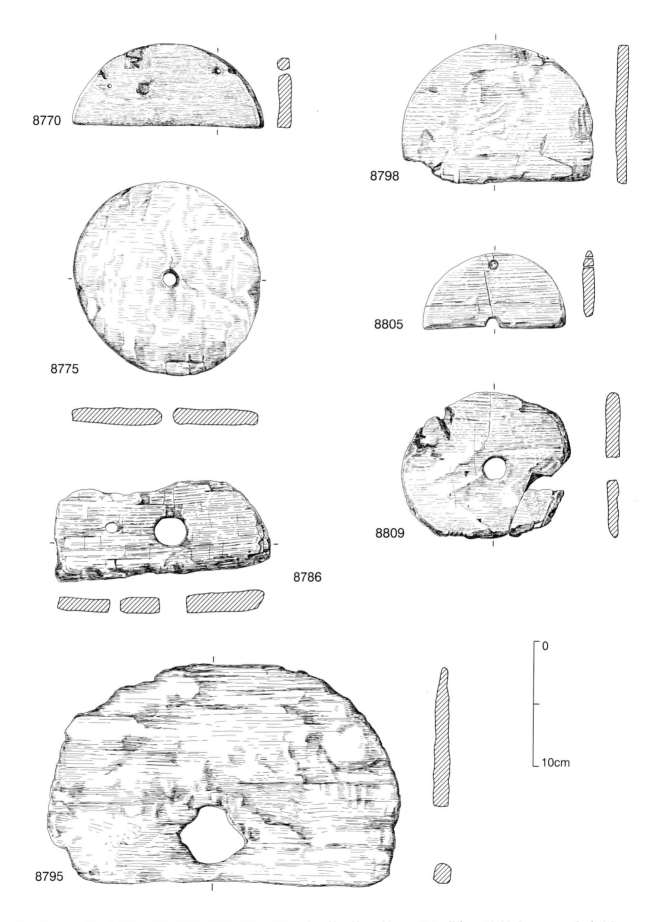

8770

8798

8775

8805

8786

8809

8795

Fig.1081 *Caskheads 8770, 8775, 8786, 8795, 8805, 8809, and caskhead/vessel base 8798, all from 16–22 Coppergate. Scale 1:3*

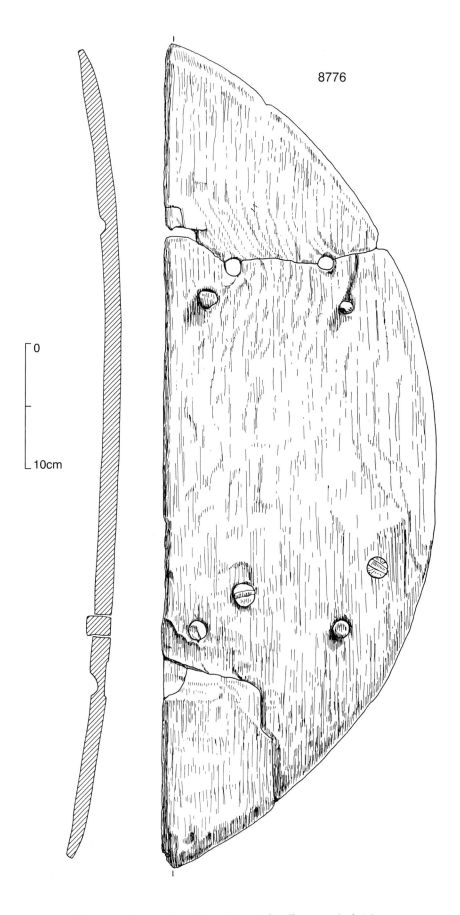

8776

0

10cm

Fig.1082 *Large oak cant stave 8776 with willow pegs. Scale 1:3*

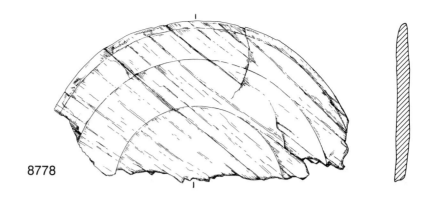

8778

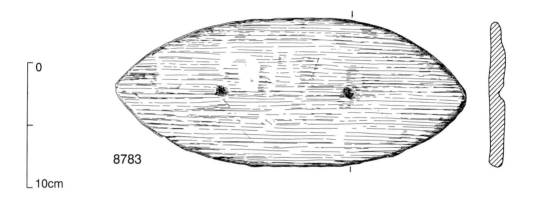

0

10cm

8783

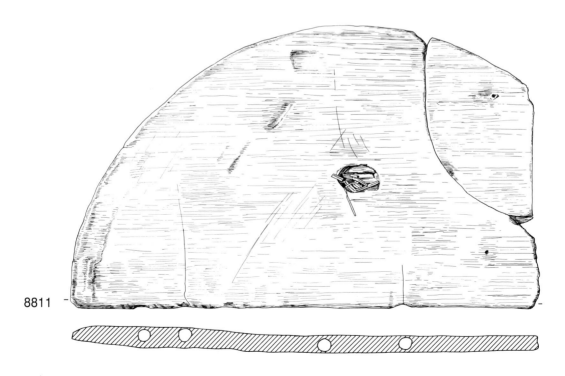

8811

Fig.1083 *Caskheads or vessel bases from 16–22 Coppergate 8778, 8783 and 8811. Scale 1:3*

2246

Fig.1084 Large oak cant stave of a circular caskhead 8789 from 16–22 Coppergate. Scale 1:3

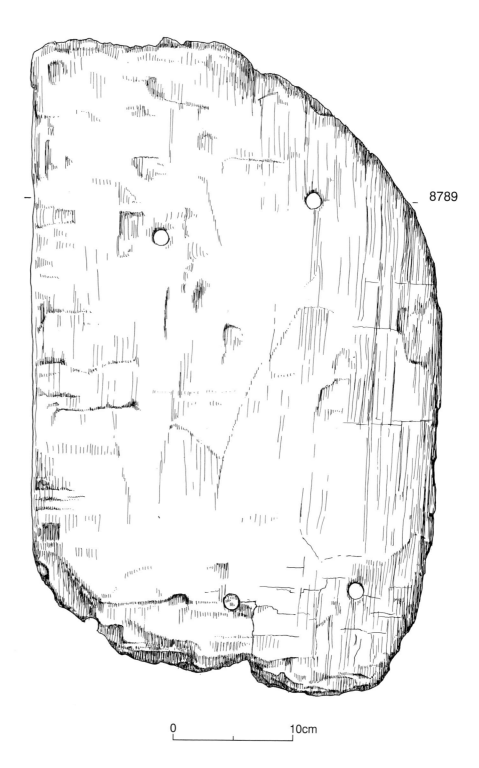

8789

0   10cm

Some of the coopered finds from Coppergate are definite caskheads because of certain distinguishing features such as vent holes and batten holes; however, neither are obligatory features in caskheads.

Plain discs such as *8771–2, 8790–1, 8798* and *8806,* cants *8773–4, 8794, 8803, 8821, 8824* and the cant and middle *8808* could be parts of caskheads or bases for vessels such as buckets or tubs.

8825

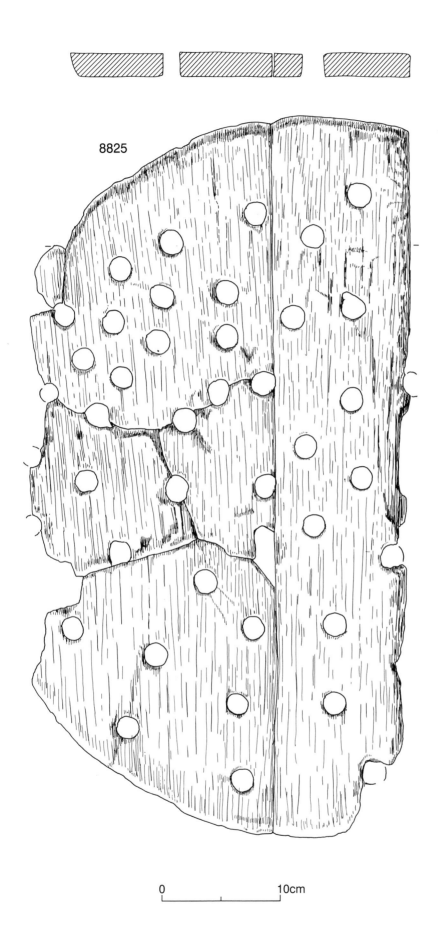

0   10cm

Fig.1085 *Fragments of two oak cant staves, 8825, perforated by circular augered holes, possibly a specialised head or lid. Scale 1:3*

Vent holes were either central as *8775, 8777, 9213* and a single-piece caskhead from Hungate (Richardson 1959, 86), or offset as on *8795* and *8809* (Fig.1081, p.2244). Most vent holes are circular and vary in diameter, but that on stave *8795* was trefoil-shaped (Fig.1081) and the pegged hole in *9213* was roughly square (Fig.1094, p.2259). Some caskheads had more than one vent hole, some of which were pegged. If a cask was to be re-used, a new vent hole may have had to be cut and the old one blocked up. This process may explain multiple pegged holes in heads such as *8776* (Fig.1082), *8805* and *8823*, and others from Threave (Good and Tabraham 1981, fig.16, 166) and Queen Street, Hull (Morris 1984a, fig.111, C275). The Threave and Hull examples had over 35 and nine holes respectively. Caskheads with vent holes similar to those from York have been found at Cork (Hurley 1982, fig.16, 4), Saddler Street, Durham (Carver 1979, fig.15, 148), Goldsmith Street and Trichay Street, Exeter (Allan and Morris 1984, figs.175, 24–5, 177, 60 and 179, 77), Weoley Castle (Morris 1984a, fig.111, C279), and Cuckoo Lane, Southampton (Platt and Coleman-Smith 1975, fig.233, 1674). Wooden bungs and spigots were used as tapping mechanisms in caskheads. These can be seen clearly in the late medieval illustration of various types of casks in Fig.1087.

Two staves of cask *8764* each have three pegged holes whose position suggests that a batten was fixed across the caskhead at each end. The cask from Goldsmith Street, Exeter, had three similar peg holes on the ends of two opposing staves which could have held pegs to fix a batten. Staves from casks *9190–2* and *9214–16* have similar peg holes for battens. *8789* is a large semi-circular cant stave 580mm in diameter with two rows of two and three peg holes, some retaining pegs, and *8776*, which would originally

have been part of the largest stave-built caskhead to have been found at Coppergate (over 727mm diameter), had two sets of three and four holes, some with willow pegs. Both *8789* and *8776* probably had battens. Rectangular battens across head staves have been found in situ on heads from 10th century Winchester (Keene 1990, fig.298, *3427*) and 11th century Dublin (Morris 1984a, fig.111, C271iii), and an impression of a single batten perpendicular to a caskhead stave was found where a cask had been used to line a late 13th century pit at Exe Bridge, Exeter (Allan and Morris 1984, fig.178, 72). *9217* from Bedern may be a caskhead batten fixed by pegs into the head rather than into the side staves (Fig.1086) and it is possible that *8944* (see pp.2302–3, Fig.1128) and *8871* are similar objects. *8872* is almost certainly a batten from a large caskhead (14th century). These battens are not repairs and medieval illustrations often show them in situ on casks in use. An English medieval illustration of c.1325–30 in the Holkham Bible Picture Book shows two casks with two-piece caskheads across which are fixed rectangular battens (British Library Add. MS 47682, fo.9). These casks also have vent holes and spigots in their heads, and bung holes in side staves. Most illustrations of casks with battens seem to be wine casks resting horizontally. It is possible that the battens are strengthening devices to reinforce heads on casks which were often used in this position.

Some caskheads from Coppergate have holes which cannot be identified definitely as vent holes or batten holes, such as two random holes 3mm diameter on cant stave *8770* (Period 3), two holes 27 × 22mm and 10mm diameter on cant stave *8786* (Period 4B), and two holes 15mm diameter on large cant stave *8807* (Period 5B). *8825* is a very large medieval head/base 620mm diameter, made up of fragments

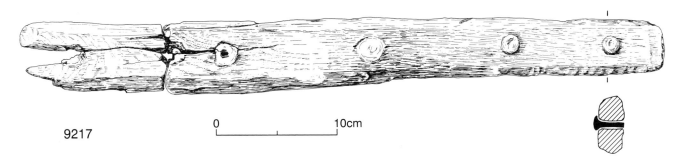

9217

0   10cm

Fig.1086 Oak batten 9217 from Bedern Foundry. It may have come from a large caskhead. Scale 1:3

Fig.1087   *Casks and dippers from a late medieval illustration, showing bungs and spigots (British Library Add. MS 27695, fo.14)*

of two semi-circular cant staves with a total of 39 circular augered holes 20mm diameter all over its surviving surface (Fig.1085). This is probably an unusual base, end or lid of a stave-built vessel which had been used for a specialised purpose such as straining liquids from solids. Cheese presses often had bases and staves perforated by many holes to let liquid run out, and it is not inconceivable that *8825* is the remains of a large cheese press.

Casks intended to be emptied of liquid without broaching needed a circular or square bung hole at the girth of one stave to allow air to come in as the liquid poured out through a vent hole in one head. Staves from medieval casks *8765* and *8767* have vari-

ous bung holes at the girth of one stave, *8765* with circular holes 27 and 57mm diameter and a cluster of five smaller holes, *8767* with circular holes 25 and 65mm diameter. Sometimes offset circular bung holes are found on staves, for example, *9215* from Bedern with a bung hole 60mm diameter and *9216* with a bung hole of 56mm diameter and two smaller holes of 10 and 21mm diameter to the side of it. Two of the Piccadilly casks (*9191–2*) had surviving oak and alder bungs in bung holes, some with accompanying spile holes. Medieval casks with similar bung holes come from Covehithe (Morris 1984a, fig.108, C238) and Waltham Abbey (Huggins and Huggins 1973, fig.16). *8768* has a bung hole 70mm square similar to a bung hole 48mm square on a cask from Carlisle,

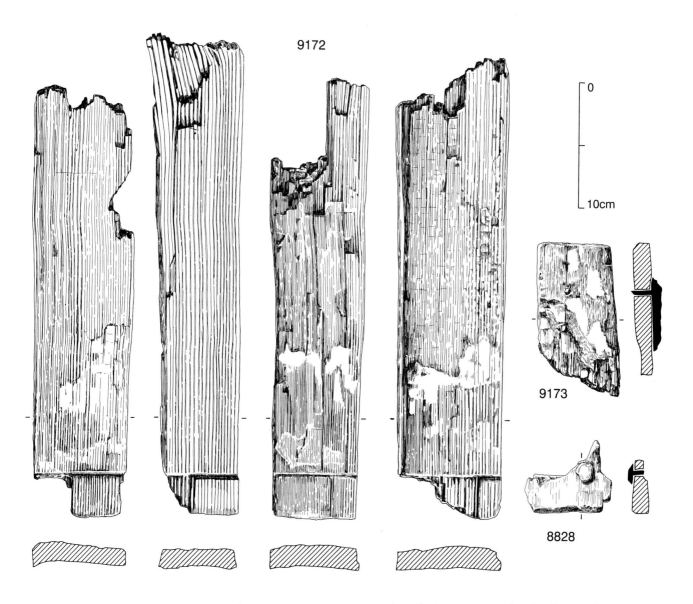

Fig.1088   Incomplete vessel staves: 8828 from 16–22 Coppergate; 9172–3 from the Coppergate watching brief site. Scale 1:3

Cumbria (Morris 1984a, fig.108, C237b). A cork bung and a willow peg were found in situ in the bung holes on *8765*, and some of the cluster of five smaller holes on *8765* also had pegs. Bungs in holes like these can be seen on the casks in Fig.1087. Holes in the side of the staves could have been used to fill a complete cask as can be seen in a carving on the Norman font at Burnham Deepdale church in Norfolk, where a man pours wine from a skin through a funnel into a cask laid on its side.

Caskheads and bases such as *8775*, *8790–1* and *8798* are discoloured on one flat surface, presumably accumulated stains from the vessels' contents.

Incomplete vessel staves

8828–49 and *9172–3* are fragments of Anglo-Scandinavian and medieval staves which are incomplete. They have no rim edge information to indicate that they belong to specific open-topped buckets or tubs, or grooves at each end to indicate that they belong to casks, and there are probably some of both kinds among the group.

8828 is a fragment of a 9th century willow stave with an iron nail attaching a fragment of wooden hoop (Fig.1088), and is likely to have belonged to a bucket like *3033*. *8837* and *9172* (Fig.1088) are Anglo-

Scandinavian and medieval silver fir stave fragments which may have come from the same type of source as the silver fir bucket and tub staves described above (pp.2226, 2236). All the rest are oak staves. Three Anglo-Scandinavian staves (*8838*) have very pronounced tool marks from a croze in their squared grooves. Medieval stave *8845* is curved in plan as a stave, but has been cut down from a stave and re-used with notches in one side. *9173* has an external concretion which is possibly a corroded iron hoop fragment since the point of a nail is visible behind it on the inside (Fig.1088).

Hoops

Anglo-Scandinavian fragments *8850–9* and medieval fragments *8860–1* were pieces of wooden hoops used with either casks or other types of open-topped stave-built vessels. *8862–4* were wooden hoop fragments found in the backfills of well pits and could have come from casks used as well linings. *8865* is almost certainly a fragment of one of the hoops from cask *8766*.

These Anglo-Scandinavian and medieval wooden hoops were made in two ways. Some were split sections of roundwood rods, D-shaped half-sections which were either split through the centre of the roundwood as in *8859*, hazel hoop *8858* and medieval birch hoop *8861*, or tangentially across the rod without going through the centre as in the willow hoops *8853* and *8865*, and the alder hoop *8851*. Others were laths with curved sub-rectangular cross-sections which had been cut down from narrow radially split sections of species such as ash or chestnut. Most of the Anglo-Scandinavian and medieval laths from Coppergate were made of ash which is strong and pliable and can be bent to a circular shape when thinned down into a lath. These include *8850* (Period 5A), *8852, 8855–7* (Period 5B) and *8864* (Period 6). Medieval lath *8863* may be ash or sweet chestnut.

Some of the hoops have surviving ends or other features which suggest how they were fastened together or fixed to the stave-built vessel; hoops with shaped ends can be seen in the late medieval illustration in Fig.1087. *8852* has a blunt, shaped end with a peg hole and other augered holes along its length, some with roundwood pegs to attach the hoop to the vessel (Fig.1090). *8855* has a similar blunt, rounded end perforated by a peg hole 11mm diameter. *8858*

has a rounded tapered end and a notch cut in the outer surface where a notch in the other end of the hoop would have slotted. Grooves in the outer surface show that smaller strands originally bound the ends together. *8857* has a shaped rectangular end with shoulders and a notch on the outer surface where a notch in the other hoop end would have slotted. It is also perforated by a peg hole 9mm diameter (Fig.1090). A hazel hoop fragment from cask *8765* also has two rectangular notches cut into one side which formed part of an interlocking device when overlapped. *8861* has a narrowed end piece and a possible notched piece, and several fragments of very thin, narrow possibly alder binding were used to overbind the ends. *8864* has the remains of a squared chiselled peg hole. Four of the seventeen staves of a late 9th century cask from Brook Street, Ipswich, had peg holes 28mm diameter close to the position of a lath hoop, and possibly associated with fixing it to the cask (Morris 1984a, fig.109, C245). All the peg holes in these hoops were designed to take wooden pegs to attach them to the vessels. *8860* and *8862–3*, however, have the remains of iron nails which were used for the same purpose (Fig.1090). The nail on *8863* was driven from the outside, while that on *8862* was driven through from the inside.

Most of the complete casks from well linings such as the three-tier wells from Coppergate and Bedern have surviving wooden hoops and allow the techniques used in their manufacture to be reconstructed. The hoops are usually split half-, third- or quarter-section rods. *8765* had half-section hazel hoops 30mm wide; *8766* and *8865* had half-section rods of hazel and willow respectively, whose ends were overlapped and bound with fine strands of withies (Fig. 1089). *9215–16* from Bedern have half-section hazel/alder hoops overlapped and bound together by very thin split strands of withies, and *9191–2* from 22 Piccadilly have split hazel hoops (internal and external), also bound with withies. Two casks from Waltham Abbey (Huggins and Huggins 1973, fig.16) had half- and third-section hoops of sweet chestnut or alder with their ends lapped over and bound with strands of fine withies like *8766* and *8865*. A cask from Goldsmith Street, Exeter, had hoops made of 6–12 year old split hazel rods bound with split strands of hazel and elder (Allan and Morris 1984, fig.178, 71) and a cask from Carlisle had half-section birch hoops similarly overlapped and bound (Morris 1984a, fig.108, C237). Some hoops were made as laths like those on

Fig.1089 *Detail of hazel hoops and withy bindings on cask 8766 of the three-tier well from 16–22 Coppergate*

a late 9th century cask from Ipswich (ibid., fig.109, C245). Fig.1087 shows casks bound with both split rods and laths.

In recent years, the manufacture of wooden hoops for casks was a separate woodland craft (Edlin 1949, 72–5; Fitzrandolph and Hay 1926, 100–7). The type of wood used for making medieval hoops was split coppiced rods. Medieval casks also had large numbers of hoops on each vessel. For example, there were

38 individual hoops on *8766*, in two groups of 17 and 21, 80 hoops on *9215* (two groups of 37 and 43), and 88 hoops on *9216* (two groups of 43 and 45). Such large numbers of wooden hoops used on large casks, as compared to smaller numbers of iron ones used in more recent times, must have been necessary to create a vessel strong enough to contain fermenting liquids. The coppiced nature of the material and the large quantities of hoops found on excavated medieval casks suggest that a separate woodland indus-

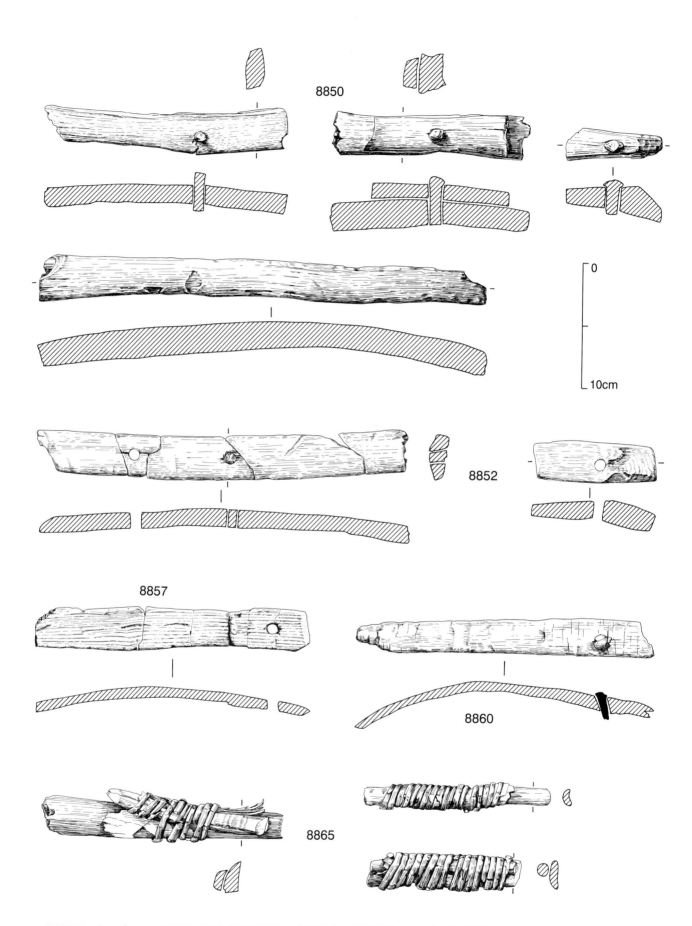

Fig.1090 *Hoop fragments 8850, 8852, 8857, 8860 and 8865 from 16–22 Coppergate. Scale 1:3*

try probably provided medieval coopers with hoops. Hoopers were certainly separate craftsmen in Bristol by 1504 from when their Company dates. They made hoops, fitted heads into position and drove hoops home on casks manufactured by coopers (Kilby 1971, 136). Many medieval illustrations show wooden hoops in groups on casks, in most cases symmetrically arranged about the girth area as in *8766*, and *9215–16*, which is left unbound for the bung hole. Three of the casks in Fig.1087 have groups of wooden hoops, some with their ends overlapped and bound with thin strands.

The account of the cost of materials and labour for building the cask-lined well at the College of the Vicars Choral in 1401 (see p.2239) includes 2s 6d for 'garthes' or wooden hoops which were presumably extra to those on the four tonnes bought. Individual hoops were certainly bought for repairs, as can be seen in the Bartoner's Accounts for Christchurch, Canterbury, where in 1414–15 hoops were bought for mending barrels (Morris 1984a, MS163).

Iron-bound casks were very rare at this period. None have been found in York. Only one example of a medieval cask bound with iron hoops has been excavated from a site in Britain — an oak cask with 22 staves dated to the second half of the 13th century, used as a pit or cistern lining at Baker Street, King's Lynn (Clarke and Carter 1977, fig.30B). It had originally been bound with iron hoops but only traces of one of these survived. In 1158 the Chancellor, Thomas à Becket, wrote to France to demand a princess in marriage for Prince Henry. His chaplain wrote that he prepared lavishly to display the wealth of England and took two chariots laden solely with iron-bound barrels of ale (Kilby 1971, 110). This 12th century reference shows that iron-bound casks were manufactured at this time, but were rare and prestigious items. Most Anglo-Scandinavian and medieval casks, whether wet or dry, would have been bound with wooden hoops like *8850–65*, and those surviving in situ on casks *8765–6*. This is in contrast with more recent years when wooden hoops were used mainly for dry casks (Edlin 1949, 72), and iron hoops were commonly used for wet casks.

Lids

Five radially split oak objects found at 16–22 Coppergate are lids which were probably used with various types and sizes of stave-built vessels. There are two different types of lid.

The first type includes *8866* and *8867* which are circular and have rectangular notches cut into their edges on opposite sides to fit around two raised staves on open-topped vessels (Fig.1091). Anglo-Scandinavian lid *8867* is only 69mm maximum diameter, is perforated by a small central circular hole 8mm diameter, and could have been used to cover a very small stave-built drinking vessel. Three similar small single-piece lids have been found in 11th century levels at Christchurch Place and Fishamble Street in Dublin, measuring between 93 and 102mm diameter (Morris 1984a, C335vii–viii and fig.117, C336x). All had notches cut into opposite sides, and were perforated by two circular or rectangular holes between the notches. The holes may have held different types of handles made of cordage or wood.

8866 is a larger Anglo-Scandinavian lid 168mm in diameter with a small iron rod of D-shaped cross-section inserted horizontally into one of the notches in the lid edge. This rod may have passed through a hole on the vessel's raised stave and helped to fix the lid in position. *8866* also has two rectangular holes cut through the lid, with wear marks on one surface (probably the underside) across and perpendicular to the holes, either from roperunners on a rope handle or from pegs used to secure a solid wooden handle. Roperunner *9024* (Fig.1157, p.2348) was found in the same context as *8866* and could be associated with it. The edges of *8866* have a deliberately rounded chamfer cut on what must be the uppermost side.

Similar notched Viking period lids to compare with *8866* (but without the iron rod) have been found at Christchurch Place and Fishamble Street, Dublin (Morris 1984a, C335i–vi and C336ix). They are either single-piece circular lids or two-piece lids made of two cant staves, and measure between 120 and 235mm in diameter. An 11th century oak lid 353mm diameter from Goldsmith Street, Exeter, has two rim notches with two holes 12mm diameter between them and two incised marks in the form of a pentacle and a cross on one flat surface (Allan and Morris 1984, fig.174, 16). An illustration of a woman carrying a bucket with a lid in the 14th century Luttrell Psalter shows how such lids may have been used (British Library Add. MS 42130, fo.163v). The lid has a curved organic handle rising from its flat surface (probably

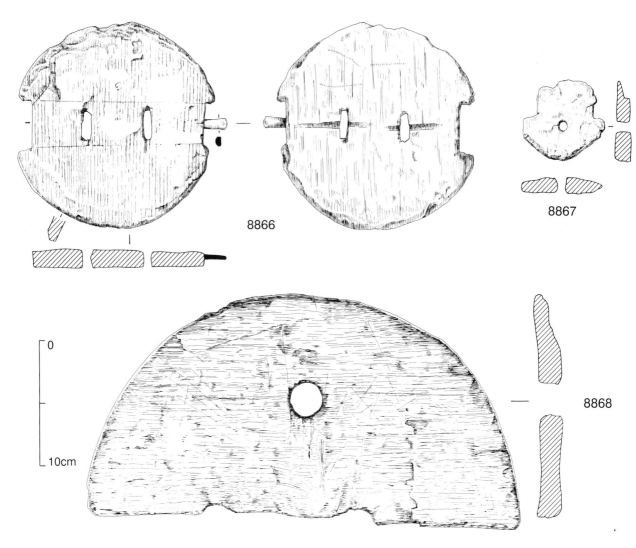

8866

8867

8868

Fig.1091 *Lids for coopered vessels, 8866–8, from 16–22 Coppergate. Scale 1:3*

fixed in two holes), and what appears to be a pin or peg fastening the lid at one side through an arched staple. The woman is apparently carrying milk in the bucket, and balances the vessel on her head with one hand. A 12th century oak lid from Lund, 190mm diameter, has two rim notches and a single central hole 25mm diameter (Nilsson 1976, fig.207). Since this type of notched lid would have been used with various kinds of upright open-topped stave-built vessels such as buckets and churns, large central holes may have been to accommodate spouts (see below) or the poles attached to churn dashers rather than rope handles.

8868–70 are examples of the second type of lid which is much larger and heavier, and was probably used with large upright open-topped vessels such

as tubs or casks stood on end without a fitted cask-head at the upper end. *8869* is a large semi-circular Anglo-Scandinavian lid with rounded edges. Its long edge has the remains of four worn, irregularly cut holes which may originally have held hinges of some organic material such as leather to allow the lid to be lifted up but not removed from its vessel (Fig.1092). The hinges presumably fastened this semi-circular lid to another fixed semi-circular board across the rest of the open vessel. Centrally placed opposite the long edge of *8869* is an oval handle hole, now broken, by which the lid was lifted. The lid's upper surface is abraded by many blade cuts where it had perhaps been used as a cutting board in situ. The lower surface has an uneven curved wear mark on one side where the lid had rested on the vessel below. Medieval lid *8870* may be a similar lid of this

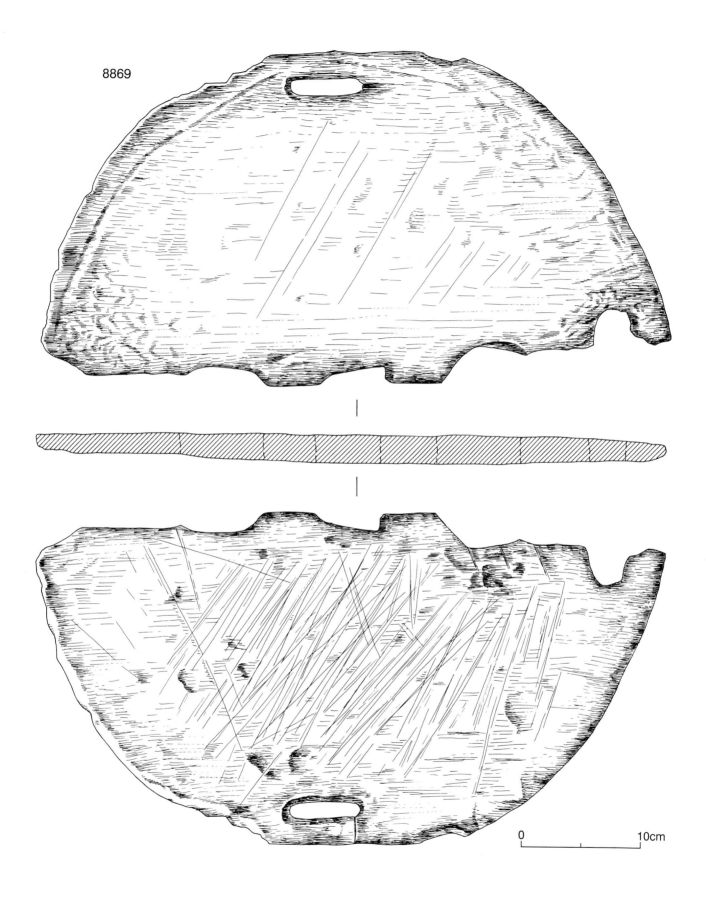

8869

0   10cm

Fig.1092 *Lid 8869 from a coopered vessel; it has been used as a cutting board, possibly in situ. Scale 1:3*

type, or a broken circular lid. At 37mm thick it is too thick and heavy to have been a normal caskhead fitted in a groove and it may have rested on the top of an open vessel. It has four irregularly spaced augered holes, and was found in the same context as broken stave *8847*. Anglo-Scandinavian lid *8868* was originally circular but is now broken across two augered holes 29mm diameter, with a third hole nearer the curved edge. One surface is very worn and abraded with blade cuts where it had been used as a cutting board, probably in situ on the top of a stave-built vessel (Fig.1091).

Spouts and spigots

8873 and *8875* are Anglo-Scandinavian elder and maple spouts which may have been used with a special type of stave-built bucket with a fitted lid (Fig. 1093). Evidence for this type of vessel has been found in York, Dublin and Lund dating to the 10th–12th centuries. The most complete vessel of this kind is a 10th century bucket from High Street, Dublin, which has straight sides, wooden hoops, two raised staves each perforated by two holes for an organic handle, and both a base and a lid fitted like caskheads into squared grooves (National Museum of Ireland 1973, pl.12). The vessel was an enclosed container like a cask, but was intended for use like a bucket. Its lid had a central hole (presumably for filling the bucket) covered with a swivel lid, and another hole near the

edge had a cylindrical, hollow, wooden spout (presumably for emptying). *8873* and *8875* are probably spouts of this kind, as is a wooden object from 6–8 Pavement in York, originally identified as a handle (Fig.77, 477, *AY* 17/3), and another 11th century spout from Christchurch Place, Dublin (Morris 1984a, fig.102, C167). All three of the York spouts have narrower bands at one end where they were fitted into the hole on top of a lid, the wider part of the spout preventing the object from slipping down through the hole. Spout *8873* also has a stopper peg which protrudes at least 55mm beyond the spout's wider end. Both *8873* and *8875* were made from roundwood which had been hollowed with a tapering auger to create a hole wider at one end. A possible fourth spout of this kind from Anglo-Scandinavian York is the bone object which has been faceted at one end and deliberately hollowed by boring a tapering hole down the centre. A wooden peg carved from roundwood, *8874*, was inserted in the wider end of the bone spout.

Staves for Viking period lidded buckets have been found at Christchurch Place (ibid., fig.102, C170v–ix), and swivel lids have been found at Winetavern Street and Christchurch Place, Dublin (ibid., fig.102, C164–5), and in a 12th century context in Lund (Nilsson 1976, fig.190). Lidded buckets which had spouts and swivel lids like these must have been constructed to prevent spillage of the contents, and it

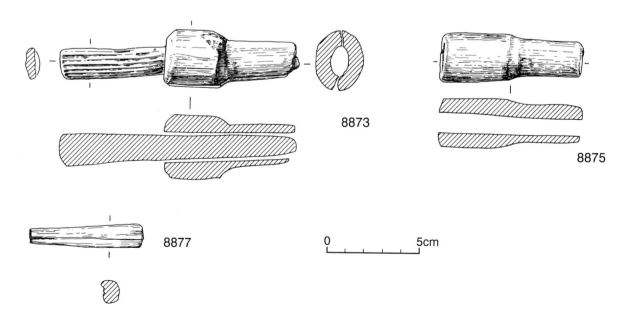

8873

8875

8877

0   5cm

Fig.1093 Spouts 8873 and 8875; spigot 8877. Scale 1:2

has been suggested that the complete bucket from Dublin could have been for use on a ship (National Museum of Ireland 1973, 48–9). A mid 8th century Anglo-Saxon stave-built vessel found at Granville Street, Southampton, at first identified as a small cask, could be a lidded bucket of this kind (Holdsworth 1976, fig.20, 1). It originally had eleven staves which tapered towards one end. The staves had roughly cut V-sectioned croze grooves at each end, but only one circular end/base survived. A re-used perforated lathe-turned core found with the vessel probably acted as a bung hole (equivalent to the spouts on the later vessels) and could have been fixed in the missing end.

8877 is a small spigot of oak roundwood, with a tapering shaft, circular cross-section and cut flat at both ends (Fig.1093), and *8876* is probably a fragment

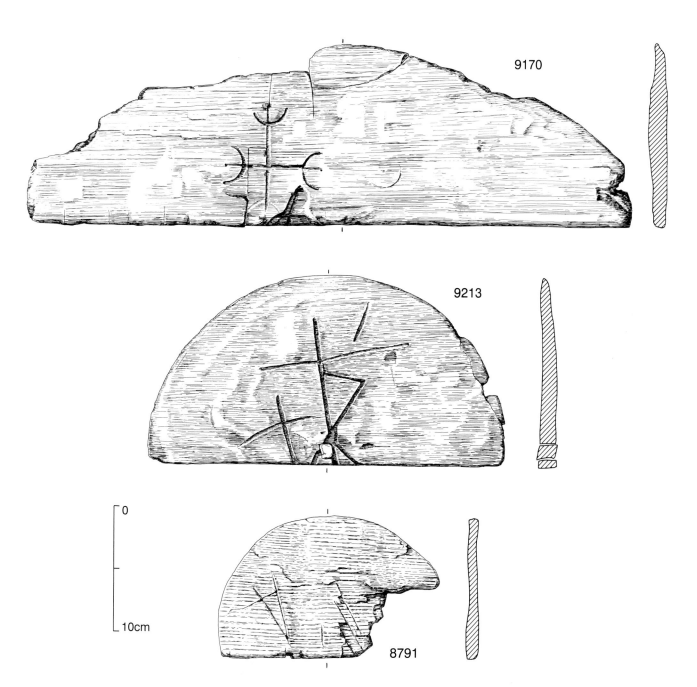

Fig.1094 *Head or base fragment 8791 from 16–22 Coppergate with an incised 'A' cut into one surface; cant stave fragment 9170 from the Coppergate watching brief site with an incised cross on one surface; cant stave 9213 from Bedern Foundry with part of an incised merchant's mark of intersecting lines. Scale 1:3*

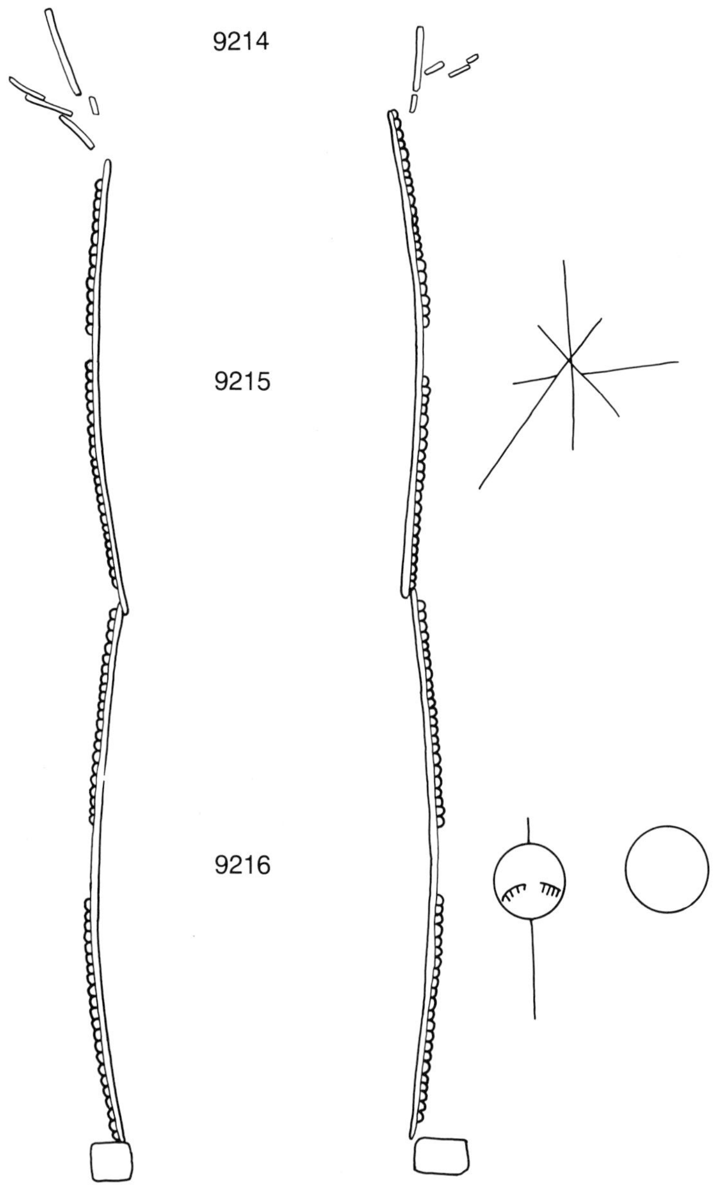

9214

9215

9216

Fig.1095 *Schematic section through three-tier cask-lined well 9214–16 at Bedern Foundry, showing marks found on casks 9215 and 9216. Scale 1:20, details of marks 1:4*

of an alder spigot. Both are Anglo-Scandinavian. This type of peg is usually associated with stave-built casks, and was used in bung holes and vent holes in the side staves or caskhead (cf. pp.2250–1), although neither of the Coppergate examples were found associated with any vessel. Tapering spouts with bungs or spigots were also used in medieval caskheads and cask staves, which are usually found isolated from their original casks. Medieval spigots have been found singly and associated with a wooden spout at High Street/Blackfriargate, Hull (Watkin 1987, fig.124, 352 and 355), and they appear in a late medieval illustration in three different types of stave-built casks (Fig.1087, p.2250).

8199 is a half-finished medieval ash object which may have been intended as a lathe-turned spout (Fig.997, p.2137).

Marks on stave-built vessels

Incised, stamped and branded marks found on stave-built vessels are usually one of three types: construction marks, makers'/merchants' marks, or symbolic marks (Morris 1984a, 156–7). Several of the Coppergate vessels have examples of these marks (Figs.1094–7).

One stave of cask *9191* from 22 Piccadilly has a possible cooper's mark in the form of an incised circle

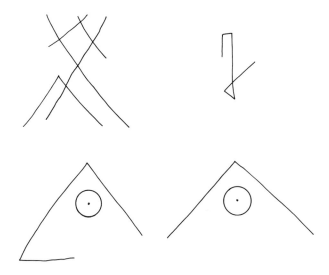

Fig.1096 *Three cooper's marks on cask 9192 and mark on cask 9191 (bottom right) from 22 Piccadilly. Scale 1:4*

an elaborate incised cross with the ends of its four arms cut by semi-circles made with a compass (Figs.1094 and 1097). Anglo-Scandinavian head *8777* has a small stamped oval mark, medieval head *8821* has a stamped H-shaped mark encircled by two grooves or compression marks in the centre of each flat surface, and cant *9213* from Bedern has part of a complex incised mark (Fig.1094). All six marks could be makers' or merchants' marks, although there is very little evidence for the use of merchants' marks in England before the late 13th century (Girling 1964, 9), and those on the four Anglo-Scandinavian heads could be some of the earliest yet found in Britain. It is possible that some of the marks are symbolic, and, like the crosses on box *8933*, pot-lid *8883* and the pentacle and cross on the lid from Exeter (Allan and Morris 1984, fig.174, 16), they may have been devices thought to protect the contents of the vessels.

within a triangle, a mark also seen on a stave from cask *9192* which suggests they could have been made by the same craftsman. Another stave from *9192* has a possible cooper's or construction mark (Fig.1096). Five staves of medieval cask *8767* have incised marks which presumably also helped the cooper in the cask's construction and assembly. Three of these staves had bung holes or batten holes of various kinds. Other stave-built vessels with such construction marks are the complete 13th century bucket from Castell-y-Bere (Butler and Dunning 1974, fig.10) and one of the 15th–early 16th century casks from Westwick Street, Norwich (Morris 1993a, 95).

Seven other caskheads or vessel bases have incised or stamped marks. *8785*, *8791* and *8806* (Periods 4B and 5B) have incised marks on one surface in the form of intersecting lines, a debased capital A, and a simple cross respectively (Fig.1094). *9170* has

Fig.1097 *Cooper's marks on caskhead 9170 from the Coppergate watching brief site*

Everyday Life

Domestic Equipment and Utensils (not lathe-turned or coopered)

The domestic wooden vessels and utensils excavated from the Coppergate, Bedern and 22 Piccadilly sites give a tantalisingly slight insight into the enormous number and range of wooden items which were made for and used in Anglo-Scandinavian and medieval households in York. The wide range reflects both the versatility of wood as a raw material, different species having properties suitable for different tasks, and also the lack of standardised production of some types of everyday objects. The preceding sections were concerned with items produced by specialised craftsmen such as the lathe-turner and cooper, but some Anglo-Scandinavian woodworking was carried out on a do-it-yourself basis, and small wooden household utensils were produced when needed if the wood and tools were available. Some items which every household would have used are well represented on English sites. In York these include wooden pot-lids 8878–89 and knife handles 2812, 2863, 2898, 2938, 8925–8, 9175. Others, such as the bread peel 8922, are unique finds or survive only in very small numbers which are unrepresentative since they would also have been common pieces of equipment.

Pot-lids (Figs.1098–9)

Twelve wooden pot-lids were found at 16–22 Coppergate, dating from the three phases with the most intensive occupation on the site, Periods 4B, 5B and 6. They are small circular or sub-circular discs with squared or rounded/squared edges. Eleven were made from riven boards of oak, their edges cut with an axe or similar bladed tool, but 8881 was made from part of a discarded lathe-turning roughout or waste product from a face-turned bowl and has traces of turning lines and a profile with a chamfered edge (Fig.1098). Most of the pot-lids were probably homemade items utilising flat boards, staves or planks of riven oak which happened to be available. 8880 and 8883 (both Period 4B) are plain discs, whereas the other ten are perforated by an approximately central hole, some of them circular and augered (8879, 8881–2, 8884–6, 8888–9), some squared and probably cut with a chisel (8878 and 8887). The augered holes

range from 13–31mm in diameter and were made with a variety of auger bits with different blade widths.

Wooden pot-lids comparable to those from York, some plain, some with central holes, have been found at various English and continental sites, dating mainly to the 10th–12th centuries. These include an 8th century pot-lid from Melbourne Street, Southampton (Morris 1984a, fig.77, M141), 10th century pot-lids from Brook Street, Winchester (Keene 1990, fig.377, 4455), and Craigywarren, Co. Antrim (Coffey 1906–7, pl.VII, 9), 10th/11th century examples from Southgate Street, Gloucester (Morris 1984a, M143), and Saddler Street, Durham (Carver 1979, 26), an 11th century example from Charavines in France (Colardelle and Colardelle 1980, fig.49, 4), a late Saxon example from Milk Street, London (Morris 1984a, fig.77, M156), six Viking Age ones from Christchurch Place and Fishamble Street, Dublin (ibid., M146–51), and a 12th century one from Goldsmith Street, Exeter (Allan and Morris 1980, fig.174, 19). Medieval examples (mainly 13th/14th century in date) have been found at King's Lynn (Clarke and Carter 1977, fig.172, 167), Austin Friars, Leicester (Mellor and Pearce 1981, fig.53, 86), Ludgate Hill and Trig Lane in London, Perth and Coventry, W. Midlands (Morris 1984a, fig.77, M155, M157, M158 and M160). Pot-lids with or without holes seem to have been used as early as the 4th century at Wijster (Van Es 1967, fig.66, 2–3) and Feddersen Wierde (Haarnagel 1979, Taf.41,1), and as late as the mid 16th century at Norton Priory, Runcorn (Morris 1984a, fig.177, M159). The shape and features of these wooden discs remained constant over a long period of time because they were ideally suited for a particular task.

8775 and 8805 (Fig.1081, p.2244) are two other Anglo-Scandinavian wooden items which may be either caskheads or pot-lids and measure 163mm and 120mm in diameter respectively.

8878–89 and all the pot-lids listed above measure between 70 and 165mm in diameter, but most have diameters between 100 and 130mm. They are likely

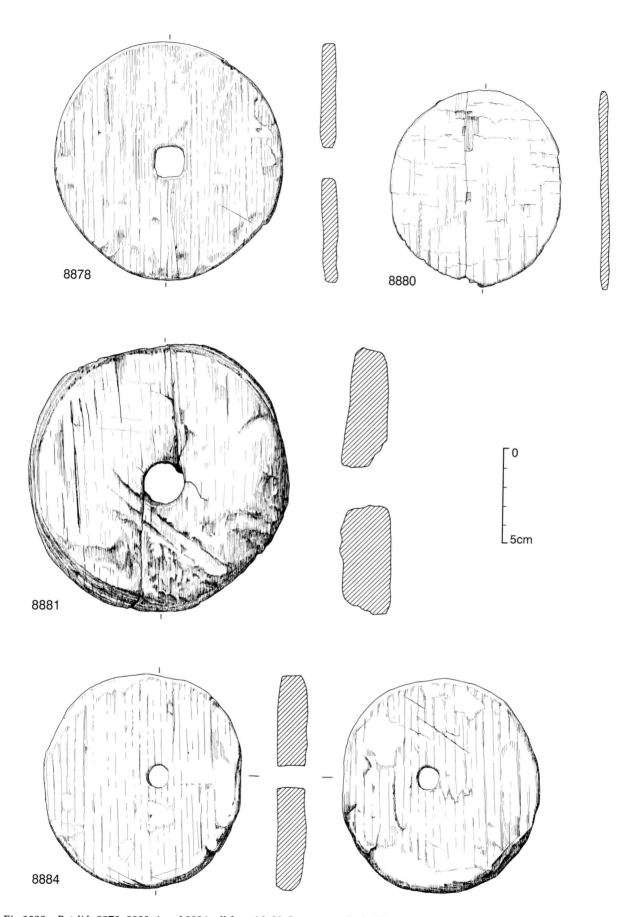

Fig.1098 *Pot-lids 8878, 8880–1 and 8884, all from 16–22 Coppergate. Scale 1:2*

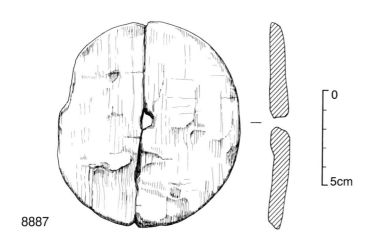

8885

8887

⌈ 0

⌊ 5cm

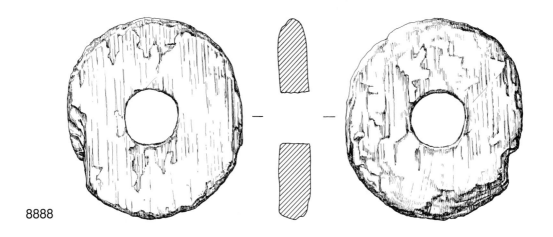

8888

to have been wooden lids for ceramic vessels, especially storage jars and cooking pots. The average diameter of the wooden lids corresponds well to the mouth diameters of pottery storage jars and cooking pots with slightly rebated lid seatings (e.g. some of the York ware, shelly ware, Torksey ware and early glazed ware vessels found at 16–22 Coppergate; *AY* 16/5). Most storage jars with an everted rim of some kind could have been fitted with a flat wooden disc lid. Pottery lids are not common (Jope 1949, fig.11, 1 and 7), and although stone lids have been found in northern Britain (Evans and Jarrett 1987, fig.111, 15 and 17; see p.2188), and linen and parchment were also used (Morris and Evans 1992, 190), wood was obviously considered the material best suited for making flat lids for jars. Wooden lids were mentioned in medieval domestic inventories (Moorhouse 1978, 14) and were used for cooking and craftsmen's recipes such as an early 15th century recipe for making vermilion which instructed 'see that you have a lid of tree upon the pot's mouth well closed' (British Library Sloane MS 73, fo.138v).

Features found on various wooden pot-lids may explain some of the ways in which they were used. Ten of the twelve lids from Coppergate have a central hole. These provide a means of lifting the lid from the jar or pot. It is known that for cooking, wooden lids could be sealed to pots using a lute of thick batter made from egg and flour, whilst alchemists used a *luteum sapientum* of flour, egg white, chalk and clay. A lid secured in this way would need some means of releasing it after use, and these central holes, which themselves may have been temporarily stoppered during use, would have been ideal for this, and also perhaps for letting out steam. The pot-lid from King's Lynn and one of the Dublin lids had two such holes, perhaps for a more elaborate rope handle. Dark staining on one surface of *8886* (and *8775*) may have occurred on the underside of the lid when it was being used in cooking; charring on the edges of *8881* may have had a similar cause. *8885* has a notch cut into the side edge perhaps to allow the handle of a spoon or ladle to remain in the jar (Fig.1099). Similar notches are found on the pot-lids from Winchester, Milk Street, London, Charavines and Perth.

Two of the York lids dating to Period 4B have incised lines cut into one surface. Two faint incised parallel lines run across one flat side of *8879* through the central hole, and there are faint incised lines on one surface of *8883* in the form of a debased saltire cross. A similar cross was incised on a hinged wooden lid for a stave-built container found on the late Norse site at The Biggings, Papa Stour, Shetland (Morris 1999, fig.101). Other pot-lids with incised decoration are two from Christchurch Place, Dublin, one of which had a six-petalled floral design with a hole at its centre (Lang 1988, fig.86) and the other had a cruciform design with the arms of the cross radiating from a central hole, and the panels between the arms decorated with other incised designs (Morris 1984a, M151). In an age of superstition, incised crosses on lids such as *8883* may have been symbolic marks to ward off evil from the contents. The cross is probably the most common symbol to be found in folk art throughout the world, and it has a long history as a protective device (Brears 1989, 26).

Stoppers (Fig.1100)

These are small wooden stoppers or bungs, some Anglo-Scandinavian and some medieval, which were used with larger vessels, wooden or otherwise. *8890–2* and *8894* were carved from alder, ash or hazel roundwood, the bark still remaining in three places on *8894*; *8893* was made from cork and *9193* was carved from radially split oak.

8894 has a conical lower end, circular in cross-section, and a narrow tapering spindle-like grip above this, square in cross-section. It is probably a stopper for a vessel with a narrow neck or spout (rather than a bung for a cask) because of its conical lower end. Although the vessels could conceivably have been made of leather, wood, pottery or even glass, few have survived. Merovingian wooden costrels with narrow necks found at Oberflacht (Paulsen and Schach-Dörges 1972, Abb.56) and Cologne Cathedral, Germany (Doppelfeld 1963, Taf.12), are rare examples of wooden vessels which would have had wooden stoppers. Wooden stoppers may have been used in the spouts of ceramic spouted pitchers, or in the narrow necks of ceramic costrels and bottles. York-type ware and Torksey-type ware spouted pitchers and narrow-necked vessels were found in the Coppergate excavations (*AY* 16/5, figs.160, 185, 187 and 193), and similar Thetford ware spouted pitchers, costrels and bottles were found in excavations at Thetford (Rogerson and Dallas 1984, figs.158–63 and 176). Ceramic cisterns such as one found during excavations at 1–5 Aldwark, York (*AY* 16/3, 794, fig.76), were common in the 15th and 16th

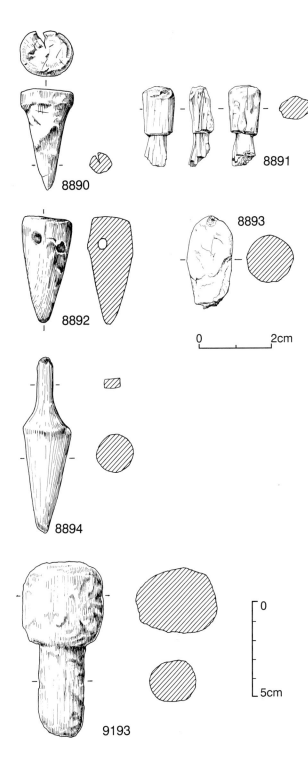

8890

8891

8892

8893

8894

9193

0   2cm

0

5cm

Fig.1100   *Stoppers 8890–4 from 16–22 Coppergate; 9193 from 22 Piccadilly. Scale 1:2, 8893 1:1*

Dublin stoppers had incised decoration in the form of a band of interlace round the widest part, and scrolls and clipped leaves in six triangular panels on the tapering grip which was hexagonal in cross-section. The lower conical part was undecorated.

8892 is a plain conical stopper with a flat top, whittled from an ash branch, then smoothed. It has a neatly augered hole 4mm in diameter slanting through the body at one side, the entry and exit of which are roughened by splitting. It would have served the same purpose as *8894*. The hole would have provided a means of extracting the stopper from and attaching it to the vessel by a thong or cord. Other wooden stoppers have provision for cord of this kind including two from Winetavern Street and Christchurch Place, Dublin (Morris 1984a, fig.76, M117–M118), which were both biconical in outline with thick, truncated conical upper parts (reminiscent of the tapered grip of *8894*), conical lower sections and four holes cut diagonally through the sides at cardinal points, an early–mid 10th century stopper from Brook Street, Winchester, which had a square upper end with a hole through one of its corners (Keene 1990, fig.110, *976*), and a carved 13th century maple stopper from London which has an oval plug below a slightly wider collar and a small flat grip with a pointed top, perforated by an augered hole (Egan 1998, BIG82 2938, sf2413).

8890 has a slightly convex top and a plain collar with a vertical edge below which the main body tapers to a point. Although it does not have the tapered grip of *8894* or the thong hole of *8892*, the collar would presumably have protruded above the neck of the bottle and allowed the stopper to be gripped and twisted out. *8891* is a peg-like stopper with a cylindrical head which would also provide a grip, and *8893* is a small cork bung or spigot which may have been used with a vial or even a small stave-built cask. The 10th century stopper *9193* from 22 Piccadilly had a large bulbous head which could have been used as a grip to remove it from a vessel such as a leather bottle.

centuries and may have used wooden bungs to shut off the flow of liquid through their bung holes. Conical wooden stoppers like *8894* have been found in mid–late 10th century and early–mid 11th century houses at Brook Street, Winchester (Keene 1990, fig.112, *989–90*), and in 10th and 11th century levels at Fishamble Street in Dublin (Lang 1988, fig.7; Morris 1984a, fig.32, T191 and fig.76, M119). One of the

Spoons (Fig.1101)

Wooden spoons would have been the main Anglo-Scandinavian and medieval eating and cooking utensil after the knife, but it is only in recent excavations that wooden spoons have been found in any quantity in Britain. Fifty years ago, surviving early medieval spoons were extremely rare (none of them made of wood), but despite this it was suggested that in the 12th and 13th centuries, spoons of bone, horn and wood were in common use (Ward Perkins 1940, 127–8). When two decorated Anglo-Scandinavian wooden spoons from Clifford Street were published twenty years later, there were still no wooden parallels to cite (Waterman 1959, fig.15, 1–2). *8895–9, 9174* and *9234* (the latter from Bedern) are seven examples, from both Anglo-Scandinavian and medieval levels, among a growing number of wooden spoons which have recently been excavated on English and Euro-

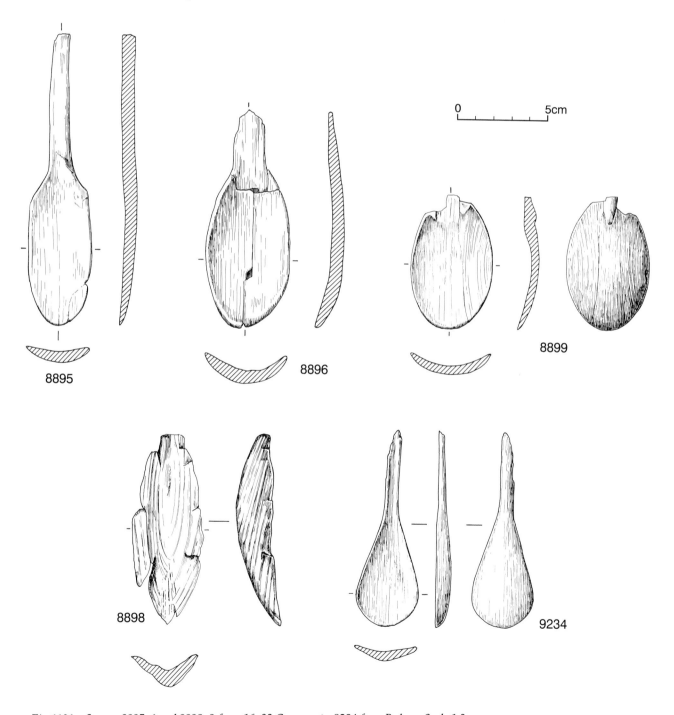

Fig.1101   Spoons 8895–6 and 8898–9 from 16–22 Coppergate; 9234 from Bedern. Scale 1:2

pean sites and are now redressing the balance. Six hundred and fifty wooden spoons dating from the 10th to the 15th centuries were found at Novgorod (Kolchin 1989, 63–6, pls.58–61i).

Wooden spoons had a much greater variety of bowl shapes than metal ones, and although it is possible to classify medieval non-ferrous metal spoons according to their bowl typology (Ward Perkins 1940, fig.41a–c), this is inappropriate for wooden ones since each was individually carved, not cast in a pre-designed mould. Wooden spoons from English sites show no apparent chronological variations in their bowl shapes. *8896–7* and *8899* are oval with rounded sides, as are 11th and 13th century spoons from Lund (Blomqvist and Mårtensson 1963, fig.153; Nilsson 1976, fig.185), a late Norse spoon from Papa Stour (Morris 1999, 100, 405), a 14th century spoon from King's Lynn (Clarke and Carter 1977, fig.171, 1), two 13th century spoons from Cork (Hurley 1982, fig.16.2, 1 and 3), a medieval example from Coventry and a 15th century one from Covehithe (Morris 1984a, fig.67, M33 and M32i). *8895* and *9174* are oval with straight sides, as is a 9th century spoon bowl from Westgate Street, Gloucester (Morris 1979, fig.17,13), whereas *8898* is leaf-shaped with a pointed end, as are examples from High Street, Dublin, and High Street, Perth (Morris 1984a, fig.67, M9 and fig.68, M23ii), 11th century Charavines (Colardelle and Colardelle 1980, fig.44, 2–3 and 5) and Cork (Hurley 1982, fig.16.2, 2 and 4). The oval and leaf-shaped bowls are forms easily produced by woodcarving and are common for wooden spoons. *9234* is a finely carved small pear-shaped spoon. Bone spoons (Collis and Kjølbye-Biddle 1979; Waterman 1959, fig.15, 3) were often pear-shaped with long narrow bowls, while medieval bronze, latten and pewter spoons were usually leaf-shaped, circular and fig-shaped (Ward Perkins 1940, fig.41, a–c). Two bone spoons were found in Anglo-Scandinavian deposits at Coppergate, one originally a double-ended example (*7062–3*, Fig.929, *AY 17/12*).

The handles of wooden spoons also varied. *8896* and the two spoons from Clifford Street have thin, flat handles; in the latter case these were wide enough for decorative carving. The handles surviving on *8895* and *9234* are rounded or rounded rectangular in cross-section, and the handle of *8898* was probably thicker and triangular in cross-section.

Different techniques of carving produced a range of cross-sections in wooden spoons. *8896–9* and *9174* have shallow, rounded profiles and thin bowl walls, whereas *8898*, *9234* and one of the Clifford Street spoons (Waterman 1959, fig.15, 1) have deeper V-shaped or U-shaped and keeled cross-sections with thicker walls. The bowl of *8895* is hardly hollowed at all and has an almost flat profile. The York spoons were made from yew, maple, hazel, fruitwood (*Prunus* sp., probably cherry or blackthorn) and oak. Like recent English and Welsh spooncarvers (Geraint Jenkins 1978, 66–70 and pls.56–61), the makers of spoons in Anglo-Scandinavian and medieval York seem to have chosen split sections of roundwood of suitable length, used an axe to cut an appropriate roughout spoon and then completed the final bowl and handle shaping with knives, and the hollowing out of the bowl with small gouges, chisels, hand-adzes or a crooked or hollowing knife. No examples of these latter tools have been found in Britain yet, but examples of hulknive (hollowing knives) from 10th–13th century contexts in Århus (Andersen et al. 1971, 133, EKU and EQE) and the 10th century Viking camp at Trelleborg (Nørlund 1948, pl.XLV, 4), both in Denmark, show what they could have looked like.

8895 and *8898* may have been home-made items, but a greater degree of skill and craftsmanship would have been needed to make the other five, suggesting that at least some of them were made by specialist spoon/ladle carvers, a craft which in recent years has been associated with lathe-turners (Geraint Jenkins 1978, pl.49). In particular, the medieval yew spoon *8899* is a finely smoothed, delicate utensil with very thin walls; although its handle is missing, the fragmentary remains of the end of the handle carved in relief on the underside of the bowl suggests that it also would have been of the same high-quality workmanship.

Decorative carving on spoons seems to have been applied mainly to their handles, but only *8895* and *9234* have part of their plain original handles surviving, and it is impossible to be certain whether any of the other wooden spoons from the York sites were decorated in the same way as the two from Clifford Street, two from Dublin (Morris 1984a, fig.67, M8 and M16), one from Hedeby (Jankuhn 1936, fig.14) and twelve from Trondheim in Norway which were the products of professional carvers (Fuglesang 1981, 23–5, pls.5–11).

Wooden spoons would have been used mainly for eating and food preparation, depending on their size. Four spoons from Dublin (Morris 1984a, fig.67, M13–M16) were large enough to have been for culinary rather than table use, whereas the York spoons were all probably small enough for eating. Dark staining on the surface of spoon bowls *8895* and *8897* is the result of scorching and the long accumulation of grease during use, a feature also noted on many lathe-turned bowls from York (p.2185 and Fig.1041).

Double-ended spoon-spatulae (Fig.1102)

8900 is a double-ended spoon-spatula, probably birch, with a broken flat spatula blade at one end and a broken keeled spoon bowl at the other end; the handle has a rounded rectangular cross-section. *8901* is a similar but more delicate object carved from yew with small flat oval blades, one larger than the other, at each end of a square cross-sectioned handle. *8900* dates to Period 4B; although *8901* was found in a Period 6 context, this was a dump layer and the double-ended spoon-spatula could be Anglo-Scandinavian in date but redeposited in the later layer. A double-ended spoon-spatula with a complete rounded oval flat blade at one end and traces of another possible blade at the other end of an oval cross-sectioned handle was found in layers associated with Anglo-Scandinavian timber buildings at 6–8 Pavement (Fig.77, *479*, *AY* 17/3).

These three wooden implements seem to be part of a distinct group of small double-ended implements of the late Saxon/Anglo-Scandinavian period in England which were made in a variety of materials and sizes. Two mid 9th century silver implements from Sevington, Kent, also belong to this group, a double-ended spoon-spatula and a fork-spatula (Wilson 1964, pl.29, 67–8), as do six double-ended tin-plated iron spoons found at 16–22 Coppergate, all dated to Period 4B (Fig.249, *2998–3003*, *AY* 17/6), a copper alloy spoon-fork found in Southampton in the 19th century (Roach Smith 1857, 62) and a double-ended copper alloy spoon found at 16–22 Coppergate, unstratified but probably Anglo-Scandinavian in date (*10366*, *AY* 17/14). A double-ended implement with a spoon at one end and the other end broken from Period 5B levels at Coppergate (Fig.929, *7063*, *AY* 17/12) and a 10th/11th century double-ended spoon and a spoon-fork from Winchester (Collis and Kjølbye-Biddle 1979, figs.2, 2 and 3, 6) were made of bone. The blades, handles and decoration on the lat-

ter two implements are very similar to the single-ended bone spoons or spoon fragments found at Winchester, Chichester, London and Norwich (ibid., figs 1–4; Kjølbye-Biddle 1990, fig.247, *2620, 2624*; Waterman 1959, fig.15, 3; Ward Perkins 1940, pl.25; Williams 1987, fig.81, 15), and there is no reason to suppose that the dating or purpose of the double-ended ones was in any way different.

Although they share a double-ended form, the implements in different materials need not necessarily have been made for the same function. They do, however, seem to be a curiously homogeneous group dating to the 9th to 11th centuries. Wilson thought that the function of the Sevington spoons was debatable and that these (and the bone examples) were probably domestic implements (1964, 62). Study of the bone spoons found in Winchester suggests that the type dates from the late 10th to the first half of the 11th century and that they possibly had an ecclesiastical use (Kjølbye-Biddle 1990, 830). A specialised use has also been suggested for the tin-plated iron spoons in view of their high-quality finish (p.603, *AY* 17/6). It is entirely feasible, however, that all the implements, and especially the wooden ones, were used in domestic contexts, and that the difference in their size is more important to their function than the materials of which they were made. Since the working ends have shallow spoon bowls, flat spatulate blades and forks, they may have been small multi-purpose tools, but were probably not intended to spoon liquid in the same way as *8895–9, 9174* and *9234*.

Spatulae (Fig.1102)

8895–9, 9174 and *9234* are described as spoons because they would have had straight, thin handles with wider hollowed bowls. *8902–5* and *9218* are classified as spatulae since each has a flat cross-section without genuine hollowing of the blade to form a bowl. The distinction between the two can often become blurred especially when items were home-made and intended for similar tasks such as stirring, scooping and spreading. *8902–5* are Anglo-Scandinavian, but vary considerably in shape and size, so were intended for different household tasks in cooking and food preparation.

8903 is a complete small spatula 129mm long, made from a half-section branch of yew. It has a narrow elongated oval flat blade, and the handle tapers to a point. In size and form it could be a single-ended

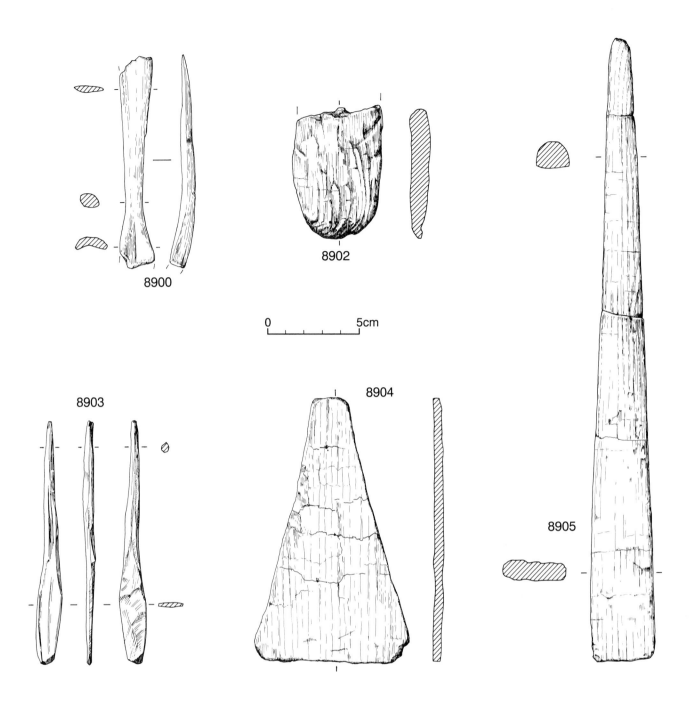

Fig.1102 *Double-ended spoon-spatula 8900; spatulae 8902–5, all from 16–22 Coppergate. Scale 1:2*

version of the double-ended spoon-spatula type *8900–1*. It was found in a Period 4B context, as were *8900* and the six tin-plated iron double-ended spoons mentioned above, and its tapering pointed handle is remarkably similar to those on the complete bone single-ended spoons from King William Street, London (Ward Perkins 1940, pl.25, 4), and Winchester (Collis and Kjølbye-Biddle 1979, figs.1, 1 and 4, b) which are related to the double-ended ones.

8902, 8904–5 and *9218* are larger, more conventional spatulae. *8902* is a fragment of an oak spatula blade 49mm wide, with a rounded end. *8905* is a large spatula, now broken into six fragments, but complete. It was carefully shaped from a tangentially split ash board and tapers from a flat blade with a straight end, to a rounded pointed handle with a thicker, semicircular cross-section. *9218* is similar to *8905* but was made of a split oak lath, and is now broken into three fragments. *8904* has a flat, fan-shaped oak blade which tapers to a narrower handle end. There are four small holes which do not fully perforate the blade in a line down the centre, possibly made by an awl; their purpose is unknown. Various types of spatula to compare with these from Coppergate have been found on other British sites, including two 15th century yew spatulae, one from Newbury in Berkshire similar to *8905* and a smaller one from Trig Lane, London, which was found inside a lathe-turned wooden bowl (Morris 1984a, fig.69, M44 and M42), and three wider spatulae with small handles, a pine one of late Norse date from The Biggings, Papa Stour (Morris 1999, 184), a medieval oak one from London with a chamfered edge (Egan 1998, BIG82 2152 sf2179) and a mid 16th century oak one from Norton Priory, Runcorn (Morris 1984a, fig.69, M45).

Basketry (Fig.1103)

Basketry containers woven of slender wooden rods were made in a variety of shapes and sizes. They usually had a framework of rods (either fixed in holes round the edges of a solid circular, oval, rectangular or square wooden base or radiating from the centre of a woven base) interwoven with finer rods. Woven basketwork is rarely preserved in archaeological contexts and it is usually found as tantalising fragments such as *8909–12*, but solid wooden basket bases such as *8906–8* and *8914* without their rods are becoming increasingly common finds.

8906 is a fragmentary sub-circular basket base or end made from a section which was tangentially cut from the edge of a piece of roundwood, but is mainly bark with very little timber. Its edges were squared and a hole 24mm wide was cut with a chisel through the centre. Around the edges are fifteen surviving evenly spaced holes 5mm in diameter for the upright rods, although there were probably originally nearer twenty. *8908* is a fragment of a much larger circular or oval basket base, also with squared edges, with five surviving circular holes 10mm diameter evenly spaced around the edge for the rods. *8907* is a similar fragment of a large round or oval basket base, probably made from a re-used oak caskhead. It has three augered holes of various sizes through the main part and six surviving holes of the same diameter arranged around the edges for the upright rods. *8914* is a complete small rectangular oak basket base with squared edges and 22 circular holes 6mm in diameter spaced evenly around the edges (between the four corner holes, two sides have five, two have four holes).

Solid basket bases seem to have been used over a long period of time in the British Isles. A basket made entirely of one-year-old rods of common osier (*Salix viminalis*), dated by radiocarbon to AD 520 ± 40 years, was found lining a well at Odell (Morris 1984a, M162). It was originally woven on a solid, probably circular, base with 49 uprights, but prior to re-use in the well, the base had been removed by cutting through the bottom of most of the stakes and tearing off the remainder. The base would probably have been similar to *8907* or *8908*. A 9th century oval oak basket base was found at Westgate Street, Gloucester (Morris 1979, fig.16, 7–8), and four Viking period basket bases, two rounded rectangular and two circular, were found at Christchurch Place and Fishamble Street in Dublin (Morris 1984a, M166–M169). *8906* dates from the second half of the 9th century, the earliest phase of Anglo-Scandinavian occupation on the Coppergate site, *8907–8* are also Anglo-Scandinavian but from 10th century levels, while *8914* is medieval. Fragments of a circular base dated to c.1100 were found in gravel pits at Colwick, Nottinghamshire, near a Norman fish weir (Morris 1984a, fig.78, M173). All the excavated examples of wooden basket bases vary in shape and size. A 4th century oval base found at Vimose in Denmark is 940mm long (Engelhardt 1869, pl.15, 30), while a small 13th century circular one found at High Street, Perth, measures only 117mm across (Morris 1984a, fig.78, M174). All the bases, however, have small circular holes around their edges for the upright rods. Some bases retain fragments of rod, for example, the bases from Gloucester and Colwick, and two from Dublin, one of which had seven pairs of holes with one rod looped through two holes to make two uprights. No fragments of rods have survived in any of the York bases.

Many split strands and roundwood rods of hazel no more than 4–6mm in diameter were found in a context dating to Period 5B and may be parts of a basketry container made of woven rods and uprights (*8912*). Four other sets of fragments of twisted roundwood rods have been found — three between 7 and 12mm diameter were found in Anglo-Scandinavian contexts at Coppergate and could also be parts of baskets or handles or both (*8909–11*), and a fourth

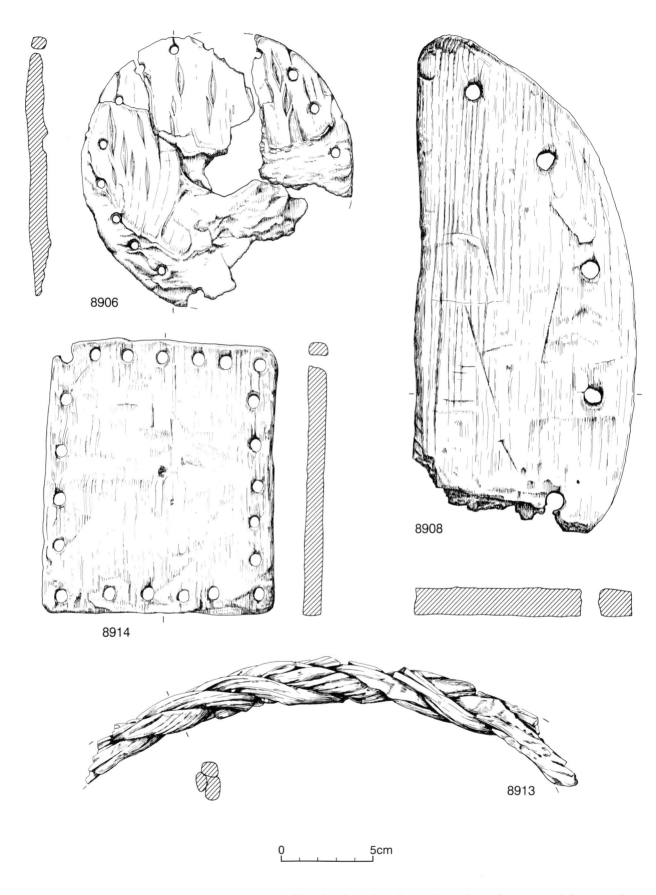

Fig.1103 *Basket bases 8906, 8908 and 8914; fragment of lengths of roundwood twisted together to form a curved three-strand 'rope' 8913. Scale 1:2*

was found in 10th century levels at 22 Piccadilly (*9194*). Fragments of roundwood rods twisted together to make a curved three-strand 'rope' which had holes from nails, pegs or other rods splitting the strands (*8913*) were found in a medieval pit with fibres. This 'rope' could be part of a handle or the twisted rim of a basketry container. Fragments of a similar twisted and plied cord of woody material were found in waterfront silts dated to the first half of the 11th century at New Fresh Wharf in London (Pritchard 1991, fig.3.132) and fragments of a twisted willow cord which could have formed part of a basket were found in a Norman pit at Pevensey Castle (Dunning 1958, 217). There are very few other surviving archaeological examples of woven basketry. The finest is the 6th century container from Odell which was re-used to line a well shaft. The rods used were one-year-old osiers, while rods used in a second basket frame lining another well at Odell, dated by radiocarbon to AD 551 ±40, were willow uprights and smaller dogwood rods for the weave (Morris 1984a, 218). Remains of a possible hazel basket were found in a 7th century burial at Hurdlow in Derbyshire (Bateman 1861, 54) and fragments of two late 13th century baskets were found in a pit at Cuckoo Lane, Southampton (Wright 1975, pl.146, 1–2). Willow, dogwood and hazel are light and pliable and can be grown to provide narrow, straight rods. All these examples show that basket makers were deliberately selecting certain species and sizes of roundwood rods and that woodland management was being practised to provide them with this particular kind of raw material.

Baskets must have been made for many different purposes as general household and farm containers, and this helps to explain why there are such a variety of shapes and sizes among the wooden basket bases. The Colwick base and a 13th/14th century wooden skep with a woven rush base found in fish-breeding tanks at Washford, Worcestershire (Wilson and Hurst 1969, 285), could have been fishing baskets. Some woven containers could have been used for traps, which may have been the function of *8906* with its central hole. Medieval illustrations show a variety of baskets. For example, in a mid 13th century manuscript a basket with an arched handle is being hoisted on a winch to lift material on a building site (Trinity College Dublin MS E i 40, fo.60r). In a 14th century Flemish manuscript, one illustration shows someone picking fruit and placing it in a

basket very similar to the one used on the 13th century building site, and another shows a large flat-bottomed basket with a handle at each side of the rim being used by a person to carry what appears to be a heavy load (Bodleian Library MS Douce 6, fos.3 and 22). In a late 15th century Book of Hours, probably from Bruges, a two-handled flat basket is used for winnowing (British Library Add. MS 17012, fo.12).

Troughs

Fragments of three large rectangular or elongated oval troughs have been found at 16–22 Coppergate, two Anglo-Scandinavian (*8915–16*) and one medieval in date (*8917*). The largest is *8915* which survives as many fragments of poplar and can be reconstructed as a rectangular vessel up to 1m in length and probably 460mm wide (Fig.1104). It was hollowed from a section of roundwood with a semi-circular cross-section but which did not include the immediate heartwood of the tree. It could either have been a proper half-section of a tree trunk which then had its heartwood removed before the vessel was hollowed out, or a piece which was tangentially split from roundwood deliberately without the heartwood. The original roundwood would have been over 500mm in diameter. The trough was U-shaped in cross-section, probably with a flat bottom, and had thick, heavy end walls 60mm thick with everted horizontal lip handles 80mm wide, and thinner side walls and bottom 15–25mm thick. Both ends survive more or less intact, but many of the wall and bottom fragments are now broken and missing. Toolmarks on the internal and external surfaces show that it was probably shaped with an axe, and possibly hollowed with an adze-like tool. The original appearance of the trough would have been similar to a post-medieval one in the author's collection (Fig.1106).

8916 is a fragment of part of one end and bottom of an alder trough, now very worn and abraded. It was probably originally rectangular and U-shaped in cross-section like *8915*, and also hollowed from half-section roundwood, with axe-cuts visible on some surfaces. It is not possible to reconstruct its dimensions, but it was probably a smaller vessel than *8915*. *8917* is a fragment of an elongated oval alder trough found in a medieval layer (Fig.1105). It was also hollowed from half-section roundwood and was U-shaped in cross-section, but had rounded ends, straight sides and a flat bottom. It would also have been smaller than *8915*.

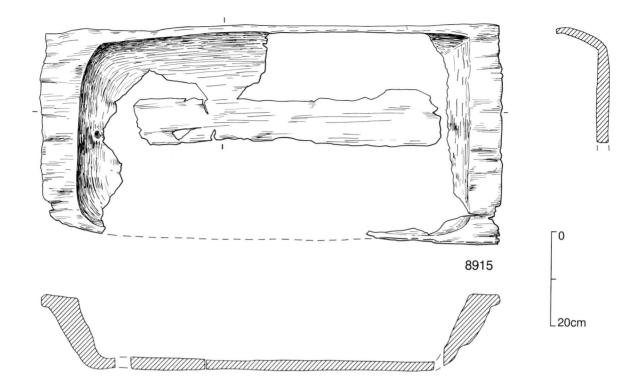

Fig.1104 Poplar trough 8915. Scale 1:8

Only one other fragment of a similar trough has been found in England, in an 11th century context at New Fresh Wharf in London (Pritchard and Morris 1991, 240–2, fig.3.126, 372), but it is invaluable in showing how the troughs were made since its internal end wall surface displays marks from the downward strokes of an adze used for hollowing and there are marks from a cutting tool such as a chisel at the sharply defined junction between the end side walls, and on the underside of the handle. There are many examples from continental sites dating from the 4th to 15th centuries. A 4th/5th century roughout for a small trough with one of the lip handles roughly formed and a finished vessel from Wijster show stages in trough manufacture (Van Es 1967, figs.64 and 65, 1). The best parallels for the York and London troughs are four 9th century examples found in the Oseberg ship burial (Brøgger and Shetelig 1928, pl.11 and figs.77–9), one of which was more than twice as large as *8915* at 2·20m in length, while the other three were more modest at 245–340mm in

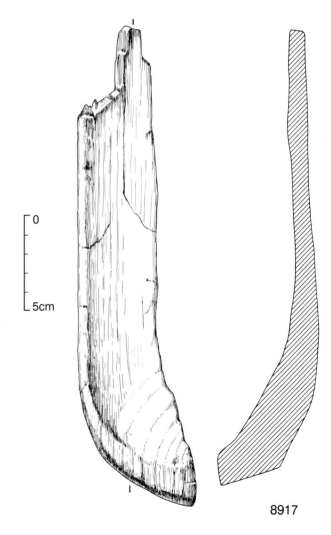

Fig.1105 Fragment of an alder trough 8917. Scale 1:2

8917

Fig.1106 *Post-medieval trough similar to 8915*

length, made from beech and fir, and an 11th century oak example from Lund (Mårtensson and Wahlöö 1970, fig.75). Fragments of other troughs have been found in 6th–9th century layers at the Irish crannogs at Ballinderry 2 and Lagore (Hencken 1942, fig.25, W187; Hencken 1950, fig.78, W189), 9th–11th century levels at Hedeby (Schietzel 1970, Abb.4), Viking levels at Christchurch Place in Dublin (Morris 1984a, M72–M73), 13th and 14th century levels at Novgorod (Kolchin 1989, pl.69, 7–8), and 15th century Lübeck (Neugebauer 1954, Abb.7, F).

Troughs may have had a variety of uses depending on their size, but some of them (perhaps the larger ones like *8915*) were traditionally bread making utensils in north-west Europe used for kneading dough (Brøgger and Shetelig 1928, 142, fig.80). Traces of rye flour were found in the largest of the Oseberg troughs. Troughs for kneading and washing are mentioned in a mid–late 7th century Irish document, the 'Crith Gablach' (Trinity College Dublin MS H.3.18), and in the 11th century manuscript commonly referred to as the 'Gerefa', troughs (OE *trogas*) are among the wooden vessels which the 11th century Anglo-Saxon reeve should provide for the manor (Cunningham 1910, 573–5). Here troughs are listed alongside vessels associated with seeds, sieving and winnowing which supports the idea that some troughs were used in tasks associated with flour, grain, kneading and bread making. In the 'Golf Book of Hours', a Flemish

manuscript dated to c.1500, a woman kneads dough in a large wooden trough with a U-shaped cross-section, while bread is baked in a nearby oven (British Library Add. MS 24098, fo.29v). The inside of the London trough was stained the dark colour associated with accumulated grease from culinary use and also found on lathe-turned bowls and spoons from York (see Fig.1041, p.2190). In the 'Tacuinum Sanitatis', an Italian manuscript of c.1385, a smaller wooden trough with everted lip handles is being used to hold tripe in a kitchen (Österreichische Nationalbibl. Vienna MS s.n. 2644, fo.81r). The shape of this sort of vessel changed little over time and illustrates the conservatism commonly found where wooden utensils evolve a useful form and are then manufactured over a wide area with little alteration for a long period of time.

Carved bowl (Fig.1107)

8918 is a large sub-circular bowl, approximately 340mm in diameter and 160mm deep, which was carved from a block of oak burrwood and is now very fragmentary and badly distorted. It was found in a post-hole firmly dated to the second half of the 9th century (Period 3). Tool marks on the internal surface show that it was hollowed with a bladed tool such as a hand-adze or chisel, not with a round-shave (Roesdahl et al. 1981, 123), a technique for which there is no evidence in Anglo-Saxon, Anglo-Scandinavian

Fig.1107 Carved oak bowl 8918 from 16–22 Coppergate. Scale 1:4

8918

0 |_____| 10cm

or medieval England. By comparison with the normal lathe-turned bowls, *8918* is a rare vessel and there is only one example of similar size from England to compare it with — a late 11th to late 12th century ash bowl 336mm in diameter and 145mm high found at Milk Street in London, which was probably not lathe-turned, and which had been repaired with an iron staple (Pritchard and Morris 1991, 276). *8918* is also rare because of its size. There are only five lathe-turned bowls from 16–22 Coppergate and one from the Bedern Foundry site over 300mm in diameter, and of these, only the medieval bowl *8583* is larger than *8918*, making *8918* the largest Anglo-Scandinavian bowl from any of the York sites. Its size probably determined that it was carved rather than lathe-turned. The largest hollowed round/oval vessel of a bowl-like form found in England was also carved from a solid block — the 12th century oak vat from Eastgate, Beverley, measuring 925 × 800mm (Morris and Evans 1992, 199, fig.96).

Carved oval and round vessels with flat or outcurving ladle-like handles made using similar techniques have been found in the 9th century Oseberg ship burial (Brøgger and Shetelig 1928, figs 88–9), in 9th–11th century Hedeby (Schietzel 1970, Abb.5, 1–2; Elsner 1990, 25, Abb.1 and 27, Abb.5) and Elisenhof, northern Germany (Szabo et al. 1984, Abb.73–4), and at Christchurch Place in Dublin (Morris 1984a, fig.74, M83). A curved handle from a similar ladle-like vessel was found at New Fresh Wharf in London (Pritchard and Morris 1991, fig.3.126, 370).

Churns (Figs.1108–9)

Cream has to be coagulated before it will form butter, a task carried out using either a plunge churn inside which a wooden dasher on a pole was beaten up and down, or a swinging churn like the 9th century stave-built one found at Lissue Rath (Bersu 1947, fig.13), which was suspended and swung to and fro. *8919* is probably an Anglo-Scandinavian churn dasher, *4421* is an Anglian or Anglo-Scandinavian churn dasher, and *8920* is a medieval churn lid, all three used in plunge churns. The history of the plunge churn in Europe is outlined in Myrdal (1988).

Churn dashers used in plunge churns are most often found without their poles or the churn with which they were used, and both archaeological and recent folk examples varied in shape and size. Two basic types of churn dasher were used in Anglo-Saxon, Anglo-Scandinavian and medieval Britain.

One type of dasher was sub-rectangular with an upstanding cylindrical core perforated to fix the dasher to the pole, of which *8919* is probably an example. It is a small oak dasher with an upstanding cylinder 57mm in diameter perforated by an augered hole 25mm in diameter (Fig.1108). Other examples include a larger 9th century oak dasher from Westgate Street, Gloucester (Morris 1979, fig.17, 11), an undated example found in Selby in 1847, now in the Yorkshire Museum (Morris 1984a, fig.74, M86), and a 13th/14th century one from Århus, whose cylindrical core was perforated by two small peg holes possibly to fix the pole in place (Andersen et al. 1971, 261, AKB).

The second type of dasher was a wooden disc perforated by multiple holes, of which *4421* from the Coppergate watching brief is a good example. It is an oak disc 137mm in diameter with squared edges (Fig.1109). There is a central augered hole for the pole surrounded by four others at the cardinal points, all the holes being 15–16mm in diameter and probably cut with the same auger bit. *4421* was found in the wood-lined pit 1778 which also contained the Anglian helmet (pp.889–91, *AY* 17/8), and although it has been examined dendrochronologically and could be as early as 6th century in date, this is as yet unconfirmed (ibid., 870–81). Similar circular dashers with multiple holes have been found in 8th/9th century levels at Elisenhof (Szabo et al. 1984, Taf.16–17), Viking period levels at Christchurch Place, Dublin, and Lund (Morris 1984a, fig.74, M89; Blomqvist and Mårtensson 1963, fig.162), and in an early–mid 11th century house at Brook Street, Winchester (Keene 1990, fig.239, *2536*).

In Irish folk material, both churns and dashers show considerable regional variation (Estyn Evans 1967, fig.67), but discs with multiple perforations like *4421* continued in use in Co. Galway and in parts of Denmark until recent times. The presence of the outer holes increases the effectiveness of this kind of dasher to agitate cream since the liquid not only swirls around the outside of the disc as it moves up and down within the confines of the churn, but is also forced through the holes (Fig.1109 inset). The pattern of holes varied. The Winchester dasher had four surrounding holes like *4421*, the Dublin dasher had six, and the Lund dasher had eight smaller ones. Both dashers from Elisenhof are fragmentary, but one has four surviving holes (probably originally eight) while the other has eight surviving holes (probably originally sixteen).

Since the dasher might not fit snugly inside the churn, its diameter need not necessarily reflect that of the churn. The diameter of a churn might be more accurately predicted by its lid, of which *8920* is an example. It is a riven oak object 171mm in diameter and although it is similar in appearance to caskheads with vent holes, it is far too thick to have been a caskhead, and the central hole of 31mm in diameter is big enough to have accommodated the pole of a

dasher (Fig.1109). Unlike an 8th/9th century churn lid from Elisenhof (Szabo 1984, Taf.16–17) which had two rectangular slots to fix it in place over raised staves at each side of the churn rim (as in Fig.1109), the Coppergate lid may have sat on a rebated ledge cut into the top of the staves or just on top of the staves themselves. A 14th century wooden lid described as 'similar to ones on old butter churns' was found at Trim Castle in Co. Meath (Sweetman 1978, 184). The only other plunge churn lid to have been found in England is a late 13th century lathe-turned ash lid 195mm in diameter and 95mm high with a hollow interior, found in a stone-lined pit at Cuckoo Lane, Southampton (Platt and Coleman-Smith 1975, fig.227, 1619, and pl.114). The size of recent folk churns varied, often according to the number of cows

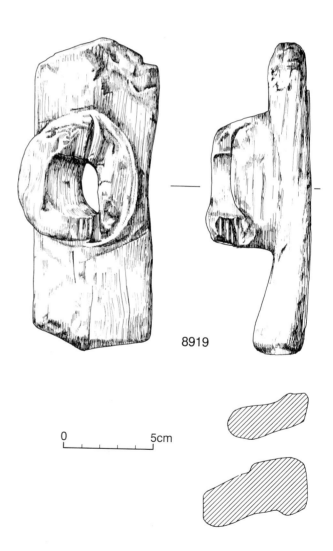

8919

0 _____ 5cm

Fig.1108 *Oak churn dash or spout 8919 from 16–22 Coppergate. Scale 1:2*

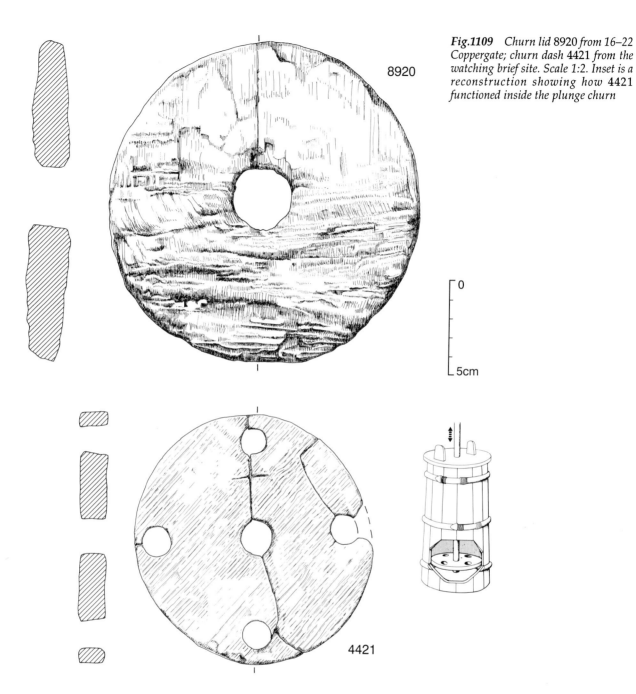

8920

4421

Fig.1109 Churn lid 8920 from 16–22 Coppergate; churn dash 4421 from the watching brief site. Scale 1:2. Inset is a reconstruction showing how 4421 functioned inside the plunge churn

0

5cm

kept on a farm and the amount of cream to be proc-essed (Estyn Evans 1967, 121). The wooden churn-ing equipment found on the Coppergate sites shows that butter was probably made in the Anglo-Scandinavian and medieval town, not just brought in from outlying farm settlements.

Possible cresset (Fig.1110)

8921 is an unusual Anglo-Scandinavian object carved from poplar roundwood. It has four adjacent circular ridges, now broken, below which is a frag-mentary rectangular tenon to fix the object into a mortice hole on another object. Above the ridges is a broken trumpet-shaped cup with traces of a hollowed interior. It is possibly a wooden cresset or type of lamp in which a wick could be floated in oil, although this is a very tentative identification. Contemporary stone (*9663, 9665, 9667, 9669, AY* 17/14) and pottery (*AY* 16/5, *1818, 1845–6, 1855–6, 2136–9*, figs.154, 156, 158, 186) lamps have been recovered from 16–22 Coppergate and are similar in basic form. A lime-stone lamp (*9663*) has a decorated carinated plinth, as do some of the pottery lamps (*1818, 2137*) and it may be that the wooden form is attempting to replicate these. *8921* has no direct parallels, but two other wooden objects which could have been taper- or wick-holders are a lathe-turned late 11th century maple object from New Fresh Wharf in London (Pritchard and Morris 1991, fig.3.127, 374) and a similar 13th century lathe-turned object found at High Street, Perth (Morris 1984a, M413). Both had globular heads with small hollows cut into the top and small circular augered holes leading from the hollow part down their length, possibly to hold wicks, tapers or even candles. Lighting equipment made of wood is not necessarily impractical. A wooden candle-holder with a cruciform base and small hollow in the upper stem was found in medieval Lübeck (Neugebauer 1973, Abb.27).

Bread peel (Fig.1110)

8922 is most probably the blade of an Anglo-Scandinavian bread peel, an all-wooden implement usually used to put bread into and remove it from an oven. It was made from a tangentially converted plank of alder (an outer split, see Fig.973b, p.2103) and has a roughly U-shaped blade with straight shoulders at right angles to a handle fragment carved all in one piece with the blade. The original

handle would have been over 23mm in diameter and long enough to reach into the back of the oven. The blade has a flat upper surface to support the bread and a convex lower surface which is scorched where it has been pushed repeatedly across a hot oven shelf. *8922* dates from the earliest phase of Anglo-Scandinavian occupation on the Coppergate site, but is one of a type of tool which has continued in use right down to the present day. Many medieval illustrations show the use of wooden bread peels like *8922*. For example, in a 14th century Flemish manuscript a person uses a peel with a rectangular blade and sloping shoulders to put bread in a small beehive-shaped oven (Bodleian Library MS Douce 6, fo.181), while in a French manuscript dating to c.1500 a baker uses a peel with a rounded blade to put bread into a much larger oven (Bodleian Library MS Canon Liturg. 99, fo.16).

8922 dates from the second half of the 9th century, the earliest period of Anglo-Scandinavian occupation on the site, and shows that daily domestic chores such as bread making were being carried out somewhere in the vicinity at this date, but it is uncertain what sort of oven was being used. There are two incised marks on the flat upper surface: a circle enclosing a cross and a cross with a bar across the

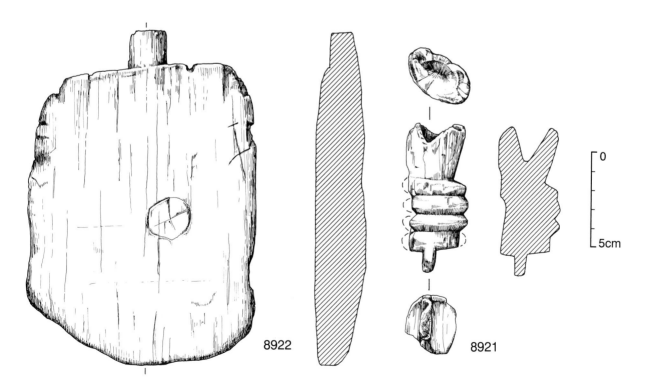

Fig.1110 *Possible cresset 8921 and bread peel 8922, both from 16–22 Coppergate. Scale 1:2*

end of one arm. Using symbols such as crosses to mark a bread peel in this way could be related to the marking of pot-lids such as *8883*, in an effort to 'protect' the bread.

The only other bread peel which can be compared to *8922* was found at an 11th century site at Charavines (Colardelle and Colardelle 1980, fig.45, 1). It had a flat, rounded blade 324mm in diameter and a broken handle 36mm wide.

Hollowed vessels

8923 is a large, deep cylindrical domestic vessel made from a hollowed length of poplar roundwood found re-used as a well lining in Period 3 (mid 9th–early 10th century) (Fig.1111). *8924* is represented by six fragments of a smaller cylindrical vessel (probably a bucket), made from a hollowed length of alder, willow or hazel roundwood, found in a gully dated to Period 5B. *8924* has walls 18mm thick and a squared groove cut 23mm above the inside bottom edge into which a separate circular solid base was slotted (Fig.1112). The groove is 6mm wide and 3mm deep and was made as a continuous cut rather than being chiselled out. It was probably cut with a tool such as a cooper's croze. Fragments of the solid base are encrusted with a crystalline substance and have compressed edges where they were fixed into the groove. An incised mark in the form of an arrow had

been cut into the base on the internal surface. Seven fragments of flat rectangular ash laths 38mm wide with tapering cross-sections are radially cleft strips which would have been used as horizontal bands on the bucket. Most of the fragments were heavily charred and the vessel had probably been discarded in the gully since it was burnt and broken. *8923* is a much larger vessel with a complete cylindrical body whose walls vary between 33mm and 58mm in thickness, and although there was a crudely cut V-sectioned basal groove near the internal bottom of the vessel, no base was found as it was presumably discarded before the vessel was re-used in the well (Fig.1111 and Hall 1984, 32–3).

Most buckets and larger cylindrical tubs of this period were stave-built with basal grooves for a separate, normally circular, base (e.g. *3033*, *8727–63*). *8923* and *8924* are examples of a rarer type of wooden vessel which would have functioned like stave-built buckets, tubs and churns, but whose bodies were hollowed from roundwood with no joints or overlaps and which had separate bases to fit into a groove cut in a similar way to their stave-built counterparts. Some of the earliest British examples of this technique are several 'buckets' found in the Wilsford Shaft Pond Barrow, probably dating from the later 2nd millennium BC (Ashbee et al. 1989, figs. 51–3). Most examples of this type of vessel of a similar date to those from Coppergate have been found on Irish rath,

Fig.1111   Large bucket 8923 re-used as a well lining at 16–22 Coppergate. Scale unit 10cm

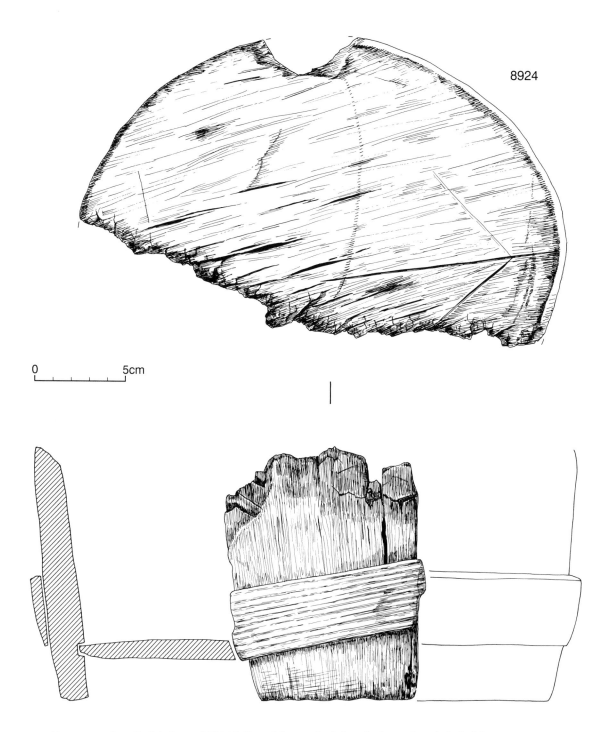

8924

0   5cm

Fig.1112 *Fragments of a cylindrical vessel 8924 hollowed from a single length of roundwood. Scale 1:2*

crannog or bog sites, including a hollowed 10th century willow vessel from Ballinderry Crannog 1 (Hencken 1936, fig.10C), a fragment of a 7th–10th century hollowed yew vessel from Lagore Crannog (Hencken 1950, fig.78) and a 7th–11th century oak vessel with an alder base from Cavancarragh, Co.

Fermanagh (Gaskell-Brown and Brannan 1978, fig.3, 5). A vessel, probably 10th century, was found at Winetavern Street, Dublin (Morris 1984a, fig.75, M101). There are many more undated examples from Ireland, but the few dated Irish vessels, an 8th century bucket from Southampton (Holdsworth 1976,

Fig.1113 *Ninth–eleventh century bucket from Hedeby, similar to 8924*

fig.20, 2) and a 9th–11th century bucket from Hedeby (Fig.1113; Elsner 1990, 25, Abb.4) are the nearest dated parallels for *8924* in form and method of construction. A roughout for a hollowed vessel found 12ft deep in a bog at Derrymullin in Ireland (unpublished, National Museum of Ireland no.1968:223) illustrates the preliminary stages of manufacture of this type of vessel. A piece of roundwood had been roughly shaped. Both ends were cut flat and a hole bored into each. The two holes missed each other, although they were almost certainly intended to join up and could then have been enlarged and the vessel hollowed from the middle outwards. A similar technique would have been used on *8923* and *8924*. A recently excavated Saxon well lining at the Number 1 Poultry site in London (Treveil and Rowsome 1998, fig.24) may also be of a similar form to *8923*, although it was made from a single length of oak roundwood which had been split, hollowed out, then rejoined with wooden pegs, a technique which may have been suitable for a well lining, but may not have functioned as well for a domestic vessel such as *8923*. There are other similarities, however, between *8923* and the Poultry well lining, as both had been placed in well

shafts of comparable dates which had themselves been reinforced with a wattle support lining (compare Fig.1111 and Treveil and Rowsome 1998, fig.24).

The Southampton bucket was hollowed from oak roundwood whose external surface had not been dressed and traces of bark remained. There were traces of adze or chisel marks on the inside walls, and the thickness of the walls varied considerably, probably indicating an inexperienced hand. The vessel was sub-circular and the base, which had an edge roughly chamfered on both sides, had to be carved to fit into a rough groove which was V-sectioned in places and a step-like ledge in others. A double-strand of half-section hazel binding was plaited and fastened around the vessel which can only be described as a poor quality object, and probably home-made. *8924*, by comparison, was a much finer vessel. The squared basal groove was made with a specialised woodworking tool normally used by a cooper and the radially split ash bands were such as a cooper would have used on a stave-built bucket. It was probably made by a craftsman who also made coopered vessels. No trace of a handle or lugs to fasten one was found on either *8924* or the Southampton vessel, although there were two broken perforated lugs on opposite sides of the rim of the Hedeby bucket, for a missing handle. This vessel was bound with two twisted organic hoops. The poplar vessel *8923* was also crudely made, and the basal groove was poorly cut. Tool marks from the hollowing are visible on Fig.1111.

Knife handles (Figs.1114–15)

Knives are composite tools generally made of at least two materials: the iron blade and tang, and a separate organic handle. The latter was sometimes made of bone, antler, ivory or horn (Waterman 1959, fig.7, 10–12; pp.1970–3, *AY* 17/12), but the majority of Anglo-Saxon, Anglo-Scandinavian and medieval knife handles may have been made of wood, whether the knives were for domestic or personal use. Although many iron knife blades or tangs have been found at 16–22 Coppergate, 218 belonging to the Anglo-Scandinavian period alone (pp.558–99, Figs.227–35, *AY* 17/6), knife handles have not survived in the same quantities. *2812, 2863, 2898, 2938, 8925–8, 9175, 9195* and *9219* (and possibly *8986*) are the only wooden knife handles to have been found on the Coppergate, Bedern and 22 Piccadilly sites, nine Anglo-Scandinavian, two medieval and one undated. Horn did not survive well in the Coppergate soil, and it has been found in the corrosion products of only two knife tangs, 2760 and 2855 (p.582, AY 17/6); the friable nature of wooden handles is more likely to have been the reason for their poor survival than the suggestion that most handles would have been made of horn.

Wooden knife handles were made in one of three ways: by whittling a branch or split section of roundwood, probably with another knife, to produce a smooth and serviceable handle with a circular or oval cross-section, a method used to make 2812, 2863, 2898, 2938, 8925–7, 9175 and 9195; by carving a more irregular outline as in 8928, a medieval ash handle with a grooved grip; or by lathe-turning as in 9219. Wood of many different species was used for the York handles, including spindlewood (*Euonymus euro-*

paeus), the Pomoideae family of trees (apple, pear, hawthorn etc.), ash, poplar, birch and boxwood. *9219*, although an unidentified hardwood, was a beautifully whorled and figured burrwood. Species used to make handles found with medieval knives in London include box, maple, Pomoideae, alder, yew and holly (Cowgill et al. 1987, 78–93). Most plain handles could have been home-made by the owner who obtained a knife blade and fitted it with a handle. All the surviving wooden handles have tang holes down part or all of their length and were made for whittle tang knives. *2812, 2863, 2898, 2938, 8926–7, 9175, 9195* and *9219* still have a blade and/or a tang in situ. *8925, 8927–8* and *9219* show that the tang hole was probably cut (or partially cut) as a slit before the knife was fixed in place. Some tangs, such as those in handles *2812, 2898, 8927* and *9219*, passed completely through the handles and were hammered over or cut off at

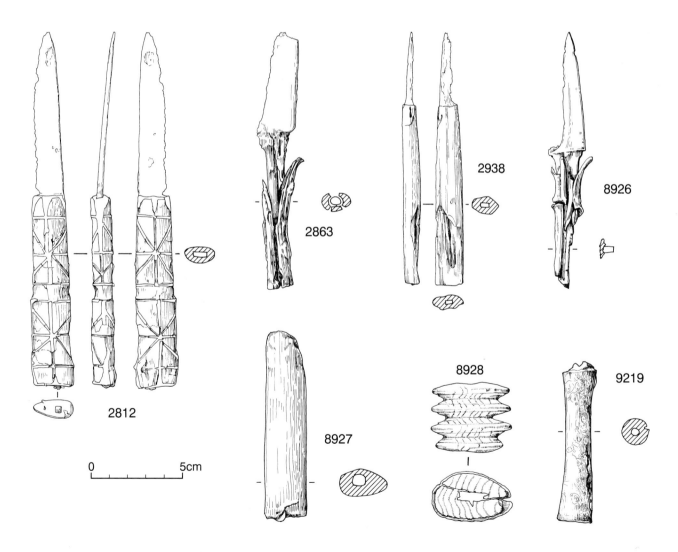

Fig.1114   Knife handles 2812, 2863, 2938 and 8926–8 from 16–22 Coppergate; 9219 from Bedern Foundry. Scale 1:2

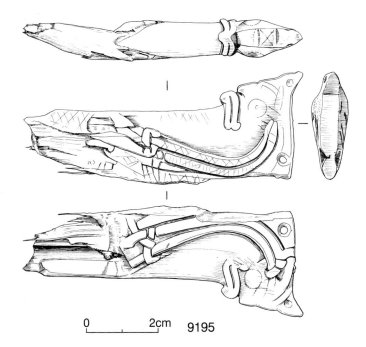

Fig.1115 *Decorated boxwood knife handle 9195 from 22 Piccadilly. Scale 1:1*

0 _____ 2cm   9195

the end, whereas the ends of tangs on *2863* and *8926* were buried within the wooden handle. Knives of this period with plain wooden handles have been found at Hungate in York (Richardson 1959, fig.18, 8), Thetford (Goodall 1984a, fig.123, 67, fig.124, 76 and fig.125, 96), High Street, Dublin (National Museum of Ireland 1973, 40), and various sites in London (Cowgill et al. 1987, figs.54ff).

Knife handles made by lathe-turning are often finer, smoother and more decorative, but none of the Coppergate wooden knife handles were made in this way, and only one from Bedern was lathe-turned (*9219*). Fine 11th–13th century examples have been found at Lund (Nilsson 1976, fig.199; Blomqvist and Mårtensson 1963, fig.222) and King's Lynn (Clarke and Carter 1977, fig.133, 20). Some of them have a waisted grip like *9219* where the middle part is narrower than the ends. This sort of wooden handle would not have been home-made.

9195 is a tantalisingly incomplete 10th/11th century knife handle carved from boxwood, with the remains of a whittle tang knife in situ (Fig.1115). Its incised and relief decoration in the Scandinavian Ringerike style make it unique in several ways. It is the first piece of woodcarving in this style ever to have been found in England on a domestic artefact,

although there are various pieces of woodcarving in this and related styles from Dublin (Lang 1988, figs. 26–34). It is a valuable addition to the very small number of decorated wooden artefacts so far found in York. The importance of the art and style has been discussed elsewhere (Tweddle 1988, 27–30). With a suspension hole at the end of the handle, and the high quality of the decoration, *9195* is more likely to have been a personal knife slung at the belt than a kitchen knife. The quality of the decoration also suggests it was a craftsman-made piece rather than home-made. The handle grip had been smoothed and worn by use (obliterating some of the decoration) before it broke and was discarded.

2812, a knife complete with its whittled spindlewood handle, is also unlikely to have been a home-made item since the wood was carefully inlaid with decorative brass strips. *2812* and *9195* are the finest Anglo-Scandinavian wooden-handled knives to have been found in Britain. *2812* was made using a species which is not often identified among collections of wooden artefacts and may have been perceived as special. Knives with inlaid wooden handles have been found in several Viking graves at Birka (Arbman 1940a, Taf.177–9) and in a 10th century grave at Fyrkat in Denmark (Roesdahl 1977, fig.185). The Fyrkat knife was inlaid with silver and was also made using an unusual species of wood, in this case bullace (*Prunus institia*).

The use of knives found at Coppergate has been discussed elsewhere (p.583, *AY* 17/6), although the medieval ridged handle *8928* may have had a more specialised, albeit unknown, use.

Other domestic utensils

8377 is a lathe-turned core which may have been re-used as a funnel, *9124* is a fragment of a perforated oak disc which could have been part of a cheese press, the caskhead fragment *8791* and lid *8869* were re-used as cutting boards, and *9116* may be part of an alder vessel base or board.

Boxes and Enclosed Containers

In Anglo-Saxon, Anglo-Scandinavian and medieval Britain boxes with lids and other enclosed containers existed in a range of shapes and sizes, varying according to material, method of construction, function and fashion. Many were made of wood, although some were made of bone, ivory or whalebone, for example the Frank's casket (Dalton 1923, 96–8, pl.VIII), some were made entirely of metal, for example Anglo-Saxon 'needlecases' like that from Burwell grave 42, Cambridgeshire (Lethbridge 1931, pl.III), and others must have been made of leather or textiles. Ceramic containers often had wooden lids (see pp.2262–5). In the absence of cupboards, boxes provided a means for storing and securing both small personal items and household goods.

3386, 6964, 8929–42 and *9235–6* from the York sites under consideration are fragments of different types of wooden boxes in varying states of survival, dating from the very earliest phase of Anglo-Scandinavian settlement through to the medieval period.

Wooden boxes were not always rectangular or square. Some were cylindrical, oval, flat or even spherical (Morris 1984a, 72–3). Most, however, were composite wooden artefacts with a body or lower part in one or several pieces and a lid or upper part, again in one or several pieces. The lid and the body were fixed together either by fittings such as hinges, hasps or pegs, or by a tight fit between them. When the terms fittings and mounts are used in this section, they refer respectively to constructional and decorative pieces attached to boxes. Many boxes were made without constructional fittings, relying on relatively sophisticated woodworking joinery and/or glueing. Some were simple in form, whilst others were highly decorated, luxury items, but the woodworking techniques involved in making boxes such as *8930, 8931* and *8935* show that they were made by craftsmen and were not home-made items. Boxes which have metal, bone or antler fittings and mounts could have been the products of more than one craftsman or a single craftsman with multiple skills.

Composite boxes

6964 and *8930–1* are three lids from rectangular boxes each probably made from at least six individual pieces of wood (lid, base and four sides). *8929* is a fragment of a wooden box with an attached decorative copper alloy strip. Without the other pieces, it is not possible to reconstruct exactly how the boxes which went with these particular lids and fragments were put together, but study of contemporary boxes and fittings and of woodworking techniques and tools allows us to make some suggestions as to the methods which could have been used in their construction. *6964* and *8929* are Anglo-Scandinavian, *8930–1* are medieval in date.

Metal constructional fittings such as angle-irons, staples and nails can be used to hold separate wooden pieces together, sometimes in conjunction with jointing and/or glueing. This was certainly true of many boxes found in 6th–7th century Anglo-Saxon graves (Morris 1984a, 67–71). Many Anglo-Scandinavian iron staples, hinges and hasps which could have been used as fittings to link box lids and bases have been found at Coppergate (pp.622–46, *AY* 17/6), but there are very few constructional fittings except for nails (none of which are directly associated with box construction) and three identifiable angle-irons or corner brackets (Fig.269, *AY* 17/6) which are too large to have been used on small boxes such as *6964*. This suggests that most of the bodies and lids of composite wooden boxes used in Anglo-Scandinavian York were constructed solely with pegging, jointing and glueing, and the lids and bodies fastened together by hinges and hasps.

There are no traces of either hinges or hasps on box lid *6964* which is a single riven board of oak 6mm thick onto which an arrangement of decorated bone mounts has been fixed with iron rivets (Fig.1116; see p.1954, *AY* 17/12 for a discussion of the mounts). A series of 10th–12th century wooden box lids decorated with bone or antler mounts provide good parallels for *6964*. An oak box lid over 250mm long was found during excavation for building work in York in 1906 in the Coppergate 'A' deposit (YORYM 500.1–6.48) which contained material of largely 10th century date (Smith 1907–9, 9, fig.4; Waterman 1959, 86–7, pl.XVII). It was decorated with a concentric rectangular arrangement of bone mounts, some backed with thin pieces of sheet copper alloy (Fig.917, *AY* 17/12). Other possibly 11th/12th century decorative bone and antler box mounts were found during excava-

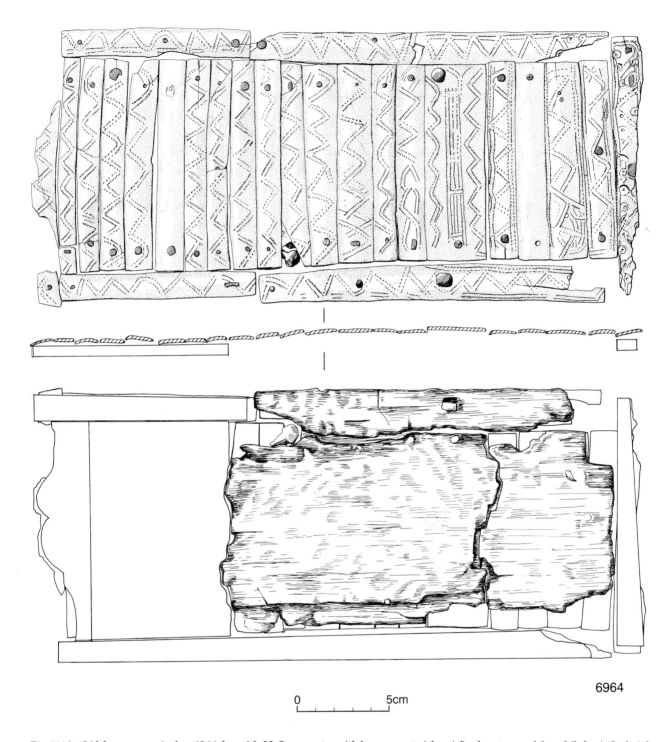

Fig.1116   *Lid from composite box 6964 from 16–22 Coppergate, with bone mounts (above) fixed on to an oak board (below). Scale 1:2*

tions under York Minster (Phillips and Heywood 1995, 418–20, fig.158). An early–mid 11th century rectangular oak box lid 340mm long and 95mm wide was found in a brushwood bed in house F253/1 in Christchurch Place, Dublin (Morris 1984a, fig.49, B85). It was originally decorated over its entire sur- face with rectangular antler mounts arranged side by side across the lid, surrounded by a frame of nar- rower mounts. This arrangement is similar to that used on *6964*. A 12th century box lid decorated over its entire surface with rectangular bone mounts was found in the excavation of a double ringwork castle

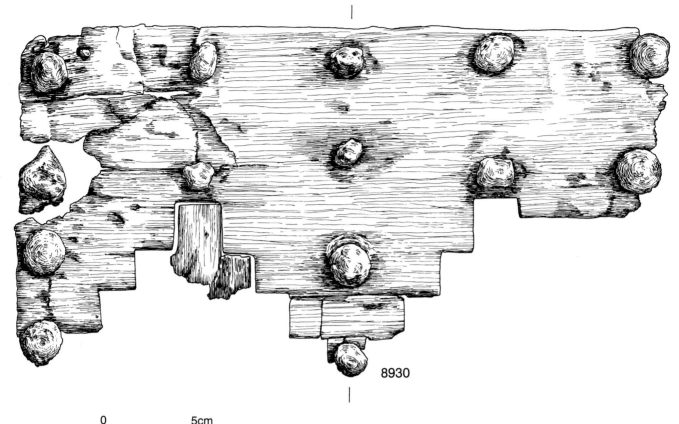

8930

0   5cm

Fig.1117   *Decorated oak lid of composite box 8930 from 16–22 Coppergate. Scale 1:2*

at Ludgershall in Wiltshire (Fig.918, *AY* 17/12; Wilson and Hurst 1966, 192, pl.XV). It is 266mm long and 185mm wide, and has two iron hinges and two iron hasps in their original positions. Some of the mounts are backed with thin sheets of lead alloy. Fragments of a wooden box lid (originally identified as a 17th century book cover) with two decorated bone mounts in situ fixed by iron rivets was found in 1913 at Telegraph Street in London, inside the north medieval town wall south of Moorgate (Morris 1984a, fig.50, B88). Its date is uncertain, but it is probably early medieval like the other examples described.

All these box lids have characteristics in common. They are made from flat, rectangular riven boards, usually in one piece, which would have been fastened directly onto the box body by hinges. The Dublin box originally had three iron hinges and there

are iron hinge rivets in three circular holes 5–6mm in diameter along the back of the lid. The wood grain of the box lids invariably runs along the length of the box and the positions of the fittings on the Dublin and Ludgershall boxes show that the bone mounts were fixed to the wooden lids before the lids were attached to the box bodies since the hinges are fitted over the bone mounts.

Some box bodies may have been fixed together using wooden dowels or pegs. Fragments of a small mid 6th century wooden box found in association with a small long brooch in the inhumation cemetery at Fonaby in Lincolnshire had peg holes near the edges and the site report recorded 'two pins of wood' which did not survive (Cook 1981, 55, 80, fig.23, 16, pl.VI, C). This is very rare evidence for a technique which may have been quite common in Anglo-Saxon and later box construction. Many Anglo-Saxon inhumations have various iron fittings such as hasps, hinges, locks and catches without constructional fittings, suggesting that the boxes were pegged or jointed (Morris 1984a, 61). The sides of the much larger Viking Age oak chest from Mästermyr were pegged to the ends and the base plank (Arwidsson and Berg 1983, 7, fig.14 and pl.15). There is evidence from Europe that some wooden boxes were pegged in the later medieval period, for example a late 13th–14th century salt box found at Buda in Hungary had its sides and base pegged together (Holl 1966, 47–8, Abb.48 and 56).

In woodworking, jointing is the technique of shaping components so as to produce a close fit between them. Joints often enable pieces to be firmly slotted into one another, but even in modern cabinet making joints are seldom the sole fixing mechanism, and most joints are glued. Where there is evidence for the use of joints such as dovetails on smaller Anglo-Saxon and medieval objects, glue might also have been used. Joints were also often used in combination with other fixing techniques.

Joints on small wooden objects such as boxes are usually cut with saws. It has been suggested that joints were not commonly used by the Anglo-Saxon joiner because he lacked accurate saws (Wilson 1976, 254). However, although saws are rarely recognised in the archaeological record (their teeth are fragile and sometimes unrecognisable as a result of heavy wear and corrosion), there are some fine examples from Anglo-Saxon England. A possible Anglo-Saxon saw fragment found at Leyland's Farm, Hockwold, Norfolk, has eight teeth per 20mm (Morris 1984a, fig.162, W91), another fragment from Icklingham, Suffolk, has eight or nine teeth per 20mm (Wilson 1968, 149, fig.4a), a fragment of a double-edged early 9th century saw from Thetford has eight teeth per 20mm on one edge and eleven per 20mm on the other (Goodall 1984a, fig.117, 77), and a fragment of an 8th century saw with three cross-set teeth was found at Six Dials, Southampton (Morris 1984a, fig.162, W97). These are comparable to a modern tenon saw which has eleven teeth per 20mm and could have been used to cut fine joints.

Fine saws were almost certainly used in Anglo-Scandinavian York in bone and antler comb making (7704, Fig.906, AY 17/12) and would also have been

available to the Anglo-Scandinavian joiner. Metalworking technology was advanced enough to provide steel for different grades of blades (pp.483–5, AY 17/6), and a blade with a very fine serrated edge was found at Coppergate (Fig.245, 2983, AY 17/6). With 26–8 teeth per 20mm this blade is the finest of its kind to have been found anywhere in Anglo-Saxon or Anglo-Scandinavian England and saws with teeth coarser than 2983 could have cut very fine joints on small wooden boxes. 2983 is more likely to have been used for bone and antler work. Fine saws come from sites contemporary with Anglo-Scandinavian York. Fragments of Viking Age saws have been found at Christchurch Place, Fishamble Street and High Street in Dublin, one with twelve teeth per 20mm (Morris 1984a, fig.162, W90i–iv). A fragment of an 11th century saw with seven teeth per 20mm was found on the site of a motte and bailey castle at Pinsley in Hampshire (ibid., W95), fragments of four saws have been found at Lagore Crannog (Hencken 1950, fig.42C), and two Viking Age saws were found in the Mästermyr toolchest, one of them with cross-set teeth and retaining its wooden handle (Arwidsson and Berg 1983, 13, 15, figs.26, 41 and 27, 42).

Judging from some contemporary wooden finds, dovetail joints were used in England at least by the 10th century and could have been used to construct the York boxes. They are strong joints cut with a fine saw, mallet and chisel, and are usually glued. A late 10th–early 11th century possible box base from Whitefriars, Norwich, has two edges with traces of dovetail joint cuts (Ayers and Murphy 1983, fig.20, 1), and when the author first examined the late Anglo-Saxon possible box side from Milk Street, London, before illustration and conservation, it had two very definite dovetail joint cuts along one edge (Pritchard and Morris 1991, fig.3.130, 393).

Mortice and tenon joints can take different forms but all involve a carved projection or tenon fitted into a similarly shaped hole or mortice. These are sometimes glued or pegged in place. The 13th/14th century lid 8931 had a rectangular wooden frame made of mortice and tenoned pieces supporting the infill of rods woven over laths stretched between the long frame sides (Fig.1118; see also Fig.971, p.2099). It is possible that the corresponding box which did not survive was constructed in a similar way, with wooden frames and woven infills making up the side panels and base. This lid has no parallels in either

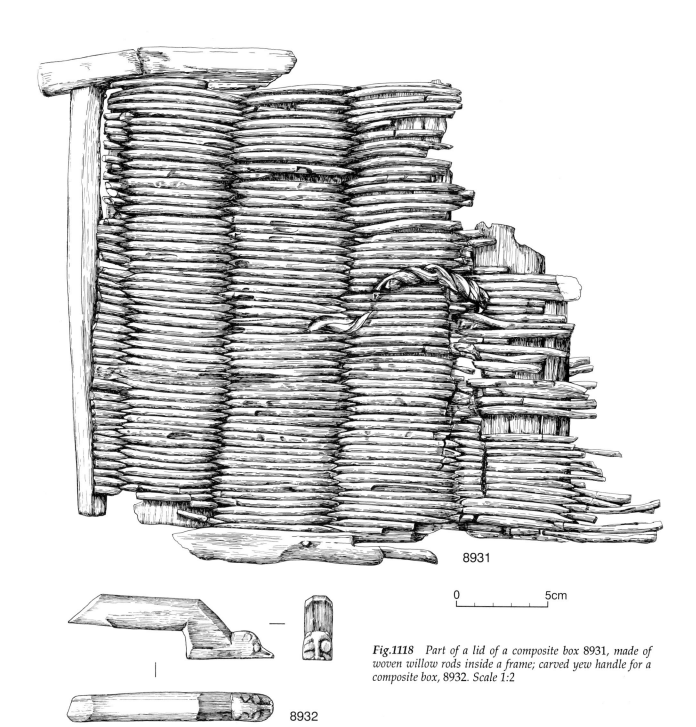

8931

8932

Fig.1118 *Part of a lid of a composite box 8931, made of woven willow rods inside a frame; carved yew handle for a composite box, 8932. Scale 1:2*

England or Europe and reconstructing the original form of the box is almost impossible. The woven lid may have been attached to a more conventional wooden body which had been jointed or nailed together. There are no metal components in *8931*, and even the hinges may have been organic, threaded through holes (one of which survives) in the back of the lid frame.

There are no surviving Anglo-Saxon or Anglo-Scandinavian boxes with mortice and tenon joints, but the base of the larger Viking Age oak chest from Mästermyr was jointed to the ends by a rectangular tenon at each end which fitted into a mortice in the ends (Arwidsson and Berg 1983, 7, figs.1 and 15). Other finely carpentered objects from England and Europe, mainly pieces of furniture, show that mortice and tenon joints were known and used by joiners. Two 4th century bench or chair components from Feddersen Wierde (Haarnagel 1979, Taf.39, 2 and 3), the 6th century chair from Cologne Cathedral (Werner 1964, fig.7), and one of the beds from the 9th century Oseberg ship burial (Brøgger and Shetelig 1928, pl.VII) have pegged mortice and tenon joints. Fragments of 11th century oak furniture from Westgate Street, Gloucester (Morris 1979, fig.16, 15 and 16), a 12th century possible bench end from Lurk Lane, Beverley (Foreman and Hall 1991, fig.123, 963A), a 9th century chair from the Oseberg ship burial (Brøgger and Shetelig 1928, pl.IX), an 11th century chair from Lund (Mårtensson and Wahlöö 1970, fig.33), a 10th century chair rail from Brook Street, Winchester (Keene 1990, fig.301, 3442), and a Viking Age chair rail from Christchurch Place, Dublin (Morris 1984a, M323), all have parts for unpegged mortice and tenon joints. The wooden reading desk now in St Radegund's convent in Poitiers, France, was probably not made in western Europe (Lasko 1971, 74, figs.59 and 60), but displays a wealth of mortice and tenon joints as they may have been used in box construction at the time.

Other joints which may have been used to construct the Anglo-Scandinavian and medieval boxes were mitred joints, as used together with dovetails on the 3rd century Roman box found at Bradwell, Buckinghamshire (Musty and Manning 1977, fig.4), and rabbeted joints as used on St Manchan's wooden shrine or reliquary, now kept at Boher, Co. Offaly (Kendrick and Senior 1937, fig.2). This is an Irish gabled box made with nails and rabbet or rebate joints by means of which the triangular ends of the box are sunk flush with the longer sides. Although there are no surviving parallels for its use in Anglo-Saxon or Anglo-Scandinavian England, this reliquary shows a contemporary type of joint which would have been useful for box construction, perhaps in conjunction with nails. It has been proposed that a rebate plane was used in England at least by the 11th century (Hewett 1982, 341) and such a tool would have been invaluable to a joiner if he used rebate joints on boxes. The base plank of the Mästermyr chest was not only morticed and tenoned to the ends, but also set into rebates in the ends and sides (Arwidsson and Berg 1983, fig.26).

Box lid *8930* was made from a riven oak board decorated with five rows of dome-headed iron nails running from back to front, and two stepped triangular panels of marquetry inlay set into corresponding slots cut into the back edge (Fig.1117). The complete lid was probably originally thicker than the surviving 10mm, judging by the length of the clenched nails which measure up to 25mm between the bottom of the nail head and the clench. The front edge is intact, but the back edge is broken and missing, along with most of the evidence for how the inlays were set into the slots. There could originally have been a second board underneath the first, fastened by the clenched nails and onto which the inlay panels were glued. Only a small fragment of inlay survives as a thin piece of oak with its grain set perpendicular to the grain of the box lid. There are saw cuts visible along the stepped edges of the inlay and the slots suggesting that medieval joiners in York were using fine saws to cut marquetry and presumably joints as well. This is a very rare piece of mid 14th century woodworking using an inlay technique, and there are no parallels. The hinges were probably fixed at the back of the inlay panels.

There are several surviving box fragments from other English sites which also suggest how the boxes corresponding to lids *6964* and *8930–1* may have been put together. Two possible 10th/11th century oak box sides were found at Brook Street, Winchester (Keene

Fig.1119 Yew handle 8932 with a carved zoomorphic head. Actual length 114mm

1990, fig.302, *3445–6*). One has two nails driven into the end grain at one end, another driven into the end grain at the opposite end, and three nails driven vertically into the lower edge originally to secure the base. The second side has two nails driven into one end, one into the opposite end and four driven vertically into the lower edge. Part of the upper edge of the latter board is cut away perhaps to form a handhold or a position for a hasp. The box would have been approximately 380mm long, 325mm wide and 215mm high, somewhat wider but only a little longer than *6964*, and approximately the same size as the boxes to which lids *8930–1* would have been fixed. A late 13th century box side found at Cuckoo Lane, Southampton (Platt and Coleman-Smith 1975, fig.234, 1683), also has traces of five nails driven vertically into one long edge from underneath and the upper edge has a rectangular notch, presumably for a hasp. The lid and back of a wooden box 350mm long, 124mm wide and 110mm high were found in the 9th century Oseberg ship burial (Brøgger and Shetelig 1928, 198–200, fig.132). Splits in the lid had been repaired by decorated copper alloy mounts and the lid was fastened to the back by two looped hinge fittings similar to *3480* found at 16–22 Coppergate (Fig.268, *AY* 17/6). The corners of the back piece have small rectangular slots cut into them, possibly as joint seatings for the short sides, joints which were used in conjunction with nails or pegs since each short side of the back was perforated by two holes and there were four holes along the lower edge of the back.

The evidence for the use of glues or resins is sparse. However, the inlays from box lid *8930* were probably glued down and the carved yew handle *8932* (Figs.1118–19) might either have broken from a box on which it had been carved all in one piece or glued in position. Many joints were probably glued. A box found in a late 13th century pit at Cuckoo Lane, Southampton (Platt and Coleman-Smith 1975, 235, fig.234, 1682 and 1684), was almost certainly glued together. Four sides, a base and a separate lid survive, roughly made from re-used oak bucket staves. The pieces are complete but there are no joints, pegs, nails or other constructional fittings, although corrosion adhering to the outside front of the box next to a carved key hole suggests that there was originally an iron lock mechanism. There is no technique other than glueing which can explain how this box was fixed together.

Solid box

8933 is a solid rectangular lid cut from the thick end of a larger radially split oak plank (Fig.1120). It was carved with a flat upper surface and a rebated lower edge, giving a flange around a central rectangular block 56 × 46mm whose measurements probably define the dimensions of the interior of the box which does not survive. A small box which matched the lid could also have been made from a solid block with a central rectangular hollow. There was no hinging mechanism for the lid, which was kept in place by the fit between lid and body. The incised cross on the lid could have been an owner's or maker's mark, or even a symbolic mark to keep evil away from the contents of the box.

The lid is undated as it was found in an unstratified context. There are no exact parallels for this particular type of fitted lid and box construction from England or Scandinavia, but fragments of small Viking Age hollowed boxes found at Fishamble Street in Dublin (Lang 1988, figs.10 and 83) may be from boxes of this kind. They do not have ledges or rebates for sliding lids, and must have had fitted lids which have not survived. Another 11th century box fragment from Christchurch Place in Dublin (ibid.,

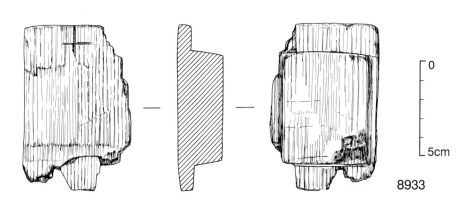

0

5cm

8933

Fig.1120   Part of a carved lid from a solid box, 8933. Scale 1:2

fig.65) is fragmentary and could be from a box with either a fitted or sliding lid. Making small one-piece solid boxes with one-piece lids seems to have been a common practice over a long period of time, and *8933* could be either an Anglo-Scandinavian or a medieval box.

A late Saxon (possibly 10th/11th century) house-shaped box with solid boxwood lid and body hinged together and carved with relief scenes from the life of Christ measures 152 × 70 × 89mm (Nelson 1936, 91–100, fig.1 and pls.XX–XXI), while a similar early 14th century house-shaped box made from boxwood with its lid and body hinged together measures 115 × 41 × 32mm (Westwood 1876, 399–400, figs.1–6). This box was carved with relief 'grotesques'. Both these boxes are in private collections. Some of the iron and non-ferrous metal hinges found on Coppergate (e.g. pp.640–2, *AY* 17/6; Ottaway and Rogers *AY* 17 in prep., sfs1019, 1624, 2036, 2519, 2729, 3536) could have been used on solid boxes like these or on boxes with a composite construction (box fragment *8929*, for example, had a copper alloy strip attached, *10374, AY* 17/14).

Boxes with sliding lids were hollowed from single blocks of wood with a groove or ledge cut around the top of the box to act as a runner for a thin, flat rectangular lid. Sometimes the external surfaces were carved with patterns. No examples have yet been found on English sites, but there are Migration period examples from Vimose (Engelhardt 1869, pl.17, 9 and 10), Garbolle, Stenmagle, in Denmark (Baeksted 1947, 202–10, fig.1) and Dyster, Akerhus, in Norway (Rygh 1885, 9, fig.180a–c), and Viking Age ones from 10th/11th century contexts at Christchurch Place, Fishamble Street and High Street, Dublin (Morris 1984a, fig.62, B141–2; Lang 1988, figs.6, 26 and 98), and Birsay on Orkney. The latter is dated to the 8th to 10th centuries on account of its decoration (Cursiter 1885, figs.1 and 2; Stevenson 1951–2, 187–90, figs.1–2, pl.XL).

Lath-walled boxes

Six boxes from 16–22 Coppergate, *8934–9*, and one from the College of the Vicars Choral, Bedern, *9235*, are of a type which have no metal or other fittings and were constructed only of wood. They are examples of circular or oval boxes often called chip boxes in Europe but which will be referred to here as lath-walled boxes after the way their walls are made. The York boxes and parallels found at other sites in Eng-

land and Europe are constructed from several pieces of wood, and in the cases where more than one part survives, as in *8935*, it appears that they are often made of different forms and species of wood due to the woodworking techniques involved and the properties of the species used for each piece.

The bases are thick, flat, circular or oval pieces made from radially or tangentially split boards which can form a rigid support for the walls. *8934–5, 8937* and *8939* are radially split oak boards, as are bases on the 9th–11th century Hedeby box (Fig.1121; Schietzel 1970, Abb.6, 1), two bases dated to the 12th/13th and 14th century from two sites in King's Lynn (Clarke and Carter 1977, fig.172, 62 and 60A–C), and the base of a 13th century box from Lydford Castle, Devon (Saunders 1980, fig.27, 1). *8938* is a tangentially split maple board. Oval bases found in 7th century levels at Lagore Crannog and 6th–9th century levels at Ballinderry Crannog 1 were made of yew boards (Hencken 1950, fig.78; 1942, fig.26), and an oval base found near Ballinderry Crannog 2 (Morris 1984a, fig.63, B148) was made of willow.

The walls can be narrow or broad and are formed from a single lath of wood which has either been radially or tangentially split, or tangentially sawn, then probably thinned and smoothed further by shaving. The species used for the walls had to be strong, pliable and flexible. The walls of *8935–6* are made from ash laths only 4mm thick, but whereas the ash lath in *8935* had been radially split, *8936* had been tangentially split or sawn, then smoothed. Other boxes with ash walls are the two 9th–11th century boxes from Hedeby (Schietzel 1970, Abb.6, 1 and 2).

Fig.1121 Lath-walled box from Hedeby, very similar to 8935

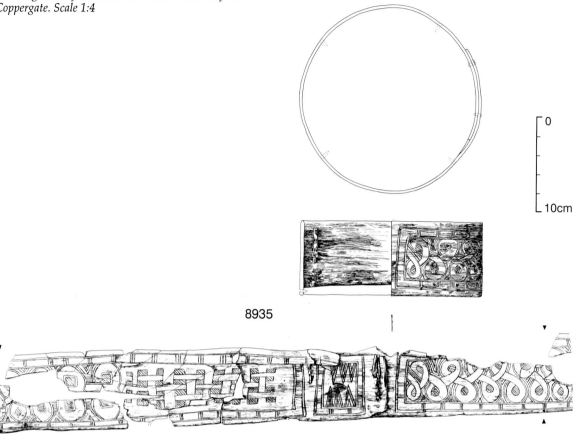

Fig.1122 *Fragments of a circular lath-walled box 8935 from 16–22 Coppergate. Scale 1:4*

8935

The 14th century box from King's Lynn had birch walls, the 13th century box from Lydford had willow lath walls and 12th and 14th century boxes from Novgorod had birch bark walls which were used in the same way as the laths (Kolchin 1968, fig.41, 2 and 1; 1989, pls.70–3). The oak lath fragments of *9235* from Bedern may be parts of a lath-walled vessel.

The thin laths may have been soaked in water or perhaps steamed to make them pliable. The lath would then have been bent (perhaps round a block) to form a circular or oval shape and the overlapping ends sewn or pegged together. The ends of the ash lath in box *8935* were overlapped and sewn together by two vertical rows of an unidentified organic stitching (separated by a rectangular panel of incised ornament), one of which was an elaborate row of looped chain stitches (Fig.1122). The two boxes from Hedeby are extremely similar to *8935*, especially in that each has two vertical rows of organic stitching separated by a rectangular panel of incised ornament. The stitching is threaded through regular circular holes probably augered through the lath (Fig.1121).

Lath *8936* is very fragmentary but the pieces can be reconstructed and three very fine slits and a circular hole in a vertical line show where the ends of the lath were stitched together. Fragments of a lath with a row of five circular stitch holes decorated with incised lines was found in the 9th century Oseberg ship burial, and fragments of another lath with similar decoration was found in the Gamlebyen excavations in Oslo (Weber 1990, figs.40b and a). A 1st/2nd century lath found at Feddersen Wierde had its overlapping ends sewn together by two vertical rows of bast fibre stitching (Haarnagel 1979, Taf.44, 3). The lath from the small 14th century oval box from King's Lynn had its ends tapered to a narrow strip which was then overlapped and fitted through a slot in the lath, then secured by being folded round itself. The 13th century box from Lydford had its overlapping ends pegged together.

The lower edges of the completed lath circle would have been fixed to the rigid base by wooden pegs through holes or slots in the lath and into the base edges. The base of *8935* has slightly thinned

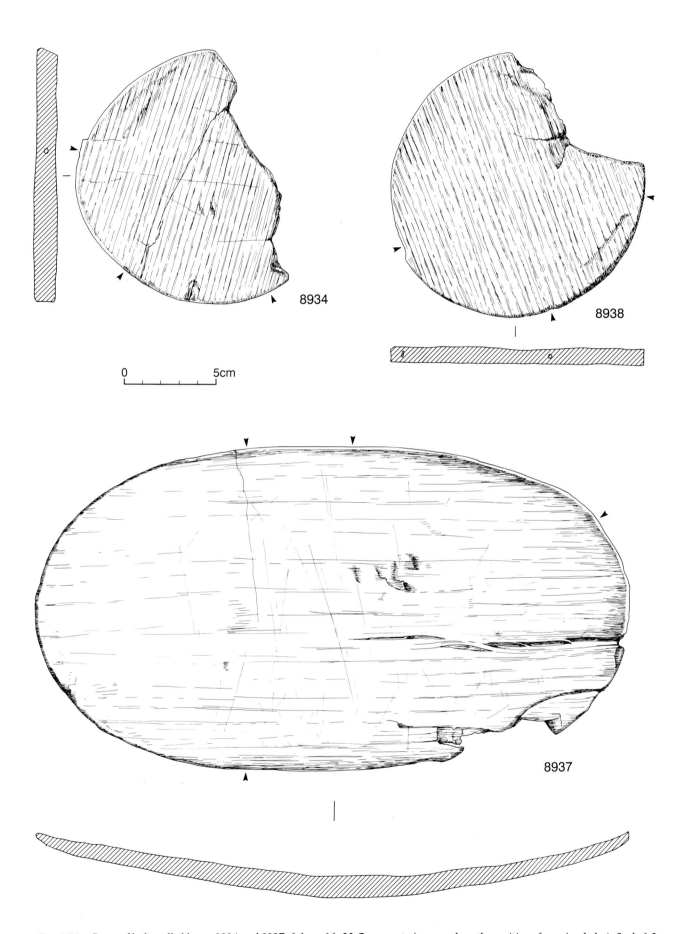

0   5cm

8934

8938

8937

Fig.1123   *Bases of lath-walled boxes 8934 and 8937–8 from 16–22 Coppergate (arrows show the position of pegs/pegholes). Scale 1:2*

edges and is pegged to the walls by five wooden pegs, one piercing two thicknesses of wall at the overlap. The Bedern lath wall fragments *9235* retain a fragment of peg or organic stitching in one of the holes. Lath *8936* has only a small section of lower edge surviving with possibly two peg holes. The maple base *8938* and the oak base *8934* each had three surviving peg holes, the latter with at least one surviving wooden peg (Fig.1123). The oak base *8937* had at least four pegs in situ in its edges (Fig.1123), and the oak base *8939* had twelve pegs, one square, one rectangular and the others probably circular in cross-section (Fig.1124). The boxes from Ballinderry Crannogs 1 and 2 and Lagore Crannog each had six pegs, and the box from Lydford had at least six tapering pegs 27mm long to secure the walls to the base.

Bases for lath-walled boxes could easily be mistaken for bases of stave-built vessels unless they have pegs or peg holes surviving in their edges, or a characteristic V-sectioned notch cut into the edge of the base to allow one of the overlapping ends of the lath wall to be seated and to prevent the overlap standing out too much. The bases of *8934–5* and *8938–9* all have the characteristic notch, as do the bases on the boxes already described from Lagore, Hedeby, Lydford, a 15th century box from Lübeck (Falk 1981, Abb.8, 6) and at least two bases from Oslo (Weber 1990, fig.38a and c).

Lids for lath-walled boxes have not been found in York. The two birch bark boxes from Novgorod, constructed in exactly the same way as those from York, did have lids without hinges or fixing mechanisms, made in a similar fashion to the boxes, but shorter and fitted over the rim edge. These lids would leave no evidence on the box walls apart from possible discolouration or wear marks. A small oval lath-walled box found with a bone spindle whorl 4ft below the surface of an undisturbed bog at Maumnahaltora in Co. Kerry is unusual in that both the oval base and a similar lid are firmly pegged in (Morris 1984a, fig.63, B149). The fragments of wall which survive show that the box was about 50mm high, 140mm long and 55mm wide. Unless it was a permanently closed case, this box must have had a different opening and closing mechanism to the York boxes, perhaps a flap in the side.

The York boxes vary in shape and size. *8937* is oval, whereas the other five were circular (Figs.1123–4).

8934, 8936 and *8938–9* would have been small circular containers approximately 140–150mm in diameter, *8935* was slightly larger at 200mm diameter, but *8937* was a large oval box over 320mm long. It is uncertain what these boxes would have contained, but the lath walls of both *8935* and *8936* have dark colouration on the external and internal surfaces which is revealed on *8935* in a broken section where the wood is markedly lighter in colour, and on the external walls of *8936* where one end was overlapped and the surface which was under the overlap is lighter in colour and preserves the outline of the overlapped end. Also on *8936*, where there is a fragment of pegged lower edge, the thickness of the base can be measured in a lighter-coloured band which is not stained.

Lath-walled boxes appear to have been made and used in north-west Europe over a long period of time. Fragments of a decorated lath-walled box were found at the Iron Age site of Hallstatt in Austria (Kramer 1960, Taf.2). The way they were all made is sophisticated enough to have required specialised woodworking skills, but is simple and effective enough to have required no metal components and could have provided a range of sizes of circular and oval wooden enclosed containers. The tradition of using thin laths of wood whose grain runs around the box has continued to the present day and there are many recent examples of lath-walled boxes, measures and sieves (Pinto 1949, pls.37 and 67). The earliest English examples are two laths which were found in the Late Iron Age lake village settlement at Glastonbury (Bulleid and Gray 1911, 311ff; Weber 1990, fig.40d–e). Each has incised geometric decoration on the external surface and a clear undecorated lower edge which is peforated by peg holes; although there are no surviving Anglo-Saxon examples of lath-walled boxes, the same technique was still being used in medieval England as shown by *8939* and the two examples from King's Lynn.

The late 9th century box *8935* and the complete 9th–11th century box from Hedeby (Figs.1121–2) are very similar indeed. Both are 180–200mm in diameter and 70–80mm high and are constructed of exactly the same species of wood (oak for the base and ash for the walls). They are both decorated with incised designs which in themselves are different but which are laid out in the same pattern, a long continuous panel and a smaller rectangular panel between the two vertical rows of stitches. They even

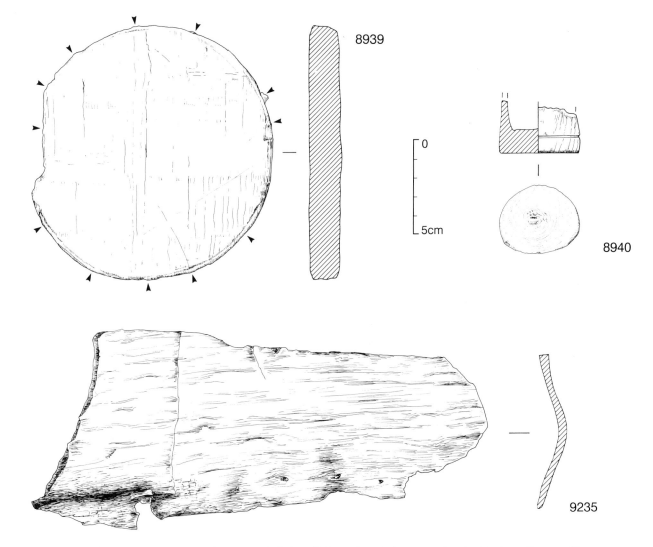

Fig.1124 *Base of a lath-walled box 8939; fragments of a lath-walled vessel 9235; fragment of a cylindrical spindle-turned box 8940 (arrows show the position of pegs/pegholes). 8939–40 are from 16–22 Coppergate, 9235 is from Bedern. Scale 1:2*

have similarities of detail in that the corners of the overlapping ends are truncated. It seems very likely that these similarities stem not only from the same tradition, but possibly from the same site — perhaps they were even made in the same workshop. Whether they were made in Hedeby and brought to York, or vice versa, is uncertain. Lathe-turned wooden bowls with incised decoration on flat, everted rims have also been found at both York (8553) and Hedeby (Jankuhn 1943, Abb.85–6). There is evidence for contact between the two centres in the form of a fragment of a silver coin minted at Hedeby c.850 and found at 16–22 Coppergate (*AY* 18/1, 55, pl.IV, 45). Three of the six lath-walled boxes from York (8934–6) date from the earliest phase of Scandinavian settlement on the site and could have been brought there

by Danish settlers rather than being made in York. *8937–8* date to Period 5B when there was intense occupation and manufacturing activity on the 16–22 Coppergate site, and these two boxes are more likely to have been made in Anglo-Scandinavian York. Incised decoration on the lath found at Oseberg consists of cross-hatched lines and a curved line infilled with straight parallel lines (Weber 1990, fig.40b). This pattern of incised decoration is present on the ash spindle-turned cup *8614* (Fig.1031, p.2180) which also dates from the earliest phase of Anglo-Scandinavian settlement on the site.

Lathe-turned box (Fig.1124)

8940 is a base/wall fragment of a distinct type of cylindrical spindle-turned container shown by excavated examples to have been common in Britain and northern Europe in the 12th to 15th centuries (Morris 1984a, 184), although Roman examples do survive (Marsden 1966, fig.19). They were made as matching box and lid sets, with a small cylindrical lid fitting tightly over the flange/rebate on the box rim, but the two pieces rarely survive together as they do on a late 14th–mid 15th century set from Westwick Street, Norwich (Morris 1993a, fig.63, 598). *8940* would originally have had a matching lid but this was not found during the excavation, and it is not possible to reconstruct its original height since the box rim does not survive. Most of these boxes are very small, measuring only 40–60mm in diameter; at 43mm diameter, *8940* is among the smallest. Further English parallels for *8940* have been found at various London sites (Henig 1975, fig.25, 9; Morris 1984a, fig.152, L246ii–iv, L247v–vi and L248; Egan 1998, nos.613–20), at Kewstoke church in Somerset where a box without a lid was used as a container in a 12th–13th century stone reliquary built into a 14th century wall under the sill of a nave window (Morris 1984a, fig.152, L252), in Southampton (Platt and Coleman-Smith 1975, fig.229, 1638–9) and at Aldwark in York (1976.15, sf209; Morris 1984a, fig.152, L250). The latter is much larger than the Coppergate box, measuring 123mm in height and 93mm in diameter, and must have had a completely different function although the techniques used to manufacture both were exactly the same (see pp.2122, 2136–42).

The boxes were probably made to contain a variety of small objects, ointments, powders or similar substances, but only rarely does any trace of the contents survive. A fragment from Baynard's House, Queen Victoria Street, London, contained a yellow deposit with a fine hair in it which has been interpreted as possibly paint with the hair from a brush (Egan 1998, no.620).

Chests

8941 and *3386* are single heavy riven boards of oak now measuring 268mm and 325mm wide respectively (although *3386* could have been larger). They are parts of solid plank-built chests which were a common and versatile method of transporting and storing goods and valuables in the Anglo-Scandinavian period. They were both cut from large, thick planks which had been radially split from felled oak trees originally exceeding 650mm in diameter. Each board is 21–23mm thick. *9236*, found in mid–late 14th century levels at Bedern, is also a heavy tangentially split board which may have been part of a chest. It split along the grain and was repaired by a smaller radially split oak board nailed across and perpendicular to the split (Fig.1126).

An iron looped hinge strap attached to the surviving intact edge of *3386* suggests that it is either the back panel or lid of a chest, but there are no sur-

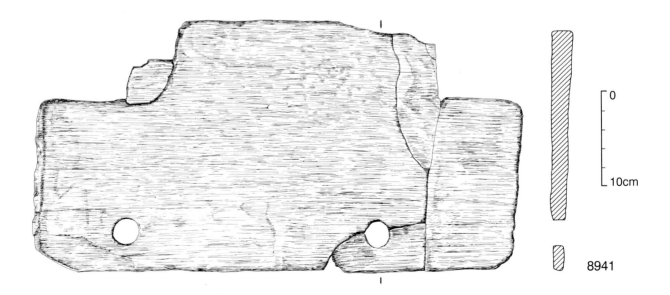

Fig.1125   Lid or side of oak chest 8941 *from 16–22 Coppergate. Scale 1:4*

viving edges which can give information as to how the chest was constructed (Fig.1127). *8941* may be the lid or side of a chest (Fig.1125). Many iron fittings found at Coppergate may have been used on similar large wooden chests, including nails, staples, hinge straps and hasps (pp.608–46, *AY* 17/6). Surviving Viking Age chests are usually jointed together using a mixture of techniques, but their fittings are often nailed on. Only three corner brackets were found at 16–22 Coppergate (Fig.269, *AY* 17/6), and since this type of iron fitting was sometimes used to strengthen

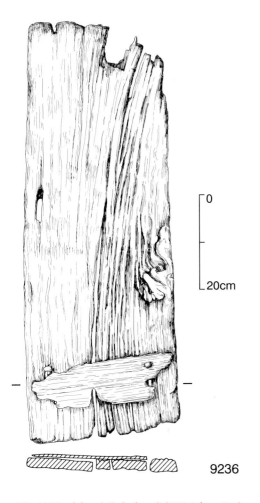

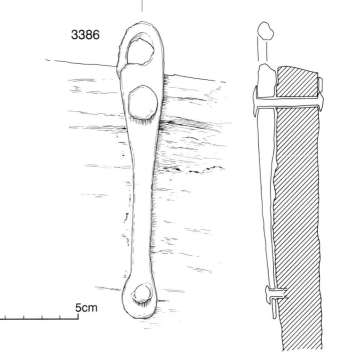

3386

Fig.1126 (above) Oak chest lid 9236 from Bedern. Scale 1:8

9236

Fig.1127 (right and below) Oak chest lid or back fragment 3386 from the Coppergate watching brief site. Scale 1:5, detail of hinge and section through wood 1:2

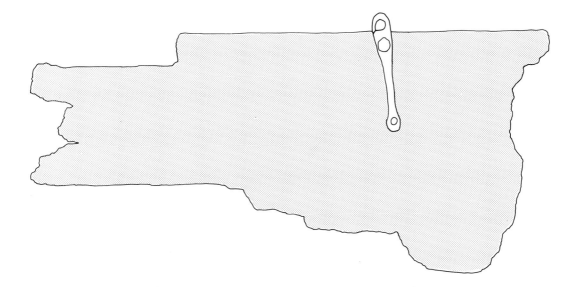

2299

coffins, wagons and other structural woodwork (ibid., 642), it is by no means certain that these were chest fittings.

Hinge straps are found on the Viking Age Mästermyr oak chest, the closest parallel for *8941* and *3386*, and suggest how they could have been made without the use of metal constructional fittings. As already described in the discussion of smaller boxes, its sides, ends and base are jointed together using a combination of mortice and tenon and rebate joints and wooden pegs. The ends and the sides are also slotted together using half-lap joints as corner seatings where alternating rectangular notches in the top and bottom of the ends and sides fit into each other (Arwidsson and Berg 1983, pl.15). *8941* has two deeply cut squared notches at two corners which could be part of a lap joint system of fixing it to the other sides, if it were a chest side and not a lid. The two circular holes could also be large mortice holes for tenons in the base. Alternatively, if *8941* were a lid, the notches may fit around corner posts, and the circular holes may have held organic hinges, perhaps of rope. Berg considers that without metal constructional fittings, the all-wooden jointed construction of the Mästermyr chest is rather weak, and that 200 years later in Norway this type of construction was replaced by a stronger one where side planks were slotted into corner posts (ibid., 26). If *8941* is a chest lid which would have fitted around square corner posts, it may belong to an early chest made in this stronger fashion.

A riven panel with deeply cut squared notches at two corners, similar to *8941*, was used in the back of a box-construction chair from Torpe, Hallingdal, Sweden, now in the Nordiska Museet in Stockholm (Brøgger and Shetelig 1928, 114, fig.60). The panel is much later than *8941*, dating from the second half of the 13th century, and was jointed into the chair legs and back struts, but it is not impossible that panels like *8941* could have been used in a similar way.

Three chests found in the Oseberg ship burial were also constructed using joints (ibid., figs.65–8, 149, 156 and 178). Oseberg chest 149 has ends and sides seated at the corners using half-lap joints, and its base is rebated into the wall panels as on the Mästermyr chest, but it also has metal strapping which is nailed on.

Nothing is known about *8942* except that it was a lid with two bars, one ash and one oak, and could have been a chest lid.

Furniture

Furniture in the British Isles dating to before the 12th century is very rare, represented by surviving examples such as the plank-built 'Bede's chair' in St Paul's church in Jarrow, Tyne and Wear, and a few excavated components. Three possible furniture components (*8943–5*), stool seat fragments (*8946–7*) and evidence for the manufacture of garderobe seats and lids (*8684, 8689* and *8951*) are welcome additions from pre-12th century York. Medieval furniture, especially dating to the 12th to 15th centuries, has been studied from surviving non-excavated pieces and pictorial and documentary references (Eames 1977). A stool seat (*8948*) and two garderobe seats (*8949–50*) are examples of medieval furniture found at Coppergate. Garderobe seat *9176* came from an unstratified level on the Coppergate watching brief site.

Most surviving, unexcavated pieces of furniture are prestigious items with ecclesiastical, royal or noble connections, and are very different in character from the few pieces of furniture which would have been used in the majority of Anglo-Saxon, Anglo-Scandinavian and medieval households. Chairs were very unusual items in lower status households, although in an 11th century document they are listed among the items which the good reeve should provide for the Anglo-Saxon manor (Cunningham 1910, 573 and 575). Chests, seats, foot-stools and chairs (OE *cyste, hlydan, sceamelas, stolas*) are mentioned in this list. Some indication as to the small range and simplicity of the majority of furniture is shown by probate inventories and *principalia* lists (Field 1965), where the most usual forms of furniture mentioned are benches and stools.

Most of the furniture of this period was made using one of two methods: either an open-, post- or stick-construction where legs, arms, panels and uprights were joined by stretchers, themselves sometimes joined by smaller rods, or a box- or panel-construction where sides, backs, seats and legs were made from squared baulks or flat boards of timber jointed together. The stretchers and rods of open-construction furniture were either carved or lathe-turned.

Furniture components (Fig.1128)

The augered holes in *8943–5* suggest they were parts of furniture made using an open-construction.

8943 is probably the flat arm of a chair. It is a riven board whose sides have been tapered so that one end is wider than the other, but both ends have been smoothed and rounded. Four augered holes 23mm in diameter along its length provided the means of fixing upright stretchers or rods from below; one of the holes retains fragments of the tenon from one of these rods. This suggests that the chair, which was found in late 9th/early 10th century levels, was made using an open-construction. The closest parallel for *8943* is a similar 9th century chair arm found in the ditch of rath 1 at Lissue in Co. Antrim (Bersu 1947, fig.114, 7). This was slightly larger than *8943* but had tapering sides, one surviving rounded end, and three holes along its length, an oval hole at the wide end and two circular holes further along.

Open-construction chairs were made from carved and/or lathe-turned components. Spindle-turned rods can be made from small lengths of roundwood or split sections and could have been used for most of the structure of a chair except for the seat as in the 6th century chair from Cologne Cathedral (Doppelfeld 1963, 50–1; Werner 1964, fig.7) and the 12th century chair in Hereford Cathedral (Barrett 1980, 6; Morris 1984a, fig.84, M325). Although no spindle-turned stretchers or rods have been found at 16–22 Coppergate, some of the pieces of spindle-turned end-waste (e.g. *8224–8*) are the kinds of waste products which could have been produced in the turning of such components, and *8943* could have been used in conjunction with either turned or carved stretchers. Two examples of turned stretchers have been excavated from English sites: an early–mid 10th century beech rail 302mm long and 45mm in diameter, with two mortice holes in one side and broken tenons at each end, and decorated with incised grooves, was found in house XII at Brook Street, Winchester (Keene 1990, fig.301, *3442*); and a late 12th–early 13th century oak rail from Eastgate Street, Beverley, which had only one intact end with a circular tenon, and a mortice hole on one side (Morris and Evans 1992, fig.95, 648). Other open-construction chairs include an 11th century example from Lund (Mårtensson and Wahlöö 1970, 28, fig.33), a carved 10th century ash chair leg/upright from Brook Street, Winchester (Keene 1990, fig.301, *3439*), a Viking Age chair rail and a possible seat and backrest from Christchurch

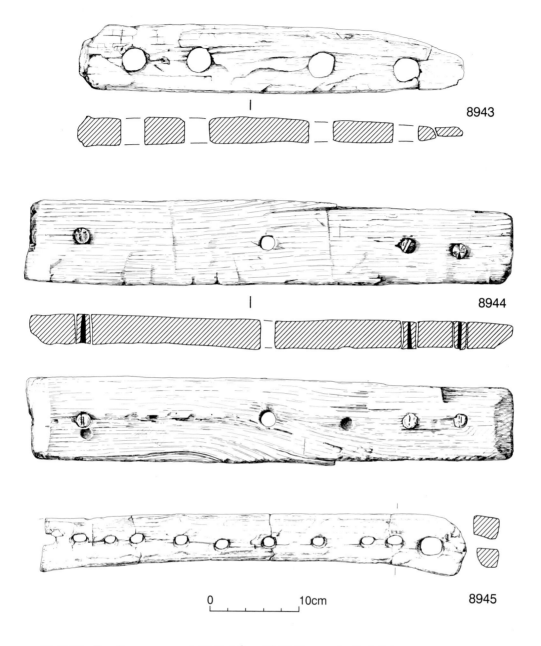

Fig.1128 *Furniture components 8943–5 from 16–22 Coppergate. Scale 1:4*

Place, Dublin (Morris 1984a, M323–4), 11th–12th century panel fragments from Westgate Street, Gloucester (Morris 1979, fig.16, 15–16), and a possible chair leg from Perth (ibid., M326).

8944–5 are 10th century furniture components, probably made using the open-construction method, but in the absence of other pieces it is impossible to be certain exactly what the complete pieces of furniture were. *8945* is a maple baulk which has been squared down from roundwood and has a hole 29mm in diameter at one end, traces of a similar large hole at the other end which is broken, and nine more holes 16–18mm in diameter along its length. These smaller holes were drilled at an oblique angle, suggesting that the stretchers which were fixed in them were also set at an angle. It is possibly the back or side piece of a chair, bench or rack. Leather thonging with stitch holes found in three of the holes also suggests that the furniture may have been upholstered in some way, perhaps with leather. *8944* is a tangentially split board whose short ends are both chamfered on one side. There are four complete augered holes 16–17mm in diameter spaced unevenly along the board, three of which still contain fragments of wedged tenons which have probably broken off the ends of stretchers with tenons similar to those from Winchester and Beverley described above. There are also two unfinished holes which do not fully perforate the board. 8944 is possibly a batten for a caskhead or a lid such as 8951, but the wedged tenons leave open the possibility that it is a furniture component.

'Bede's chair' in Jarrow, two 11th century bench ends from Christchurch Place, Dublin (Lang 1988, 65, 75, figs.38 and 56), an 11th–12th century bench end from Beverley (Foreman and Hall 1991, fig.123, 963A), and a 12th century boarded chair in Stanford Bishop church, Hereford and Worcester (Eames 1977, pl.56), are examples of panel-construction furniture found in the British Isles, and two panels from the Migration period site at Feddersen Wierde (Haarnagel 1979, Taf.39, 2 and 3), the boarded beechwood chair and three beds from the Oseberg ship (burial dated 843) (Brøgger and Shetelig 1928, figs.40, 42–3

and 53 and pls.VII–IX) and five beds from the Gokstad ship (burial dated c.900) (Nicolaysen 1882, pl. VII, 2) are examples from continental sites.

Stools (Fig.1129)

During the Anglo-Scandinavian and medieval periods stools were made using an open- or stick-construction. 8946–8 are single, heavy boards of oak and possibly burrwood, shaped to form semi-circular or D-shaped seats for stools. 8947 is the smallest and was made from a riven board with roughly squared edges. It is possible that the original seat was much rounder in plan (possibly even circular), and fragments are now missing from the edges. Three holes 22mm in diameter were augered through the seat in a triangular arrangement, each retaining a fragment of the end of the stool leg which was fitted into it from below. 8948 was made from a thicker, tangentially split board and is much larger than 8947. One surface which is slightly hollowed and also very battered, worn and criss-crossed by linear cuts is likely to have been the upper surface. The stool may have

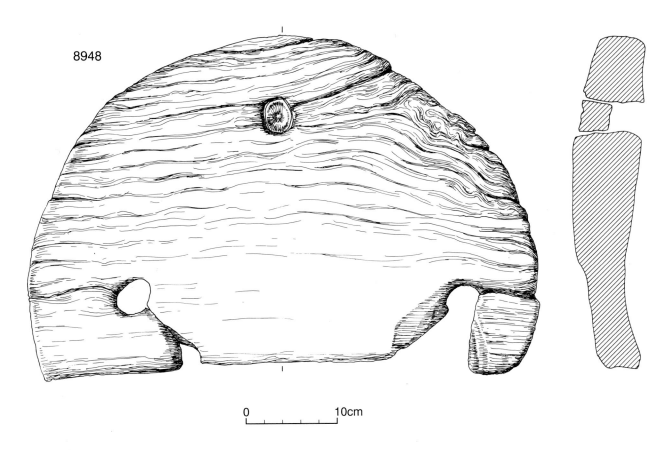

8948

0   10cm

Fig.1129   Oak three-legged stool seat 8948 from 16–22 Coppergate. Scale 1:4

ended its life as a work bench or it could have been intermittently used as a cutting surface while still serving as a stool. It has three holes 36mm in diameter in a triangular arrangement, with a fragment of a roundwood tenon 33mm in diameter remaining in one hole. *8946* is a fragment of a larger stool, possibly originally sub-rectangular, and with a concave upper surface like *8948*. Only two holes survive in two corners — 26–28mm and 30mm diameter. A large four-legged oak stool/bench found in the early 9th century Oseberg ship burial (Brøgger and Shetelig 1928, fig.104) is a similar piece of furniture which may have served a dual purpose as a work bench and a seat.

Similar three-legged stools with semi-circular seats have been found in early–mid 10th century levels in house IX at Brook Street, Winchester (Keene 1990, fig.301, *3441*), in 11th century levels at Fishamble Street, Dublin (Morris 1984a, M338), and in 11th century levels in house II in Lund (Blomqvist and Mårtensson 1963, fig.115). The Winchester stool had two surviving legs, one of beech, one of sweet chestnut. They were roughly carved and one was secured at the top with a wedge in the same way as the tenons on component *8944*. D-shaped holes in the centres of the Winchester and Dublin seats would have provided handholds for lifting the stools. Other stools of the period have rounded rectangular seats with four legs, one in each corner. For example, an 11th century four-legged stool seat was found at High Street, Dublin (Morris 1984a, M339), and a small four-legged stool was found in Viking Age levels at Hedeby (Graham-Campbell 1980, 14, pl.29).

Garderobe seats and lid (Fig.1131)

8949 and *8950* are single heavy riven boards of oak 0·98m and 1·07m long respectively; *9176* from the Coppergate watching brief site is a fragment of a similar board, now 365mm long. All three are seats from medieval garderobes which were made using

Fig.1130   Garderobe seat 8950 from 16–22 Coppergate in situ. Scale unit 10cm

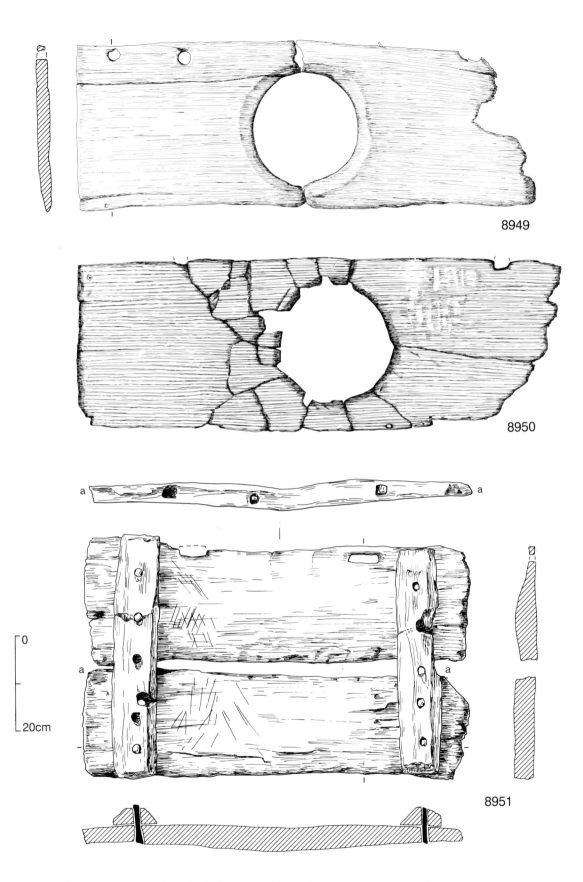

Fig.1131 *Garderobe seats 8949–50 and garderobe lid 8951, all from 16–22 Coppergate. Scale 1:8*

a box- or panel-construction and each has evidence for a single large circular hole, 230–50mm diameter. Like chests *3386* and *8941*, the seats were cut from large, thick planks of oak which had been radially split from felled oak trees. In the case of *8949* and *8950*, however, the trees originally exceeded 740mm in diameter and the radially split boards are 28–42mm thick, so they are generally much bigger and heavier than those used to make the chests. *8950* was found within a circular pit (Fig.1130).

There are several other garderobe seats from British sites to compare with those from York, some of which were also found discarded in the cess pits or garderobes over which they were probably used. The earliest is a semi-circular seat made from an oak board over 20mm thick which had been re-used as part of a pit revetment at Trichay Street in Exeter (Allan and Morris 1984, fig.179, 76). Dendrochronological analysis shows that the tree from which it was made had been felled around AD 949 ± 9 years. A late 13th–early 14th century stone-lined latrine pit excavated on the Brooks site, Winchester, contained not only structural timbers from a latrine building, but also oak timbers from the garderobe itself and its walnut tongue-and-grooved plank seat (Scobie et al. 1991, fig.40; Hillam 1992, 18). Another early 14th century seat made from two tongue-and-grooved oak boards was found on the High Street/Blackfriargate site in Hull (Watkin 1987, fig.125, 372). A 14th century seat made from a pine board 792mm long, 366mm wide and 42mm thick was found in occupation material over a cobbled path in King's Lynn (Clarke and Carter 1977, fig.174, 88), while another 14th century oak seat found at Kirk Close, Perth (and now in Perth Museum), was found in a cess pit (Morris 1984a, M345). A fragment of a 15th century oak seat made from a board 29mm thick was found in the fill of a garderobe pit at Lurk Lane, Beverley (Foreman and Hall 1991, fig.123, 966).

8949–50, 9176 and these six garderobe seats had evidence for only one large circular hole like *8949* and *8950*. A very long 11th/12th century oak seat found on the Fleet Valley site in London, however, had three circular holes lined up along its length making it a three-seater (McCann and Orton 1989, fig.4; DUA site PWB 88A, sf821). It was a radially split plank 1·85m long and 370mm wide, and was apparently still in situ over a small rectangular wattle-lined pit. Such multiple wooden seats known collo-

quially as 'two-ers' and 'three-ers' (at least in East Anglia) were used in rural areas of England until recent times.

The large central holes on most of the seats, including *9176* and *8949*, have edges chamfered on both sides, giving an hourglass shape to the hole when looked at in cross-section. The hole on *8950*, however, is chamfered on one side only. Recent wooden seats with chamfered edges around their holes often have circular wooden lids with a corresponding chamfer which can be snugly fitted over the hole, then lifted when necessary with a wooden handle on the lid. The chamfers on the medieval examples could also have provided seating for removable wooden lids.

8951 is a very thick, heavy rectangular garderobe lid (Fig.1132) which was originally hinged, presumably by leather strap hinges, to the wooden box-like seat structure below, which does not survive. A rectangular notch in medieval seat *8950* suggests the use of a similar leather-hinged lid. Although possible, *8951* is less likely to be a chest lid as there is no provision for a hasp or lock, and it is far too heavy and impractical to be a shutter.

Although none of the York seats is Anglo-Scandinavian in date, two Anglo-Scandinavian oak objects found at 16–22 Coppergate (*8684* and *8689* dated to Period 5C) are waste products from the cutting of large circular holes in radially split boards. Another example of this kind of object was excavated from High Street in Perth. They are exactly the sort of offcut which would have been produced when holes were made in the garderobe seats *8949–50* and *9176*. A circle of the size required would have been inscribed on the surface of the plank, then a series of small holes augered through the plank, following the line of the circle and each practically conjoining with its neighbour so that when the last hole was cut the cog-like offcut could easily be cut out with a chisel. *8684* has traces of eighteen adjoining curves from holes augered with a spoon bit approximately 20mm in diameter (see Fig.1064, p.2221); *8689* is a semi-circular offcut with traces of three holes on its curved edge and a central one on its broken straight edge. In the making of this hole, the circle may have been cut between the augered holes. The Perth offcut has traces of 31 holes. *8684* and *8689* came from the making of large holes over 175mm and 195mm in diam-

Fig.1132 *Garderobe lid 8951 from 16–22 Coppergate in situ. Scale unit 10cm*

eter. The large holes in seats *8949–50* and *9176* were 245, 250 and 230mm respectively, whilst other seats had holes measuring 192mm (King's Lynn), 204mm (Beverley), 210mm (Hull) and 220mm (Exeter). After the waste cog was removed, the internal edge of the large hole would have been smoothed and chamfered. Lid *8951* is also Anglo-Scandinavian.

An early 18th century three-seater earth closet from Townsend House near Leominster, Hereford and Worcester, has been reconstructed at the Avoncroft Museum of Buildings at Bromsgrove. Its seat is

plank-built with three holes cut through the conjoined planks unlike *8949–50* and *9176* and some of the other medieval seats which are single boards. However, the box bench onto which it is fixed gives some idea as to how the medieval seats could have been fitted onto similar plank-built superstructures over their deep cess pits. The timbers found with the Winchester seat may have been part of such a structure. Three separate hinged rectangular lids, one over each hole, on the Leominster box bench may also help to explain some features found on medieval seats. A nail hole in the corner of *8950* and two probable peg holes 12mm in diameter near the long edge on the opposite side could have been used to fix the seat down onto the supporting wooden box bench below. A rectangular notch cut into the long edge opposite the peg holes may be a seating for some kind of hinged lid like *8951* which has not survived, or it could be a seating for a joint with the planks below. *8949* has three augered holes 23mm in diameter near one long edge which are probably too big to have been peg holes, but could have been used for organic (possibly rope) hinges for a lid or as mortices for tenons on the planks below. The 10th century semi-circular seat from Exeter has traces of at least eleven peg holes around its edges which could have been used to fasten it to a box bench. The King's Lynn seat has two rectangular notches cut into one long edge, similar to that on *8950*. It is the only seat with a rectangular notch cut into the chamfer around the large hole. If this hole had a circular lid/cover which was shaped to fit this notch, there would be no need for a larger rectangular lid as on the Leominster earth closet, suggesting that the notches on the long edge (and that on *8950*) are more likley to have been for jointing with the planks below.

Personal Items

Pins (Fig.1133)

8952 and *8955–9* are unusual for decorated pins (and pins with shaped heads) in that they were carved from wood. *8953–4* and *8960* are broken wooden pin points included here, rather than with the bale pins in the textile section, since it is uncertain what type of pin they come from. All nine pins were whittled from small roundwood or split sections of wood, and, where the species can be identified, they are scots pine, alder, hazel and yew.

8952 is an unfinished pin which someone had begun to carve from a length of debarked yew branch. It has a carved thistle-shaped head at one end and the beginnings of a pin shaft 7mm in diameter below, but the rest of the branch is unworked. There are no wooden parallels for this thistle-shaped head, but it is reminiscent of the thistle-shaped terminals on silver thistle-brooches and penannular brooches dating to the late 9th/10th centuries found in Britain (Graham-Campbell 1980, 54–5, pls.195 and 197).

8955–9 were all found in levels of medieval date. Although *8958* has little of its shaft remaining, it is by far the most elaborate of the pins, with a smooth globular head surmounting three carved mouldings, square, biconical and cylindrical, each with incised geometric decoration. There are no other elaborately carved pins to compare with *8958*, but wooden pins with plain globular or onion-shaped heads have been found on Viking Age and medieval sites at Lagore Crannog (Hencken 1950, fig.81, W38, W87, W129), Ballinderry Crannog 2 (Hencken 1942, fig.26), Vicar Lane, Hull, Trig Lane, London (Morris 1984a, fig.92, M420 and M422), and Austin Friars, Leicester (Mellor and Pearce 1981, fig.53, 89). *8959* has no head as such, but its head end is carved in a series of unequal step-like slots and notches which would perhaps have helped prevent it pulling through fabric. *8956* has a plain expanded trumpet-shaped head with a concretion adhering to one side. A small bone pin with a similar trumpet-shaped head was found at Hungate in York (Richardson 1959, fig.19, 18). *8955* has a square head with facets cut across the corners making it resemble a cornerless cube, a feature also found on a wooden pin from Lagore Crannog (Hencken 1950, fig.81, W100), Anglo-Scandinavian bone pins from Clifford Street and Goodramgate in York

(Waterman 1959, fig.12, 7–9), and copper alloy ring-headed pins of an Irish type found in Nessgate and Pavement, York (ibid., fig.11, 13–14 and fig.25, 1), and also on the 16–22 Coppergate site (*10472*, AY 17/14).

Most surviving Anglian, Anglo-Scandinavian and medieval pins were made from bone, antler or metal, and many examples of all these three materials (bone and copper alloy in particular) have been found at 16–22 Coppergate and other sites in York (Fig.48, *448–506*, AY 17/3; Fig.101, *742*, *972* and *1233*, AY 17/4; pp.148–50, Fig.907, AY 17/12; *10472*, *10497*, AY 17/14; Waterman 1959, figs.11–12 and 14). Many of the bone and metal pins were used to fasten garments, whilst others could have been used in textile crafts or even in the dressing of hair. Some wooden pins with carved heads such as *8952* and *8955–9* could have been used as alternatives to bone, antler and metal pins or for different purposes. Wooden pins may not have had the strength of those made of other materials, but they were quicker and easier to whittle and carve than bone and antler, and would have been cheaper than either these or metal ones. Intricately carved and polished yew pins such as *8958*, however, would have been just as impressive as those in other materials.

Combs (Fig.1133)

Using the terminology standardised by Galloway in her discussion of bone and antler combs, *8962* is a double-sided simple comb type (Galloway 1976, fig.48). It has one surviving very worn end bar and fragments of 54 fine and fifteen coarse teeth over a length of 74mm. *8961* is a single-sided simple comb type (ibid.), with one surviving end bar, a solid back with a slot carved along one side, and traces of 24 surviving teeth, whole or fragmentary. Both combs were recovered from Period 6 contexts, *8962* from 15th century levels and *8961* from a 16th–19th century well fill.

Double-sided combs such as *8962* were made from small cleft or tangentially sawn boards shaved finely on each side of a central bar or back into elongated lozenge-shaped cross-sections. They vary from very thick combs such as one found at Trig Lane,

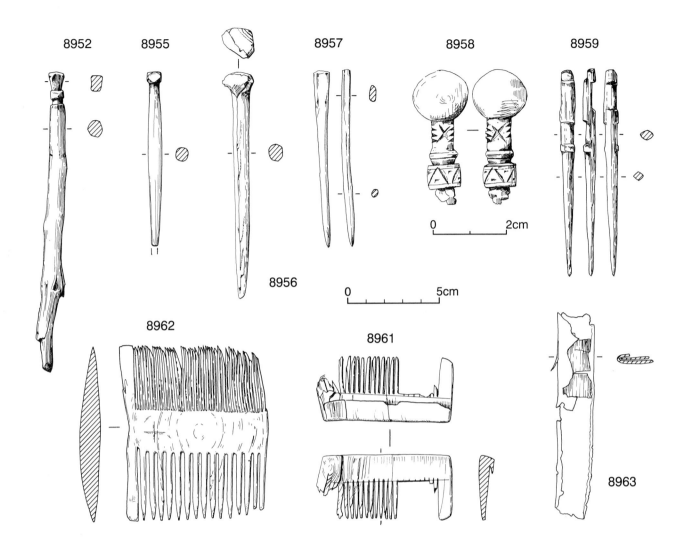

Fig.1133 *Wooden pins 8952, 8955–9; combs 8961–2; scabbard lining 8963, all from 16–22 Coppergate. Scale 1:2, 8958 1:1*

London, 18mm thick (Morris 1984a, fig.90, W400ix), to very thin combs such as the one found at Scale Lane, Hull, which was only 6mm thick (Armstrong 1980, fig.28, 50). Most have fine teeth cut into one side and coarse teeth cut into the other side. A fragment of another medieval double-sided comb was found at 1–5 Aldwark in York (YAT 1976.15, sf231). 8961 is unusual in that it was made from a tangentially sawn board 8mm thick, cut and shaved into a triangular cross-section. The slot carved along one side of the back may indicate that the comb, now broken, originally had a case or cover which fitted into the slot and over the teeth to protect them. One end of the comb is missing so that there is no trace of a possible handle or hinged case fitting. Two scenes in the early 14th century Luttrell Psalter (British Li-

brary Add. MS 42130, fos.63r and 70v) show double-sided combs being used for combing hair. In the first, a woman combs another's hair while a second comb rests on the latter's knee; in the second, a mermaid holds a comb in her left hand. The extremely close spacing of the fine teeth on medieval combs suggests that they could have been effective in removing lice, whilst the coarser teeth would have had a more general use. Two late medieval double-sided bone combs from Scale Lane and Sewer Lane, Hull (Armstrong 1977, fig.29, 141; Armstrong 1980, fig.28, 54), have been identified as beard combs.

The teeth of all archaeologically excavated wooden combs (at least 72 examples from eighteen sites) were cut with very fine saws (Morris 1984a,

122, M394–M411). Examination of the teeth of *8961* and other later medieval combs such as ones from the High Street and Goldsmith Street sites, Exeter (Allan and Morris 1984, fig.176, 38–9), and Sewer Lane, Hull (Armstrong 1977, fig.29, 132), show that the saw cuts had been straight down and across, whereas other combs such as another from Trichay Street, Exeter (Allan and Morris 1984, fig.176, 40), and two others from Sewer Lane, Hull (Armstrong 1977, fig.29, 131 and 135), show that two saw cuts had been made, one from each side, leaving an inverted V-shaped profile. On *8961*, an incised line had been drawn along the length of the comb back, and the teeth had been cut approximately to this line, with some of the saw cuts going up to and over it on both sides. There were no marking out lines on *8962*, however, and the depth of the cuts between both the fine and coarse teeth are unequal.

Both *8961* and *8962* were made from boxwood, the species traditionally associated with comb-making because it is hard with a dense smooth grain and can be split or sawn into boards, then sawn into extremely thin slivers when making fine teeth. It is a mellow light yellow colour and can be polished to look like bone or ivory. Other double-sided boxwood combs similar to *8962* include a 13th century comb from Cuckoo Lane, Southampton (Platt and Coleman-Smith 1975, fig.229, 1641), four 15th century combs from Trig Lane, London (Morris 1984a, fig.90, M400viii–xi), and a 15th century comb from High Street, Exeter (Allan and Morris 1984, fig.176, 38). Similar double-sided combs made of other species are a 14th century possibly hazel comb from Upper Thames Street, London (Hill, Millett and Blagg 1980, fig.51, 133), two 15th century combs from Goldsmith Street and Trichay Street, Exeter, made from *Malus* sp. or apple/pear (Allan and Morris 1984, fig.176, 39–40), two 15th century combs made probably from ash and apple/hawthorn found at Narrow Quay, Bristol (Morris 1984a, fig.91, M408i–ii), a late 13th–mid 14th century oak comb found at Custom House, London (Henig 1975, fig.25, 4), and a 15th/16th century apple/hawthorn comb found at Austin Friars, Leicester (Mellor and Pearce 1981, fig.53, 91). Nearly 300 double-sided combs dating from the 10th to 14th centuries were found in the excavations at Novgorod, most of which were made from boxwood which had to be brought into Novgorod from the Caucasus region as it does not grow locally (Herteig 1975, 81; Kolchin 1989, 163–5, pls.153–4). No wooden combs

have been found in Britain as early as the 10th century, but even in Novgorod they were especially fashionable in the 13th and first half of the 14th centuries when many of the English examples were made. At Bergen, boxwood and yew were also imported as raw materials for making combs (Herteig 1978, 53); although boxwood now grows in Norway, in medieval Europe its distribution was limited, and botanists consider the Bergen box to be of sufficient dimensions for it to have come from the Mediterranean area (Herteig 1975, 81). Boxwood would not have had to be imported into England, where it was grown locally and specially chosen for making various wooden items, including combs.

8962 has a small incised cross at one end of the central bar, possibly an owner's or maker's mark rather than decoration, as the usual forms of decorating wooden double-sided combs are openwork shapes punched out with a metal die, ring-and-dot motifs incised with a compass, or fretwork along the edges using a fret-type saw (Morris 1984a, 122).

Wooden comb-making seems to have been mainly a later medieval craft, possibly associated with the development of very fine fret saws. *8961* and *8962* are two examples of this craft which obviously carried on into the post-medieval period. Wooden double-sided combs had been made in the Roman period, for example boxwood combs were found at Castleford in W. Yorkshire (Morris 1998a, fig.154, 20), London (Chapman 1980, fig.73, 678) and *Vindolanda* (Birley 1977, 123–4, pl.60), but Anglo-Saxon and Viking Age combs in Britain were made almost exclusively of bone and antler (many were uncovered at Coppergate and other York sites; pp.1923–40, Figs.883–96, *AY* 17/12), materials which seem to have been mainly replaced by wood from the 13th century onwards. In Britain, archaeological evidence from the 72 combs previously mentioned suggests that these wooden combs have an extremely limited date range (for wooden artefacts) from the 13th to 16th centuries. No Anglo-Saxon or Viking Age wooden combs have been found in Britain, even on sites with large collections of surviving wood. Examples of bone and ivory double-sided combs of the same type as *8962* have been found in 15th–16th century levels at Scale Lane, Hull (Armstrong 1980, fig.28, 54), 16th–17th century levels at various sites in Southampton (Platt and Coleman-Smith 1975, fig.249, 1944, 1946–7, 1949), in 16th–19th century levels in Winchester (Galloway

1990, 676–7, fig.185) and in 17th–18th century levels on several sites in Exeter (Allan 1984, fig.195, 9–15), suggesting that bone and ivory generally replaced wood again as a comb-making material in post-medieval England.

Possible scabbard lining (Fig.1133)

8963 comprises very thin fragments of a veneer-like strip of wood found inside two folds of leather on an incomplete narrow strap in levels dating to Period 5B. The wood is now compressed and less than 1mm in thickness, but may originally have been slightly thicker. It may have been part of the wooden stiffening or lining for a small leather knife scabbard, since the strip narrows from 19 to 16mm along its length, although neither end survives intact. There appear to be no Viking Age parallels to compare with *8963*, but fragments of 14th century wooden knife linings were found at Goldsmith Street, Exeter (Allan and Morris 1984, 305, fig.175, 28), and a 17th century knife/dagger sheath lined internally with a very thin strip of wood was found at Trichay Street in Exeter (Friendship-Taylor 1984, 331, fig.187, 62), showing that *8963* is an early example of a technique which was still being used in post-medieval England.

Other personal items

A tiny Anglo-Scandinavian wooden bead fragment *9151* may originally have been part of a piece of inexpensive jewellery such as a necklace, or even possibly a rosary.

Manual and Agricultural Implements

Separate-bladed shovels (Fig.1135)

8964–7 from 16–22 Coppergate and *9177* from the Coppergate watching brief are blades from a now well-recognised composite tool which has been called a separate-bladed shovel (Morris 1981). It is usual on archaeological sites to find only the blade and perhaps the pegs which fixed it to a separate handle; the handle itself is rarely found.

The shovel blades which have been found on sites in England, Ireland and northern Europe (cf. Morris 1980a; 1981) have common characteristics including a sub-triangular or sub-rectangular shape, a flat blade, generally sloping shoulders, one or two peg holes and a rectangular slot below these. The slot almost invariably has channels cut into the wood which led down to it on the front of the blade and away from it on the reverse. The handle was fitted into the rectangular slot, the sloping channels giving the required angle, and it was secured by pegs. At least two later medieval manuscripts have illustrations of separate-bladed shovels in use (Morris 1981, figs.10–11), and the method of fixing the handle and blade illustrated in Fig.1134 is based on these and surviving examples.

Only five blades from over 40 examples in Britain and Ireland have surviving pegs. One of these is *8965*; the others are from King's Lynn (Morris 1980a, fig.2e), Exeter, Carlisle and Dublin (Morris 1981,

figs.7–9) and these seem to have been trenails with expanded heads. Although no British shovel has a surviving handle, a blade found in Durham (originally interpreted as a roof shingle) was reported to have had its slot made by 'a post driven through the shingle at glancing incidence' (Carver 1979, 24). This could well have been the original handle. Blades from Dublin, Lübeck, and Tommarp in Sweden all retain fragments of their original shafts (Morris 1981, 67–8, fig.7).

The shape of the end to which the handle was fixed ('fixing end') could vary and five distinct shapes have been identified (Morris 1981, fig.5b); two of these are represented in the York group. *8966, 9177* and two other shovel blades found at St Saviourgate and Castlegate/Coppergate in the city (ibid., fig.8, 20–1) have diamond-shaped fixing ends. Other examples of this type were found in Chester (Morris 1980a, fig.2a), Dublin and Ballymacaldrack (Morris 1981, fig.8, 3 and 9). These could have been specially designed to fasten a cord around the restriction below the diamond. *8965* has a truncated fixing end, with parallels in five blades from Dublin and others from Chester, Lund and London (ibid., fig.7), whilst *8964* and *8967* are too broken for a particular shape to be recognised.

These tools are definitely shovels, not spades (see below), and the obtuse angle between the handle and blade would have been an advantage in shovelling

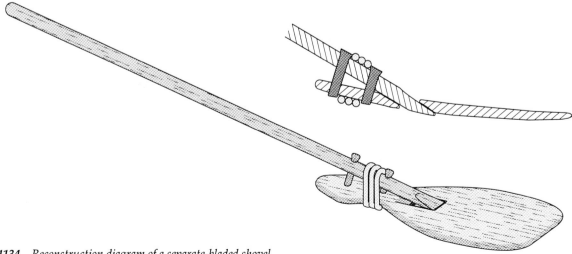

Fig.1134 Reconstruction diagram of a separate-bladed shovel

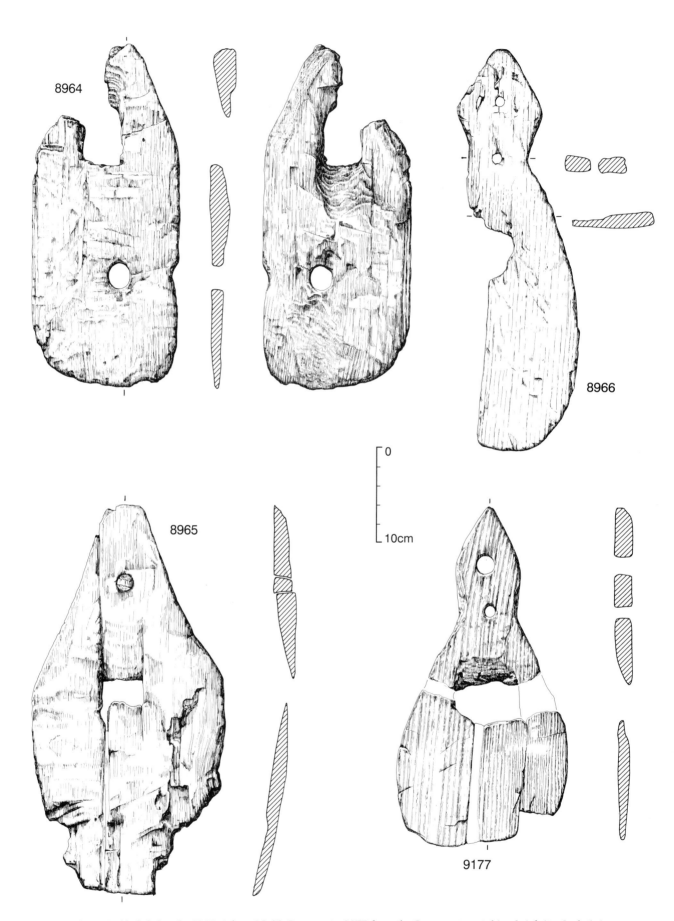

Fig.1135 *Separate-bladed shovels: 8964–6 from 16–22 Coppergate, 9177 from the Coppergate watching brief site. Scale 1:4*

soft, loose materials such as earth, mortar, grain, dung and mud. They seem to conform to a specific pattern and the people who manufactured them held a common mental template of the tool they were producing over a long period of time. An 8th/9th century blade was found at Moynagh Lough Crannog in Co. Meath (Bradley 1982), and the manuscript illustrations already mentioned show that separate-bladed shovels were still in use in north-west Europe in the 14th and 15th centuries. Some undated Cornish tools now in the Truro and Penzance museums (Morris 1981, 68) may even be post-medieval in date. Thus, although they have been discovered in quantity in Anglo-Scandinavian York and Viking Age Dublin, since the earliest dated example comes from a native Irish site, it does not now seem that the separate-bladed shovel was a specifically Scandinavian type of tool. Rather, it was a very efficient composite tool which had its origins in northern Europe sometime in the first millennium AD and continued to be used for at least another 600 years.

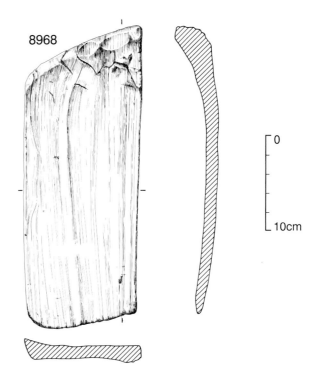

Fig.1136 *Part of the blade of a shovel from 16–22 Coppergate, 8968. Scale 1:4*

Shovel (Fig.1136)

A fragment of a large shovel (*8968*) whose handle and blade were shaped from the same tangentially sawn oak board was found in post-medieval backfill of a medieval stone-lined well at 16–22 Coppergate. It is identified as a shovel and not a spade by its sloping shoulder which would be useless for putting the foot on to exert pressure for digging. Most spades (e.g. *8969*) have straight shoulders perpendicular to the handle. The blade fragment of *8968* is very worn and abraded through use and was obviously discarded when it split from the main tool. An unusual feature is the pronounced hollowing of the blade, which would not only have made the tool more efficient for shifting loose materials, but, since it was made of oak, would have made a large, heavy implement considerably lighter to handle. Tool marks show that the hollowing was done with a chisel, gouge or hand adze.

There are very few one-piece English shovels to compare with this fragment in shape, size or date, perhaps the nearest being a somewhat earlier 11th or 12th century example found at Pevensey Castle (Dunning 1958, fig.6, 2). A Viking period shovel with similar sloping shoulders and square blade was found with the Oseberg ship burial (Brøgger and

Shetelig 1928, pl.XVII, m). Both, however, had flat, unhollowed blades, and this feature is repeated in all the separate-bladed shovels (*8964–7* and *9177*).

The general shape and the hollowing of the blade on the Coppergate shovel are very reminiscent of English malt and grain shovels (cf. Edlin 1949, fig.46) although these are usually carved from much lighter timber such as beech. Since it is made of oak, it is possible that the Coppergate shovel was intended for external work.

Spade (Fig.1137)

A spade with its handle and elongated wooden blade made from a single board of oak (*8969*) was found in the floor levels of one of the semi-basement workshop buildings, Structure 5/4. Although its shoulders are straight and perpendicular to the handle, one is cut 32mm lower than the other giving the spade an asymmetrical appearance. It would originally have had a separate iron shoe, and, although this has not survived, two features in the wooden blade suggest where it would have fitted. These are two steps cut into each side of the blade approximately 160mm from the end, and a chamfer 15mm wide cut into the

Fig.1137 *Spade 8969 after conservation. Actual length 631mm*

rounded blade edge from step to step. As there are no nail holes in the wood, the chamfered blade edge and sides must have been fitted into a groove round the internal mouth of the iron shoe. Most surviving late Saxon spade shoes were attached without nails or clenched lugs, features often found on later medieval shoes, and they were presumably heated and shrunk on to their wooden blades. The Coppergate spade is a very important addition to our knowledge of these tools because it is the only English example of its date (Period 5B) where most of the wooden part has survived.

It is uncertain what shape the Coppergate iron shoe would have been, but there is a good reason for suggesting it would have been rounded. In Saxon and medieval Britain, there seem to have been three shapes of iron spade shoe — rounded, triangular and rectangular — and nearly two-thirds of them are dated more or less accurately to within a century (Morris 1984a, 9). Most dated rounded shoes are pre-1100 in date, and this appears to be confirmed by manuscript illustrations, whereas archaeological and documentary evidence suggest that most triangular and rectangular shoes are 13th to 16th century in date (ibid., fig.3.5). The Coppergate spade is dated to Period 5B, and so it fits well with the dates of other rounded shoes.

Although each shoe would conform to a general type, for example rounded, it would be different from all the others of a similar date because it was manufactured by an individual blacksmith. Examples of late Saxon rounded shoes similar in date to the Coppergate spade have been found at Ufton Nervet,

Berkshire (Manning 1973–4, fig.31, 3), Thetford (Goodall 1984a, fig.121, 44 and 45), Portchester Castle (Cunliffe 1976, fig.134, 31) and Southampton (Addyman and Hill 1969, fig.24, 13), and give some indication as to the general shape of the iron shoe originally fastened to *8969*. There is also an undated rounded iron shoe from York in the collections of Sheffield Museum.

Contemporary illustrations also show what the complete Coppergate spade may have looked like, although most show implements with a much shorter blade. Examples are the 11th century Bayeux Tapestry (Wilson 1985, pl.49), the Caedmon Manuscript dated c.1000 (Bodleian Library MS Jun.XI, fos.45, 46 and 49), Aelfric's Paraphrase of the Pentateuch and Joshua dated c.1025–50 (British Library Cotton Claud. B IV, fo.22v), and an 11th century Anglo-Saxon Calendar (British Library MS Tit. B V pt.1, representation of March). In addition to the rounded iron shoes, all these illustrations seem to be depicting asymmetrical spades which have a single shoulder, and their handles are flush with the blade at one side. The asymmetry of the Coppergate spade is slightly different, however, and it definitely has two shoulders. Although contemporary artists may sometimes have represented objects in stylised or abstract ways, it does not seem to have been the case with these asymmetrical spades. An excavated example from Jelling in Denmark, almost identical to the illustrated ones, is dated to c.950 (Lerche 1970, 152 fig.4e), whilst another much larger asymmetrical spade with an elongated triangular blade was found in a peat hole during gravel extraction at Bawburgh in Norfolk in 1987 (Barbara Green, pers. comm.). Although it is as yet undated, the blade length of the Bawburgh spade at 410mm is very close to that of the Coppergate spade, and since the former had a complete surviving handle and an overall length of 1·41m, it could indicate the original size of the Coppergate spade.

Forked tool (Fig.1138)

8970 is a complete fork whose handle and tines were made from a single board of oak. Its wide, solid shovel-like blade (curved in longitudinal section), sloping shoulders and unworn tines suggest it was not a digging fork to compare with the Irish 'gowl gob' forks typified by one found at Bartrauve, Co. Mayo (Lucas 1978, fig.3a). It has no nail holes or wear marks to suggest that the tines were ever covered with iron shoes. Comparison with forked tools found in the 9th century Oseberg ship burial (Brøgger and Shetelig 1928, 225–6, pl.XVIIo — identified as a 'mok-grep') and in 13th century levels in Lund (Nilsson 1976a, figs.162 and 163 — identified as a 'godsel-grep'), suggests a possible identification as a manure fork. The Oseberg and Lund forks have two and three tines respectively and the Oseberg fork in particular was identified as a manure fork by comparison with other known examples. These tools, and the Coppergate fork, would have been much more suitable for the task than a straight-bladed shovel. There are plenty of references in 13th and 14th century farm accounts to forked tools specifically used as dung forks (Rogers 1866; Morris 1984a, fig.3.13).

There are no archaeological English parallels for this fork, but it is remarkably similar to a fork illustrated in the 14th century Luttrell Psalter (British Library Add. MS 42130, fo.162). This is held by a 'man-monster', and its rounded blade with sloping shoulders is divided into two pointed tines. The Coppergate fork is itself 13th century in date and could therefore be an example of the type of tool illustrated in the Psalter.

Mattocks (Fig.1139)

Another composite manual tool with a separate wooden head and handle was the mattock, and two types of wooden mattocks with no iron components have been found at Coppergate. These are a double-ended type which has a long head with curved sides, a combination of blunt or pointed ends and an approximately central hole for a handle (*8972–5*), and a single-ended type which has a long head with only

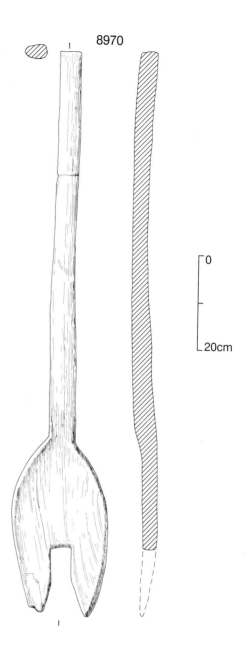

Fig.1138   Forked tool 8970 from 16–22 Coppergate. Scale 1:8

one pointed working end and the handle hole set towards the other end of the head (*8971*).

8971 dates from the earliest Anglo-Scandinavian levels on the Coppergate site (Period 3), whereas the more efficient double-ended mattocks (*8972–5*) come from later Anglo-Scandinavian and medieval levels (Periods 4B, 5B and 6).

It is quite likely that early mattocks were made from one naturally forked branch, although none

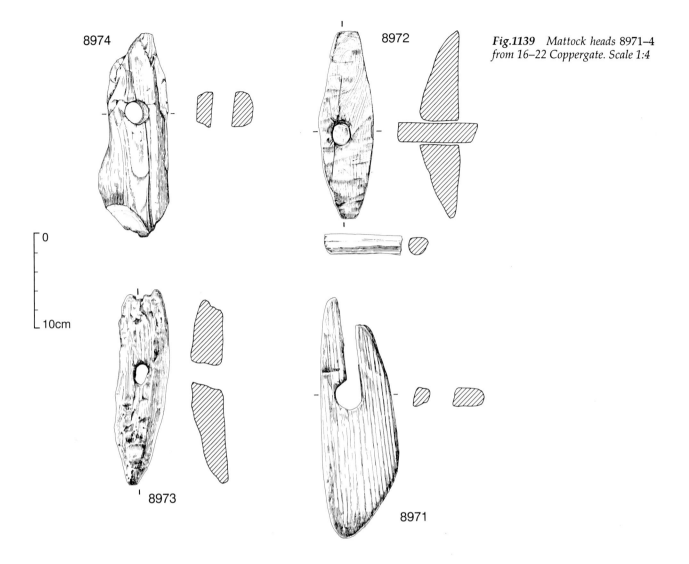

8974

8972

Fig.1139 *Mattock heads 8971–4 from 16–22 Coppergate. Scale 1:4*

0

10cm

8973

8971

have been found on English sites. An early 9th century simple forked branch mattock from the Oseberg ship burial (Brøgger and Shetelig 1928, fig.144) may be the forerunner to the single-ended type represented by *8971*. The advantage of having a separate handle and head lies in being able to make the head much wider by using a separate split section of timber, and being able to fix the head at any angle. Also, timber from different parts of a tree or even from different species of tree can be selected for their strength and resilience. However, if the handle hole is set at one end of the head, the area of wood between the hole and the non-working end will be weaker and liable eventually to split. This happened to *8971* and presumably caused the tool to be discarded.

A further development of this type of tool can be seen in *8972–5* where separate split sections or pieces of squared roundwood timber have been shaped into double-ended mattock heads; the handle hole is centrally placed in a stronger position, and both ends can be used for working.

Double-ended mattocks of varying dates which are similar to these from Coppergate have been found on other British sites. For example, there are late Saxon oak mattock heads from Gloucester (Morris 1983a, fig.118, 5) and Lurk Lane, Beverley (Morris 1984a, fig.16), and medieval ones from Hall Garth, Beverley (ibid., fig.16), and King's Lynn (Clarke and Carter 1977, fig.172, 65). A complete all-wooden mattock with a double-ended oak head (similar to *8972–5*) and a larch shaft was found in a peat bog in North Unst, Shetland, in 1965 (Morris 1984a, fig.16). Larch is reputed not to have arrived in Britain from its native Alps until the 16th century, so unless the

Shetland tool was made from timber imported from the Continent, it may be post-medieval in date and shows not only how these tools were hafted, but also that they continued to be used in some areas for a very long time. A representation of March in an 11th century Calendar (British Library MS Tit. B V pt.1) includes a man breaking clods of earth with a double-ended tool. Its head is very similar to the Coppergate tools and the parallels cited above, and it is hafted exactly as the one from Unst.

All the mattock heads have rounded, blunt or pointed functional ends, useful for cutting into the ground or breaking clods by impact. In an agricultural sense, the term hoe is often used to cover all implements of the mattocking type, and hoe cultivation is contrasted with plough cultivation. Ground can be prepared for sowing by breaking up the soil either on a large scale with a plough and harrow or on a smaller scale with a spade and mattocks such 8971–5. In 19th century Ireland, where spades were used on farms for tillage, a blunt-ended mattock/mallet called a mell was used to break up clods left by a wooden plough (Estyn Evans 1967, 90, fig.44), and similar blunt-ended mattocks can be seen in the 14th century Luttrell Psalter (British Library Add. MS 42130, fo.171b) where a man and a woman are using double-ended mattocks whose handles are fixed in a central hole in the head. These tools are very similar to 8975 which is medieval in date.

Rakes (Fig.1140)

8977 is a very fine example of a medieval toothed hay rake which had a separate handle and head. It was found in fragments in a post-medieval backfill of a medieval stone-lined well, but the head is complete and would originally have had eleven wooden teeth, although traces of only five survive. Three of these were definitely cleft pegs which provide much stronger teeth than lengths of roundwood.

Two holes augered through the head perpendicular to the row of teeth are positioned each side of the middle three teeth. The end of the handle would have been split or sawn for about 2ft, then opened out into a Y-shape and the ends of the arms fixed into the two holes. This method of fixing a hay rake handle was used extensively in the Midlands and south of England until recent times (Edlin 1949, 32) and is still in use at the rake factory at Sicklesmere in Suffolk. Edlin

notes that in the north and west of England the end of the handle was driven through a single hole in the centre of the head and strengthened by connecting pieces. All these rakes were made of ash, whereas the Coppergate rake was poplar or aspen. 8977 had the initials 'SR' branded twice into one flat side between teeth, a mark, probably of ownership, which was also found on a lathe-turned bowl (8586) and another fragment (8694). 8694 and fragment 9148 could have been part of the rake handle. All four items were found in the same well.

Two other objects which could possibly be toothed rakes have been found on English sites, but these are very fragmentary and incomplete and in no way as informative as the Coppergate rake. They are an 11th century ash beam with four oak teeth from Lineacre College, Oxford (Henig 1977, 155, fig.2), and a 13th century beam with five holes, two with teeth, from Norton Priory, Runcorn (Morris 1984a, A97).

A different type of raking tool is represented by 8976, 8978–9 (and possibly 9129; see p.2387), three solid oak rake heads which had no separate teeth. Each tool would originally have had a handle fixed in the circular hole in the centre of the head, which itself often has a curved upper edge. Anglo-Scandinavian 8976 may originally have had an iron shoe. They could have been used for moving loose, dry or even semi-liquid materials. Two rake heads were found on the High Street/Blackfriargate site in Hull (Watkin 1987, fig.122, 339–40). One was found lying at the bottom of a brick-lined garderobe pit and had part of its handle intact. 8978, from a 14th–15th century context, was heavily charred on one side and along the straight raking edge, suggesting it was probably an oven rake for raking embers and ash. Two 11th century rakes found in Lund were similarly scorched (Blomqvist and Mårtensson 1963, figs.157–8), and many rakes of this kind were found in the 9th to 11th century settlement at Hedeby where they had been used to rake out embers and ashes before bread or pots of food were put in to bake or simmer (Elsner 1990, 26). The original iron shoe on 8976 would have extended its life in such conditions.

Other possible uses for rakes of this kind are suggested by parallels. An early–mid 11th century oak rake head with a wedged hazel handle from Winchester (Keene 1990, fig.113, 991) was not scorched, and could have been used to rake tan in a tannery on

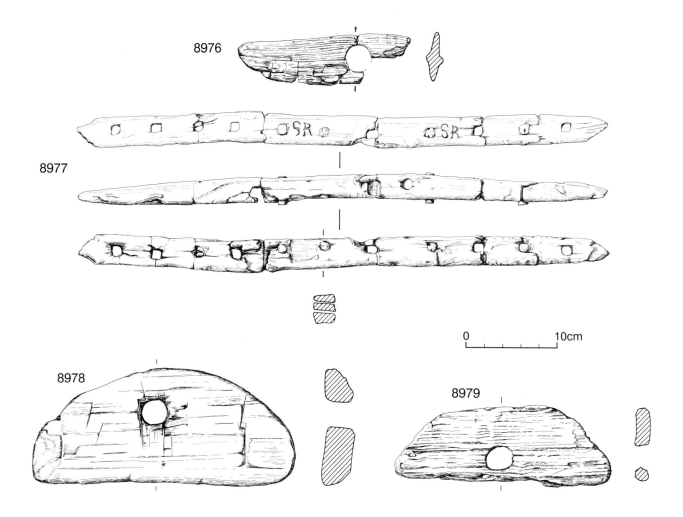

Fig.1140 *Rake heads 8976–9 from 16–22 Coppergate. Scale 1:4*

the site. Rake heads of the same type were found on medieval saltworking sites at Seasalter in Kent (Thompson 1956, figs.4–5) and Nantwich in Cheshire (McNeill Sale 1981, 187). In Nantwich they were used to rake salt to the side of pans in which brine was heated.

Ladders (Fig.1141)

Excavations at 16–22 Coppergate yielded fragments of four Anglo-Scandinavian ladders, represented by rungs (8982–3) and uprights (8980–1). These fragments and examples from other sites suggest that most late Saxon and medieval ladders differed little from modern ones in their general construction and had two uprights with horizontal rungs between them.

The Coppergate uprights (from Periods 3 and 4B) were squared half-section lengths of timber with

augered holes for the tapered ends of rungs such as 8982–3 (from Period 5B) to be fitted through. They are incomplete and their original length cannot be calculated; however, some indication as to the lengths of early medieval ladders can be gained from examples such as that from Pevensey Castle (Dunning 1958, 211–12) which was over 3·5m long. In addition, we know that in 1353 the constable of Nottingham Castle bought two ladders of 28ft and two of 22ft (Pipe Rolls M43 27 Edw III).

There is no evidence to suggest that any of the Coppergate rungs was pegged to secure it against an upright as on an 11th/12th century rung found at Pevensey Castle (Dunning 1958, fig.3), and a 13th century one from Winchester (Cunliffe 1964, fig.55). A ladder found in a late 12th–mid 13th century deep feature during excavations adjacent to 1–5 Aldwark (YAT 1976–7.15, timber 8088) had two uprights made from longitudinally split stems of alder, with oak

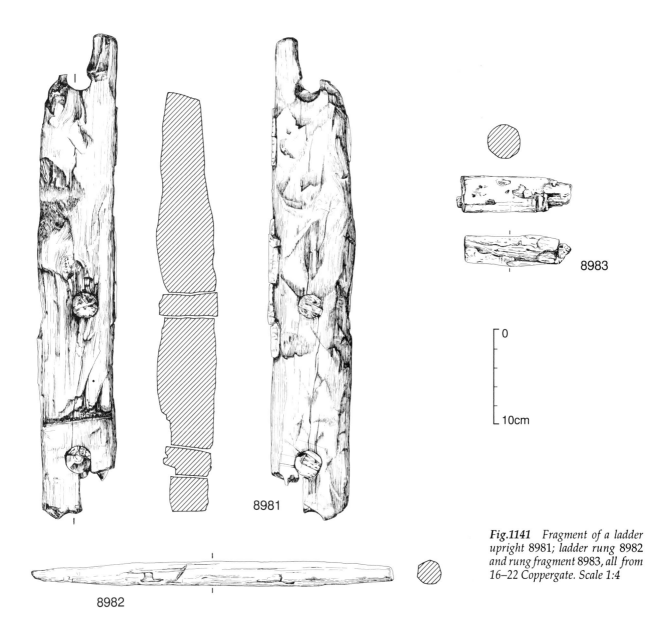

8981

8982

8983

Fig.1141 *Fragment of a ladder upright 8981; ladder rung 8982 and rung fragment 8983, all from 16–22 Coppergate. Scale 1:4*

rungs (*AY* 10/2, 71, 81, pl.XXI). These rungs were secured in the holes in the uprights by wooden wedges. The reconstructed ladder was c.3·80m long, the uprights c.150mm wide and c.70mm thick, with nine pairs of holes for the rungs c.32mm in diameter. The rungs were c.470mm long and c.36mm diameter in the middle. They were spaced along the uprights at c.450mm intervals.

Handles (Fig.1142)

Many different crafts and activities required tools with metal blades or heads and wooden handles. Fragments of these wooden handles are often found without their metal parts since these were valuable as recyclable raw material, even when broken. *8984–*

9002 are fragments of various types of wooden handles for small manual tools; most of them originally had a metal blade or head which is now missing.

8993–4 and *8999* are Anglo-Scandinavian and medieval handles with a rebated or tapered end shaped to fit inside a sheet metal flanged socket such as are found on chisels, gouges and similar tools. A wooden handle with a similarly shaped end would have been used with the woodworking slice found on the 16–22 Coppergate site (*2258*; Fig.977, p.2109). *8990* is a knee-shaped handle whose tapered end to fit into a metal socket is set perpendicular to the main handle. It was probably used with a small hand-adze or similar tool.

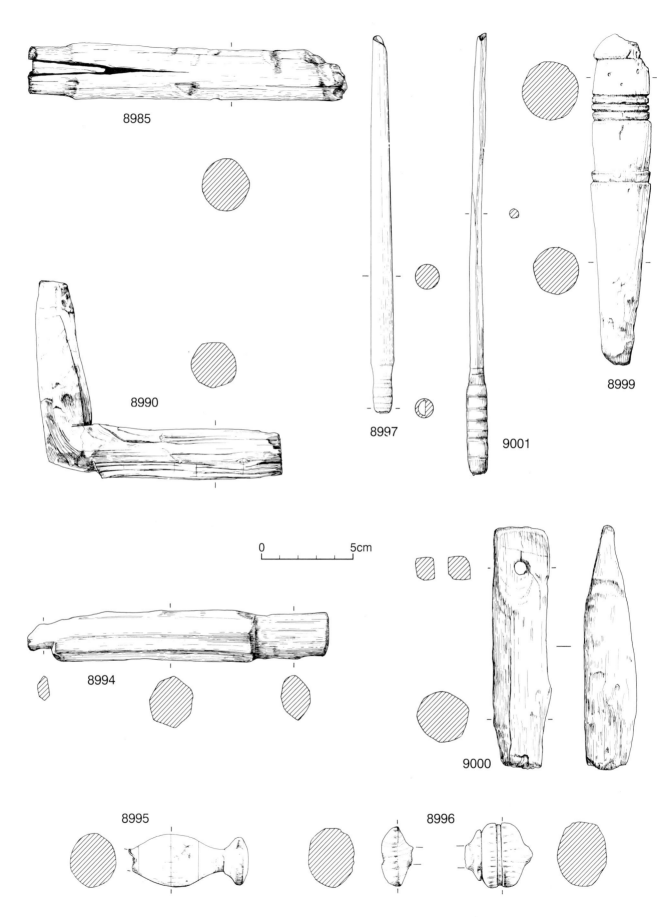

8985

8990

8997

9001

8999

0   5cm

8994

9000

8995   8996

Fig.1142   *Handles 8985, 8990, 8994–7, 8999–9001, all from 16–22 Coppergate. Scale 1:2*

8985 is an Anglo-Scandinavian handle for a small metal hammer head or similar tool with a vertical socket hole through the main solid part of the head. The rebated end of the wooden handle was firmly fixed inside the socket by a wooden splaying wedge hammered into a pre-cut groove.

8997, a very narrow tapering, lathe-turned handle from a 14th century context, is probably a brush handle. It has one hollow rebated end which would originally have contained brush hairs but is now empty. A binding cord or metal collar would have held the hairs in place as on a modern paint brush. It is possible that this is a medieval paint brush handle, and it is unparalleled anywhere in Britain. *9001* is also yew and finely lathe-turned; it could be a similar tool, but it does not have a hollow end. Several medieval manuscript illustrations show similar brushes being used for painting, for example in Giovanni Boccaccio's two 15th century works 'Le Livre des Femmes Nobles et Renommés' (Bibl. Nat. Paris MS Fr. 598, fos.86 and 100v) and 'Le Livre des Cleres et Nobles Femmes' (Bibl. Nat. Paris MS Fr. 12420, fos.86 and 101v).

From 14th–16th century levels at 16–22 Coppergate came *9000*, an example of a type of handle which must have been suspended on a cord in a similar way to the handle on the end of a modern lavatory chain, although its actual use is uncertain.

Three fragments (*8984, 8989, 8991*) are sections of larger hafts used for tools such as axes, adzes, sickles and scythes. All three are Anglo-Scandinavian in date. *8989* is interesting in that it is made of a radially split section of ash, the form and species of timber which has traditionally been used for tool handles because of its strength, resilience and elasticity down to the present day (Edlin 1949, 30–1).

Small handles with tang holes designed for metal tools with various sizes of whittle tang are represented by fragments *8986–8, 8992, 8995–6* and *8998*. Some of them could be knife handles. The two 16th–19th century handles *8995–6*, turned from alder and ash respectively, are particularly attractive handles with pommels and bulbous grips, but it is impossible to be certain what sort of tool they were designed for.

Plough

Fragments of *9178*, which is probably an Anglo-Scandinavian oak plough, were found on the Coppergate watching brief site. These consist of a roughly squared, naturally angled beam and six other fragments. There are perhaps two ways of interpreting these fragments in the light of our knowledge of ploughs in early medieval Europe (see Fig.1143).

The beam, which is 1·54m in length, could be interpreted as a one-piece stock-and-stilt with a straight handle or stilt 870mm long, and a slightly curved foot or stock projecting at an obtuse angle from it. The stock is the wooden beam whose leading point (with or without an iron ploughshare) did the actual breaking of the ground. If it is a stock-and-stilt, a rectangular slot on the upper surface of the stock may originally have received the end of a draught beam. The other fragments may have been parts of the draught beam, wooden handles and fittings which unfortunately cannot be reconstructed.

Simple ploughs with a stock-and-stilt formed in one piece from a tree branch and its junction with the trunk may have been used in prehistoric Europe (Jope 1956, 82). An Early Iron Age plough found at Donnerupland in central Jutland had a stock, set at an angle, which was carried up to form a handle in a combined stock-and-stilt (ibid., fig.44), but another Early Iron Age plough found at Vebbestrup in Jutland had a horizontal stock and a separate handle-stilt curving away from it (ibid., fig.46) showing that at this period the two forms could have existed simultaneously.

Ethnographic examples of ploughs with a combination of a stock-and-stilt in one integral piece have also been studied, for example the Ropas plough of Corfu (Sordinas 1978). Sordinas was of the opinion, however, that the combination of the two parts in one piece of timber was an attribute of fragile and functionally primitive ploughs (ibid., 142). As such they would have been 'scratch' ploughs which did little more than disturb the surface of the soil.

It is not clear whether this type of primitive plough with a one-piece stock-and-stilt was still being used in northern Europe in the Viking period, and the Coppergate fragments are not well enough

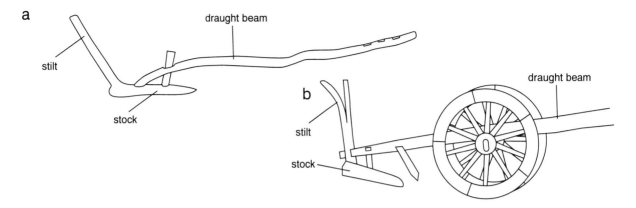

Fig.1143 *(a) Simplified drawing of a one-piece stock-and-stilt plough, based on the Ropas plough (cf Sordinas 1978, fig.3); (b) simplified composite drawing based on medieval square-framed ploughs in 10th and 12th century illustrations (cf. Jope 1956, figs.52–3)*

preserved to be unequivocally identified as these parts of a plough.

An alternative interpretation is that the main beam is possibly the draught beam of a more sophisticated heavy square-framed plough of the type developed by the Romans and common in medieval Europe. These ploughs have separate stocks and stilts, and examples can be seen in many early medieval illustrations (Jope 1956, figs.51–57). In most cases the draught beam is fixed through the stilt, and itself has slots for a coulter and a bracing bar. If the Coppergate beam is a draught beam of this kind, perhaps the slot cut into it was intended for one of these implements, but was never finished.

Discussion

Wood was the main material used in the manufacture of most implements used for tillage and manual work. Manual tools from 16–22 Coppergate such as shovels, spades, mattocks and rakes suggest that wood alone was often durable enough to cope with the tasks involved. Metal was used when necessary, but in small quantities such as the iron shoe which would originally have been fitted to spade *8969*. Other iron components which have not survived include a share and coulter for plough *9178* and a shoe for rake *8976*.

There is a persistence of tradition in the form of some of the tools being used, for example, the separate-bladed shovel. This probably implies the dominance of functional utility and the continuity of traditional types of tillage and manual work.

Tools such as the mattocks, hay rake, spade, dung fork and shovels indicate that small-scale tillage could have been carried out in limited areas of Anglo-Scandinavian and medieval York, perhaps in gardens or yards. The plough *9178* suggests that even larger, open plots of land might have been cultivated within the town. The Coppergate finds and parallels from other urban sites show that these two forms of tillage need not have been restricted to rural areas.

Implements used in the Production and Handling of Fibres and Textiles

An extensive range of tools was used in Anglo-Scandinavian and medieval textile manufacturing processes, whether for domestic production or as part of a larger textile industry. Many of the tools must have been made of organic materials, especially wood, but only a small, probably unrepresentative, sample has survived. Many implements are absent from the York assemblage, for example, weaving swords/beaters, a common find in Viking Age and medieval Dublin (cf. Ó Ríordáin 1971, fig.22 and Lang 1988, figs.68, 79, 88–9), but this pattern of survival is the same on other English sites. It is significant that many of the tools which have survived were probably thrown away as useless because they had broken or worn out, for example, the flax pounders *6642–3*, the weft-beater blade *6653*, and the heddle cradle and heddle rod *6654–5*. The 47 wooden textile tools from the York sites considered in this report are a valuable source of information about the techniques used to produce the wide range of fibres and textiles from these sites which have already been published (*AY* 17/5).

The wooden implements are discussed in three sections, each related to a stage in the production or handling of fibres and textiles.

Raw material and fibre preparation

The natural fibres used to produce textiles in Anglo-Scandinavian and medieval York were of two kinds: animal fibre, especially sheep's wool, and vegetable bast fibres from the stems of certain plants, especially *Linum usitatissimum*, flax for linen. Sometimes the same kind of tool was used to process these different fibres, for example, spindles. However, wool and flax fibres require different techniques to separate them from the animal or plant respectively and then prepare them for spinning; hence some wooden tools are specific to one fibre or the other, and these will be discussed below.

Flax stems have a thick woody core and an outer bark. Between these lie the linen fibres which must be isolated by a complicated series of processes including rippling, retting, beating and/or breaking, scutching and heckling. Most of these were still part of English flax production in the 16th century and were listed in the 'Booke of Husbandrie' of 1523 (Fitzherbert 1979, 922–4). Wooden tools would have been used at most stages to prepare the linen fibres, and several of these have been found in Anglo-Scandinavian and medieval York.

Rippler (Fig.1144)

When flax has been harvested, tied into bundles and dried, the seeds can be removed by pulling the heads through a wooden rippler or comb with long coarse teeth. *6641*, dated to the mid 13th century, is probably an example of a medieval flax rippler with five coarse teeth; it is now broken. The handle would originally have been longer and set in a stand.

It is very similar to flax ripplers found in medieval Bergen (Herteig 1975, fig.10) which have five or seven teeth and small holes through the body below the teeth. Apart from the hole, one of the Bergen tools is so similar to the York rippler in size and form that both could have been manufactured in the same place. Fragments of 33 possible flax ripplers have been found in excavations in Bergen (dated c.1170–1332), all with holes cut through at a slant, including two with fragments of wooden handles set in the hole and joining the tool head at an acute angle (Øye 1988, 29–31, fig.I.5). It is possible that *6641* originally had a hole for a separate handle, but broke across the head leaving no trace. Apart from the lack of a hole, *6641* fits well with the features and dimensions of the Bergen tools, which measure 90–320mm in length (*6641* is 142mm), and 68–160mm wide (*6641* is 75mm). They have between four and eight teeth with an average of five (*6641* has five). The thickness of the head, length of teeth and distance between them all fit well within the range of the Bergen tools. Another tool similar to the York and Bergen finds was excavated recently at Tonsberg in Norway (ibid., 29). There are no other close parallels, apart from a group of Roman tools found at Vindonissa in Switzerland and dated to the 1st century AD (Wild 1970, 124, table D). These were wooden tools 100–140mm long and 100mm wide, with between eight and twelve teeth, and holes augered perpendicularly through the heads, not at a slant; they were identified as flax ripplers (Øye 1988, 28).

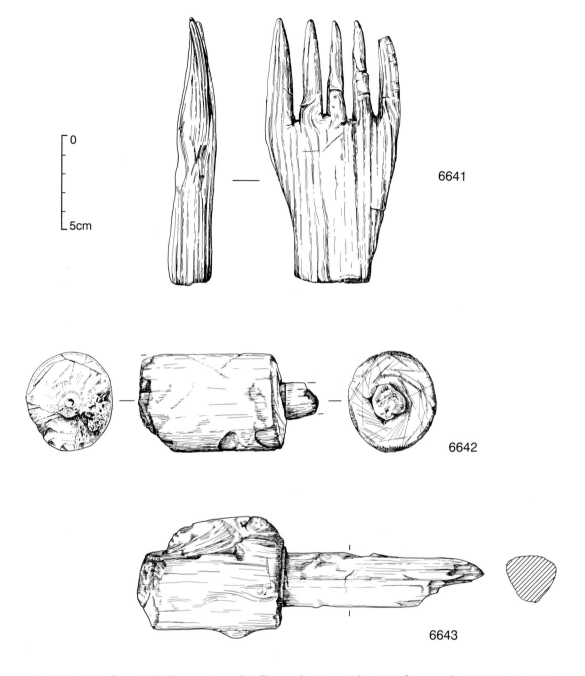

0
5cm

6641

6642

6643

Fig.1144   *Tools from 16–22 Coppergate used in fibre production: rippler 6641; flax pounders 6642–3. Scale 1:2*

6641 is made of pine, a species which was used extensively in Viking Age and medieval Scandinavia to manufacture small wooden objects, but not as commonly used in England and not well represented among the other York wooden finds, so it is possible that it was made in Norway and imported to York. Only three of the Bergen tools were made of pine, 28 were oak, one beech and one an unidentified hardwood (ibid., 30).

No other wooden flax ripplers have been excavated from English sites, but a large wooden comb from High Street, Dublin, is possibly a flax rippler (Morris 1984a, fig.20, T53). It is 278mm long, 83mm wide and has nine carved teeth 85mm long with circular cross-sections. The teeth are spaced too far apart for a wool comb, and the object is far too big to have been a personal hair comb. It is not closely dated, however, having been found during cellar clearance on a site whose stratigraphy dates from the 10th to 14th centuries. Walton Rogers suggests that ripplers more commonly had iron teeth and that some of the sturdier iron spikes found at Coppergate may have come from this type of tool (pp.1727–31, *AY* 17/11).

Flax pounders and scutching knife
(Figs.1144–5)

Flax needs to be retted or soaked in slowly moving water to soften the woody core and outer bark. This can be done in natural or man-made pools, tanks or even bogs; Askham Bog was evidently sometimes used for the retting of hemp (cf. Greig 1988, 122–7). Recent research in north-west England (Higham 1989) has identified several 12th–13th century flax-retting sites with watercourses, sluices and raised banks for drying flax. All were associated with either lay or monastic demesne holdings. Such sites have not been identified for Anglo-Scandinavian or medieval York, and evidence from the wooden tools suggests that flax processing after the retting stage was carried out by hand.

After retting and drying (p.1725, *AY* 17/11), bundles of flax stems were beaten with mallets or pounders. *6642–3* are probably fragments of Anglo-

Scandinavian flax pounders, heavy tools with cylindrical heads and handles projecting from one end of the head, carved from full stem roundwood willow and alder (Fig.1144). These were used to break up the flax stems by repeated pounding, probably against a stone or boulder (for an 18th century Irish illustration see Fig.799, *AY* 17/11). This type of tool was very common in Viking Age and medieval Europe, and complete examples have been found in Viking Age Dublin and 12th century Perth (Morris 1984a, fig.17), the 9th century Oseberg ship burial (Brøgger and Shetelig 1928, figs.111–12), late 11th century Lund (Nilsson 1976b, fig.210), Viking Hedeby (Schietzel 1970, Abb.7,1), Viking and medieval Novgorod (Kolchin 1968, pl.4, 1–3; 1989, pls.13–14), medieval Bergen (Øye 1988, 27) and medieval Cork (Hurley 1982, fig.16.2, 9). One was also found in an actual retting pit at Westbury, Buckinghamshire (Ivens et al. 1995, 393, 395). Most of these, like the Coppergate tools, were made of species which could be easily shaped and would withstand constant pounding, for example willow, beech and ash.

The broken flax stalks and bark were almost certainly removed from the fibres with all-wooden scutching knives. These had narrow, flat blades and were worked up and down the flax bundles against a verti-

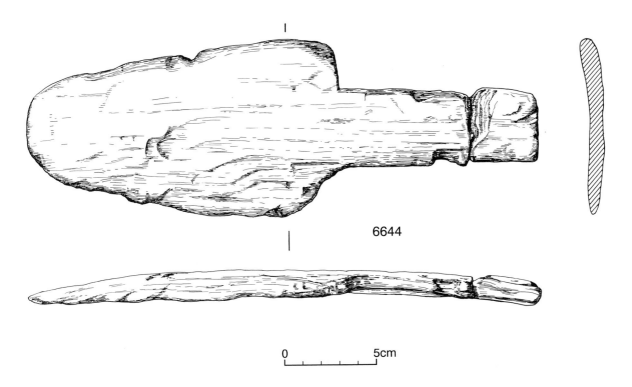

6644

0   5cm

Fig.1145 Tools from 16–22 Coppergate used in fibre production: scutching knife 6644. Scale 1:2

cal wooden board. *6644* is an Anglo-Scandinavian oak scutching knife (Fig.1145), and is well paralleled by similar Viking Age and medieval oak tools from Hedeby (Jankuhn 1943, Abb.82a), Macclesfield in Cheshire (Morris 1984a, fig.18) and King's Lynn (Clarke and Carter 1977, fig.173, 83 and 84). Four wooden scutching blades found in 2nd/3rd century levels at Feddersen Wierde (Haarnagel 1979, Taf.36, 1 and 5, Taf.37, 6 and 7) and 33 from 10th to 15th century levels in Novgorod (Kolchin 1989, 108–9 and pl.110) show that, in its general form, this flax-breaking tool changed little over time. On the evidence of the wooden tools, scutching was a process used after pounding in northern Europe at least by the early first millennium AD. Since these tools have spatulate blades, they may easily be mistaken for kitchen tools, spatulae or stirrers. Most have rectangular cross-sections and flat, blunt edges. *6644* is very worn along one edge and corner where it has been used against a board.

There are no English medieval illustrations of these tools, but two early 16th century illustrations, a French one in the 'Heures de la Bienheureuse Vierge Marie' in the Petit Palais, Paris (Fox 1985, entry for November), and the other a woodcut of Virgilius Solis's Activities of the Months: November, in the British Museum (Patterson 1956, fig.158), show scutching with a bat-like wooden blade against a vertical wooden board or block.

The Anglo-Scandinavian pounders and scutching knife, along with the medieval rippler, are rare survivals of wooden tools which indicate that various stages of flax processing were being carried out in the city of York from at least the 10th century onwards. This is supported by finds of flax seeds and capsules (*AY* 14/4, 205; *AY* 14/7, 687) and broken fragments of flax stems from scutching. The subject of flax waste found at Coppergate and its significance is discussed in *AY* 17/11 (p.1719). Large quantities of these were found in a single Anglo-Scandinavian pit dated to Period 4B (context 32185 in cut 32190; *AY* 14/7, 562, 773). An important group of linen textiles from Coppergate which could have been made from this locally produced flax have already been published (pp.312–13, 345–59, *AY* 17/5).

Wool comb

After wool has been shorn from the sheep and scoured to remove most of the dirt and impurities, it must be prepared in one of two ways before being spun into thread. The two operations are combing and carding; both require tools which, although not entirely made of wood, have basic wooden parts which ought to be distinguishable archaeologically.

Combing wool removes short fibres and aligns long staples parallel to each other, whereas carding only roughly aligns fibres of any length in a mixed, criss-cross fashion. Both processes were in use contemporaneously, at least in later medieval Europe (Morris 1984a, 33). The Coppergate excavations produced the iron case and teeth of a wool comb which would originally have had multiple rows of long, pointed iron teeth set into a wooden head (*2272–3*, Fig.212, *AY* 17/6). The wooden handle of this type of comb was set into the head at 80 or 90 degrees to the axis of the teeth (Ling Roth 1909, fig.6), but no wood has survived on the Coppergate comb. Although the wooden parts of these composite tools have not been found in Britain, there are many medieval illustrations of them (e.g. from the early 14th century Holkham Bible, British Library Add. MS 47682, fo.6, and the Decretals of Gregory IX, British Library Royal MS 10 E IV, fo.138) and they always appear to have been used in pairs. Many of these combs have been found in Viking graves in Norway (Petersen 1951, 524) and they are often found in pairs. An almost complete Viking Age wool comb with a limewood handle 175mm long was found at Fyrkat (Roesdahl 1977, fig.21). It has been suggested, however, that *2272–3* represent a typical Anglo-Saxon form of tool, and not a Viking type comb (pp.1720–1, *AY* 17/11).

No wooden pieces of wool carders have been positively identified archaeologically, but the first known use of them from manuscript evidence is in 13th century France (Baines 1977, 35). The earliest English illustration of wool carders is in the Luttrell Psalter dated to c.1340 (British Library Add. MS 42130, fo.193). However, the metal backing plate from a mid–late 12th century wool card has been identified at Eastgate, Beverley (Goodall 1992, 289, fig.79); this pushes their use in England back even earlier.

Bale pins (Fig.1146)

6656–61, 9003–14, 9196–8, 9220–3, 9238–41 are almost certainly wooden bale pins used in the handling and packaging of raw wool which in medieval England was exported in sacks. For example, in the decade 1280–90, Boston exported an annual average of 10,000 sacks of wool (Pipe and Chancellor's Rolls PRO E372 and E352). Until recent times in the woollen district of the West Riding of Yorkshire bales of raw wool were held together by sacking attached with wooden bale pins. Walton Rogers illustrates the tools of the medieval packman in a 15th century stained glass window in Cumbria as consisting of bale pins or pack pricks, a wool hook and a bundle of rope (Fig.794, *AY* 17/11). The York bale pins would have been used to fasten the outer wrapping of bales of wool.

All the pins have tapering, straight, whittled shafts, rounded or blunt points and no heads. They would have been easy to manufacture by whittling split billets of small roundwood. They are undecorated and utilitarian, and wooden pins such as these from York are very common on some later medieval sites where wood is well preserved. A total of nearly 300 of them have been found at large inland trading centres such as Oxford, or at ports on rivers and on the British coast such as London, King's Lynn, Perth, Gloucester and Hull which would have handled wool in its raw state as a commodity en route for Europe (Morris 1984a, 35–6, fig.19). King's Lynn in particular was the outport for the wool of East Anglia and the Midlands, whilst a large number of bale pins have been found at the waterfront Custom House site in London (Henig 1974, 201, fig.42; 1975, 153), a site known as the 'Wool Quay', at least from 1376 (Dyson 1974, 144), where customs were levied on exported wool.

Bale pins vary in length from 53mm (Custom House, London) to 275mm (*9005*). This variation occurs not only from site to site, but also within large groups; for example, the London pins varied from 53 to 158mm, whilst those from Coppergate ranged from 89 to 275mm. Most, however, measure between 100 and 150mm. The species of wood used to manufacture bale pins also varied, between sites as well as within large groups, but do not include the major 'constructional' species of oak, ash and beech. Rather, small roundwood from small trees was selected. Those from York were made from yew, elder, birch, *Prunus* sp. and maple, whilst additional species from other sites include hazel, holly and pine (Morris 1984a, fig.10.3). Four of the York pins (*6656* and *9012–14*) were made of elder and all were found in the same context. Elder (*Sambucus nigra*) is rarely used to manufacture small wooden objects because its small

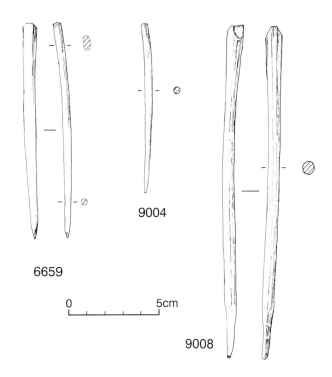

Fig.1146   Bale pins 6659, 9004 and 9008 from 16–22 Coppergate. Scale 1:2

branches and twigs are pithy, but the heartwood is extremely hard, and this part of the timber must have been used to manufacture these pins which were presumably used together.

None of the pins from British sites are dated earlier than the 12th century, and most are 13th to 15th century in date, a period when English wool was prized as a commodity (Power 1941). Sixteen bale pins similar to these York examples were found in 13th/14th century levels in Århus (Andersen et al. 1971, 245). The Coppergate pins dating from the 12th/13th century to the 16th century indicate that bales of raw wool, probably for export, were being handled in medieval York when the wool trade was very important.

Thread production

After heckling, flax fibres were prepared into bundles, and after combing (or carding), wool fibres were prepared into rovings or rolags. Each then had to be converted into thread by spinning. The process of spinning involves twisting together a number of drawn-out fibres, whether flax or wool, into a strong continuous thread. If the fibres are drawn out in one direction, they begin to form a thread, and by continuing to twist, the thread lengthens. If let go, the thread unwinds, but if wound onto a stick it remains twisted. Many Anglo-Scandinavian and medieval spinning tools were made of wood, and examples from York include a possible distaff (*6645*) and spindles (*6646–9, 6697*).

Distaff (Fig.1147)

Although the rolags of shorter-stapled wools could simply be held in the hand for spinning (p.1735, *AY* 17/11), prepared bundles of flax or longer-stapled wools were fastened to a distaff. In post-Roman Europe three types of distaff seem to have been used (e.g. Morris 1984a, 37–9): a small one which was held in the hand, an intermediate length one which could be tucked under the arm (see p.1735, *AY* 17/11) and a much longer one which took the form of a wooden rod which could be slotted into a belt to allow the spinner to move around, held between the knees or set in a stand.

6645 could be either a small hand distaff or the upper end of a long distaff. It was made from a length of elder which has a very hard heartwood and was also used for making the bale pins *6656, 9012–14*. Although its complete original length is unknown, the surviving piece was 334mm long and had been carefully squared along its length, expanding towards a maximum thickness of 12mm approximately 120mm from one end which is now broken. Beyond this point, the distaff tapered to a blunt tip only 7mm square and the edges had been grooved in many places over a distance of approximately 200mm where threads had been tied or secured. If we presume that the blunt tip was the upper end, and the fibres were attached below this but not beyond the point of maximum thickness, then the ungrooved part was either the handhold (if it was a hand distaff) or part of the long rod which went through the belt.

Hand distaffs were first recognised in north-west Europe by Patterson (1955, 81–2) who compared wooden ones found on Early Christian Irish sites, for example, Lough Faughan (Collins 1955, fig.12), Lagore Crannog (Hencken 1950, figs.82 and 84) and Ballinderry Crannog 2 (Hencken 1942, fig.26), with hand distaffs depicted on Greek vases and which have also been found on Roman sites (Wild 1970, 31; 1988, fig.17c–e). Some of these Roman hand distaffs were made of unusual materials, such as amber and

jet examples from Dorweiler and Cologne in Germany (ibid.).

There were two types among the Irish group. One was single-ended, typified by the Lough Faughan example which is 166mm long and has one pointed end and one decorated flat end. The fibres were attached to the pointed end, and it was held at the other. This type has only been found on Irish sites dating from the 7th to 10th centuries. The second was double-ended, typified by an example from Lagore Crannog (Hencken 1950, 163, fig.82A) which is a rod of circular cross-section, 204mm long, with an approximately central grooved moulding. The rod tapers to a point on each side of this moulding. The double-ended tool from Ballinderry Crannog 2 (Hencken 1942, fig.26) is broken at one end, but also has a central carved moulding, rectangular in cross-section, with two notches cut into each corner, and the rod tapers away from this moulding on one side to an intact point.

Although the York tool *6645* is larger, it could have been used in a similar way to these Irish hand distaffs. The threads attaching the fibres would have been secured to the moulding on the Irish examples, whereas on *6645* they were secured to the shaft itself over the grooves. The Lagore and Ballinderry tools date from the 6th to 10th centuries; *6645* is 10th century in date, found in a trench fill dating to Period 4B. Two more Viking Age double-ended hand distaffs of a similar size to *6645* were found in chest 149 in the 9th century Oseberg ship burial (Brøgger and Shetelig 1928, figs.109–10). Both had handholds, plain mouldings and rods tapering above the mouldings to carved tips. A double-ended spindle complete with whorl was found in the same chest.

This type of tool, which must have had its origins in the Classical world and spread to north-west Europe, was still being used in the 11th century. An illustration in a Classical manuscript dating to c.1023, Hrabanus Maurus's 'De Universo' (Monte Cassino Library MS 132), shows a person standing up, using a short hand distaff in her left hand.

If *6645* is not a hand distaff, it could have been the upper part of a long distaff whose use is well documented in medieval English illustrations, although most give very little information about the shapes of the upper ends. A carving on a late Anglo-Saxon or Saxo-Norman marble font at East Meon in

Hampshire shows Eve sitting with a long distaff supported in her belt. It has a pointed lower end, but the upper end is covered in fibre. This is probably the earliest English illustration of a long distaff and indicates that they were in use at least by the 11th century. Illustrations in the 14th century Holkham Bible (British Library Add. MS 47682, fos.4v and 6) show long distaffs being held either at the belt or in the crook of the knee, and in the latter case, the upper end of the distaff has a carved knob.

If the grooves from the securing threads had not helped to identify *6645* as a probable distaff, it could have been overlooked and described as a wooden rod. Equally, unless distaffs were deliberately shaped at the upper end or had holes for attaching prepared fibres as on the bat-like distaffs found in Gdansk in Poland (Kaminska and Nahlik 1960, 92, figs.2a and b) or Novgorod in Russia (Kolchin 1968, 66–7, pl.66; 1989, pls.114–16), most would have looked like simple wooden poles, which explains why few have been identified among the archaeological finds of northwest Europe.

Spindles (Fig.1147)

Spindle whorls are very common artefacts on Anglo-Saxon, Viking Age and medieval sites and they show that the usual form of spinning throughout this period was suspended-spindle spinning (see p.2333 for discussion of spindle wheels). The spindle was a rod of wood, or very occasionally bone (Roesdahl et al. 1981, 119, 122), to which a length of drawn-out fibre from the hand or distaff was hitched at the top. When the spindle, weighted by a disc-shaped weight/whorl acting as a fly wheel, was rotated with one hand and suspended in the air by the twisted yarn, the whorl kept the spindle vertical and gave it momentum. The fibre was drawn out with one hand and twisted with the other until the spindle's rotation stopped, when the yarn could be unhitched, wound onto the spindle, and the process repeated. It is important to include this description of the basic method in discussing the wooden spindles from York because several features on the tools reflect variations in the basic method.

The majority of wooden spindles found in northwest Europe which date from the 4th to the 15th century are double-ended with an off-centre maximum diameter and tapered ends. *6646–9* and *6697* fall into this category, *6646–8* are Anglo-Scandinavian (Periods 3, 4B and 5B respectively) whilst *6649* is medieval (Period 6) and *6697* is unstratified. Another complete Anglo-Scandinavian double-ended spindle was found at 6–8 Pavement (*510*, Fig.54, *AY* 17/3). A whorl is usually fixed on the shorter end of an asymmetrical double-ended spindle. Sometimes a whorl is found in situ on a spindle, however, as on examples from Leicester (Mellor and Pearce 1981, fig.51, 71), medieval Lund (Mårtensson and Wahlöö 1970, fig.147), Novgorod (Kolchin 1989, fig.113, 8–10) and the 9th century Oseberg ship burial (Brøgger and Shetelig 1928, fig.108). In the case of three wooden spindles from Meols (Morris 1984a, fig.21) and one from 9th–11th century Hedeby (Graham-Campbell 1980, pl.67), wear marks around the spindle indicate the whorl's position, or spiral marks from the thread indicate which end held the thread.

Double-ended spindles can be used either way up, with the maximum diameter and whorl above or below the centre. In either mode, the spindle works well since thread can be wound on the spindle below the whorl or above it. Different methods of using a spindle are illustrated in Figs.811a–c, *AY* 17/11. On some double-ended spindles, it is possible to identify which end was used uppermost by a single notch cut into the wood for hitching (as *6647* and *6697*), or a hook fixed into the wood for the same purpose, a feature which can be seen on one of the Meols spindles. On some spindles, there are notches at both ends. *6649* has an incised slit 10mm from one end and a V-sectioned notch cut into the side at the opposite end. Four possible spindles with parallel sides and V-sectioned notches cut into each end were recovered from Vimose. These date from the 4th century and would presumably have been used in the same way as *6649*. Another similar medieval example was found at Trig Lane in London (Morris 1984a, fig.22). One notch could have been for hitching, the other for securing the initial thread. The spindles may even have been used with either end uppermost, at different times, for different weights of thread. Most double-ended spindles do not have the maximum thickness in the centre, but often two-thirds of the way along the length, giving optional positions.

Spindles such as *6648* have no slot or notch at either end for hitching the thread which would have been wound in a loop round the spinner's thumb and slipped over the top of the spindle.

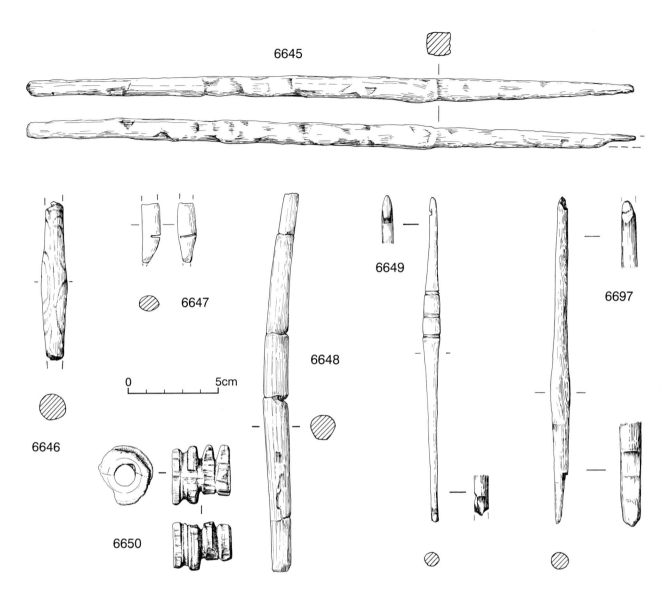

6645

6646

6647

6648

6649

6650

6697

Fig.1147 *Tools used in thread production: distaff 6645; spindles 6646–9 from 16–22 Coppergate and 6697 from the Coppergate watching brief site; whorl for a spindle wheel 6650. Scale 1:2, enlargement of notches on spindles 6649 and 6697 1:1*

The weight, and therefore the size and length of a spindle varies with the length of fibre, thickness of thread required and amount of twist (Baines 1977, 41). This fact, and also the differences in sizes, weights and material of whorls (see pp.1735–45, *AY* 17/11), may help to explain the great variation in the size of wooden spindles found. A single-ended type with a carved all-in-one whorl found at Christchurch Place, Dublin (Morris 1984a, T85), was only 130mm long, whereas a large Viking Age double-ended type from Hedeby (Schietzel 1970, Abb.8.3) was almost three times longer at 356mm.

Wooden spindles in their crudest form were sticks smoothed and shaped with a knife or other bladed

tool and are likely to have been home-made items. The Anglo-Scandinavian spindles *6646–8* were made from oak and ash and may fall into this category. Certain spindles, however, were very finely crafted by a lathe-turner and decorated with groups of turned grooves. The medieval spindle from Coppergate was finely turned from a Rosaceae species (*6649*), and decorated with three pairs of grooves. This dichotomy of manufacturing technique may be a chronological one. Double-ended spindles to compare with the Anglo-Scandinavian ones from York have been found at 9th–11th century Hedeby (Schietzel 1970, Abb.8, 3; Graham-Campbell 1980, pl.67), Ribe (ibid., pl.68), in the 9th century Oseberg ship burial (Brøgger and Shetelig 1928, fig.108), at

Christchurch Place, Dublin (Morris 1984a, fig.21, T68), in a 10th century building at St Peter's Street, Northampton (Williams 1979, 319), and from 7th to 10th century levels at Lagore Crannog (Hencken 1950, fig.82B). None of these have been positively identified as lathe-turned products, and are all likely to have been hand-carved. We can be absolutely certain that work of superb quality was being produced by the lathe-turners in York in the 10th century, but it is possible that at this period small items such as spindles were not a usual part of the turner's repertoire. A finely turned yew bobbin dating to Period 5B (see below, *6651*), however, would seem to suggest otherwise.

More than 800 spindles were found in the excavations in Novgorod, dating from the mid 10th to 15th centuries (Kolchin 1989, 111–12 and fig.113). These were also either handmade or lathe-turned, but Kolchin does not make any chronological distinction.

Whorl for spindle wheel (Fig.1147)

6650 is a whorl for a spindle wheel. It is a circular lathe-turned poplar or alder cylinder with a hole 11mm diameter augered through its central axis and the remains of three deeply turned grooves in its circumference. The well-defined ridges between the grooves were broken in many places and the object could well have been discarded and replaced.

The composite device known as a spindle wheel is the earliest type of spinning wheel in which spinning and winding on were separate processes. It was made from individual components of wood, mounted in a bench. At one end, one or two uprights supported a horizontal spindle and its bearings, the spindle passing through a hole in a small wooden whorl positioned between the bearings. Its circumference had to be deeply grooved to take the driving band from the large wheel supported by uprights at the other end of the bench. Turning the wheel with one hand and drawing out fibres from a rolag in the other hand, the spinning process is similar to suspended spindle spinning (for a reconstruction see Fig.810, *AY* 17/11).

6650 may have functioned as a whorl for a spindle wheel with the drive band for the large wheel passing around one of the three grooves. Such whorls often had multiple grooves so that as one wore out,

the others could be used. Only one groove of *6650* was still relatively intact. Spindle wheels were certainly in use in north-west Europe in the later 13th century: in 1298 the use of wheel-spun yarn was forbidden for warp threads in Speyer in Germany (Baines 1977, 53). It was almost certainly used in medieval England and well established there by at least 1340, since there is a representation of one in the Luttrell Psalter (British Library Add. MS 42130, fo.193). *6650* was found in a 17th/18th century deposit which contained earlier material, and so could be medieval in date, a unique object with as yet no excavated parallels.

Thread handling and fabric production

After spinning, thread was removed from the spindle and reeled into skeins. When it had been washed and dyed, a skein would then have been placed on a swift and the thread transferred onto spools, bobbins or shuttles for use in weaving and other textile manufacturing processes. No pieces of wooden reels, swifts or spools have been found in the Coppergate excavations, although 9th century reels and a swift found in the Oseberg ship burial (Brøgger and Shetelig 1928, figs.119, 121–2) suggest the form such tools might have had.

Tapestry flutes and possible two-beam loom (Fig.1148)

6651 is a fine, smooth, lathe-turned yew bobbin with a flat disc-shaped head below which is a rebate 2mm deep and 8mm wide. The other end has a smoothly rounded point. Although it resembles in shape and size the South Buckinghamshire 'thumper' type of lace bobbin used in England throughout the later 18th and 19th centuries (Huetson 1983, 141), it is very unlikely to have been a lace bobbin since bobbin lace-making was probably not invented until the end of the 15th century either in Flanders or Italy (Palliser 1911, 109–11). A small amount of thread would have been wound around the rebate, and it would almost certainly have been used in textile production of some kind, the most likely being as a weft bobbin in tapestry weaving. For an illustration of a modern example see Fig.818, *AY* 17/11.

One of the techniques in tapestry weaving involved using small amounts of different coloured threads on a vertical two-beam loom to create different pictures or patterns (Wild 1970, 71). The differ-

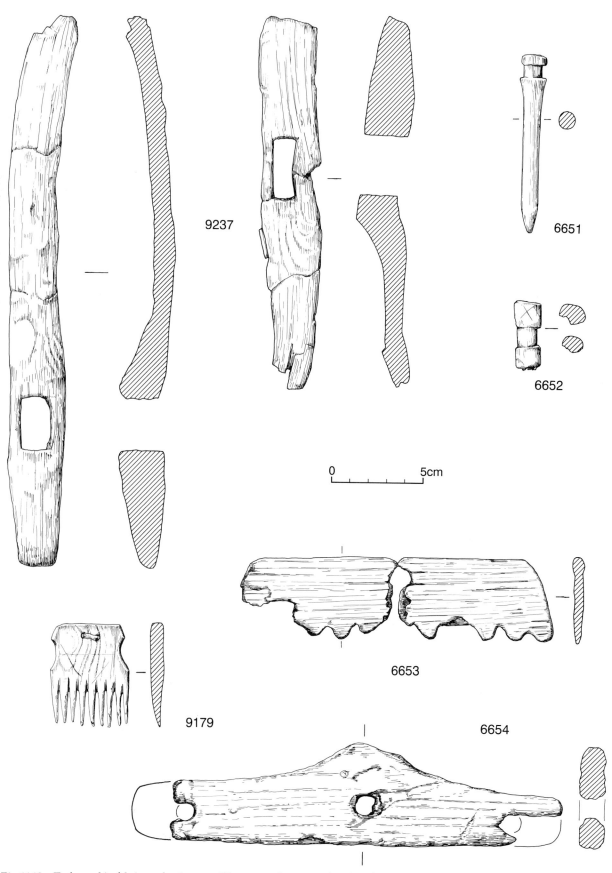

Fig.1148 *Tools used in fabric production: possible tapestry loom or embroidery frame from the College of the Vicars Choral at Bedern 9237; weft bobbins 6651–2, weft-beater blade 6653 and heddle cradle 6654 from 16–22 Coppergate; weaving comb 9179 from the Coppergate watching brief site. Scale 1:2*

9237

6651

6652

0   5cm

6653

9179

6654

ent colours were wound onto wooden tapestry flutes, and a Dutch illustration in Christine de Pisan's 'Cité des Dames' dated to 1475 (British Library Add. MS 20698, fo.90), shows a woman using a wooden tapestry flute on a tapestry loom. Two men working at tapestry looms also used wooden flutes in an old Testament Picture Book from northern Italy dated to c.1400 (British Library Add. MS 15277, fo.15v). The 12th century tapestry from Skog Church in Halsingland, Sweden (Magnusson 1976, 54–5), was probably woven on a loom using this technique, but it was already a well-established technique in Viking Age north-west Europe. Tapestries (Foote and Wilson 1970, pl.13) and two-beam looms (Brøgger and Shetelig 1928, 176–9, pl.XIV) were found in the 9th century Oseberg ship burial. There are representations of these vertical looms in the 9th century Utrecht Psalter (Utrecht Library, fo.84) and the 12th century Eadwine Psalter (Trinity College, Cambridge) (both manuscripts derived from earlier versions which probably originate in a late Roman or possibly Byzantine original; p.1761, *AY* 17/11) and in Hrabanus Maurus's 'De Universo' (Monte Cassino Library MS 132) dated c.1023.

Fragments of one of the horizontal beams from an ash frame (*9237*) were found in late 14th–early 15th century levels at Bedern. There would originally have been tenons from two side bars fixed into the mortice holes at each end of the beam, and another beam at the other end to complete a rectangular frame. Comparison with a pre-Norman beam fragment found in the excavations at Dublin Castle (R.A. Hall, pers. comm.), almost certainly part of a two-beam tapestry loom like that from Oseberg, suggests that the Bedern fragment may also be part of a similar frame.

Both the York and Dublin beams have rounded oval ends perforated vertically by rectangular mortice holes to hold side frames; both have a central bar between these two ends — that on *9237* is D-shaped, whereas the bar on the Dublin fragment is elliptical in cross-section. The differences between the two pieces lie in their size and the fact that the Dublin fragment has a series of equidistant but closely spaced nicks/grooves along what is probably the top edge, suggesting the positions where the warp threads were fastened on the loom beam. *9237* could have been used in this way but there are no surviving marks from warp threads, and it is not incon-

ceivable that it is part of a different type of frame, for example, one used for stretching an embroidery canvas. The Dublin beam was 680–700mm wide, whereas *9237* is only 485mm wide and may have been a hand-held frame.

6651 could have been used as a tapestry flute, along with others, each carrying a different coloured thread. *6652* could be a broken flute used in the same way. Although its shaft and point have not survived, it has a shallow rebate 2mm deep and 10mm wide for holding thread. The closest parallels for the York flutes are a group of over 200 carved Roman bone flutes dating to c.365, found at Kourion in Cyprus (Soren 1988, 47 and 53). They were mistakenly identified by the excavator and local Cypriots as lace bobbins. Different types of wooden flutes used in Europe are illustrated by Whiting (1928, 307), the York flutes resembling those used on Gobelin tapestries.

Weft-beater blade (Fig.1148)

6653 is a 14th century coarse-toothed wooden weft-beater blade which would originally have been hafted with a wooden handle (see reconstruction in Fig.816, *AY* 17/11). This type of beater is usually associated with a two-beam loom, and Walton Rogers suggests this wooden example could have been used in the manufacture of coarse sacking (ibid., 1762).

Heddle cradle and heddle rod (Figs.1148–9)

Two wooden objects found in Period 6 levels at 16–22 Coppergate (*6654–5*) are small parts of a large, composite wooden device, the horizontal treadle loom. This type of loom is discussed at length elsewhere (pp.386–91, *AY* 17/5) in relation to fragments of textiles found on the site which can only have been made on a horizontal treadle loom.

On this loom, the warp was stretched between two beams which were held in place horizontally by a framework. Multiple heddle rods (marked as shafts in Fig.162, *AY* 17/5) were suspended from the roof or superstructure by pulleys, and sometimes additional heddle cradles (not shown in Fig.162). The heddle rods opened and closed the sheds using treadles below the loom. Walton Rogers has also discussed the possibility that some textiles with patterned weaves, for example *1336*, may have been produced on a horizontal loom without treadles but with multiple heddle rods (p.358, *AY* 17/5). A reconstruction of a horizontal

6655

0   10cm

Fig.1149 *Tools used in fabric production: possible heddle rod 6655. Scale 1:3*

loom with heddle rods and heddle cradles is shown in Fig.820, *AY* 17/11.

A heddle cradle is a wooden bar, usually with three points of attachment, one in the centre to suspend it from a pulley, and one at each end to suspend the heddle rod below. *6654* is a late 11th–early 13th century oak heddle cradle with three holes 10mm diameter, one at each end and a third set below a central rounded projection. The latter hole has been worn on the upper edge where the suspending thread was attached and one of the others has broken where the thread has pulled downwards. Large and small heddle cradles similar to *6654* are shown in the Ypres Kuerboek, c.1310 (see Patterson 1956, fig.183), and six heddle cradles are shown in an early 15th century manuscript (Milan Bibl. Ambrosiana Cod. G 301, fo.3r).

Several parallels for the York heddle cradle have been found on sites in northern Europe, including two from 3rd century layers at Feddersen Wierde (Haarnagel 1979, 331, Taf.30, 4 and 5), one from medieval Bergen dated to 1248–1332 (Øye 1988, 75, fig.III, 11) and a 15th century one from Novgorod (Kolchin 1989, pl.120, 14). Kolchin also identified another type of heddle cradle which he termed 'dog'. More than 40 of these were found at Novgorod (ibid., 119, pl.119, 7–8, pl.120, 7–13) and took the form of cylindrical rods with a wide groove in the centre and one at each end to function in the same way as the three holes on *6654*. If the Feddersen Wierde objects are heddle cradles, they are extremely early in date, since horizontal looms are usually considered to have reached Europe only in the 10th or 11th century (pp.1763–6, *AY* 17/11). They may have been used for some other purpose; for example, the author has seen objects similar to heddle cradles being used in Shet-

land for hanging two sheep carcasses, the weight of one balancing the other.

6655, from an early 13th century context, is almost certainly a heddle rod with a deep V-sectioned groove and an adjacent shallower one cut into each end. Knob-like ends prevented the heddles from coming off the rod, and cords fastened to the grooves were used to suspend the heddle rod from pulleys or heddle cradles. It was carved from a roundwood alder pole 20mm diameter. If the rods for a particular loom had to be a specific length (in this case, reconstructed at approximately 445mm), this rod may have been rejected since one end was broken. Over 35 heddle rods with knob-like ends and deep grooves dating to the late 13th to 15th centuries were found at Novgorod (Kolchin 1989, 116–17, pl.118). These were very similar to but longer than *6655*, in two groups averaging 600–50mm and 750–80mm. Ten of the rods were found in pairs, lying together. Since the York and Novgorod heddle rods were quite short, they could have been used on narrow horizontal looms operated by one person in the home, and this suggests that they were used in domestic textile production rather than a professional industry. In her discussion of some of the medieval textiles found at Coppergate, Walton Rogers is in no doubt that a horizontal loom had been used to make some of them (p.389, *AY* 17/5). Fragments of two more possible heddle rods of indeterminate length, but with one end carved with the same knob-like projection and deep groove as those from York and Novgorod, were found in late medieval Lübeck (Falk 1983a, Abb.4, 7 and 7, 7).

6655 was found in the same Period 6 context as the finely turned spindle *6649*, suggesting that spindle-spun thread and the narrow horizontal loom were being used at the same period in 13th century York.

Weaving comb (Fig.1148)

Weaving combs were used to beat the weft threads and needed to be smooth, polished and straight with well-spread short teeth (Hoffman 1988, 234). These qualities are all present in *9179*, which is an exceptionally fine, smooth Anglo-Scandinavian implement made from a tangentially sawn piece of a Pomoideae species such as apple, pear, hawthorn or rowan. It is a tool specially made for the purpose by a woodworking craftsman. Not only are there saw marks on one flat side, but there are marks at the base of the wooden teeth at each side showing the use of a cross-set saw. There are nine teeth, oval in cross-section, and small curved hollows cut into the sides at the other end to act as fingerholds. Two small holes pierced through the handle end with an awl retain fragments of a small leather carrying strap. In antiquity this tool would have had a smooth, polished surface which was absolutely essential for ensuring the threads were not torn and distorted. It is therefore possibly a weaving comb.

The closest wooden parallels for *9179* are five combs from Novgorod dating from the 12th–14th centuries (Kolchin 1989, pl.112, 4 and 6), although they are larger than *9179* and have 21–23 much finer teeth. They also have curved hollows cut into the sides and top to act as fingerholds but they are 130mm long and 100mm wide. Another Viking Age parallel, made in bone with a longer handle, is a comb with ten teeth from the Oseberg ship burial (Brøgger and Shetelig 1928, fig.126c). An alternative interpretation is that *9179* is a hair or beard comb.

Artefacts used in Non-Woodworking Crafts and Activities

Business transactions: tally sticks (Fig.1150)

9015–16 are fragments of medieval wooden tally sticks, marked with notches to indicate sums of money owed, to act as a counting record or to serve as duplicated accounts, tags or labels. The word tally is derived from the Latin *talea*, meaning a bar, rod or stick of wood. *9015*, dating to the mid/late 14th century, was made from a half-section alder branch which had been whittled flat, but both ends are broken and bark remains in places. Seventeen notches were cut on one flat surface and fifteen notches were cut into one side edge; since not all the notches of each group correspond, they were probably separate sets. *9016*, dating to the mid/late 13th century, is a roughly carved sliver of oak, rectangular in cross-section, with four wide and 27 narrow notches cut across the same flat surface.

Several medieval wooden tally sticks found on other English sites are comparable to *9015–16*. A 13th–15th century notched wooden tally stick was found in rubbish dumped as reinforcement for a waterfront causeway at Hungate in York (Richardson 1959, 102), although no details of its dimensions or species are known. A small tally stick with seven notches on one side in groups of three and four, and eight notches on the other side, was found with late Saxon/early medieval pottery at Milk Street, London (Morris 1984a, fig.81, M263), a large 14th century tally carved from a curved branch with two groups of eight and nine notches on one side and two groups of nine and ten notches on the other was found in King's Lynn (Clarke and Carter 1977, fig.172, 78), and eight late 13th century tally sticks roughly carved from small branches of alder and poplar with varying numbers of notches were found in a stone-lined cess pit at Cuckoo Lane in Southampton (Platt and Coleman-Smith 1975, fig.229, 1647–54). By far the largest group of excavated medieval tallies comes from Bergen, where approximately 600 items have been found dating from 1130–1350 (Grandell 1988, 66–70). Some of these may have been used for checking ships' cargoes as they were loaded or unloaded and for counting skins and furs.

Tally sticks have been used all over the world in all kinds of trades (Jenkinson 1911, 368). However, it seems that only the English Exchequer formalised the use of tallies as an official accounting procedure. Many of the medieval tallies which the Exchequer used survive in the Public Records Office, and date from the 12th century until 1826 (Jenkinson 1911; 1925). They were essentially physical wooden receipts for payments made, and were extremely important items at a time when most people could not read and parchment was a costly material. A prepared stick was marked with different-sized notches corresponding to values of pounds, shillings and pence. The stick was then split in two by inserting a cutting tool from one side and turning it to follow the grain for the rest of the length. This left a broad butt end on one piece (the stock) and only the genuine smaller piece (the foil) could be matched against it in the pattern of notches and wood grain. The stock would be given to the payer as a receipt and returned to the Exchequer when the account was finally made up. A split tally which was a stock of this type was found in Bergen (Grandell 1988, fig.3).

9015–16 and their English parallels are not stocks, and it is difficult to ascertain if any of them are foils in the sense described. They are more likely to be private tallies used to record transactions or keep simple accounts. An example of private use of tallies is recorded in the Kitchener's Roll for Selby Abbey (N. Yorkshire) in 1416–17, where 'the granger answers

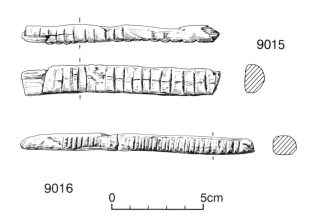

9015

9016

0   5cm

Fig.1150 *Tally sticks 9015–16 from 16–22 Coppergate. Scale 1:2*

for 282 quarts of wheat for the household as shown by seven tallies, examined, and he also answers for 625 quarts of malt as shown by tallies'. The granger could presumably answer for his payments because of the tallies he obtained as receipts. The use of private tallies was fairly universal in the 13th and 14th centuries in England (ibid., 313); York, Southampton, King's Lynn and London were four large medieval centres where commerce was highly developed. Although the sizes of the notches on Exchequer tallies was regulated, there is no way of calculating the values represented by the notches on *9015–16*. Private tallies would have varied with date, area, trader and goods. *9016* and the tally from Milk Street, London, have wide and narrow notches which may represent different values.

Leatherworking: awls and last (Fig.1151)

Tools made of wood or incorporating wooden elements were used by leatherworkers. Two of these have been found at two sites in York: awls with narrow iron points and tangs set in small circular holes in wooden handles which were used as general leatherworkers' tools, and lasts used specifically by shoemakers as blocks for shaping leather shoes and boots.

From 16–22 Coppergate, *9017* is a small Anglo-Scandinavian wooden awl handle made of beech or *Prunus* sp. with a circular hole for the tang of an iron awl which is now missing. *9018* is 12th–13th century in date but is a type of iron awl whose form was the same from the Roman period to the present day, and would have been the type originally fitted into *9017*. On *9018*, only traces of the wooden handle survive, and the species is unidentifiable. Similar Anglo-Scandinavian awls have been found at 6–8 Pavement (Fig.41, *422–6*, AY 17/3), two of which were complete with their wooden handles. Thirty-nine Anglo-Scandinavian iron awls without handles have been found on the 16–22 Coppergate site (pp.552–4, Fig.222, AY 17/6). A Viking awl with a complete wooden handle and suspension loop, and another awl handle, were found in the 9th century Oseberg ship burial (Brøgger and Shetelig 1928, figs.146–7), Viking Age and 13th century awls with wooden handles were found at Fishamble Street and Winetavern Street, Dublin (Lang 1988, pl.XII; National Museum of Ireland 1973, 41), and Anglo-Scandinavian and medieval wooden awl handles without their iron points have been found at Lagore Crannog (Hencken

1950, fig.84), High Street, Dublin, Norton Priory, Runcorn (Morris 1984a, fig.80, M242–3 and M253), King's Lynn (Clarke and Carter 1977, fig.171, 3), Westgate, Oxford (Henig 1976, fig.16, 2), and six sites in London — Custom House, Milk Street, Trig Lane, Blossoms Inn, Worship Street and Seal House (Henig 1974, fig.42, 247; Morris 1984a, fig.80, M247–51). Some awls may have been fitted with antler or bone handles, like the antler handle on an awl found in Århus (Andersen et al. 1971, 220, BCS). Iron awl points without handles have been found at many other sites in England, some with other leatherworking tools and heavy concentrations of manufacturing waste, for example, at Eastgate, Beverley (Atkinson and Foreman 1992, 175, fig.80, 303–11).

Awls like these were used for making channels and small holes in leather prior to stitching, among other tasks, but it is possible that some of the awls listed above were also used in crafts such as woodworking. A 15th century illustration of a cobbler (Stadtbibl. Nürnberg MS Mendel I Amb. 317) shows how an awl was used to make holes in a leather sole (Grew and de Neergaard 1988, fig.71b). Most of the wooden handles were made from small roundwood and were whittled or lathe-turned. It is not possible to identify whether *9017* was lathe-turned since it is too abraded.

9019 is a post-medieval last carved from a split section of willow. It has a narrow, rounded toe end, a wide body with curved sides and is waisted at the instep with vertical grooves cut down each side. The heel end is square and rounded, and narrows vertically to a flat top with no provision for a peg or socket to attach it to a bench. It was presumably held between the knees, a method shown in a 15th century illustration in fo.48v of the Mendel Housebook (Treue et al. 1965, pl.84). The overall outline of *9019* with its sharply cinched waist is very different from the three Anglo-Scandinavian lasts found at 6–8 Pavement (Figs.74 and 77, *492–4*, AY 17/3), and other earlier medieval lasts such as those from Charavines (Colardelle and Colardelle 1980, fig.47, 3), Hedeby (Graham-Campbell 1980, pl.476), Wolin in Poland (Kostrzewski 1949, fig.149), Lagore Crannog (Hencken 1950, fig.86) and Oslo in Norway (Schia 1977, fig.36). This, along with its date, suggests that *9019* was used in the production of later designs of shoes with entirely different shapes of leather sole. The closest parallels for *9019* come from Novgorod,

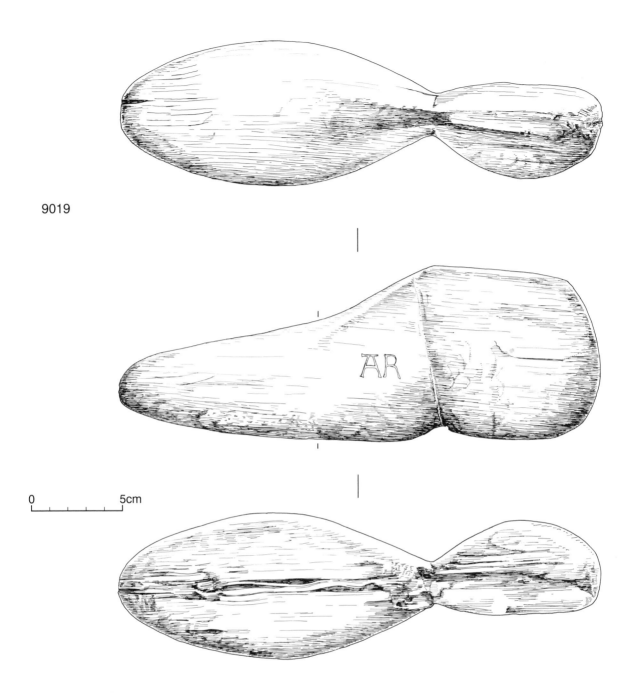

9019

0   5cm

Fig.1151 *Willow last for shoe- or patten-making 9019, from 16–22 Coppergate. Scale 1:2*

where 102 lasts were found dating from the 10th to the 15th century (Kolchin 1989, 28–30). Several have narrow waists and shaped insteps like *9019* (ibid., pl.16, 5).

Although the Coppergate last has a slightly rounded toe, it could probably still have been used to make narrow waisted shoes with pointed toes as well as rounded ones. Two more 15th century illustrations from the Mendel Housebook (fos.68v and 93v) show pairs of lasts with narrow waists and pointed toes in racks on the wall (Treue et al. 1965, pls.108 and 142). Shoes with this distinct waisted sole outline constructed using the turnshoe method (Thomas 1980, 8–10; Grew and de Neergaard 1988, 47–8) have been found at many medieval sites in England including Parliament Street in York (Fig.110, *AY* 17/4), Coventry (Thomas 1980, figs.1, 5, 7, 9–18), Austin Friars, Leicester (Mellor and Pearce 1981, figs.55–60), Southampton (Platt and Coleman-Smith

1975, figs.260–1, 264), Eastgate, Beverley (Atkinson and Foreman 1992, figs.87 and 89–90), London (Grew and de Neergaard 1988, figs.106–8) and Hull (Armstrong 1977, figs.20–4; 1980, figs.29–30). It is a common medieval shoe sole shape with wide joint, narrow waist, small seat and an oval or rounded toe (Thomas 1980, 10).

Lasts were often used in pairs and were asymmetrical to make distinct left- and right-foot shoe shapes. *9019* is symmetrical, however, and could have been used to make shoes for both feet. Lasts were not necessarily the exact outline of the finished product, although some were probably made to fit a particular person's feet. *9019* has the letters 'AR' branded into the side at the toe end, which may be the initials of the person it was made for or even owned by. The last is only one of many wooden objects of a similar date which were found in 16th–19th century layers in the same well, but three of these objects were branded with the initials 'SR' — rake *8977*, fragment *8694* and lathe-turned bowl *8586*. These initials are probably owner's marks on wooden items used by the same household, possibly the same household which marked the last with 'AR'.

On the evidence of the leather finds themselves (Carlisle *AY 17/–*, in prep.) and leatherworkers' tools such as *9017–19*, shoe making was probably carried out in the vicinity of 16–22 Coppergate during the Anglo-Scandinavian and medieval periods. Similar evidence has also been found at three other sites in York, 6–8 Pavement (pp.80, 138–42, 144–5, *AY 17/3*), Feasegate (Dyer and Wenham 1958, 422) and Hungate (Richardson 1959, 63–4), and one of the awls from High Street, Dublin (Morris 1984a, fig.80, M242), was found with much scrap leather.

Riding: saddle bow (Figs.1152–5)

9020 is a broken fragment of a much larger one-piece saddle bow found discarded in a layer dating to Period 5B. A rounded extension forming a wing on one side of the saddle bow is perforated horizontally by two augered peg holes 6mm diameter. Fragments of the arched front pommel and a lower bar survive, which can be reconstructed above and below a crescent-shaped hole. The lower bar is not carved in a straight line with the wing, and one possible reconstruction shows a shallow arch below the bar (Fig.1153). Another possible reconstruction shows a steeper arch (Fig.1152). The complete saddle bow

was one component of a com-posite wooden saddle (see Fig.1154), the rest of which has not survived.

Examination of the grain on the piece which does survive reveals that one of two types of timber could potentially have been used to make the saddle bow. It could have been carved from a radially split section of oak such that the wood grain would run obliquely through the saddle bow. If this was the case, the grain would run along one wing, but across the other, making the latter extremely weak. The much more likely alternative is that the saddle bow was made from a specially selected piece of timber taken from the junction of a large side branch with the main stem, and carved such that the grain would run in two directions from the centre of the pommel arch down each wing. This was almost certainly the type of timber used for a 10th century saddle bow found at Fishamble Street in Dublin (Lang 1988, fig.113) and 12th and 13th century examples from Novgorod (Kolchin 1989, pl.90, 6–7), and would have been the strongest form of timber available to make this curved shape.

Every surface of *9020* is decorated, except for one flat side and the underside of the surviving wing (Fig.1152). The decoration involves three different materials: shallow relief carving in the wood with tiny hand gouges and chisels, reed inlay and rows of tiny tin nails with a silvery appearance. Small interlocking triangular panels containing triquetra knots were carved along each side of the pommel arch and lower bar and one side of the wing. Each triangle was surrounded by three concentric triangular borders, two plain with a carved beaded moulding in between. A sub-rectangular panel on the upper surface of the wing was filled with simple three-strand interlace, surrounded by a plain-beaded-plain concentric border. Each triangular panel with its border was separated from its neighbour by a strip of split reed set in a shallow groove, held down by a row of tin nails, identified as tin alloy by X-ray fluorescence analysis. Similar reed strips were laid in grooves across the top and bottom edges of the pommel arch, lower bar and the top of the decorated side of the wing. Only fragments of the reed inlay now survive.

The surface of the saddle bow is very worn on the front and back faces of the arch and the front face of the wing, and some of the decoration has been almost worn off in places, suggesting that the saddle

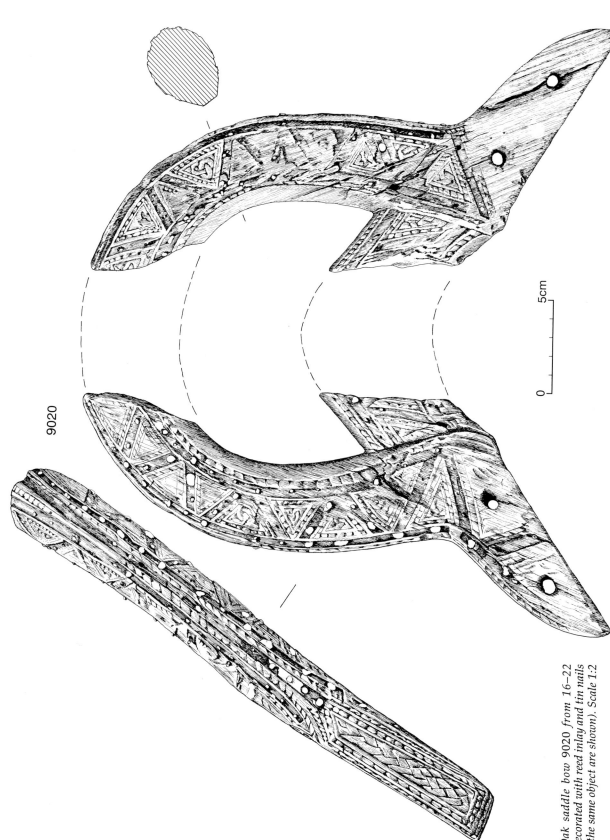

9020

0 _____ 5cm

Fig.1152 *Oak saddle bow 9020 from 16–22 Coppergate, decorated with reed inlay and tin nails (both sides of the same object are shown). Scale 1:2*

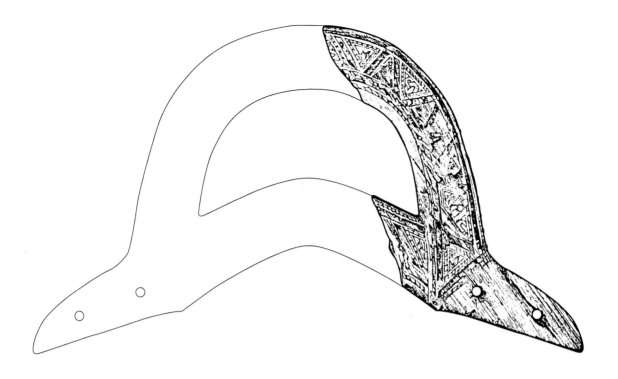

Fig.1153   *Wide reconstruction of saddle bow 9020*

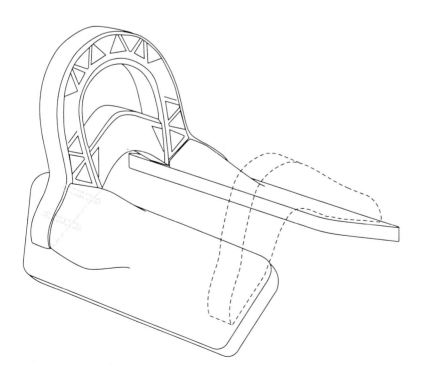

Fig.1154   *Reconstruction showing how saddle bow 9020 would have fitted on to a composite wooden saddle*

2343

Fig.1155   *Detailed views of saddle bow fragment 9020*

had served a useful life and was probably quite old when it finally broke and was discarded.

Interlocking triangular fields with interlace ornament and beaded borders are also found on a leather sheath for a small knife found in Parliament Street (*755*, pl.XIII, *AY* 17/4), and it has been suggested that the sheath is possibly earlier than Anglo-Scandinavian in date (ibid., 241) especially since small sub-triangular fields and beaded borders are particularly characteristic of the 9th/early 10th century Trewhiddle style. Although *9020* was found in a context dating to Period 5B (c.975 to early/mid 11th century), the amount of wear shows it was old when it was deposited. A 9th century date has already been suggested for the saddle bow (Wilson 1984, 111), but triangular fields with interlaced knots also appear on bone motif pieces from London (Pritchard 1991, figs.3.62 and 3.66), one of them firmly dated to the 10th century, and on a bone motif piece from Viking Age Dublin (Lang 1988, fig.120). These are very similar to those on *9020*. Lang suggests that knots composed of interlaced strands are part of a continuing tradition which is so conservative that there is an overlap between earlier and later use (ibid., 15). If this is so, an Anglo-Scandinavian date and origin for the saddle bow must not be ruled out.

The overall decoration on *9020* suggests that at least the saddle bow on this type of saddle (if not the rest of the wooden components) was not covered in any way by leather, padding or fabric. Wooden parts of a 6th century arched saddle bow from grave XII at Vendel in Sweden were also decorated with carving, and this saddle bow (along with others such as those from grave XIV at Vendel, grave 7 at Valsgärde in Sweden and grave 1782 at Krefeld-Gellep in Germany) also had decorative metal binding strips and/or mounts (Arrhenius 1983, figs.13–15). Even though the decorative elements on *9020* are in themselves quite simple, the panels, borders, inlay and nails were combined to create one of the finest pieces of decorated woodwork of this period to have been found in England. It was a fine piece of craftsmanship and would have been an ostentatious and expensive item for its owner in Anglo-Scandinavian York.

The basic saddle tree (or wooden frame) of the composite wooden saddle used in early medieval Europe seems to have had four wooden components — two side boards, a back or cross-piece at the cantle

and a saddle bow at the pommel (Fig.1154). In some parts of northern Europe it continued in use to the present day, for example in Russia and Poland (Kolchin 1989, pl.90, 4–5; Kostrzewski 1949, fig.151, 1). The shape of the pieces may have varied through time and in different areas, but these folk examples and surviving archaeological fragments of saddles help to suggest the kind of construction of which *9020* was part.

The use of wooden frames seems to be a long-established method of making the structure of saddles. Saddles found in burials at Pazyryk in Siberia dated to the 5th and 4th centuries BC were made with two cushions held on either side of the horse's back by wooden back pieces and saddle bows (Rudenko 1970, 129). Reconstruction of Roman cavalry saddles has suggested that their leather covers and horns would probably have been mounted on an internal wooden structure (Connolly and Van Driel-Murray 1991). Stirrups do not appear in north-west Europe until about the 6th century, and the type of saddle used would have been suited to a method of riding without stirrups. Saddles found in Hunnic and Frankish graves of the 5th–6th century are unlike Roman horned saddles and had high wooden back pieces, arched wooden saddle bows with extra semi-circular elevations and wooden side boards. Examples have been found in a grave at Derkul, South Ural (Vierck 1972, 213–17; Arrhenius 1978, fig.14a), grave 446 at Wesel-Bislich (Jannsen 1981, 149–69, Abb.8) and grave 1782 at Krefeld-Gellep (Pirling 1974, Abb.12; Arrhenius 1983, fig.15). This kind of saddle with a high frame to give the rider a steady seat has also been found in early Vendel period graves at Vendel and Valsgärde (Arrhenius 1983, 63–4, figs.13–14; Arwidsson 1977, 61ff).

Parts of an early 11th century saddle, closer in date to *9020*, were found in Novgorod and consist of a back piece and two side boards which would have been jointed and pegged into the back piece (Kolchin 1989, pl.90, 1–3). The saddle bow did not survive. An early 9th century saddle found in the Oseberg ship burial also had fragments of a back piece which was jointed and pegged onto two side boards (Brøgger and Shetelig 1928, fig.157 and pl.XVIII). The front edges of the side boards rise abruptly upwards and curve inwards, following the shape of the horse's withers, and there are lines of small holes along the inside and front edges of the side boards, presumably to fasten down a covering. There are no joints or holes which seem specifically intended for fixing on a wooden saddle bow of the Coppergate kind. The arched saddle bow from Coppergate would have been part of a saddle similar in construction to those from Vendel, Valsgärde and Novgorod, rather than the Oseberg saddle. Conventionalised depictions of 11th century saddles on the Bayeux Tapestry (Wilson 1985, pls.14 and 52ff) consistently include a high back and saddle bow, and would appear to be saddles of the type to which *9020* would have been attached.

The positioning of the decoration on *9020* helps to suggest how it was fitted to the saddle. One side of the surviving wing and its upper surface are decorated and were meant to be seen from the front. Joints would have been cut in the front of the two side boards so that the underside of the wings would have stood on the side boards and the undecorated backs of the wings would have butted against vertical surfaces, as on the Russian peasant saddle already described. Wooden pegs fixed horizontally through the two holes in the wing would have fastened the bow to the side board (Fig.1154).

Saddle bows to compare with *9020* have been found at several European sites. The closest in shape and size is an almost complete mid 10th century one from Fishamble Street in Dublin which has a solid arch decorated with a simple incised arch and cross design on one flat side, and two wings, each perforated horizontally by the remains of four peg holes

(Lang 1988, fig.113). It differs from *9020* in that it does not have the crescent-shaped hole below the upper arch, but it is otherwise remarkably similar in outline, and both would have been used on similar saddles. A wide reconstructed outline of *9020* (Fig.1153) shows it could have been up to 400mm wide and 240mm high, while the Dublin saddle bow was probably 260mm wide and 180mm high. A steeper, narrower reconstructed outline of *9020* (Fig.1152) is based on a saddle bow 320mm wide and 290mm high.

A much smaller saddle bow with the same general outline as *9020* and wings perforated by two peg holes was found in the bottom of a lake at Ballincarriga, Co. Westmeath, Ireland (Fig.1156; Day 1879–82, 345, figs.2–3; Morris 1984a, fig.92, M427). It is carved from a solid block of holly and has an arched pommel perforated by a sub-circular hole with an upward-pointing projection, forming a semi-circular space. The wings are plain but the pommel is decorated with carved relief interlace and knots in panels. It is undated by its context, but the interlace ornament suggests an early medieval date. Although it is smaller at only 184mm wide and 64mm high, it would have been fastened to side boards in exactly the same way as *9020*. The difference in size of saddle bows is probably due to the fact that wooden saddles were made specifically to fit individual horses. Other early medieval saddle bows to compare with *9020* include one from Gostkow in Poland (Kostrzewski 1949, fig.151) which has two wings perforated by two horizontal peg holes, and an arch surmounted by a solid

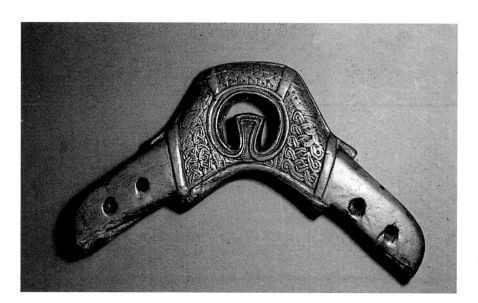

Fig.1156 Saddle bow found at Ballincarriga, Co. Westmeath, Ireland

oval pommel, and one from Christchurch Place, Dublin, which has two wings perforated by three peg holes and a solid angular arched pommel (Morris 1984a, fig.92, M429).

The projection under the arch of the Ballincarriga saddle bow (Fig.1156) may have been a reins holder, a facility which may also originally have been present on *9020* but did not survive. The crescent-shaped hole between the arch and lower bar would allow space for one, but the reins could just as easily have been fastened to the arch through the hole. A metal mount found in Vendel grave XIV which was placed directly on the saddle bow, and triangular knobs on the saddle from Valsgärde 7, may have had the same function (Arrhenius 1983, figs.13a and 14b).

Handling of cord and rope: ropewoods and roperunner (Fig.1157)

Small carved wooden objects were sometimes used in conjunction with ropes for purposes such as tethering, rigging and line-stretching. Four objects from the 16–22 Coppergate excavations are examples of these simple but essential items.

9021–3 are rectangular or sub-rectangular blocks made from radially split sections of oak and ash, perforated by one or two circular holes. *9021* and *9023* are Anglo-Scandinavian and late 11th century in date respectively, with two holes each, 20mm and 16mm in diameter respectively, both now broken through one or both holes. Other two-hole ropewoods of various materials have been found to compare with *9021* and *9023*. The closest parallel is an early medieval wooden ropewood 170mm long from Christchurch Place, Dublin (Morris 1984a, M270). Wooden ropewoods with an S-shaped outline and two circular ends perforated by holes have been found in medieval Bergen (Christensen 1985, fig.9, 24), four wooden ropewoods were found in the 9th century Oseberg ship burial (Petersen 1951, fig.154) and two 11th century ropewoods each with three holes were found in Lund (Nilsson 1976, fig.169). A bone ropewood with two holes was found in a well-equipped Norwegian boat grave at Kaupang (Christensen 1985, 136), and similar whalebone ropewoods were found at Vestfold and Rogaland in Norway (Petersen 1951, 522) and the Brough of Birsay (Curle 1982, fig.50, 279). An 11th century antler example was also found in Lund (Nilsson 1976, fig.170). The blocks with two holes

would have been used as tightening devices on ships' rigging, for tethering animals, for tent guy ropes or as burden ropes for making bundles. Wooden ropewoods similar to *9021* and *9023* have been used until recent times as tightening devices (Estyn Evans 1967, fig.81). The blocks with three holes are more likely to have been parts of swivelling tethers (Morris 1984a, 114).

9022 was found in an early 12th century context, and had only one hole 24mm in diameter. A 9th century oak ropewood from Westgate Street, Gloucester (Morris 1979, fig.17,12), an early 12th century oak ropewood from All Saints Street, King's Lynn (Clarke and Carter 1977, fig.172, 73), and a 13th century one from Cork (Hurley 1982, fig.16.3, 4) would all have functioned similarly to *9022*. Blocks with one hole such as these were possibly used next to knots in rope to prevent the ropes going through certain-sized openings, or as footholds.

The sizes of the holes in both one- and two-hole types indicate the maximum diameter of the rope which was used with the ropewoods; in the York examples this appears to have been 15–24mm.

9024 is a much smaller hazel object which could have been a roperunner, a wooden object fastened onto rope or cord at a specific point to limit its movement. It has a central rectangular hole flanked by two smaller circular holes, and the remains of a small projection at each short end. This type could have functioned in various ways: in the same way as the larger one-hole ropewood, by providing a block too wide to go through an opening, as a toggle to prevent knots in ropes undoing, or as a useful way of linking or fastening ropes by passing the roperunner through a loop in another rope like a button. *9024* was found in the same context as the stave-built vessel lid *8866*, an object which had residual wear marks in the wood from two roperunners which had originally been set perpendicular to two rectangular slits in the lid (Fig.1091, p.2256). Roperunners could have been fastened to the ends of a rope handle which would then have been secured in place on *8866*. *9024* may have been used with *8866*, although it was not found in situ. A similar object, 60mm long with a central hole 7mm in diameter and small pointed extensions projecting from each short end, was found at Winetavern Street, Dublin (Morris 1984a, fig.82, M284).

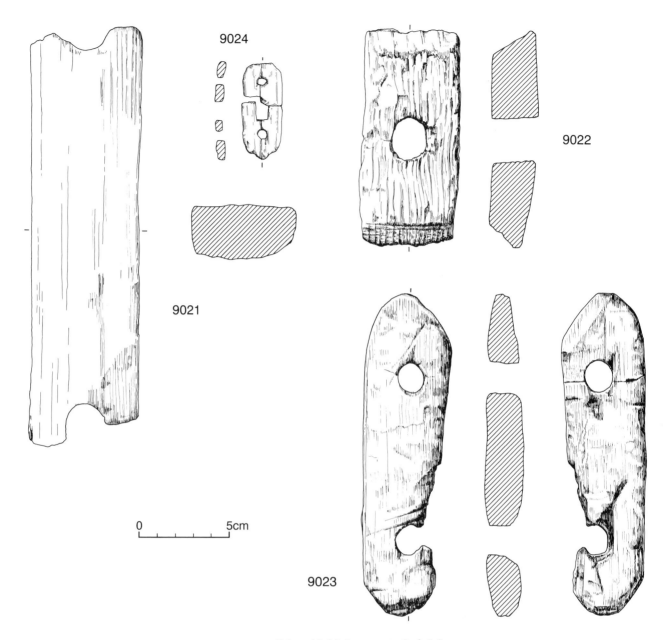

Fig.1157 *Ropewoods 9021–3 and roperunner 9024, all from 16–22 Coppergate. Scale 1:2*

Tanning or glue production: birch bark rolls

Fragments of small strips of tightly rolled birch bark (*Betula* sp.) have been found in levels dating to all phases of occupation on the 16–22 Coppergate site from Period 4A onwards, although not in large quantities or in any concentrations. *9025–31* are single or multiple (up to seven in a group) finds. Some or all of them may be the waste products of debarking birch timber in advance of working it into objects such as roughouts for turned vessels (*8194*) and turned ves-

sels themselves (*8559, 8584–5, 8615*). However, the bark of other species has not been found so consistently on the site over such a long period of time and it is more likely that the bark was collected for a particular purpose.

Birch bark can be readily peeled from the tree in thin strips and used in various ways. In medieval Novgorod, wide strips of birch bark were used to make round and rectangular containers with or without lids in a similar way to the lath-walled boxes *8934–9* (Kolchin 1989, 75–6, pls.70–3), and for documents where letters were made by pressing a hard pointed instrument into the soft fibre of the bark (Thompson 1967, 55–63, figs.55–66). Birch bark has also been used for insulation, roofing material and making canoes (Edlin 1949, 41, 45).

The two most probable uses for the small rolls found on the Coppergate site, however, are either as a tanning material or for making glue. As late as the 19th century in Scotland, birch bark was harvested and used for tanning hides, sails, nets and cordage; the inner bark was whittled from the wood and chopped up into little pieces to be sold to the tanner. When dried and twisted into a rope, birch bark could also function as a candle (ibid., 45). Birch bark contains a high proportion of pitch and rolled pieces burn with a clear flame. If the pitch is extracted and prepared it can be made into a resin-like glue (Taylor 1981, 47). Birch bark rolls, and larger pieces of unrolled birch bark, have been found on the late Norse site at The Biggings, Papa Stour (Morris 1999, 191–3, fig.109).

Games and Pastimes

Games which are played on a specially designed surface with pieces, counters or 'men' are usually referred to as board games. The board does not necessarily have to be an artefact; the playing surface can be scratched on the ground. Pieces need not be specially made; pebbles or seeds can suffice. Certain boards and pieces used in Anglo-Scandinavian and medieval York, however, were specially manufactured items.

Gaming board (Fig.1158)

9032 is a part of a much larger composite wooden gaming board found in a context dating to Period 5B. It is a rectangular riven oak plank 481mm long and 109mm wide which would have been one of probably five such pieces, laid side by side and fastened together by two raised strips nailed across the ends of the planks, making a large square gaming board. Two more strips laid along the edges of the two outer planks would have completed a square frame to help keep the pieces on the board as well as battening the five planks together. One of the latter strips survives in situ on the board, held on by an iron nail with a flat head hammered in from the top of the strip and clenched under the plank. This wooden strip had straight rectangular ends which did not reach the edge of the plank since it butted against the two missing side strips. The two outer corners both have nail holes (one retaining a flat-headed nail clenched under the plank) where the missing strips were attached. Another similar unclenched nail survives near one of the short edges, nailed from underneath the plank, its point probably originally hidden in the missing wooden strip, and there is another nail hole in a similar place on the opposite edge. There is an inlay of beeswax, probably used as a binder or glue (AML report 209/87 by John Evans).

This composite method of constructing gaming boards can be seen on five other boards from three European sites. A single plank found in the ship burial at Gokstad (c.900–5) was probably one of the middle pieces of a four- or five-plank board (Nicolaysen 1882, pl.VIII, 1). It had nail holes down each short end where battening edge strips which did not survive had originally been fastened across it. Three fragmentary, possibly 4th century, gaming boards from a bog at Vimose had some surviving decorated edge strips, each butted at the corner in a mitre joint (Engelhardt 1869, pl.3, 9–11). A nearly complete 12th century board from Trondheim had the remains of three edging strips, also butted at the corners in mitre joints (Christophersen 1987, 55).

The upper playing surface of 9032 was marked out by intersecting incised lines forming three rows of fifteen squares/rectangles. These cells are unequal in size, the rows towards one short end of the plank being much narrower than those at the other end. The lines were scored with a sharp, pointed implement before the edge strips were nailed into place, since their ends were covered by the two missing side strips. When complete, the board would have had fifteen rows and probably fifteen columns. Although it was specially made as a gaming board, probably by a woodworking craftsman, it is not a piece of fine-quality workmanship.

Six other wooden gaming boards found on Scandinavian and Viking Age sites in Europe have rows of square cells incised into the playing surface like 9032. One of the three boards found at Vimose had traces of two rows of eighteen squares (Engelhardt 1869, pl.3, 9); the single plank of a composite gaming board found in the Gokstad ship burial had traces of four rows of fifteen squares; fragments of two Viking Age boards from Fishamble Street and Christchurch Place, Dublin, had ten rows of seven squares and a grid of incised lines forming rows of squares (number unknown) respectively (Morris 1984a, M300 and M398); a board from excavations at Tyskebryggen in Bergen had thirteen rows of thirteen squares (Klindt-Jensen 1970, 165) and the board from Trondheim had eight rows of eleven squares (Christophersen 1987, 54–5).

Other Viking Age gaming boards have rows of augered holes in their playing surface, typified by the decorated 10th century yew board found at Ballinderry 1 Crannog which had seven rows of seven holes (Hencken 1936, 135–6, 175–90, pl.XXV). This fine-quality board was made from a single piece of wood, its raised frame-like edge carved all-in-one-piece with the board. A fragment of an 11th century

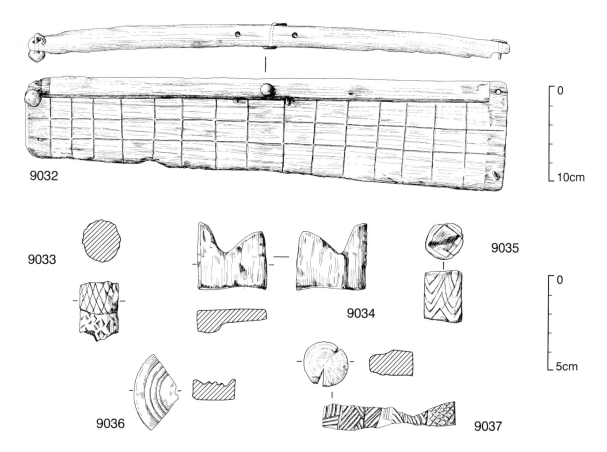

9032

9033

9034

9035

9036

9037

0
10cm

0
5cm

Fig.1158 *Fragment of a gaming board 9032; gaming pieces 9033–7, all from 16–22 Coppergate. Scale 1:2, gaming board 1:4*

wooden board with two surviving rows of seven holes was found at Christchurch Place, Dublin (Morris 1984a, M299), some of the holes retaining fragments of the wooden pegs used in the game, and a fragment of a whalebone board with four rows of five holes was found in a building beside the church on the Brough of Birsay (Curle 1982, fig.50, 274). Two of its sides were incomplete, but the surface remaining was clearly marked out into rough squares by incised lines, with holes roughly at the intersections. A gaming board of Ballinderry type, not closely dated but perhaps 6th–12th century, came from Knockanboy, Co. Antrim (Simpson 1972).

Games would often have been played on square boards where the surface was divided up into equal numbers of 'ranks' and 'files' (terms used in Bell 1980, fig.1). These could have been incised squares or peg holes, and similar games may have been played on both types, the difference being in the form of playing pieces used. Various forms of the game of *tafl* were popular in north-west Europe throughout the first millennium. *Hnefatafl* is referred to in the early

literature (Murray 1913, 444–5), as are the Scandinavian games of *halatafl*, *hnetafl* and *hnottafl* (Fiske 1905, 156; Bell 1960, 75–82). In the *Kroka Refs Saga*, an Icelandic saga written in the 14th century but based on earlier works, 'Gunnar sent from Greenland to King Harald Fairhair a board of walrus bone (*tann-tafl*)', to which a later writer has added 'it was both a *hnefatafl* and a *skaktafl*' (Murray 1952, 58). *Hnefatafl* and its variations could be played on boards with a lattice either eighteen cells square or an odd number of cells square (ibid., 55). *9032* with fifteen squares, the Gokstad and Bergen boards with thirteen squares, the Ballinderry board with seven holes, the Trondheim board with eleven squares and the Vimose board with eighteen squares could all have been used to play various forms of *tafl*. The board referred to in the *Kroka Refs Saga* was a double board, with facilities for two games, and although *9032* had only one pattern on one playing surface, the Gokstad board had a merels (or nine-men's-morris) pattern on its other flat surface, and the board from Fishamble Street, Dublin, had a pattern of incised semi-circles on its flipside.

Gaming counters and playing pieces
(Fig.1158)

The form of pieces used with board games varied considerably, as did the material from which they were made. *9033–7* are Anglo-Scandinavian and medieval wooden pieces, but examples made of antler, stone and re-used Roman tile have also been found at 16–22 Coppergate (Roesdahl et al. 1981, 111–12; pp.1981–2, Fig.940, *AY* 17/12; *9752–8, AY* 17/14). *9033–7* were individual isolated finds, but Viking Age playing pieces have also been found in sets, for example the glass, horn and bone pieces from burials at Birka and Valsgärde (Arbman 1940b, Taf.147–9; Graham-Campbell 1980, 24, pl.95).

Three types of wooden gaming pieces were found at 16–22 Coppergate: counters, upright cylinders and 'men'. *9036* is a fragment of a 15th–16th century counter or small circular lathe-turned disc of a type which is often decorated with grooves or incised ornament on the upper and lower surfaces. *9036* has the remains of four concentric circles on its upper face, a feature also found on a slightly larger late 14th century wooden counter from Trig Lane, London (Morris 1984a, fig.83, M307). Other medieval decorated wooden counters have been found in Lund (Persson 1976, fig.331), Trig Lane (Morris 1984a, fig.83, M308), High Street/Blackfriargate, Hull (Watkin 1987, fig.123, 348–9), Trondheim (Christophersen 1987, 106–7) and Threave Castle (Good and Tabraham 1981, fig.15, 151–3).

9033, 9035 and *9037* are all charred fragments of taller, upright, cylindrical pieces, 22–24mm in diameter, which were decorated on the sides. Since most small wooden objects would have ended their useful lives as fuel, these three partially burnt items are rare examples of decorated wooden objects which do not normally survive. *9033* is broken at both ends and was found in Period 4B levels. It is possibly hazel roundwood decorated with bands of incised cross-hatched lines and stamped triangles. *9035* was found in Period 5B levels, and has tool marks on one flat end showing it had been sawn, and traces of a lozenge-shaped extension at the other. Its species is not identifiable, but its sides were decorated with an incised concentric arched pattern, some of which is now missing. *9037* is similar to *9033*, but was found in late 12th–13th century levels. It was made from hazel or possibly alder roundwood, decorated with

groups of incised parallel lines aligned in different directions, and is now broken at each end. There are no wooden parallels for this kind of playing piece, but a mid 10th century oblong playing piece of jet, found at Bawdsey in Suffolk, is of a similar size and is decorated on the sides, top and bottom (Wilson 1970).

Some gaming pieces were shaped, anthropomorphic or zoomorphic and can be termed 'men'. The different shapes may reflect the games in which they were used. For example, the *hnefi* or king-piece and *hunn* or men in *hnefatafl* could have been anthropomorphic in shape (Murray 1952, 60). *9034* is an example of a specifically shaped Anglo-Scandinavian wooden gaming piece dated to Period 5B. Like *9033, 9035* and *9037*, it has been burnt and the wood species is unidentifiable. It is rectangular with vertical sides and has a U-shaped notch cut into the upper end, giving it a bifurcated shape.

This shape is not uncommon among medieval wooden gaming pieces. A 13th century bifurcated piece was found during excavations near Nantwich Castle ditches (Morris 1984a, fig.83, M310), and a 13th–14th century piece with a deep V-shaped notch in the upper end and a small perforation below, giving an exaggerated bifurcation, was found on the Castle Street/Fisher Street site in Carlisle (D. Neal, pers. comm.). Different types of wooden bifurcated pieces dating from the 13th to 15th centuries have been found in Novgorod, where this particular bifurcated form is interpreted as the rook in chess (Kolchin 1989, 204, pl.218, 17–22; Rybina 1992, fig.V.5, 9–10). In Novgorod and the rest of western Europe, medieval chessmen seem to have been made in geometrical shapes borrowed from the Near East (Kolchin and Linder 1961). Linder argues that chess first came to Russia via the Arab world no later than the 9th–10th centuries (Linder 1975, 54), but none of the Novgorod chessmen can be dated reliably to earlier than the second half of the 13th century (ibid., 108). A bifurcated jet piece found in Nessgate, York, was considered by Waterman to be a chess rook (warder or castle) based on a conventional Arab form, although its date is uncertain (1959, 94, fig.21, 1), as is the date of a similar jet piece found at Grimes Graves, Norfolk (ibid., 94). Another bifurcated jet piece of probable Anglo-Scandinavian type was found in a 13th century deposit in the Castle ditch in York (Ottaway 1981, 17, 19). If *9034* were a chessman, it would be one of the earliest datable wooden chessmen found in western Europe.

Syrinx (Figs.1159, 1161)

9038 is an incomplete wooden syrinx, a musical instrument often referred to as panpipes. It was made from a board tangentially converted from boxwood roundwood at least 170mm in diameter, but it is impossible to be certain whether the original board was converted by splitting or sawing. Fig.1160 shows the approximate position in the roundwood where the board was taken from. Boxwood timber of this size is very unusual in Britain as it grows very slowly, puts on very thin annual rings, and the roundwood of young trees is very small. *9038* represents a rare and probably expensive piece of raw material, from a tree probably 100–200 years old. It was found in a pit dated to Period 5B and is not a common, home-made item, but rather a fine, expensive instrument, made by a craftsman using a specially selected piece of wood. Large items made of boxwood are not com-

mon finds. *8578* (Fig.1023, p.2172) is the only box-wood lathe-turned vessel from 16–22 Coppergate, from levels of the same date as *9038*, made from roundwood over 120mm in diameter. A bowl 138mm in diameter, dating to the second half of the 10th century, was found on the Brook Street site, Winchester (Keene 1990, fig.296, *3411*). All three artefacts show that in England in the 10th and 11th centuries, mature box trees were being selected to provide unusually large tangential boards or half-sections for making musical instruments and turned vessels.

In its present outline, the syrinx is sub-rectangular, but it would originally have been more trapezoidal in shape, with a narrower side extension for the shorter tubes which have not survived. It has been carefully smoothed on both flat sides, its lower edge is straight, each side shaved so that it tapers towards a squared edge in cross-section, and the completely intact side edge is straight and rounded. The other side edge is only complete on the lower 35–40mm, above which the syrinx has split through the fifth

Fig.1159   Front and back of boxwood syrinx 9038. *Actual length 97mm*

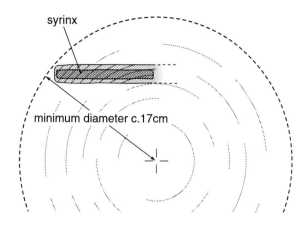

Fig.1160 *Diagram showing the tangential conversion of the roughout for syrinx 9038*

tube; the fragment which had split away was not found during excavation. The upper edge has an undulating outline where holes were bored into it to form tubes of different depths. Five evenly spaced tubes survive, their upper edges chamfered slightly perhaps to allow the player to sound each note more easily and comfortably. The tubes were bored into the end grain of the syrinx using a very sharp auger bit with a rounded end and parallel sides less than 8mm apart. Among the Anglo-Scandinavian spoon bits found at 16–22 Coppergate, none has such a narrow blade, but *2264* is the kind of tool which would have been used. Boxwood is hard, dense and close grained, allowing very accurate cuts to be made into its end grain. These qualities explain why it was easy to make each tube exactly 8mm in diameter, and separated from its neighbour by a wall only 2mm thick. The accuracy of the size, depth and separation of the tubes must have been of great importance when making this sort of musical instrument, determining

Table 220 The dimensions of *9038* from Coppergate compared with four Roman syrinxes (W1 = width at top; W2 = width at bottom; Th1 = maximum thichness; Th2 = minimum thickness)

	H	W1	W2	Th1	Th2
York (*9038*)	97	56	61	12	6
London	118	46	46	10	9
Barbing-Kreuzhof	100	45	40	10	6
Alesia	115	77	43	11	6
Shakenoak	124	96		11	6

the accuracy of the notes produced. A hole 5mm in diameter bored through a solid part of the syrinx below the fourth tube is chamfered on both sides and would have held a thong by which the syrinx could be suspended. An incised cross on each flat surface of the syrinx may be simply for decoration rather than maker's or owner's marks.

9038 is only the fourth wooden syrinx to have been found in north-west Europe and is unique in being the only one of any material to be firmly dated to the Viking period (c.975 to early/mid 11th century). It is obviously incomplete and had probably been discarded after it was broken. The others are all made of boxwood but are Roman in date. One was an almost complete syrinx found in a well at Mont-Auxois in Alesia, France, in 1906 (Reinach 1906–7, 161–9, 180–5, pl.XXI; 1907–8, 201–2); a fragment of another was found in a well at Barbing-Kreuzhof, Regensburg, Germany (Ulbert 1961, 56–60, Taf.1), and a third fragment was found in waterlain deposits in front of the Roman waterfront at the Thames Exchange site in London (Geoff Egan, pers. comm.; unpublished DUA TEX88 1767 sf1327). All three were made from tangentially split or sawn boards and are very similar to each other in shape, size, surface decoration and the size of the roundwood from which they were made, but different from *9038*. Ulbert calculated the diameter of the roundwood from which the Barbing-Kreuzhof syrinx was made to have been approximately 85mm (1961, 56), only half that of *9038*. The Alesia and London syrinxes were made from similarly small roundwood. All three are also longer than the Anglo-Scandinavian syrinx from York (Table 220), but are similar in thickness, each being thinner at the lower edge. Each Roman syrinx has the same type of impressed decoration on one flat surface in the form of three sets of horizontal parallel lines between which are various sets of concentric semi-circles, and although the patterns vary slightly, they all appear to be conforming to a Roman decorative convention. Each has either a complete or broken suspension hole below the fourth tube, however, as in *9038*. The tube diameters and depths vary (Table 221), and are similar to those from York, but they all have conical ends showing they were bored with pointed bits rather than bits with rounded ends. A pottery syrinx with seven surviving tubes also with conical ends was found at Shakenoak Farm (Brodribb et al. 1973, 44–6, fig.23). The remarkable similarities between the Roman

Table 221 The number of tubes surviving on *9038* and the four Roman syrinxes; also tube diameters and depths

		Deepest						Shallowest	
	Diam	1	2	3	4	5	6	7	8
York (*9038*)	8.0	91	83	76	70	59	x	x	x
London	7.5–8.0	90	?	70	60	52	x	x	x
Barbing-Kreuzhof	8.5	65	57	51	47	x	x	x	x
Alesia	9.0	71	63	55	50.5	43.5	39	35.5	31.5
Shakenoak	7.0–8.0	105	102	97	86	84	71	67	x

wooden syrinxes make them at least part of the same Roman fashion, perhaps even products of the same workshops, but unrelated to the York syrinx except as forerunners of a continued musical tradition.

Table 221 shows the number of tubes surviving on *9038* and the four Roman syrinxes. The Alesia syrinx has eight tubes and the Shakenoak syrinx has seven tubes, both possibly complete, whereas the others are incomplete and it is not possible to be certain exactly how many tubes they originally had. Details of other Roman syrinxes appearing on figural representations or in Classical writings have already been published (Reinach 1906–7, 164–9, 180, 201–2). The classical number of tubes (and also the minimum number) is seven like the strings on a lyre, according to Virgil and Ovid (ibid., 180), but there is evidence that syrinxes were made with up to thirteen holes (Brodribb et al. 1973, 46). An illustration of musicians in a 12th century manuscript, now in St John's College, Cambridge, shows one musician holding what appears to be a syrinx like *9038*. It has a straight top showing seven holes and straight parallel vertical

sides (Hawthorne and Stanley Smith 1979, pl.XV). The musician is holding the syrinx in his left hand only, leaving his right hand free. His left hand holds the longer, extended part of the syrinx, and the exposed part which he is not holding is a shorter extension with a lower edge which curves slightly upwards, projecting beyond his hand. It is likely, therefore, that *9038* had at least seven holes, two of which are completely missing in the shorter extension which has broken off. This manuscript gives us some idea how *9038* would have been held and played — possibly with other instruments in an ensemble.

After excavation and removal of the soil in the tubes, a five-note scale running from top A to top E could be played, along with simple tunes (Hall 1984, 116). The scales in Table 222 show the range of the York syrinx compared with those from Alesia and Shakenoak.

Lyre bridge (Fig.1161)

9039 is a wooden bridge for a six-stringed musical instrument, probably a round lyre, found in levels dating to Period 5B. In a previous publication, it was wrongly identified as lignite (Roesdahl et al. 1981, 111). Although complete and intact, it is very heavily charred and it has proved impossible to establish which species of wood it was carved from. No other parts of a lyre were found with it, or anywhere else on the site. However, it has been suggested that the craftsmen who made musical instruments were the makers of boxes, bowls and other fine domestic utensils (Lawson 1981, 98), and it is possible that *9039* was the product of a woodworker's workshop in Coppergate rather than simply a lost or discarded artefact.

Table 222 Scales showing the range of the York syrinx compared with those from Alesia and Shakenoak

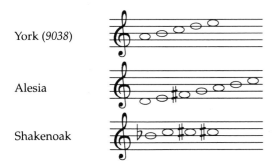

On a lyre, a free-standing bridge like *9039* was positioned approximately centrally on the wooden body of the instrument and was the lowest point of contact between the strings and the soundboard. Its function was to transmit vibration, and it was stressed under compression. The strings passed over the bridge and were attached to the end of the lyre via a separate tailpiece as in the modern violin family (ibid., iii and vii). Both the bridge and tailpiece of a lyre were completely separate items from the main wooden body and can be found, as *9039*, independently from the main instrument. A 13th century tailpiece illustrating the type of object which may have been used in conjunction with the York bridge was found at Winchester (Lawson 1990, fig.203, 2253).

Bridges for lyres and related instruments were made from a variety of materials including wood, bone, antler, amber and copper alloy, but only two other wooden bridges have been found to compare with *9039*, excavated from an 11th century dwelling at Charavines (Colardelle and Colardelle 1980, fig.51, 3) and in a 13th century house on the Mindets tomt site in Gamlebyen, Oslo, in 1971 (Kolltveit 1997, fig.1). Whereas *9039* had six notches along its upper edge for six evenly spaced strings, the Charavines bridge had only three notches, asymmetrically placed with two over to one side and a single notch at the other side. It could be a wooden bridge for a bowed instrument of comparatively simple form that was not a lyre (Lawson 1990, 716), but since a fragment had

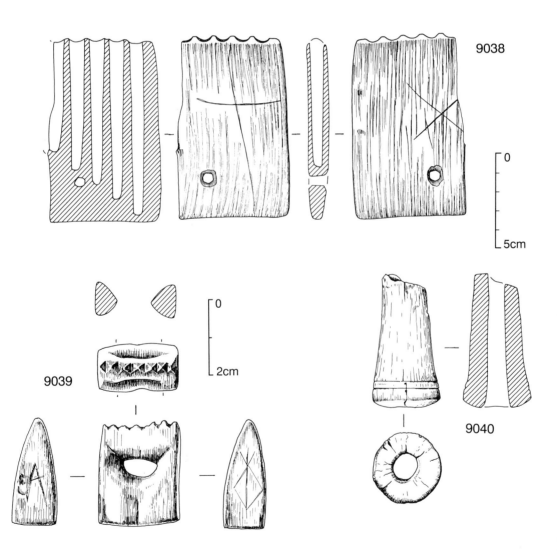

Fig.1161 *Boxwood syrinx 9038; bridge for a six-stringed instrument 9039; fragment of a woodwind instrument 9040, all from 16–22 Coppergate. Scale 1:2, 9039 1:1*

broken away from one corner, leading from one of the notches, it is also possible that the bridge broke during manufacture before all the notches were completed. The medieval Oslo bridge was made of pine and had seven evenly spaced notches. Other bridges to compare with *9039* are a 7th/8th century amber bridge from Broa i Halle, Götland, Sweden (Andersson 1930, 174–7), two 8th/9th century amber bridges from Dorestad (Werner 1954, pl.II), two 8th century amber ones from Elisenhof (Bruce-Mitford and Bruce-Mitford 1970, fig.2), a 9th century bone or antler bridge from Birka (Arbman 1939, 129) and a 5th/6th century copper alloy bridge from Concevreux in France (Pilloy 1889, pl.E3).

The York bridge is rectangular in profile, triangular in cross-section with convex outline, and is perforated through the body by a roughly D-shaped hole chamfered round the edges on each side. It is unusual in that it does not have an arch hollowed out below the notches, dividing the lower edge into two feet, and it does not have curved splaying sides, features which can be seen on all the other nine bridges already mentioned. None of the others have a single perforation through the body, although the Concevreux bridge has an approximately rectangular hole between the notches and the arch. The arches appear to have been typological rather than functional characteristics of lyre bridges, and the D-shaped hole on the York bridge could be a debased arch form.

The York bridge was probably intended for use on a round lyre whose form had not substantially changed in England since the early Anglo-Saxon period and which is typified by that reconstructed by Lawson (1978, pl.IV). This instrument shows the position of a lyre bridge. In England, lyres have been found in a 5th century grave at Abingdon, Oxfordshire (Leeds and Harden 1936, pl.IXb), the 7th century ship burial in Mound 1 at Sutton Hoo (Bruce-Mitford and Bruce-Mitford 1983), the 7th century Taplow barrow (ibid., 701–20), and the 6th–7th century grave 97 at Morningthorpe and grave 22 at Bergh Apton, both in Norfolk (Lawson 1978, 87–97, figs.78–9 and 102–9). No bridges had been preserved in any of these burials. Six 8th–13th century manuscript illustrations of round lyres and three substantially complete 6th–8th century wooden lyres (also without bridges) from Oberflacht and Cologne in Germany (Lawson 1981, fig.10.1 and pls.23A and B; Bruce-Mitford and Bruce-Mitford 1970, 8–10, pl.VII)

also help suggest the form of lyre *9039* was made for. Bridges for lyres are discussed elsewhere by Bruce-Mitford and Bruce-Mitford (1983, 693–5).

Most round lyres had between four and six strings (Lawson 1990, 714). One of the Dorestad bridges, and the Broa and Concevreux bridges, had six notches like *9039* for six strings, whereas the Birka bridge had a row of five shallow grooves with a deeper groove at each end, for either five or seven strings, and the Oslo bridge had seven notches. Eighth, 10th, 12th and 13th century manuscript illustrations show five-, six- and seven-stringed lyres (Lawson 1981, fig.10.1). Early Germanic lyres were plucked not bowed like their later relatives, and the design of some of the bridges, with projections extending above the plane of the strings, makes them unsuited to bowing, along with the considerable width and flat bellies of the lyres themselves (ibid., 153–4). *9039* does not have projections like those on the Concevreux, Broa, Dorestad, Elisenhof and Birka bridges, but has a straight, flat upper edge into which the string notches were cut, as do the other wooden bridges from Charavines and Oslo. It would still have been difficult, however, to use a bow on an instrument where the strings were arranged side by side on a *flat* bridge.

The Anglo-Saxon and Germanic lyre of the 5th to 8th centuries was essentially an instrument played by specialists and the wealthy, and was not the popular instrument of its day (ibid., 97). It would have been used for formal vocal accompaniment (ibid., 98). The York bridge, along with remains of lyres such as the 9th century bridge from Birka and a fragment of a 9th–10th century yew lyre arm from Hedeby (ibid., pl.24B), shows that the round lyre continued in use in Viking Age Europe. It has been suggested that there was a fundamental change in the role of lyres in north-west European music culture from the early 11th century onwards, from being instruments of specialist performers to part of the popular orchestration of common folk music, a niche which before the 11th century had probably been filled by bone and wooden pipes and simple percussion instruments (ibid., 98, 265). Iconographic evidence suggests that lyres were used in Norway later than many other places in Europe and the context of the Oslo bridge in a house occupied by ordinary citizens reinforces the popularisation of the instrument. The somewhat debased arch form of *9039* may be a consequence of the popularisation of the lyre in Anglo-Scandinavian York.

Musical pipe (Fig.1161)

9040 is probably a fragment of a wooden musical pipe, but it is uncertain what type of instrument is represented. It was found in post-medieval layers in a well and the workmanship is fine-quality spindle-turning using alder. The pipe has a flaring trumpet-shaped mouth, and is perforated down its length by an augered tube widening from 10mm to 14mm at the mouth end. It was decorated with two turned grooves near the mouth, but no traces of finger holes survive as it had been broken beyond the place where the holes may have ended. It is possible that 9040 is part of a spout used in the head of a coopered cask like 8873–5 (pp.2258–60), but its fine quality would suggest otherwise.

Wooden pipes are not common finds on archaeological sites, but 9040 is one of several different types which have been found, all the others earlier in date. A decorated Anglo-Scandinavian pipe of hawthorn or apple (Crataegus sp.) with straight sides but a flared mouth came from Hungate, York (Richardson 1959, fig.19, 20), while two similar 9th/10th century pipes were found at Achlum and Blija in Friesland (Boëles 1951, pl.XXXI, 4–5), and another was found at Mechelen in the Netherlands (Vandenburghe 1981, fig.14, 9). Two intact wooden pipes were found in the excavations in Novgorod, a late 11th century one with four finger holes and an early 15th century one with three finger holes (Kolchin 1989, 143, pl.142, 4–5). Both had straight sides without a flared mouth. A boxwood pipe 306mm long was found in the 1938 excavations at Weoley Castle in layers in the bottom of the castle moat dated post-1280. It had a cylindrical bore but no finger holes and was interpreted as possibly the drone of a bagpipe-style instrument (Baines 1973, 145).

Bowling ball (Fig.1162)

Recovered from 15th century levels at Coppergate, 9041 is a spindle-turned ash ball with spur centre marks visible as V-sectioned holes 2–3mm across in each end grain (cf. Figs.1004–9, pp.2147–52, for similar holes in lathe-turned cores). It is oblate, an elongated sphere, and has the characteristic concentric grooved tool marks of turning at each end, and a wide band left rough and unturned around the centre. It is 110mm in diameter and 100mm wide and was turned from a roundwood blank, the position of the tree centre clearly visible in each end. 8229 is the

sort of end waste which would have been produced after turning a ball such as 9041 (see Fig.1000, p.2141).

This ball is almost like a cylinder with rounded ends, so it is unlike a modern ball used in the game of bowls whose profile has a smooth curve from the tall to the short axis. 9041 has a flatter circumference on which it would have run when bowled, whereas the modern bowling ball runs on a narrower section of the widest part of the circumference. Two 17th century balls of this kind were found in a well at St Paul-in-the-Bail, Lincoln (Morris forthcoming a, 632–3, WAG).

There are six other English parallels for the Coppergate ball, the most similar being a 15th/16th century lathe-turned ball 96mm in diameter and 84mm wide found at Trichay Street in Exeter (Allan and Morris 1984, fig.177, 65) which also has a flatter circumference on which it would have run. A 13th century lathe-turned ball found at the High Street/ Blackfriargate site in Hull was also of a similar size to 9041, at 100mm in diameter, but more spherical in shape (Watkin 1987, fig.123, 346), as was a ball of 108mm diameter dated to the Civil War period (before 1649), found at Pontefract Castle (Morris forthcoming c, sf868). Two more medieval wooden balls were found in the moat of a manor house at Marton in Cheshire (Webster and Cherry 1972, 193). A fossilised 16th century bowling ball was found sealed beneath the floor of the Henrician bowling alley at Whitehall during excavations in 1962 (Thurley 1993, 190). A medieval parallel from a European site is a spindle-turned ball 77mm in diameter from Lübeck (Falk 1983a, Abb.3, 8).

These nine balls were almost certainly used in games, and the oblate shape of 9041 and the Exeter ball means that they do not have a deliberately created bias (a tendency resulting from shaping to divert from a straight line in movement), unlike their modern counterparts. The earliest reference to the use of a bias seems to be the middle of the 16th century (Donaghey 1979, 37). Balls like 9041 could have been used in various medieval games, including variants of modern bowls and skittles. Three 13th–14th century manuscript illustrations show balls being used singly in bowling games, not in sets (Strutt 1830, pl.30); the earliest shows two men, one aiming a ball at a small cone, the other standing beside him (Royal Library MS 20 E iv).

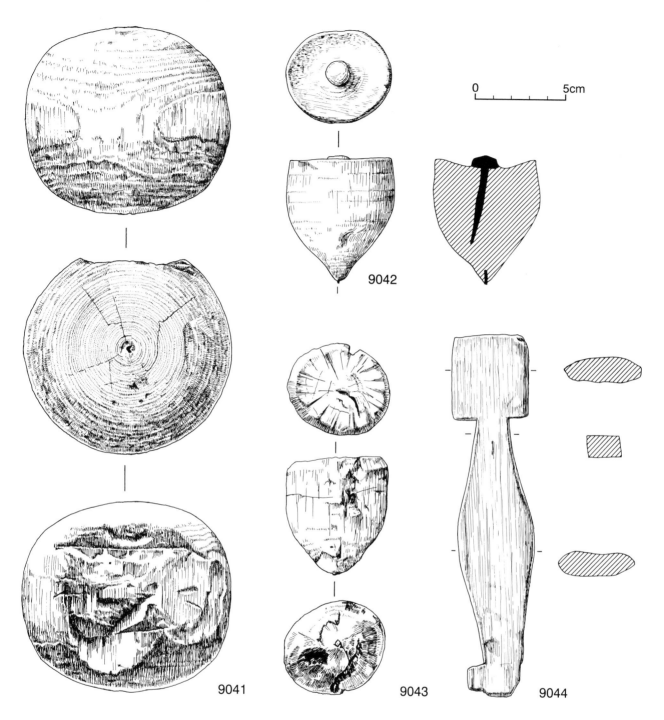

Fig.1162 *Spindle-turned bowling ball 9041; spinning tops 9042–3; possible toy sword handle 9044, all from 16–22 Coppergate. Scale 1:2*

Spinning tops (Fig.1162)

Originally *9042–3* were curved conical lathe-turned cores, waste products from the spindle-turning method of making wooden bowls (cf. Figs.1006–7, pp.2148–9), but they were re-used and adapted into Anglo-Scandinavian toy spinning tops

65 and 59mm long (*9042* comes from Period 4B, *9043* from Period 5B levels). X-ray photography shows that small spikes (possibly headless nails) with square shafts had been driven into the pointed ends of each top to provide solid metal points on which they could

spin. The end of the spike protruding from the bottom of *9043* is now very worn. A tinned dome-headed nail had been driven into the top of *9042* which was the more elaborate of the two since it had also been enhanced by red pigment (possibly haematite) on the external surface. The sides of *9043* had been faceted in places to narrow the point, and also had an incised groove scored into the sides 17mm below the top possibly as an anchor point for the lash of a whip.

There are no excavated wooden spinning tops from Britain to compare with the two from York. A lathe-turned biconical maple object from Winchester, dated to the early–mid 11th century, was identified as a whipping top (Keene 1990, 706, fig.197, *2245*), but this is extremely unlikely as the two pointed ends are very thin and show no sign of wear from spinning. An object of this kind would have needed iron points such as those on *9042–3* and on modern spinning tops to allow them to function correctly. One side of the Winchester object has a deliberately flattened area, and when the object is positioned on its side with this area on a flat surface, it can be spun around by pushing on one of the ends, making it probably another kind of spinning toy. The nearest parallels for the York tops are two bone lathe-turned spinning tops, 52mm and 63mm long, dated to the 11th and 13th centuries respectively, and decorated with turned grooves, which were found at Winetavern Street, Dublin (National Museum of Ireland 1973, 34), and a medieval wooden top from Lübeck (Falk 1983b, Abb.1, 9).

Possible toy sword (Fig.1162)

Dating from the early 13th century, *9044* is possibly the hilt of a toy sword or dagger, broken across the hilt with its original all-in-one-piece blade missing. It was hand-carved from willow and has shallow angled sides giving it an elongated lozenge-shaped grip; it also has a large square pommel and a small wing-like hilt fragment. The pommel and the centre of the grip have smoothly rounded edges and were carefully shaped to an oval cross-section. Traces of black paint were found on both the pommel and the grip. The closest parallels to *9044* are fragments of more than 50 toy wooden swords found at Novgorod (Kolchin 1989, 203). Four are illustrated, but these have straight rather than lozenge-shaped grips (ibid., pl.26) and date from the 10th to the 14th century. Two others, also with straight grips, were found in the Gamlebyen excavation in Oslo (Weber 1990, fig.63c–d).

Building Accessories and Structural Fragments

Wooden objects such as *9045–66* and *9242* were made as individual parts of larger structures. While components such as locks and door fasteners, shutters and window openings, sluices and panels were used singly or in small numbers, others, for example shingles, were used in great quantities. In both cases these accessories are most often found only singly on archaeological sites, unassociated with the building or structures in which they were used, a situation which can often cause problems in identification.

Lock housings (Fig.1163)

9045 is a post-medieval rectangular wooden lock housing made from a riven oak plank. It is thinner at one end where the outer surface is also faceted. On the reverse it is hollowed to contain an iron lock mechanism (see Ottaway and Rogers *AY* 17 in prep. for details). Patches of discolouration in two corners and remains of holes in the other corners show that the housing was originally fixed by four iron nails. A key hole of usual shape is cut through the housing. *9242* is a similar post-medieval oak lock housing with sawn surfaces and edges, made from either a radial or tangential section. It is hollowed to contain an iron lock mechanism which is now missing, and once had a lock plate at one end where the hollowing is open at the edge. These two lock housings are large, heavy objects and were almost certainly used to secure the doors of a building rather than a box or chest. An Anglo-Scandinavian wooden lock housing found at 6–8 Pavement in York (*430*, Fig.42, *AY* 17/3) was a much smaller, lighter object and more likely to have secured a chest or small door.

Brackets for fastening doors (Figs.1164–7)

9046–52 are seven wooden hooked or slotted brackets associated with the type of wooden door fastening mechanism illustrated in Fig.1166. A pivoted latch bar moved up and down within an enclosed bracket. The latch rested on a hooked bracket fixed in the door jamb and was restrained by the peg's carved vertical end. If the latch was lifted up it could move over the peg and the door would open. This mechanism is simple and effective, and has survived in wooden or metal forms until the present day. The brackets from Coppergate are both Anglo-Scandinavian and medieval in date.

The hooked brackets were made from various forms of timber, and were either fastened to the door jambs by iron nails or by a carved wooden tenon on the bracket which fitted into a mortice hole on the door jamb. Two brackets were nailed on, Anglo-Scandinavian *9050* which was made from a riven section of oak, and *9051* from a 16th–19th century context which was squared from a quarter-section of oak (Fig.1167). *9050* has a long rectangular slot cut in one side to form a gap between the door and the bracket. Below the slot two iron nails fixed it to a door jamb. It was found in a Period 5B build-up deposit outside and east of Structure 5/5. *9050* is broken and could be part of an enclosed bracket within which a latch bar moved up and down. *9051* has a flat back edge and a rectangular notch cut vertically into a rounded convex front edge. Two nail holes above and three below the slot were used to fasten it to a door jamb. It was found in the same post-medieval well deposits as lock housing *9045*.

Five remaining brackets have carved tenons. On three Anglo-Scandinavian (*9046–7* and *9049*) and one late 12th–early 13th century (*9052*) bracket, these tenons have circular cross-sections (Figs.1164–5). *9046* is carved from a tangentially riven length of birch. It has a broken triangular vertical end and a short circular tenon with a blunt point. *9049* is made from oak roundwood taken from the junction of main stem and branch; it has a large triangular vertical end and a tenon with a blunt point. *9047* is carved from field maple roundwood taken from the junction of main stem and branch, and has an L-shaped functional end with a triangular terminal and a short horizontal shaft of square cross-section beyond which is a broken circular tenon. *9052* is a large solid bracket which was shaped from a length of alder roundwood. It has an L-shaped functional end and a circular tenon which tapers to a rounded point. Anglo-Scandinavian oak bracket *9048* has an L-shaped functional end with a horizontal shaft of rectangular cross-section and a straight shoulder cut perpendicular to the main shaft, beyond which is a tenon 33mm square.

There are few parallels for this type of bracket. An example found in a 12th century context at Christchurch Place in Dublin has a narrow, curving triangular functional end and a broken tenon with a D-shaped cross-section (Lang 1988, 65, fig.40). This

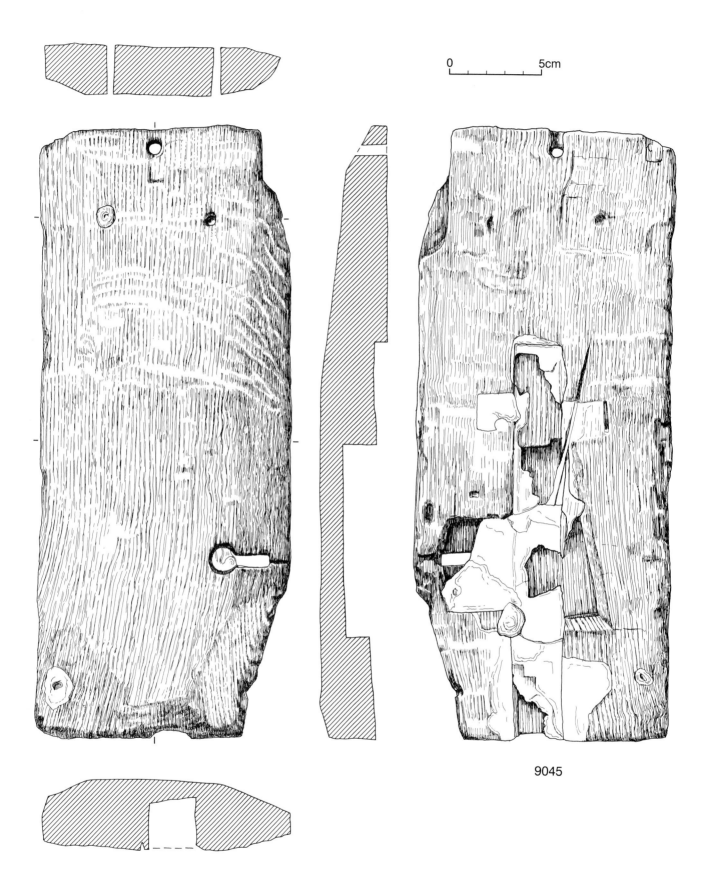

Fig.1163   *Lock housing 9045 from 16–22 Coppergate. Scale 1:2*

9045

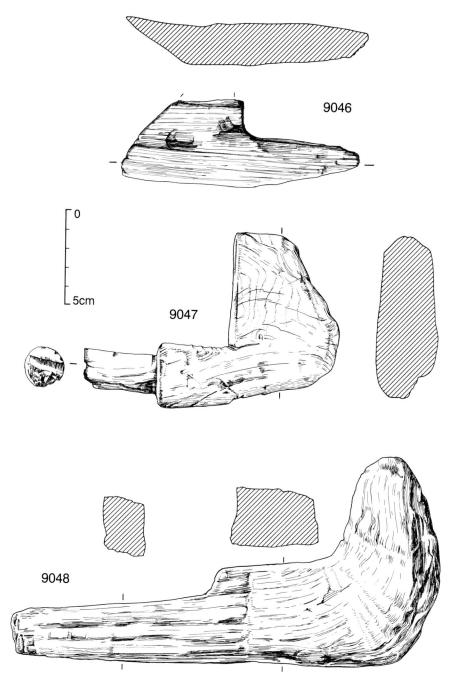

9046

0

5cm

9047

9048

Fig.1164 *Brackets for door fastening mechanisms, 9046–8. Scale 1:2*

bracket was decorated by carving in the form of grooved rings and a three-dimensional volute tendril. It is very similar to the undecorated Anglo-Scandinavian bracket *9049* from Coppergate, and both objects may have been used as shelf supports rather than as latch rests, although there is no evidence to suggest how they could have been fixed vertically with the triangular end downwards. A mid–late 12th century bracket made from a riven section of oak was found at Eastgate, Beverley (Morris and Evans 1992, fig.95, 645). It had an L-shaped terminal and a long tenon with a circular cross-section.

Variations of the wooden door-fastening device may have had a latch bar which slid sideways within one or more enclosed brackets on the door and could

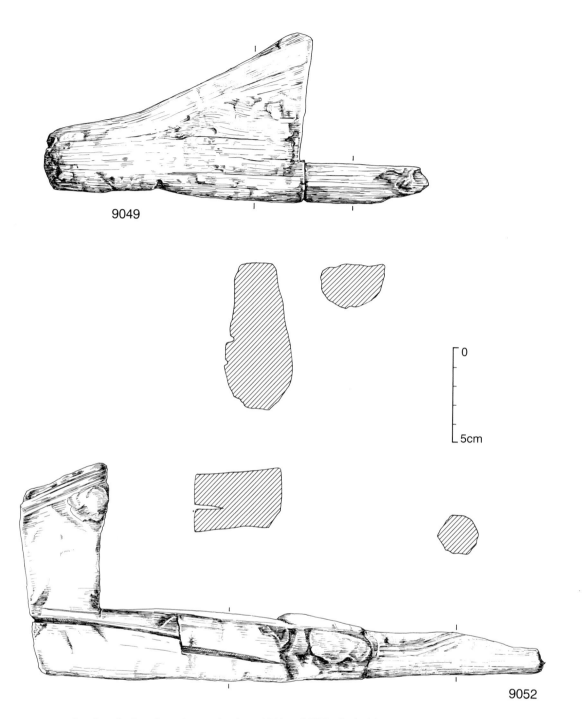

9049

5cm

9052

Fig.1165 *Brackets for door fastening mechanisms, 9049 and 9052. Scale 1:2*

have slid into either an enclosed bracket or a hooked bracket on the door jamb. A complete door with a device of this kind was found in the 9th–11th century Viking settlement at Hedeby (Elsner 1990, 33, fig.8), with a latch bar sliding between two enclosed brackets fixed to the door by wooden pegs at top and bottom. A 13th century oak enclosed bracket of a type which would have been used in conjunction with brackets of the Coppergate hooked type was found in Cork (Hurley 1982, fig.16.2, 8).

Considering the large amount of evidence for lathe-turning in the Coppergate area, it is possible that some of the Coppergate hooked brackets, espe-

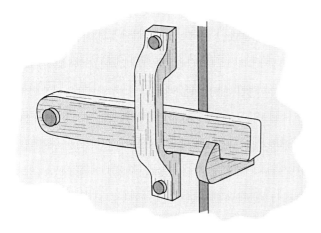

Fig.1166 *Diagram explaining how brackets such as 9046–52 were used for fastening doors*

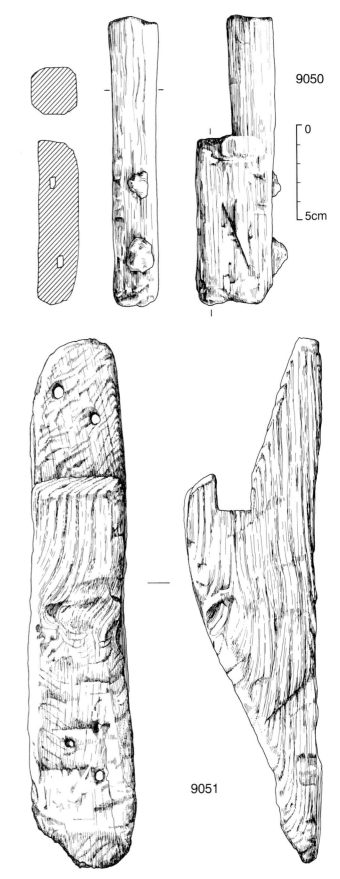

Fig.1167 *Brackets for door fastening mechanisms, 9050–1. Scale 1:2*

cially those with tenons, could have acted as supports for lathe-turners' tool-rests, rather than door brackets. As such they would have functioned as simple, unadjustable versions of *8237*. They are included with the distribution plots of lathe-turned evidence in Figs.1043–9, pp.2199–205.

Shingles (Fig.1168)

9054–5 are nearly complete examples of medieval shingles or wooden roof tiles, both made from riven oak boards. *9054* is narrow and parallel-sided with a rounded pointed upper end perforated by a circular hole 10mm diameter and dates to the late 12th–13th century; *9055* is a wider spade-shaped board with sloping shoulders and is late 14th century in date. It has two incised parallel lines across the shoulders between which and over to one side is an augered hole 9mm diameter containing a wooden peg 7mm diameter. Both shingles are worn and broken at one lower corner. *9053* could be a shingle fragment.

Other roof shingles to compare with *9054–5* have been found on British and European sites. Although there are none with exactly the same shape as *9055*, a possible trapezoidal oak shingle found at Blake Street, York, has small peg holes in each corner (YAT 1975.6, sf724). Similar to *9054* are a 10th century oak shingle with one rounded pointed end and one rectangular end found at the Viking camp at Trelleborg (Schmidt 1973, fig.35), a 10th century oak shingle with sloping shoulders and an offset peg hole from Brook

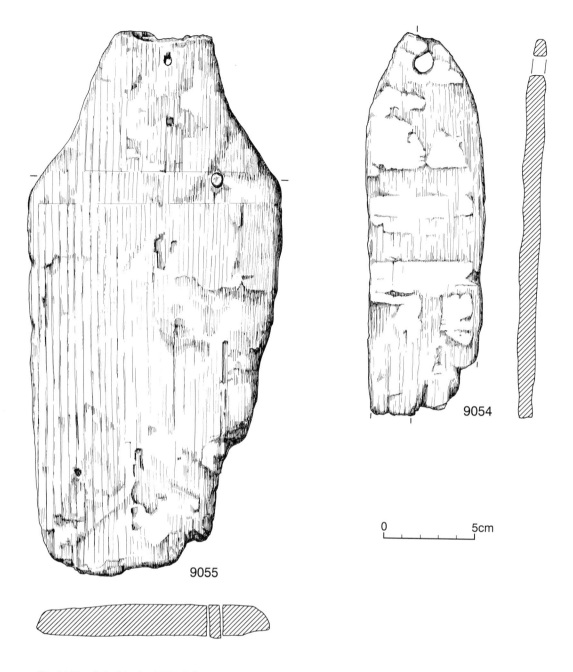

Fig.1168 *Oak shingles 9054–5 from 16–22 Coppergate. Scale 1:2*

Street, Winchester (Keene 1990, fig.73, *443*), and a 12th century oak shingle with sloping shoulders and a rounded/pointed end perforated by two nail/peg holes from King's Lynn (Clarke and Carter 1977, fig.172, *59*). Other late Saxon and medieval rectangular shingles have been found at Winchester (Biddle and Quirk 1962, fig.11, *1–4*; Keene 1990, figs.73–5), Norwich (Williams 1987, fig.85, *6*), Oxford (Morris 1980b, fig.32, *21*), Southampton (Platt and Coleman-Smith 1975, fig.232, *1670–1*), Rickmansworth, Hertfordshire (Biddle et al. 1959, fig.18, *26* and *28*), Perth (Bogdan, Curteis and Morris forthcoming, sf119/A11257), Almondbury and Milk Street, London (Morris 1984a, fig.88, *M376–8*).

Shingles such as *9053–5* were made from wood obtained from managed forests and woodland. For example, in 1252 the manufacture and carriage of

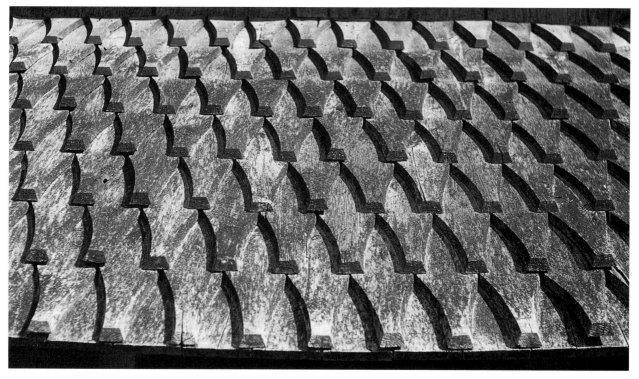

Fig.1169   Experimental oak shingles on the roof of a reconstructed 10th century timber house at Trelleborg

60,000 shingles from the Forest of Dean for the works of Gloucester Castle cost £23 17s 7d (Calendar of Close Rolls); in the 12th century Salisbury Cathedral (Wiltshire) was roofed with shingles using wood from Bramshaw Woods in the New Forest, Hampshire; and in 1281 twelve oak trees were sent from Sherwood Forest, Nottinghamshire, to the Franciscan friars at Lincoln for shingles (Innocent 1916, 184).

The late Saxon/Viking period hogback tombstone series in Britain is a possible source of information for the use and shapes of shingles at the time. Hogbacks occur mainly in Cumbria, North Yorkshire, and Tyne and Wear (Lang 1984, fig.1), and are usually thought to represent buildings. Some of their roofs have representations of shingles. On the hogbacks, when studying a representation of a complete roof, only the lower ends of the shingles can be seen, and some patterns may be more artistic than realistic representations of shingles. Eleven different shapes have been identified (ibid., fig.5). If, as seems most likely, *9054* was fixed with the peg hole at the upper end, it would have had a rectangular lower end, a type of shingle seen on hogbacks from Brigham in Cumbria,

and possibly Ormesby in North Yorkshire (ibid., 117, 157) and Govan in Glasgow, Scotland (Schmidt 1973, fig.32a). On all three hogbacks, the rows of rectangular shingles are aligned so that the end of one shingle overlaps the division between the two shingles in the next row down, in an offset pattern. If *9055* was also fixed with the peg hole towards the upper end, it would have had a trapezoidal lower end, a common type seen, for example, on hogbacks from Burnsall, Gosforth, Lythe and Sockburn (Lang 1984, 125, 135, 149–53, 163), where the same pattern of offset alignment applies. Although this is also the usual way of laying rectangular roof slates today, it is not possible to be certain this is how the York medieval shingles would have been laid. It has been suggested that many of the rectangular wooden shingles found in Winchester, for example, were not laid in such a pattern, but in a rectilinear fashion (Keene 1990, 321; shingles in figs.73–5). However, experiments with the laying of wooden shingle roofs on plank-built Viking buildings at the Museum of Danish Prehistory at Moesgård, and at the site of the 10th century Viking camp at Trelleborg, have shown that the offset alignment described above is very efficient. The roof of oak shingles on the reconstructed timber house at Trelleborg (Fig.1169) is still in good condition after nearly 50 years exposure to the elements.

In 1966 the upper part of the arcade structure in the great hall of the bishop's palace at Hereford was examined and evidence for the fixing of wooden shingles like 9054–5 was found in situ. The 12th century aisle roof had been independently constructed, with its rafters slotted into the main hall's vertical beams. Shingles had originally been fastened onto laths/battens between the rafters, with the upper ends of the upper row of shingles slotted into a groove in the main horizontal beam (Ralegh Radford et al. 1973, fig.36). Where a peg hole by which a shingle was fixed to a roof batten survives (as 9054–5), it is usually offset or centrally placed at the upper end. Shingles such as 9055 and an 11th century shingle from Brook Street, Winchester (Keene 1990, fig.73), were fixed to battens by small wooden pegs. Others, such as the 12th century rectangular oak shingle from St Martin-at-Palace Plain in Norwich (Williams 1987, fig.85, 6) and a mid 12th century triangular shingle from Nantwich (Morris 1984a, fig.89, M379), were nailed on, a practice which Salzman suggested was common from the medieval period onwards (1967, 311). 'Shingul nails' were used to repair the roof of the tower of Nottingham Castle in 1312 (Acct. Excheq. Q.R. Bundle 477.M.20 6 Edw II).

Roofing with wooden shingles is only one of several medieval alternative methods. In the 12th century De Naturis Rerum, Alexander Neckam lists straw, rushes, shingles and tiles (Walton 1954, 69). Salzman argued that wooden shingles were used extensively in England up to the early 14th century when the increase in the price of timber made stone and ceramic tiles more economical (Salzman 1967, 228–9). Nearly all the surviving archaeological examples of shingles date from the 10th to 13th centuries (Morris 1984a, 123–5, M364–81) and seem to reinforce Salzman's argument, but 9055 is a late 14th century survival. Wooden shingles are durable but have few advantages over stone and ceramic tiles other than their relative lightness in weight which makes them very suitable for steeply pitched roofs, for example church steeples, some of which are still roofed with shingles today.

Shingles were not merely a poor man's alternative to ceramic or stone tiles. Many were used on royal and ecclesiastical buildings (ibid., 125). They were expensive to manufacture and the rights to use large quantities of good oak timber from forests was restricted. Wooden shingles such as 9053–5, therefore, would have been a valuable commodity, and probably a prestigious alternative to thatch before ceramic tiles became more popular. They must have been used on buildings of some importance in the Coppergate area. Shingles were probably only thrown away when completely useless, such as the quantities of broken, worn and battered medieval shingles discarded in pits in Winchester (Keene 1990, figs.73–5). Shingles were definitely re-used. For example, in 1260 Henry III ordered shingles to be taken from a kitchen roof and used to repair the tower of Marlborough Castle, Wiltshire (Lib. Roll. 44 Henr III). It is not surprising, therefore, that only two complete wooden shingles were found on the entire Coppergate site. As boards of riven oak, shingles could be re-used for making smaller objects such as pot-lids, or as fuel.

Possible shutter (Fig.1170)

The heavy oak composite object 9056, made from two or three radially split planks originally fixed together by wooden battens, may be part of an early 15th century window shutter, or possibly a chest lid. The complete end of one of the two surviving iron strap hinges has a circular terminal which would either have swivelled on a hinge pivot in a window if 9056 was a shutter or have been connected to a second iron strap on the chest back if 9056 was a lid. The hole in the terminal is aligned perpendicular to the main axis of the hinge strap and so would have functioned well as a shutter hinge, used with a hinge pivot. For examples of the latter and how they are used, see pp.635–7, Fig.266, AY 17/6. The hole on the hinge on wooden chest lid or back 3386 (Fig.1127, p.2299) is not aligned in the same direction as that on 9056 and could not have functioned as a shutter hinge. In its final form 9056 is a much repaired and re-used object which was probably originally fixed together with wooden battens (like lid 8951), then at a later date fixed by a combination of wooden battens and iron hinges.

Frame/rack (Fig.1171)

9057 comprises several fragments of squared ash roundwood with a curving grain which can be reconstructed into one complete large rectangular beam 587mm long. It has a projecting rectangular block at each end between which the timber has been cut

9056

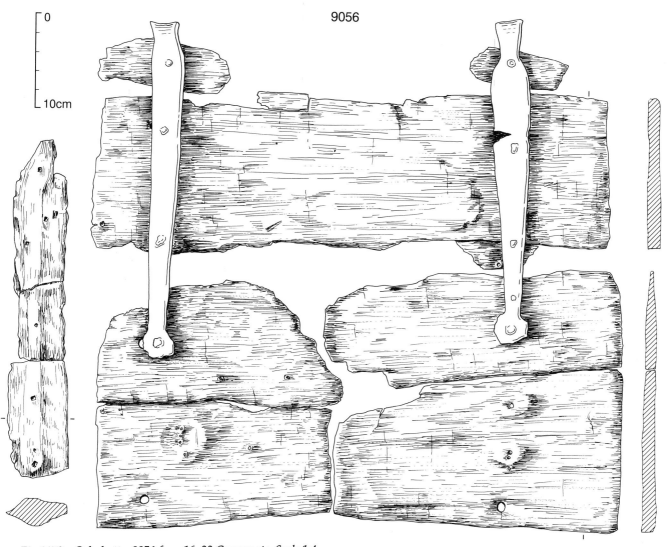

Fig.1170 *Oak shutter 9056 from 16–22 Coppergate. Scale 1:4*

away to a depth of 30mm. An incised line was cut across the beam 84mm from each block and a circular hole 15mm diameter augered through the beam at each end between the block and the line, each containing a peg of faceted roundwood. Two augered holes 34mm diameter and two 15mm diameter were positioned symmetrically between the lines. The flat surfaces at the ends of the beam show signs of having been sawn straight across. *9057* was recovered from Period 4B levels.

The entire object was carefully measured out and shaped and may be part of an Anglo-Scandinavian free-standing frame, rack, bench or other construction. The pegs may have fastened the beam to two uprights 84mm wide which fitted against the blocks,

or perhaps across two horizontal beams. The exact function of the other holes is uncertain, but they probably fastened other pieces of wood to beam *9057* in a symmetrical arrangement.

Window openings (Fig.1172)

Two fragmentary Anglo-Scandinavian objects made of radially split oak boards are probably the surrounds for window openings. Each is 17mm thick and has the remains of a rectangular or sub-rectangular central opening whose internal edges are chamfered on both sides. Each panel has evidence for one broad end and much narrower side bars. *9058* from Period 4B has the remains of a side bar and a wide end surrounding a central rectangular space. *9059*

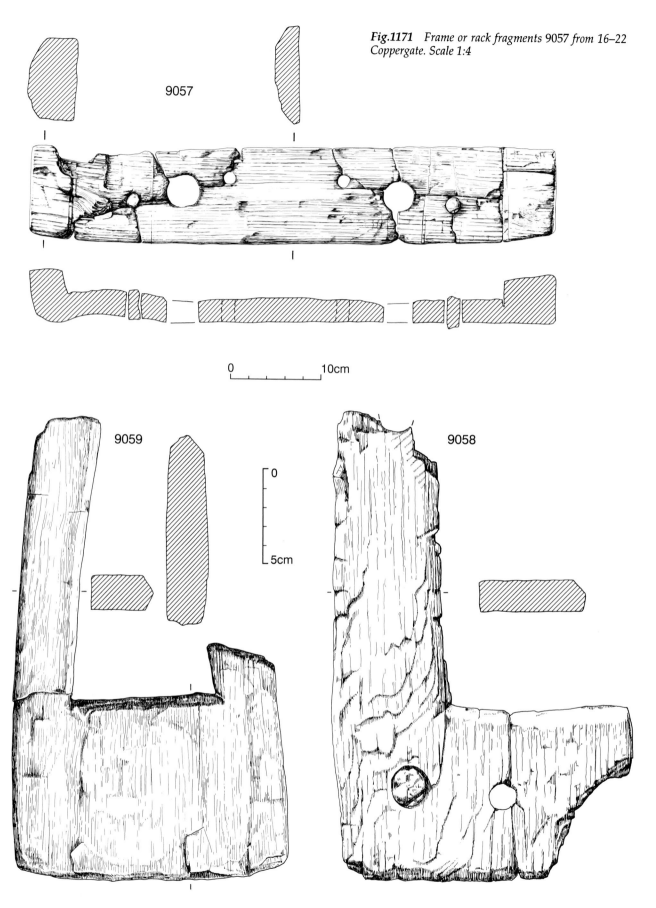

Fig.1171 *Frame or rack fragments 9057 from 16–22 Coppergate. Scale 1:4*

9057

0   10cm

9059

9058

0

5cm

Fig.1172 *Oak window opening fragments 9058–9 from 16–22 Coppergate. Scale 1:2*

from Period 5B has the remains of two side bars and a wide end, the vertical sides sloping inwards slightly, and possibly forming a more triangular-shaped opening. The surviving end of *9058* is perforated by two augered holes, one retaining a peg fragment, but that on *9059*, although complete, has no peg holes. The missing end would probably have been as wide as the surviving end to provide structural strength.

The panels would have been pegged to upright planks, presumably in plank-built structures, to provide small window openings. They may have functioned as shutters in that they could have been pegged temporarily over much larger openings to reduce the window size and restrict the effect of the weather on the inside of a building.

A complete window opening of this kind was found in the excavations at the 9th–11th century Viking settlement at Hedeby and is now exhibited at the Wikinger Museum there. It was made from a split oak board of a similar size to the two Coppergate examples, had a small triangular opening and peg holes to fasten it to the upright planks of a plank-built structure.

Possible sluices/filters (Fig.1173; see Fig.972)

9061 is a large, heavy, tangentially converted board of oak, but it is not possible to be certain whether it was tangentially split or sawn. One end had rounded squared corners while the other, probably the upper, end had sloping shoulders meeting at a rounded point. This end has many fragments of iron nail points embedded in the wood. The main rectangular body is perforated by six columns of seven augered holes 20mm diameter. The first four holes in each column are regularly spaced and form straight lines, and the lower three holes in each column are regularly spaced and line up with each other but do not line up with the first four. This suggests that the two sets of holes were cut as two distinct groups. The holes appear to have been cut by the woodworker's eye rather than to a pre-measured grid. *9060* is a broken fragment probably from an object similar to *9061* although it is a radially split oak board with sloping shoulders and a roughly broken extension. Only three large holes survive, 24–38mm diameter.

9061 was found in the fill of a 15th century rectilinear pit while *9060* was found in a Period 3 con-

text, the earliest phase of Anglo-Scandinavian occupation on the site, but both may be parts of a sluice gate or filter which had been used in a drain or channel. The grid of holes on *9061* would allow the passage of water but restrain objects wider than 20mm diameter. The larger holes on *9060* would allow the passage of slightly larger objects than *9061* and water. The lower ends suggest that the channels were probably rectangular in profile so that the boards could stand upright with their bottom and sides snug to the channel's floor and walls, possibly in a wooden frame or slots. The remains of iron nails on *9061* may indicate that some sort of lifting device such as a leather strap had been fixed to the board's upper end, while the upper end of *9060* is broken, suggesting it originally had a larger all-in-one-piece wooden handle. A fragment of a smaller object similar to *9060–1* was found at Hedeby (Schietzel 1970, Abb.10, 2) and an early 14th century perforated board used as a sluice mechanism in a drain was found at High Street, Perth (Bogdan, Curteis and Morris forthcoming, fig.39, A05–0113). The wide date range of *9060–1* and the Hedeby and Perth objects shows a continuity of use of this sort of efficient wooden device over time.

Panels (Fig.1174)

Fragments of three panels dating to Period 5B were found at 16–22 Coppergate. *9064* consisted of thirteen fragments of a panel of riven oak 16mm thick, at least four of which conjoin, showing that one long edge was chamfered. The panel was decorated on one flat surface only with a pattern of cross-hatched incised grooves 2–3mm wide, rectangular in cross-section, probably cut with a chisel or gouge. Although the four conjoined pieces measured 143 × 59mm, it is not clear how large the original panel was or where it could have been used. It may have been part of an internal wall panel, a furniture panel such as a chair back or side, or even a chest panel.

9062 is a narrow rectangular pine panel with a sub-rectangular cross-section, broken at both ends. One long edge has been shaped with four long grooves to produce a tripartite moulded effect. This was possibly achieved using a moulding-iron with a distinct pattern corresponding to the outline of the panel edge cut into the tool blade. A tool of this kind was found in the Mästermyr tool chest, dated to c.1000 (Arwidsson and Berg 1983, pl.27, 57). In Norway, such tools were commonly used up to the present day, especially in boat-building to decorate

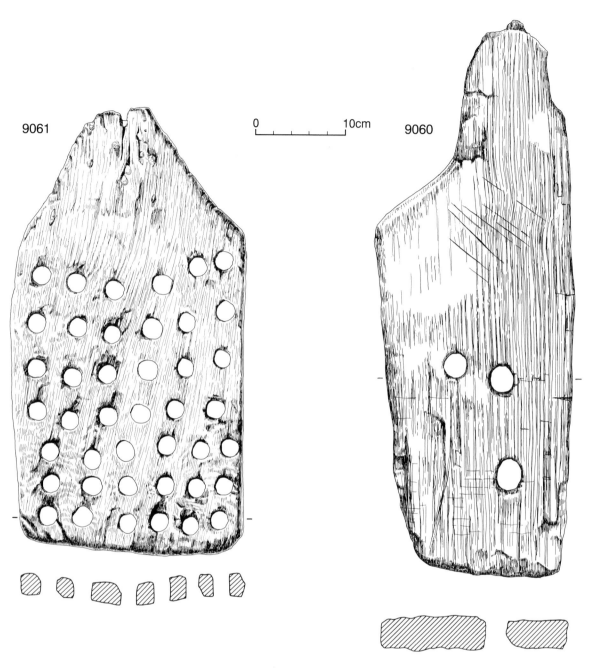

9061

0   10cm

9060

Fig.1173   *Oak sluices 9060–1 from 16–22 Coppergate. Scale 1:4*

the gunwale (ibid., 35). Complicated mouldings occur in finds from the Viking and medieval period, such as the boat find from Årby, Uppland, Sweden (Arbman 1940b, 38ff). Mouldings also occur on furniture and buildings (Krogh and Voss 1961, 27ff), which is a more likely use for *9062*.

9063 is a narrow rectangular pine panel with a rectangular cross-section. Cut into one long edge is a rectangular cross-sectioned groove 10mm wide and

9mm deep, possibly cut with a grooving-iron in a similar way to the moulding on *9062*. This may have been used in a tongue-and-groove method of joining two panels or planks together. This method was used in the construction of some of the Viking timber buildings at Hedeby where radially split planks with triangular cross-sections had deep grooves cut into their flat edges into which were slotted the pointed edges of the planks (Elsner 1990, 34, Abb.2). *9063* would not have been used in the construction of a building,

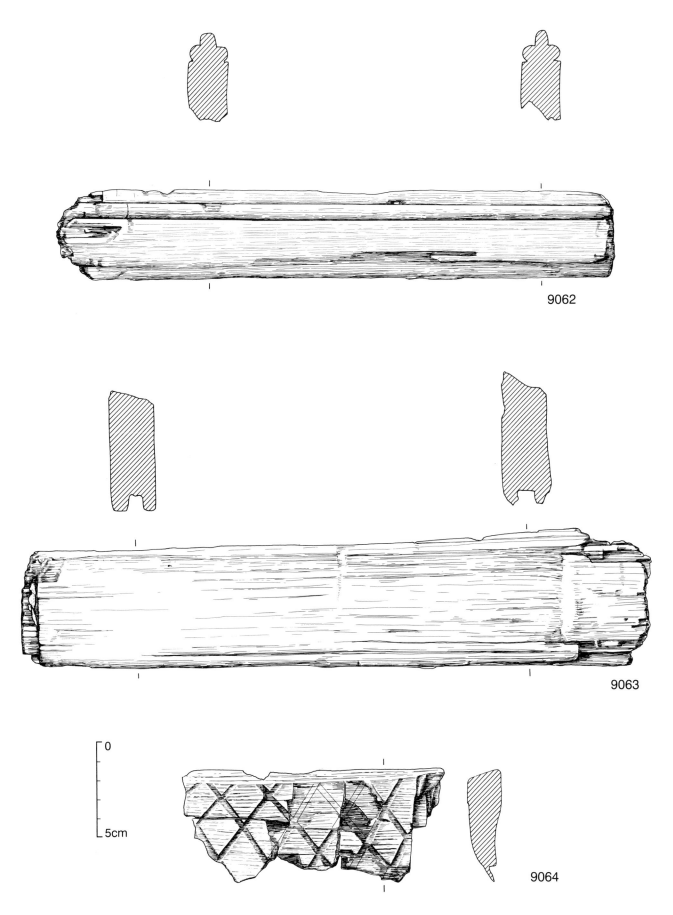

Fig.1174 *Panels 9062–4 from 16–22 Coppergate. Scale 1:2*

9062

9063

9064

0

5cm

however, and is much more likely to have been part of an internal panel. At one end of *9063* is a rectangular tenon offset to one side, to fix the panel into another panel or structure.

9062 and *9063* were both found in the same context firmly dated to Period 5B (975–mid 11th century), and appear to be related in their function, even if they did not fit together. They are unusual in that they are made of pine, a species uncommon among the wooden finds from Anglo-Scandinavian York, and in that they are made from tangentially sawn boards using an advanced conversion technique unusual not only in Anglo-Scandinavian York, but in the rest of northern Europe at this time where radial and tangential splitting was the normal method.

There are as yet no other Viking examples from northern Europe to compare with *9062* and *9063*. However, internal wooden panels made from smaller geometric pieces, with or without tongue-and-grooving, come from the Islamic world. The earliest dated examples of polygonal strapwork and tongue-and-grooved wooden panels come from a minbar (or preaching pulpit) in Haramm al-Khalili in Hebron dated to 1091–2. The construction of such panelling was an established technique in Egypt by the 12th century, where it saw its greatest usage (information from the Metropolitan Museum of Art, New York). Wooden panels with tongue-and-grooving not unlike *9063*, taken from a minbar in the mosque of Ahmed ibn Tulun in Cairo, dated to 1296, are on display at the Metropolitan Museum (Rogers Fund 07.236.6.43.51). A magnificent wooden decorated minbar with many individual wooden panels (made in Cordoba in Spain in 1137) can be seen on display at the Badi' Palace, Marrakech, Morroco (Bloom 1998). If *9062* and *9063* were parts of internal interlocking wooden panels, they are probably the earliest dated examples of this technique in northern Europe. Fine woodworking using unusual, exotic and imported timbers was not uncommon in the Moslem world, and one of the oldest surviving minbars is in the Great Mosque of Kairouan in Tunisia, made in the mid 9th century (ibid., 5). It used pieces of Javanese teak, probably carved in Iraq and shipped to north Africa. Viking York's trade with the Islamic world has been well demonstrated (e.g. Hall 1994, fig.59) and it is not inconceivable that both timber and techniques were imported and copied.

Floor planks

9065–6 are fragments of floor planks. *9066* is silver fir with squared edges and a nail through the intact end; *9065* is a tangentially sawn pine plank with a rectangular cross-sectioned groove 6mm wide down one long edge. They both resemble modern tongue-and-grooved floor planking but date from Period 5B. As mentioned above, tangential sawing is an unusual technique at this period, and both pine and silver fir are uncommon species among the wooden finds from York. The possibility that these are imported objects must not be overlooked. Floor planks recovered in their primary structural position will be considered in the reports on structures at 16–22 Coppergate (*AY* 8/4 in prep.; *AY* 10/6 in prep.).

Pegs

Wooden pegs are essential elements of timber technology where wooden planks, boards, blocks or beams need to be fastened together. Wooden pegs were mainly used as components of large objects or structures, but small wooden pegs and dowels were also used to make composite wooden objects such as separate-bladed shovels *8964–7* and *9177*, rake *8977*, stave-built vessel hoop *8852*, lath-walled boxes *8934–9*, saddle bow *9020*, and the Mästermyr chest (Arwidsson and Berg 1983, fig.14, pl.15). Pegs found singly at Coppergate could have been used in holes measuring 5–32mm in diameter, giving some indication as to the range in size of the auger bits used to make the holes.

Pegs were often needed in large quantities but are generally found singly or in small groups on archaeological sites, unassociated with the object or structure with which they were used, a fact which can often cause problems in identifying a specific use. Four types of pegs were found at Coppergate, and within three of these types pegs were often made from either radially split sections or roundwood, each with different properties and strengths.

Trenails (Fig.1175)

9067–72 and *9180* are trenails (or treenails). They have smooth, parallel-sided, cylindrical shafts, blunt ends and characteristic, slightly flaring, round heads with flat tops, faceted sides and shoulders which slope gradually into the shaft with no abrupt division. When a trenail was hammered into a hole, it would have fitted tightly and its head would not usually project much beyond the hole.

The Coppergate trenails were made from oak, willow or ash billets cut down from radially split sections, and hazel and willow roundwood whittled to shape. *9067* and *9069* have deliberate splits or notches cut vertically into their flat blunt ends, measuring 25mm and 28mm deep respectively. These were for small wooden wedges which would be hammered into the slots after the trenail was in place, to expand the end and secure the trenail in place. A small wedge and a sliver of wood survive in *9069* which expanded the shaft from 20mm to 25mm. Although the peg heads range from 13 to 33mm in diameter, the shafts

measure only 10–25mm in diameter, giving a good indication of the size of holes in which the pegs were used.

Six trenails from 16–22 Coppergate and the watching brief site are Anglo-Scandinavian and have a wide date range from Periods 3 to 5B (*9067–71* and *9180*), whilst *9072* is mid–late 12th century in date, showing that this type of peg was used over a long period of time. Similar trenails have been found at 9th–11th century Hedeby (Schietzel 1970, Abb.9, 3) and in medieval contexts at High Street/Blackfriargate in Hull (Watkin 1987, fig.125, 365, 367–9).

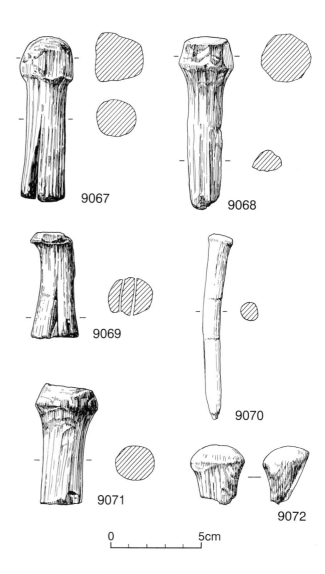

Fig.1175 *Trenails 9067–72 from 16–22 Coppergate. Scale 1:2*

Various 18th and 19th century dictionary definitions of 'trenail' describe these pegs as long cylindrical wooden pins which were driven into ships' sides to hold planks together or used to fasten planks to timbers. Modern definitions describe trenails as pins of wood for securing wooden planks. Since the site is close to the River Foss, it is possible that some of the seven Coppergate trenails could have been used in ships (see pp.2379–82), or otherwise for securing planks in structures on land.

Pegs with differentiated heads (Fig.1176)

Fifteen pegs of various sizes have differentiated heads, narrower parallel-sided or slightly tapering shafts, and blunt points. Like the trenails, they were made from either billets of wood cut down from radially split sections, or roundwood whittled to shape; unlike trenails, they have an abrupt division between the head and the shaft. Species chosen were hazel, alder, poplar/aspen, willow, oak and ash. Pegs made from radially split sections of timber are stronger and more resistant to sheer stress than those made from roundwood, but since this type of peg is likely to have had many uses, some with little or no stress, in some cases roundwood would have provided suitable raw material.

The head shapes differ. *9075–7, 9080, 9082, 9084* and *9200* have rough expanded heads with whittled and faceted sides; *9073–4, 9078–9* and *9081* have straight-sided heads with flat or rounded tops and triangular, oval, octagonal or circular cross-sections;

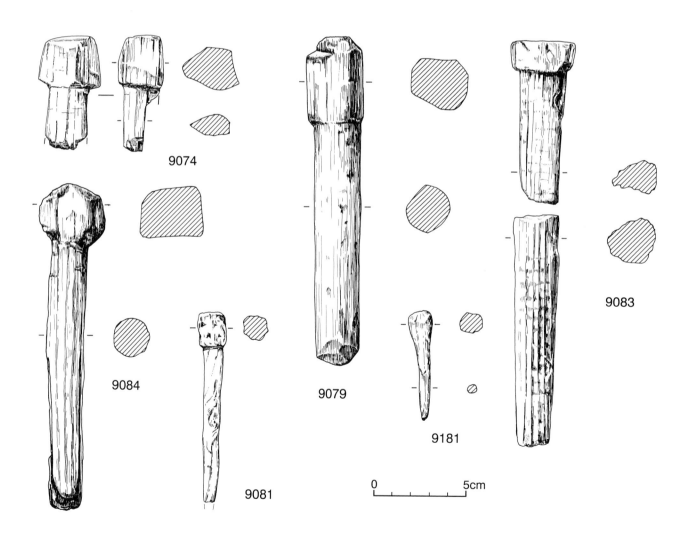

9074

9084

9081

9079

9181

9083

0   5cm

Fig.1176   Pegs with differentiated heads: 9074, 9079, 9081, 9083–4 from 16–22 Coppergate; 9181 from the Coppergate watching brief site. Scale 1:2

9083 has a flat disc-like head with straight sides and flat top; *9243* has a rounded triangular head and *9181* has an expanded, bulbous end. Although the heads range from 12 to 43mm in diameter, the shafts measure only 5–27mm in diameter, giving an indication of the size of holes in which the pegs were used.

Ten of the 'headed' pegs from 16–22 Coppergate and 22 Piccadilly are Anglo-Scandinavian (*9073–82*) and have as wide a date range as the trenails (Periods 3 to 5B), and three are medieval (*9083–4* and *9200*), showing that this type was also used over a long period of time. *9243* was found in pit 25 on the site of the College of the Vicars Choral at Bedern. This pit contained 10th century pottery, so *9243* is almost certainly Anglo-Scandinavian.

These pegs have a definite division between the head and the shaft, and, unlike trenails, the heads would have projected beyond the peg hole. Many headed pegs would have been used in the construction of timber buildings, doors, paths, fences and vehicles, but some were probably intended for slotting into holes in objects so that they could be easily removed and replaced. Headed pegs could have been used with frames, racks, easels, warping boards and looms. *9073* has a small hole in the shaft which could have originally held a small securing peg. On the Coppergate site, headed pegs were used to fasten the cross-beams of a 10th century plank pathway into axial beams below (Hall 1984, fig.70), and peg holes in the uprights of a collapsed 10th century sunken building show that wooden pegs had been used in its construction (ibid., fig.76). These could have been headed or plain pegs.

Headed pegs are quite common. Three 9th/10th century headed pegs were found in a pit on the Eastgate Street site in Gloucester (Morris 1983a, fig.118, 1, 2 and 4), and there are medieval examples from Norwich (Williams 1987, fig.85, 1–2 and 4–5), Oxford (Morris 1980b, fig.32.20), Beverley (Morris and Evans 1992, fig.94, 635), Exeter (Allan and Morris 1984, fig.176, 41) and King's Lynn (Clarke and Carter 1977, fig.171, 9). Headed pegs were used in 9th–11th century Hedeby in buildings, on pathways and for fixing two horizontal bars across the three upright planks of a door (Elsner 1990, 32–3, Abb.1, 2, 5 and 8). Individual pegs found at Hedeby have carved heads similar to those from Coppergate (Schietzel 1970, Abb.9, 1–2, 4–5).

Pegs with no heads (Fig.1177)

Twenty-three plain pegs (not including *8698*) of various sizes have straight-sided shafts (some parallel-sided, some tapering), blunt or rounded points and no heads. Like the trenails and headed pegs, they were made from either billets of wood cut down from radially split sections, or roundwood whittled to shape. Species chosen were hazel, alder, oak, yew, ash, willow and Rosaceae, and since this type of peg is also likely to have had many uses, some with little or no stress, in some cases roundwood would have been a suitable raw material. Many of them, for example *9087*, *9089* and *9182*, have roughly faceted shafts, where a knife or other bladed tool has been used to shape the pegs with long sweeping cuts.

The plain pegs differ in cross-section: *9102* is hexagonal, *9086* and *9225* are rectangular, *9091*, *9094* and *9182* are square, *9096–7* and *9103* are oval and *9093*, *9095*, *9100–1* and *9199* are circular in cross-section. These cross-sections may reflect the shapes of the holes in which the pegs were used, although octagonal, circular and oval pegs were probably used in circular holes. The pegs have maximum widths between 9 and 32mm, giving an indication of the size of holes in which they were used.

Eleven of the plain pegs from 16–22 Coppergate and 22 Piccadilly are Anglo-Scandinavian (*9085–94* and *9199*) and have as wide a date range as the trenails and headed pegs (Periods 3 to 5B), and ten are medieval (*9095–103* and *9244*), showing that this type was also used over a long period of time.

These pegs have no definite division between the 'head' end and the shaft, and, unlike headed pegs, the top of most plain pegs would probably not have projected beyond the peg hole. Most would have been used in the construction of timber buildings and other structures. *8698* comprises a group of eighteen medieval offcut rods made from billets cut down from radially split sections which shows how some of the plain pegs may have been used. Each has faceted sides and one end which is sawn straight across, while the other end is either broken or faceted. They are probably the waste ends of longer pegs used in joints to fasten two timbers together, then trimmed so that the pegs were flush with the surface of the timbers. As a group, *8698* are probably the waste products of a single event. Pegs *9089* and *9091–2* may

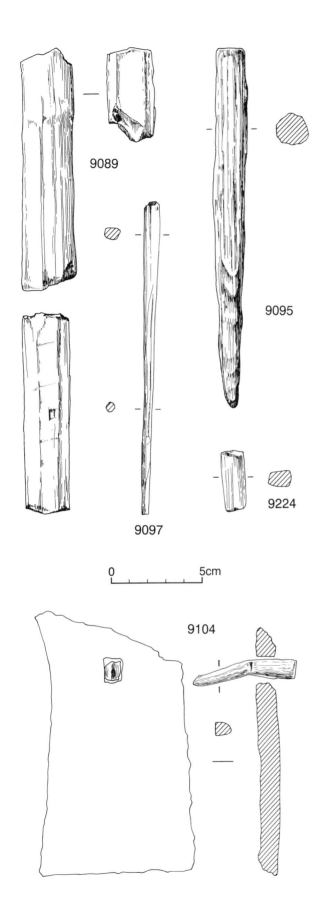

be similar offcuts, but most of the other pegs are complete in themselves. A similar sawn-off peg fragment was found on the High Street/Blackfriargate site in Hull (Watkin 1987, fig.125, 366). Some pegs have features which may have given them specialised uses, for example the hole and knotted leather thong on *9225* from Bedern Foundry may have fastened the peg to something so that it could hang freely when removed from its hole. *9244* has a rectangular rebate (perhaps also for a cord) just below the top.

Plain pegs are common finds where wood is preserved on archaeological sites. Pegs similar to those from Coppergate have been found in a late Saxon context at Whitefriars, Norwich, used to secure brushwood (Ayers and Murphy 1983, fig.20, 2), and on medieval sites such as St Martin-at-Palace Plain, Norwich (Williams 1987, fig.85, 3), Shackerley Mound, where they were used in the construction of a timber bridge (Morris 1987, fig.10, 1–4), High Street/Blackfriargate in Hull (Watkin 1987, fig.124, 353) and Eastgate, Beverley (Morris and Evans 1992, fig.94, 632–4, 636–8). Peg holes for this type of plain peg are found on many excavated structural timbers, such as *9054* and *9056–7* from the Coppergate sites. Pegs sometimes survive in situ, for example, two oak joints from Lurk Lane, Beverley (Foreman and Hall 1991, fig.124, 970 and 971A).

Tile pegs (Fig.1177)

Of all the pegs found individually on the Coppergate and Bedern sites, *9104*, *9224* and *9245* are the only ones whose purpose is certain. *9104* is a small oak peg now 10mm square found in situ in a hole 15mm square in a 15th century ceramic tile, and *9224* and *9245* are almost identical 13th century pegs which would have been used for a similar purpose.

The tradition of making small square wooden pegs like *9104*, *9224* and *9245* to hang tiles has continued down to the present day. Oak pegs like *9104*, measuring 58mm in length, were collected from the debris of a 17th century barn at Flixton near Manchester (Cripps 1973, 97). A Cotswold slater uses a peg splitter, a small axe-like tool with a wooden handle, to convert a block of wood 100mm square into 144 pegs exactly like *9104* (ibid., 97–8). Medieval peg splitters exactly like the one used by the Cotswold slater have been found in a 13th century context at Clough Castle in Co. Down (Waterman

Fig.1177 *Pegs with no heads: 9089, 9095 and 9097 from 16–22 Coppergate; tile pegs 9104 from 16–22 Coppergate and 9224 from Bedern Foundry. Scale 1:2*

1954, fig.11, 3) and at Montgomery Castle in Powys (Lewis 1968, fig.8, 19). Similar tools could have been used to make the Coppergate tile pegs. The Cotswold pegs were not tapered, but driven into the hole in the tile with a wooden mallet, the wood 'reeving up' or swelling round the constricting tile (in this case made of stone) to form an adequate 'head' (Cripps 1973, 97).

Re-used medieval boat timbers found at Coppergate

by D.M. Goodburn (Museum of London Specialist Services), with contributions by Penelope Walton Rogers (Textile Research in Archaeology)

A small group of medieval boat timbers were found during machine clearance work on the Coppergate watching brief site, re-used as part of a low revetment (context 1618) to the edge of the River Foss. They were conserved prior to examination; all dimensions cited in this report are post-conservation.

The material comprised three main re-used fragments of clinker boat boards. They do not now clearly articulate with each other but are so similar that they probably derive from the same vessel. They had several diagnostic features such as the use of iron rivets (rove nails) to hold all the overlapping boards together. The laps were waterproofed (caulked) with tarred animal hair. Traces of closely spaced trenails that originally fastened the framing timbers were also found, suggesting strong construction in the parent vessel which is therefore more likely to have been a trading craft than a fast, light longship. Each original hull board was much patched (tingled), indicating that the parent vessel was old and worn, perhaps barely river-worthy, when broken up for re-use.

Timbers 71b/75/74 (Fig.1178)

After refitting conjoining sections, the original hull board of this group was found to have a length of 3·08m, with a surviving thickness of 30mm and truncated width of c.280mm. The original width was probably around 300mm. The proportions are typical of many 13th–14th century clinker boat boards from England. Both ends were cut to a through-splayed scarf with the ends left about 11mm thick

inboard. The boards, joined end to end, made a course of boards or strake. The direction of the scarf opening suggests the board came from the starboard side of the parent hull (they are almost always cut so as to open aft). The original lap (land) fastenings were spaced on c.200mm centres which is roughly a span and a very common spacing for medieval clinker land nails.

Penelope Walton Rogers comments on the caulking:

It consists of, firstly, two or more long sausage-shaped rolls of fibre, which are single strands twisted in the S direction, running lengthways along the lap between the hull boards; and secondly, a thin layer of fibre inside two scarf joints, probably the remains of a felt. The S-twist rolls are made from black goat hair, but the fibres inside the two scarf joints are a good quality white wool which has been dyed blue with woad. Single strand S-twist rolls of this sort are typical of English caulkage of the 12th to 17th centuries. Wool was used in the early finds and no animal hair has yet been identified in caulking rolls from northern England dated earlier than the 13th century. This ties in well with the dendrochronology dates supplied for the timbers (see below).

The trenails left in situ appeared to be of cleft oak. They had the typical medieval form with sightly bulbous heads outboard. They originally fastened in position the framing elements in the hull and sometimes other fittings. The placing of the holes indicates the rough spacing of the framing. Repairs have clearly been carried out on this board, but a frame element spacing of c.360–400mm centres is indicated. There is no clear suggestion of the placing of intermediary frames. The use of closely spaced framing is indicative of a cargo vessel function in the parent craft.

The main board 75 had one thin tingle (D) added to the outboard face, and two fastened to its inboard face, the long thick tingle (B) amounting to a second board and fragments of another thinner tingle (C) along the lap. At its aft end the main board had a fragment of the next board aft attached which was in turn tingled inboard (tingle A). The tingles were fastened mainly with small, flat-headed, square-shanked iron blind-nails; occasional larger iron rove nails were also used of the same form as those in the land. When the larger tingles were fitted inboard the parent vessel was massively repaired as the framing had to be lifted and refastened. Each tingle had been bedded down on a mat of fine dyed wool felt.

2379

The surfaces of the original board were generally abraded and had clearly been subject to some ancient decay prior to excavation. The tingles were slightly better preserved, with a few tool signature mark striations surviving on the chamfered ends, and occasional patches of possible tar coating.

Timbers 71a/73 (Fig.1178)

Timber fragment 71a was found to fit Timber 73, a fragment of board edge 0·95m long. The combined section of hull boards was 1·83m long, and included the edge of one board and the edge and central section of another. The general characteristics of these articulated fragments were similar to those described above. However, the land nails were spaced a little closer together on c.160mm centres, although they were apparently the same as those used in 75. This variation in spacing may be due to an origin in a different part of the parent hull and/or repair. **Penelope Walton Rogers** comments:

In situ on Timber 71a, between overlapping strakes, were two or more caulking rolls, each twisted in the S direction, made from pigmented (light brown) hair, perhaps goat hair (young kid). Behind a tingle was a layer of non-pigmented (white) wool, with no detectable dye.

A thin chamfered tingle (A) was fitted to the outboard face of the largest board and a thicker example (B) to the inboard face. Tingle A was fastened with small iron dead nails (that is, nails which do not pass completely through the two pieces of timber being joined), whilst B was fastened with a mixture of small dead nails and rove nails.

Timber 72

Timber 72 was a very small fragment of clinker planking similar to the above but not clearly refitting anywhere. It had one iron rove nail, with two land fragments. **Penelope Walton Rogers** comments:

In situ on Timber 72, between overlapping strakes, were two or more caulking rolls, each twisted in the S direction, made from pigmented (black) goat hair.

Timber 69

This small board fragment (c.300mm long) may have been a fragment of a tingle or lap. It had thick rolls of tarred hair adhering and two iron nails. **Penelope Walton Rogers** comments:

S-twist rolls of fibre were found with Timber 69, in this instance made from light brown cattle body hair.

A detailed report by Penelope Walton Rogers on all the caulking materials associated with these re-used boat timbers, including a full catalogue, is available for consultation in the York Archaeological Trust archive or direct from the author at Textile Research in Archaeology.

A possible fragment of trenail-fastened clinker boat planking

A tracing of Timber 70 was examined and seen to exhibit features suggesting a possible origin in a clinker built vessel. The small board fragment, c.300mm long and 20mm thick, was pierced by several small peg holes along the edge. It is just possible that these were holes for small trenails fastening a clinker boat lap. More substantial fragments of trenail fastened clinker vessels of 8th and 10th century date have been found in the south of England on several sites (Goodburn 1994).

Woodworking features

Raw materials: the boards

All the board material was radially faced, of a cross-section suggesting that it was cleft and trimmed with axes as is typical of most English medieval clinker boat finds. The tingles were of similar material. Where clearly visible the boards were straight grained and slow grown, suggesting origin in oaks of wildwood type. An exception was the main board of the Timber 71a group which was clearly tangentially faced and had been cut from a fairly fast grown

Fig.1178 (facing, foldout) Simplified drawings of re-used boat timbers 71a, 71b, 73, 74 and 75 from the Coppergate watching brief site. Scale 1:8

oak and the parent log contained some large knots. In the late 14th century sawing is known, so the board may have been either cleft and hewn from half a log or sawn out by hand. This method of making timbers was usually reserved for the thicker, longer reinforcing strakes in the upper parts of a hull (Goodburn 1991, 111). The fast growth of the main board of 71a may suggest an English origin as much native oak of later medieval date in England is fast grown (see tree-ring analysis report in *AY* 10/6 in prep.). The combination of local oak for longer structural elements and imported wildwood-type boards is known from buildings in England (G. Simpson, pers. comm.). By the late 14th century wildwood quality boards were not available in England but enclaves of oak wildwood still existed in the south-east Baltic region and this wood is known to have been exported to western Europe.

Tool marks

Relatively few survived on the timbers, but the undulating surfaces and cross-sections suggest the boards were all axe hewn, with the exception perhaps of board 71a. Exceptions are the survival of axe stop marks and striations (signature marks) in the aft scarf of board 75. The best-preserved stop mark indicated the use of an axe with a slightly curved thin blade over 90mm wide, with which the shipwright had skilfully cut the long scarf joint. The ends of some of the tingles had been neatly chamfered with an axe which left some small flats and striations behind. The ends of several of the tingle boards, for example Timber 75 (B), were slightly stepped and had clearly been axe cross-cut, as had the main board of Timber 71a when it was cut up for re-use. No evidence for the use of saws or planes of any kind was found as is typical of material from clinker built keel-type craft of 12th to 14th century date.

Fastenings

The lap and scarf fastenings were wrought iron rove nails with square or rectangular shanks about 8mm across; the roves were rectangular to diamond shaped c.30–40mm square and about 4mm thick. The heads were slightly domed sub-rectangular to round, about 25–30mm across. The tingle nails were small, flat-headed, square shanked with tapered tips, too corroded to be measured accurately in most cases; in Timber 74 (A) an example had a head of c.10mm di-

ameter with a rectangular to square shank of 2–3mm. The oak trenails had slightly enlarged heads at least 28mm in diameter with shanks of about 24mm, very similar to trenails *9067–9* and *9071* found on the main Coppergate site.

Dating and source of the timbers

The technological features of the fragments are consistent with a later medieval date. The scarf length or slope of c.1:7 is more than would be expected on most early medieval finds. In sum, a date between c.1150 and c.1500 is implied. The post-conservation tree-ring study in 1998 on samples from six of the timbers (see report by C. Groves in *AY* 10/6 in prep.) indicated felling dates between 1276 and 1376, the majority in the second half of the 14th century for the radially cleft boards. The timbers were dated by comparison with reference chronologies produced from other groups of timbers imported into various parts of north-west Europe and sourced by dendrochronology to the eastern Baltic region. The vast majority of timbers analysed from Coppergate were of local origin, but oak planking is known to have been extensively exported from the eastern Baltic from the early 14th century until c.1650.

Comparison with other finds

A section of articulated hull planking was found during excavations in the 1950s at Hungate in York (Richardson 1959). This appears to have been broadly contemporary, but with narrower boards and closer spaced land nails. The scarf and caulking were similar to those of the main Coppergate material. The trenail pattern shown in the drawings of the Hungate material is erratic and cannot be easily compared.

The Coppergate material may also be compared with London finds, such as those from Hays Wharf where boards from a large ship were found, all provenanced by tree-ring studies to the south-east Baltic. They also date to the late 14th century (Marsden 1996, 118). The Coppergate material clearly derives from a smaller vessel. Perhaps the scale of the parent vessel was more like that of a small trader, such as the c.11m long clinker built keel-type vessel Kingston No.1 boat from south-west London (Goodburn 1991, 109). That vessel dates to c.1300 and the boards are local but of similar proportions to the Coppergate examples.

The importance of the finds

The collection of re-used boat boards from Coppergate is small but regionally important since archaeological evidence for boats and ships is still relatively rare. Very few accounts of such finds from later medieval England have been published in any detail at all outside London (Goodburn 1988, 1991, 1994; Marsden 1994, 1996), despite broadly similar finds having been made at Hull, Grimsby, Lincoln, Doncaster, Norwich, Yarmouth, Bristol and elsewhere. The eastern Baltic origin of many of the Coppergate hull boards is interesting, but it is not clear whether the parent vessel was built in the Baltic or simply built in England of predominantly imported boards.

Miscellaneous Objects

There are a number of wooden objects from the Coppergate, Bedern and 22 Piccadilly sites (*9105–62, 9201* and *9246*) whose exact uses cannot be easily identified. Difficulties in determining the function of a wooden object often arise because a small find may be merely a broken fragment of an object which, in itself, is only a component of a larger composite device. As wooden artefact research progresses, many of these objects may nevertheless be identified. They are described here in period order according to the primary conversion of the wood. Where possible, a tentative use is suggested.

Objects made from radially split sections of wood

The majority of unidentified objects (36) were made from radially split sections of wood. Two came from Period 4A contexts: *9105*, a very thin pine board with its edge rounded where intact, and a row of very fine stitching holes approximately 7mm apart, 5mm inside this edge, may be part of a sewn vessel; *9106*, an oak board with axe-cut chamfers at each short end, a notch cut into one long side and an augered hole 29mm diameter, is unlikely to be a cask stave (Fig. 1180).

There are seven objects from Period 4B: *9107* is an oak object with a rounded curved edge and a rectangular notch in one side, and could be a vessel handle fragment (Fig.1180); *9108* is an oak stake point made from a quarter-section; *9109* is a strip of maple perforated by at least five small nail holes (Fig.1180); *9110*, an oak object similar to *9046–52* but too thin to have been a bracket, may have functioned as a latch-lifter (Fig.1180); *9111* is an oak board with a chamfer at one end, perforated by an augered hole 22mm diameter; *9112* is possibly a worn oak rake head with a rounded rectangular hole 32mm wide; *9113* is a heavy triangular oak object perforated by an augered hole 33mm diameter, and, although it has traces of a rough groove, it is probably not a re-used stave.

Two objects were found in Period 5A levels: *9114* is a charred oak beam perforated by an augered hole 25mm diameter; *9115* is an oak rod with a square cross-section, curving towards the ends and thinner in the middle (Fig.1180).

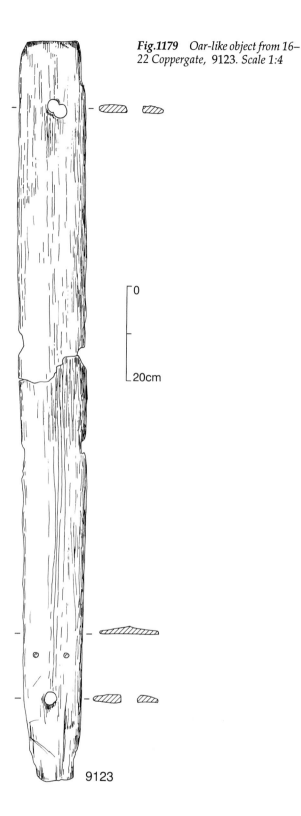

Fig.1179   Oar-like object from 16–22 Coppergate, 9123. Scale 1:4

0

20cm

9123

There are seven objects from Period 5B: *9116* consists of fragments of what may have been a flat sub-circular or oval alder board with squared edges; *9117* is a thin oak plank with one surface flat and smooth, perforated by an augered hole 25mm diameter; *9118* is a rounded oval ash object perforated by a hole

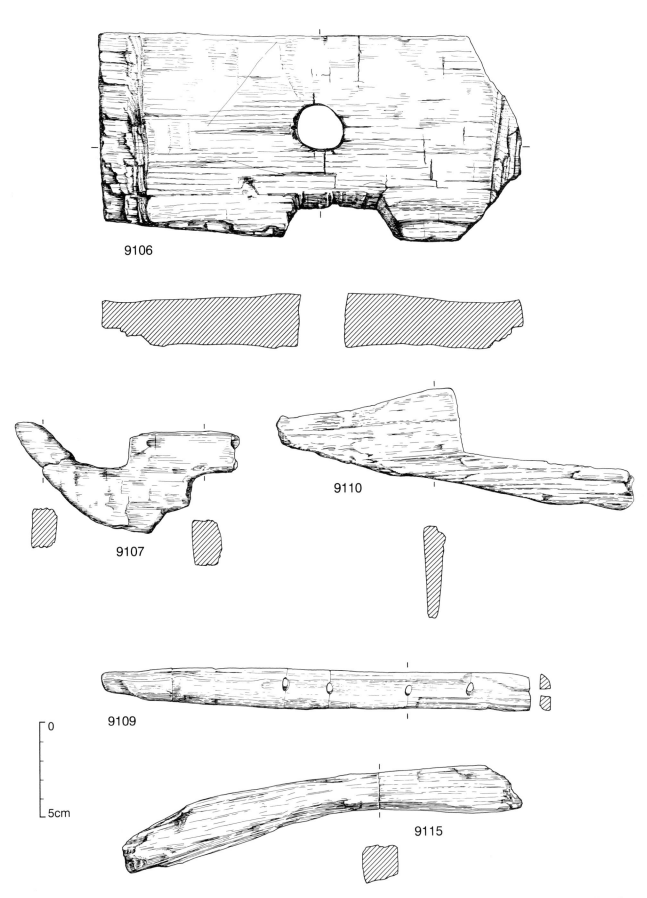

9106

9107

9110

9109

0

5cm

9115

Fig.1180 *Miscellaneous objects from 16–22 Coppergate made from radially split sections of wood: 9106–7, 9109–10, 9115 and 9118. Scale 1:2*

13mm diameter (Fig.1180); *9119* is an alder plank with two holes, one 18mm diameter and the other 17 × 20mm; *9120* comprises two oak beam fragments, which originally overlapped, made from quarter-sections, perforated by two augered holes and fastened together by wedged pegs (Fig.1181); *9121* is part of a broken oak beam with an augered hole and surviving peg 27mm diameter, 65mm long; *9122* is

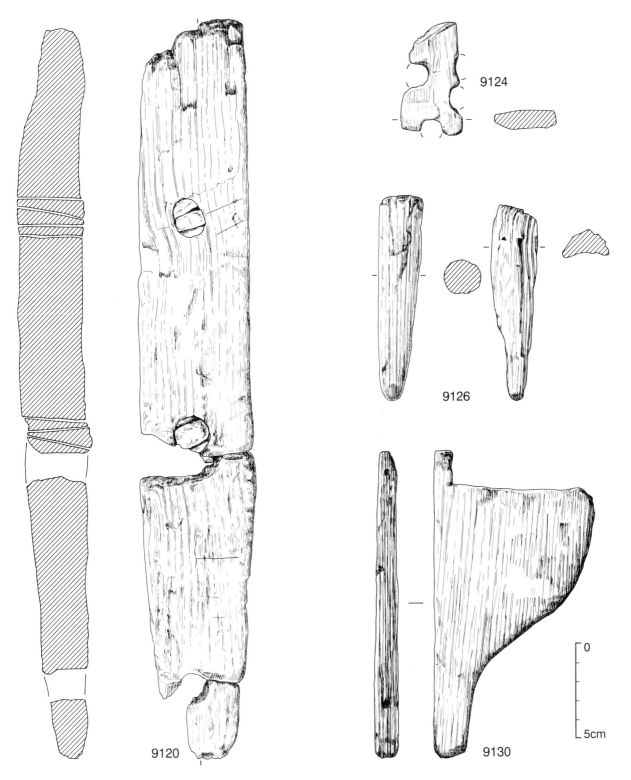

Fig.1181 *Miscellaneous objects from 16–22 Coppergate made from radially split sections of wood: 9120, 9124, 9126 and 9130.*
Scale 1:2

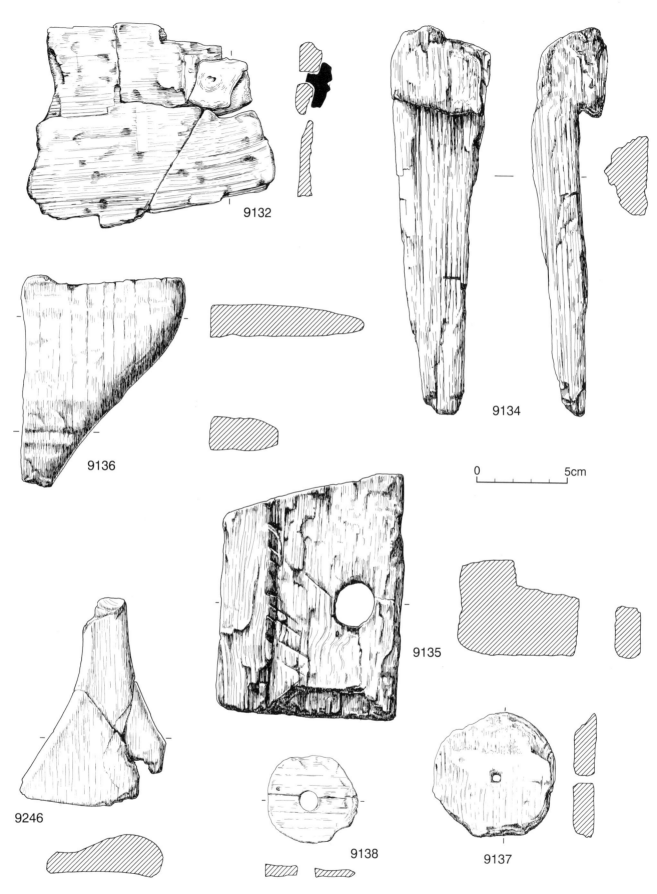

Fig.1182 *Miscellaneous objects made from radially split sections of wood: 9132, 9134, 9135–8 from 16–22 Coppergate and 9246 from Bedern. Scale 1:2*

2386

an oak board with pointed ends, with sapwood and heartwood present, and perforated by a central augered hole 29mm diameter.

9123, an oak paddle/oar-like object, came from P5Cf levels (Fig.1179). *9124*, an oak fragment with a squared edge which was possibly originally circular, perforated by multiple holes 12mm diameter, may have been part of a cheese press (Fig.1181). This was recovered from a P5Cr context.

Twelve objects were found in Period 6 levels: *9126* is an oak rod of oval cross-section with one rounded end, the other broken (Fig.1181); *9127* is an oak plank with at least five nail holes along one edge with iron fragments in situ; *9128* is an oak plank with a rectangular cross-section, deliberately squared across the grain and with broken iron nails at each end; *9129* may be an oak rake head with one edge curved, the other broken but with the trace of a hole across which the wood has split; *9131* is a sub-rectangular oak block perforated by an augered hole 15mm diameter; *9132* is an oak plank fragment with a clench nail (Fig.1182), the wood surface pitted by small marks at one side of the lozenge-shaped iron rove (cf. pp.615–18, *AY* 17/6, for other clench nails from Coppergate and a discussion of the use of clench nails); *9133* is an oak stake fragment, and *9134* is an oak stake with a rough, asymmetrical rectangular head (Fig.1182); *9125* and *9135* are sub-rectangular oak blocks with steps/ledges perforated by one and two augered holes 23mm and 26mm diameter respectively (Fig.1182); *9130* and *9136* are oak rudder-shaped objects, with pronounced curved profiles and small terminals at each end (Figs.1181–2). In some of their features they resemble *9047* (Fig.1164, p.2363) and a 12th century bracket from Christchurch Place, Dublin (Lang 1988, fig.40), and could be shelf supports. One of the terminals of *9130* is perforated by a hole which may have been used to fasten it in an upright position, with its flat edge horizontal.

Three objects were recovered from unstratified contexts: *9137* is a disc of oak 66mm diameter, perforated by an augered hole 5mm diameter, and *9138* is a small willow disc perforated by an augered hole 11mm diameter, with an incised line cut across the hole, but they are neither spindle whorls nor pieces of lathe-turning base waste (Fig.1182); *9139* is an oak strip fragment with a large iron nail.

9246 is possibly a handle fragment made from radially split alder or hazel. It has a fish-tail shape and its smooth, worn surface suggests it has been hand-held (Fig.1182). *9246* was found in pit 25 on the site of the College of the Vicars Choral at Bedern. This pit contained 10th century pottery, so *9246* is almost certainly Anglo-Scandinavian.

Objects made from tangentially converted boards

Four objects were made from tangentially converted boards. *9140* from Period 3 is a yew disc with an irregular cross-section, perforated by an augered hole 7mm diameter (Fig.1183). *9141* from Period 4B comprises two thin, almost identical, willow strips, with triangular cross-sections, and holes in various places (Fig.1183). *9142*, found in a Period 5B build-up deposit outside and east of Structure 5/5, is a D-shaped ash object with a rounded end, perforated by an augered hole 10mm diameter, with two V-shaped notches cut into one rounded side; it is possibly the end of a stave-built vessel hoop with an elaborate fastening device (Fig.1183). *9143*, found in a Period 6 layer, is a sub-rectangular oak block with an augered hole in one corner containing a squared peg 18 × 15mm in cross-section, and has a sloping-sided mortice cut into one long edge (Fig.1183).

Objects made from roundwood

Seven objects were made from roundwood. Two were found in Period 3 levels. *9144* is a hazel ring or collar made from a short section of roundwood perforated by an augered hole 25mm diameter (Fig. 1184). *9145*, a length of alder roundwood cut flat on two opposing sides, with bark on the other two sides, has one pointed and one flat end and is perforated by a central augered hole 28mm diameter (Fig.1184). It is possibly a mattock or mell head with a function similar to *8971–5* (see Fig.1139, p.2318). *9146* is a willow rod from Period 4B but is unlikely to be a spindle. It has an oval cross-section, a chamfer cut at the widest end and tapers to a rounded point at the other end. The primary conversion of *9147*, from a Period 5A context, is very unusual at this period since it is a fragment of a disc of sawn roundwood 114mm diameter, with the centre of the tree offset from the centre of the disc, possibly cut from a turned cylinder (Fig.1184). Both flat surfaces are smoothed, and one has traces of concentric grooves 18mm and 53mm

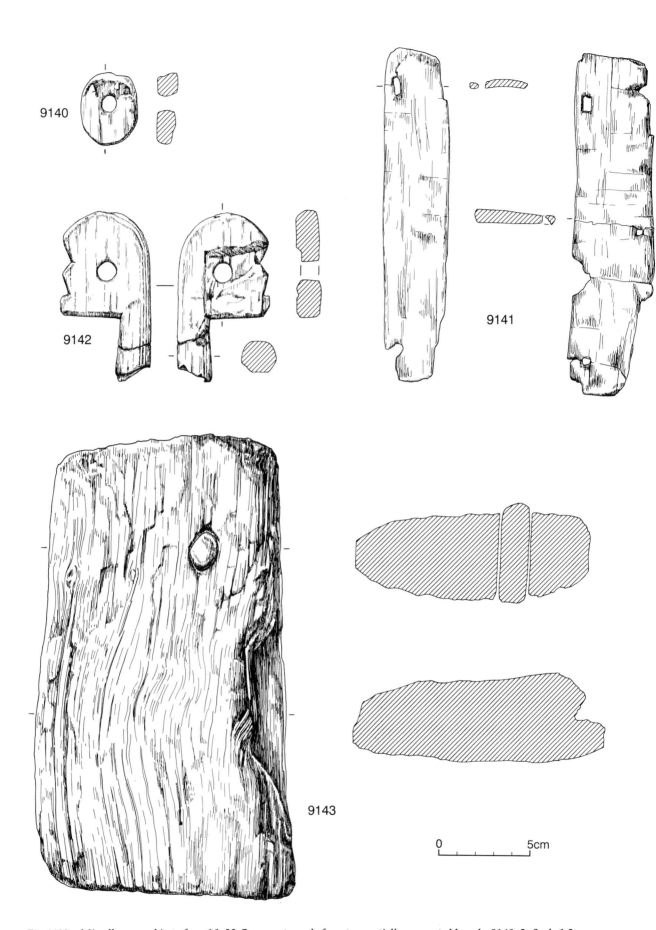

Fig.1183   Miscellaneous objects from 16–22 Coppergate made from tangentially converted boards: 9140–3. Scale 1:2

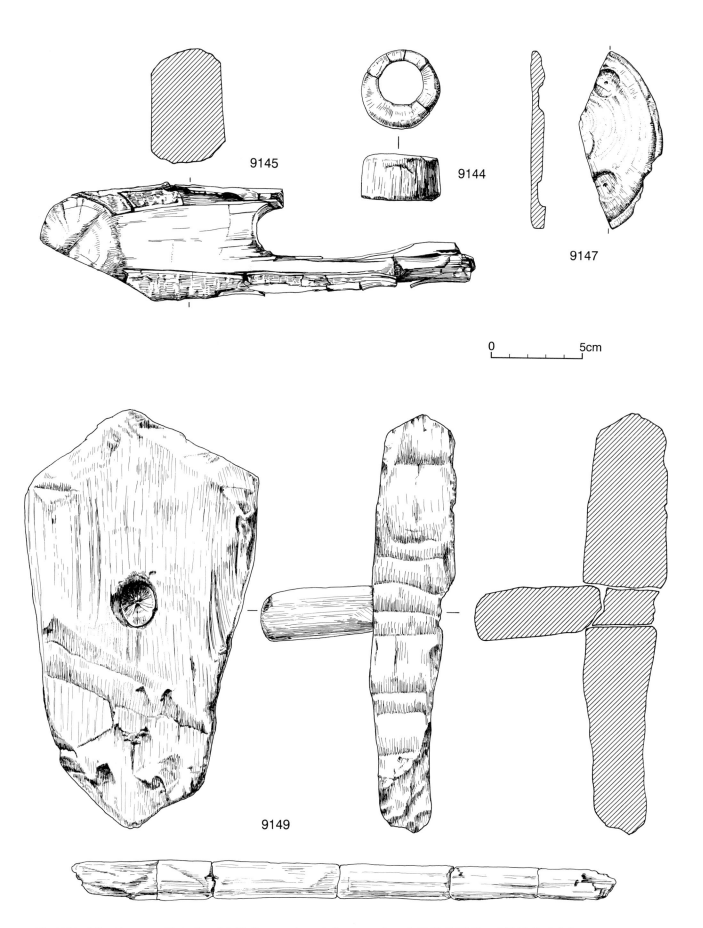

9145

9144

9147

0   5cm

9149

Fig.1184 *Miscellaneous objects from 16–22 Coppergate made from roundwood: 9144–5, 9147 and 9149. Scale 1:2*

diameter. Two circular depressions (with centre point marks made perhaps by the tool which marked or cut them) 3mm deep and 15mm diameter are placed at two cardinal points between the grooves. Two objects are dated to Period 6. *9148* is an oak branch fragment with the bark removed, one end faceted, perforated by two large dome-headed nails driven through the branch where it had been shaved flat on one side; it is possibly part of the handle of rake *8977* found in the same well. *9149* is a hazel block which was possibly intended for suspension (Fig.1184). It is sub-triangular, squared down on all sides by axe cuts and perforated by an augered hole 24mm diameter. Six fragments of a whittled roundwood shaft survive, one still in the hole, but the shaft tapers markedly away from the hole and was probably not a handle.

9201, from a late 10th–mid 11th century context at 22 Piccadilly, is possibly the head of a mallet-like tool perforated by an oval shaft hole. It was made of shaped alder or hazel roundwood.

Objects made from wood whose primary conversion cannot be ascertained

Thirteen objects were made from wood whose primary conversion cannot be ascertained. These include *9150*, an alder rod with a lead ferrule (Fig.1185), and *9151*, a small wooden bead from Period 4B. Six objects came from Period 5B contexts. *9152* is an oak object, *9153* a charred wooden object, *9154* an alder object and *9155* a wooden object attached to an iron

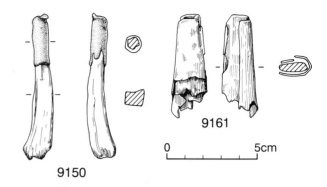

Fig.1185 Miscellaneous objects from 16–22 Coppergate made from wood whose primary conversion cannot be ascertained: 9150 and 9161. Scale 1:2

spike. *9156* is a thick, heavy plank, possibly eroded by water, which tapers from a wide rectangular end to a rounded point, now broken across a small circular hole; a large circular hole 24mm diameter perforates the plank near the wide end and the long edges are rebated with tapering slots cut out of each side. *9157* is a large stake or offcut probably cut down from a quarter-section or smaller; it tapers to a rounded point and there are three incomplete augered holes, 13–14mm diameter, cut into the side of the stake probably with the same boring tool (Fig.1186).

Five objects were found in Period 6 levels: *9158*, an oak lath with five holes; oak object *9159*; a beech object, *9161*, with a copper alloy strip folded over the end (Fig.1185); two items were of unidentified wood, stake *9162* and object *9160*.

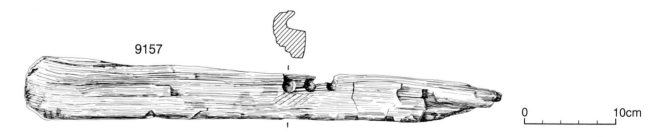

Fig.1186 Large stake or offcut 9157 from 16–22 Coppergate. Scale 1:4

Conclusion

This report presents a large, impressive corpus of excavated wooden material as evidence for the crafts, activities and daily lives of ordinary people in the city of York from the 9th to the 16th century. It is an unprecedented collection, not only from York itself where wooden finds have been found in small quantities in the past, but from any site at any period in Britain. The rare survival of such a large quantity of objects made of wood — a material which was so very common, but has such a poor survival rate on British archaeological sites of any period — has given us a remarkable reference set, especially for the lathe-turning of wooden vessels. It will certainly stand as a point of reference and research for all future studies of Anglo-Scandinavian and medieval wooden artefacts in Britain.

Many of the artefacts are unique in Britain at this period, for example, saddle bow *9020*, syrinx *9038* and the lathe-turner's tool rest and hook-ended tool *8237* and *9183*. Others are fairly common and can occur in larger numbers, for example, fragments of lathe-turned bowls or coopered staves. These types of wooden finds (including the 301 lathe-turned waste cores) have allowed comparative and quantitative analyses to be made, and more generalised conclusions to be drawn about woodland exploitation and species selected for various products, woodworking techniques used, styles, types and fashions etc. Typologies and descriptive terms have been established here for items such as cores and lathe-turned vessels, and methods have been suggested for calculating the capacities of stave-built casks and buckets. These should provide a means of standardising future studies of such artefacts, which were central to people's everyday lives, and which will be found on other British sites.

The six sites from which this assemblage of wooden material derives differ in terms of their main chronological span, their location within the city of York and their character. Similarities and differences in the function and status of the sites are reflected in some of the ranges of wooden objects found or in the evidence for their manufacture.

For example, the lathe parts, tools, waste products, roughouts, unfinished and finished turned items from 16–22 Coppergate, the Coppergate watching brief site, 22 Piccadilly and Castlegate/Coppergate, in addition to strong street-name evidence, indicate that this entire sector of the Anglo-Scandinavian city of York (Fig.962) was an area of intense specialist lathe-turning activity, on either a semi-permanent or seasonal basis, for over 200 years in the 9th–11th centuries. This woodworking craft, producing and selling wooden tablewares, had to share the tenements of this thriving manufacturing area of York with many other crafts using a variety of materials. Lathe-turners had certainly worked in or around some of the structures on the 16–22 Coppergate site from the earliest Anglo-Scandinavian activity in Period 3 right through until Period 5B. Evidence for medieval lathe-turning in the area, although sparse, is still present showing that the craft continued in this area. The sites of the College of Vicars Choral (11th/12th century to post-medieval) and the Foundry (late 12th century to post-medieval), both at Bedern, have a smaller range of wooden finds by comparison with the Coppergate area, due mainly to variable preservation conditions. There is no real evidence for specific woodworking crafts on either of the Bedern sites, but the range of wooden objects found suggests some general carpentry, domestic occupation and possibly some fibre handling (in the form of bale pins for raw wool bales from both sites, items also found in medieval Coppergate). There are no wooden objects of a specifically ecclesiastical nature, however.

Much of the material from all the sites is domestic in character, and the bowls, spoons, stave-built vessels, pot-lids, boxes, troughs and churns etc. would have been used by the craftsmen of Coppergate, the ecclesiastical residents of Bedern and the domestic tenants of both areas alike. Later medieval cask-lined wells dug into the water tables of the 16–22 Coppergate, 22 Piccadilly and Bedern Foundry sites are large surviving wooden containers helping to supply a common domestic need of all areas of the city. Many of the artefacts presented here also shed some light on the range of non-domestic activities carried out in Anglo-Scandinavian and medieval York which relied on wood in some way — riding, accounting, leatherworking, textile production, games and pastimes, agriculture/horticulture and shipbuilding to name but a few.

As stated at the beginning of this work, considering that most wooden objects would have been reused or burnt as fuel when they were worn out or broken, the 1,500 or more artefacts which were deposited and which have subsequently survived for us to study must represent only the tip of an enormous wooden iceberg of artefacts which were made and used in Anglo-Scandinavian and medieval York. It is hoped that this fascicule has gone some way to uncover a little more of that wooden iceberg, and that future excavations will reveal further wooden material which can be compared with it. Future finds of perhaps coopers', carpenters' or shipbuilders' workshops would add greatly to our knowledge of specialist woodworking craftsmen, as would looms and equipment for textile production, and perhaps more of the furniture and fittings of the interiors of domestic houses.

Catalogue

The catalogue numbers follow consecutively those on p.2059, *AY* 17/12, except for items previously catalogued in fascicules in *AY* 17 which appear at the start of relevant sections. Each entry ends with the small find number, prefixed sf, preceded by context number. If a catalogue entry incorporates more than one item or fragment, the dimensions given relate to the largest item. Entries for items attributed to Period 6 are followed by a code denoting Tenement (A–D), Period (6), phase and sequence. It should be noted that since 1994 the Yorkshire Museum accession codes have been prefixed YORYM.

Abbreviations: L. = length; W. = width; T. = thickness; D. = diameter; H. = height.

Finds from 16–22 Coppergate (1976–81.7)

Woodworking tools

See also *AY* 17/6 for further discussion of *1843, 2143, 2253–70*. See also *8237* (ash tool-rest support) and *9046–50, 9052* (possible tool-rest supports/brackets)

Axes

2253 Iron; wide symmetrical flaring blade, edge sharpened on both sides; butt and socket broken off and missing. L.152, W.123, T.35mm. 22789 sf7991 (P4B) (*Fig.975*)

2254 Iron; neck and socket fragment; upper and lower edges curve towards narrow broken neck with rectangular cross-section. L.82, W.56, T. (neck) 33mm. 24556 sf8646 (P4B) (*Fig.975*)

2255 Iron; blade tip fragment which flares slightly towards blade edge; butt and socket missing; blade edge sharpened on both sides. L.63, W.73, T.11mm. 14925 sf6369 (P5A) (*Fig.975*)

2256 Iron; neck and socket fragment; upper and lower edges curve towards narrow broken neck; blade missing; cross-section shows blade set asymmetrically to butt. L.72, W.57, T. (neck) 20mm. 14973 sf6732 (P5B) (*Fig.975*)

Wedges

2257 Iron; burred head; tapers in profile to chamfered point. L.62, W.27, T.8mm. 32676 sf13396 (P3) (*Fig.976*)

8170 Iron; heavily burred head; shaft tapers to narrow squared tip. L.100, W.5 2, T.27mm. 5348 sf1999 (C6e1, D6a16; 12th/13th century, mid 12th century) (P6)

8171 Iron; flat, rectangular head; slightly burred; straight shaft which expands to wider tip. L.70, W.23, T.18mm. 15136 sf4109 (A6n2, B6a5; 11th/12th century) (P6)

8172 Iron; shaft tapers slightly, head slightly burred. L.47, W.15, T.6mm. 17551 sf5930 (C6c3; early 12th century) (P6)

8173 Oak; radially split timber; rectangular cross-section. L.65, W.29, T.11mm. 18168 sf4827 (P4B)

8174 Oak; radially split timber; head slightly rounded; parallel-sided shaft compressed; rectangular cross-section. L.62, W.16, T.15mm. 25270 sf8318 (P4B)

8175 Oak; tangentially split timber. L.143, W.117, T.31mm. 25808 sf9704 (P4B) (*Fig.976*)

8176 Possible oak wedge. 8168 sf951 (P5A)

8177 Oak; manufactured from re-used stave; radially split timber; sides taper slightly towards tip; traces of groove re-main at head; rectangular cross-section. L.123, W.41, T.14mm. 22128 sf7493 (P5A)

8178 Oak; radially split timber; rectangular cross-section; facet cut from one side to tip. L.83, W.31, T.10mm. 2463 sf170 (P5B) (*Fig.976*)

8179 Oak; radially split timber; rectangular cross-section; long faceted cut from one side to tip. L.135, W.35, T.26. 1473 sf453 (P5B) (*Fig.976*)

8180 Possible oak wedge. 7348 sf1107 (P5B)

8181 Possible oak wedge. 6170 sf2428 (P5B)

8182 Possible oak wedge. 6170 sf2430 (P5B)

8183 Oak; radially split timber; rectangular cross-section; tapers to rounded tip. L.135, W.26, T.18mm. 15179 sf4060 (P5B)

8184 Oak; radially split timber; squared cross-section; small facet cut from side to tip. L.88, W.20, T.17mm. 15619 sf4575 (P5B) (*Fig.976*)

8185 Oak; narrow radially split section; tapers to rounded tip; rectangular cross-section; compressed at head. L.141, W.26, T.13mm. 15731 sf5270 (P5B) (*Fig.976*)

Slice

2258 Iron; flaring symmetrical blade; open, circular flanged socket; blade edge is sharpened on upper (socket) side; blade now curves downwards slightly in cross-section. L.155, W.67, D. (socket) 32mm. 28187 sf10108 (P3) (*Fig.977*)

Chisel

2143 Iron paring chisel with thin triangular blade; narrow tang with rectangular cross-section, tapers to point; tang would originally have been straight, but is now bent to one side. L.92, W.17, T.3mm. 18744 sf5668 (P5Cr) (*Fig.978*)

Small hand gouges

2269 Iron; parallel-sided blade, curved in cross-section; tang is rectangular in cross-section and tapers to point, but is bent perpendicular to the gouge blade, then bent back to lie in the same plane but offset 20mm. L.100, W.20, T.11mm. 24520 sf8272 (P4B) (*Fig.978*)

2270 Iron; triangular blade, curved in cross-section, but now distorted; tang is rectangular in cross-section and tapers to point. L.78, W.9, T.6mm. 14787 sf6598 (P5A) (*Fig.978*)

Mallet head

8186   Willow, with hazel handle; head is cylindrical with flat circular ends which are well worn, compressed and burred; head now broken; handle is roundwood with circular cross-section; lower end is intact, but tang which fitted into socket in head is now broken. L. (head) 120, D.36mm; L. (handle) 175, D.18mm. 27093 sf9604 (P4B) (*Fig.979*)

Bow-drill parts

8187   Alder handle of bit possibly used with bow-drill; circular head with deep groove cut around it, presumably for cord of bow; circular shaft below head is broken across and no trace of metal bit or tang hole. L.39, D.13mm. 5714 sf2346 (P5B) (*Fig.980*)

8188   Yew bow for bow-drill or bow-powered lathe; rod of rectangular cross-section tapering slightly towards each end; rounded triangular terminals with notches cut below them as shoulders for cord. L.330, W.10, T.6mm. 9058 sf868 (D6e8; early 14th century) (P6) (*Fig.980*)

Spoon bits

Note: 2260–5 have been catalogued as augers in *AY* 17/6

1843   Iron blade; one side straight, shape otherwise roughly oval. L.49, W.8mm. 25923 sf9954 (P4B)

2260   Iron; broken rounded tang; square cross-sectioned shank; blade broken and missing. L.122; L. (tang) 33, W.12mm. 26434 sf8991 (P4A)

2261   Iron; flat, tapering lozenge-shaped tang; heavy rectangular cross-sectioned shank; blade broken and missing. L.241, T.10; L. (tang) 61, W.21; W. (shank) 13mm. 22660 sf7957 (P4B) (*Fig.981*)

2262   Iron; flat, tapering lozenge-shaped tang; heavy square cross-sectioned shank; rounded spoon-shaped blade with U-shaped cross-section and rounded tip. L.326; L. (tang) 71, W.22; W. (shank) 14; L. (blade) 65, W.24, T.15mm. 25350 sf8542 (P4B) (*Fig.981*)

2263   Iron blade, now distorted; rounded spoon-shaped with shallow U-shaped cross-section and rounded tip; shank fragment has rectangular cross-section. L.97; L. (blade) 78, W.35, T.13mm. 21143 sf8668 (P4B) (*Fig.981*)

2264   Iron; expanded lozenge-shaped tang; square cross-sectioned shank; almost parallel-sided blade with U-shaped cross-section and rounded tip. L.211; L. (tang) 48, W.17; L. (blade) 58, W.12, T.8mm. 19390 sf9071 (P4B)

2265   Iron blade; rounded spoon-shaped with U-shaped cross-section and rounded tip. L.76, W.27, T.13mm. 18988 sf9439 (P4B) (*Fig.981*)

2266   Iron; straight-sided tang tapering slightly to squared end; rectangular cross-sectioned shank; tapering blade with shallow U-shaped cross-section and pointed tip. L.200; L. (blade) 36, W.13, T.6mm. 22124 sf10853 (P5A)

2268   Iron; expanded lozenge-shaped tang, now curved upwards; square cross-sectioned shank; distorted blade with broken tip; originally spoon-shaped with U-shaped cross-section. L.141; L. (tang) 55, W.12; T. (shank) 7; L. (blade) 26, W.9mm. 19320 sf6947 (P5B)

8189   Iron; tang missing; rectangular cross-sectioned shank; spoon-shaped blade with U-shaped cross-section and rounded tip. L.137; L. (blade) 33; W. (bit) 12, T.7mm. 4788 sf797 (C6e13; mid 13th century) (P6)

8190   Iron; expanded lozenge-shaped tang; square cross-sectioned shank; almost parallel-sided blade with U-shaped cross-section and rounded tip. L.140; L. (blade) 36, W.8,

T.6; W. (shaft) 6; L. (tang) 36, W.11mm. 4850 sf854 (C6e11; mid 13th century) (P6)

8191   Iron; blade only; shallow U-shaped cross-section, tapers to a near pointed tip and the sides are slightly convex; broken at the junction with the shaft; slightly twisted suggesting a clockwise motion. L.77, W.16, T.5mm. 9641 sf3222 (D6e1; 13th/14th century) (P6)

8192   Iron; blade only; shallow U-shaped cross-section and rounded; roughly parallel sides and, viewed from the front, appears slightly worn on the lower right-hand side. L.55, W.45, T.15mm. 16534 sf4179 (D6a13; mid 12th century) (P6)

Twist bits/gimlets

2267   Iron fragment; rounded square shank; blade has three twists and pointed tip. L.35, W.6, T.5mm. 19196 sf6390 (P5B) (*Fig.982*)

8193   Iron; expanded lozenge-shaped tang; square cross-sectioned shank; blade has five twists and pointed tip. L.171; L. (blade) 40; L. (tang) 33, W.12; W. (shank) 8mm. 5348 sf1561 (C6e1, D6a16; 12th/13th century, mid 12th century) (P6) (*Fig.982*)

Round shave

2259   Iron; with curved semi-circular blade, triangular in cross-section and sharpened on one side of one edge only; two long tangs (originally 124mm long) with straight sides and pointed tips are set perpendicular to blade but aligned in same direction as blade edge; tangs are parallel and one is now broken. L.135, W.103, T.71; W. (blade) 30mm. 22081 sf7278 (P5A) (*Fig.982*)

Lathe-turning manufacturing waste

8194   Birch blank for lathe-turning; length of roundwood, debarked, with ends sawn straight across. L.255, D.150mm. 27864 sf16267 (P4B)

8195   Alder offcut waste from preparing roughout for face-turning; fragment from the side of a length of half-section timber; bark adhering; axe cuts visible. L.99, W.96, T.45mm. 21510 sf9159 (P5B) (*Fig.991*)

Roughouts for spindle-turning

8196   Maple; roundwood; originally cylindrical but now oval in cross-section; base column of circular cross-section 54mm diameter at one end tapers slightly towards main body; both have sides faceted by axe cuts. L.148, D.75mm. 22103 sf7303 (P5B) (*Fig.997*)

8197   Maple; also an end waste product of a stacking technique; roundwood; roughly faceted circular piece with profile rounded into a bowl shape; deep facet cut into circumference; flat surface has slight hollowing and incipient core with turning lines and central knob where previous bowl in the stack removed; cylindrical base column 51mm long and 48mm diameter with V-sectioned centre hole. L.100, D.117mm. 21510 sf9404 (P5B) (*Fig.997*)

8198   Maple; roundwood; cylindrical body with two deep radial splits; cylindrical base column 53mm diameter at one end, tapers slightly towards main body. L.245, D.88mm. 7527 sf16249 (P5B) (*Fig.997*)

8199   Ash; cylindrical; V-sectioned holes 18mm and 33mm deep in opposite ends and slightly offset; no turning lines visible. L.95, D.30mm. 4769 sf881 (C6g19; mid 14th century) (P6) (*Fig.997*)

Unfinished spindle-turned cups

8200 Maple; rounded globular profile; small squared base; circular broken base knob 26mm diameter; no spur centre mark; no rim or internal shaping; V-sectioned cup centre hole in incipient core rising above intended rim; sides of core roughly turned and top has axe marks; two splits in external surface and fragment broken from one side. H.64, D.72mm. 36184 sf13661 (P3) (*Fig.996*)

8201 Maple; fragment; rounded globular profile; small base knob; external surface probably completed since there is a decorative groove below rim with applied pigment; cup centre surface remaining has turning marks. H.60, D.76mm. 27341 sf10288 (P4B) (*Fig.996*)

Unfinished spindle-turned bowl

8202 Maple; almost vertical walls with rounded angled corner with convex bottom; small knobs at spur and cup centres; interior has beginnings of shaping and incipient core 42mm diameter; two fragments split from sides. H.62, D.115mm. 32589 sf13289 (P4B) (*Fig.996*)

Unfinished face-turned bowl

8203 Alder; rounded profile; flat bottom with remains of small knob perforated by V-sectioned spur centre hole; rounded rim with external step; interior turned but has wide uncleaned area where core broken out and removed; bowl distorted and split. D.110, H.51, T.6mm. 7204 sf980 (P5B) (*Fig.996*)

Base waste

15 pieces in the form of discs or circular shavings cut from the bottoms of face-turned bowls after turning.

Centres: * V-sectioned round metal point; = two metal plates; # triangular, lozenge-shaped or rectangular metal point; NO no traces or no evidence; o mandrel hole.

Cat. no.	Status	Species	D.	T.	sf. no.	Context	Phase	Centre	Fig.
8204	Shavings	Alder			10477	28092	4B	NO	
					10480	28092	4B	NO	
					10497	28092	4B	NO	
8205	Sloping sides	Alder	92	11	12860	29459	4B	NO	
8206	Thin disc/ shaving	Willow	61	5	7233	20877	5A	NO	
8207	Sloping sides	Alder	56	14	7508	22267	5A	NO	
8208	Sloping sides	Alder	77	26	438	1473	5B	=	995
8209	Uneven thickness	Alder	65	16	2348	5714	5B	=	
8210	Section split off	Alder	70	27	3757	14184	5B	=	
8211	Uneven thickness	Alder	68	15	3786	14184	5B	=	
8212	Sloping sides	Alder	55	27	3871	14297	5B	=	995
8213	Sloping sides	Alder	68	28	5281	6434	5B	=	
8214	Uneven break	Alder	85	17	5319	6287	5B	*	995
8215	Thin disc	Maple	38	8	5502	6578	5B	*	995
8216	Parallel sides	Alder	60	20	10378	29191	5B	=	
8217	Fragment	Alder	88	18	10719	29457	5B	=	
8218	Two fragments	Charred	54	12	135/138	2193	6 (A6z4; 13c)	NO	

End waste from spindle-turning

17 pieces; usually cylinders with or without wide circular collar making them 'mushroom-shaped'; faceted sides; broken knob at one end and usually a centre mark at the other.

Cat. no.	Status	Species	L.	D.	sf. no.	Context	Phase	Centre	Fig.
8219	Cylinder	Maple	60	59	9617	24753	3	*	
8220	Mushroom-shaped	Maple	85	72	13178	32530	3	*	1000
8221	Cylinder	Maple	65	58	12917	34377	4B	#	
8222	Cylinder	Maple	54	49	13223	34292	4B	*	
8223	Iron centre in situ	Alder	45	38	13244	32585	4B	*	1000
8224	Mushroom-shaped	Alder	106	100	13617	32742	4B	*	1000
8225	Cylinder	Alder	63	48	13652	35060	4B	*	1000

Cat. no.	Status	Species	L.	D.	sf. no.	Context	Phase	Centre	Fig.
8226	Cylinder	Maple	52	48	13685	35225	4B	*	
8227	Cylinder	Maple	35	54	13697	35137	4B	*	1000
8228	Cylinder	Birch	85	58	1361	8453	5A	NO	1000
8229	Wide, flat cylinder	Alder	47	103	682	8044	5B	NO	1000
8230	Cylinder	Birch?	57	54	4321	15473	5B	NO	
8231	Cylinder	Maple/*Prunus*?	60	41	7302	22102	5B	NO	
8232	Cylinder	Maple	66	65	9345	19625	5B	*	
8233	Cylinder	Maple	89	53	9737	21846	5B	*	1000
8234	Mushroom-shaped	Maple	90	115	9756	21249	5B	NO	1000
8235	Cylinder	Maple	54	61	10676	21925	5B	NO	

Middle waste

8236 Alder; cylindrical with faceted sides; each end has turning lines and central knob where two pieces of work have been broken off after turning, one from each end; sides have wide smooth grooves round circumference for cord attached to pole and treadle. L.80, D.82mm. 35451 sf13938 (P4B) (*Fig.998*)

Tool-rest support

8237 Ash; riven section; rectangular in cross-section; one end has straight shoulders at right angles to grain and a circular cross-sectioned rod, now broken; other end had one long edge curving upwards to meet other straight edge at point; three rounded V-shaped notches cut out of upper long edge 62, 77 and 63mm wide; now broken below two of the notches; sloping curves of notches and long edges smoothed; possibly cut with drawknife. L.562, W.72, T.20mm. 1606 sf1735 (P5B) (*Fig.987*)

Cores (grouped according to shape)

294 pieces of centre waste in the form of cores cut from the interiors of face- and spindle-turned vessels after turning.

Centres: * V-sectioned round metal point; = two metal plates; # triangular, lozenge-shaped or rectangular metal point; o mandrel hole; NO no traces or no evidence.

Core shapes: C conical; TC truncated conical; CC curved conical; TCC truncated curved conical; SS S-shaped; TSS truncated S-shaped; CYL cylindrical; C/C cylindrical and conical; I irregular; ? shape unknown.

S/F: S spindle-turned; F face-turned.

Cat. no.	S/F	Shape	Species	L.	D.	sf. no.	Context	Phase	Centre	Fig.
8238	S	C	Ash	40	47	11118	30274	4A	*	1004
8239	S	C	Maple	51	26	8156	22996	4B	*	
8240	S	C	Maple	70	37	9085	21479	4B	*	
8241	S	C	Alder?	75	36	9088	21479	4B	*	
8242	S	C	Alder	62	30	9193	19626	4B	*	
8243	S	C	Maple	50	26	9194	19626	4B	*	1004
8244	S	C	Maple	62	30	9592	27271	4B	*	
8245	F	C	Alder	67	102	10944	29470	4B	=	1004
8246	F	C	Alder	68	77	11183	28901	4B	=	1004
8247	F	C	Maple?	58	58	11646	26157	4B	o	1004
8248	S	C	Maple	50	31	13252	29954	4B	*	
8249	S	C	Alder	57	33	1467	8453	5A	*	
8250	S	C	Maple	37	33	7347	22140	5A	*	
8251	S	C	Maple	63	42	440	1473	5B	*	1004
8252	S	C	Alder	40	51	998	7232	5B	*	

Cores *contd*

Cat. no.	S/F	Shape	Species	L.	D.	sf. no.	Context	Phase	Centre	Fig.
8253	F	C	?	59	55	5330	6425	5B	o	1004
8254	F	C	Alder	43	75	6471	20277	5B	o	1004
8255	F	C	Maple	36	51	7321	22103	5B	o	
8256	F	C	Maple?	35	65	7323	22107	5B	o	
8257	F	C	Alder	46	69	7324	22107	5B	o	
8258	S	C	Alder	50	35	8310	21244	5B	*	
8259	S	C	Maple	60	24	9374	21510	5B	#	
8260	F	C	Alder	64	81	9015		u/s	=	1005
8261	F	TC	Maple	27	57	7661	22447	4B	o	
8262	F	TC	Alder	30	79	7694	22490	4B	o	
8263	F	TC	Alder	37	84	1509	8454	5A	o	1005
8264	F	TC	Alder	39	62	439	1473	5B	=	
8265	F	TC	Alder	60	71	443	1473	5B	=	
8266	F	TC	Alder	37	55	446	1473	5B	=	
8267	F	TC	Alder	32	58	449	1473	5B	=	1005
8268	F	TC	Alder	56	75	457	1473	5B	=	
8269	F	TC	Alder	24	59	540	1473	5B	=	
8270	F	TC	?	34	41	600	2875	5B	o	
8271	F	TC	?	30	50	611	2875	5B	=	
8272	F	TC	Alder	33	58	775	2876	5B	=	
8273	F	TC	Alder	35	51	844	8107	5B	o	
8274	F	TC	Alder	36	56	1026	7205	5B	=	
8275	F	TC	Maple	44	72	1178	1478	5B	=	
8276	F	TC	Maple	39	51	2272	9721	5B	=	
8277	F	TC	Alder	42	65	2351	5714	5B	=	1005
8278	F	TC	Alder	38	51	2360	6119	5B	=	
8279	F	TC	Alder	60	100	2431	5692	5B	=	
8280	F	TC	Maple	22	48	3750	14184	5B	=	
8281	F	TC	Alder	29	34	3756	14184	5B	NO	
8282	F	TC	Alder	35	62	3785	14184	5B	=	
8283	F	TC	Alder	40	68	4152	15189	5B	=	
8284	F	TC	Alder	41	76	4409	15470	5B	=	
8285	F	TC	Alder	36	67	4730	14625	5B	=	
8286	F	TC	Alder	36	68	5259	14667	5B	o	
8287	F	TC	Alder	45	54	6946	19326	5B	=	
8288	F	TC	Alder	35	85	7037	20552	5B	=	
8289	F	TC	Maple?	37	47	7301	22102	5B	o	
8290	F	TC	Alder	45	75	7312	22102	5B	=	
8291	F	TC	Alder	43	68	8165	21037	5B	=	
8292	F	TC	Alder	32	53	8288	21244	5B	=	
8293	F	TC	Alder	42	70	8578	21375	5B	=	
8294	F	TC	Alder	48	80	9134	21510	5B	o	
8295	F	TC	Alder	45	74	9141	21510	5B	=	
8296	F	TC	Alder	42	88	9142	21510	5B	=	
8297	F	TC	Maple	39	65	9202	21510	5B	o	1005
8298	F	TC	Alder	57	76	9203	21510	5B	=	
8299	F	TC	Alder	55	83	9532	6287	5B	=	
8300	F	TC	Alder	24	57	9796	21854	5B	o	
8301	S	TC	Maple	40	25	10100	21925	5B	*	
8302	F	TC	Maple	43	60	10206	21925	5B	=	
8303	F	TC	Alder	43	83	10365	14515	5B	=	
8304	F	TC	Alder	34	72	3582	14069	5Cf	=	
8305	F	TC	Alder	31	62	3583	14069	5Cf	=	1005
8306	F	TC	Alder	37	56	3590	14069	5Cf	=	
8307	F	TC	Alder	33	53	3591	14069	5Cf	=	
8308	F	TC	Alder	35	57	6657	6908	5Cr	=	
8309	F	TC	Alder	74	78	6997	6926	5Cr	=	1005
8310	F	TC	Alder	49	76	7006	21088	5Cr	=	
8311	F	TC	Alder	34	64	2129	1404	6 (D6y1; late 12–13c)	=	
8312	F	TC	Alder	25	75	2156	5412	6 (C6e1, 12/13c)	o	

Cores *contd*

Cat. no.	S/F	Shape	Species	L.	D.	sf. no.	Context	Phase	Centre	Fig.
8313	F	TC	Alder	35	57	9402		u/s	=	
8314	S	CC	Ash	60	43	11334	30337	4A	*	
8315	S	CC	Alder	42	23	1762	8665	4B	*	
8316	F	CC	Alder	71	99	4649	8856	4B	o	1006
8317	S	CC	Alder	64	34	7289	20881	4B	*	
8318	S	CC	Maple	57	27	7504	23366	4B	*	
8319	S	CC	Birch	53	30	7671	22452	4B	*	
8320	S	CC	Birch	58	28	7712	22490	4B	*	
8321	S	CC	Maple	66	29	7721	22574	4B	*	
8322	S	CC	Maple	42	31	10025	21887	4B	*	
8323	S	CC	Maple	46	26	10040	27560	4B	*	
8324	S	CC	Alder	57	28	10393	29193	4B	*	
8325	S	CC	Maple	71	27	11047	28494	4B	*	
8326	S	CC	Maple	42	26	11645	27503	4B	*	
8327	S	CC	Maple	45	26	13407	29926	4B	*	
Also 9042	S	CC	Maple	65	57	8174	25102	4B	NO	1162
8328	S	CC	Maple	49	28	160	2317	5A	*	
8329	F	CC	Maple	33	79	1481	8453	5A	o	1006
8330	S	CC	Maple?	69	48	7265	20877	5A	*	
8331	S	CC	Maple	41	28	7491	22128	5A	#	
8332	S	CC	Alder	47	43	7544	22358	5A	*	
8333	S	CC	Elder?	60	28	7739	20808	5A	*	
8334	S	CC	Hazel	89	47	155	2369	5B	*	1006
8335	S	CC	Maple?	48	27	649	2875	5B	*	
8336	F	CC	Maple	32	40	1709	8520	5B	o	1006
8337	S	CC	Maple	50	30	2344	5673	5B	*	
8338	F	CC	Alder	58	63	4075	14403	5B	=	
8339	S	CC	Birch	60	35	4146	14420	5B	*	
8340	F	CC	Alder	42	61	4289	14433	5B	=	
8341	F	CC	Alder	81	86	4580	15640	5B	=	1006
8342	S	CC	Maple	80	42	5375	5532	5B	*	1007
8343	S	CC	Alder	43	34	5758	15999	5B	*	
8344	F	CC	Alder	54	67	6371	14575	5B	=	
8345	S	CC	not ident.	50	30	6467	20277	5B	*	1007
8346	F	CC	Alder	53	71	6473	20277	5B	o	
8347	F	CC	Alder	65	65	6714	14666	5B	o	
8348	S	CC	Maple?	57	31	7315	22102	5B	*	
8349	S	CC	Maple	49	35	7316	22103	5B	*	
8350	S	CC	Alder	59	30	7328	22107	5B	#	
8351	F	CC	Alder	60	75	8256	19600	5B	=	
8352	S	CC	Maple	50	30	8282	21244	5B	*	
8353	S	CC	Alder	35	26	9038	21507	5B	*	1007
8354	F	CC	Alder	40	71	9269	21510	5B	o	
8355	S	CC	Oak	58	34	9282	21627	5B	NO	1007
8356	S	CC	Alder	60	31	9289	21510	5B	*	
8357	S	CC	Maple	60	29	9303	19625	5B	*	
8358	S	CC	Maple	61	30	9320	19625	5B	*	
8359	S	CC	Maple	64	30	9375	21510	5B	#	
Also 9043	S	CC	Alder	59	56	9419	21682	5B	*	1162
8360	S	CC	Alder	56	25	10165	21857	5B	*	
8361	S	CC	Maple	59	30	10417	29156	5B	*	
8362	S	CC	Maple	54	28	10507	29156	5B	*	
8363	S	CC	Maple	58	28	10641	21925	5B	#	
8364	S	CC	Maple	48	29	10913	29263	5B	*	
8365	F	CC	Maple	59	53	10921	29263	5B	=	1007
8366	S	CC	Maple	44	26	11602	22107	5B	#	1007
8367	S	CC	Maple	48	34	3619	3521	4/5	*	1007
8368	S	CC	Holly/Lime	62	43	2396	11020	6 (C6e6; early 13c)	*	
8369	S	CC	Poplar	72	37	4837	17275	6 (C6d11; late 12c)	*	
8370	F	CC	Alder	70	84	11289		u/s	o	

Cat. no.	S/F	Shape	Species	L.	D.	sf. no.	Context	Phase	Centre	Fig.
8371	F	TCC	Alder	28	111	8879	26715	3	o	1007
8372	F	TCC	Alder	25	55	2255	1363	4B	NO	
8373	F	TCC	Alder	36	72	7281	20918	4B	o	
8374	F	TCC	Alder	71	85	7666	22452	4B	o	
8375	F	TCC	Alder	39	66	8488	25380	4B	o	
8376	F	TCC	Alder	44	69	9195	19626	4B	=	
8377	F	TCC	Alder	53	82	10243	28088	4B	o	1007
8378	F	TCC	Alder	58	68	10329	30002	4B	o	
8379	F	TCC	Alder	31	70	10394	29193	4B	o	
8380	F	TCC	Alder	23	73	10545	21903	4B	o	
8381	F	TCC	Alder	61	93	10546	21903	4B	=	
8382	F	TCC	Alder	35	62	10552	28054	4B	o	
8383	F	TCC	Alder	35	66	10767	28362	4B	o	
8384	F	TCC	Alder	70	94	10858	28230	4B	o	
8385	F	TCC	Alder	42	75	11559	21903	4B	=	
8386	F	TCC	Alder	60	90	12094	28912	4B	=	1007
8387	F	TCC	Alder	40	83	12304	28904	4B	o	
8388	F	TCC	Alder	55	63	12447	28967	4B	o	
8389	F	TCC	Alder	37	50	12553	32032	4B	o	
8390	F	TCC	Alder	55	94	13272	29954	4B	o	
8391	F	TCC	Alder	81	120	13539	35118	4B	o	1007
8392	F	TCC	Alder	40	77	13651	35060	4B	o	
8393	F	TCC	Alder	31	56	1121	8281	5A	=	
8394	F	TCC	Maple	38	82	1124	8281	5A	o	
8395	F	TCC	Maple	54	72	8153	22197	5A	=	1008
8396	S	TCC	not ident.	38	28	171	2475	5B	*	
8397	F	TCC	Alder	36	70	456	1473	5B	=	
8398	F	TCC	Alder	45	68	539	1473	5B	=	
8399	F	TCC	Alder	29	33	618	2875	5B	o	
8400	F	TCC	Maple	36	36	627	2875	5B	o	
8401	F	TCC	Alder	38	50	637	2875	5B	=	
8402	F	TCC	Alder	35	50	640	2875	5B	=	
8403	F	TCC	Alder	36	51	693	8033	5B	=	
8404	F	TCC	Alder	31	44	846	8107	5B	=	
8405	F	TCC	Alder	45	60	849	8110	5B	=	
8406	F	TCC	Alder	30	60	1778	8525	5B	=	
8407	F	TCC	Alder	38	51	2342	5673	5B	=	
8408	F	TCC	Alder	35	60	3787	14184	5B	=	
8409	F	TCC	Alder	26	61	4077	14403	5B	o	
8410	F	TCC	Maple	58	56	4133	15131	5B	=	
8411	F	TCC	Alder	30	67	4614	15314	5B	=	
8412	F	TCC	Alder	55	81	4677	14575	5B	=	
8413	F	TCC	Birch	31	45	5231	14666	5B	o	
8414	F	TCC	Alder	51	85	5260	14667	5B	o	
8415	F	TCC	Alder	41	65	5346	6429	5B	o	
8416	F	TCC	Alder	34	45	5614	6425	5B	=	
8417	F	TCC	Alder	24	46	5626	6425	5B	=	
8418	F	TCC	Alder	30	49	6950	19326	5B	=	
8419	F	TCC	Alder?	30	45	6953	19326	5B	=	
8420	F	TCC	Alder	40	69	6957	20441	5B	o	
8421	F	TCC	Alder	27	65	8182	21198	5B	=	
8422	F	TCC	Alder	32	55	8233	21204	5B	=	
8423	F	TCC	Alder	54	85	8257	19600	5B	=	
8424	F	TCC	Alder	33	62	8283	21244	5B	=	
8425	F	TCC	Alder	45	47	8382	21270	5B	=	1008
8426	F	TCC	Alder	57	87	8392	19615	5B	=	
8427	F	TCC	Alder	42	84	8395	21069	5B	=	
8428	F	TCC	Alder	21	48	8404	21182	5B	=	
8429	F	TCC	Alder	42	59	8830	21482	5B	=	
8430	F	TCC	Alder	40	77	8984	21464	5B	NO	

Cat. no.	S/F	Shape	Species	L.	D.	sf. no.	Context	Phase	Centre	Fig.
8431	F	TCC	Alder	71	80	9190	21510	5B	=	1008
8432	F	TCC	Alder	48	67	9197	21510	5B	=	
8433	F	TCC	Alder	54	86	9257	21511	5B	=	
8434	F	TCC	Alder	38	68	9307	21510	5B	o	
8435	F	TCC	Maple	53	75	9328	19625	5B	=	
8436	F	TCC	Alder	39	85	9356	19625	5B	=	1008
8437	F	TCC	Alder	33	74	9406	21510	5B	=	
8438	F	TCC	Alder	46	65	9459	21033	5B	=	
8439	F	TCC	Alder	40	65	9986	21916	5B	=	
8440	F	TCC	Alder	28	55	10012	21554	5B	=	
8441	F	TCC	Alder	43	85	10257	21863	5B	=	
8442	F	TCC	Alder	47	48	10801	29263	5B	=	1008
8443	F	TCC	Alder	48	70	11607	22107	5B	o	
8444	F	TCC	Alder	40	60	5082	3612	4/5	=	
8445	F	TCC	Alder	28	48	6658	6908	5Cr	=	
8446	F	TCC	Alder	37	58	6694	6926	5Cr	=	
8447	F	TCC	Alder	39	63	6994	6926	5Cr	=	
8448	F	TCC	Alder	50	82	7017	21088	5Cr	=	
8449	F	TCC	Maple	35	56	1063	4636	6 (C6e12; mid 13c)	=	
8450	F	TCC	Alder	25	54	1717	5638	6 (D6a2–15; late 11–mid 12c)	=	
8451	F	TCC	Maple	45	56	5470	11112	6 (B6a6; 11/12c)	o	1008
8452	F	TCC	Alder	38	66	705		u/s	=	
8453	F	TCC	Yew	20	56	2821		u/s	=	1008
8454	F	SS	Alder	50	77	1839	9450	4B	=	
8455	F	SS	Alder	48	75	7844	23635	4B	o	1008
8456	F	SS	Alder	55	72	9877	27118	5A	o	1008
8457	F	SS	Maple?	40	60	530	2494	5B	o	
8458	F	SS	Alder	50	60	1183	1478	5B	o	1009
8459	F	SS	Alder	36	72	7322	22107	5B	o	1009
8460	S	SS	Maple	58	31	9191	21592	5B	*	1009
8461	F	TSS	Alder	82	76	7647	22495	4B	o	1009
8462	F	TSS	Alder	50	75	10598	21903	4B	o	
8463	S	TSS	not ident.	18	20	5862	18594	5A	*	
8464	F	TSS	Maple	52	52	229	1546	5B	=	
8465	F	TSS	Alder	31	69	1862	5714	5B	=	1009
8466	F	TSS	Alder	38	75	2349	5714	5B	=	
8467	F	TSS	Alder	38	58	3771	14184	5B	=	1009
8468	F	TSS	Alder	58	77	4689	14469	5B	=	
8469	F	TSS	Alder	47	72	5340	6472	5B	=	
8470	F	TSS	Alder	56	79	9158	21510	5B	=	
8471	F	TSS	Maple	41	62	9405	21510	5B	=	
8472	F	TSS	Alder	41	75	9504	27094	5B	=	
8473	F	TSS	Alder	38	70	9699	21748	5B	o	
8474	F	TSS	Alder	50	76	9750	21846	5B	=	
8475	F	TSS	Alder	40	68	10407	29156	5B	=	
8476	F	TSS	Alder	52	90	10775	29458	5B	=	
8477	F	TSS	Alder	34	60	10878	29263	5B	=	
8478	F	TSS	Alder	50	77	10911	29463	5B	=	
8479	F	TSS	Alder	51	65	19522		u/s	=	
8480	S	I	Birch	79	36	7729	22574	4B	*	1009
8481	S	I	Birch	76	39	7734	22574	4B	*	1009
8482	S	I	Maple	59	25	10326	27503	4B	#	
8483	S	I	Maple	57	26	10451	28092	4B	*	1009
8484	S	I	Maple	65	26	13260	29954	4B	*	
8485	S	I	Alder	57	27	13369	29926	4B	*	
8486	S	I	Maple	56	29	13429	29926	4B	*	
8487	S	I	Maple	62	22	210	2463	5B	*	
8488	S	I	Maple	59	27	462	1473	5B	*	
8489	S	I	Alder	75	27	1882	8666	5B	*	1009

Cores *contd*

Cat. no.	S/F	Shape	Species	L.	D.	sf. no.	Context	Phase	Centre	Fig.
8490	S	I	Alder	53	23	2140	7672	5B	*	
8491	S	I	Alder	56	30	9814	21863	5B	*	1009
8492	S	I	Maple	55	26	2394	11018	6 (C6e6; early 13c)	*	
8493	S	CYL	Maple	46	31	7465	22200	4B	*	
8494	S	CYL	Alder	58	28	7634	23366	4B	*	
8495	S	CYL	Willow?	58	28	7711	22490	4B	NO	
8496	S	CYL	Alder	54	28	8248	22970	4B	*	
8497	S	CYL	Maple	51	26	8308	25241	4B	*	
8498	S	CYL	Alder	75	28	9217	19626	4B	*	
8499	S	CYL	Maple	60	30	10027	21887	4B	*	
8500	S	CYL	Maple	49	21	11144	31279	4B	*	
8501	S	CYL	Maple	60	24	12821	29459	4B	*	
8502	S	CYL	Pomoideae?	49	22	13527	35118	4B	#	1009
8503	F	CYL	Alder	45	69	621	2875	5B	o	
8504	S	CYL	Maple?	56	25	6078	14887	5B	*	
8505	S	CYL	Maple	74	33	8624	21381	5B	*	
8506	S	CYL	Maple	61	27	9300	19625	5B	*	
8507	S	CYL	Alder	60	29	9890	21854	5B	*	
8508	S	CYL	Maple	39	25	10011	21554	5B	*	
8509	S	CYL	Maple	57	26	10632	21925	5B	*	
8510	S	C/C	Maple	49	22	10548	21903	4B	*	
8511	S	C/C	Alder	61	32	11045	28941	4B	*	
8512	S	C/C	Alder	46	48	13710	35085	4B	*	
8513	S	C/C	Pomoideae?	43	29	13848	35323	4B	*	
8514	S	C/C	Alder	47	31	7293	20877	5A	#	1009
8515	S	C/C	Birch	43	34	4436	15550	5B	*	
8516	S	C/C	Birch?	55	23	4474	15561	5B	*	
8517	S	C/C	Alder?	48	20	4501	15622	5B	*	
8518	S	C/C	Birch?	58	25	4513	15622	5B	*	
8519	S	C/C	Maple	61	33	8765	21432	5B	*	
8520	S	C/C	Maple	80	30	8822	21478	5B	*	
8521	S	C/C	Maple	58	24	9229	24888	5B	*	
8522	S	C/C	Alder	54	28	10117	21863	5B	*	
8523	S	C/C	Birch?	56	35	10347	29156	5B	*	
8524	S	C/C	Maple	62	21	10550	21746	5B	*	
8525	S	C/C	Maple	39	28	11810		u/s	*	
8526	F	?	Alder	70	87	14039	35483	4B	NO	
8527						450	1473	5B		
8528			Alder			451	1473	5B		
8529			Birch			4407	15530	5B		
8530	F	?	Alder	20	52	6012	6433	5B	=	

Middle cores

3 pieces of waste; cut from the centre of one bowl and the base of another after turning using a spindle-turned stacking process.

Cat. no.	S/F	Shape	Species	L.	D.	sf. no.	Context	Phase	Fig.
8531	S	C	Maple	55	27	12995	29844	4B	1010
8532	S	CC	Birch	58	40	4185	16507	6 (B6c1; 12/13c)	1010
8533	S	I	Birch	66	24	7756	22574	4B	1010

Lathe-turned vessels

Bowls

See also *8671* (includes charred fragment of turned bowl)

8534 Alder; face-turned; deep rounded profile; rounded rim; flat base with angled edge and rough circle 37mm diameter where base waste removed but not cleaned down. D.190, H.58, T.10mm. 3698 sf9817 (P3) (*Fig.1018*)

8535 Ash; fragments; face-turned; deep rounded profile; rounded rim; rounded bottom; thin walls; one split had been repaired with organic stitching (probably wood, species unidentified); two sets of four external grooves 33mm and 59mm below rim. D.184, H.c.90; T. (wall) 5; T. (bottom) 7mm. 28431 sf11009 (P3) (*Fig.1018*)

8536 Fragments. 19763 sf13052 (P3)

8537 Maple; fragments; face-turned; rounded profile; rounded rim with external groove underlining slight lip; flat base with rounded edges. D.130, H.37, T.7–8mm. 19763 sf13058 (P3) (*Fig.1018*)

8538 Alder; face-turned; rounded profile; rounded rim; flat bottom, now very worn; dark stained internal surface with many cuts/scratches. D.280, H.82; T. (wall) 12; T. (bottom) 20mm. 36265 sf13800 (P3) (*Fig.1018*)

8539 Alder; face-turned; rounded profile; rounded rim; rounded bottom; two internal grooves; two sets of two external grooves; small hole for repair staple has metal salts but no surviving metal. D.215, H.40, T.8–9mm. 22417 sf7581 (P4B) (*Fig.1018*)

8540 Charred base fragment; face-turned; footring base. T. (wall) 5; T. (base) 6mm. 22433 sf7621 (P4B)

8541 Maple (or Pomoideae); face-turned; rounded profile; rounded rim; flat base 64mm diameter with rounded edge and central disc 30mm diameter showing where base waste removed. D.125, H.38, T.6mm. 22440 sf7625 (P4B) (*Fig.1019*)

8542 Maple; face-turned; rounded profile; rounded rim, now very worn and broken; two external grooves; flat bottom, now very worn; raised internal base disc 75mm diameter; split in five places on rim, one of which was repaired with rectangular metal rim clip (tin with small amounts of lead and zinc) held by two rivets; to side of this, corrosion suggests a previous iron repair staple; circular hole in wall opposite repair may have caused one of the splits. D.193, H.49, T.6mm. 22523 sf7758 (P4B) (*Figs.1019, 1041*)

8543 Alder; fragments; charred; face-turned; rounded profile; rounded base with pronounced hollowing groove emphasising base edge. T.7mm. 22745 sf8009 (P4B)

8544 Charred fragments; face-turned. T.9mm. 22845 sf8025 (P4B)

8545 Charred fragments; face-turned. T.5mm. 22848 sf8034 (P4B)

8546 Ash; face-turned; rounded profile; rounded rim; rounded bottom; dark stained internal surface. D.300, H.90; T. (wall) 5; T. (bottom) 16mm. 29193 sf10425a (P4B)

8547 Ash; fragment; face-turned; rounded profile; rounded bottom; two sets of four external grooves. T. (wall) 10; T. (bottom) 16mm. 29193 sf10425b (P4B)

8548 Maple; fragment; face-turned; footring base with chamfered edge. D. (base) 100, T.10mm. 21807 sf10431 (P4B) (*Fig.1019*)

8549 Alder; face-turned; rounded profile; rounded rim; slightly concave worn base, probably originally with footring 7mm wide; rounded base edge; dark stained internal surface; two sets of two external grooves. D.202, H.81, T.9mm. 27503 sf10557 (P4B) (*Fig.1019*)

8550 Charred alder fragment; face-turned; slightly concave base with rounded edge and disc visible where base waste removed. T.12mm. 29470 sf11506 (P4B)

8551 Alder; fragments; face-turned; rounded profile; no rim survives, but possible internal and external rim flange 75mm above base; base 4mm high with rounded edges. T.7–12mm. 32185 sf12700 (P4B) (*Fig.1020*)

8552 Alder; face-turned; very worn external and internal surfaces; deep rounded profile; rounded rim; slightly convex base with rounded edge; small hole 8mm square in wall, deliberately chiselled from both sides; two small holes and a linear stain near rim indicate bowl was repaired with iron staples (not extant); two sets of two external grooves. D.200, H.80, T.9–10mm. 29844 sf13057 (P4B) (*Fig.1020*)

8553 Alder; face-turned; straight-sided; flat everted rim 18mm wide with incised interlocking step pattern above and below; flat bottom with traces of what may be an incised triquetra in double outline on external surface; small hole in wall is possibly for repair staple (not extant). D.240, H.55, T.8mm. 34703 sf13160 (P4B) (*Fig.1021*)

8554 Alder; face-turned; rounded profile; rounded rim; thick rounded bottom; dark stained internal surface with cuts/scratches in all directions. D.185, H.c.65, T. (wall) 10; T. (bottom) 19mm. 35147 sf13626 (P4B)

8555 Alder; fragment; face-turned; rounded profile; rim thinned on interior; dark stained internal surface. T.9mm. 35447 sf14053 (P4B)

8556 Charred ash fragment; face-turned. T.8mm. 18594 sf5878 (P5A)

8557 Alder; face-turned; rounded profile with very worn external surface; rounded rim with external ridge and groove underlining slight lip; footring base; dark stained internal surface. D.320, H.65, T.10mm. 22153 sf7452 (P5A) (*Fig.1020*)

8558 Alder; fragments; face-turned; charred on inside; footring base 6mm wide and 5mm high, worn down on inside. D. (base) 95, T.10mm. 22256 sf7500, sf7511 (P5A) (*Fig.1020*)

8559 Birch; face-turned; rounded profile; rounded rim; flat bottom; dark stained internal and external surfaces; external base very worn; internal surfaces cut and gouged; deliberate roughly cut hole through wall at base/wall junction; bowl split in half and repaired along crack with four iron staples, three clenched on inside; split again before being discarded. D.256, H.86, T.9mm. 1611 sf375 (P5B) (*Fig.1040*)

8560 Maple?; fragment; charred; face-turned. T.9mm. 2875 sf591 (P5B)

8561 Willow?; fragment. 2875 sf596 (P5B)

8562 Fragment. 7348 sf1096 (P5B)

8563 Alder; face-turned; rounded profile; rounded rim; wide turned groove just inside squared base edge makes footring base; crescent-shaped split repaired with individually stitched copper alloy loops. D.180, H.48, T.7mm. 7473 sf1383 (P5B) (*Fig.1040*)

8564 Alder? burrwood?; very knotty wood; probably lathe-turned; thick walls, rounded profile; rounded rim; rounded bottom. D.200, H.63, T.13mm. 7467 sf1459 (P5B)

8565 Alder; fragment; thick walls; rounded profile; rounded bottom; internal bottom has raised centre. T.14–16mm. 7589 sf2101 (P5B)

8566 Alder?; face-turned; rounded profile; rounded rim; external ridge between two grooves; flat bottom. D.210, H.72, T.9mm. 7473 sf2283 (P5B)

8567 Alder; face-turned; rounded profile; rounded rim; external groove; flat bottom; dark stained internal surface; very badly worn and abraded on both surfaces; split in half and repaired with iron staples, fragments of two survive in holes on base. D.220, H.65; T. (base) 14; T. (wall) 5mm. 13916, 13921 sfs3654–5 (P5B)

8568 Ash; face-turned from almost half-section roundwood (bowl centre approximately 30–50mm from tree centre);

rounded profile; rounded rim; very rough and worn on both surfaces; rounded bottom, no real base. D.335, H.110–20, T.14mm. 15195 sf4085 (P5B) (*Fig.1022*)

8569 Alder; face-turned; S-shaped profile; rounded pointed rim; slightly concave bottom; dark stained internal surface; both surfaces very worn and abraded. D.130, H.50, T.7–10mm. 18470 sf5208 (P5B) (*Fig.1022*)

8570 Maple burrwood; fragments; rounded base edge. D. (base) 65, T. 13; T. (wall) 7mm. 19446 sf6928 (P5B)

8571 Maple; face-turned; rounded profile; rounded rim with single grooves on inside and outside; external groove/ledge further down walls; slightly concave base with angled edges and base circle 35mm diameter which was unturned and shaved off; dark stained internal surface. D.216, H.60, T.7mm. 21258 sf8311 (P5B) (*Fig.1022*)

8572 Alder; fragment; face-turned; shallow rounded profile; slightly concave base with angled edges and base circle 32mm diameter left unturned; small V-sectioned spur centre hole; dark stained internal surface. D. (base) 80, T.10mm. 21834 sf9706 (P5B) (*Fig.1022*)

8573 Alder; fragment; face-turned; rounded profile; flat bottom; external surface worn and abraded; dark stained internal surface. D. (base) 82, T.10mm. 21554 sf9902 (P5B)

8574 Alder; fragments; face-turned; rounded rim; two groups of three and four external grooves; dark stained internal surface. T.9mm. 29104 sf10155 (P5B)

8575 Alder; fragment; face-turned; base edge rounded; external surface very worn and abraded. T.11mm. 29104 sf10322 (P5B)

8576 Base fragment; face-turned; charred; slightly concave base with angled edges. D. (base) 60–3, T.15mm. 21746 sf10554 (P5B)

8577 Alder; face-turned; rounded profile; rounded squared rim; flat bottom; very worn and abraded externally, and dark stained internal surfaces which are also heavily cut and scratched. D.160, H.72, T.13mm. 21925 sf10722 (P5B)

8578 Boxwood; fragment; rounded profile; footring base; dark stained external and internal surfaces. D.>120; D. (base) 80, T.7mm. 21925 sf10730 (P5B) (*Fig.1023*)

8579 Maple; face-turned; shallow rounded profile, now distorted; rounded rim; internal groove just below rim; flat bottom; dark stained internal surface; exterior very worn and abraded. D.270–80, H.60, T.6mm. 29562 sf10793 (P5B)

8580 Alder; face-turned; rounded rim with internal groove; slight external lip 25mm below rim; rounded base, now very worn with central disc where base waste cleaned off; internal base disc remains where core removed but not cleaned down. D.214, H.50, T.6mm. 29463 sf10902c (P5B) (*Fig.1023*)

8581 Maple; face-turned; rounded profile; high footring base with chamfered edges. D. (base) 50, T.7; T. (wall) 3mm. 22107 sf11603 (P5B)

8582 Rosaceae?; fragments; face-turned. T.4mm. 6785 sf6182 (P5Cr)

8583 Alder; thick-walled bowl fragments; face-turned; rounded profile; squared rim; two deep grooves on external surface below rim; rounded convex base; split in bowl originally repaired with continuous stitches of iron wire; fragment of wire, flattened oval in cross-section, in situ near rim. D.360, H.115, T. (wall) 12, T. (rim) 20mm. 4385 sf536 (C6i4; 16th–19th century) (P6) (*Fig.1023*)

8584 Birch; fragments; face-turned; rounded profile; rounded rim; decorative external ridge; base is 9mm deep and has chamfered edges. D. (base) 48, T.5mm. 4385 sf542a (C6i4; 16th–19th century) (P6)

8585 Birch; fragments; face-turned; rounded profile; rim thinned on outside; rough, worn external surface. T.9mm. 4385 sf542b (C6i4; 16th–19th century) (P6)

8586 Alder; fragments; face-turned; inturned profile; convex base with angled edges; branded with 'SR' on external base. D.c.150, T.10mm. 4385 sf562, sf566b (C6i4; 16th–19th century) (P6) (*Fig.1023*)

8587 Maple; fragment; face-turned; rounded profile; rounded rim; decorative external ridge. T.7–8mm. 4385 sf566c (C6i4; 16th–19th century) (P6)

8588 Ash; fragment; face-turned; rounded profile; two external grooves; rounded base edge; dark shiny stained internal surface. D. (base) 105, T.4–6mm. 4434 sf646 (C6g19; mid 14th century) (P6)

8589 Ash; fragment; face-turned; rounded profile; flat bottom which is very worn. D. (base) 130, T.7mm. 1842 sf689 (D6f8; 15th/16th century) (P6)

8590 Ash; fragment; face-turned; rounded profile; rounded rim with internal groove; concretion and charring on external surface. T.8mm. 1842 sf690 (D6f8; 15th/16th century) (P6)

8591 Alder; plate/bowl fragments; face-turned; shallow, straight-sided profile; rounded pointed rim; flat base with rounded edge emphasised by two grooves; interior has dark organic concretion with hairs and vegetable matter including human hair. D.207, H.21, T.4–5mm. 1944 sf840 (D6e10; mid 14th century) (P6)

8592 Ash; small; face-turned; rounded profile; everted rim; rounded base edge; trace of V-sectioned spur centre mark. D.106, H.31, T.9mm. 4885 sf859 (C6f5; 13th/14th century) (P6)

8593 Ash; face-turned; stepped profile; rounded rim; flat bottom; one external groove; internal surface dark stained and shiny. D.145, H.45, T.5–8mm. 4885 sf883 (C6f5; 13th/14th century) (P6)

8594 Ash; fragment; face-turned; rounded profile. T.9mm. 9129 sf912 (D6e9; mid 14th century) (P6)

8595 Ash; fragment; face-turned; rounded profile; convex base with squared edges and central disc 38mm diameter where base waste removed but not cleaned down; charred and broken. D. (base) 65, T.6mm. 3235 sf1205 (A6g1; 13th/14th century) (P6)

8596 Alder; fragments; face-turned; rounded profile; squared rim. T.6mm. 5749 sf1856 (C6c6; mid 12th century) (P6)

8597 Ash; half survives; face-turned; rounded profile; rounded rim with internal groove; flat bottom; dark stained internal surface; knife cuts across external lower walls. D.248, H.57, T.9mm. 5655 sf1864 (D6a17–23; 12th/13th century) (P6)

8598 Alder; fragments; face-turned; rounded profile; rounded rim; flat base with squared edge and groove 5mm inside edge. T.6mm. 5755 sf1878 (D6a17–23; 12th/13th century) (P6)

8599 Alder; face-turned; rounded profile; rim thinned on outside; rounded bottom. D.206, H.52, T.7mm. 9765 sf2299 (D6a5; 11th/12th century) (P6)

8600 Ash; face-turned; rounded profile; rim thinned on outside; concave base with rounded edge; worn and abraded on external and internal surfaces. D.235, H.52, T.7mm. 11050 sf2400 (B6c7; early 13th century) (P6)

8601 Maple; small; face-turned; rounded profile; flanged rim; two external grooves below flange; flat base with rounded edge; now distorted. D.122, H.43, T.4mm. 10758 sf2662 (B6g6; 15th century) (P6) (*Fig.1024*)

8602 Ash; face-turned; rounded profile; rounded rim; flat base with rounded edge; two external grooves. D.188, H.58, T.7mm. 11052 sf2695 (B6c7; early 13th century) (P6) (*Fig.1024*)

8603 Ash; fragments; face-turned; rounded profile; rounded rim with internal groove. T.5–6mm. 11342 sf2749 (B6f7; 14th century) (P6)

8604 Ash; face-turned; rounded profile; rounded rim; external groove; very worn rounded bottom and external walls; dark stained internal surface; interior and exterior criss-crossed by knife cuts. D.192, H.40, T.8mm. 12548 sf3288 (D6a25; 12th/13th century) (P6)

8605 Alder; fragments; face-turned; rounded profile; rounded rim. T.6mm. 12276 sf3408 (D6e5; early 14th century) (P6)

8606 Ash; face-turned; rounded profile; rim thinned on outside; flat bottom; many knife cuts on external bottom. D.180, H.67, T.5–10mm. 15026 sf3718 (B6c8; early 13th century) (P6) (Fig.1024)

8607 Ash; face-turned; rounded profile; rounded rim; flat base with rounded edge; grooves on internal and external base 90–95mm diameter; dark stained interior and very abraded. D.180, H.42, T.9mm. 15041 sf4008 (B6c6; early 13th century) (P6) (Fig.1024)

8608 Ash; face-turned; rounded profile; rounded rim with internal groove; flat base with rounded edge emphasised by groove; two parallel slits in external base, offset to one side, are remains of spur centre mark; dark stained internal surface. D.171, H.55, T.7mm. 18153 sf4747 (B6c3; 12th/13th century) (P6) (Fig.1024)

8609 Alder; fragment; face-turned; rounded profile; rounded rim; light brown stained internal surface. D.220, T.9mm. 17890 sf5437 (B6a1, C6a1; late 11th century) (P6) (Fig.1025)

8610 Ash; face-turned; rounded profile; rounded rim; rounded bottom; split in half and repaired by an iron staple clenched on inside; very worn and abraded. D.170, H.55, T.7mm. 5750 sf5869 (C6e6; early 13th century) (P6) (Fig.1025)

8611 Fragments. L.49, W.30, T.6mm. 10763 sf19038 (D6f1; mid–late 14th century) (P6)

8612 Ash; face-turned; rounded profile; rounded rim; flat bottom; charred interior. D.182, H.65, T.7mm. u/s sf9595

Cups

8613 Alder; spindle-turned from half-section roundwood; vertical straight-sided profile; deep external groove 15mm wide, possibly for metal band. D.83, T.6mm. 20590 sf7015 (P3) (Fig.1031)

8614 Ash; fragments; spindle-turned; very short beaded rim; walls are almost vertical, then curve inwards slightly; three rim fragments have incised decoration in form of two parallel lines with diagonal hachures between them, below which are two curved lines with the space between divided into small squares; seven wall fragments have further incised lines. T.5mm. 26721 sf9079 (P3) (Fig.1031)

8615 Birch; spindle-turned from roundwood; vertical walls turning into slightly globular profile; rounded rim; probably flat bottom. D.96, H.75–80; T. (base) 11mm. 32751 sf13630 (P3) (Fig.1031)

8616 Alder; face-turned; globular profile; rounded rim; flat base with rounded edge. D.110, H.60, T.5–8mm. 30031 sf10373 (P4A) (Fig.1031)

8617 Maple; spindle-turned; globular profile; rounded rim; flat base with squared edges; two external grooves. D.90, H.70–5; T. (base) 20; T. (wall) 5mm. 30286 sf11181 (P4A) (Fig.1031)

8618 Maple; fragment; spindle-turned; globular profile with slightly out-turned rounded rim; possible area of dark staining/pigment below external rim edge, 30mm wide. T.6–7mm. 18602 sf5358 (P4B) (Fig.1031)

8619 Maple; spindle-turned; globular profile; flat base with squared edges. D.100; T. (base) 10; T. (wall) 7mm. 18602 sf5359 (P4B) (Fig.1031)

8620 Maple; fragment; spindle-turned; globular profile with everted rounded rim; possible area of dark staining/pig-ment below external rim edge. H.65–70, T.8mm. 22490 sf7830 (P4B) (Fig.1031)

8621 Alder; spindle-turned; thin vertical walls; thick bottom with probably flat base. T. (base) 19; T. (wall) 2–3mm. 22846 sf8022 (P4B)

8622 Maple; spindle-turned; globular profile; rim thinned on inside; two pairs of external grooves; flat base with angled edges; convex internal bottom. D.84, H.62, T.6mm. 18988 sf9478 (P4B)

8623 Alder; spindle-turned; thick walls; globular profile; rounded rim with external groove; three more grooves lower down; probably flat bottom. D.95, H.50, T.5–10mm. 18988 sf9479 (P4B) (Fig.1031)

8624 Maple; spindle-turned; globular profile with thin walls and rounded rim; rounded bottom with rough central knobs on outside and inside where cores/end waste removed. D.108, H.65, T.5mm. 28987 sf12196 (P4B) (Fig.1031)

8625 Alder; spindle-turned from half-section roundwood; globular profile; rounded rim; flat bottom. D.100–5, H.65, T.10mm. 27093 sf12805 (P4B) (Fig.1032)

8626 Alder; fragment; spindle-turned from half-section round-wood; globular profile with wall turning sharply inwards towards bottom; rounded rim. D.126, H.c.45, T.8mm. 32465 sf13099 (P4B)

8627 Base fragment; charred; spindle-turned from roundwood. T.10mm. 29930 sf13131 (P4B)

8628 Alder; spindle-turned from half-section roundwood; globular profile with slight out-turned rim thinned on inside; rounded bottom. D.96, H.85, T. (bottom) 19, T. (wall) 10mm. 29926 sf13296 (P4B) (Fig.1032)

8629 Maple; spindle-turned from roundwood; globular profile; rounded rim with external groove; two external grooves just above rounded bottom; rough central external knob where core/end waste removed; dark staining and concretion on internal surface. D.124, H.65; T. (bottom) 18; T. (wall) 6mm. 35079 sf13427 (P4B) (Fig.1032)

8630 Alder; spindle-turned from possible half-section round-wood; globular profile; rounded rim; rounded bottom; external and internal central knobs where cores/end waste removed; charred, but concretion deposited on internal surface before charring. D.100; T. (bottom) 12; T. (wall) 6mm. 36116 sf13703 (P4B) (Fig.1032)

8631 Maple; spindle-turned; globular profile with very thin walls; rounded bottom. D.80, H.60–5; T. (wall) 3; T. (bottom) 10mm. 20808 sf7267 (P5A) (Fig.1032)

8632 Alder; spindle-turned; globular profile; flat base with squared edge emphasised by groove. D.105; T. (base) 14; T. (wall) 7mm. 22089 sf7290 (P5A)

8633 Yew; spindle-turned from roundwood; globular profile; rounded pointed rim with two external grooves; flat base with squared edge. D.111, H.81, T.4–9mm. 7473 sf1384 (P5B) (Figs.1032, 1038)

8634 Maple; spindle-turned from roundwood; globular profile; two external grooves; flat base with squared edges; external and internal knobs where cores/end waste removed. D.76; T. (base) 18; T. (wall) 5mm. 24916 sf8519 (P5B) (Fig.1032)

8635 Maple; spindle-turned; globular profile; rounded, slightly everted rim with deep external groove 4mm wide; two more external grooves; convex base with rounded edge. D.100, H.86; T. (base) 13; T. (wall) 3mm. 21510 sf9179 (P5B) (Fig.1032)

8636 Maple; spindle-turned; vertical straight-sided profile; deep external groove 12mm wide, possibly for metal band; traces of iron in three places from possible repair staples. T.5mm. 22107 sf11605 (P5B) (Fig.1032)

8637 Maple; spindle-turned; globular profile; flat bottom. T. (bottom) 12; T. (wall) 3mm. 29841 sf12894 (P5B)

Lids

8638 Maple; fragment; spindle-turned; rounded profile; flanged rim; interior hollowed. D.128, H.50, T.10mm. 26631 sf12525 (P3) (Fig.1039)

8639 Fragment; charred; spindle-turned from roundwood; flanged rim with squared flange 12mm wide; sloping, straight-sided profile?; interior hollowed. T.10mm. 27621 sf10962 (P4A) (Fig.1039)

8640 Maple; spindle-turned from roundwood; solid; angled edge has prominent lathe-turned grooves; upper surface has rounded sloping profile and central knob where end waste removed or handle broken off. D.130, T.32mm. 22941 sf8121 (P4B) (Fig.1039)

8641 Alder; spindle-turned; rounded profile; upper surface has seven grooves; flanged rim; central disc-like handle with sloping sides; interior hollowed with central knob where core/end waste removed. D.97, H.60mm. 25808 sf9700 (P4B) (Fig.1039)

8642 Maple?; spindle-turned from half-section roundwood; solid; angled edge; upper surface has rounded sloping profile and central knob where end waste removed and then rounded off. D.91, T.32mm. 21746 sf9717 (P5B) (Fig.1039)

Fragments and woodworking offcuts

8643 Pomoideae wood fragment. 27088 sf9621 (P3)

8644 Alder; possibly hurdle fragments. 30304 sf11543 (P3)

8645 Blackthorn or hawthorn thorn fragment. L.22mm. 32549 sf13412 (P3)

8646 Pomoideae offcut; irregular block, probably cut down from roundwood or half-section roundwood or tangentially split timber. L.80, W.65, T.45mm. 20506 sf16253 (P3)

8647 Alder offcut; irregular shape; straight sides, some probably showing axe cuts; rectangular cross-section. L.80, W.39, T.20mm. 27921 sf11764 (P4A) (Fig.1064)

8648 Oak fragment; radially split timber; D-shaped cross-section; rounded at one end; broken across augered hole at the other end. L.70, W.30, T.25mm. 20747 sf7555 (P4B)

8649 Wood fragments adhering to iron/iron corrosion. 25144 sfs8216 (iron) and 19022 (wood) (P4B)

8650 Willow offcuts; one is radially split timber with rectangular cross-section; the other has an elliptical cross-section. L.103, W.50, T.9mm. 28362 sf10761 (P4B)

8651 Oak fragment; radially split timber. L.61, W.20, T.10mm. 27887 sf11046 (P4B)

8652 Fragment. 31195 sf11179 (P4B)

8653 Oak fragments; radially split timber; thicker block at one end separated from thinner part by marked step; not a stave. L.108, W.75, T.18mm. 29736 sf11196 (P4B)

8654 Willow offcut; roundwood; similar to lathe-turning end waste but not from turning; roughly faceted cylinder with shoulders sloping steeply to narrower faceted knob fragment. L.70, W.51, T.41mm. 35060 sf13653 (P4B) (Fig.1064)

8655 Fragment with small hole 1–2mm diameter (possibly woodworm). 34412 sf14497 (P4B)

8656 Ash burr fragment. L.60, W.44mm. 22309 sf7533 (P5A)

8657 Maple block fragment; made from radially split timber (possibly one-sixth section); perforated by augered hole 30mm diameter; sides shaped with sloping facets. L.74, W.66, T.44mm. 22124 sf10859 (P5A)

8658 Oak board fragment; radially split timber; no intact edges; perforated by augered hole 23mm diameter. L.280, W.210, T.20mm. 22381 sf16096 (P5A)

8659 Oak offcut; sub-rectangular cross-section. L.45, W.10, T.9mm. 2475 sf171a (P5B)

8660 Alder fragment; woodworm holes. L.68, W.28, T.17mm. 2477 sf220 (P5B)

8661 Fragment; now curved, but not part of a lathe-turned bowl. L.26, W.21, T.5mm. 2875 sf595 (P5B)

8662 Two alder offcut fragments; one charred. L.90, W.65, T.23mm. 2875 sf647 (P5B)

8663 Oak offcut; part of radially split board; rectangular cross-section. L.176, W.25, T.15mm. 7061 sf744 (P5B)

8664 Oak offcut; one surface rough with traces of bark; opposite surface smooth. L.43, W.43, T.10mm. 8696 sf1794 (P5B)

8665 Oak offcut; part of radially split plank. L.63, W.40, T.27mm. 8666 sf1802 (P5B)

8666 Oak fragment. 6119 sf2347 (P5B)

8667 Oak offcut; two smooth axe-cut facets. L.82, W.53, T.23mm. 6170 sf2432 (P5B)

8668 Oak fragment; part of radially split timber. L.103, W.34, T.9mm. 8525 sf2530 (P5B)

8669 Oak fragment of radially split board; very worn and charred; remains of large chiselled hole over 65mm diameter at one broken end. L.180, W.138, T.15mm. 6238 sf3043 (P5B) (Fig.1064)

8670 Wooden fragment; naturally L-shaped piece with curved grain. L.57, W.46, T.12mm. 14253 sf4059 (P5B)

8671 Three oak chips/offcuts and possibly a charred fragment of lathe-turned bowl. 14420 sf4145 (P5B)

8672 Two poplar fragments with knot hole; probably unworked. 14535 sf4310 (P5B)

8673 Bark fragment; cut straight across at one end. L.65, W.40, T.2mm. 14543 sf4380 (P5B)

8674 Alder offcut; charred. L.57, W.48, T.31mm. 15561 sf4478 (P5B)

8675 Three oak offcuts from larger radially split timber; square or rectangular cross-section; some axe cuts visible. L.127, W.37, T.29mm. 14573 sfs4708–10 (P5B)

8676 Oak offcut; radially split timber; rectangular cross-section; one end has axe-cut facet. L.67, W.24, T.14mm. 11125 sf5123 (P5B)

8677 Bark fragments. 14973 sfs6748, 6777 (P5B)

8678 Oak offcut from larger radially split timber. L.126, W.31, T.8mm. 21925 sf10592 (P5B)

8679 Oak or sweet chestnut fragment; roundwood; circular cross-section; whittled sides; tapers slightly; broken at both ends. L.81, D.17mm. 29263 sf10605 (P5B)

8680 Ash fragment; roundwood; charred. L.46, W.39, T.18mm. 21925 sf10710 (P5B)

8681 Ash fragments and slivers of wood; some could be fragments of split sections of timber; others appear to be waste from whittling the outside surface of roundwood. 29463 sf10912 (P5B)

8682 Alder? fragment. 15176 sf19024 (P5B)

8683 Ash fragment. 6437 sf19025 (P5B)

8684 Oak circular offcut, a waste product from the technique of making a large circular hole in a radially split board; circumference has eighteen adjoining curves from augered holes giving the object a cog-like appearance. L.172, W.168, T.14mm. 7954 sf3630 (P5Cf) (Fig.1064)

8685 Oak fragment; radially split timber; augered hole 32mm diameter. L.130, W.87, T.16mm. 20178 sf6243 (P5Cr)

8686 Bark fragment. 6573 sf6279 (P5Cr)

8687 Oak offcut/fragment of larger radially split timber; all sides have chamfered axe cuts; perforated by augered hole 23mm diameter. L.73, W.50, T.19mm. 16889 sf6998 (P5Cr) (Fig.1064)

8688 Maple object; roundwood; faceted cone with roughly broken pointed end and faceted knob at wider end; not a lathe-turned core or end waste; probably an offcut. L.67, W.60, T.51mm. 6926 sf6999 (P5Cr) (*Fig.1064*)

8689 Oak semi-circular offcut, a waste product from the technique of making a large circular hole in a radially split board; rounded edge has at least three curves from augered holes and is split and gouged in places; one flat surface is covered with linear axe cuts. L.195, W.100, T.22mm. 21088 sf7009 (P5Cr)

8690 Oak fragment from radially split board; perforated by hole 14 x 12mm. L.54, W.17, T.14mm. 1002 sf3 (D6y1; late 12th–13th century) (P6)

8691 Oak fragment with iron. 2195 sf33 (A6z4; 13th century) (P6)

8692 Oak fragment; roundwood; facet cut at one end. L.199, D.19mm. 2195 sf48 (A6z4; 13th century) (P6)

8693 Three lengths of birch or alder roundwood; bark in situ; one end of one piece has facet cut. D.12mm. 2235 sf57 (A6z4; 13th century) (P6)

8694 Alder or hazel branch split into quarter-section; fragment of side branch and junction between the two survives; main stem branded with the letters 'SR'; possibly part of the handle of toothed rake *8977*. L.160, W.24, T.12mm. 4385 sf553 (C6i4; 16th–19th century) (P6) (*Fig.1065*)

8695 Oak fragment. 4385 sf555 (C6i4; 16th–19th century) (P6)

8696 Length of elder roundwood with hollow centre (no pith remaining); split and broken at one end; oblique facet cut at other end. L.466, D.16mm. 1506 sf605 (D6e9; mid 14th century) (P6)

8697 Oak offcut from larger radially split timber; now lozenge-shaped cross-section. L.98, W.24, T.24mm. 7064 sf670 (C6x2–6; 11th/13th century) (P6)

8698 Eighteen offcut rods; made from radially split timber which is smooth-grained and hard; all have faceted sides and one end which is sawn straight across; the other ends are either broken or faceted circular or oval cross-sections. L.103, D.46mm. 4872 sf808 (C6g6; late 14th century) (P6)

8699 Oak offcut; radially split timber. L.85, W.13, T.8mm. 9125 sf898 (D6e9; mid 14th century) (P6)

8700 Two conjoining oak fragments; radially split board; perforated by augered hole 23mm diameter. L.170, W.54, T.15mm. 4915 sf915 (C6e11; mid 13th century) (P6)

8701 Oak fragment. 5245 sf1250 (D6d3; late 13th century) (P6)

8702 Twig with iron deposit. L.104, W.13, T.10mm. 5585 sf1674 (C6e2; 12th/13th century) (P6)

8703 Alder fragment; half-section roundwood; semi-circular cross-section with groove 10mm wide down the flat surface; groove may not be man-made. L.167, W.34, T.15mm. 9362 sf1689 (D6a25; 12th/13th century) (P6)

8704 Oak fragment; radially split plank; facet cuts down one long side and at one end; perforated by hole 14mm diameter with fragment of trenail 35mm long; charred on one side. L.235, W.61, T.25mm. 5667 sf1835 (D6a8–15; 11th/12th century) (P6) (*Fig.1065*)

8705 Two decayed oak fragments. 5906 sf2136 (C6c3, D6a5; early 12th century, 11th/12th century) (P6)

8706 Bark fragment? 11020 sf2398 (C6e6; early 13th century) (P6)

8707 Oak fragment. 11004 sf2399 (B6c8; early 13th century) (P6)

8708 Two ash offcuts; one has narrow D-shaped cross-section and is cut down from roundwood or half-section; the other is roughly square in cross-section with truncated corners. L.69, W.30, T.11mm. 10033 sf2446 (D6k1; late 17th/18th century) (P6)

8709 Oak offcut/sliver. L.201, W.8, T.6mm. 10033 sf2456 (D6k1; late 17th/18th century) (P6)

8710 Oak fragment with iron nail. 10521 sf2568 (C6g10; early 15th century) (P6)

8711 Oak fragment with iron. 12126 sf2828 (D6e9; mid 14th century) (P6)

8712 Fragment. 12389 sf3031 (C6e6; early 16th century) (P6)

8713 Alder fragment from radially split section; remains of 30–40 copper alloy nails/rivets. L.75, W.39, T.24mm. 11995 sf3142 (B6y1; 16th–17th century) (P6) (*Fig.1065*)

8714 Fragment. 11953 sf3164 (B6f3; early 14th century) (P6)

8715 Fragment. 12548 sf3315 (D6a25; 12th/13th century) (P6)

8716 Ash fragment; radially split section; iron flat-headed nail embedded in it. L.66, W.37, T.25mm. 13456 sf3399 (B6d5, C6f6; 13th century, late 13th century) (P6)

8717 Fragment with iron. 11991 sf3410 (B6f3; early 14th century) (P6)

8718 Two oak offcuts; radially split timber; rectangular cross-sections. L.121, W.30, T.7mm. 13385 sf3588 (B6c1; 12th/13th century) (P6)

8719 Oak fragment. 13184 sf3807 (B6y1, C6i1; 16th–17th century, late 17th century) (P6)

8720 Birch offcut; radially split timber; three sides faceted, other side cut straight across. L.75, W.60, T.25mm. 16605 sf4290 (B6b4; late 12th century) (P6)

8721 Oak offcut; radially split timber; two opposite sides faceted. L.76, W.72, T.22mm. 16605 sf4291 (B6b4; late 12th century) (P6)

8722 Oak fragment; rounded but not lathe-turned; possibly burrwood. L.85, W.46, T.10mm. 10763 sf16086 (D6f1; mid–late 14th century) (P6)

8723 Wood fragment with leather. 5331 sf19026 (D6a17; late 12th century) (P6)

8724 Wood fragment with iron. 11513 sf19029 (B6g4; early 15th century) (P6)

8725 Fragment with iron. 11514 sf19031 (B6c2; 12th/13th century) (P6)

8726 Oak fragment with large flat-headed iron nail 60mm long embedded in it. L.70, W.27, T.26mm. u/s sf2323

Coopered vessels

Bucket staves

Note: see also *AY 17/6* for further discussion of *3033*

3033 Willow; radially split board; broken at upper end; parallel-sided; squared basal groove; fragments of three ash bands in the form of laths 32mm wide attached to external surface by dome-headed iron rivets whose points are just visible on the inside; rivet heads were tinned; lower band shows that the laths were overlapped and riveted; two other rivets and Y-shaped iron strips associated with *3033*. L.168, W.84, T.10mm. 28362 sf10755 (P4B) (*Fig.1068*)

8727 Yew; tangentially split board; wider at top edge which is rounded in cross-section; bottom edge squared; shallow V-sectioned basal groove; pressure marks on external surface made by three bands 28, 22 and 20mm wide; internal surface has dark reddish-brown stain which can also be seen in section. L.159, W.38, T.7mm. 28600 sf10931 (P3) (*Fig.1068*)

8728 Oak; radially split board; parallel-sided; roughly chiselled V-sectioned basal groove; linear cuts on internal and external surfaces. L.280, W.68, T.13mm. 31595 sf12404 (P3)

8729 Oak; radially split board; parallel-sided; top edge rounded, bottom edge squared; long edges chamfered; squared basal groove. L.247, W.100, T.12mm. 26632 sf8850 (P4A) (*Fig.1068*)

8730 Pine; tangentially split board; parallel-sided with carefully chamfered long edges allowing diameter to be reconstructed; stepped rectangular lug rises above rounded rim edge; lug is partially perforated by small V-sectioned hole; squared basal groove. L.132, W.65, T.12mm; D. (reconstructed) 194mm. 23062 sf7349 (P4B) (*Fig.1068*)

8731 Oak?; radially split board; parallel-sided; broken across squared basal groove. L.201, W.80, T.8mm. 22733 sf7915 (P4B)

8732 Yew; tangentially split board; wider at top end; rim edge is pointed in cross-section with a smoothly cut chamfer on inside; roughly cut V-sectioned basal groove; dark stains on external surface at top and bottom where bands had been attached. L.172, W.28, T.7mm. 32025 sf12503 (P4B)

8733 Oak; fragments of two circular bases, five staves and tangentially split organic bands 23mm wide, 9mm thick; one base complete, the other survives only as a fragment; both are radially split, have squared edges and are 270mm in diameter; staves are slightly wider at the bottom with squared basal grooves, widths ranging from 69–118mm, and all are radially split; one stave has remains of rounded lug with sloping sides rising above rim edge. D.280, H.237; T. (base) 10; T. (stave) 11mm. 29916 sf12996 (P4B) (*Fig.1069*)

8734 Oak; radially split board; parallel-sided; rectangular lug (with sides sloping inwards slightly) rises above rim edge; lug is perforated by circular hole 13mm diameter below which is an arc-shaped depression, possibly made by a handle or escutcheon. L.290, W.84, T.9mm. 14932 sf6235 (P5A) (*Fig.1068*)

8735 Yew; tangentially split board; wider at bottom end; rounded top edge and squared bottom edge; shallow V-sectioned basal groove; linear cuts on internal surface. L.330, W.52, T.9mm. 8666 sf1812 (P5B)

8736 Oak; five fragments of circular base made from radially split board; rounded edge chamfered on one side only; diameter is not recoverable; fragments of two staves, one broken above squared basal groove, the other broken at top and bottom; both are radially split. Largest stave fragment: L.180, W.79, T.20mm. 14420 sf4144 (P5B)

8737 Oak; radially split board; parallel-sided; top edge is thinned and pointed in cross-section; squared basal groove. L.270, W.70, T.9mm. 18826 sf5326 (P5B)

8738 Oak; fragment; radially split board; parallel-sided with possible foot below bottom edge; foot has flat bottom edge and sloping sides; very narrow linear basal groove which retains a tiny fragment of oak base and fibrous caulking material. L.174, W.68, T.12mm. 9016 sf871 (D6e10–11; mid 14th century) (P6)

8739 Oak; fragment; radially split board; broken at upper end; parallel-sided; V-sectioned basal groove; two circular holes 5mm diameter, one 78mm above groove, one below groove; third (rectangular) hole with iron rivet below groove. L.130, W.63, T.10mm. 9068 sf896 (C6e11; mid 13th century) (P6) (*Fig.1068*)

8740 Silver fir; radially split board; very worn and abraded; parallel-sided; tapers in cross-section towards the top edge which is very thin; squared basal groove. L.270, W.53, T.15mm. 7782 sf3138 (D6y1; late 12th–13th century) (P6)

8741 Oak; radially split board; parallel-sided with chamfered long edges; top edge rounded, bottom edge squared and chamfered on inside; V-sectioned basal groove; internal surface at top scored by 4–5 deeply chiselled lines. L.272, W.67, T.15mm. 12257 sf3421 (D6e5; early 14th century) (P6) (*Fig.1068*)

8742 Oak; radially split staves and base; nine staves, two of which have raised rounded upper ends perforated by augered circular holes; two internal iron plate escutcheons reinforce handle holes and each is fixed around a hole by four iron rivets; angular U-shaped basal groove; one-piece circular base with rounded edges; three iron bands 40mm wide, the middle one with an iron rivet below it; arched

iron handle with straight horizontal ends fixed through holes in raised staves; centre of handle arch has hole through which is fixed an iron swivel mechanism with closed loop; three figure-of-eight links of iron chain attached to latter; bucket wider at top. Found inside cask *8766*. H.424, D. (top) 365, D. (bottom) 265, T. (staves) 21–8, T. (base) 16mm. 15300 sf4176 (B6g4; early 15th century) (P6) (*Figs.966, 1066–7*)

8743 Oak; radially split board; parallel-sided with long edges chamfered; worn, squared basal groove. L.176, W.57, T.14mm. 11641 sf4424 (B6a7; early 12th century) (P6)

8744 Oak bucket; fragments of three complete and ten incomplete staves; radially split boards; bucket wider at top end; rounded/squared top edges; neatly crozed square basal groove; two of the complete staves have circular holes 7mm diameter just below top edge, one retaining a peg made from split section timber. L. (largest stave) 260, W.81, T.8mm. 17360 sf4691 and sf4699 (C6d1; mid 12th century) (P6) (*Fig.1068*)

8745 Oak; unfinished; radially split board; tapers slightly towards thicker bottom end; no basal groove; long edges chamfered; top edge pointed in cross-section and broken at corner. L.235, W.50, T.5mm. 17449 sf4700 (C6c4, D6a6; early 12th century, 11th/12th century) (P6) (*Fig.1068*)

Tub staves

8746 Oak bucket/tub stave; radially split board; wider at bottom end; broken at upper end; squared basal groove. L.247, W.90, T.15mm. 30340 sf11353 (P4A) (*Fig.1073*)

8747 Fragments of two oak tub/bucket staves; radially split boards; parallel-sided; rim edge pointed in cross-section; asymmetrical V-sectioned basal groove. L. (complete stave) 397, W.90, T.10mm. 22714 sfs7913–14 (P4B)

8748 Oak; radially split board; slightly wider at bottom end; rim edge pointed in cross-section; broken across basal groove. L.345, W.133, T.10mm. 24073 sf8116 (P4B)

8749 Oak tub/bucket stave; radially split board; wider at bottom end; long edges smoothed and chamfered; squared rim edge below which is augered handle hole 11mm diameter; broken across squared basal groove; it is possible that the circular base *8780* is from the same vessel as this stave. L.345, W.90, T.12mm. 22936 sf8149 (P4B) (*Fig.1073*)

8750 Oak tub/bucket stave fragments; radially split board; parallel-sided; squared rim edge; pronounced squared basal groove 12mm wide, 5mm deep. L.494, W.119, T.11mm. 35300 sf13804 (P4B)

8751 Oak; very large and heavy radially split board; slightly wider at the top end; long edges smoothed and chamfered; pronounced squared basal groove 15mm wide; upper end is perforated by large D-shaped handle hole 65 x 65mm; shallow V-shaped notch cut into each long edge just above handle hole. L.570, W.159, T.14mm. 22668 sf16097 (P4B) (*Fig.1074*)

8752 Oak; radially split board; tapers towards lower end; squared basal groove 5mm deep; upper end is perforated by large D-shaped handle hole 71 x 59mm; shallow V-shaped notch cut in each long edge just above handle hole. L.545, W.157, T.19mm. 35669 sf16098 (P4B) (*Fig.1074*)

8753 Oak; fragments; radially split board; no upper or lower edge remains; possibly from same vessel as *8750*. L.252, W.120, T.15mm. 35300 sf19040 (P4B)

8754 Oak tub stave in six fragments; radially split board; tapers towards lower end; squared basal groove 19mm wide, 6mm deep. L.680, W. (top) 120, W. (bottom) 101, T.12mm. 29778 sf19541 (P4B) (*Fig.1075*)

8755 Oak; fragment; radially split board; part of stave which rises above rim edge and is perforated by D-shaped hole; shaped outline with concave sloping sides. L.134, W.53, T.16mm. 5651 sf1760 (P5B)

8756 Oak tub/bucket stave; radially split board; parallel-sided; roughly rounded rim edge; bottom edge pointed in cross-section; long edges roughly chamfered; shallow squared basal groove 20mm wide. L.415, W.110, T.17mm. 15538 sf4364 (P5B)

8757 Oak tub/bucket stave; radially split board; parallel-sided; squared top edge, rounded bottom edge; asymmetrical V-sectioned basal groove; possibly part of same vessel as 8758. L.380, W.98, T.15mm. 15554 sf4390 (P5B)

8758 Oak tub/bucket stave; radially split board; narrower and thinner at top end; asymmetrical V-sectioned basal groove; possibly part of same vessel as 8757. L.380, W.103, T.10mm. 15566 sf4462 (P5B)

8759 Silver fir tub/bucket stave; radially split board; parallel-sided; long edges and bottom edge smoothly chamfered; asymmetrical V-sectioned basal groove. L.510, W.77, T.11mm. 27323 sf12471 (P5B) (Fig.1073)

8760 Oak; fragments; radially split board; parallel-sided; D-shaped handle hole 70 x 58mm at top end. L.525, W.170, T.20mm. 6583 sf16260 (P5B)

8761 Oak tub stave; tangentially split board; worn and thinned towards upper end; squared basal groove 12mm wide, 2mm deep, cut 33mm above bottom edge. L.441, W.65, T.14mm. 5253 sf19531 (P5B)

8762 Oak tub stave fragment; radially split board now broken along grain with longitudinal section missing from one edge; circular hole 11mm diameter near rim edge, chamfered slightly; basal groove 16mm wide, 4mm deep, cut 33mm above lower edge. L.620, W.123, T.14mm. 7543 sf19536 (P5B) (Fig.1075)

8763 Oak tub or possibly a cask which had been cut in half; eighteen staves, all radially split boards; wider at top end; squared rim edge; V-sectioned basal groove; small circular holes in some staves below groove, presumably for organic binding hoops; one hole near rim edge. Found in a three-tier cask-lined well with cask 8765 above it and 8767 below. H.600, W. (largest stave) 160, T.15mm. 13682 sf14523 (B6g4; early 15th century) (P6)

Casks

8764 Oak; five radially split staves survive; roughly parallel-sided; some ends hollowed; narrow squared croze-cut grooves; two staves each have three pegged holes whose position suggests they held two hoops and a batten across the head at each end. L.521, W.110, T.11mm. 4385 sf572 (C6i4; 16th–19th century) (P6)

8765 Oak; 20 staves, all radially split boards which are listed and taper towards both ends; internal surfaces of staves are hollowed at both ends, but one end badly preserved; narrow, shallow, V-sectioned grooves at each end for caskheads (not extant); chamfered chimes; hazel hoops are split half-section rods 30mm wide whose ends were narrowed and thinned then overlapped and bound with strands of fine withies; timber 8427 is an end fragment of hazel hoop with two rectangular notches cut into one side, presumably to interlock when overlapped; a cork bung (27 x 50mm) and a willow peg (34 x 31mm) were found in situ in circular holes 27mm and 57mm diameter in the middle of one stave; next to these were a cluster of five smaller holes, some with pegs. Cask found in three-tier cask-lined well with 8763 and 8767 below it. H.1.21m, D. (girth) 700mm, D. (end) 500, W. (average stave) 120, T. (average stave) 18mm. 11531 sf14521 (B6g4; early 15th century) (P6)

8766 Oak; 20 staves, all radially split boards which are listed and taper towards both ends; chamfered chimes; V-sectioned grooves at each end for caskheads (not extant); two groups of 21 and 17 organic hoops made from split-section hazel rods whose ends are overlapped and bound over 100mm with fine strands of withies (Fig.1089); the

two groups of hoops are separated by a small unbound area at cask girth. Bucket 8742 found inside this cask. H.1.45m, D. (girth) 0.95m, D. (end) 720mm, W. (staves) 132–70mm, T. (staves) 10–16mm. 15299 sf14524 (B6g4; early 15th century) (P6) (Fig.966)

8767 Oak; 22 staves; all radially split boards which are listed and taper towards both ends; internal surfaces of staves are hollowed at both ends; shallow, V-sectioned grooves at each end for caskheads (not extant); one stave has central bung hole 60mm diameter, now empty; another stave has three circular holes 10mm diameter below the groove at one end; a third stave has groups of three and two holes 10mm diameter at each end; these three staves, and two others, have various incised marks, presumably used in the cask's construction; a sixth stave has two bung holes 25mm and 65mm diameter. Cask found in a three-tier cask-lined well below 8765 and 8763. It was placed on a frame of two rectangular oak timbers (timber 8587) set at right angles with their centres overlapped in halved lap joint; timbers 1.06 and 1.08m long. H.1.50m, D. (girth) 1.08m, D. (ends) 0.95m, W. (staves) 110–70mm, T. (staves) 10–15mm. 18419 sf14525 (B6g4; early 15th century) (P6)

8768 Oak; fourteen staves, all radially split boards which are listed and taper towards both ends; staves incomplete as one end of the cask is not preserved; very narrow groove 55mm from end; one stave has a hole 70mm square; if this hole is centrally placed, the cask's height can be calculated. H. (reconstructed) 740, D. (end) 530, D. (girth) 596, W. (stave) 140, T.10mm. 19813 sf16176 (D6e10; mid 14th century) (P6)

Caskheads or vessel bases

See also 8907 (cant stave re-used as basket base)

8769 Oak fragment of cant stave or one-piece head; radially split board; edges roughly chamfered on one side only. L.142, W.36, T.13mm. 34758 sf13169 (P3)

8770 Oak cant stave of head or base; radially split board; edges are steeply chamfered on one side only; two small holes 3mm diameter, randomly spaced; dark stained on one flat side. L.160, W.65, T.10mm. 33144 sf13358 (P3) (Fig.1081)

8771 Pine head or base; tangentially split board; now oval, but probably originally more circular; edges chamfered on one side only. L.150, W.123, T.9mm. 25250 sf8278 (P4A)

8772 Oak head or base; radially split board; oval/sub-circular; edges have prominent blade cuts where they have been roughly squared. D.170–80mm. 25276 sf8331 (P4A)

8773 Oak cant stave or fragment of head/base; radially split board; edges roughly squared. L.280, W.83, T.11mm. 25278 sf8344 (P4A)

8774 Oak cant stave; radially split board; fragment missing from circumference; edges chamfered on both sides and very charred in places. L.153, W.61, T.11mm. 1363 sf2254 (P4B)

8775 Oak caskhead; radially split board; sub-circular with roughly rounded edges; perforated by approximately central vent hole 11mm diameter; discoloured on one flat side. L.163, W.156, T.11mm. 23111 sf7369 (P4B) (Fig.1081)

8776 Large oak cant stave; radially split board; edges chamfered on one side only; two sets of three and four circular holes, four of which have willow trenail pegs. L.727, W.250, T.14mm. 22551 sf7761 (P4B) (Fig.1082)

8777 Oak caskhead broken across central vent hole 27mm diameter; radially split board; squared edges; impressed oval mark on one flat side 14 x 10mm. D.290, T.21mm. 22732 sf7862 (P4B)

8778 Oak head or base fragments; radially split board; squared edges; charred in places. Three incised concentric circles, c.135, 200 and 235mm diameter on one flat surface. D.250, T.10mm. 22856 sf8050 (P4B) (Fig.1083)

8779 Large oak head/base fragments; edges rounded but also chamfered in places; two fragments have circular holes. T.10mm. 22855 sf8052 (P4B)

8780 Oak head or base; radially split board; sub-circular; squared edges; possibly same vessel as *8749*. D.280, T.9mm. 22936 sf8140 (P4B)

8781 Possible oak caskhead fragments. 22988 sf8183 (P4B)

8782 Oak semi-circular cant stave; radially split board; edges chamfered; two holes 8mm diameter in straight edge containing wooden dowels. L.238, W.120, T.14mm. 25215 sf8245 (P4B)

8783 Oak pointed oval one-piece caskhead; radially split board; rounded edges. Two circular depressions approximately 10mm diameter, 90mm apart, aligned between the points on one flat surface. L.295, W.124, T.16mm. 25350 sf8551 (P4B) (*Fig.1083*)

8784 Oak head or base fragment; radially split board; edges chamfered on one side only. D.290, T.12mm. 24787 sf8779 (P4B)

8785 Oak caskhead or cant stave fragment; squared edges; broken across vent hole 27mm diameter which is cut at an angle through the radially split board; hole contains roundwood oak peg 77 x 27mm, broken at both ends and constricted in middle; incised mark of crossed lines on one flat side. L.264, W.82, T.16mm. 26249 sfs9100–1 (P4B)

8786 Oak cant stave fragment; radially split board; edges chamfered on one side only; very worn and broken; perforated by two holes 27 x 22mm and 10 x 9mm. L.180, W.74, T.16mm. 22807 sf9246 (P4B) (*Fig.1081*)

8787 Large oak cant stave fragment; radially split board; edges chamfered on one side only; broken across circular vent hole 12–15mm diameter. L.193, W.146, T.13mm. 34612 sf13151 (P4B)

8788 Large oak cant stave; radially split board; straight edge broken at points where two dowel holes cut into it; edges roughly squared/pointed but no deliberate chamfering. L.480, W.213, T.13mm. 29931 sf13156 (P4B)

8789 Large oak semi-circular cant stave of circular caskhead; radially split board; rounded edges; broken at one end; one dowel hole cut into long edge; two rows of two and three peg holes 13mm diameter (one retaining a peg), probably for battens. L.580, W.380, T.28mm. 29939 sf13201 (P4B) (*Fig.1084*)

8790 Oak head or base; tangentially split board; circular with fragments missing; three or four peg holes cut into squared edge; dark stained on internal? surface. D.211, T.8mm. 35249 sf13714 (P4B)

8791 Oak head or base fragment; radially split board; edge chamfered on one side only; incised 'A' and blade cuts on one flat surface; many blade cuts, charring and dark staining on other flat surface. L.178, W.113, T.8mm. 35264 sf13764 (P4B) (*Fig.1094*)

8792 Two large oak semi-circular cant staves of circular caskhead; radially split boards; roughly rounded/squared edges; one cant has circular vent hole. D.400, T.14mm. 36482 sf14087 (P4B)

8793 Oak semi-circular cant stave; radially split board; edges chamfered on both sides in places but squared in others; large vent hole 35mm diameter cut at an angle through head. L.259, W.136, T.12mm. 8801 sf1998 (P5A)

8794 Yew cant stave fragment; radially split board; edges chamfered on one side only. L.285, W.140, T.14mm. 15173 sf4191 (P5A)

8795 Oak semi-circular cant stave; radially split board; trefoil-shaped vent hole near straight edge; squared edges. L.290, W.180, T.10mm. 14933 sf6236 (P5A) (*Fig.1081*)

8796 Oak cant stave fragment; radially split board; uneven, rounded edges. L.265, W.85, T.15mm. 14883 sf6237 (P5A)

8797 Large oak cant stave fragments; radially split board; rounded edges; circular vent hole 16mm diameter; two dowel holes cut into straight edge. L.360, W.142, T.14mm. 22141 sf7354 (P5A)

8798 Oak head or base fragment; radially split board; circular; squared edge; dark stained on one flat surface. D.160, T.9–10mm. 22128 sf7387 (P5A) (*Fig.1081*)

8799 Oak cant stave fragments, perhaps part of same object as *8797*; radially split board; rounded edges; circular vent hole 13mm diameter; two dowel holes 5mm diameter cut into long edge. L.309, W.140, T.14mm. 22141 sf16083 (P5A)

8800 Oak cant stave fragment; radially split; very worn and broken; edges roughly chamfered. L.205, W.68, T.16mm. 2875 sf635 (P5B)

8801 Oak cant stave fragments; radially split board; squared edges. L.180, W.77, T.12mm. 7040 sf742 (P5B)

8802 Oak cant stave; radially split board; edges roughly rounded; vent hole 18mm diameter near straight edge. L.230, W.76, T.9mm. 7616 sf2032 (P5B)

8803 Large oak cant stave fragments; radially split board; rounded edges. L.585, W.170, T.25mm. 15425 sf4365 (P5B)

8804 Oak cant stave, possibly broken across vent hole; radially split board; edges chamfered on one side only. L.342, W.85, T.15mm. 15553 sf4389 (P5B)

8805 Oak semi-circular cant stave; radially split; part of circular vent hole at centre of straight edge with incised line running from it towards curved edge; smaller hole 8mm diameter with fragment of peg 7mm diameter. L.120, W.60, T.6mm. 6434 sf5277 (P5B) (*Fig.1081*)

8806 Oak circular head or base fragments; radially split board; squared edges; incised cross on one flat side. D.250, T.11mm. 21554 sf9959 (P5B)

8807 Large oak cant stave fragments; radially split board; squared edges; two circular holes 15mm diameter. L.510, W.190, T.19mm. 29128 sf10244 (P5B)

8808 Large alder cant and middle staves of piece-built head or base; radially split board; rounded pointed edges; circular hollow cut across both staves and small sections cut from edges suggesting possible re-use. L.421, W.219, T.23mm. 29263 sfs10513–14 (P5B)

8809 Oak caskhead; radially split board; circular with broken edges originally chamfered on one side only; off-centre vent hole 18mm diameter; gouged and broken in places. D.145, T.10mm. 29263 sf10699 (P5B) (*Fig.1081*)

8810 Large middle stave of piece-built caskhead; radially split board; edges squared; circular hole near one curved edge. L.565, W.156, T.10mm. 6881 sf16095 (P5B)

8811 Large oak cant stave fragments; radially split board; squared edges; area on both sides which is gouged and broken but has not fully perforated the stave as a hole; four unevenly spaced dowel holes in straight edge. L.393, W.223, T.13mm. 7008 sf16099 (P5B) (*Fig.1083*)

8812 Large oak semi-circular cant stave fragments; radially split board; incised lines of concentric semi-circles (310 and 246mm diameter) on both flat sides whose centre is the same as the cant; rounded squared edges; two dowel holes in straight edge with dowels 48mm long and 10mm diameter. L.490, W.136, T.17mm. 7310 sf16250 (P5B)

8813 Fragment of oak cant stave; radially split board; part of curved outer edge survives; perforated by circular augered hole 19mm diameter. L.216, W.81, T.14mm. 5280 sf19529 (P5B)

8814 Oak; radially split board fragment, partially burnt; possibly part of a cant stave; perforated by circular augered hole 18mm diameter. L.424, W.105, T.7mm. 5286 sf19530 (P5B)

8815 Oak cant stave, incomplete at one end; radially split board; part of circular augered hole 20mm diameter cuts long straight edge. L.487, W.146, T.10mm. 5259 sf19532 (P5B)

8816 Large oak cant stave, now in three fragments; radially split board; perforated by three circular augered holes 9, 10 and 12mm diameter. L.417, W.134, T.12mm. 5252 sf19537 (P5B)

8817 Fragment of semi-circular oak cant stave; radially split board; very small length of curved outer edge survives; perforated by circular augered hole 18mm diameter. L.340, W.163, T.13mm. 5255 sf19538 (P5B)

8818 Fragment of oak cant stave; radially split board; part of curved outer edge survives. L.320, W.147, T.9mm. 5256 sf19539 (P5B)

8819 Middle stave of caskhead; radially split board; one curved edge intact, other broken; perforated by two circular augered holes 11 and 12mm diameter; burnt. L.473, W.63, T.13mm. 5288 sf19540 (P5B)

8820 Fragment of cant or middle stave of caskhead; radially split board. L.260, W.130, T.13mm. 5290 sf19547 (P5B)

8821 Oak cant stave (greater than semi-circle); radially split board; roughly rounded edges; two dowel holes cut into long edge; at centre on each side is a stamped mark encircled by two grooves or compression marks. D.266, T.13mm. 4385 sf537a (C6i4; 16th–19th century) (P6)

8822 Large oak cant stave; radially split board; edges chamfered on one side only but not continuously. L.497, W.106, T.14mm. 4385 sf558 (C6i4; 16th–19th century) (P6)

8823 Large oak cant stave fragments; radially split board; edges roughly squared; two vent holes; one is 12mm diameter, the other was drilled twice, once at 7mm diameter, then adjacent to this at 11mm diameter with a 10mm peg in situ. L.376, W.108, T.13mm. 9305 sf2056 (D6a24; 12th/13th century) (P6)

8824 Oak semi-circular cant stave; radially split board; squared edges; three holes cut into straight edge; holes have remains of iron rivets/pegs. L.140, W.61, T.11mm. 11883 sf3014 (B6f3; early 14th century) (P6)

8825 Two large oak semi-circular cant staves; radially split boards now in fragments; edges chamfered on one side only; perforated all over surviving surface by 39 circular augered holes 20mm diameter; cant staves originally joined by dowels in two holes cut into straight edges; possibly a specialised head or lid. D.620, T.22mm. 13949 sf4104 (B6c1; 12th/13th century) (P6) (Fig.1085)

8826 Large oak cant stave; radially split board; edge chamfered on one side only; ends broken. L.474, W.117, T.17mm. 16382 sf14522 (B6c5; early 13th century) (P6)

8827 Fragment of very large oak cant stave; radially split board; part of curved outer edge survives. L.482, W.350, T.16mm. u/s sf19548

Incomplete staves

8828 Willow; fragment; radially split board; broken across squared basal groove 12mm wide; squared bottom edge; large iron dome-headed rivet through wood from exterior into groove, attaching a fragment of organic binding hoop; curved in plan; diameter reconstructable. L.60, W.72, T.15; D. (vessel) 240mm. 24273 sf8192 (P3) (Fig.1088)

8829 Oak; fragments; radially split board; roughly cut squared basal groove. L.305, W.120, T.13mm. 32259 sf12729 (P3)

8830 Oak; fragment; radially split board, now charred and broken above narrow, irregular basal groove; pronounced curve in plan allows diameter to be reconstructed. L.83, W.95, T.15; D. (vessel) 230mm. 22460 sf7655 (P4B)

8831 Oak; fragments; slightly wider at top end; broken at top end and across 5mm deep basal groove. L.124, W.26, T.7mm. 28904 sf12422a (P4B)

8832 Oak fragments, possibly of a base or head and two staves; radially split boards; no edge, rim or groove information. L. (base) 315, W.80, T.16mm; L. (largest stave) 195, W.55, T.16mm. 22122 sf7539 (P5A)

8833 Oak; fragment; radially split board; parallel-sided; broken at both ends; no groove information. L.405, W.127, T.20mm. 15535 sf4366 (P5B)

8834 Oak; fragment; radially split board; broken at top end; possible trace of basal groove. L.158, W.129, T.11mm. 15540 sf4367 (P5B)

8835 Oak; fragments; radially split board; top end broken; broken below and across roughly cut squared basal groove; long edges chamfered; axe marks on internal and external surfaces. L.220, W.160, T.13mm. 15539 sf4369 (P5B)

8836 Oak; fragment; radially split board; parallel-sided; broken at top end; squared basal groove; hole 6mm diameter just above groove fully perforates the stave; marked curvature in plan allows reconstruction of vessel diameter. L.145, W.87, T.12; D. (vessel) 182mm. 18709 sf5218 (P5B)

8837 Silver fir; fragment; radially split board; parallel-sided; broken or cut above and below shallow, squared basal groove. L.120, W.73, T.23mm. 21510 sf9091 (P5B)

8838 Fragments of three oak staves; radially split boards; all broken above squared basal groove; charred external surfaces; pronounced tool marks from croze in grooves. L.197, W.73, T.20mm. 19623 sf9170 (P5B)

8839 Oak; fragment. 21918 sf9960 (P5B)

8840 Oak; fragment; charred, radially split board; broken above squared basal groove; rounded bottom edge. L.66, W.59, T.16mm. 29465 sf10925 (P5B)

8841 Stave? L.232, W.127, T.20mm. 19623 sf14526 (P5B)

8842 Oak; fragment; radially split board; parallel-sided; one end broken; other end has squared groove whose width tapers from 16 to 13mm; end of stave is squared, but is cut obliquely. L.635, W.136, T.15mm. 29153 sf16092 (P5B)

8843 Oak; fragment; radially split board; parallel-sided; roughly cut, very shallow squared basal groove; broken or cut at top end which is roughly squared. L.620, W.140, T.15mm. 7209 sf16248 (P5B)

8844 Oak; fragment; radially split; broken above and below basal groove of which a trace survives. L.29, W.43, T.11mm. 4385 sf566a (C6i4; 16th–19th century) (P6)

8845 Oak; fragment; radially split board; curved in plan as a stave but re-used/cut down with notches in one side. L.115, W.99, T.11mm. 4398 sf574 (C6f6; late 13th century) (P6)

8846 Oak; fragment; radially split board; broken just above squared basal groove; curved in plan with characteristic profile of a hollowed and backed stave. L.45, W.105, T.15mm. 10993 sf2733 (D6g2; mid 16th century) (P6)

8847 Oak; fragment; radially split board; broken above squared basal groove; found with lid 8870. L.104, W.84, T.14mm. 16474 sf4401b (B6c2; 12th/13th century) (P6)

8848 Fragments. 4385 sf19016 (C6i4; 16th–19th century) (P6)

8849 Oak; fragments. u/s sf16387

Hoop fragments

8850 Ash; curved rectangular in cross-section and probably cut down from narrow radially split sections; some fragments show the ends were overlapped and pegged by trenails 10mm diameter. W.28–40, T.13–18mm. 31304 sf16245 (P5A) (Fig.1090)

8851 Alder; narrow D-shaped cross-section, probably tangentially split from edge of roundwood; charred. L.69, W.24, T.6mm. 15176 sf4016 (P5B)

8852 Ash; curved rectangular in cross-section and probably cut down from narrow radially split sections; one fragment has blunt, shaped end with peg hole; other augered holes along length, some with roundwood pegs; charred in places on outside surface. W.37, T.13mm. 6437 sf5295 (P5B) (Fig.1090)

8853 Willow; narrow D-shaped cross-section indicates it is tangentially split from the edge of roundwood and is not a half-section. L.152, W.50, T.21mm. 14722 sf5647 (P5B)

8854 Charred; half-section timber shaped to square cross-section; thinner rectangular head with slight shoulders and rectangular cross-section. L.49, W.17, T.12mm. 29104 sf10080 (P5B)

8855 Ash; sub-rectangular cross-section; cut down from narrow radially split section; blunt, rounded end perforated by peg hole 11mm diameter. L.47, W.28, T.13mm. 21925 sf10751 (P5B)

8856 Ash; rectangular cross-section; cut down from narrow radially split section. L.137, W.23, T.8mm. 29463 sf10902a (P5B)

8857 Ash; radially split with rounded rectangular cross-section; tapers towards shaped rectangular end with slight shoulders and notch on outer surface where a notch in the other end of the hoop would have fitted; end perforated by discoloured (perhaps charred) peg hole 9mm diameter. L.228, W.35, T.10mm. 29263 sf10914 (P5B) (Fig.1090)

8858 Hazel; split half-section timber with narrow D-shaped cross-section; one fragment has rounded tapered end, is curved in plan and has a notch cut in its outer surface where a notch in the other end of the hoop would have fitted; grooves in the outer surface where smaller strands bound the ends together; charred. L.134, W.26, T.10mm. 29465 sfs11765, 11768 (P5B)

8859 Charred; split half-section timber with D-shaped cross-section; one fragment has broken tapered end. L.89, W.16, T.7mm. 29465 sfs11766, 11769 (P5B)

8860 Two strips of radially split lath, one with iron rivet. L.246, W.30, T.10mm. 1755 sf601 (D6i3; mid–late 17th century) (P6) (Fig.1090)

8861 Birch; some retaining bark; split half-section roundwood; one rounded, narrowed end piece and one possible notched piece; several fragments of very thin, narrow alder? binding possibly used to overbind the hoop ends; split half-section roundwood 7 x 2mm. W.26, T.12mm. 5777 sf2134 (D6a17–23; 12th/13th century) (P6)

8862 Ash; cut down from radially split section; sub-rectangular in cross-section with curved outer surface; iron nail driven through hoop from inside. L.190, W.45, T.16mm. 13575 sf3489 (B6g4; early 15th century) (P6)

8863 Ash or sweet chestnut; cut down from radially split section; D-shaped cross-section; iron nail driven through hoop from outside. L.161, W.37, T.13mm. 13575 sf3490 (B6g4; early 15th century) (P6)

8864 Ash; cut down from radially split section; rectangular in cross-section; one end perforated by squared, possibly chiselled, peg hole. L.85, W.36, T.12mm. 15041 sf4045 (B6c6; early 13th century) (P6)

8865 Fragment of hoop, perhaps from cask 8766; split-section willow rods whose ends are overlapped and bound with fine strands of withies. 15299 sf19545 (B6g4; early 15th century) (P6) (Fig.1090)

Lids

See also 8825 (specialised head or lid)

8866 Oak; circular; radially split board; two rectangular notches cut into rim edge on opposite sides; small iron rod of D-shaped cross-section inserted in one notch; two rectangular holes cut through lid between notches; marks in the lid on one surface across and perpendicular to the holes were probably caused by roperunners on a rope handle (e.g. 9024 which was found in same context); lid edges rounded by chamfer on one side only. D.168, T.15mm. 32484 sf19028 (P3/4B) (Fig.1091)

8867 Oak; circular; radially split board; rectangular notches cut into rim edge on opposite sides; circular hole 8mm diameter between notches but off to one side; squared edges. L.69, W.64, T.13mm. 22370 sf7993 (P4B) (Fig.1091)

8868 Oak; radially split board; originally circular but now broken across two circular augered holes 29mm diameter; third complete hole nearer the rounded edge; very worn and abraded with blade cuts between three holes where used as cutting board, possibly in situ as lid; squared edges. D.360, T.20mm. 25630 sf9415 (P4B) (Fig.1091)

8869 Oak; semi-circular; radially split board; rounded edges; long edge has remains of four irregular holes, possibly for leather hinges; centrally opposite long edge is rounded oval handle hole, now broken; upper surface is worn and abraded by blade cuts where lid used as cutting board, possibly in situ; other surface has uneven asymmetrical curved mark on one side where lid rested on vessel. L.545, W.285, T.22mm. 29262 sf14527 (P5B) (Fig.1092)

8870 Oak; fragments; circular (or semi-circular); perforated by at least four irregularly spaced augered holes; rounded edge; found with broken stave 8847. L.380, W.310, T.37mm. 16474 sf4401a (B6c2; 12th/13th century) (P6)

Battens

8871 Possible oak batten; radially split section; tapers towards each end, one of which is split across one of two circular peg holes; also split across larger peg hole nearer to other end; carefully shaped squared long edges, chamfered in places. L.583, W.116, T.29mm. 30347 sf19533 (P4A)

8872 Batten for large caskhead made from re-used radially split plank or stave, now in two fragments; the tapering long sides, the curved edge at one end and notched edge at the other end are features of the original piece and irrelevant to the batten; perforated by one single and three pairs of peg holes along the length, none retaining pegs. L.485, W.70, T.25mm. 1628 sf19546 (D6e10; mid 14th century) (P6)

Spouts

See also 8199 (possible half-finished spout)

8873 Elder; roundwood; cylindrical, with narrower band at one end; hollow along length; hole (now oval in cross-section) tapers from 17 to 12mm diameter and contains a long peg or stopper cut down from radially split section; peg tapers and protrudes at least 55mm beyond spout's wider end. Spout: L.71, W.32, T.26mm; peg: L.131, W.17, T.5mm. 29835 sf13067 (P4B) (Fig.1093)

8874 Possible spout (sf8152) made from animal bone deliberately hollowed by boring a tapering hole down the centre; narrower end also faceted; tapering wooden peg, carved from roundwood, inserted at wider end. L. (peg) 40, D.12mm. 22956 sf19020 (P4B)

8875 Maple; roundwood; cylindrical, with narrower band at one end; hollow along length; hole tapers from 13 to 10mm diameter. L.72, W.25, T.20mm. 7554 sf1929 (P5B) (Fig.1093)

Spigots

8876 Possible spigot fragment; alder; oval cross-section but probably originally circular; tapers towards one end which is broken. L.58, W.18, T.9mm. 2463 sf167 (P5B)

8877 Oak spigot/peg; roundwood; cut flat at both ends but tapers from 'head' end; circular cross-section. L.61, W.12, T.8mm. 8110 sf877 (P5B) (Fig.1093)

Domestic equipment and utensils

See also *8377* (possible alder funnel); *8775* and *8805* (possible pot-lids or caskheads); *8986* (possible boxwood knife handle); *9116* (possible alder vessel base fragment); *9124* (possible cheese press fragment)

Pot-lids

8878 Oak; circular riven board; flat, squared edges; central rounded square hole probably chisel-cut. D.125, T.8mm. 22552 sf7696 (P4B) (*Fig.1098*)

8879 Oak; circular riven board; squared edges; perforated by central augered hole 15mm diameter; two faint incised parallel lines run across one flat side through perforation. D.112, T.7mm. 22867 sf8060 (P4B)

8880 Oak; thin sub-circular riven board; squared edges. D.103 x 94, T.5mm. 34428 sf13310 (P4B) (*Fig.1098*)

8881 Alder; traces of turning lines and chamfered profile on edge suggest that it was made from a discarded lathe-turning roughout of a face-turned bowl or a core or a piece of base waste; perforated by central augered hole 19mm diameter; edge charred in places. D.140, T.19mm. 35012 sf13324 (P4B) (*Fig.1098*)

8882 Oak; fragment; sub-circular riven board, half remains; broken across central augered hole 25mm diameter; edges roughly squared possibly with axe. D.160, T.15mm. 29926 sf13384 (P4B)

8883 Oak; sub-circular riven board; squared edges; faint incised lines on one flat side possibly in form of debased saltire cross. D.131 x 117, T.7mm. 36094 sf13664 (P4B)

8884 Oak; circular riven board; perforated by central augered hole 13mm diameter; rounded squared edges. D.112, T.14mm. 5772 sf2004 (P5B) (*Fig.1098*)

8885 Oak; roughly circular riven board; edges rounded squared and incomplete in places with angular notch cut into edge; perforated by central circular hole 22mm diameter. D.143, T.21mm. 15361 sf4234 (P5B) (*Fig.1099*)

8886 Oak, two fragments; circular riven board; split across central circular hole 14mm diameter; rounded edges; dark staining on one flat side only. D.13, T.8mm. 6434 sf5288 (P5B)

8887 Oak; sub-circular riven board, now split across central roughly squared hole 10mm wide; rounded squared edges. D.110 x 101, T.8mm. 29156 sf10284 (P5B) (*Fig.1099*)

8888 Oak; riven board; sub-circular; roughly carved; central circular hole 31mm diameter; rounded edges. D.105 x 96, T.16mm. 4705 sf762 (C6g3–5; mid–late 14th century) (P6) (*Fig.1099*)

8889 Oak; thick, circular riven board; split across central augered hole 16mm diameter; approximately half survives; rounded edges. D.164, T.25mm. 4867 sf815 (C6g6; late 14th century) (P6)

Stoppers

8890 Alder; conical; carved from roundwood; slightly convex top below which is plain collar with straight vertical edge; oval cross-section. L.55, D.29 x 24mm. 28092 sf10458 (P4B) (*Fig.1100*)

8891 Hazel peg-like stopper; carved from roundwood; cylindrical head with oval cross-section; narrower body expands slightly away from the head but is broken. L.42, D. (head) 17 x 11mm. 28967 sf12189 (P4B) (*Fig.1100*)

8892 Ash; conical; carved from roundwood; flat top; circular cross-section; neatly augered hole 4mm diameter slants through body at one side; entry and exit of hole are rough and split. L.55, D.26mm. 34385 sf12926 (P4B) (*Fig.1100*)

8893 Cork stopper/bung; rounded head; other end broken; circular in cross-section. L.22, D.11mm. 9793 sf3015 (D6a25; 12th/13th century) (P6) (*Fig.1100*)

8894 Alder; carved from roundwood; conical body, slightly oval in cross-section; other end has faceted shoulder and thin projecting grip, rectangular in cross-section; retains traces of bark on shoulder. L.90, D.24 x 22mm. 13147 sf3505 (B6u1; late 11th–early 13th century) (P6) (*Fig.1100*)

Spoons

8895 Hazel; elongated oval bowl with straight sides and rounded end; sloping shoulders; slightly hollowed; handle rounded rectangular in cross-section and broken; dark stained bowl showing lighter wood underneath where scratched. L.154, W.35, T.7mm. 23292 sf7462 (P4B) (*Fig.1101*)

8896 Maple; wide, oval bowl split into three fragments with traces of flat handle 20mm wide; shallow curved cross-section. L.123, W.50, T.7mm. 22714 sf7924 (P4B) (*Fig.1101*)

8897 Maple bowl fragment; oval with shallow curved cross-section and profile; no trace of handle; dark stained surface. L.63, W.22, T.6mm. 29459 sf12816 (P4B)

8898 Oak; narrow, pointed oval, keeled bowl; V-shaped in cross-section; traces of triangular cross-sectioned handle 12mm wide. L.99, W.38, T.7mm. 8524 sf1625 (P5B) (*Fig.1101*)

8899 Yew; thin-walled, rounded oval bowl; broken handle has carved rectangular terminal below bowl, 7mm wide; shallow, curved cross-section. L.68, W.45, T.3mm. 9362 sf1666 (D6a25; 12th/13th century) (P6) (*Fig.1101*)

Double-ended spoon-spatulae

8900 Birch?; rounded rectangular cross-sectioned shaft with broken flat spatula blade at one end and broken keeled spoon bowl at the other. L.113, W. (spatula) 17, W. (spoon) 18, W. (shaft) 10, T.8mm. 25350 sf8555 (P4B) (*Fig.1102*)

8901 Yew; square cross-sectioned shaft with small, flat oval blade at each end, both broken; one blade was larger. L.106, W.4, T.4mm. 10979 sf2801 (D6e7; early 14th century) (P6)

Spatulae

8902 Oak; blade fragment; rounded end; straight sides; plano-convex in cross-section. L.73, W.49, T.9mm. 22845 sf8042 (P4B) (*Fig.1102*)

8903 Yew; half-section roundwood with trace of heartwood on blade; narrow, elongated oval, flat blade; plano-convex in cross-section; handle tapers to rough point and has rectangular cross-section 7 x 6mm. L.129, W.14, T.3mm. 34663 sf13545 (P4B) (*Fig.1102*)

8904 Oak spatula/scoop; flat with fan-shaped blade tapering to narrower handle end; cut flat at both ends; rectangular cross-section; tapers in thickness to 3mm at blade end; four small awl? holes in line down centre of blade. L.138, W.85, T.7mm. 14184 sf3793 (P5B) (*Fig.1102*)

8905 Ash; in six fragments; carefully shaped from tangentially split board; tapers from flat blade with straight end and rectangular cross-section to rounded pointed handle with semi-circular cross-section. L.329, W.35, T.11mm. 29263 sf10936 (P5B) (*Fig.1102*)

Basketry

8906 End or base of basketry vessel; mainly bark; sub-circular with squared edges; central chisel-cut hole 24mm wide; fifteen circular holes for uprights (probably originally c.20), 5mm diameter, evenly spaced round circumference. D.165 x 150, T.11mm. 26939 sf9408 (P3) (*Fig.1103*)

8907 Oak basket base fragment probably made from re-used caskhead stave; riven board; squared edges; three augered holes of various sizes through main part and six holes of same diameter arranged round circumference; edges broken and split. L.395, W.150, T.15mm. 23795 sf8096 (P4B)

8908 Oak circular basket base fragment; squared edges; traces of five circular holes 10mm diameter arranged around circumference. L.270, W.120, T.15mm. 25090 sf8258 (P4B) (*Fig.1103*)

8909 Fragments of lengths of roundwood, twisted together; possible basketry or handle fragments. D.9–10mm. 2325 sf154 (P5A)

8910 Fragments of twisted roundwood; possibly basketry or handle fragments. D.7–12mm. 2475 sf173 (P5B)

8911 Fragments of plaited roundwood; possibly basketry. 1473 sf423 (P5B)

8912 Many fragments of hazel twisted strands made from half-section and roundwood rods; probably from basketry vessel. D.4–6mm. 29465 sf10924 (P5B)

8913 Fragments of lengths of roundwood twisted together (not plaited) to form a curved three-strand 'rope'; some strands have possible nail or peg holes; a note at the time of excavation connected these strands with fibres; possibly part of a handle or the rim of a basket. L.280, D.20–4mm. 1842 sf165 (D6f8; 15th/16th century) (P6) (*Fig.1103*)

8914 Oak rectangular basket base; riven board; squared edges; 22 small circular holes 6mm diameter spaced evenly around the edges (between the four corner holes, two sides have five, two have four holes); one corner broken. L.144, W.128, T.10mm. 12159 sf2804 (C6e9; mid 13th century) (P6) (*Fig.1103*)

Troughs

8915 Poplar; fragments; rectangular; hollowed from half-section roundwood; originally U-shaped in cross-section; thick heavy ends with horizontal everted lips; thinner side walls and bottom which have broken and only some fragments survive. Reconstructed dimensions possibly L.1.0m, W.400, H.140–50, T. (end) 60, T. (side) 15–25mm. 32518 sf13159 (P4B) (*Fig.1104*)

8916 Alder; fragment; very worn and abraded; hollowed from half-section roundwood; originally U-shaped in cross-section; traces of bottom and one end remain; axe cuts visible. L.150, T.35mm. 29463 sf10902b (P5B)

8917 Alder; fragment; hollowed from half-section roundwood; elongated oval in outline and U-shaped in cross-section; rounded ends; straight sides; flat bottom. L.228, W.68, H.67mm. 10758 sf2666 (B6g6; 15th century) (P6) (*Fig.1105*)

Bowl

8918 Oak; sub-circular, possibly originally oval; rounded sides; carved from burrwood with no clear grain; end walls flattened square and thicker than side walls; tool marks on internal surfaces from bladed tool; made using similar techniques to troughs *8915–17*; deep slash cut in external wall near rim; small subcircular plug 10 x 12mm fixed in a hole in lower wall; another hole plugged with a piece of oak of radially split section c.38 x 15mm whose medullary rays are perpendicular to the irregular grain of the bowl body; fragmentary and badly distorted. L.c.450, W.c.300, H.c.160, T.10–25mm. 27202 sf9537 (P3) (*Fig.1107*)

Churns

8919 Oak churn dash or spout; sub-rectangular; short sides have obtuse-angled points; one face has upstanding 'core' 57 x 52mm through which is an augered hole 25mm diameter; badly distorted. L.165, W.66, T.20mm. 1473 sf455 (P5B) (*Fig.1108*)

8920 Oak circular churn lid; heavy riven board, thicker at the centre; squared edges; rough surfaces; perforated by central circular hole 31mm diameter. D.171, T.21mm. 12375 sf3115 (C6e6; early 13th century) (P6) (*Fig.1109*)

Possible cresset

8921 Poplar; carved fragment; roundwood; four adjacent circular ridges, now broken, below which is a fragmentary rectangular tenon; above ridges is broken trumpet-shaped cup with traces of hollowed interior. H.75, D. (cup) 36mm. 14469 sf4690 (P5B) (*Fig.1110*)

Bread peel

8922 Alder; tangentially split board; roughly U-shaped blade with plano-convex cross-section, scorched underneath; fragment of handle at least 23mm diameter in middle of straight side; incised marks on upper side include a circle enclosing a cross. L.177, W.127, T.30mm. 32530 sf13176 (P3) (*Fig.1110*)

Possible buckets

8923 Cylindrical vessel hollowed from single large roundwood length of poplar; very thick walls; crudely cut V-sectioned continuous groove for original base which does not survive; found re-used as a well lining. H.800, D.590, T. (wall) 42–58, T. (bottom edge) 33–40mm. 27231 sf19542 (P3) (*Fig.1111*)

8924 Six fragments of cylindrical vessel hollowed from single large roundwood length, probably alder, willow or hazel; heavily charred; thick walls; squared groove for separate base cut 23mm above bottom edge; continuous groove, not chiselled out; approximately two-thirds of circular base with compressed edges, encrusted with crystalline substance; incised mark in the form of an arrow on internal base surface; seven fragments of radially cleft ash binding laths 38mm wide. D.304, H.135, T.18; D. (base) 280mm. 29463 sf10789 (P5B) (*Fig.1112*)

Knife handles

Note: see also *AY 17/6* for further discussion of *2812, 2863, 2898, 2938*

2812 Spindlewood; with whittle tang knife; carved; handle oval in cross-section (originally circular) perforated along entire length by tang hole; decorated with inlaid strips of copper alloy in panels of criss-cross lines; end of handle has copper alloy stud fixing tang in place. L. (handle) 103, D.25mm. 22679 sfs7948 (iron) and 19003 (wood) (P4B) (*Fig.1114*)

2863 Apple/pear/hawthorn (Pomoideae); with broken whittle tang knife; carved; circular cross-section; perforated along part of length by tang hole. L. (handle) 82, D.14mm. 22806 sfs8078 (iron) and 19004 (wood) (P4B) (*Fig.1114*)

2898 Birch; with whittle tang knife; carved; oval cross-section (originally circular); tang hole down entire length for tang which is bent over and fixed at end of handle. L. (handle) 96, D.22mm. 7260 sf1518 (iron) and 19008 (wood) (P5B) (*Fig.233, AY 17/6*)

2938 Ash; with whittle tang knife; carved; oval cross-section (originally circular); handle tapers towards where blade is fixed in tang hole. L. (handle) 95, D.15 x 10mm. 29623 sfs10917 (iron) and 19009 (wood) (P5B) (*Fig.1114*)

8925 Ash; fragment; carved from split section; traces of tang hole down length. L.65, D.20mm. 25241 sf8264 (P4B)

8926 Ash; fragments with S-shaped whittle tang knife; carved; circular cross-section. L. (handle) 75, D.20mm. 26902 sfs9285 (iron) and 19006 (wood) (P4B) (*Fig.1114*)

8927 Poplar; with iron whittle tang knife fragments; carved from split section; oval cross-section with lower edge flattened by tool cuts; both ends have rectangular slot where cut made for tang; tang hole down entire length with tang end protruding. L.101, W.25, T.14mm. 35678 sfs15514 (iron) and 19007 (wood) (P4B) (*Fig.1114*)

8928 Ash; fragment?; carved; oval cross-section; four prominent ridges separated by wide grooves; narrow rectangular cross-sectioned slit, 14mm wide, down entire length for whittle tang. L.33, D.46 x 25mm. 10448 sf2565 (C6g8; 14th/15th century) (P6) (*Fig.1114*)

Boxes and enclosed containers

Note: see also *AY 17/12* for further discussion of *6964*

Composite boxes

6964 Oak rectangular lid; single riven board; decorated over entire surface with arrangement of rectangular bone mounts decorated with patterns of zig-zag lines; nineteen mounts arranged side by side across lid, surrounded by border of six mounts; mounts fixed by iron rivets; no traces of hinges or handle. L.336, W.144, T.6mm. 14063 sf3572 (P5Cf) (*Fig.1116*)

8929 Box fragment with copper alloy strip. 22590 sfs7736 and 19021 (P4B)

8930 Rectangular oak lid; most of one short and one long side intact; radially split board; decorated with five rows of domed clenched iron rivets (fourteen survive); also decorated with two pieces of marquetry inlay in form of stepped triangles along incomplete long side; each has four steps cut with a saw and set with wood grain perpendicular to main lid. L360, W.182, T.10mm. 4599 sf743 (C6g19; mid 14th century) (P6) (*Fig.1117*)

8931 Lid; fragments of three sides of rectangular willow frame supporting infill of woven willow? rods aligned with long sides; rods woven under and over laths stretched between long frame sides; approximately central plaited willow handle; circular hole in one long frame side. L.330, W.273mm; D. (rods) 4mm. 4704 sf778 (C6f5; 13th/14th century) (P6) (*Figs.971, 1119*)

8932 Carved yew D-shaped handle with small hollow to fit two fingers; possibly originally carved in one piece with flat surface or side of box; one end has carved zoomorphic head with bulbous eyes, ears and snout, other end incomplete; upper surface faceted/angular, underside rounded. L.114, W.32, T.15mm. 4830 sf796 (C6g6; late 14th century) (P6) (*Figs.1118–19*)

Solid boxes

8933 Oak carved rectangular lid; radially split section; rebated giving flange with squared edges; latter broken on three sides; only one corner intact; incised cross on upper surface at one end. L.83, W.60, T.24mm. u/s sf2486 (*Fig.1120*)

Lath-walled boxes

See also *8790* and *8824* (possible bases of lath-walled boxes)

8934 Oak sub-circular base; radially split board; squared edges; large section missing; three surviving peg holes in edge, at least one with peg; deep notch in edge where wall overlap seated. L.c.155, W.137, T.14mm. 26721 sf9036 (P3) (*Fig.1123*)

8935 Fragments of circular lath-walled box; walls formed of radially split ash lath bent to a circle and overlapping ends sewn together by two vertical rows of organic stitching;

one row has looped chain stitches; overlap 113–15mm; circular oak base with thinned edges is pegged to lath by five pegs, one piercing the overlap; base has notch in edge where overlap seated; exterior wall surface decorated with incised geometric looped ornament; between two stitch rows is rectangular panel with chevron design; external and internal surfaces darker than broken section and possibly stained. D.200, H.79, T.4mm. 28066 sf9974 (P3) (*Fig.1122*)

8936 Fragments of small circular lath-walled box; walls formed of smoothed, tangentially split/sawn ash lath bent to a circle whose overlapping ends were originally sewn together; interior surface has dark staining except where ends overlapped and where separate base (not extant but probably 10mm thick) was fixed by pegs; traces of three fine slits and one peg hole in vertical unstained stitching line, and traces of peg holes near bottom of walls. D.c.140, H.70, T.4mm. 33144 sf13362 (P3)

8937 Oak oval base; radially split board; squared edges; at least four pegs in edges; heavily charred on one surface. L.322, W.171, T.8mm. 5277 sf701 (P5B) (*Fig.1123*)

8938 Maple; circular base of lath-walled box; tangentially split board; squared edges; edge broken in one place; three surviving peg holes in edge; notch in edge where wall overlap seated. D.138, T.10mm. 6532 sfs5459 (P5B) (*Fig.1123*)

8939 Oak circular base of lath-walled box; radially split board; squared edges; twelve pegs (one square, one rectangular, the others probably round) in edges; trace of notch in edge where wall overlap seated. D.132, T.15mm. 15013 sf3696 (B6c8; early 13th century) (P6) (*Fig.1124*)

Lathe-turned box

8940 Base/wall fragment of cylindrical ash spindle-turned box; vertical sides, now slightly sloping inwards; flat bottom; external groove just above base. D.43, T.4mm. 10977 sf2724 (D6g2; mid 16th century) (P6) (*Fig.1124*)

Chests

See also *9056* (shutter or chest lid)

8941 Oak lid or side; heavy riven board, now in five fragments; next to one long edge are two augered holes 27–8mm diameter, evenly spaced and possibly for organic hinges or mortice and tenon joint; large square notches cut into corners opposite these holes making lid outline T-shaped. L.539, W.268, T.23mm. 9640 sf2167 (P5B) (*Fig.1125*)

8942 Possible oak lid; two bars, one ash, one oak. L.710, W.490, T.20mm. 10877 sf2688 (B6g6; 15th century) (P6)

Furniture

Furniture components

8943 Oak; possible arm of chair or bench; riven board; straight sides taper towards one end; both ends rounded; perforated along length by four augered holes 23mm diameter; broken across one hole; peg/tenon fragment remains. L.426, W.76, T.30mm. 27621 sf11078 (P4A) (*Fig.1128*)

8944 Oak batten; tangentially split board axed to rectangular shape; both short ends chamfered on one side only; group of three augered holes 16–17mm diameter (and one unfinished hole) at one end, two of which have fragments of circular wedged tenons; similar sized hole at other end with fragment of circular wedged tenon and small unfinished hole by side. L.538, W.91, T.31mm. 28904 sf12422b (P4B) (*Fig.1128*)

8945 Maple; possible back or side piece of chair, bench or rack; shaped from length of roundwood; rectangular in cross-section but slightly wider at one end which is complete and is perforated by circular hole 29mm diameter; nine more holes 16–18mm diameter along length, and traces of another larger hole at other broken end; all smaller holes drilled obliquely; leather thonging with stitch holes in three of the holes. L.479, W.52, T.24mm. 32480 sf13180 (P4B) (*Fig.1128*)

Stools

8946 Burrwood?, possible stool seat fragment; flat, sub-rectangular block with a very irregular whorled grain; burnt and fragmentary on what may be the underside; probable upper surface smoother and more regular; slightly concave; toolmarks on both surfaces; perforated by circular holes in two surviving corners, one 30mm diameter, the other tapering from 26–8mm diameter. L.540, W.232, T.44–53mm. 34787 sf19535 (P4B)

8947 Oak stool seat; thick, heavy, riven board; possibly originally circular, but now split and D-shaped in plan; edges roughly squared; perforated by three augered holes 22mm diameter in triangular arrangement; holes taper in profile, and retain fragments of stool legs. D.285, T.27mm. 28912 sf11204 (P5B)

8948 Oak three-legged stool seat; D-shaped; thick, heavy, tangentially split board; three holes 36mm diameter, one with fragment of leg made from roundwood 33mm diameter; one side slightly hollowed and very worn with linear cuts in surface. L.565, W.385, T.56mm. 1504 sf16085 (D6f1–7; mid 14th–late 15th century) (P6) (*Fig.1129*)

Garderobe seats

See also *8684* and *8689* (waste from manufacturing garderobe seats)

8949 Oak; sub-rectangular, slightly wider at one end; riven board; central sub-circular hole 217 x 229mm which has its edges chamfered on both sides; three augered holes 23mm diameter near one long edge at wider end; other end broken. L.977, W.366mm. 16654 sf4293 (B6b4; late 12th century) (P6) (*Fig.1131*)

8950 Oak; rectangular riven board; central sub-circular hole 230–45mm in diameter with edges chamfered on one side only; rectangular notch 30mm wide cut into one long side 123mm from corner; two holes 12mm in diameter near long edge on the opposite side; nail hole in one corner. L.1.07m, W.360, T.28mm. 5512 sf16280 (C6e2–6; 12th/13th century) (P6) (*Figs.1130–1*)

8951 Garderobe lid. Two large heavy tangentially split planks pegged together by three pegs/dowels at their abutting long edge; pegs 15mm diameter, probably made from cut down radially split sections; dowel holes irregularly spaced, one now very worn and broken; planks further held together by two transverse wooden battens made from radially split planks, each with five wooden pegs/dowels made from radially split sections, originally roughly square in cross-section, c.13mm square, set in roughly augered round holes; sixth hole in one batten, slightly offset, and another hole in one of the lid planks suggests that the batten may have been re-set at one time; multiple linear cut marks on both planks near one batten; battens have chamfered ends and sides on upper surface and squared flat edges. One plank has been damaged at its outer long edge; originally there were two small rectangular hinge slots, c.60 x 20 and 70 x 20mm, the former now incomplete. Each plank L.850, W.220–50, T.50mm. 20728 sf19520 (P5B) (*Figs.1131–2*)

Personal items

See also *9151* (wooden bead fragment)

Pins

8952 Yew; unfinished; length of debarked roundwood branch with carved thistle-shaped head at one end; rest unworked. L.157, D.12; D. (head) 10 x 8mm. 31534 sf11374 (P3/4A) (*Fig.1133*)

8953 Alder?; point fragment; circular cross-section. L.58, D.6mm. 15659 sf4600 (P5B)

8954 Point fragment; charred; circular cross-section. L.28, D.6mm. 21796 sf10396 (P5B)

8955 Scots pine; whittled; square faceted head; circular cross-sectioned shaft thickens then tapers to pointed end which is broken. L.91, D.7mm. 1585 sf270 (C6v1; late 11th–early 12th century) (P6) (*Fig.1133*)

8956 Whittled from split section, species not identifiable; circular cross-section shaft with straight sides and rounded point; trumpet-shaped head with hard concretion at one side. L.117, D.8; D. (head) 16mm. 2830 sf506 (B6w2; early 15th century) (P6) (*Fig.1133*)

8957 Whittled from split section; circular cross-section; tapers from expanded head of oval cross-section to point. L.93, D.4; D. (head) 9 x 4mm. 4416 sf597 (C6e13; mid 13th century) (P6) (*Fig.1133*)

8958 Yew; elaborately decorated globular head with three carved mouldings below (square, biconical and cylindrical); each has incised geometric decoration; below is broken but plain and circular cross-sectioned shaft. L.37, D.5; D. (head) 15mm. 10546 sf2580 (C6g6; late 14th century) (P6) (*Fig.1133*)

8959 Yew; no actual head, but head end carved in series of unequal steps/slots; oval cross-section; rounded point. L.109, W.8, T.7mm. 10464 sf2585 (C6g7; 14th/15th century) (P6) (*Fig.1133*)

8960 Hazel point fragment; circular cross-section. L.77, D.9mm. 15166 sf4039 (B6a7; early 12th century) (P6)

Combs

8961 Boxwood; single-sided; made from tangentially split board; triangular in cross-section; one end bar 10mm wide; solid back with carved slot on one side; 24 teeth survive; incised line at junction of back and teeth. L.74, W.35, T.8mm. 4385 sf567 (C6i4; 16th–19th century) (P6) (*Fig.1133*)

8962 Boxwood; double-sided; one very worn end bar; midrib 23mm wide; fragments of 54 fine and 15 coarse teeth (both triangular-shaped) over length of 74mm. L.78, W.91, T.9mm. 10758 sf2657 (B6g6; 15th century) (P6) (*Fig.1133*)

Scabbard lining

8963 Fragments of wooden lining for small leather scabbard (possibly for a knife); very thin veneer-like strip of wood laid between two strips of leather, one of which narrows from 19 to 16mm in width. Now less than 1mm thick. 5673 sf18993 (P5B) (*Fig.1133*)

Manual and agricultural implements

Separate-bladed shovels

8964 Oak blade; riven board; concave sloping shoulders; broken fixing end; remains of sloping channel and rectangular slot; no peg holes survive; made from re-used caskhead stave with two residual vent holes and squared edge. L.373, W.167, T.23mm. 35465 sf14180 (P4B) (*Fig.1135*)

8965 Oak blade; riven board; fixing end truncated; concave sloping shoulders; rounded blade, both corners of which are broken away; peg hole D.20mm with fragments of wedged peg D.17mm; rectangular slot 47 x 28mm. L.407, W.211, T.20mm. 7510 sf700 (P5B) (*Fig.1135*)

8966 Oak blade; riven board; diamond-shaped fixing end; rounded oval blade of which half is split away and now missing; two peg holes D.10mm; incomplete irregular slot L.54mm. L.425, W.190, T.14mm. 5669 sf1772 (P5B) (*Fig.1135*)

8967 Oak blade, two halves survive but fixing end broken; riven board; convex sloping shoulders; traces of rectangular slot and one peg hole below slot; two other holes in line with peg hole but not functional; timber probably re-used to make shovel blade. L.330, W.230, T.10mm. 11011 sf16090 (B6a6; 11th/12th century) (P6)

Shovel

8968 Oak; half of blade survives; carved from tangentially split/sawn board; originally all-in-one-piece with handle (no trace survives); blade is hollowed out and thicker at handle end, with convex sloping shoulders and straight sides perpendicular to straight blade edge. L.325, W.130, T.45mm. 4385 sf556 (C6i4; 16th–19th century) (P6) (*Fig.1136*)

Spade

8969 Oak; four fragments of all-in-one shaft; elongated rounded blade with two steps 150mm above blade edge for attachment of iron shoe (not extant); straight shoulders perpendicular to shaft, one 32mm lower than the other, giving spade an asymmetrical appearance. L.631, W.135, T.35mm. 8225 sf1079 (P5B) (*Fig.1137*)

Forked tool

8970 Oak; all-in-one shaft tapers towards end; rounded spade-like blade with sloping shoulders; blade edge divided into two wide tines by rectangular slot; tines have rounded points, one broken; blade curved in longitudinal section. L.1.21m, W.173, T.26mm. 3386 sf699 (A6f3; 13th century) (P6) (*Fig.1138*)

Mattock heads

8971 Oak; single-ended; long narrow blade with thicker rounded blade end; other end has circular shaft hole 30mm diameter with section of timber split out along grain. L.253, W.84, T.26mm. 36024 sf16266 (P3) (*Fig.1139*)

8972 Poplar/aspen; double-ended; solid and heavy; curved sides; roughly pointed ends; in cross-section the ends are chisel-like since timber is chamfered in both directions from centre; central augered shaft hole 23mm diameter with remains of shaft 20mm diameter. L.200, W.60, T.49mm. 8760 sf5037 (P4B) (*Fig.1139*)

8973 Maple?; double-ended; slightly curving sides and narrow blunt ends, one broken; rounded rectangular shaft hole; chamfered from centre, giving ends a chisel-like cross-section. L.210, W.58, T.44mm. 23706 sf8075 (P4B) (*Fig.1139*)

8974 Ash; possible mattock head; length of roundwood squared off along two edges and faceted to form chisel-like ends; circular shaft hole D.24mm. L.213, W.74, T.37mm. 7261 sf16251 (P5B) (*Fig.1139*)

8975 Oak?; double-ended; solid and heavy; carved from quarter stem; very charred on one surface; rounded blunt ends; central augered shaft hole 27mm diameter. L.180, W.91, T.38mm. 3401 sf3334 (A6e2; early 13th century) (P6)

Rake heads

8976 Oak; two fragments; radially split timber; upper edge curved; blade edge straight and squared; latter is compressed from both sides in cross-section suggesting an iron shoe (not extant); shaft hole D.29mm. L.191, W.53, T.19mm. 32526 sf13365 (P4B) (*Fig.1140*)

8977 Poplar/aspen; toothed; squared off half-section timber; rectangular cross-section; head fragmentary but both ends intact and cut to points; eleven more or less evenly spaced holes along length, five of which retain fragments of rake teeth; three of these are split section timber, two are roundwood; two circular holes for rake handle (possibly represented by fragments 8694 with 'SR' branded into it, or 9148) augered through head perpendicular to teeth holes and positioned each side of the middle three; initials 'SR' branded twice into flat side between teeth. L.594, W.34, T.27mm. 4385 sf546 (C6i4; 16th–19th century) (P6) (*Fig.1140*)

8978 Oak; thick section of radially split timber; hemispherical upper edge; straight lower edge, pointed in cross-section; circular shaft hole next to upper edge tapers in cross-section, D.25–9mm; charred on one side and discoloured along bottom edge and on other side. L.289, W.121, T.31mm. 10840 sf16252 (C6g4–14; mid 14th–mid 15th century) (P6) (*Fig.1140*)

8979 Oak; upper edge curved; blade edge straight but battered and rounded in cross-section; circular shaft hole. L.234, W.92, T.16mm. 10560 sf16263 (B6g10; 15th/16th century) (P6) (*Fig.1140*)

Ladders

8980 Oak upright; six fragments of split half-section timber; roughly rectangular cross-section; traces of four or five augered rung holes irregularly spaced. L.c.850, W.93, T.42mm. 34801 sf16262 (P3)

8981 Alder upright fragment; half-section timber roughly axed and faceted to rectangular cross-section; bark still adheres in places; three augered holes D.27mm, irregularly spaced, two with fragments of rung in situ. L.520, W.95, T.70mm. 36011 sf16254 (P4B) (*Fig.1141*)

8982 Possible maple rung; whittled and roughly faceted; circular cross-section; tapers towards blunt rounded ends. L.391, D.26mm. 14184 sf3769 (P5B) (*Fig.1141*)

8983 Possible hazel rung fragments; four full-stem roundwood lengths with bark still in situ; circular cross-section; ends narrowed and faceted. L.118, D.36mm. 21882 sf16265 (P5B) (*Fig.1141*)

Handles

8984 Willow; fragment; roundwood carved to oval cross-section shaft; broken at one end, shaped to point at other. L.168, D.38 x 22mm. 31595 sf12403 (P3)

8985 Young oak roundwood handle for hammer, axe or adze; straight-sided; circular cross-section; functional end has carved tang which is split and wedged with small oak wedge; handle broken at other end. L.175, D.29mm. 22316 sf7629 (P4B) (*Fig.1142*)

8986 Boxwood, possibly turned, handle fragment; originally circular cross-section; trace of a facet at one end and a small circular tang hole at other. L.10, W.21mm. 22574 sf7751 (P4B)

8987 Fragment; dried out; groove along inside is tang hole; found with small iron tool blade. L.41, W.12, T.5mm. 22590 sf7768 (P4B)

8988 Willow; fragment; circular cross-section; broken at one end where there are traces of hollowing possibly for a tool tang; other end is faceted like a trenail. L.44, D.22mm. 8801 sf2301 (P5A)

8989 Ash; fragment; radially split section carved to oval cross-section shaft; broken or cut at both ends. L.104, D.37 x 25mm. 14873 sf6010 (P5A)

8990 Maple?; knee-shaped handle for socketed tool; split half-section timber from joined main stem and branch; both parts faceted along length with roughly circular cross-sections. L.139, D.23mm. 22267 sf7507 (P5A) (*Fig.1142*)

8991 Willow or possibly poplar; fragment; circular cross-section; broken at one end; tapers towards other end which is flat. L.90, D.32mm. 6170 sf2429 (P5B)

8992 Oak; fragment; faceted roundwood; broken at one end, charred and exfoliated at other. L.65, D.26mm. 14535 sf4309 (P5B)

8993 Maple handle for socketed tool; radially split section whittled to oval cross-section; smooth and worn; three rough grooves round carved tang at functional end; other end rough and faceted. L.107, D.25 x 20mm. 22107 sf11604 (P5B)

8994 Birch; with smooth oval cross-section tang for socketed tool; faceted hexagonal cross-section shaft, now very split, charred and abraded. L.164, W.27, T.25mm. 1113 sf177a (D6f1; mid–late 14th century) (P6) (*Fig.1142*)

8995 Alder; turned from split section; prominent pommel end which narrows to waist and expands to wide bulbous grip; broken at functional end. L.66, D.29mm. 4385 sf552 (C6i4; 16th–19th century) (P6) (*Fig.1142*)

8996 Ash; two fragments; turned from split section; oval cross-section; probably originally waisted but middle part missing; pommel and bulbous fragment with two turned grooves survive. D.35 x 24mm. 4385 sfs568–9 (C6i4; 16th–19th century) (P6) (*Fig.1142*)

8997 Yew lathe-turned handle for brush-like tool; wider at functional end where wood is rebated perhaps for binding; end is hollow perhaps for brush hairs; no hairs or binding extant; tapers towards other end which has a twisting spiral groove. L.199, D.13mm. 4874 sf825a (C6g6; late 14th century) (P6) (*Fig.1142*)

8998 Willow; two fragments; rounded sub-rectangular cross-section; broken at one end; expands towards other end which is flat. L.84, D.24 x 17mm. 11106 sf2508 (B6c8; early 13th century) (P6)

8999 Poplar/aspen lathe-turned handle for socketed tool; shaft tapers towards slightly faceted functional end away from two groups of two and four deeply turned decorative grooves; other end broken, but originally turned to rounded point. L.178, D.32mm. 10515 sf2564 (C6g8; 14th/15th century) (P6) (*Fig.1142*)

9000 Hazel handle for suspension on cord; whittled from roundwood; circular cross-section; upper end chamfered on two sides and perforated by circular suspension hole D.8mm; both ends cut flat. L.131, D.30mm. 10334 sf2618 (C6g3, D6g1; mid 14th, early–mid 16th century) (P6) (*Fig.1142*)

9001 Yew lathe-turned handle for a tool; single-ended; upper end broken; lower end wider over 50mm with gently curving sides; narrows abruptly to straight-sided shaft; circular cross-section. L.231, D.10mm. 4874 sf18992 (C6g6; late 14th century) (P6) (*Fig.1142*)

9002 Possible handle with iron fragment. 8305 sf19001 (A6z4; 13th century) (P6)

Textile implements

See *AY* 17/11 for further discussion of *6641–61*, and see also *8503* (possible alder loomweight)

Rippler

6641 Pine; radially split board; thick, rounded rectangular shaft, broken; functional end expands from shaft to five pointed teeth 56mm long, one tip broken; teeth taper to point in cross-section. L.142, W.75, T.21mm. 12159 sf2805 (C6e9; mid 13th century) (P6) (*Fig.1144*)

Flax pounders

6642 Willow; carved roundwood; cylindrical head with circular cross-section; fragment of all-in-one handle projecting from centre of one end of head. L.99, D.51mm. 21512 sf9057 (P5B) (*Fig.1144*)

6643 Alder; carved roundwood; small roughly cylindrical head with sub-circular cross-section; all-in-one handle projects from side of one end of head. L.188, D.59 x 55mm. 20191 sf6282 (P5Cr) (*Fig.1144*)

Scutching knife

6644 Oak; rounded, wide flat blade; shoulders originally perpendicular to handle, one very worn; all-in-one flat rectangular handle, now broken, with unknown length missing; end of handle survives. L.243, W.92, T.9mm. 8750 sf1901 (P5B) (*Fig.1145*)

Bale pins

See also *8953–4* and *8960* (pin point fragments)

No heads; all have tapering straight shafts, wider at 'head' end; most made from split billets, not roundwood; approximately circular cross-section; whittled.

Cat. no.	Status	Species	L.	D.	sf. no.	Context	Phase	Fig.
6656	Broken point	Elder	150	7	5174	13902	6 (B6c3; 12/13c)	793
6657	Complete	Yew	134	5	2796	12125	6 (D6e7; early 14c)	793
6658	Complete	Yew	125	6	2830	12126	6 (D6e9; mid 14c)	793
6659	Rectangular 'head'	Yew	113	7	2566	10511	6 (C6g8; 14/15c)	1146
6660	Rectangular 'head'	Yew	130	9	2584	10557	6 (C6g6; late 14c)	793
6661	Complete	Yew	113	6	2732	10093	6 (D6m1; early 18c)	793
9003	Incomplete?	Birch	127	8	644	4548	6 (C6g18; 15/16c)	
9004	Complete	Yew	89	4	810	4797	6 (C6g6; late 14c)	1146

Bale pins *contd*

Cat. no.	Status	Species	L.	D.	sf. no.	Context	Phase	Fig.
9005	Complete; broken	Yew	275	9	2543	10447	6 (C6g13; mid 15c)	
9006	Complete	Yew	106	5	2590	10464	6 (C6g7; 14/15c)	
9007	Rectangular 'head'	Maple	149	8	2658	10821	6 (C6g4–14; late 14–mid 15c)	
9008	'Head' chamfered	Yew	175	7	2663	11120	6 (B6f4; early 14c)	1146
9009	Rectangular 'head'	Yew	138	9	3036	11919	6 (B6f3; early 14c)	
9010	Rectangular 'head'	Yew	111	6	3107	11920	6 (B6f3; early 14c)	
9011	Rectangular 'head'	Yew	137	6	3152	11883	6 (B6f3; early 14c)	
9012	Rectangular section	Elder	90	7	5165	13902	6 (B6c3; 12/13c)	
9013	Complete	Elder	114	5	5167	13902	6 (B6c3; 12/13c)	
9014	Rectangular section	Elder	120	8	5168	13902	6 (B6c3; 12/13c)	

Distaff

6645 Elder; square cross-section rod tapering in both directions from maximum width; one end pointed; other end broken; edges are compressed in places as if bound. L.334, W.12, T.12mm. 36241 sf13808 (P4B) (*Fig.1147*)

Spindles

6646 Oak fragment; double-ended; both ends broken; tapers in both directions from maximum diameter; made from split section, not roundwood. L.82, D.14mm. 31101 sf11021 (P3) (*Fig.1147*)

6647 Oak; charred fragment; probably double-ended; circular cross-section; originally rounded pointed end, broken at tip; neatly incised slit 4mm deep 20mm from original end. L.30, D.10mm. 1363 sf1627 (P4B) (*Fig.1147*)

6648 Ash; five fragments; made from radially split section; double-ended; circular cross-section; tapers in both directions from approximately central maximum diameter to flat blunt ends. L.201, D.14mm. 21886 sf9827/sf9834 (P5B) (*Fig.1147*)

6649 Rosaceae lathe-turned spindle; double-ended; upper end has rounded point with incised slit 10mm from tip; other end broken with trace of V-sectioned notch cut into side; tapers in both directions from maximum diameter two-fifths of way down length; three pairs of decorative grooves. L.172, D.10mm. 15026 sf3702 (B6c8; early 13th century) (P6) (*Fig.1147*)

Whorl for spindle wheel

6650 Poplar or alder; lathe-turned; circular cross-section; augered hole 11mm diameter through central axis; three deeply turned grooves; broken. L.31, D.32mm. 10033 sf2440 (D6k1; late 17th/18th century) (P6) (*Fig.1147*)

Bobbins

6651 Yew; lathe-turned; circular cross-section; flat head end with rebate 2mm deep; waisted; tapers to rounded point. L.94, D.13mm. 21845 sf9786 (P5B) (*Fig.1148*)

6652 Elm; broken; carved cylindrical head with incised cross on side; rebate 2mm deep; second cylindrical section below rebate; shaft below this is circular in cross-section but broken. L.35, D.15mm. 8132 sf1034 (P5B) (*Fig.1148*)

Weft-beater blade

6653 Oak; serrated; broken in two fragments across what may be a central circular shaft hole 10mm diameter; originally eleven pointed teeth 12mm wide, now worn and broken. L.171, W.45, T.5mm. 12018 sf2798 (D6e9; mid 14th century) (P6) (*Fig.1148*)

Heddle cradle

6654 Oak; rectangular; rounded projection from centre of one long side; perforated by three circular holes 10mm diameter, one at each end and other below projection; latter hole is worn on upper edge and one of others is broken. L.219, W.55, T.14mm. 13147 sf3509 (B6u1; late 11th–early 13th century) (P6) (*Fig.1148*)

Possible heddle rod

6655 Alder roundwood; circular cross-section; symmetrical; at each end, flat cylindrical knob separated from rod by deep V-sectioned groove; one knob missing; shallower groove 63mm inside deep groove at each end. L.429, D.20mm. 15026 sf3719 (B6c8; early 13th century) (P6) (*Fig.1149*)

Implements used in non-woodworking crafts and activities

Tally sticks

9015 Alder; half-section roundwood whittled flat; 17 horizontal notches on flat side; both ends broken; one edge has 15 notches, not all corresponding to other 17 and probably a separate set; bark still adheres in places. L.106, W.15, T.9mm. 1113 sf177b (D6f1; mid–late 14th century) (P6) (*Fig.1150*)

9016 Oak; in two fragments; roughly carved sliver; rectangular cross-section; four wide and 27 narrow notches cut across width on one flat side. L.128, W.10mm. 5289 sfs2885 and 2890 (D6d3; mid–late 13th century) (P6) (*Fig.1150*)

Awl handles

9017 Beech/*Prunus*?; fragment; very abraded; circular cross-section; rounded end; small circular tang hole 2–3mm diameter augered down 29mm of length. L.47, D.17mm. 22806 sf8047 (P4B)

9018 Wood traces on tang of iron awl. L.>40mm. 9305 sf1700 (D6a24; 12th/13th century) (P6)

Last

9019 Willow last for shoe- or patten-making; carved from split section of timber; narrow rounded toe end; wide body with curved sides; narrows again to 'waist' at instep with vertical grooves cut down each side; rounded square heel end which is high and has flat top; letters 'AR' branded into side of toe end. L.264, W.94, T.74mm. 4385 sf548 (P6) (C6i4; 16th–19th century) (*Fig.1151*)

Saddle bow

9020 Oak; fragment; carved from split section of timber; rounded extension on one side is perforated by two augered peg holes; fragments of arched front grip and a lower bar remain; decorated on all surfaces except underside of extension with shallow relief carving of plaits and knot interlace in triangular and rectangular panels; strips of reed inlay fixed on by tin nails. W.200, H.240, T.40mm. 1611 sf1745 (P5B) (*Figs.1152, 1155*)

Ropewoods

9021 Possible ash ropewood; shaped from half-section roundwood; straight sides; both ends broken across circular holes 20mm diameter; plano-convex in cross-section. L.223, W.63, T.31mm. 15537 sf4437 (P5B) (*Fig.1157*)

9022 Oak; either tangentially split or shaped from radially split section so that the width of the object is now perpendicular to tree radius; rectangular; each end chamfered on one side; perforated by central hole 24mm diameter. L.111, W.50, T.25mm. 13243 sf3437 (B6a7; early 12th century) (P6) (*Fig.1157*)

9023 Oak; riven board; sub-rectangular with rounded ends; each end perforated by circular hole 16mm diameter, one broken. L.173, W.48, T.21mm. 3561 sf3907 (A6a1; late 11th century) (P6) (*Fig.1157*)

Possible roperunner

9024 Hazel; rectangular with rounded corners; small extensions, now broken, projecting from each end; perforated by central rectangular hole and two flanking circular holes; possibly used in conjunction with lid *8866* which had marks from roperunners and was found in the same context. L.50, W.21, T.5mm. 32484 sf19028 (P3/4B) (*Fig.1157*)

Birch bark rolls

9025 Tightly bound; made from large strip. L.58, W.24, T.25mm. 27915 sf10580 (P4A)

9026 With small twig/branch in centre around which bark had been tightly rolled. L.33mm. 25253 sf8299 (P4B)

9027 L.37, W.11mm. 29193 sf11642 (P4B)

9028 Seven, silver birch. L.62, D.22mm. 2149 sf102 (P5A)

9029 L.20mm. 20764 sf7406 (P5A)

9030 Three. W. (largest) 35–40mm. 11720 sf3959 (B6c2; 12th/13th century) (P6)

9031 Fragments. 13523 sf3960 (B6a3; 11th/12th century) (P6)

Games and pastimes

Gaming board

9032 Oak; fragment; riven board; frame formed by raised strips nailed round sides; one side of frame held by central iron nail survives and two other iron nails remain in corner holes; one flat side of board has three rows of 15 squares or rectangles formed by intersecting incised lines; two holes in side of board, either side of central nail. L.481, W.109, T.23mm. 20342 sf6609 (P5B) (*Fig.1158*)

Gaming pieces

9033 Hazel?; fragment; roundwood; charred; cylindrical; broken at both ends; external surface decorated with two patterns, a band of incised cross-hatched lines and a band of stamped triangles. D.22, H.30mm. 27452 sf11682 (P4B) (*Fig.1158*)

9034 Charred; rectangular cross-section; vertical sides; U-shaped notch at upper end gives bifurcated shape. L.37, W.35, T.9mm. 21203 sf8260 (P5B) (*Fig.1158*)

9035 Charred; cylindrical; one end sawn flat; other end has faint traces of rectangular extension; external surface decorated with incised concentric arched pattern, some of which is missing. D.23 x 20, H.28mm. 29462 sf10799 (P5B) (*Fig.1158*)

9036 Yew; fragment; lathe-turned; circular; approximately a quarter survives; concentric decorative grooves on upper surface. D.26, T.5mm. 10148 sf2519 (C6g17; 15th/16th century) (P6) (*Fig.1158*)

9037 Hazel or alder; fragment; roundwood; charred; cylindrical; broken at both ends; external surface decorated with groups of incised parallel lines aligned in different directions. D.24, H.13mm. 7782 sf3127 (D6y1; late 12th–13th century) (P6) (*Fig.1158*)

Musical instruments

9038 Boxwood syrinx (panpipes); tangentially split or sawn board from roundwood c.170mm diameter; smoothed carefully on both flat sides; lower edge straight and squared; intact side edge straight and rounded; upper edge has undulating outline where five evenly spaced holes 8mm diameter bored into it to form tubes; each is a different depth; fourth edge broken; incised cross motifs on both flat sides; small hole 5mm diameter bored through syrinx below tubes. L.97, W.61, T.12mm. 6358 sf5083 (P5B) (*Figs.1159, 1161*)

9039 Bridge for six-stringed instrument, probably a lyre; charred; rectangular in profile, triangular in cross-section with convex sides; upper edge has row of six notches; perforated through body by roughly D-shaped hole chamfered round edges on each side; incised decoration on each flat end surface in the form of a capital 'A' and a lozenge-shaped device respectively. L.29, W.22, T.13mm. 20387 sf6870 (P5B) (*Fig.1161*)

9040 Alder woodwind instrument fragment; trumpet-shaped mouth intact; spindle-turned; perforated down entire length by augered hole 10mm diameter which had been widened at mouth end to 14mm; two lathe-turned decorative grooves near mouth; other end broken; no finger holes survive. L.71, D.39mm. 4385 sf551 (C6i4; 16th–19th century) (P6) (*Fig.1161*)

Bowling ball

9041 Ash; spindle-turned from roundwood; elongated sphere with wide central band and rounded ends; central band is probably not turned; centre marks visible at both ends; fragment broken from one side. D.110, W.100mm. 10758 sf2665 (B6g6; 15th century) (P6) (*Fig.1162*)

Spinning tops

9042 Maple; curved conical; probably a re-used spindle-turned core; X-ray shows that a square shafted spike has been driven into the pointed end, and a tinned dome-headed nail has been driven into the top; external surface has red pigmentation applied, possibly haematite. L.65, D.57 x 48mm. 25102 sf8174 (P4B) (*Fig.1162*)

9043 Alder; curved conical; probably a re-used spindle-turned core; sides faceted in places; incised line 17mm below top; X-ray shows that a square shafted spike (now worn down) has been driven into pointed end. L.59, D.56 x 49mm. 21682 sf9419 (P5B) (*Fig.1162*)

Possible toy sword handle

9044 Willow; shaft has shallow angled sides giving elongated diamond-shaped form; tapers in each direction from centre; rounded rectangular cross-section; carved all-in-one square piece at each end of shaft (one broken) with straight shoulders perpendicular to it; penannular impression 16mm diameter on one side of shaft. Traces of black paint on complete square piece and minute traces on diamond-shaped shaft. L.192, W.43, T.11mm. 11018 sf2393 (C6e6; early 13th century) (P6) (*Fig.1162*)

Building accessories and structural fragments

Rectangular lock housing

9045 Oak; riven board, thinner and faceted on front surface at right-hand side; hollowed on reverse to contain iron lock mechanism; two patches of discolouration in upper corners and remains of two other holes in lower corners where iron rivets held lock to door; key hole of usual shape cut through housing at lower left corner. L.320, W.138, T.36mm. 4385 sfs561 (iron) and 18997 (wood) (C6i4; 16th–19th century) (P6) (*Fig.1163*)

Brackets for door fastening mechanism

9046 Birch; tangentially riven; short L-shaped functional end with triangular extension; upper end of latter broken; short roughly circular cross-sectioned shaft tapering to blunt point. L.130, W.50, T.22mm. 26632 sf8849 (P4A) (*Fig.1164*)

9047 Maple; made from roundwood at junction of main stem and branch; L-shaped functional end with triangular extension; short shaft of roughly square cross-section beyond which is tenon of circular cross-section with broken end. L.141, W.89, T.34mm. 29835 sf13028 (P4B) (*Fig.1164*)

9048 Oak; L-shaped functional end with triangular extension and rectangular cross-section; straight shoulder cut perpendicular to main shaft, beyond which is square cross-sectioned tenon 33mm square. L.240, W.120, T.33mm. 20372 sf6772 (P5B) (*Fig.1164*)

9049 Oak; made from roundwood at junction of main stem and branch; large triangular functional end; shaft of roughly circular cross-section with blunt end. L.210, W.90, T.35mm. 21510 sf9124 (P5B) (*Fig.1165*)

9050 Oak fragment; carved from riven section; rectangular shape with long rectangular notch cut from one corner to form gap between door and bracket; wider part perforated by two holes retaining iron dome-headed nails. L.151, W.47, T.24mm. 29156 sf10293 (P5B) (*Fig.1167*)

9051 Oak; squared from quarter-section timber; rounded rectangular in outline with back edge flat to fit against door jamb and front edge rounded and convex; rectangular notch for door latch cut vertically into front edge; two nail holes at top and three at bottom, all made with awl-like tool then nailed. L.280, W.78, T.57mm. 4385 sf547 (C6i4; 16th–19th century) (P6) (*Fig.1167*)

9052 Alder; shaped from length of roundwood; axe marks visible; L-shaped functional end with rectangular extension and rectangular cross-section; other end has circular cross-section and tapers to rounded point. L.290, W.108, T.53mm. 5755 sf1865 (D6a17–23; late 12th/13th century) (P6) (*Fig.1165*)

Shingles

9053 Oak; fragment. 1404 sf2111 (D6y1; late 12th–13th century) (P6)

9054 Oak; rectangular riven board; parallel-sided; upper end rounded pointed and perforated by circular hole 10mm diameter; lower edge broken at one corner. L.204, W.65, T.10mm. 12375 sf3094 (C6e6; late 12th–13th century) (P6) (*Fig.1168*)

9055 Oak; riven board; spade-shaped; tapers in both directions from maximum width at a shoulder which is about one-third of the way down the length; across shoulder are two incised parallel lines between which at one side is augered hole 9mm diameter with peg 7mm diameter; upper end has sloping shoulders; lower end is rounded and broken at one corner. L.285, W.140, T.9mm. 4867 sf16247 (C6g6; late 14th century) (P6) (*Fig.1168*)

Possible shutter or chest lid

9056 Oak; large, heavy rectangular object made from at least two, possibly three, radially split planks. Traces of a row of three peg holes remain, and another close to the lower plank edge, suggesting either that the original fixing of the two planks could have been by wooden battens and wooden pegs, neither extant, or that the planks were re-used. Nail holes and iron stain/wood compression patterns suggest that the planks were at some later date fixed together by a combination of transversely positioned wooden battens and iron hinges, the latter no longer extant. Planks are plano-convex in cross-section with the flat (internal?) surface towards the battens; squared edges; remains of two iron strap hinges now nailed perpendicular to long axis on external surface, are probaly replacements for the originals described above; hinges have remains of circular terminals; little trace of hinge mechanism beyond edge of wood as iron straps are broken; extra nail holes near edge of one plank. Order of construction: wooden battens fixed first, then strap hinges nailed on. L.568, W.528, T.15mm. 3270 sf19521 (A6i3; early 15th century) (P6) (*Fig.1170*)

Frame/rack fragments

9057 Ash; shaped from length of roundwood with curving grain; rectangular beam with projecting rectangular blocks at each end between which wood cut away to depth of approximately 30mm; incised line cut across beam 84mm from each block; augered hole 15mm diameter through beam at each end between block and line, each containing peg; two holes 34mm diameter and two 15mm diameter between lines. L.587, W.102, T.55mm. 29840 sf12891 (P4B) (*Fig.1171*)

Window opening fragments

9058 Oak; radially split board; parts of two sides surrounding central rectangular space remain; internal edges chamfered; one side is wider and is perforated by two augered holes, one retaining a peg. L.240, W.178, T.17mm. 22857 sf8051 (P4B) (*Fig.1172*)

9059 Oak; radially split board; parts of three sides surrounding central rectangular space remain; internal edges chamfered on both sides; shorter edge at the end of the frame is almost three times as wide as the other two. L.246, W.153, T.17mm. 7474 sf1391 (P5B) (*Fig.1172*)

Possible sluices

9060 Oak; radially split board; heavy rectangular board, one end squared, the other end (top?) with sloping shoulders and broken tapered end; both shoulders chamfered on one side of the edge; one long side edge intact, the other broken where a large section has broken off along the grain, now missing; board is slightly curved in profile, burnt in places and perforated by three irregularly spaced holes 24, 28 and 38mm in diameter; blade cuts near one shoulder. L.590, W.215, T.32–40mm. 32872 sf19534 (P3) (*Fig.1173*)

9061 Oak; tangentially split/sawn board; heavy rectangular board, one end squared, the other (probably the top) with sloping shoulders meeting at rounded point; this end has many fragments of iron nails embedded in the timber; main part perforated by six columns of seven augered holes, 20mm diameter. L.480, W.265, T.25mm. 10758 sf2659 (B6g6; 15th century) (P6) (*Figs.972, 1173*)

Panels

9062 Pine; rectangular; tangentially sawn board; sub-rectangular cross-section; one long edge has been shaped with four long grooves to produce tripartite moulded effect; possibly shaped with moulding plane; broken at both ends. L.303, W.49, T.22mm. 21554 sf9965 (P5B) (*Fig.1174*)

9063 Pine; tangentially sawn board; rectangular with rectangular cross-section; one long edge has deep rectangular cross-sectioned groove 10mm wide and 9mm deep, possibly made with grooving plane; at one end is rectangular tenon offset to one side. L.346, W.75, T.25mm. 21554 sf10024 (P5B) (*Fig.1174*)

9064 Oak; thirteen fragments; incomplete; riven board; at least four fragments conjoin and show that one long edge was chamfered; decorated on one surface with a cross-hatched pattern of incised grooves 2–3mm wide and rectangular in cross-section. Four conjoined pieces: L.143, W.59, T.16mm. 7552 sf1782; 21746 sfs10380, 10382, 10388, 10391, 10400, 10410, 10414, 10416, 10418–19, 10422; 29465 sf10841 (P5B) (*Fig.1174*)

Floor planks

9065 Pine; tangentially sawn; split and broken at one end; other end has splintering characteristic of being sawn across the grain; one intact long edge has rectangular cross-sectioned grooving 6mm wide. L.480, W.85, T.21mm. 29140 sf10522 (P5B)

9066 Silver fir; smoothed surface; squared edges; one end broken; split along grain at one side; iron nail through plank at intact end. L.503, W.85, T.20mm. 29156 sf10531 (P5B)

Pegs

Trenails

9067 Oak; cut down from radially split section; bulbous head with rounded top, faceted sides and sloping shoulders; shaft whittled and parallel-sided; circular cross-section; flat end has a deliberate split/notch 25mm long for a wedge (not extant). L.85, D.29mm. 31101 sf11020 (P3) (*Fig.1175*)

9068 Oak; cut down from radially split section; round head with flat top, faceted sides and sloping shoulders; parallel-sided shaft which tapers in plan to rounded blunt point; circular cross-section. L.90, W.31, T.26mm. 27503 sf10289 (P4B) (*Fig.1175*)

9069 Oak; cut down from radially split section; broken round head with flat top, faceted sides and sloping shoulders; circular cross-section; flat end has deliberate split/notch

28mm long containing small wedge and sliver of wood. L.56, W.25, T.20mm. 14005 sf4000 (P5B) (*Fig.1175*)

9070 Willow; whittled from roundwood; small round head with flat top, faceted sides and sloping shoulders; finely finished with straight smooth sides and rounded blunt end; circular cross-section; charred along one side. L.97, D.13mm. 21375 sf8596 (P5B) (*Fig.1175*)

9071 Hazel; whittled from roundwood; round head with flat top, faceted sides and sloping shoulders; parallel-sided shaft with flat end; circular cross-section; head charred. L.63, W.33, T.29mm. 21678 sf9801 (P5B) (*Fig.1175*)

9072 Ash; cut down from radially split section; round head with domed top and faceted sloping shoulders; broken below head; probably parallel-sided shaft; circular cross-section. L.29, D.30mm. 16923 sf4547 (C6d9; mid–late 12th century) (P6) (*Fig.1175*)

Pegs with differentiated heads

9073 Hazel; fragment with broken, charred, cylindrical head; narrower shaft of circular cross-section, broken across possible circular hole 7–8mm diameter. L.98, D. (head) 28, D. (shaft) 23mm. 30392 sf11358 (P3)

9074 Poplar/aspen; radially split section; straight-sided head with flat top and sub-triangular cross-section; straight shoulders taper towards parallel-sided shaft; end broken. L.61, W.30, T.24mm. 34877 sf13376 (P3) (*Fig.1176*)

9075 Hazel; roundwood with facet cuts on sides where bark removed; rough expanded head retains bark and tapers towards narrower parallel-sided shaft; circular cross-section; end broken. L.143, D.38mm. 27919 sf10689 (P4A)

9076 Alder; roundwood; very worn and abraded; expanded head tapers towards narrower parallel-sided shaft; circular cross-section; flat end. L.87, W.36, T.28. 28092 sf10441 (P4B)

9077 Hazel; roundwood; faceted expanded head tapers towards narrower shaft; now oval in cross-section; end broken. L.63, W.40, T.30mm. 25934 sf12707 (P4B)

9078 Oak; roundwood; head originally octagonal in cross-section with faceted sides, now broken; fragment of circular cross-sectioned shaft remains. L.40, D.31mm. 29835 sf13066 (P4B)

9079 Willow; cut down from radially split section; straight-sided head with rounded top and oval cross-section; straight shoulders taper towards parallel-sided shaft; rounded faceted end. L.171, W.31, T.26mm. 34412 sf13375 (P4B) (*Fig.1176*)

9080 Oak; roundwood; large expanded head with faceted top and sides, and shoulders tapering into parallel-sided shaft; end broken; circular cross-section. L.119, W.43, T.37mm. 1473 sf458 (P5B)

9081 Whittled from roundwood, but long axis of peg cuts across centre of roundwood; cylindrical head with straight sides and flat top; narrower shaft tapers to blunt point; circular cross-section. L.101, D.14mm. 21245 sf8313 (P5B) (*Fig.1176*)

9082 Hazel; roundwood; head circular in cross-section with rounded top, faceted sides and sloping shoulders; now broken; fragment of probably parallel-sided shaft remains. L.47, D.34mm. 21925 sf10259 (P5B)

9083 Ash; fragments; cut down from radially split section; narrow disc-like head with straight sides and flat top, now broken; circular cross-section; shaft tapers towards broken point. L.>212, D.36mm. 4385 sf559 (C6i4; 16th–19th century) (P6) (*Fig.1176*)

9084 Oak; radially split section; large round faceted head, worn and marked as though hit by a mallet; parallel-sided shaft with rounded blunt point. L.171, W.35, T.26mm. 4797 sf793 (C6g6; late 14th century) (P6) (*Fig.1176*)

Pegs with no heads

9085 Hazel; long facet cut along one side to rounded blunt point; tapers towards rounded 'head' end. L.110, W.20, T.18mm. 25990 sf10268 (P3)

9086 Alder; carved from middle section of roundwood rod; rectangular cross-sectioned shaft; blunt point. L.110, W.22, T.11mm. 22574 sf7754 (P4B)

9087 Hazel; roundwood; roughly hexagonal cross-section; faceted sides taper from flat 'head' end to roughly faceted point. L.78, W.16, T.13mm. 27093 sf9611 (P4B)

9088 Alder; fragment; roundwood; straight-sided shaft. L.41, D.24mm. 35323 sf13870 (P4B)

9089 Fragments of three pegs; cut down from radially split section; roughly faceted shafts; one end of each is roughly cut, the other is very rough, possibly hammered; no crushed corners on facets. L.125, W.28, T.23mm. 35305 sf16082 (P4B) (*Fig.1177*)

9090 Willow? 2527 sf664 (P5A)

9091 Oak; cut down from radially split section; square cross-section; flat 'head' end; flat blunt point faceted on one side. L.73, W.18, T.17mm. 20808 sf7279 (P5A)

9092 Oak; roundwood; tapers to blunt end, no point; whittled sides. L.115, W.16, T.14mm. 27296 sf9858 (P5A)

9093 Rosaceae; split half-section roundwood; 'head' end broken; circular cross-section; parallel-sided; rounded point. L.42, W.11, T.6mm. 2875 sf642 (P5B)

9094 Alder; square cross-section; straight sides; flat 'head' end; blunt, broken point. L.90, W.20, T.16mm. 18710 sf5318 (P5B)

9095 Oak; radially split section; blunt rounded 'head' end; straight-sided shaft tapers to point; circular cross-section. L.188, D.15mm. 4260 sf521 (C6f1; late 13th century) (P6) (*Fig.1177*)

9096 Oak; radially split section; flat 'head' end; straight-sided shaft tapers to rough blunt point; oval cross-section. L.133, W.13, T.10mm. 4252 sf756 (C6i4; 16th–19th century) (P6)

9097 Yew; radially split section; expanded 'head' end; parallel-sided shaft; oval cross-section; no point. L.166, W.9, T.5mm. 4931 sf833 (C6g18; 15th/16th century) (P6) (*Fig.1177*)

9098 Ash; roundwood; narrower at one end; ends possibly cut but not shaped; nail fragments near wider end. L.168, W.32, T.26mm. 4885 sf857 (C6f5; 13th/14th century) (P6)

9099 Oak. 5906 sf2108 (C6c3, D6a5; early 12th century, 11th/12th century) (P6)

9100 Oak; wider at 'head' end; shaft tapers to blunt point; circular cross-section. L.147, D.12mm. 10557 sf2584a (C6g6; late 14th century) (P6)

9101 Alder; wider at 'head' end; shaft tapers towards other end; circular cross-section; broken. L.85, D.11mm. 10557 sf2584c (C6g6; late 14th century) (P6)

9102 Alder?; roundwood, whittled and roughly stripped of bark; hexagonal cross-section; slightly wider at 'head' end; other end broken; parallel-sided shaft. L.150, D.29mm. 12548 sf3264 (D6a25; 12th/13th century) (P6)

9103 Oak; cut down from radially split section; rectangular cross-section at 'head' end; shaft oval in cross-section tapering to rounded point. L.180, W.29, T.11mm. 13964 sf3674 (B6c8; early 13th century) (P6)

Tile peg

9104 Oak; in square hole (15 x 15mm) in ceramic tile; cut from radially split section; flat 'head' end; straight shaft; blunt point; square cross-section. L.58, W.10, T.10mm. 3140 sf894 (A6j4; 15th century) (P6) (*Fig.1177*)

Miscellaneous objects

Objects made from radially split sections of wood

9105 Pine fragments, possibly part of a sewn vessel; very thin radially split board with rounded edge intact in places; row of very fine stitching holes 5mm inside rounded edge (c.7mm apart); broken edges charred in places. L.545, W.150, T.5mm. 25276 sf8330 (P4A)

9106 Oak object; radially split rectangular board; sloping chamfer along each short end and notch with sloping sides cut into one long side, all three probably cut with an axe; central augered hole 29mm in diameter. L.234, W.115, T.22mm. 30076 sf11273 (P4A) (*Fig.1180*)

9107 Oak object; one edge is rounded and curves downwards towards narrowed end perforated on one side by sub-rectangular notch; broken at both ends; possibly part of a handle. L.125, W.53, T.15mm. 22809 sf8001 (P4B) (*Fig.1180*)

9108 Oak stake point; radially split quarter-section; roughly squared broken shaft; shaped pointed end circular in cross-section. L.105, W.34, T.27mm. 24240 sf8160 (P4B)

9109 Maple strip fragments; one end has blunt faceted point; other end broken; perforated by at least five small nail holes. L.236, W.20, T.9mm. 25350 sf8545 (P4B) (*Fig.1180*)

9110 Oak object; similar to *9046–52*, but probably too thin to be one of these brackets; triangular end with narrow rectangular bar projecting from one end of short side. L.191, W.50, T.10mm. 25860 sf9785 (P4B) (*Fig.1180*)

9111 Oak fragment; axe cuts form a chamfer at one end; other end broken but perforated by augered hole 22mm diameter. L.84, W.50, T.17mm. 32199 sf13097 (P4B)

9112 Oak object, possibly originally oval; intact edge rounded; broken across rounded rectangular hole 32mm wide. L.164, W.64, T.10mm. 32525 sf13181 (P4B)

9113 Oak object; thick, heavy, radially split board; triangular shape with convex sloping sides; perforated by augered hole 33mm diameter at apex; traces of rough groove at other end; not a stave. L.340, W.150, T.28mm. 25285 sf16088 (P4B)

9114 Oak beam; charred; perforated by augered hole 25mm diameter. L.120, W.85, T.25mm. 8801 sf2109 (P5A)

9115 Oak rod; square cross-section; curves towards both ends which are broken, but is thinner in the middle. L.220, W.29, T.23mm. 22309 sf7522 (P5A) (*Fig.1180*)

9116 Alder board fragments; possibly originally a flat sub-circular or oval board; squared edges. L.233, W.201, T.20mm. 2875 sf612 (P5B)

9117 Oak plank; thin, radially split board; one surface flat and smooth; perforated by augered hole 25mm diameter. L.225, W.99, T.9mm. 14535 sf4312 (P5B)

9118 Ash object fragment; rounded oval with one end broken; edges smooth and squared; perforated by hole 13mm diameter. L.33, W.29, T.8mm. 21643 sf9347 (P5B) (*Fig.1180*)

9119 Alder plank fragments; rectangular cross-section; squared ends; perforated at one end by two holes, one augered 18mm diameter, the other roughly cut 20 x 17mm. L.1.35m, W.202, T.18mm. 2709 sf16093 (P5B)

9120 Oak beam fragments; radially split quarter-section timber; two beam ends originally overlapped and were perforated by two augered holes, both with wedged peg fragments; wedges are driven from opposite sides; pegs are roundwood, wedges are made from radially split timber; only one beam now survives. L.390, W.63, T.39mm. 2952 sf16246 (P5B) (*Fig.1181*)

9121 Oak beam fragment; rectangular cross-section; broken at both ends; augered hole with broken peg/dowel 27mm diameter, 65mm long. L.345, W.62, T.30mm. 6869 sf16261 (P5B)

9122 Oak object; radially split board with strip of sapwood present along one long edge; this and the opposite edge are straight and parallel; ends have two sloping sides joining at a point; central augered hole 29mm diameter. L.357, W.124, T.18mm. 6717 sf16264 (P5B)

9123 Oak paddle/oar-like object; long, radially split plank; one end cut straight across and is perforated by two bisecting holes 27 and 28mm diameter; other end has sides gently tapering to truncated straight edge; this end has central augered hole 29mm diameter above two smaller augered holes with fragments of pegs 10mm diameter; cross-section at this end is plano-convex; at other end it is elliptical. L.1.57m, W.145, T.20mm. 14221 sf16087 (P5Cf) (*Fig.1179*)

9124 Oak fragment; possibly originally circular object with squared edge; perforated by at least four augered holes 12mm diameter. L.60, W.33, T.10mm. 6785 sf6238 (P5Cr) (*Fig.1181*)

9125 Oak block fragment; sub-rectangular with small ledge or step along one edge; perforated by two augered holes 26mm diameter, one broken. L.275, W.200, T.70mm. 4385 sf560 (C6i4; 16th–19th century) (P6)

9126 Oak object; oval cross-section rod with one end rounded, other broken across. L.109, W.23, T.18mm. 4385 sf564b (C6i4; 16th–19th century) (P6) (*Fig.1181*)

9127 Oak plank fragments; at least five irregularly spaced nail holes along one long edge, one with iron fragments in situ. L.311, W.71, T.10mm. 4454 sf588 (C6h1; 15th/16th century) (P6)

9128 Oak plank; deliberately squared against the grain; rectangular cross-section; tapers from squared end to narrower end cut at an angle; both ends perforated by broken iron nails. L.363, W.55, T.13mm. 4484 sf620 (C6g18; 15th/16th century) (P6)

9129 Oak object fragment; part of one curved outer edge remains; other edge broken, but has trace of circular or oval hole across which wood has split. L.239, W.85, T.20mm. 4885 sf852 (C6f5; 13th/14th century) (P6)

9130 Oak rudder-shaped object fragment; rectangular cross-section; one edge has pronounced curved profile; small terminal at one end 22mm wide, perforated from edge to edge by small hole; smaller terminal at other end, 19 x 10mm. L.163, W.89, T.13mm. 10521 sf2586 (C6g10; early 15th century) (P6) (*Fig.1181*)

9131 Oak block; sub-rectangular with sloping sides and one wider rounded end; perforated by augered hole 15mm diameter. L.158, W.131, T.17mm. 3536 sf3484 (A6c3; 12th century) (P6)

9132 Oak fragments; perforated by iron clench nail with lozenge-shaped plate still in situ; timber is pitted by many small marks at one side of iron plate. L.137, W.106, T.13mm. 3558 sf3640 (A6c4; 12th century) (P6) (*Fig.1182*)

9133 Oak stake fragment; radially split section with irregular cross-section; faceted sides whittled or axed; tapers slightly to blunt, rounded end; other end possibly broken. L.168, W.24, T.22mm. 15026 sf3727 (B6c8; early 13th century) (P6)

9134 Oak stake; rough rectangular head positioned asymmetrically at one side of shaft which tapers to blunt point. L.205, W.50, T.36mm. 17481 sf4701 (C6c4, D6a6; early 12th century, 11th/12th century) (P6) (*Fig.1182*)

9135 Oak block; sub-rectangular with small ledge or step along one edge; manufactured from larger radially split half- or quarter-section, but deliberately squared against the grain; perforated by augered hole 23mm diameter. L.130, W.102, T.41mm. 18074 sf4735 (B6c7; early 13th century) (P6) (*Fig.1182*)

9136 Oak rudder-shaped object fragment; rectangular cross-section; small broken terminals at both ends; one edge has a marked curved profile. L.115, W.91, T.17mm. 16443 sf16091 (B6c1; 12th/13th century) (P6) (*Fig.1182*)

9137 Oak; flat disc; approximately circular; edges worn and battered; charred edge; central hole 5mm diameter. D.66, T.11mm. u/s sf2612 (*Fig.1182*)

9138 Willow disc; perforated by augered hole 11mm diameter; not a spindle whorl or lathe-turning basal waste; wedge-shaped cross-section; incised line cut across hole. L.49, W.47, T.6mm. u/s sf9362 (*Fig.1182*)

9139 Oak strip; plano-convex cross-section with squared edges; both ends broken; perforated by iron dome-headed nail. L.141, W.34, T.14mm. u/s sf16089

Objects made from tangentially converted boards

9140 Yew sub-circular disc; irregular cross-section; perforated by augered hole 7mm diameter. L.38, W.30, T.12mm. 19739 sf13316 (P3) (*Fig.1183*)

9141 Two willow strips; tapering triangular cross-sections; next to the thickest edge, each strip has a circular hole in one corner and a rectangular hole in the other corner; one strip has two further holes next to the thinner edge; edges rough and broken in places. L.180, W.44, T.8mm. 29835 sf13061 (P4B) (*Fig.1183*)

9142 Ash object; probably made from tangentially split/sawn section; D-shaped, with rounded end; perforated by augered hole 10mm diameter, which is worn and rough on one surface; two V-shaped notches cut into one rounded side edge; bar with oval cross-section 20 x 16mm projects below the straight edge at the opposite side to the notches; bar broken. L.92, W.50, T.14mm. 29156 sf10292 (P5B) (*Fig.1183*)

9143 Oak block; sub-rectangular with squared ends and rounded corners; augered hole in one corner has squared peg made from split section, 18 x 15mm; sloping-sided mortice cut into one long edge. L.245, W.147, T.45mm. 4385 sf563 (C6i4; 16th–19th century) (P6) (*Fig.1183*)

Objects made from roundwood

9144 Hazel ring; short section of roundwood perforated by large augered hole 25mm diameter; not lathe-turned. D.45, H.23mm. 27088 sf9552 (P3) (*Fig.1184*)

9145 Alder object; length of roundwood cut flat on two opposing sides whilst bark remains on other two sides; rounded rectangular cross-section; one end has two sloping sides joining at a point; other end cut flat and broken; perforated by central augered hole 28mm diameter. L.237, W.60mm. 34882 sf13327 (P3) (*Fig.1184*)

9146 Willow rod, not a spindle; oval cross-section; chamfer cut at widest end; tapers to rounded point at other end. L.216, W.11, T.8mm. 25270 sf8317 (P4B)

9147 Decorated disc fragment; centre missing; very thin sawn section of roundwood, but centre of tree is offset from centre of disc, indicating object could have been sawn from a turned cylinder; flat sides smoothed; one has traces of two concentric grooves 18mm and 53mm diameter; two circular depressions (with centre point marks) 3mm deep and 15mm diameter cut at two cardinal points between grooves. D.114, T.7mm. 22104 sf7333 (P5A) (*Fig.1184*)

9148 Oak roundwood branch fragment with bark removed; faceted at one end where a side branch has been removed; other end broken; two large dome-headed nails driven into branch next to each other, and surface shaved flat between them. L.240, W.34, T.27mm. 4385 sf564a (C6i4; 16th–19th century) (P6)

9149　Hazel block possibly intended for suspension; sub-triangular roundwood block, squared down on all sides by axe cuts; ends have sloping sides joining at a point; perforated by circular augered hole 24mm diameter; seven fragments of a whittled roundwood shaft remain, one of which is still in the hole; shaft tapers dramatically away from the block and was probably not a handle. L. (block) 223, W.125, T.50mm; L. (shaft) >368, D.26mm. 11763 sf2915 (B6g4; early 15th century) (P6) (*Fig.1184*)

Objects made from wood whose primary conversion cannot be ascertained

9150　Alder rod fragment with lead ferrule; roughly rectangular cross-section; one end broken; tapers to other end which has conical lead strip hammered onto it; small circular lip bent over and crushed onto wood; possibly casket leg. L.76, D.15mm. 34412 sf12974 (P4B) (*Fig.1185*)

9151　Bead fragment; tiny cylindrical object perforated by hole 1mm wide. L.3, D.3mm. 25750 sf14399 (P4B)

9152　Oak object. 7231 sf1062 (P5B)

9153　Wooden object; charred. 8225 sf1084 (P5B)

9154　Alder object. 5772 sf1941 (P5B)

9155　Wooden object attached to iron spike (sf1032). L.17, D.8mm. 7262 sf19010 (P5B)

9156　Thick, heavy plank; plano-convex in cross-section; tapers from wide rectangular end to rounded point, now broken across small circular hole; large circular hole 24mm diameter perforates plank near wide end; long edges rebated with tapering slots cut out of each side; possibly eroded by water. L.560, W.145, T.42mm. 7207 sf19543 (P5B)

9157　Large stake or offcut probably cut down from quarter section or smaller; tapers to rounded point; three incomplete augered holes with rounded bottoms cut into side of stake probably with the same boring tool, 13–14mm diameter. L.530, W.62. 21856 sf19544 (P5B) (*Fig.1186*)

9158　Oak strip fragments; rectangular cross-section; broken at both ends; three nail holes and two augered holes along length. L.600, W.56, T.6mm. 4385 sf537b (C6i4; 16th–19th century) (P6)

9159　Oak object. 9201 sf930 (D6e10; mid 14th century) (P6)

9160　Wooden object. 10022 sf2437 (C6i1; late 17th century) (P6)

9161　Beech object fragment; oval cross-section; terminal fragment encased in copper alloy ferrule (sf2525) folded over the end. L.54, W.19, T.10mm. 10096 sf19012 (B6g13; 16th–17th century) (P6) (*Fig.1185*)

9162　Stake. 15001 sf3690 (B6c8; early 13th century) (P6)

Finds from the Coppergate watching brief site (1981–2.22)

Lathe-turning manufacturing waste

9163 Possible maple roughout for spindle-turning; roundwood; cylinder with sides and ends faceted by axe cuts, originally circular, now oval in cross-section; no turning lines visible; V-sectioned centre hole in each end. L.6, D.60mm. 2033 (Anglo-Scandinavian) sf352

9164 Alder waste core from face-turned bowl; truncated conical shape; deep groove 50mm diameter on flat top encircling two parallel slits from cup centre with two metal plates. L.62, D.82mm. 1961 (Anglo-Scandinavian) sf181

Lathe-turned vessels

Bowls

9165 Alder thick-walled bowl; face-turned; rounded profile; large unturned facet on external wall where a cut on the roughout has not been turned down; rounded rim; three external grooves (two in a pair); worn footring base, 10mm wide with convex bowl bottom; dark stained internal surface. D.298, H.102, T.10–17mm. 1205 (medieval) sf98 (*Fig.1025*)

9166 Alder; fragments; face-turned; rounded profile; rounded rim; worn, flat bottom; two external grooves. T.8mm. u/s sf182

9167 Alder; face-turned; rounded profile; rounded rim; external groove; slightly convex base with rounded edges; faint traces of V-sectioned spur centre mark; knife cuts on internal surface. D.230, H.80, T.9mm. 2093 (Anglo-Scandinavian) sf326

9168 Ash; face-turned; rounded profile; convex base with rounded edge emphasised by groove; dark stained internal surface. D.220, T.9mm. 1966 (Anglo-Scandinavian) sf350

Fragments and woodworking offcuts

9169 Fragment with iron. 2077 (medieval) sf253

Coopered vessels

Caskheads or vessel bases

9170 Large oak cant stave fragment; radially split board; rounded edges; incised mark on one flat surface in the form of a cross with outward-curving semi-circles at the end of the cross arms. L.502, W.140, T.12mm. 1600 (medieval) sf347 (*Figs.1094, 1097*)

9171 Oak cant stave fragment; radially split board; squared edges. L.159, W.73, T.18mm. 2033 (Anglo-Scandinavian) sf351

Incomplete vessel staves

9172 Fragments of four silver fir staves; radially split boards; parallel-sided; V-sectioned basal groove below which the stave ends are chamfered; other ends are broken. L.385, W.70, T.15mm. 1838 (medieval) sf345 (*Fig.1088*)

9173 Oak stave fragment; radially split board; tapers towards rim edge; broken across middle; no groove information; concretion adhering to external surface is possibly a corroded iron hoop since the point of a rivet is visible behind it on the inside, 37mm below rim edge. L.125, W.65, T.15mm. 1622 (medieval) sf346 (*Fig.1088*)

Domestic equipment and utensils

Note: see also *AY* 17/8 for further discussion of 4421

4421 Oak sub-circular churn dash; flat, riven board; central augered hole surrounded by four others at cardinal points, all 15–16mm diameter; squared edges; split in three places. D.137, T.16mm. 1777 (early Anglo-Scandinavian) sf245 (*Fig.1109*)

9174 Hazel spoon bowl fragments; oval with straight sides; shallow curved cross-section. L.72, W.17, T.5mm. 1247 (Anglo-Scandinavian) sf46

9175 Wooden handle fragments with S-shaped whittle tang knife; probably roundwood; possibly carved; oval cross-section. L.76, W.18mm. 1327 (pre-Anglo-Scandinavian) sf19

Boxes and enclosed containers

Note: see also *AY* 17/6 for further discussion of 3386

3386 Oak chest lid or back fragment; radially split rectangular board; one corner survives, others broken or missing; iron hinge with looped end projecting beyond intact edge of one long side; hinge fixed with two iron rivets. L.720, W.325, T.21mm. 1717 (Anglo-Scandinavian) sf92 (wood), sf344 (iron) (*Fig.1127*)

Furniture

9176 Oak garderobe seat fragment; originally rectangular; riven board; part of large circular hole with edges chamfered on both sides; augered circular hole 25mm diameter close to intact long edge. L.365, W.145, T.42mm. u/s sf203

Manual and agricultural implements

9177 Oak separate-bladed shovel blade; radially split board; fixing end diamond-shaped; concave sloping shoulders; rounded blade, now split; two peg holes 20mm and 10mm diameter; rectangular slot 60 x 30mm. L.355, W.180, T.18mm. u/s sf211 (*Fig.1135*)

9178 Oak plough fragments?; possible one-piece plough stock-and-stilt (or draught beam) survives intact as a single angled beam of shaped roundwood with roughly square/rectangular cross-section; straight piece 870mm long with slightly curved smaller beam 670mm long projecting at an obtuse angle from it; rectangular slot 60mm long and 15mm deep on the upper surface of the curved part; other broken fragments survive. L.1.54m, W.65, T.45mm. 2001 (Anglo-Scandinavian) sfs200–2

Textile implements

Note: see also *AY* 17/11 for further discussion of 6697

6697 Yew spindle; double-ended; made from split section; broken at both ends, but one end has traces of V-section notch cut into side; tapers in both directions away from maximum diameter. L.169, D.10mm. u/s sf72 (*Fig.1147*)

9179 Small apple/pear/hawthorn weaving comb; tangentially sawn; rectangular with smoothed surfaces; small curved hollows in each side at one end are finger holes; these and upper end are smoothed and faceted; lower end has nine teeth, oval in cross-section; at base of teeth are saw marks on each side indicating use of cross-set saw; saw marks on one flat side; two small holes made with awl near upper edge retain fragments of leather carrying strap. L.54, W.44, T.6mm. 1480 (Anglo-Scandinavian) sf56 (*Fig.1148*)

Pegs

9180   Willow trenail/peg; radially split section; circular cross-section; head has rounded top, straight sides and sloping shoulders; shaft is parallel-sided; other end broken. L.63, D.25mm. 2093 (Anglo-Scandinavian) sf329

9181   Expanded, bulbous head tapers to pointed end; whittled shaft. L.57, D.12mm. u/s sf40 (*Fig.1176*)

9182   Yew; radially split section; flat square 'head' end with facet cuts on each side sloping towards top of shaft; latter is smoothly faceted and tapers to point; square cross-section; section split from one side. L.127, W.13, T.12mm. u/s sf76

Find from Castlegate/Coppergate (Excavation by Benson in 1906)

9183   Iron hook-ended tool for lathe-turning; flanged circular socket for wooden handle (missing); shank is a bar of circular cross-section which is flattened in the upper part into a rectangular cross-sectioned bar and the last 90mm curves at approximately 110 degrees from the shank; the extreme 25–30mm of the tip are thinned into a blade edge and curve back on themselves to form a hook. This tool was found during excavations at the corner of Castlegate and Coppergate in 1906. Now in the Yorkshire Museum (YORYM: 551.48). Briefly published by Benson (1906, 73, pl.II). L.288, shank 13 x 7mm (*Fig.1014*)

Finds from 22 Piccadilly (1987.21)

Lathe-turned manufacturing waste

Waste cores from face-turned bowls

9184 Alder; truncated curved conical; circular augered mandrel hole cup centre 14mm diameter; top of core retains facet cuts from original bowl roughout; core now broken or cut with a large facet running diagonally from top to bottom. L.38, D.68mm. 2291 sf845 (P4.1)

9185 Alder; truncated S-shaped; originally two parallel slits on top from cup centre with two metal plates 20mm apart, but only one now faintly visible, 27mm long. L.30, D.50mm. 2219 sf867 (P4.1)

Fragments and woodworking offcuts

9186 Oak; small offcut/chip from tangentially converted block; rectangular; facet cuts at both ends. L.42, W.30, T.11mm. 3130 sf690 (P3)

9187 Oak; offcut/twig fragments; probably not an object, but with blue vivianite residue. 3178 sf840 (P3)

9188 Two offcuts/chips of different species; one is an oak offcut from a radially split board/lath; the other is acer and is an offcut or small fragment of a larger object possibly with the remains of an oval hole through the piece. L.50, W.25, T.10mm. 2291 sf747 (P4.1)

Coopered vessels

9189 Oak bucket base fragment, originally a very thick, one-piece circular base made from radially split oak section; deeply chamfered on only one side of the curved outside edge. D.350–60, T.24mm. 2042 sf102 (P6)

9190 Cask (upper of three-tier cask well, cf. 9191–2); 25 staves, all radially split oak boards. Truncated by modern levelling. The staves have a slight taper, and are flat. The chimes are chamfered, a number of staves have a distinct hollowing at the ends, and the groove to take the caskheads (now missing) is a narrow shallow V-profile, which has worn to a flatter U-profile in several staves. Four staves have holes below the groove for the reinforcing battens. Two staves have only one hole, one with the remains of an oak peg in situ. One stave has two holes and another has three. All holes c.10mm diameter. No binding survives, but impressions have been left in the outer surface. The archive report suggests that there was a continuous line of withy binding. A single line of nails has been hammered in from the inside, close to the base, presumably to reinforce the outer hooping. H.600 minimum, D. (girth) not known due to truncation, D. (base) 814mm, W. (staves) 80–138, T. (staves) 10–20mm, distance from groove to groove not known due to truncation. 2043 sf1304 (P6) (Fig.1078)

9191 Cask (middle of three-tier cask well, cf. 9190 and 9192); 22 staves, of which fifteen are tangential boards and seven are radially split boards. The staves taper and list, have chamfered chimes and a deep narrow V-profile groove to take the caskheads (no longer present). A number of the tangentially converted staves have a pronounced internal convex profile, and have several knots. One stave has five peg holes beneath the groove at both ends. These holes are 13–15mm in diameter and are slightly elliptical, as if worn. The remains of an oak peg survive in one of the holes. One stave has a possible cooper's mark in the form of an incised circle within a triangle, also seen on a stave from the lower barrel (Fig.1096). Two oak pegs of 8mm

diameter in holes close to this mark survive as well. Two staves have bungs surviving, one of oak, the other alder. The oak bung is 38mm diameter and its stave has a smaller spile hole filled with an oak peg of 8mm diameter close by. The alder bung is 60mm in diameter and the stave has an elliptical hole c.23mm diameter close by. This stave has a further three holes with oak pegs in situ, c.8mm diameter. A small number of nails have been hammered in from inside the barrel, usually one close to the base, at midpoint and near the top of the staves. These nails fastened three internal hoops of ash, c.50mm wide, to reinforce the staves against the weight of the external soil. The outer hoops were of split hazel rod, fastened by willow withies. H.1.45m, D. (girth) 950mm, D. (ends) 700 and 800, W. (staves) 86–189, T. (staves) 10–18mm, groove to groove distance 1.34m. 2044 sf1305 (P6)

9192 Oak cask (lower of three-tier cask well, cf. 9090–1); made up of 21 staves of which seventeen were tangentially converted and the remainder radial splits. The staves list and taper, and have chamfered chimes. The grooves for the caskhead (now missing) have a deep narrow V-profile. A number of the staves have a pronounced internal convex surface and several knots can be seen. One stave has a 10mm diameter peg hole below the groove at the top end and another has four holes of 10mm diameter, one with the remains of an oak peg in situ. Another stave has an alder bung 50mm diameter, with a smaller spile hole 20mm diameter close by. This stave also has a possible cooper's mark inscribed near the bung hole. One stave has a circle within an open triangle (similar to that on a stave from 9191) and another has a series of crossed lines carved into the surface (Fig.1096). One stave has three tiny oak pegs of 3mm, likely to be spile holes. The staves were fastened by an external hoop of split hazel bound by continuous withy binding. The cask was further reinforced during its life as a well lining by the addition of three internal hoops of ash, about 50mm width, held in place by nails. The majority of these staves have a series of very fine tool marks over both inner and outer surfaces. These consist of very fine striations within the surface and are therefore not tool signatures. They may represent marks left by either a drawknife or a plane. This was the lower cask in the three-tiered well and rested upon a platform made of oak planking set fast with sharpened alder, hazel and willow stakes. The planking has not survived very well. H.1.48m, D. (girth) 1.04m, D. (ends) 840 and 845mm, W. (staves) 85–195, T. (staves) 11–17mm, groove to groove distance 1.36m. 2051 sf1306 (P6) (Fig.1079)

Domestic equipment and utensils

9193 Possible oak stopper; made from radially split section; complete; large bulbous head with oval cross-section and short, straight-sided, oval cross-section shaft with blunt rounded point. L.95, W. (head) 48, T. (head) 33, W. (shaft) 26mm. 3130 sf688 (P3) (Fig.1100)

9194 Fragments of twisted strands of roundwood; possibly basketry or handle fragments. D. up to 25mm. 1058 sf356 (P3)

9195 Decorated boxwood knife handle with remains of iron whittle tang of knife embedded in it; made from radially split section; sub-oval cross-section; broken and split at the blade end, worn and smoothed by hand grip at other end, now obscuring some of the original incised and relief decoration which is in the Scandinavian Ringerike style; the corner of the handle behind the animal head ornament is fully perforated by a small hole countersunk on both sides, possibly for suspending the knife at a belt.

At the outer end of the handle is an inward-facing animal mask with a high forehead and short muzzle, from the top of which develop two pairs of nose lappets — long narrow extensions with clubbed ends, one falling to each side of the muzzle. The animal's eyes are indicated by very lightly incised circles, its ears are modelled forming a triangular extension to the handle. The neck of the animal is depicted on both sides of the handle and is made up of pairs of relief strands curving down and up again across the face of the handle towards its upper edge. About half way along its length, subsidiary strands interlace with each pair forming an elaborate knot. The relief strands and the body of the animal are additionally decorated with lightly incised saltires and cross-hatching. L.73, W.27, T.10mm. 3136 sf632 (P3) (*Fig.1115*)

Textile implements

Bale pins

No heads; all have tapering straight shafts, wider at 'head' end; made from split billets; approximately circular cross-section; whittled shafts.

Cat. no.	Status	Species	L.	D.	sf. no.	Context	Phase
9196	Broken tip	not identifiable	105	8	20	2007	6
9197	Tip only	not identifiable	39	6	84	2042	6
9198	Rough fragment	Oak	74	9	224	2083	6

Pegs

9199 Tip fragment which could not be identified to species; roundwood; originally circular in cross-section, now broken in half and at upper end; round blunt point. L.56, D.15mm. 2280 sf819 (P4.1)

9200 Oak; radially split section; square head end which tapers to blunt point; square cross-section; head end only is charred/darkened as if it had been the only part of the peg exposed. L.99, W.20, T.20mm. 2045 sf89 (P6)

Miscellaneous object

9201 Possible alder/hazel tool head; now broken; made from roundwood shaped on sides but centre still present; subcylindrical object perforated vertically by oval hole, leaving two narrow sides; possibly the head of a mallet-like tool with a large handle hole or the end of a larger piece like a frame which had a tenon fixed in the hole (cf. *9237*). L.82, W.47, T.34mm. 2233 sf734 (P4.1)

Finds from the Bedern Foundry (1973–6.13.II)

Lathe-turned vessels

Bowls

9202 Maple?; bowl/cup fragments; face-turned; very finely turned thin walls; fine-grained wood; steep-sided profile; rounded pointed rim; no diameter, base or height can be reconstructed; surfaces appear to have been smoothed with an abrasive. T. (wall) 3–4, T. (rim) 1–2mm. 4228 sf1273 (P2)

9203 Ash; face-turned; rounded, stepped profile, with external break in profile delineated by a groove 35mm below the rim, and a corresponding internal step 38mm below rim; rounded rim with internal groove 2mm below it; flat base 2mm high with rounded edge delineated by groove; incised turner's/owner's mark on external base in the form of a simple cross; charring on base; rough area 50mm wide in centre of bowl where core removed, and dark staining on internal surfaces. D.170, H.45, T.7, T. (base) 9mm. 2981 sf1510 (P2)

9204 Ash; face-turned (unusual in that original roughout appears to have been prepared with open bowl end to outside of tree); rounded profile with thin fine walls deeply incurving towards base; surfaces smoothed as if polished by abrasive; rounded pointed rim; flat base 1mm high with rounded edge delineated by groove; raised internal base disc 48mm diameter delineated by groove, with central disc 25mm diameter where core removed. D.160, H.46, T.2–4, T. (base) 6mm. 4227 sf1760 (P2)

9205 Ash; face-turned with smoothed, very thin, fine walls; very few turning lines visible suggesting polishing with abrasive; rounded external profile with one small and one large decorative ridge made by three grooves 42mm below the rim; internal profile stepped 20mm above base; rounded pointed rim; flat bottom with slight groove near wall/bottom junction, and hollow disc 25mm diameter at centre of bottom where basal waste removed. D.220, H.58, T.2–5mm. 4228 sf1766 (P2)

9206 Ash; thick-walled bowl fragment; face-turned; deep rounded profile; rectangular rim 23mm deep, with two external grooves 18 and 21mm below rim edge; flat rim top 18mm wide. D.c.300, T.14mm. 2482 sf1762 (P3) (Fig.1026)

Fragments and woodworking offcuts

9207 Yew sliver/offcut, not a worked object or peg fragment. L.67, W.11, T.7mm. 4077 sf1625 (P2)

9208 Oak handle or offcut; radially split section; faceted sides; rounded square cross-section; tapers slightly towards broken end which had been perforated vertically by nail hole. L.112, W.22, T.22mm. 4208 sf1745 (P2)

9209 Ash offcut of radially split section; prepared length of wood which has roughly faceted sides and sub-square cross-section; broken at both ends. L.196, W.26, T.24mm. 4228 sf1765 (P2)

9210 Oak offcut of radially split section; prepared length of wood which has roughly faceted sides and rectangular cross-section; cut across at both ends. L.138, W.30, T.23mm. 4222 sf1773 (P2)

9211 Oak offcut of radially split section; prepared length of wood which has roughly faceted sides and sub-circular cross-section; cut/broken at both ends. L.108, W.24, T.23mm. 4222 sf1779 (P2)

9212 Carbonised fragment with trace of possibly curved worked edge. L.45, W.35, T.16mm. 145 sf198 (P5)

Coopered vessels

9213 Oak cant stave of two-piece caskhead; radially split board; edges chamfered on one side only; sub-square vent hole 12 x 10mm with remains of square peg; incised merchant's mark of intersecting lines is now incomplete as it was originally cut over the entire caskhead; two holes 7mm diameter in straight edge containing wooden dowels; many knife cuts on same surface as incised mark. L.295, W.154, T.15mm. 4228 sf1778 (P2) (Fig.1094)

9214 Cask (upper of three-tier cask well, cf. 9215–16); only eight staves surviving, of radially split oak boards. The boards taper, but no longer have a list. The chimes are chamfered, and all staves have a broad deep V-shaped groove to take the caskheads which are missing. The upper lengths of the staves have been truncated during burial. Four staves have small peg holes 6–10mm diameter below the grooves to take reinforcing battens. No hoops survive. H.c.800, D. (girth and end) not known due to incompleteness of staves, W. (staves) 66–130mm, T. (staves) 10–20mm, distance from groove to groove not known due to incompleteness of staves. 4227 sf3538 (P3)

9215 Cask (middle of three-tier cask well, cf. 9214 and 9216); 22 staves, all radially split oak boards which taper towards each end and are listed. The chimes are chamfered and the staves have a shallow V-sectioned groove to take the caskheads which are missing. Several grooves appear to have worn to more of a U-profile. The internal surfaces of a number of staves have been hollowed at each end. One stave has an offset bung hole, 60mm diameter, the bung missing. Three staves have one hole each below the groove at one end, all holes slightly worn and approximately 10mm diameter. An oak peg survives in one of these holes, remains of a reinforcing batten. Another stave has two holes below the groove at one end, c.10mm diameter and elliptical in shape. There is an incised mark, possibly a cooper's mark, on another stave (Fig.1095). The barrel was bound with split hazel/alder rods, the ends of which were bound by willow withies. The bindings extended the full height of the barrel except for the central zone, thus avoiding the bung hole. Although the bindings are no longer attached to the staves, the site plan shows 37 turns in total on one side and 43 on the other. There are a number of nails hammered in from the inside to reinforce the outer hooping during use as a well lining. Many of the nails are in pairs. H.1.34m, D. (girth) 880mm, D. (ends) 770 and 750, W. (staves) 93–160, T. (staves) 10–15mm, distance from groove to groove not known due to incompleteness of staves. 4019 sf3539 (P3) (Fig.1077)

9216 Cask (lower of three-tier cask well, cf. 9214–15); 26 staves, all radially split oak boards which list and taper towards each end. The staves have a narrow, shallow V-shaped groove to take the caskheads which are missing. The chimes are chamfered and a number of the staves have hollowed internal surfaces at each end. One stave has a 56mm diameter bung hole (bung missing) with two smaller holes of 10 and 21mm diameter to the side of it. The bung hole is not centrally located along the length of the stave. Two staves have incised marks on them, possible cooper's marks, one a circle with a line either side of it, the other a plain inscribed circle (Fig.1095). Several staves have dowel/peg holes below the grooves to take the reinforcing battens. One stave has four holes at both ends, all with diameters of c.10mm (they are quite worn), whilst another stave has three holes at both ends of 8–11mm diameter. Another stave has two holes below the base groove of 10mm diameter. Two staves taper only from top to bottom — these are different from the other staves, and may represent repairs to the barrel at some time during its use. The staves were bound together with split hazel/alder rods, the ends of which were bound by willow withies. Although the bindings had become detached from the staves during recovery, the site plan shows them extending the full height of the barrel, apart from one zone around the bung hole. There are 43 turns in total on one side and 45 on the other. Many of the staves have 10–15 nails hammered in from inside to reinforce the outer hoops during its use as a well lining. The number of nails seems excessive but may indicate that the cask had had considerable use and the hoops were becoming detached. This is the lower barrel of the well and was sited on a base constructed from four slightly curving oak timbers, held together by dowelled lap joints. Two of these timbers have mortice joints surviving suggesting that they were re-used from a building. H.1.47m, D. (girth) 988mm, D. (ends) 833 and 876, W. (staves) 60–184, T. (staves) 10–15mm, groove to groove distance 1.37m. 4221 sf3540 (P3) (*Fig.1076*)

9217   Oak batten possibly from large caskhead; radially split section; one surface (underside?) is flat; other surface has edges chamfered all the way around; tapers towards one complete end; other end was possibly originally tapered but now broken and split apart; six augered holes along length, probably originally filled with wooden pegs, some of which were later pierced by iron nails with square cross-sectioned shafts; fragments of iron remain in situ and one nail hole is clearly visible; one hole (third in from broken end) is possibly a repair after the batten split through the first and second holes. L.535, W.58, T.27mm. 2670 sf1387 (P2) (*Fig.1086*)

Domestic equipment and utensils

9218   Oak spatula/stirrer in three fragments; split lath; flat rectangular cross-section; tapers along length from wider flat blade with straight end (now broken) to narrow rounded end; latter was possibly the hand-grip, and its sides are worn and rounded. L.413, W.32, T.4mm. 4228 sf1767 (P2)

9219   Hardwood (unidentified) lathe-turned knife handle; beautifully whorled and figured wood (possibly boxwood burr) which has been smoothed and polished; waisted, with wider ends; originally circular, now oval cross-section, further distorted by iron whittle tang fragment which has caused the wood to swell and split; tang originally fixed in a hole which ran the entire length of the handle, its tip visible in a small hole at the centre end. L.79, D. (near blade) 18, D. (end) 21mm. 4228 sf1749 (P2) (*Fig.1114*)

Textile implements

Bale pins

No heads; all have tapering straight shafts, wider at 'head' end; most made from split billets (*9221* is roundwood); approximately circular cross-section; whittled shafts.

Cat. no.	Status	Species	L.	D.	sf. no.	Context	Phase
9220	Complete	*Prunus* sp.	111	6	1342	2349	2
9221	Rough roundwood	not identifiable	118	8	1522	2961	2
9222	Smooth, long facets	*Prunus* sp.	160	8	1756	4208	2
9223	Facet point	*Prunus* sp.	145	10	1756	4208	2

Pegs

9224   Oak tile peg; made from radially split billet; flat upper and lower ends; sub-rectangular cross-section; straight sides. L.32, W.12, T.9mm. 4224 sf1759 (P1) (*Fig.1177*)

9225   Oak; made from radially split section; no head, but upper end has rectangular cross-section and is cut at an angle through which is a countersunk hole with the remains of a knotted leather thong; tapers to rounded point; lower end is rounded rectangular in section and worn smooth as if it had been repeatedly put into a peg hole. L.165, W.34, T.30mm. 2668 sf1398 (P2)

Finds from the College of the Vicars Choral, Bedern
(site areas specified at the end of each entry)

Lathe-turned vessels

Bowls

9226   Ash; face-turned; rounded profile; rounded rim thinned slightly on outside with internal groove 2mm below rim; external groove 28mm below rim, and corresponding internal step 30mm below rim; internal surfaces dark stained; flat bottom with rounded edge and several unturned facets at bottom/wall junction from original roughout. D.165, H.48, T.4–6mm. 1359 sf286 (P8) (1978–9.14.II)

9227   Alder; face-turned; flat everted rim 14mm wide; almost straight-sided profile; flat base 62mm diameter with rounded edge delineated by groove; possible V-notch spur centre mark visible in centre of base. D.140, H.28, T.5mm. 1359 sf288 (P8) (1978–9.14.II)

9228 Birch bowl/cup; face-turned; wafer thin fragments of very fine walls, now flattened and compressed, but probably originally a shallow rounded profile; base with rounded edge and central disc 24mm diameter where basal waste removed; traces of V-notch spur centre mark still visible. D. (base) 70, T.3–4; T. (walls) 1–2mm. 1359 sf295 (P8) (1978–9.14.II)

9229 Field maple; face-turned; flat everted rim 14mm wide; S-shaped profile; small flat base with angled edge; tool marks in two directions on external base probably from cleaning off basal waste; V-notch spur centre hole 2mm deep still visible and now at the centre of a branded or stamped turner's/owner's mark in the form of a four-armed florid cross; internal base has unturned area 15mm diameter where core removed. D.120, H.25, T.3–5mm. 1359 sf303 (P8) (1978–9.14.II) (Fig.1026)

9230 Ash; face-turned; rounded profile; squared flat rim; external groove 11mm below rim edge; two deep grooves 47 and 84mm diameter on rounded bottom, and central unturned knob/disc 16mm diameter where basal waste removed; internal base cleaned off over an area 55mm diameter. D.142, H.44, T.7mm. 1359 sf311 (P8) (1978–9.14.II)

Plate

9231 Ash; complete; face-turned; shallow profile with straight sides; rounded rim with internal and external grooves 5mm below rim; flat base 70mm diameter and 1mm high with rounded edge delineated by deep groove 5mm wide; internal base hollowed slightly over 88mm, with centre free of turning lines where core removed; internal surface criss-crossed with knife cuts and also marked by a linear scorch mark across the bottom. D.213, H.30, T.4–6mm. 1359 sf312 (P8) (1978–9.14.II) (Fig.1026)

Fragments and woodworking offcuts

9232 Unidentified species of very small shaving/offcut. L.20, W.12, T.2mm. 5501B sf2559 (P6) (1978.13.X)

Coopered vessels

9233 Willow?; bucket stave fragments; radially split board; probably originally wider at top; broken along one long edge, the other intact and slightly chamfered; originally squared basal groove, now broken; rounded top edge. L.208, W.58, T.11mm. 25 sf19 (Anglo-Scandinavian) (1976.14.I)

Domestic equipment and utensils

9234 Cherry?/blackthorn? (Prunus sp.) spoon; made from radially split section; small, pear-shaped, keeled bowl; shallow curved cross-section; handle fragment 8mm wide, possibly circular or D-shaped in cross-section, but now split and part has broken away leaving a hollow effect which is not original; toolmarks on the inside of the bowl are from the original carving. L.104, W.35, T.7mm. 1225 sf1141 (P1) (1973–5.13.III) (Fig.1101)

Boxes and enclosed containers

9235 Oak lath-walled vessel fragments; two curved conjoined pieces are possibly parts of a vessel whose walls were originally bent to form a circle/oval and sewn together (cf. 8935); one intact edge which is now rippled and distorted inwards; largest piece has possibly 4–5 small irregular awl-pierced holes running parallel to the intact edge, one containing a peg or piece of organic stitching 4mm diameter. L.254, W.101, T.5mm. u/s sf1367 (1976.13.V) (Fig.1124)

9236 Oak; possible chest lid or cover. Sub-rectangular tangentially split board from large tree; irregular oval knot hole near one long edge; short ends are rough, the longer edges are squared and straighter; no evidence for hinges, lock fittings or joints to fix the board to other components, except for the remains of one nail fixed in one corner from underneath; large split from one short end down two-thirds of length has been repaired with a separate radially split oak board nailed to the larger board in four corners and positioned perpendicular to the split. L. (lid) 880, W.325, T.17; L. (smaller board) 310, W.95, T.6mm. 5508 sf962 (P6) (1978.13.X) (Fig.1126)

Textile implements

9237 Beam from ash frame, possibly a tapestry loom or embroidery frame, made from radially split section; each end is carved into a long oval with slightly curved sides and rounded end, and is fully perforated vertically by a rectangular mortice hole; sloping shoulders taper downwards in profile from each perforated end and the latter are linked by a small beam with D-shaped cross-section; now broken across beam. L.485mm; ends: (i) W.32, T.25mm. (ii) W.30, T.28mm; holes: (i) 30 x 21, (ii) 35 x 16mm. 5342B sf2086/sf3027 (P7) (1976–9.13.X) (Fig.1148)

Bale pins

No heads; all have tapering straight shafts, wider at 'head' end; made from split billets; approximately circular cross-section; whittled shafts.

Cat. no.	Status	Species	L.	D.	sf. no.	Context	Phase	Site code
9238	Bark in one place	Yew	155	9	999	1120	1	1973–5.13.III
9239	Split near point	Yew	114	8	752	1090	6	1973–5.13.III
9240	Square cross-section	Hardwood	78	4	956	1505	6	1978–9.14.II
9241	Naturally curved	Yew	137	8	279	1359	8	1978–9.14.II

Building accessories and structural fragments

9242 Oak rectangular lock housing; either a radial or tangential section, more likely the latter since it has sawn surfaces and edges; perforated by three countersunk augered nail holes, one above and one below a rectangular hollowed section on the reverse, and a third to the left of it; fully perforated by key hole of usual shape; rectangular hollow is chiselled with irregular-shaped edges inside the basic rectangle, presumably to house a metal lock mechanism which is now missing except for small iron fragments trapped in the corners; hollow is open at one end where nail holes above and below the opening once held a lockplate. L.200, W.132, T.38mm. u/s sf2863 (1980.13.XV)

Pegs

9243   Ash; radially split section; rounded triangular head which is larger than parallel-sided shaft; latter has blunt rounded end, and is worn and compressed, now wedge-shaped in profile. L.71; W. (head) 33, T.23: W. (shaft) 23mm. 25 sf22 (Anglo-Scandinavian) (1976.14.I)

9244   Oak; radially split section; no head, but upper end is flat with rectangular rebate cut into side, perhaps for a cord or thong; rebate now broken on one side; tapers slightly to rounded blunt point. L.133, W.24, T.18mm. 1784B sf731 (P1) (1978–9.14.II)

9245   Oak tile peg; made from radially split billet; flat upper end and blunt point; square cross-section; straight sides, tapering in profile. L.48, W.10, T.10mm. 1784B sf685 (P1) (1978–9.14.II)

Miscellaneous object

9246   Hazel or alder handle end fragment?; shaped like expanded fishtail; appears to be made from a radially split section of wood with a twisted grain, possibly a branch junction; one corner broken; smooth, worn surface suggesting it has been held in the hand with broken corner lowermost. L.111, W.76, T.21mm. 25 sf15 (Anglo-Scandinavian) (1976.14.I) (*Fig.1182*)

Provenances

Finds were recovered from contexts on the sites as follows; context numbers are given in Roman type, catalogue numbers in italics.

16–22 Coppergate

1002: *8690*; 1113: *8994, 9015*; 1363: *6647, 8372, 8774*; 1404: *8311, 9053*; 1473: *8179, 8208, 8251, 8264–9, 8397–8, 8488, 8527–8, 8911, 8919, 9080*; 1478: *8275, 8458*; 1504: *8948*; 1506: *8696*; 1546: *8464*; 1585: *8955*; 1606: *8237*; 1611: *8559, 9020*; 1628: *8872*; 1755: *8860*; 1842: *8589–90, 8913*; 1944: *8591*; 2149: *9028*; 2193: *8218*; 2195: *8691–2*; 2235: *8693*; 2317: *8328*; 2325: *8909*; 2369: *8334*; 2463: *8178, 8487, 8876*; 2475: *8396, 8659, 8910*; 2477: *8660*; 2494: *8457*; 2527: *9090*; 2709: *9119*; 2830: *8956*; 2875: *8270–1, 8335, 8399–402, 8503, 8560–1, 8661–2, 8800, 9093, 9116*; 2876: *8272*; 2952: *9120*; 3140: *9104*; 3235: *8595*; 3270: *9056*; 3386: *8970*; 3401: *8975*; 3521: *8367*; 3536: *9131*; 3558: *9132*; 3561: *9023*; 3612: *8444*; 3698: *8534*; 4252: *9096*; 4260: *9095*; 4385: *8583–7, 8694, 8764, 8821–2, 8844, 8848, 8961, 8968, 8977, 8995–6, 9019, 9040, 9045, 9051, 9083, 9125–6, 9143, 9148, 9158, 9695*; 4398: *8845*; 4416: *8957*; 4434: *8588*; 4454: *9127*; 4484: *9128*; 4548: *9003*; 4599: *8930*; 4636: *8449*; 4704: *8931*; 4705: *8888*; 4769: *8199*; 4788: *8189*; 4797: *9004, 9084*; 4830: *8932*; 4850: *8190*; 4867: *8889, 9055*; 4872: *8698*; 4874: *8997, 9001*; 4885: *8592–3, 9098, 9129*; 4915: *8700*; 4931: *9097*; 5245: *8701*; 5252: *8816*; 5253: *8761*; 5255: *8817*; 5256: *8818*; 5259: *8815*; 5277: *8937*; 5280: *8813*; 5286: *8814*; 5288: *8819*; 5289: *9016*; 5290: *8820*; 5331: *8723*; 5348: *8170, 8193*; 5412: *8312*; 5512: *8950*; 5532: *8342*; 5585: *8702*; 5638: *8450*; 5651: *8755*; 5655: *8597*; 5667: *8704*; 5669: *8966*; 5673: *8337, 8407, 8963*; 5692: *8279*; 5714: *8187, 8209, 8277, 8465–6*; 5749: *8596*; 5750: *8610*; 5755: *8598, 9052*; 5772: *8884, 9154*; 5777: *8861*; 5906: *8705, 9099*; 6119: *8278, 8666*; 6170: *8181–2, 8667, 8991*; 6238: *8669*; 6287: *8214, 8299*; 6358: *9038*; 6425: *8253, 8416–17*; 6429: *8415*; 6433: *8530*; 6434: *8213, 8805, 8886*; 6437: *8683, 8852*; 6472: *8469*; 6532: *8938*; 6573: *8686*; 6578: *8215*; 6583: *8760*; 6717: *9122*; 6785: *8582*; 6785: *9124*; 6869: *9121*; 6881: *8810*; 6908: *8308, 8445*; 6926: *8309, 8446–7, 8688*; 7008: *8811*; 7040: *8801*; 7061: *8663*; 7064: *8697*; 7204: *8203*; 7205: *8274*; 7207: *9156*; 7209: *8843*; 7231: *9152*; 7232: *8252*; 7260: *2898*; 7261: *8974*; 7262: *9155*; 7310: *8812*; 7348: *8180, 8562*; 7467: *8564*; 7473: *8563, 8566, 8633*; 7474: *9059*; 7510: *8965*; 7527: *8198*; 7543: *8762*; 7552: *9064*; 7554: *8875*; 7589: *8565*; 7616: *8802*; 7672: *8490*; 7782: *8740, 9037*; 7954: *8684, 8033: 8403*; 8044: *8229*; 8107: *8273, 8404*; 8110: *8405, 8877*; 8132: *6652*; 8168: *8176*; 8225: *8969, 9153*; 8281: *8393–4*; 8305: *9002*; 8453: *8228, 8249, 8329*; 8454: *8263*; 8520: *8336*; 8524: *8898*; 8525: *8406, 8668*; 8665: *8315*; 8666: *8489, 8665, 8735*; 8696: *8664*; 8750: *6644*; 8760: *8972*; 8801: *8793, 8988, 9114*; 8856: *8316*; 9016: *8738*; 9058: *8188*; 9068: *8739*; 9125: *8699*; 9129: *8594*; 9201: *9159*; 9305: *8823, 9018*; 9362: *8703, 8899*; 9450: *8454*; 9640: *8941*; 9641: *8191*; 9721: *8276*; 9765: *8599*; 9793: *8893*; 10022: *9160*; 10033: *6650, 8708–9*; 10093: *6661*; 10096: *9161*; 10148: *9036*; 10334: *9000*; 10447: *9005*; 10448: *8928*; 10464: *8959, 9006*; 10511: *6659*; 10515: *8999*; 10521: *8710, 9130*; 10546: *8958*; 10557: *6660, 9100–1*; 10560: *8979*; 10758: *8601, 8917, 8962, 9041, 9061*; 10763: *8611, 8722*; 10789: *8924*; 10821: *9007*; 10840: *8978*; 10877: *8942*; 10977: *8940*; 10979: *8901*; 10993: *8846*; 11004: *8707*; 11011: *8967*; 11018: *8492, 9044*; 11020: *8368, 8706*; 11050: *8600*; 11052: *8602*; 11106: *8998*; 11112: *8451*; 11120: *9008*; 11125: *8676*; 11342: *8603*; 11513: *8724*; 11514: *8725*; 11531: *8765*; 11641: *8743*; 11720: *9030*; 11763: *9149*; 11883: *8824, 9011*; 11919: *9009*; 11920: *9010*; 11953: *8714*; 11991: *8717*; 11995: *8713*; 12018: *6653*; 12125:

6657; 12126: *6658, 8711*; 12159: *6641, 8914*; 12257: *8741*; 12276: *8605*; 12375: *8920, 9054*; 12389: *8712*; 12548: *8604, 8715, 9102*; 13147: *6654, 8894*; 13184: *8719*; 13243: *9022*; 13385: *8718*; 13456: *8716*; 13523: *9031*; 13575: *8862–3*; 13682: *8763*; 13902: *6656, 9012–14*; 13916: *8567*; 13921: *8567*; 13949: *8825*; 13964: *9103*; 14005: *9069*; 14069: *8304–7*; 14184: *8210–11, 8280–2, 8408, 8467, 8904, 8982*; 14221: *9123*; 14253: *8670*; 14297: *8212*; 14403: *8338, 8409*; 14420: *8339, 8671, 8736*; 14433: *8340*; 14469: *8468, 8921*; 14515: *8303*; 14535: *8672, 8992, 9117*; 14543: *8673*; 14573: *8675*; 14575: *8344, 8412*; 14625: *8285*; 14666: *8347, 8413*; 14667: *8286, 8414*; 14722: *8853*; 14787: *2270*; 14873: *8989*; 14883: *8796*; 14887: *8504*; 14925: *2255*; 14932: *8734*; 14933: *8795*; 14973: *2256, 8677*; 15001: *9162*; 15013: *8939*; 15026: *6649, 6655, 8606, 9133*; 15041: *8607, 8864*; 15131: *8410*; 15136: *8171*; 15166: *8960*; 15173: *8794*; 15176: *8682, 8851*; 15179: *8183*; 15189: *8283*; 15195: *8568*; 15299: *8766, 8865*; 15300: *8742*; 15314: *8411*; 15361: *8885*; 15425: *8803*; 15470: *8284*; 15473: *8230*; 15530: *8529*; 15535: *8833*; 15537: *9021*; 15538: *8756*; 15539: *8835*; 15540: *8834*; 15550: *8515*; 15553: *8804*; 15554: *8757*; 15561: *8516, 8674*; 15566: *8758*; 15619: *8184*; 15622: *8517–18*; 15640: *8341*; 15659: *8953*; 15731: *8185*; 15999: *8343*; 16382: *8826*; 16443: *9136*; 16474: *8847, 8870*; 16507: *8532*; 16534: *8192*; 16605: *8720–1*; 16654: *8949*; 16889: *8687*; 16923: *9072*; 17275: *8369*; 17360: *8744*; 17449: *8745*; 17481: *9134*; 17551: *8172*; 17890: *8609*; 18074: *9135*; 18153: *8608*; 18168: *8173*; 18419: *8767*; 18470: *8569*; 18594: *8463, 8556*; 18602: *8618–19*; 18709: *8836*; 18710: *9094*; 18744: *2143*; 18826: *8737*; 18988: *2265, 8622–3*; 19196: *2267*; 19320: *2268*; 19326: *8287, 8418–19*; 19390: *2264*; 19446: *8570*; 19600: *8351, 8423*; 19615: *8426*; 19623: *8838, 8841*; 19625: *8232, 8357–8, 8435–6, 8506*; 19626: *8242–3, 8376, 8498*; 19739: *9140*; 19763: *8536–7*; 19813: *8768*; 20178: *8685*; 20191: *6643*; 20277: *8254, 8345–6*; 20342: *9032*; 20372: *9048*; 20387: *9039*; 20441: *8420*; 20506: *8646*; 20552: *8288*; 20590: *8613*; 20728: *8951*; 20747: *8648*; 20764: *9029*; 20808: *8333, 8631, 9091*; 20877: *8206, 8330, 8514*; 20881: *8317*; 20918: *8373*; 21033: *8438*; 21037: *8291*; 21069: *8427*; 21088: *8310, 8448, 8689*; 21143: *2263*; 21182: *8428*; 21198: *8421*; 21203: *9034*; 21204: *8422*; 21244: *8258, 8292, 8352, 8424*; 21245: *9081*; 21249: *8234*; 21258: *8571*; 21270: *8425*; 21375: *8293, 9070*; 21381: *8505*; 21432: *8519*; 21464: *8430*; 21478: *8520*; 21479: *8240–1*; 21482: *8429*; 21507: *8353*; 21510: *8195, 8197, 8259, 8294–8, 8354, 8356, 8359, 8431–2, 8434, 8437, 8470–1, 8635, 8837, 9049*; 21511: *8433*; 21512: *6642*; 21554: *8440, 8508, 8573, 8806, 9062–3*; 21592: *8460*; 21627: *8355*; 21643: *9118*; 21678: *9071*; 21682: *9043*; 21746: *8524, 8576, 8642*; 21748: *8473*; 21796: *8954*; 21807: *8548*; 21834: *8572*; 21845: *6651*; 21846: *8233, 8474*; 21854: *8300, 8507*; 21856: *9157*; 21857: *8360*; 21863: *8441, 8491, 8522*; 21882: *8983*; 21886: *6648*; 21887: *8322, 8499*; 21903: *8380–1, 8385, 8462, 8510*; 21916: *8439*; 21918: *8839*; 21925: *8235, 8301–2, 8363, 8509, 8577–8, 8678, 8680, 8855, 9082*; 22081: *2259*; 22089: *8632*; 22102: *8231, 8289–90, 8348*; 22103: *8196, 8255, 8349*; 22104: *9147*; 22107: *8256–7, 8350, 8366, 8443, 8459, 8581, 8636, 8993*; 22122: *8832*; 22124: *2266, 8657*; 22128: *8177, 8331, 8798*; 22140: *8250*; 22141: *8797, 8799*; 22153: *8557*; 22197: *8395*; 22200: *8493*; 22256: *8558*; 22267: *8207, 8990*; 22309: *8656, 9115*; 22316: *8985*; 22358: *8332*; 22370: *8867*; 22381: *8658*; 22417: *8539*; 22433: *8540*; 22440: *8541*; 22447: *8261*; 22452: *8319, 8374*; 22460: *8830*; 22490: *8262, 8320, 8495, 8620*; 22495: *8461*; 22523: *8542*; 22551: *8776*; 22552: *8878*; 22574: *8321, 8480–1, 8533, 8986, 9086*; 22590: *8929, 8987*; 22660: *2261*; 22668: *8751*; 22679: *2812*; 22714: *8747, 8896*; 22732: *8777*; 22733: *8731*; 22745: *8543*; 22789: *2253*; 22800: *2863*; 22806: *9017*; 22807: *8786*; 22809: *9107*; 22845: *8544, 8902*; 22846: *8621*; 22848: *8545*; 22855: *8779*; 22856: *8778*; 22857: *9058*; 22867: *8879*; 22936: *8749, 8780*; 22941: *8640*; 22956: *8874*; 22970: *8496*; 22988: *8781*;

22996: *8239*; 23062: *8730*; 23111: *8775*; 23292: *8895*; 23366: *8318, 8494*; 23635: *8455*; 23706: *8973*; 23795: *8907*; 24073: *8748*; 24240: *9108*; 24273: *8828*; 24520: *2269*; 24556: *2254*; 24753: *8219*; 24787: *8784*; 24888: *8521*; 24916: *8634*; 25090: *8908*; 25102: *9042*; 25144: *8649*; 25215: *8782*; 25241: *8497, 8925*; 25250: *8771*; 25253: *9026*; 25270: *8174, 9146*; 25276: *8772, 9105*; 25278: *8773*; 25285: *9113*; 25350: *2262, 8783, 8900, 9109*; 25380: *8375*; 25630: *8868*; 25750: *9151*; 25808: *8175, 8641*; 25860: *9110*; 25923: *1843*; 25934: *9077*; 25990: *9085*; 26157: *8247*; 26249: *8785*; 26434: *2260*; 26631: *8638*; 26632: *8729, 9046*; 26715: *8371*; 26721: *8614, 8934*; 26902: *8926*; 26939: *8906*; 27088: *8643, 9144*; 27093: *8186, 8625, 9087*; 27094: *8472*; 27118: *8456*; 27202: *8918*; 27231: *8923*; 27271: *8244*; 27296: *9092*; 27323: *8759*; 27341: *8201*; 27452: *9033*; 27503: *8326, 8482, 8549, 9068*; 27560: *8323*; 27621: *8639, 8943*; 27864: *8194*; 27887: *8651*; 27915: *9025*; 27919: *9075*; 27921: *8647*; 28054: *8382*; 28066: *8935*; 28088: *8377*; 28092: *8204, 8483, 8890, 9076*; 28187: *2258*; 28230: *8384*; 28362: *3033, 8383, 8650*; 28431: *8535*; 28494: *8325*; 28600: *8727*; 28901: *8246*; 28904: *8387, 8831, 8944*; 28912: *8386, 8947*; 28941: *8511*; 28967: *8388, 8891*; 28987: *8624*; 29104: *8574–5, 8854*; 29128: *8807*; 29140: *9065*; 29153: *8842*; 29156: *8361–2, 8475, 8523, 8887, 9050, 9066, 9142*; 29191: *8216*; 29193: *8324, 8379, 8546–7, 9027*; 29262: *8869*; 29263: *8364–5, 8442, 8477, 8679, 8808–9, 8857, 8905*; 29457: *8217*; 29458: *8476*; 29459: *8205, 8501, 8897*; 29462: *9035*; 29463: *8478, 8580, 8681, 8856, 8916*; 29465: *8840, 8858–9, 8912*; 29470: *8245, 8550*; 29562: *8579*; 29623: *2938*; 29736: *8653*; 29778: *8754*; 29835: *8873, 9047, 9078, 9141*; 29840: *9057*; 29841: *8637*; 29844: *8531, 8552*; 29916: *8733*; 29926: *8327, 8485–6, 8628, 8882*; 29930: *8627*; 29931: *8788*; 29939: *8789*; 29954: *8248, 8390, 8484*; 30002: *8378*; 30031: *8616*; 30076: *9106*; 30274: *8238*; 30286: *8617*; 30304: *8644*; 30337: *8314*; 30340: *8746*; 30347: *8871*; 30392: *9073*; 31101: *6646, 9067*; 31195: *8652*; 31279: *8500*; 31304: *8850*; 31534: *8952*; 31595: *8728, 8984*; 32025: *8732*; 32032: *8389*; 32185: *8551*; 32199: *9111*; 32259: *8829*; 32465: *8626*; 32480: *8945*; 32484: *8866, 9024*; 32518: *8915*; 32525: *9112*; 32526: *8976*; 32530: *8220, 8922*; 32549: *8645*; 32585: *8223*; 32589: *8202*; 32676: *2257*; 32742: *8224*; 32751: *8615*; 32872: *9060*; 33144: *8770, 8936*; 34292: *8222*; 34377: *8221*; 34385: *8892*; 34412: *8655, 9079, 9150*; 34428: *8880*; 34612: *8787*; 34663: *8903*; 34703: *8553*; 34758: *8769*; 34787: *8946*; 34801: *8980*; 34877: *9074*; 34882: *9145*; 35012: *8881*; 35060: *8225, 8392, 8654*; 35079: *8629*; 35085: *8512*; 35118: *8391, 8502*; 35137: *8227*; 35147: *8554*; 35225: *8226*; 35249: *8790*; 35264: *8791*; 35300: *8750, 8753*; 35305: *9089*; 35323: *8513, 9088*; 35447: *8555*; 35451: *8236*; 35465: *8964*; 35483: *8526*; 35669: *8752*; 35678: *8927*; 36011: *8981*; 36024: *8971*; 36094: *8883*; 36116: *8630*; 36184: *8200*; 36241: *6645*; 36265: *8538*; 36482: *8792*

Unprovenanced: *6697, 8260, 8313, 8370, 8452–3, 8479, 8525, 8612, 8726, 8827, 8849, 8933, 9137–9*

Watching Brief

1205: *9165*; 1247: *9174*; 1327: *9175*; 1480: *9179*; 1600: *9170*; 1622: *9173*; 1717: *3386*; 1777: *4421*; 1838: *9172*; 1961: *9164*; 1966: *9168*; 2001: *9178*; 2033: *9163, 9171*; 2077: *9169*; 2093: *9167, 9180*

Unprovenanced: *9093, 9176–7, 9181–2*

Castlegate/Coppergate

Unprovenanced: *9183*

22 Piccadilly

1058: *9194*; 2007: *9196*; 2042: *9189, 9197*; 2043: *9190*; 2044: *9191*; 2045: *9200*; 2051: *9192*; 2083: *9198*; 2219: *9185*; 2233: *9201*; 2280: *9199*; 2291: *9184, 9188*; 3130: *9186*; 3130: *9193*; 3136: *9195*; 3178: *9187*

Bedern Foundry

145: *9212*; 2349: *9220*; 2482: *9206*; 2668: *9225*; 2670: *9217*; 2961: *9221*; 2981: *9203*; 4019: *9215*; 4077: *9207*; 4208: *9208, 9222–3*; 4221: *9216*; 4222: *9210–11*; 4224: *9224*; 4227: *9205, 9214*; 4228: *9202, 9209, 9213, 9218–19*; 4277: *9204*

College of the Vicars Choral, Bedern

25: *9233, 9243, 9246*; 1090: *9239*; 1120: *9238*; 1225: *9234*; 1359: *9226–31, 9241*; 1505: *9240*; 1784: *9244–5*; 5342: *9237*; 5501: *9232*; 5508: *9236*

Unprovenanced: *9235; 9242*

Acknowledgements

York Archaeological Trust and the author wish to express their thanks to all those who have helped in the preparation of this fascicule.

The excavation at 16–22 Coppergate was directed by R.A. Hall, with supervision by David T. Evans (1976–81), Shahed Power (1976–8), Mick Humphreys (1976–7) and Ian Lawton (1978–81). Post-excavation work is under the overall direction of R.A. Hall. The excavation was made possible through the generous co-operation of York City Council, the site owners, and the financial support of the then Department of the Environment and a number of generous benefactors and donors.

The excavation at 22 Piccadilly was directed by N.F. Pearson, assisted by R. Finlayson who undertook post-excavation analysis. The project was financed by Wimpey Property Holdings Limited.

The Bedern excavations were initially directed for York Archaeological Trust by B. Whitwell, then by M.J. Daniells, and finally by M. Stockwell. The Foundry site was supervised in 1973 by P. Mills (Trench I) and I. Reed (Trench II), in 1974 by P. Mills, and from 1975–6 by R. Bartkowiak. The latter also conducted some post-excavation ordering of the Foundry site archive. For Bedern south-west and Bedern north-east, initial post-excavation analysis and production of the archive report was undertaken by A. Clarke and M. Stockwell. York Archaeological Trust is most grateful to the original owner of the site, York City Council, and the subsequent owner, Simons of York, and also to the Dean and Chapter of York Minster who own the Chapel, for making the land available for excavation, and for giving every assistance during the work. The excavations were supported by grants from the Department of the Environment, now English Heritage. Many of the excavation assistants were employed on a STEP scheme administered by the Manpower Services Commission, whilst the supervisory staff were financed directly by the Department of the Environment. From 1976–8 the excavation was staffed with DOE-funded excavation assistants and supervisors who were supplemented by Manpower Services Commission Job Creation Programme staff from 1978–9. Later all employees were replaced with MSC Special Temporary Employment Programme personnel although the DOE continued to provide funding for supervision. Until 1979 additional summer help was provided by many hard-working volunteers, students from the University of Pennsylvania and the College of Ripon and York St John, and inmates from HM Open Prison at Askham Bryan.

Thanks are expressed to: Christine McDonnell and the Trust Finds Department staff, especially Bev Shaw, who supervised the transport of artefacts for study and illustration; to the many conservators, students and volunteers who have, over the years, contributed their time, skill and enthusiasm in helping to record and preserve these unique collections of wooden artefacts; to Ian Panter for writing the catalogue entries for casks from 22 Piccadilly (9190–2) and from Bedern (9214–16); to Ailsa Mainman and Sylvia Bowen for their work on the List of Provenances; to Allan Hall and others at the Environmental Archaeology Unit, University of York, for species identification; to Kurt Hunter-Mann and David Evans for help with contextual queries; to Ken Hawley for the loan of old Welsh lathe-turning tools (Fig.1016); to Penelope Walton Rogers for help with the textile tools section; to lathe-turner Gwyndaff Breeze, formerly of the Welsh National Folk Museum; and to Richard Darrah and Jim Spriggs for their friendship and generous sharing of specialist woodworking and conservation knowledge over the years.

The majority of the object illustrations are by Kate Biggs, with others by Charlotte Bentley, Glenys Boyles, Sheena Howarth, Helen Humphreys and Trevor Pearson. The maps, plans, diagrams and distribution plots were produced by Charlotte Bentley, Paula Chew, Simon Chew, Terry Finnemore, Peter Marshall and Graeme Morris. The tables were produced by Graeme Morris. All the illustrations were prepared for publication by Charlotte Bentley, with the assistance of Mike Andrews. The principal photographer was Simon I. Hill, FRPS (Scirebröc). Other photographs were taken by the author (Figs.988–9, 1013, 1016, 1041–2, 1097, 1106, 1113, 1121, 1137, 1156, 1169) or are reproduced with permission from Stadtbibliothek Nürnberg (Fig.984), the Bodleian Library (Figs.1034–5, 1037), the British Library

(Figs.1033, 1036 and 1087), the President and Fellows of Corpus Christi Library, Oxford (Figs.1070–2), Bibliothèque Nationale de France, Paris (manuscript detail on the front cover).

The summary was translated into French by Charlette Sheil-Small and into German by Mrs K. Aberg. This fascicule was edited by Frances Mee, who also prepared the text for publication. The project has been funded and the fascicule published with the assistance of a generous subvention by English Heritage.

Summary

This report presents over 1,500 domestic and utilitarian artefacts made of wood, including complete objects as well as woodworking waste, unfinished products, woodworking tools and boat timbers, from six locations in the city of York. The date range covered by the assemblage is c.850–post-medieval. The bulk of the material is of Anglo-Scandinavian date (c.850–late 11th century) and was recovered from excavations of well-preserved structures and associated features at 16–22 Coppergate, the Coppergate watching brief site and a site excavated in 1906 at the corner of Castlegate/Coppergate. Medieval material from those sites and from the College of the Vicars Choral at Bedern, the Bedern Foundry site and 22 Piccadilly is also included, as is a small amount of late/post-medieval material from some of the sites. Taken together, these sites provide a very detailed picture of the production processes of many different types of wooden artefact, but especially those produced by lathe-turning, and the many uses of different forms and species of wood in the daily life of the people of York over a period of almost a millennium.

The report includes a brief description of the sites from which the material was recovered, and the material itself. This is followed by a discussion of the particular conservation techniques used to preserve these wooden assemblages, and of the specially prepared wet wood laboratory and equipment developed to cope with the conservation of waterlogged wooden objects varying from a few centimetres to several metres in length. On-site retrieval, temporary storage, conservation, reconstruction and permanent archive storage of the artefacts are all discussed.

The rest of the report presents the material in two main sections. The first section, 'Craft and Industry', describes and evaluates the evidence for the production of wooden objects. This involves not only the exploitation of local woodland, various types of woodworking tools and general woodworking techniques, but also the two major vessel-producing crafts of lathe-turning and coopering. Most of the excavated evidence is for the manufacture of lathe-turned wooden bowls and cups during the Anglo-Scandinavian period at 16–22 Coppergate in the form of part of a lathe, roughouts, unfinished discarded vessels, waste products and an iron turning tool. Possible locations of turners' workshops in Coppergate are discussed and their craft linked with the street name 'Coppergate' — 'the street of the cup-turners'. Coopering is mainly represented by finished products.

The second section, 'Everyday Life', presents the extremely wide range of wooden artefact types which were not necessarily made on the sites under discussion, but which were used (and discarded) there for a variety of functions. These include domestic equipment and utensils; boxes and other enclosed containers of various sizes and shapes; furniture such as garderobes and stools; personal items such as pins, combs and wooden-handled knives; manual and agricultural implements from spades, shovels and mattocks to parts of a plough; implements used in the manufacture and handling of fibres and textiles, artefacts used in other non-woodworking crafts such as leatherworking, riding, the handling of rope and cord etc.; wooden components of games and pastimes such as gaming boards and parts of musical instruments; small wooden components of internal or external structures such as roof shingles, window openings, door latches and panels; pegs of various kinds and re-used boat timbers; and miscellaneous wooden artefacts whose uses are as yet unidentifed.

Finally, a short discussion attempts to bring together various general conclusions from the study of this material. A catalogue of all the wooden artefactual material recovered from the sites and a provenance concordance completes the report.

Résumé

Ce rapport présente plus de 1500 objets domestiques et utilitaires, façonnés en bois, y compris des pièces entières ainsi que des déchets de travail du bois, des objets inachevés, des outils pour le travail du bois et des poutres de bateaux, en provenance de six sites dans la ville d'York. L'ensemble couvre des dates allant d'environ 850 à la période postérieure au moyen âge. La plupart du matériel est de date anglo-scandinave (d'environ 850 à la fin du 11ème siècle) et a été récupéré lors de fouilles de structures bien préservées et d'attributs s'y rapportant au 16–22 Coppergate, le site d'observation de Coppergate et un site fouillé en 1906, au coin de Castlegate et de Coppergate. Du matériel médiéval en provenance de ces sites et du College of the Vicars Choral à Bedern, du site de Bedern Foundry et de 22 Piccadilly est également inclus, comme l'est une petite quantité de matériel de la fin du moyen âge et postérieur au moyen âge. Dans leur ensemble, ces sites fournissent un aperçu très détaillé des procédés de production de très nombreux différents types d'objets façonnés en bois, tout particulièrement ceux produits au tour, et des nombreuses utilisations de différentes formes et sortes de bois dans la vie quotidienne des gens d'York, couvrant une période de près d'un millénaire.

Le rapport inclut une brève description des sites où le matériel a été retrouvé ainsi que du matériel lui-même, à la suite duquel une discussion est engagée à propos des techniques de préservation spéciales utilisées pour la préservation de ces ensembles d'objets en bois, ainsi que du laboratoire spécialement préparé pour le bois humide et du matériel développé pour la préservation d'objets en bois trempés, dont les dimensions vont de quelques centimètres à plusieurs mètres de longueur. Ce rapport porte aussi sur la récupération sur place, l'entreposage, la préservation, la reconstruction et le rangement permanent en archive des objets façonnés.

Le reste du rapport présente le matériel en deux sections principales. La première section, 'Artisanat et Industrie', décrit et évalue les indices de production d'objets en bois. Ceci implique non seulement l'exploitation des forêts locales, les divers types d'outils de travail du bois et les techniques générales pour le travail du bois, mais aussi les deux grands métiers de production de récipients, le travail au tour et la fabrication des tonneaux. La plupart des indices récupérés lors des fouilles se rapportent à la fabrication de bols et chopes en bois travaillés au tour pendant la période anglo-scandinave sous la forme d'une partie de tour, d'ébauches, de récipients inachevés mis au rebut, de déchets et un outil de tournage en fer. Le rapport examine des emplacements possibles d'ateliers de tourneurs à Coppergate et les liens entre leur métier et le nom de rue 'Coppergate' — 'la rue des tourneurs de chopes'. La tonnellerie est principalement représentée par des produits finis.

La deuxième section, 'Vie quotidienne', présente une extrêmement large gamme de types d'objets en bois qui n'ont pas forcement été fabriqués sur les sites examinés, mais qui y ont été utilisés (et jetés) à diverses fins. Parmi ceux-ci, se trouvent du matériel domestique et des ustensiles, des boîtes et autres conteneurs fermés de diverses dimensions et formes; des meubles comme des garde-robes et des tabourets; des objets personnels comme des épingles, des peignes et des couteaux à manche en bois; des outils manuels et agricoles allant des bêches, pelles et pioches à des pièces de charrue; des outils utilisés pour la fabrication et le maniement de fibres et de textiles, des objets façonnés utilisés dans d'autres métiers que le travail du bois comme le travail du cuir, la monte d'un cheval, le maniement des cordes et cordons etc.; des éléments en bois de jeux et de passe-temps comme des tableaux de jeu et des parties d'instruments de musique; des petits éléments en bois provenant de structures intérieures ou extérieures comme des bardeaux, des châssis de fenêtre, des clenches et panneaux de porte; des chevilles de diverses sortes et des poutres de bateaux réutilisées; et divers objets façonnés en bois dont les utilisations n'ont pas encore été identifiées.

Finalement, une brève discussion tente de centraliser diverses conclusions générales tirées de l'étude de ce matériel. Un catalogue de tout le matériel d'objets façonnés en bois trouvé dans les sites et une concordance de la provenance complètent ce rapport.

Zusammenfassung

Dieser Bericht legt über 1500 aus Holz gefertigte Artefakte für den häuslichen und allgemeinen Gebrauch vor. Zu diesen gehören komplette Gegenstände sowie Abfälle aus der Holzverarbeitung, halbfertige Produkte, Werkzeuge für die Holzverarbeitung und Bootsplanken. Diese Artefakte stammen aus sechs Grabungsstätten in der City von York. Die Datierung der Sammlung reicht von circa 850 bis in die frühe Neuzeit. Der größte Teil des Materials datiert in die anglo-skandinavische Zeit (circa 850–ausgehendes 11.Jahrhundert) und wurde aus Ausgrabungen von guterhaltenen Bauten und angeschlossenen Anlagen im Gebiet 16–22 Coppergate, dem Areal der Geländebeobachtungen in Coppergate und einer Grabungsstelle aus dem Jahr 1906 an der Ecke von Castlegate und Coppergate sichergestellt. Im Bericht ebenfalls enthalten ist das mittelalterliche Material aus diesen Fundstellen und aus dem College of Vicars in Bedern, der Lokalität der Gießerei in Bedern und der Grabungsstelle 22 Piccadilly sowie eine kleine Menge spät- und nachmittelalterlichen Materials aus einigen dieser Fundstätten. Zusammengenommen bieten diese Fundstellen ein sehr detailiertes Bild der Herstellungsweisen für viele verschiedene Typen von hölzernen Gegenständen, aber ganz besonders im Bezug für die auf der Drehbank hergestellten Artefakte, sowie für den vielseitigen Gebrauch von unterschiedlichen Formen und Holzarten im täglichen Leben der Bevölkerung von York über eine Zeitspanne von beinahe einem Jahrtausend.

Dieser Bericht enthalt eine kurze Beschreibung der Fundstätten aus denen das Material sichergestellt wurde und des Materials selbst. Daran schließt sich eine Diskussion der besonderen Konservierungstechniken an, die benutzt wurden um diese Holzsammlungen zu erhalten. Hinzu kommt die Diskussion des speziell eingerichteten Naßholzlabors und der Apperaturen, die entwickelt wurden, um die Konservierung von durchnäßtem Holz mit Ausmaßen von wenigen Zentimetern bis mehreren Metern in Länge zu ermöglichen. Die Bergung auf der Fundstelle, zeitweilige Aufbewahrung, Konservierung, Rekonstruktion und die langfristige Aufbewahrung der Artefakte im Archiv werden besprochen.

Der Rest des Berichtes stellt das Material unter zwei Hauptthemen vor. Der erste Teil, 'Handwerk und Industrie', beschreibt und bewertet den Befund für die Herstellung von Holzgegenständen. Dazu gehört nicht nur die Nutzung der örtlichen Walder, die verschiedenen Typen von Werkzeugen für die Holzverarbeitung und die allgemeinen Holzverarbeitungstechniken, sondern auch die beiden Haupthandwerke in der Gefäßherstellung — der Gebrauch der Drehbank und die Arbeit des Böttchers. Der größte Teil des Grabungsbefundes bezieht sich auf die Herstellung auf der Drehbank von Holzschüsseln unf Bechern aus der anglo-skandinavischen Zeit auf dem Gebiet von 16–22 Coppergate. Dieser Befund besteht aus einem Teil einer Drehbank, grob ausgefertigten Teilen, halbfertigen unbrauchbaren Gefäßen, Werkstattabfall und einem eisernen Drechslerwerkzeug. Die mögliche Ansiedlung von Drechslerwerkstätten in Coppergate wird diskutiert und ihr Handwerk wird mit dem Straßennamen 'Coppergate' — 'die Gasse der Becherdrechsler' in Verbindung gebracht. Die Böttcherei ist hautsächlich durch Fertigprodukte vertreten.

Der zweite Teil, 'Tägliches Leben', bietet eine außergewöhnlich große Auswahl an Holzartefakten, die nicht unbedingt an Ort und Stelle hergestellt worden sind, die jedoch dort in einer Vielzahl von Anwendungen benutzt (und fortgeworfen) wurden. Zu ihnen gehören Haushaltsgegenstände und Gerätschaften, Schachteln und andere geschlossene Behälter in verschiedenen Größen und Formen; Hausinventar wie etwa Abortplanken und Hocker; persönliches Zubehör wie etwa Nadeln, Kämme und Messer mit Holzgriffen; landwirtschaftliches Gerät von Spaten, Schaufeln, und Breithacken bis zu Teilen eines Pfluges; Gerätschaften für die Herstellung und Behandlung von Fasern und Textilien; Artefakte, die bei der Ausübung von anderen, nicht Holz bearbeitenden Handwerken wie etwa Lederverarbeitung, Reiterei, die Handhabung von Seilen und Leinen usw, benutzt wurden; weiterhin hölzerne Gegenstände für Spiel und Zeitvertreib wie etwa Spielbretter und Teile von Musikinstrumenten; kleine Holzteile für die Innen- und Außenausstattung wie etwa Dachschindel, Fensteröffnungen, Türriegel und Türfüllungen; Holzpflöcke verschiedener Art und wiederverwendete Bootshölzer, außerdem verschiedentliche hölzerne Artefakte, deren Gerauch bisher noch festgestellt worden ist.

Zum Abschluß wird in einer kurzen Diskussion versucht die verschiedenen allgemeinen Schlußfolgerungen aus der Untersuchung dieses Materials zusammenzubringen. Ein Katalog allen hölzernen, bearbeiteten Materials, das aus den Fundstellen geborgen wurde und eine Konkordanz der Provinienz vervollständigen den Bericht.

Glossary

billhook
a woodworking tool in the form of a heavy curved blade with a concave cutting edge; usually tanged and set in a short wooden handle; used for lopping, pruning and general woodworking

butt
thick, back end of a tool such as an axe with a vertical socket hole; opposite end to the blade or cutting edge

cant stave
in a piece-built caskhead or stave-built vessel base, one of the two outer staves with a markedly curved edge, fixed outside the middle staves (q.v.)

celt
name often given in early publications to metal or stone chisel-edged prehistoric implement

chime
projecting rim edge at the end of a cask beyond the caskhead, often cut with a bevel or chamfer

chiming adze
a cooper's tool in the form of a small hand adze with a curved horizontal blade and short wooden handle, used for 'chiming' a cask, i.e. cutting a bevel or chamfer on the end of the staves

chisel (firmer)
a common type of woodworking chisel used for general woodwork; a robust chisel which can be used for heavy work, and can be hit with a mallet

chisel (mortice)
a woodworking chisel particularly suited for cutting mortice holes

chisel (paring)
a fine, delicate woodworking chisel particularly suited for fine paring work where a small amount of material is to be removed; not struck with a mallet, but usually pushed by hand

cross-set teeth
teeth of a saw which (when viewed from above) are 'set' at a very slight angle to the surface of the saw blade; either singly or in groups the 'set' alternates to one side, then the other

croze
a cooper's tool (in the form of a curved wooden block which holds a toothed cutting blade) for cutting the groove in the ends of staves which will receive the caskhead or vessel base; it is swung

around the inside of the vessel, keeping the groove depth constant

drawknife
a woodworking tool with a flat or slightly curved blade, a single-bevelled cutting edge and tangs at both ends of the blade for wooden handles; a shaping tool for quickly removing bark and/or quantities of rough and surplus wood from small objects, or for particular shaping, by pulling the tool towards the worker along the grain

iron
a tool or implement made of iron; turners often referred to their cutting tools as irons

jointer
a cooper's tool in the form of a long, upturned plane down which the long edges of staves are pushed to shave and shape them with the correct 'shot' (or angle) on the edge of the stave to make a particular radius of cask

middle stave
in a piece-built caskhead or stave-built vessel base, one of the inner staves with straight parallel long edges and short curved ends, fixed between the cants (q.v.)

moulding iron
a woodworking tool in the form of a drawknife with a customised, cut-out shaped blade which will cut a particular pattern or 'moulding' along the edge of a length of wood; usually used for mouldings for furniture, buildings and ships etc.

spile
wooden peg or spigot to block a spile hole (q.v.)

spile hole
hole in one of the staves of a caskhead, usually to allow liquid to flow out (cf. vent hole)

spud
a small, narrow metal spade blade for cutting the roots of weeds etc.

twybil, twybill
a specialised medieval woodworking tool used for cutting mortice holes in timber; usually shaped like a double-ended axe-adze with both cutting edges very long and narrow, and a long wooden handle

vent hole
a hole in one of the side staves of a cask which, with the cask on its side, allows air in and allows liquid out through a spile hole (q.v.) in the caskhead

Bibliography

Addyman, P.V. and Hill, D.H., 1969. 'Saxon Southampton: a Review of the Evidence. Part II: Industry, Trade and Everyday Life', *Proc. Hampshire Field Club Archaeol. Soc.* **26**, 61–96

Addyman, P.V. and Priestley, J., 1977. 'Baile Hill, York: A Report on the Institute's Excavations', *Archaeol. J.* **134**, 115–56

Allan, J.P., 1984. *Medieval and Post-Medieval Finds from Exeter, 1971–1980*, Exeter Archaeol. Rep. **3** (Exeter)

Allan, J.P. and Morris, C.A., 1984. 'Wooden Objects' in Allan 1984, 305–15

Ambrose, W., 1971. 'Freeze-drying of swamp-degraded wood' in *Conservation of Stone and Wooden Objects* **2**, 2nd edn, Preprints of New York Conference 1970 (IIC) (London), 53–7

Andersen, H.H., Crabb, P.J. and Madsen, H.J., 1971. *Århus Søndervold: en Byarkeologisk Undersøgelse*, Jysk Arkeologisk Selskabs Skrifter **9** (Århus)

Andersson, O.E., 1930. *The Bowed Harp: A Study in the History of Early Musical Instruments* (London)

Andrews, D.D., 1987. 'Shackerley Mound: A Medieval Moated Site and its Bridge', *Trans. Shropshire Archaeol. Soc.* **65**, 12–32

Anon., 1984. 'Environmental Standards for the Permanent Storage of Excavated Material from Archaeological Sites', Guidelines **3** (UKIC)

Arbman, H., 1939. 'Birka. Sveriges äldsta Handelsstad', *Från Forntid och Medeltid* **1** (Stockholm)

—— 1940a. *Birka 1 Die Gräber* (Stockholm)

—— 1940b. 'Der Årby-Fund', *Acta Archaeologica* **9**, 43–102 (Copenhagen)

Armstrong, P., 1977. *Excavations in Sewer Lane, Hull, 1974*, E. Riding Archaeol. **3**

—— 1980. *Excavations in Scale Lane/Lowgate, 1974*, E. Riding Archaeol. **6**

Armstrong, P. and Ayers, B., 1987. *Excavations in High Street and Blackfriargate*, E. Riding Archaeol. **8**

Armstrong, P., Tomlinson, D. and Evans, D.H., 1991. *Excavations at Lurk Lane, Beverley, 1979–82*, Sheffield Excavation Rep. **1** (Sheffield)

Arrhenius, B., 1978. 'Diskussion Kring Valsgärde 7', *Fornvännen* **73**, 187–93

—— 1983. 'The Chronology of the Vendel Graves' in Lamm and Nordström (eds) 1983, 39–70

Arwidsson, G., 1977. *Välsgarde 7* (Uppsala)

Arwidsson, G. and Berg, G.G., 1983. *The Mästermyr Find: A Viking Age Tool Chest from Gotland* (Stockholm)

Ashbee, P., Bell, M. and Proudfoot, E., 1989. *Wilsford Shaft: Excavations 1960–2*, English Heritage Archaeol. Rep. **11** (London)

Atkinson, D. and Foreman, M., 1992. 'The Leather' in Evans and Tomlinson 1992, 175–87

AY. Addyman, P.V. (ed.). *The Archaeology of York* (London)

8 *Anglo-Scandinavian York (AD 876–1066)*:

    4 R.A. Hall, in prep. Anglo-Scandinavian Structures from 16–22 Coppergate

10 *The Medieval Walled City north-east of the Ouse*

    2 R.A. Hall, H. MacGregor and M. Stockwell, 1988. *Medieval Tenements in Aldwark, and Other Sites*

    6 R.A. Hall and K. Hunter-Mann, in prep. Buildings and Land Use at and around 16–22 Coppergate

11 *The Medieval Defences and Suburbs*:

    1 J.D. Richards, C. Heighway and S. Donaghey, 1989. *Union Terrace: Excavations in the Horsefair*

14 *The Past Environment of York*:

    4 A.R. Hall, H.K. Kenward, D. Williams and J.R.A. Greig, 1983. *Environment and Living Conditions at Two Anglo-Scandinavian Sites*

    7 H.K. Kenward and A.R. Hall, 1995. *Environmental Evidence from 16–22 Coppergate*

16 *The Pottery*:

    3 C.M. Brooks, 1987. *Medieval and Later Pottery from Aldwark and Other Sites*

    5 A.J. Mainman, 1990. *Anglo-Scandinavian Pottery from Coppergate*

17 *The Small Finds*:

    2 A. MacGregor, 1976. *Roman Finds from Skeldergate and Bishophill*

    3 A. MacGregor, 1978. *Anglo-Scandinavian Finds from Lloyds Bank, Pavement, and Other Sites*

    4 D. Tweddle, 1986. *Finds from Parliament Street and Other Sites in the City Centre*

    5 P. Walton, 1989. *Textiles, Cordage and Raw Fibre from 16–22 Coppergate*

    6 P.J. Ottaway, 1992. *Anglo-Scandinavian Ironwork from 16–22 Coppergate*

    7 J. Bayley, 1992. *Anglo-Scandinavian Non-Ferrous Metalworking from 16–22 Coppergate*

    8 D. Tweddle, 1992. *The Anglian Helmet from 16–22 Coppergate*

    11 P. Walton Rogers, 1997. *Textile Production at 16–22 Coppergate*

    12 A. MacGregor, A.J. Mainman and N.S.H. Rogers, 1999. *Craft, Industry and Everyday Life: Bone, Antler, Ivory and Horn from Anglo-Scandinavian and Medieval York*

    14 A.J. Mainman and N.S.H. Rogers, forthcoming. *Craft, Industry and Everyday Life: Anglo-Scandinavian Finds from York*

–   P.J. Ottaway and N.S.H. Rogers, in prep. Craft, Industry and Everyday Life: Medieval Finds from York

–   I. Carlisle, in prep. Craft, Industry and Everyday Life: Leather and Leatherworking from Anglo-Scandinavian and Medieval York

18 The Coins:

1   E.J.E. Pirie, 1986. Post-Roman Coins from York Excavations, 1971–81

Ayers, B., 1987. Excavations at St Martin-at-Palace Plain, Norwich, 1981, E. Anglian Archaeol. 37

Ayers, B. and Murphy, P., 1983. A Waterfront Excavation at Whitefriars Street Car Park, Norwich, 1979, E. Anglian Archaeol. 17, 1–60

Baeksted, A., 1947. 'The Stenmagle Rune Box and the Golden Horn Inscription', Acta Archaeologica 18, 202–10

Baigent, J. (ed.), 1891. Returns, Services and Customs of the Manor of Crondall in the Customal and Rental of St Swithin's Priory, Winchester, Hampshire Record Soc. 3

Baines, A., 1973. 'The Wooden Pipe from Weoley Castle', Galpin Soc. J. 26, 144–5

Baines, P., 1977. Spinning Wheels, Spinners and Spinning (New York)

Baldwin Brown, G., 1915. The Arts in Early England: Vols III and IV, Saxon Art and Industry in the Pagan Period (London)

Barber, J.W. 1981. 'Excavations on Iona, 1979', Proc. Soc. Antiq. Scotland 111, 282–380

—— 1984. 'Medieval Wooden Bowls' in Breeze 1984, 125–47

Barrett, P.L.S., 1980. Hereford Cathedral

Bateman, T., 1861. Ten Years' Digging in Celtic and Saxon Grave Hills in the Counties of Derby, Stafford and York from 1848–1858 (London)

Bell, R.C., 1960. Board and Table Games from Many Civilizations (London)

—— 1980. Discovering Old Board Games (Princes Risborough)

Benson, G., 1906. 'Notes on an Excavation at the Corner of Castlegate and Coppergate', Yorks. Phil. Soc. Ann. Rep. for 1906, 72–6

Bersu, G., 1947. 'The Rath in Townland Lissue, Co. Antrim', Ulster J. Archaeol. 10, 30–58

Biddle, M. (ed.), 1990. Object and Economy in Medieval Winchester, Winchester Studies 7 (2 vols) (Oxford)

Biddle, M., Barfield, L. and Millard, A., 1959. 'Excavation of the Manor of the More, Rickmansworth', Archaeol. J. 116, 136–99

Biddle, M. and Quirk, R.N., 1962. 'Excavations near Winchester Cathedral, 1961', Archaeol. J. 119, 150–94

Birley, R.E., 1977. Vindolanda: A Roman Frontier Post on Hadrian's Wall (London)

Black, M., 1992. The Medieval Cookbook (London)

Blanchette, R.A. and Hoffmann, P., 1993. 'Degradation Processes in Waterlogged Arcahaeological Wood' in P. Hoffmann (ed.), Proc. 5th ICOM Group on Wet Organic Archaeological Materials Conference (Portland, Maine)

Blomqvist, R. and Mårtensson, A.W., 1963. Thulegrävningen 1961, Archaeol. Lundensia 2 (Lund)

Bloom, J.M., 1998. 'The Masterpiece Minbar', Aramco World 49/3, 2–11 (Houston)

Boëles, P.C.J.A., 1951. Friesland, Tot de Elfde Eeuw ('S-Gravenhage)

Bogdan, N.Q., Curteis, A. and Morris, C.A., forthcoming. Perth High Street Archaeological Excavation 1975–77, Fascicule V: The Worked Wood (Oxford)

Boon, G.C., 1974. Silchester: The Roman Town of Calleva (Newton Abbot)

Boothby, C. and Boothby, N., 1980. 'The Bowlmaker. The Turner's Art in Ethiopia', Fine Woodworking 21, 12–13

Bradley, J., 1982. 'A Separate-bladed Shovel from Moynagh Lough, County Meath', J. Royal Soc. Antiq. Ireland 112, 117–22

Brears, P., 1989. North Country Folk Art (Edinburgh)

Breeze, D., 1984. Studies in Scottish Antiquity (Edinburgh)

Brent, J., 1868. 'An Account of the Society's Researches in the Anglo-Saxon Cemetery at Sarre', Archaeol. Cantiana 7, 307–21

Brodribb, A.C.C., Hands, A.R. and Walker, D.R., 1972. Excavations at Shakenoak Farm, near Wilcote, Oxfordshire: Part III, Site F (Oxford)

—— 1973. Excavations at Shakenoak Farm, near Wilcote, Oxfordshire: Part IV, Site C (Oxford)

Brøgger, A.W. and Shetelig, H., 1928. Osebergfundet. Band II: Kongsgaarden (Kristiania)

Bruce-Mitford, R., 1983. The Sutton Hoo Ship-Burial Volume 3 (London)

Bruce-Mitford, R. and Ashbee, P., 1975. The Sutton Hoo Ship-Burial Volume 1 (London)

Bruce-Mitford, R. and Bruce-Mitford, M., 1970. 'The Sutton Hoo Lyre, Beowulf, and the Origins of the Frame Harp', Antiquity 44, 7–13

—— 1983. 'The Musical Instrument' in Bruce-Mitford 1983, 611–726

Bulleid, A. and Gray, H. St G., 1911. The Glastonbury Lake Village. A Full Description of the Excavations and the Relics Discovered, 1892–1907, Vol. I (Glastonbury)

Butler, L.A.S. and Dunning, G.C., 1974. 'Medieval Finds from Castell-y-bere, Monmouth', Archaeol. Cambrensis 123, 78–112

Butler, L.A.S. and Evans, D.H., 1979. 'The Old Vicarage, Conway: Excavations 1963–64', Archaeol. Cambrensis 128, 40–103

Büttner, H., Feger, O. and Meyer, B., 1954. Aus Verfassungs und Landesgeschichte (Festschrift für Theodore Mayer) 1

Carver, M.O.H., 1979. 'Three Saxo-Norman Tenements in Durham City', Medieval Archaeol. 23, 1–81

Casparie, W.A. and Swarts, J.E.J., 1980. 'Wood from Dorestad, Hoogstraat I' in Van Es and Verwers 1980, 262–85

Chapman, H., 1980. 'Roman Wood' in Jones and Rhodes 1980, 128–31

Chauffers, W., 1850. 'On Medieval Earthenware Vessels', *J. Brit. Archaeol. Assoc.* **5**, 22–39

Christensen, A.E., 1985. *Boat Finds From Bryggen*, The Bryggen Papers Main Series **1**, 47–280

Christophersen, A., 1987. *Trondheim — en By i Middelalderen* (Trondheim)

Clarke, C.H.M., 1976. *Notes for the Guidance of Excavation Supervisors and Finds Supervisors* (York Archaeological Trust)

Clarke, H. and Carter, A., 1977. *Excavations in Kings Lynn, 1963–70*, Soc. Medieval Archaeol. Monogr. **7**

Claus, M. et al., 1968. *Studien zur Europäischen Vor- und Frügeschichte* (Neumünster)

Coffey, G., 1906–7. 'Craigywarren Crannog', *Proc. Royal Irish Acad.* **26C6**, 109–18

Colardelle, R. and Colardelle, M., 1980. 'L'Habitat Médiéval Immergé de Colletière, à Charavines (Isère). Premier Bilan des Fouilles', *Archéologie Médiévale* **10**, 167–269

Coles, J.M., Coles, B.J. and Dobson, M.J. (eds), 1990. *Waterlogged Wood: The Recording, Sampling, Conservation and Curation of Structural Wood* (WARP/English Heritage)

Collins, A.E.P., 1955. 'Excavations in Lough Faughan Crannog, Co. Down, 1951–52', *Ulster J. Archaeol.* **18**, 45–82

Collis, J. and Kjølbye-Biddle, B., 1979. 'Early Medieval Bone Spoons from Winchester', *Antiq. J.* **59**, 375–91

Connolly, P. and Van Driel-Murray, C., 1991. 'The Roman Cavalry Saddle', *Britannia* **22**, 33–50

Cook, A., 1981. *The Anglo-Saxon Cemetery at Fonaby, Lincolnshire*, Occ. Papers in Lincs. Hist. and Archaeol. **6**

Cowgill, J., de Neergaard, M. and Griffiths, N., 1987. *Medieval Finds from Excavations in London: 1 Knives and Scabbards* (London)

Cripps, A., 1973. *The Countryman: Rescuing the Past* (Newton Abbot)

Cunliffe, B., 1964. *Winchester Excavations, 1949–1960* 1 (Winchester)

—— 1976. *Excavations at Portchester Castle, Hants, 1961–71. Vol II: Saxon*, Soc. Antiq. London Res. Rep. **33**

Cunningham, W., 1910. *The Growth of English Industry and Commerce* (Cambridge)

Curle, C.L., 1982. *Pictish and Norse Finds from the Brough of Birsay 1934–74*, Soc. Antiq. Scotland Monogr. Ser. **1** (Edinburgh)

Cursiter, J.W., 1885. 'Notice of a Wood-Carver's Tool Box, with Celtic Ornamentation, Recently Discovered in a Peat Moss in the Parish of Birsay, Orkney', *Proc. Soc. Antiq. Scotland* **20**, 47–50

Dalton, O.M., 1923. *A Guide to the Anglo-Saxon and Foreign Teutonic Antiquities in the Department of British and Medieval Antiquities, British Museum* (Oxford)

Darby, H.C. and Maxwell, I.S. (eds), 1962. *The Domesday Geography of Northern England* (Cambridge)

Darrah, R., 1982. 'Working Unseasoned Oak' in McGrail 1982, 219–29

Day, R., 1879–82. 'Pommel of an Ancient Irish Saddle', *J. Royal Soc. Antiq. Ireland* **15**, 345

Desvallées, A., 1976. 'A Propos de l'Invention du Tour à Bois en Auvergne et de l'Invention du Puisoir à Petitlait: Invention Fortuite ou Recherche de Fonctionnalité?', *Revue de la Haute-Auvergne* **45**, 577–600

Donaghey, B.S., 1979. 'A Singular Find; an Unbiased Report', *Interim: Archaeology in York* **6/2**, 33–7

Doppelfeld, O., 1963. 'Die Domgrabung XIV. Das Inventar des Fränkischen Knabengrabes', *Kölner Domblatt* **21–2**, 49–68

Dunning, G.C., 1937. 'A 14th Century Well at the Bank of England, London', *Antiq. J.* **17**, 414–18

—— 1958. 'A Norman Pit at Pevensey Castle, and its Contents', *Antiq. J.* **38**, 205–17

Durbridge, P., 1977–8. 'A Late Medieval Well at Covehithe', *Lowestoft Archaeol. and Local Hist. Soc. Ann. Rep.* **10**

Durham, B., 1977. 'Archaeological Investigations at St Aldates, Oxford', *Oxoniensia* **42**, 83–203

—— 1984. 'The Thames Crossing at Oxford: Archaeological Studies 1979–82', *Oxoniensia* **49**, 57–100

Dyer, J. and Wenham, L.P., 1958. 'Excavations and Discoveries in a Cellar in Messrs. Chas. Hart's Premises, Feasegate, York, 1856', *Yorkshire Archaeol. J.* **39**, 419–25

Dyson, T., 1974. 'Early Development of the Customs, and the Topography and Descent of Wool Quay' in Tatton-Brown 1974, 143–7

Eames, P., 1977. 'Furniture in England, France and the Netherlands from the 12th to the 15th Century', *J. Furniture Hist. Soc.* **13**

Edlin, H.L., 1949. *Woodland Crafts in Britain* (London)

Egan, G. (ed.), 1998. *Medieval Finds from Excavations in London 6: The Medieval Household, Daily Living c.1150–c.1450* (London)

Elsner, H., 1990. *Wikinger Museum Haithabu: Schaufenster einer Frühen Stadt* (Neumünster)

Engelhardt, C., 1869. *Vimosefundet*, Fynske Mosefund **11** (Copenhagen)

Erith, F.H., 1972. 'The Well at Bramford', *Colchester Archaeol. Group Ann. Bull.* **15**, 1–11

Esteban, L., Spriggs, J.A. and Crawshaw, A., 1998. 'Is Acetone/Rosin Treatment for Wood Reversible?', *ICOM/WOAM Newsletter* **29**, 3–4

Estyn Evans, E., 1967. *Irish Heritage* (Dundalk)

Evans, D.H. and Jarrett, M.G., 1987. 'The Deserted Village of West Whelpington, Northumberland: Third Report, Part One', *Archaeol. Aeliana* (5th series) **15**, 199–308

Evans, D.H. and Tomlinson, D.G., 1992. *Excavations at 33–35 Eastgate, Beverley, 1983–6*, Sheffield Excavation Rep. **3** (Sheffield)

Evans, E., 1905. 'Bucket from Ty'r Dewin, Caernarvonshire', *Archaeol. Cambrensis* **5**, 255–6

Evison, V.I., 1968. 'The Anglo-Saxon Finds from Hardown Hill', *Proc. Dorset Nat. Hist. and Archaeol. Soc.* **90**, 232–40

Falk, A., 1981. 'Holzgeräte und Holzgefässe des Mittelalters und der Neuzeit aus Lübeck', *Zeitschrift für Archäologie des Mittelalters* **9**

—— 1983a. 'Holzgeräte und Holzgefässe des Mittelalters und der Neuzeit aus Lübeck', *Zeitschrift für Archäologie des Mittelalters* **11**, 31–48

—— 1983b. 'Hausgeräte aus Holz' in Pohl-Weber 1983, 55–63

Fehring, G.P., 1980. 'Ein Kastenbrunnen aus Eichenbohlen vom Jahre 1155 — Grabungsbefund aus der ehemaligen Burg zu Lübeck', *Brunnenbau Bau von Wasserwerken Rohrleitungsbau* **31.1**, 5–12

Fell, C.E., 1975. 'Old English beor', *Leeds Studies in Old English* **8**, 76–95

Fellows-Jensen, G., 1979. 'The Name Coppergate', *Interim: Archaeology in York* **6/2**, 7–8

Fenton, A. and Myrdal, J. (eds), 1988. *Food and Drink and Travelling Accessories. Essays in Honour of Gösta Berg* (Edinburgh)

Field, R.K., 1965. 'Worcestershire Peasant Buildings, Household Goods and Farming Equipment in the Later Middle Ages', *Medieval Archaeol.* **9**, 105–45

Fiske, W., 1905. *Chess in Iceland* (Florence)

Fitzherbert, J., 1979. *Booke of Husbandrie* (Amsterdam)

Fitzrandolph, H.E. and Hay, M.D., 1926. *The Rural Industries of England and Wales. Vol I: Timber and Underwood Industries and Some Village Workshops* (Oxford)

Foote, P.G. and Wilson, D.M., 1970. *The Viking Achievement* (London)

Foreman, M. and Hall, A., 1991. 'The Wood' in Armstrong et al. 1991, 174–82

Fox, S. (ed.), 1985. *The Medieval Woman. An Illuminated Book of Days* (London)

Freke, D.J., 1978. 'Excavations in Church Street, Seaford, 1976', *Sussex Archaeol. Collections* **116**, 199–224

Friendship-Taylor, D.E., 1984. 'The Leather' in Allan 1984, 323–33

Fuglesang, S.H., 1981. 'Woodcarvers — Professionals and Amateurs — in 11th century Trondheim' in Wilson and Caygill 1981, 21–31

Galloway, P., 1976. 'Note on Descriptions of Bone and Antler Combs', *Medieval Archaeol.* **20**, 154–6

—— 1990. 'Combs of Bone, Antler and Ivory' in Biddle 1990, 665–90

Gaskell-Brown, C. and Brannan, N.F., 1978. 'The Rath in Hillsborough Fort, Co. Down', *Ulster J. Archaeol.* **41**, 78–87

Gelling, M., 1984. *Place Names in the Landscape* (London)

Geraint Jenkins, J., 1978. *Traditional Country Craftsmen* (London)

Gille, B., 1956. 'Machines' in Singer et al. 1956, 629–62

Girling, F.A., 1964. *English Merchants' Marks* (London)

Godwin, H. and Bachem, K., 1959. 'Appendix III: Plant Material' in Richardson 1959, 109–13

Good, G.L. and Tabraham, C.J., 1981. 'Excavations at Threave Castle, Galloway, 1974–78', *Medieval Archaeol.* **25**, 90–140

Goodall, I.H., 1977. 'Iron Objects' in Durham 1977, 142–8

—— 1980. 'The Iron Objects' in Wade-Martins 1980, 509–16

—— 1984a. 'Iron Objects' in Rogerson and Dallas 1984, 77–106

—— 1984b. 'Iron Objects' in Allan 1984, 337–8

—— 1990. 'Woodworking Tools' in Biddle 1990, 273–7

—— 1992. 'The Iron Objects' in Evans and Tomlinson 1992, 151–61

Goodburn, D., 1988. 'Recent finds of ancient boats from the London area', *London Archaeologist* **5/16**, 423–8

—— 1991. 'New light on early ship and boatbuilding in the London area' in G. Good et al. (eds), *Waterfront Archaeology*, Counc. Brit. Archaeol. Res. Rep. **74**, 105–15

—— 1994. 'Anglo-Saxon boat finds from London; are they English?' in C. Westerdahl (ed.), *Crossroads in Ancient Shipbuilding*, ISBSA **6** Roskilde, 97–104

Goodman, W.L., 1964. *The History of Woodworking Tools* (London)

Graham-Campbell, J., 1980. *Viking Artefacts: a Select Catalogue* (London)

—— 1995. *The Viking Age Gold and Silver of Scotland, AD 850–1100* (Edinburgh)

Grandell, A., 1988. *Finds from Bryggen Indicating Business Transactions*, The Bryggen Papers Supp. Series **2**, 66–72 (Oslo)

Greig, J., 1988. 'Plant Resources' in G. Astill and A. Grant (eds), *The Countryside of Medieval England* (Oxford), 108–27

Green, B. and Rogerson, A., 1978. *The Anglo-Saxon Cemetery at Bergh Apton, Norfolk*, E. Anglian Archaeol. Rep. **7** (Gressenhall)

Grew, F. and de Neergaard, M., 1988. *Medieval Finds from Excavations in London: 2 Shoes and Pattens* (London)

Griffiths, R., 1979. 'Rescue Excavation of a Medieval House at Whaddon, Buckinghamshire', *Records Bucks.* **21**, 40–76

Haarnagel, W., 1979. *Die Grabung Feddersen Wierde. Methods, Hausbau, Seidlungs- und Wirtschaftsformen Sowie Sozialstruktur Band II* (Wiesbaden)

Hall, R.A. (ed.), 1978. *Viking Age York and the North*, Counc. Brit. Archaeol. Res. Rep. **27** (London)

—— 1984. *The Viking Dig* (London)

—— 1994. *Viking Age York* (London)

Hamerow, H., 1993. *Excavations at Mucking Volume 2: The Anglo-Saxon Settlement*, English Heritage Archaeol. Rep. **21** (London)

Hassall, T.G., 1976. 'Excavations at Oxford Castle, 1965–1973', *Oxoniensia* **41**, 232–308

Hawkes, J.W. and Heaton, M.J., 1993. *Jennings Yard, Windsor. A Closed-Shaft Garderobe and Associated Medieval Structures*, Wessex Archaeol. Rep. **3** (Salisbury)

Hawkes, S.C., Campbell, J. and Brown, D. (eds), 1984. *Anglo-Saxon Studies in Archaeology and History* **3** (Oxford)

Hawthorne, J.G. and Stanley Smith, C. (trans.), 1979. *Theophilus' On Divers Arts: The Foremost Medieval Treatise on Painting, Glassmaking and Metalwork* (New York)

Heighway, C.M., Garrod, A.P. and Vince, A.G., 1979. 'Excavations at 1 Westgate Street, Gloucester', *Medieval Archaeol.* **23**, 159–213

Hencken, H. O'N., 1936. 'Ballinderry Crannog No.1', *Proc. Royal Irish Acad.* **43C5**

—— 1942. 'Ballinderry Crannog No.2', *Proc. Royal Irish Acad.* **47C1**, 1–76

—— 1950. 'Lagore Crannog: an Irish Royal Residence of the 7th to 10th Centuries AD', *Proc. Royal Irish Acad.* **53C**, 1–247

Henig, M., 1974. 'Medieval Finds' in Tatton-Brown 1974, 189–201

—— 1975. 'Medieval Finds' in Tatton-Brown 1975, 153–4

—— 1976. 'Wood' in Hassall 1976, 270–1

—— 1977. 'Wood' in Durham 1977, 155

Herteig, A.E., 1975. 'Bryggen' in A.E. Herteig, H.E. Liden and C. Blindheim (eds), *Contributions to the Early History of Urban Communities in Norway* (Oslo)

—— 1978. *Handbook to the Cultural History of the Middle Ages — Supplementary to the displays and Exhibits in Bryggen Museum* (Bergen)

Hewett, C.A., 1982. 'Toolmarks on Surviving Works from the Saxon, Norman and Later Medieval Periods' in McGrail 1982, 339–48

Higham, M.C., 1989. 'Some Evidence for 12th- and 13th-century Linen and Woollen Textile Processing', *Medieval Archaeol.* **33**, 38–52

Hill, C., Millett, M. and Blagg, T., 1980. *The Roman Riverside Wall and Monumental Arch in London*, London Middlesex Archaeol. Soc. special paper **3**

Hillam, J.A., 1992. 'Winchester Tree-Ring Chronology and a Medieval Walnut Toilet Seat', *Newsletter Wetland Archaeol. Res. Project* **11**, 16–20

Hodges, H., 1964. *Artefacts. An Introduction to Early Materials and Technology* (London)

Hoffman, M., 1988. 'Textile Implements: Identification in Archaeological Finds and Interpretation in Pictorial Sources' in L. Bender Jørgesen and K. Tidow (eds), *Archaeological Textiles: Report from the 2nd NESAT Symposium, Bergen 1984* (Copenhagen), 232–46

Holdsworth, P., 1976. 'Saxon Southampton: a New Review', *Medieval Archaeol.* **20**, 26–61

Holl, I., 1966. 'Mittelälterliche funde aus einem Brunnen von Buda', *Studia Archaeologica* **4**

Holtzapffel, C., 1846. *Turning and Mechanical Manipulation, Intended as a Work of General Reference and Practical Instruction, on the Lathe, and the Various Mechanical Pursuits Followed by Amateurs Vol II* (5 vols) (London)

Holtzapffel, J.J., 1881. *Turning and Mechanical Manipulation, Intended as a Work of General Reference and Practical Instruction, on the Lathe, and the Various Mechanical Pursuits Followed by Amateurs Vol IV* (5 vols) (London)

Hope, W.H. St J. and Fox, G.E., 1899. 'Excavations on the Site of the Roman City of Silchester, Hants, in 1898', *Archaeologia* **56i**, 103–24

Huetson, T.L., 1983. *Lace and Bobbins*, 2nd edn (Newton Abbot)

Huggins, P.J. and Huggins, R.M., 1973. *Excavation of a Monastic Forge and Saxo-Norman Enclosure, Waltham Abbey, Essex, 1972–3*, Essex Archaeol. and Hist. **5**, 127–84

Hughes, T. McK., 1888–91. 'On Some Antiquities found near Hauxton, Cambs.', *Proc. Cambs. Antiq. Soc.* **7**, 24–8

Hume, A., 1863. *Ancient Meols: Some Accounts of Antiquities found near Dove Point on the Sea Coast of Cheshire* (London)

Hurley, M., 1982. 'Wooden Artfacts from the Excavations of the Medieval City of Cork' in McGrail 1982, 301–11

Innocent, C.F., 1916. *The Development of English Building Construction* (Newton Abbot)

Ivens, R., Bushby, P. and Shepherd, N., 1995. 'Tattenhoe and Westbury. Two Deserted Medieval Settlements in Milton Keynes', *Bucks. Archaeol. Soc. Monogr.* **8**

Jackson, K.H., 1969. *The Gododdin. The Oldest Scottish Poem* (Edinburgh)

Jankuhn, H., 1936. *Die Ausgrabungen in Haithabu, 1935–6*, Offa **1**, 96–140

—— 1943. *Die Ausgrabungen in Haithabu, 1937–39* (Berlin/Dahlem)

Jannsen, W., 1981. 'Die Sattelbeschlage aus Grab 446 des Fränkischen Gräberfeldes von Wesel-Bislich, Kreis Wesel', *Archäologisches Korrespondenzblatt* **11**, 149–69

Jenkinson, H., 1911. 'Exchequer Tallies', *Archaeologia* **62**, 367–80

—— 1925. 'Medieval Tallies, Public and Private', *Archaeologia* **74**, 289–351

Jensen, S., 1991. *The Vikings of Ribe* (Ribe)

Jones, A.K.G., Jones, J. and Spriggs, J.A., 1980. 'Results of a marker Trial', *Conservation News* **11** (UKIC), 6–7

Jones, D.M. and Rhodes, M. (eds), 1980. *Excavations at Billingsgate Buildings 'Triangle', Lower Thames Street, 1974*, London Middlesex Archaeol. Soc. special paper **4**

Jones, J., 1980. 'The Use of Polyurethane Foam in Lifting Large, Fragile Objects on Site', *The Conservator* **4**, 31–3

Jope, E.M., 1949. 'Medieval Pottery Lids and Pots with Lid-seating', *Oxoniensia* **14**, 78–81

—— 1956. 'Agricultural Implements' in Singer et al. 1956, 81–102

Kaminska, J. and Nahlik, A., 1960. 'Etudes sur l'Industrie Textile du Haut Moyen Age en Pologne', *Archaeol. Polona* **3**, 89–119

Keene, D., 1990. 'Shingles; Whipping Top; Butter Churn; Wooden Vessels; Wooden Furniture; Unidentified Wooden Objects' in Biddle 1990, 320–6, 706, 817, 959–66, 969–70, 1147–50

Kendrick, T.D. and Senior, E., 1937. 'St Manchan's Shrine', *Archaeologia* **86**, 105–18

Kenward, H.K., Williams, D., Spencer, P.J., Greig, J.R.A., Rackham, D.J. and Brinklow, D., 1978. 'The Environment of Anglo-Scandinavian York' in Hall 1978, 58–73

Kilby, K., 1971. *The Cooper and His Trade* (London)

Kjølbye-Biddle, B., 1990. 'Early Medieval Spoons' in Biddle 1990, 828–31

Klindt-Jensen, O., 1970. *The World of the Vikings* (London)

Kolchin, B.A., 1968. 'Novgorod Excavations — the Wooden Artifacts', Archaeology of USSR E-155 (Moscow)

—— 1989. *Wooden Artefacts from Medieval Novgorod*, Brit. Archaeol. Rep. Int. Ser. **495**

Kolchin, B.A. and Linder, I.M., 1961. 'Shakhmaty v Drevnem Novgorode' in *Shakhmaty v SSSR* **8** (Moscow)

Kolltveit, G., 1997. 'Traces of the Medieval Musical Life: Two Bridges excavated in Gamlebyen, Oslo', *Viking* **LX**, 70–83 (Oslo)

Kostrzewski, J., 1949. *Les Origines de la Civilisation Polonaise*, Publs. de l'Institut Occidental **1** (Paris)

Kramer, K., 1960. 'Bericht über Neuere Untersuchungen im Salzberg zu Hallstatt', *Mitteil. d'Anthrop. Ges. Wien* **90**, 33–8

Krogh, K.J. and Voss, O., 1961. *Fra Hedenskab til Kristendom*, Fra Nationalmuseets Arbejdsmark (Copenhagen)

Lamm, J.P. and Nordström, H.-A. (eds), 1983. *Vendel Period Studies 2*, Transactions of the Boat Grave Symposium in Stockholm, February 2–3, 1981 (Stockholm)

Lang, J.T., 1984. 'The Hogback: A Viking Colonial Monument' in Hawkes et al. 1984, 85–176

—— 1988. 'Viking-Age Decorated Wood. A Study of its Ornament and Style', *Medieval Dublin Excavations 1962–81 Series B Vol.1* (Dublin)

Lasko, P., 1971. *The Kingdom of the Franks: North West Europe before Charlemagne* (London)

Lawson, R.G., 1978. 'The Lyre from Grave 22' in Green and Rogerson 1978, 87–97

—— 1981. (unpublished) *Stringed Musical Instruments; Artefacts in the Archaeology of Western Europe 500 BC to AD 1200*, Ph.D. thesis, University of Cambridge

—— 1990. 'Pieces from Stringed Instruments' in Biddle 1990, 711–18

Leeds, E.T., 1923. 'A Saxon village at Sutton Courtenay, Berkshire', *Archaeologia* **73**, 147–92

Leeds, E.T. and Harden, D.B., 1936. *The Anglo-Saxon Cemetery at Abingdon, Berks* (Oxford)

Lefebvre, G., 1923. *Le Tombeau de Petosiris* (Paris)

Le Patourel, H.E.J., 1976. 'Pottery as Evidence for Social and Economic Change' in Sawyer 1976, 169–79

Lerche, G., 1970. 'The Cutting of Sod and Heather Turf in Denmark' in A. Gailey and A. Fenton (eds), *The Spade in Northern and Atlantic Europe* (Belfast), 148–54

Lethbridge, T.C., 1931. *Recent Excavations in Anglo-Saxon Cemeteries in Cambridgeshire and Suffolk* (Cambridge)

—— 1933. 'Anglo-Saxon Burials at Soham, Cambs', *Proc. Cambs. Antiq. Soc.* **33**, 152–63

Lethbridge, T.C. and Tebbutt, C.F., 1933. 'Huts of the Anglo-Saxon Period', *Proc. Cambs. Antiq. Soc.* **33**, 133–51

Lewis, J.M., 1968. 'The Excavation of the "New Building" at Montgomery Castle', *Archaeol. Cambrensis* **117**, 127–56

Linder, I.M., 1975. *Chess in Rus* (Moscow)

Ling Roth, H., 1909. *Hand Woolcombing*, County Borough of Halifax, Bankfield Museum Notes **6** (Halifax)

Lucas, A.T., 1953–4. 'Two Recent Bog Finds', *J. Galway Archaeol. Hist. Soc.* **25**, 86–9

—— 1978. 'The "Gowl-Gob": an Extinct Spade Type from Co. Mayo, Ireland' in *Tools and Tillage* 3/3, 191–9

Lynn, C.J., 1978. 'A Rath in Seacash Townland, Co. Antrim', *Ulster J. Archaeol.* **41**, 55–74

McCann, B. and Orton, C., 1989. 'The Fleet Valley Project', *London Archaeologist* **6/4**, 102–7

MacGregor, A., 1978. 'Industry and Commerce' in Hall (ed.) 1978, 37–57

McGrail, S., 1977. 'Axe, Adze, Hoe or Slice?', *Internat. J. Nautical Archaeol.* **6**, 62–4

—— (ed.), 1982. *Woodworking Techniques Before 1500 A.D.*, Brit. Archaeol. Rep. **S129**

McKerrell, H., Roger, E., and Varsanyi, A., 1972. 'The Acetone/Rosin Method for Conservation of Waterogged Wood', *Studies in Conservation* **17** (IIC), 111–25

McNeil Sale, R., 1981. 'Nantwich', *Current Archaeol.* **77**, 185–7

MacManus, M. 1983. 'Joseph Hughes: an Armagh Woodturner' in *Tools and Trades* **1**, 43–8

Magnusson, M., 1976. *Hammer of the North* (London)

Manning, W.H., 1973–4. 'Excavations on Late Iron Age, Roman and Saxon Sites at Ufton Nervet, Berkshire in 1961–63', *Berks. Archaeol. J.* **67**, 1–61

Manning, W.H. and Saunders, C., 1972. 'A Socketed Axe from Maids Moreton, Buckinghamshire, with a Note on the Type', *Antiq. J.* **52**, 276–92

Margeson, S. (ed.), 1993. *Norwich Households: The Medieval and Post-Medieval Finds from Norwich Survey Excavations 1971–78*, E. Anglian Archaeol. **58** (Gressenhall)

Marsden, P.R.V., 1966. *A Ship of the Roman Period, from Blackfriars, in the City of London*, Guildhall Museum Publication (London)

—— 1994. *Ships of the Port of London, First to Eleventh Centuries AD* (London)

—— 1996. *Ships of the Port of London, Twelfth to Seventeenth Centuries AD* (London)

Mellor, J.E. and Pearce, T., 1981. *The Austin Friars, Leicester*, Counc. Brit. Archaeol. Res. Rep. **35** (London)

Moorhouse, S., 1978. 'Documentary Evidence for the Uses of Medieval Pottery: an Interim Statement', *Medieval Ceramics* **2**, 3–22

Morris, C.A., 1979. 'The Wooden Objects' in Heighway et al. 1979, 197–200

—— 1980a. 'A Group of Early Medieval Spades', *Medieval Archaeol.* **24**, 205–10

—— 1980b. 'Wooden Objects' in Palmer 1980, Microfiche C12

—— 1981. 'Early Medieval Separate-Bladed Shovels from Ireland', *J. Royal Soc. Antiq. Ireland* **111**, 50–69

—— 1982. 'Aspects of Anglo-Saxon and Anglo-Scandinavian Lathe-turning' in McGrail 1982, 245–61

—— 1983a. 'The Wooden Objects' in C.M. Heighway, *The East and North Gates of Gloucester and Associated Sites. Excavations 1974–81*, Western Archaeol. Trust Monogr. **4** (Bristol), 206–10

—— 1983b. 'A Late Saxon Hoard of Iron and Copper-alloy Artifacts from Nazeing, Essex', *Medieval Archaeol.* **27**, 27–39

—— 1984a. (unpublished) *Anglo-Saxon and Medieval Woodworking Crafts: the Manufacture and Use of Domestic and Utilitarian Wooden Artifacts in the British Isles, 400–1500 AD*, Ph.D. thesis, University of Cambridge

—— 1984b. 'The Wooden Objects' in Durham 1984, 74–6 and Microfiche E04

—— 1987. 'Wooden Artefacts' in Andrews 1987, 25–6

—— 1990a. 'Wooden Finds from Enclosure 1 and Well 1' in Wrathmell and Nicholson 1990, 206–23

—— 1990b. 'Recording Ancient Timbers: The Technologist's View' in Coles et al. 1990, 9–15

—— 1992. 'Mill Paddles from Nailsworth, Gloucestershire and the Wooden Bowl from Tamworth' in Rahtz and Meeson 1992, 102–7

—— 1993a. 'Furniture and Household Equipment — Wooden Vessels and Spoons; Occupations, Industry and Crafts — Wooden Awl Handle and Shovel' in Margeson 1993, 95–6, 136–7, 190–1 and 195

—— 1993b. 'Tools' in Hamerow 1993, 69–70

—— 1993c. 'Wooden Artefacts and Off-Cuts' in Hawkes and Heaton 1993, 60–2

—— 1994. 'Finds Connected with Wooden Artefacts, Woodworking and Other Tools' in C. Hills et al., *The Anglo-Saxon Cemetery at Spong Hill, North Elmham Part V: Catalogue of Cremations and Specialist Reports*, E. Anglian Archaeology 67, 30–5

—— 1998. 'The Wooden Artefacts' in H.E.M. Cool and C. Philo (eds), *Roman Castleford Excavations 1974–85. Volume 1, The Small Finds*, Yorkshire Archaeol. **4** (Wakefield), 335–46

—— 1999. 'Late Norse and Medieval Woodworking and Wooden Artefacts and Products' in B.E. Crawford and B. Ballin Smith (eds), *The Biggings, Papa Stour, Shetland: The History and Excavation of a Royal Norwegian Farm*, Soc. Antiq. Scotland / Det Norske Videnskaps Akademi Monogr. Series **15** (Edinburgh), 182–93

—— forthcoming a. '17th Century Wooden Artefacts and Woodworking Report from Excavations at St Paul-in-the-Bail, Lincoln', *Post-Medieval Archaeol.*

—— forthcoming b. 'A Saxo-Norman Burrwood Bowl from Hemington, Leics' in P. Clay (ed.) *Trans. Leics. Archaeol. and Hist. Soc.*

—— forthcoming c. 'Wooden Artefacts and Other Turned Items from Pontefract Castle', *Yorkshire Archaeol.* (Wakefield)

Morris, C.A. and Evans, D.H., 1992. 'The Wood' in Evans and Tomlinson 1992, 189–209

Murray, H.J.R., 1913. *History of Chess* (Oxford)

—— 1952. *A History of Board Games Other than Chess* (Oxford)

Musty, J. and Manning, W.H., 1977. 'A Wooden Box from the Roman Villa at Bradwell, Milton Keynes, Bucks.', *Antiq. J.* **57**, 330–2

Myrdal, J., 1988. 'The Plunge Churn from Ireland to Tibet' in Fenton and Myrdal 1988, 111–37

Myres, J.N.L. and Dixon, P.H., 1988. 'A Nineteenth-Century Grubenhaus on Bucklebury Common, Berkshire', *Antiq. J.* **68**, 115–22

Mårtensson, A.W. (ed.), 1976. *Uppgrävt Förflutet för PKbanken i Lund. E Investering i Arkeologi*, Archaeol. Lundensia **7** (Lund)

Mårtensson, A.W. and Wahlöö, C., 1970. *Lundafynd: en Bilderbok*, Archaeol. Lundensia **4**

National Museum of Ireland, 1973. *Viking and Medieval Dublin. Catalogue of Exhibition: National Museum Excavations 1962–73* (Dublin)

Nelson, P., 1936. 'An Ancient Boxwood Casket', *Archaeologia* **86**, 91–100

Neugebauer, W., 1953–5. 'Eine Drechslerwerkstatt in Alt-Lubeck aus der Zeit um 1100', *Hammaburg* **9/10**, 71–8

—— 1954. 'Typen Mittelalterliche Holzgeschirrs aus Lübeck' in *Frühe Burgen und Städte. Beiträge zur Burgen- und Stadtkernforschung. Festschrift fr W. Unverzagt, Deutsche Akad. der Wissenschaft, Berlin, Schriften der Sekt. für Vor- und Frühgeschichte* **2**, 174–90

—— 1973. 'Arbeiten der Böttcher und Drechsler aus den Mittelalterliche Bodenfunde der Hansestadt Lübeck', *Rotterdam Papers* **2**, 117–37

Neville, R.C., 1852. *Saxon Obsequies, Illustrated by Ornaments and Weapons from the Cemetery near Little Wilbraham, Cambs* (Cambridge)

Nicolaysen, N., 1882. *Langskibet fra Gokstad ved Sandefjord* (Kristiania)

Nilsson, T., 1976. 'Stadsbornas bin Aringar: Jordbruk, Jakt och Fiske' and 'Något om Hushållet och Dess Inventarium' in Mårtensson (ed.) 1976, 223–8 and 233–50

Nørlund, P., 1948. 'Trelleborg', *Nordiske Fortidsminder* **4**, 1

O'Brien, M., 1978. *Viking Settlement to Medieval Dublin* (Dublin)

Ó Ríordáin, B., 1971. 'Excavations at High Street and Wine-tavern Street, Dublin', *Medieval Archaeol.* **15**, 73–85

Ó Ríordáin, S.P., 1940. 'A Pole-lathe from Borrisokane, Co. Tipperary', *J. Cork Hist. Archaeol. Soc.* **45**, 28–32

Organ, R.M., 1959. 'Carbowax and Other Materials in the Treatment of Waterlogged Paleolithic Wood', *Studies in Conservation 4* (IIC), 96–105

Ottaway, P., 1981. 'Castle Garage', *Interim: Archaeology in York* **8**/1, 14–19

Palliser, Bury, Mrs, 1911. *History of Lace* 4th edn (New York)

Palmer, N., 1980. 'A Beaker Burial and Medieval Tenements in the Hamel, Oxford', *Oxoniensia* **45**, 124–225 and microfiche

Patterson, R., 1955. 'Hand Distaffs from Lough Faughan, Lagore and Ballinderry Crannogs', *Ulster J. Archaeol.* **18**, 81–2

—— 1956. 'Spinning and Weaving' in Singer et al. (eds) 1956, 191–220

Paulsen, P. and Schach-Dörges, H., 1972. *Holzhandwerk des Alamannen* (Stuttgart)

Peate, I.C., 1935. *Guide to the Collection Illustrating Welsh Folk Crafts and Industries* (Cardiff)

Perring, D., 1981. *Early Medieval Occupation at Flaxengate, Lincoln, Archaeology of Lincoln* **9**/1

Persson, J., 1976. 'Spel och Dobbel' in Mårtensson 1976, 379–82

Petersen, J., 1951. *Vikingetidens Redskaper* (Oslo)

Phillips, D. and Heywood, B., 1995. *Excavations at York Minster 1: From Roman Fortress to Norman Cathedral* (HMSO, London)

Pilloy, J., 1889. *Études sur d'Anciens Lieux de Sepultures dans l'Aisne* (Saint Quentin)

Pinto, E.H., 1949. *Treen or Small Woodware Throughout the Ages* (London)

Pirling, R., 1974. *Das Römisch-fränkische Gräberfeld von Krefeld-Gellep 1960–63* (Berlin)

Platt, C. and Coleman-Smith, R., 1975. *Excavations in Medieval Southampton 1953–1969. Vol 2: The Finds* (Leicester)

Plenderleith, H.J. and Werner, A.E.A., 1971. *The Conservation of Antiquities and Works of Art* (Oxford)

Pohl-Weber, R., 1983 (ed.). *Aus dem Alltag der Mittelalterlichen Stadt* (Bremen)

Power, E., 1941. *The Wool Trade in English Medieval History* (Oxford)

Pritchard, F., 1991. 'Small Finds' in Vince 1991, 120–278

Pritchard, F. and Morris, C.A., 1991. 'Wooden Artefacts' in Pritchard 1991, 240–6

Rackham, O., 1975. *Hayley Wood: Its History and Ecology* (Cambridge)

—— 1976. *Trees and Woodland in the British Landscape* (London)

—— 1980. *Ancient Woodland: its History, Vegetation and Uses in England* (London)

—— 1982. 'The Growing and Transport of Timber and Underwood' in McGrail 1982, 199–218

Radley, J. and Simms, C., 1971. *Yorkshire Flooding: Some Effects on Man and Nature* (York)

Rahtz, P. and Meeson, R., 1992. *An Anglo-Saxon Watermill at Tamworth*, Counc. Brit. Archaeol. Res. Rep. **83** (London)

Ralegh Radford, C.A., Jope, E.M. and Tonkin, J.W., 1973. 'The Great Hall of the Bishop's Palace at Hereford', *Medieval Archaeol.* **17**, 78–86

Reinach, T., 1906–7. 'La "Flûte de Pan" d'Alesia', *Pro Alesia* **1**, 161–9, 180–5

Reinach, T., 1907–8. 'Note Additionelle à la Flûte de Pan d'Alesia', *Pro Alesia* **2**, 201–2

Rhodes, M., 1980. 'Wood and Woody Tissue' in Jones and Rhodes 1980, 144

Richardson, K.M., 1959. 'Excavations in Hungate, York' *Archaeol. J.* **116**, 51–114

Roach Smith, C., 1857. *Collectanea Antiqua IV*

Robinson, P., 1973. 'A small wooden dish of medieval date near Stafford', *Staffordshire Archaeol.* **2**, 4–5

Roesdahl, E., 1977. *Fyrkat, en Jysk Vikingeborg. Vol II: Oldsagerne og Gravpladsen* (Copenhagen)

—— 1982. *Viking Age Denmark* (London)

Roesdahl, E., Graham-Campbell, J., Connor, P. and Pearson, K. (eds), 1981. *The Vikings in England* (London)

Rogers, J.E.T., 1866. *A History of Agriculture and Prices in England, Volume I: 1259–1400* (Oxford)

Rogerson, A. and Dallas, C., 1984. *Excavations in Thetford 1948–59 and 1973–80*, E. Anglian Archaeol. Rep. **22** (Gressenhall)

Rudenko, S.I., 1970. *Frozen Tombs of Siberia. The Pazyryk Burials of Iron Age Horsemen* (London)

Rudstrom, J., 1983. 'Turning Tools that Cut', *Fine Woodworking for 1983*, 92–4

Rybina, E.A., 1992. 'Recent Finds from Excavations in Novgorod', *Soc. Medieval Archaeol. Monogr.* **13**, 160–92

Rygh, O., 1885. *Norske Oldsager* (Kristiania)

Salzman, L.F., 1967. *Building in England down to 1540* (Oxford)

Saunders, A.D., 1980. 'Lydford Castle, Devon', *Medieval Archaeol.* **24**, 123–86

Savory, H.N., 1960. 'Excavations at Dinas Emrys, Beddgelert, Caernarvonshire, 1954–6', *Archaeol. Cambrensis* **109**, 13–77

Sawyer, P.H. (ed.), 1976. *Medieval Settlement: Continuity and Change* (London)

Schia, E., 1977. 'Sko som Arkeologisk Kildemateriale', *Hikuin 3*, 303–24

Schia, E. and Molaug, P.B. (eds), 1990. *De Arkeologiske Utgravninger i Gamlebyen, Oslo. Bind 7: Dagliglivets Gjenstander-Del 1* (Øvre Ervik)

Schietzel, K., 1970. 'Holzerne Kleinfunde aus Haithabu: Ausgrabung 1963–64' in K. Schietzel (ed.), *Berichte über die Ausgrabungen in Haithabu* **B4** (Neumünster)

Schmidt, H., 1973. 'The Trelleborg House Reconsidered', *Medieval Archaeol.* **17**, 52–77

Scobie, G.D., Zant, J.M. and Whinney, R., 1991. 'The Brooks, Winchester. A Preliminary Report on the Excavations 1987–88', *Winchester Museums Service Archaeol. Rep.* **1** (Winchester)

Sheppard, T., 1939. 'Viking and Other Relics at Crayke, Yorkshire', *Yorkshire Archaeol. J.* **34**, 273–81

Simpson, W.G., 1972. 'A Gaming Board of Ballinderry-Type from Knockanboy, Derrykeighan, Co. Antrim', *Ulster J. Archaeol.* **35**, 63–4

Singer, C., Holmyard, E.S., Hall, A.R. and Williams, T.I. (eds), 1956. *A History of Technology. Volume II: The Mediterranean Civilisations and the Middle Ages c.700 BC to AD 1500* (London)

Small, A., 1964–6. 'Excavations at Underhoull, Unst, Shetland', *Proc. Soc. Antiq. Scotland* **98**, 225–48

Smith, R., 1907–9. 'Notes on Some Objects of the Viking Period, Recently Discovered in York', *Proc. Soc. Antiq. London* (2nd series) **22**, 5–9

Sordinas, A., 1978. 'The Ropas Plough from the Island of Corfu, Greece' in *Tools and Tillage* 3/3, 139–49

Soren, D., 1988. 'The Day the World ended at Kourion: Reconstructing an Ancient Earthquake', *National Geographic* **174/1**, 30–53

Spannagel, F., 1940. *Das Drechslerwerk* (Ravensburg)

Sparkes, I.G., 1977. *Woodland Craftsmen* (Princes Risborough)

Spearman, R.M., 1995. 'The wooden "bowl" found with the Burray hoard, Orkney' in Graham-Campbell 1995, 141–2

Spriggs, J.A., 1977. 'Roll out the Barrel', *Interim: Archaeology in York* 4/4, 11–15

—— 1980. 'The Recovery and Storage of Waterlogged Material from York, *The Conservator* **4**, 19–24

—— 1981. 'Filling a Gap', *Conservation News* **15** (UKIC), 7–8

—— 1982. 'The Conservation of Timber Structures at York — a Progress Report' in D.W. Grattan (ed.), *Proc. ICOM Waterlogged Wood Working Group Conference* (Ottawa)

—— 1991. 'The Treatment, Monitoring and Display of Viking Structures at York' in P. Hoffmann (ed.), *Proceedings of the 4th ICOM Group on Wet Organic Archaeological Materials Conference* (Bremerhaven), 53

Stamper, P.A., 1979. 'Wood' in Griffiths 1979, 66–9

Stenton, D.M., 1952. *English Society in the Early Middle Ages (1066–1307)* (Harmondsworth)

Stenton, F., 1957. *The Bayeux Tapestry: a Comprehensive Survey* (London)

Stevens, J., 1884. 'On the Remains found in an Anglo-Saxon Tumulus at Taplow, Bucks', *J. Brit. Archaeol. Assoc.* **40**, 61–71

Stevenson, R.B.K., 1951–2. 'A Celtic Carved Box from Orkney', *Proc. Soc. Antiq. Scotland* **86**, 187–90

Strutt, J., 1830. *The Sports and Pastimes of the People of England* (London)

Swanton, M., 1973. *Spearheads of the Anglo-Saxon Settlement* (London)

Sweetman, P.D., 1978. 'Archaeological Excavations at Trim Castle, Co. Meath, 1971–74', *Proc. Royal Irish Acad.* **78C6**, 127–98

Szabo, M., Grenander-Nyberg, G. and Myrdal, J., 1984. *Elisenhof in Eiderstedt: Die Holzfunde* (Frankfurt-am-Main)

Tatton-Brown, T., 1974. *Excavations at the Custom House Site, City of London, 1973*, Trans. London Middlesex Archaeol. Soc. **25**

—— 1975. *Excavations at the Custom House Site, City of London, 1973: part 2*, Trans. London Middlesex Archaeol. Soc. **26**

Taylor, M., 1981. 'Wood in Archaeology', *Shire Archaeol.* **17** (Princes Risborough)

Thomas, G.W., 1887. 'Excavations in an Anglo-Saxon Cemetery at Sleaford, Lincs', *Archaeologia* **50ii**, 384–406

Thomas, S., 1980. *Medieval Footwear from Coventry. A Catalogue of the Collection of Coventry Museums* (Coventry)

Thompson, M.W., 1956. 'A Group of Mounds on Seasalter Level near Whitstable and the Medieval Imbanking in this Area', *Archaeol. Cantiana* **70**, 44–67

—— 1967. *Novgorod the Great: Excavations at the Medieval City* (London)

Thurley, S., 1993. *The Royal Palaces of Tudor England: Architecture and Court Life 1460–1547* (New Haven and London)

Treue, W. et al., 1965. *Das Hausbuch der Mendelschen Zwölfbrüderstiftung zu Nürnberg (2 vols)* (Munich)

Treveil, P. and Rowsome, P., 1998. 'Number 1 Poultry — the Main Excavation: Late Saxon and Medieval Sequence', *London Archaeologist* **8/11**, 283–91

Tweddle, D., 1988. 'Ringerike', *Interim: Archaeology in York* **12/4**, 27–30

Ulbert, G., 1961. 'Ein Römischer Brunnenfund von Barbing-Kreuzhof (Ldkr. Regensburg)', *Bayerische Vorgeschichtsblätter* **26/1**, 48–60

Vandenberghe, S., 1981. 'Houten Gebruiksvoorwerpen in Vlaanderen: Mechelen', *Stads Archeologie* **5/1**, 27–34

Van Es, W.A., 1967. *Wijster: a Native Village Beyond the Imperial Frontier 150–425 AD*, Palaeohistoria **11**

—— 1968. *Excavation of Frustrated Terps 200 BC–250 AD*, Palaeohistoria **14**, 187–352

Van Es, W.A. and Verwers, W.J.H., 1980. *Excavations at Dorestad: 1. The Harbour in Hoogstraat*, R.O.B. Nederlandse Oudheden **9**

Vierck, H., 1972. 'Prunksattel aus Gellep und Ravenna', *Archäologisches Korrespondenzblatt* **2**, 213–17

Vince, A.G. (ed.), 1991. *Aspects of Saxon and Norman London 2: Finds and Environmental Evidence*, London Middlesex Archaeol. Soc. special paper **12**

Wade-Martins, P., 1980. *Excavations in North Elmham Park 1967–72*, E. Anglian Archaeol. **9** (Gressenhall)

Walton, J., 1954. 'Hogback Tombstones and the Anglo-Danish House', *Antiquity* **28**, 68–77

Ward Perkins, J.B., 1940. *London Museum Medieval Catalogue* (London)

Warhurst, A., 1955. 'The Jutish Cemetery at Lyminge', *Archaeol. Cantiana* **69**, 1–40

Waterman, D.M., 1954. 'Excavations at Clough Castle, Co. Down', *Ulster J. Archaeol.* **17**, 103–63

—— 1959. 'Late Saxon, Viking and Early Medieval Finds from York', *Archaeologia* **97**, 59–105

—— 1971. 'A Marshland Habitation Site near Larne, Co. Antrim', *Ulster J. Archaeol.* **34**, 65–76

Watkin, J., 1987. 'Objects of Wood' in Armstrong and Ayers 1987, 209–16

Weber, B., 1990. 'Tregjenstander' in Schia and Molaug (eds) 1990, 11–180

Webster, L.E. and Cherry, J., 1972. 'Medieval Britain in 1971', *Medieval Archaeol.* **16**, 147–212

—— 1973. 'Medieval Britain in 1972', *Medieval Archaeol.* **17**, 138–88

Werner, J., 1954. 'Leier und Harfe im Germanischen Frühmittelalter' in Büttner et al. 1954, 9–15

—— 1964. 'Frankish Royal Tombs in the Cathedrals of Cologne and St Denis', *Antiquity* **38**, 201–16

West, S., 1985. *West Stow: The Anglo-Saxon Village*, E. Anglian Archaeol **24** (Ipswich)

Westwood, J.O., 1876. 'The "Hopkins" Casket', *Archaeol. J.* **33**, 399–400

Wharton, A., 1978. *Excavation of the 14th Century Well at Tong Castle, Shropshire*, Tong Archaeol. Group Rep. **1**

Wheeler, R.E.M., 1927. *London and the Vikings London Museum Catalogue 1* (London)

Whitelock, D., 1930. *Anglo-Saxon Wills* (Cambridge)

Whiting, G., 1928. *Tools and Toys of Stitchery* (New York)

Wild, J.P., 1970. *Textile Manufacture in the Northern Roman Provinces* (Cambridge)

—— 1988. *Textiles in Archaeology* (Princes Risborough)

Williams, J.H., 1979. *St Peters's Street, Northampton. Excavations 1973–76* (Northampton)

Williams, V., 1987. 'Wooden Objects' in Ayers 1987, 108

Wilson, D.M., 1960. *The Anglo-Saxons* (Harmondsworth)

—— 1964. *Anglo-Saxon Ornamental Metalwork 700–1100 in the British Museum* (London)

—— 1968. 'Anglo-Saxon Carpenters' Tools' in Claus et al. 1968, 143–50

—— 1970. 'An Anglo-Saxon Playing Piece from Bawdsey', *Proc. Suffolk Instit. Archaeol.* **32**, 38–42

—— 1976. *The Archaeology of Anglo-Saxon England. Chapter 6: Craft and Industry* (Cambridge)

—— 1984. *Anglo-Saxon Art* (London)

—— 1985. *The Bayeux Tapestry* (London)

Wilson, D.M. and Caygill, M.L., 1981. *Economic Aspects of the Viking Age*, British Museum Occasional Paper **30** (London)

Wilson, D.M. and Hurst, D.G., 1966. 'Medieval Britain in 1965', *Medieval Archaeol.* **10**, 168–219

—— 1969. 'Medieval Britain in 1968', *Medieval Archaeol.* **13**, 230–87

Wrathmell, S. and Nicholson, A., 1990. *Dalton Parlours Iron Age Settlement and Roman Villa*, Yorkshire Archaeol. **3** (Wakefield)

Wright, D., 1975. 'The Baskets' in Platt and Coleman-Smith 1975, 342

Øye, I., 1988. *Textile Equipment and its Working Environment, Bryggen in Bergen, c.1150–1500*, The Bryggen Papers Main Series **2** (Oslo)

Index

By Susan Vaughan

Illustrations are denoted by page numbers in *italics* or by *illus* where figures are scattered throughout the text. Places are in York unless indicated otherwise. The following abbreviations have been used in this index: C – century; E. Riding – East Riding of Yorkshire; E. Sussex – East Sussex; f – following; *illus* – illustrated; N.E. Lincolnshire – North East Lincolnshire; N. Yorks – North Yorkshire; W. Mids – West Midlands; W. Sussex – West Sussex.